W9-BRA-722

Mary Shelley

Mary Shelley

MIRANDA SEYMOUR

GROVE PRESS
New York

First published in 2000 by John Murray (Publishers) Ltd., London, England

Printed in the United States of America

FIRST AMERICAN EDITION

Library of Congress Cataloging-in-Publication Data

Seymour, Miranda.
   Mary Shelley / Miranda Seymour.
      p. cm.
   Originally published: London : John Murray, 2000.
   Includes bibliographical references and index.
   ISBN 0-8021-1702-3
   1. Shelley, Mary Wollstonecraft, 1797–1851. 2. Women and literature—England—History—19th century. 3. Authors, English—19th century—Biography. I. Title.

PR5398 .S47 2001
823'.7—dc21
[B]   2001035094

Grove Press
841 Broadway
New York, NY 10003

01 02 03 04   10 9 8 7 6 5 4 3 2 1

'The sleep of reason produces monsters.'

Goya, *Los Caprichos* (1799)

CONTENTS

ILLUSTRATIONS

PREFACE

Mary Shelley's course was set from that early morning in the summer of 1814 when she and her stepsister Claire Clairmont left their home in dingy Holborn to run away with Percy Shelley across war-ravaged France to Switzerland, seen by them as the romantic birthplace of the Enlightenment. Mary was only sixteen, her stepsister was fifteen. Shelley, just twenty-one, had left his young pregnant wife behind. The following spring, Mary gave birth to his child, a little girl who died a few weeks later.

Eight years on, Mary miscarried her fifth child. Only one survived. She was not yet twenty-five when Shelley drowned in a sailing accident with a friend off the north-west coast of Italy. Shelley's death was the scene to which Victorian painters were drawn, and one can see why. His friends Edward Trelawny, Byron and Leigh Hunt were there to see the fish-eaten remains of the poet's body burned on a lonely shore while Mary, shocked and grief-stricken, shut herself away in her room to mourn alone. After her death, a sculptor would show her as the *mater dolorosa*, her husband's body stretched over her knees.

Today, the most famous scene from Mary's life and, perhaps, in literary history is the stormy summer night at the Villa Diodati on Lake Geneva when Byron, his handsome young doctor John Polidori, the Shelleys and Mary's stepsister, who was carrying Byron's child, decided to write horror stories for fun. This was the night on which *Frankenstein*, that best known of all Romantic works, was born. Its author was not yet nineteen.

Frankenstein has become part of our lives. The ambitious young scientist who, in Mary's bold imagination, became the first creator of a living human being without divine assistance – a shocking idea in her day and an extraordinary one for a young woman to choose for her first subject – is invoked almost daily in debates on the ethics of genetic engineering. Cartoonists from George Cruikshank to Gary Larsen have made use of *Frankenstein*; a recent survey among American children showed his name to be more familiar than that of the President.

Many books have been written about *Frankenstein*. The subject is of endless fascination. Where did the idea come from? Why did Mary choose to make the Creature a monster? Was she, as as some have suggested, exorcizing her own demons? Mary Wollstonecraft died a few days after giving birth to Mary; did Mary see herself as the monstrous child who killed her mother, or does the Creature represent her tormented relationship with Mary Jane Clairmont, the stepmother who made her feel an exile in her own home?

In the course of research, new possibilities presented themselves. As a sickly and troubled young girl, Mary was sent away from her family to live among strangers at Dundee, then one of the biggest whaling ports in Britain. The story which encloses the tale of Victor Frankenstein and his scientific experiment is of an ambitious young man who sets off to find a new land beyond the North Pole, following the route taken by the whaling vessels which were a feature of Mary's life at Dundee. It was there, she wrote later, 'that my true compositions, the airy flights of my imagination, were born and fostered'. Here, it appears, she began work on a story which was later adapted to frame the story of *Frankenstein*.

A further and intriguing possibility emerged as I was considering the summer of 1815, when Mary was temporarily on her own, staying in lodgings at Clifton. Living within strolling distance of Bristol, a town which had grown prosperous on the slave trade, Mary read books on the subject with increasing horror and indignation. Slavery, although formally abolished in England, remained a thriving industry; in England, slaves were still being rescued from service in the mid-nineteenth century. At Bristol, the evidence was all around her. Here, surely, was the explanation for the Creature's carefully described and decidedly un-English appearance, his hair of 'a lustrous blackness', his 'yellow' skin and teeth 'of a pearly whiteness', features which, when combined with his strength and muscular build, suggest that the author was deliberately evoking the African and West Indian, while his yellow skin hints at the Eastern 'lascars' whom she would have seen on her journeys from the London docks. Here, too, was a clue to why Mary, whose sympathies as an author are with the Creature, lays so much emphasis on the fact that Victor Frankenstein judges him – misjudges him – by his appearance. She was, it seems, covertly attacking a society which still believed that the physical appearance of the Africans indicated their moral inferiority to Europeans.

My interest in Mary began with the woman, not the subject. Twenty-five years ago I wrote a historical novel about Byron. This led me to the Shelleys. Richard Holmes's enthralling life of the poet had just been published; there, I encountered Mary as a sulky, bad-tempered young woman, a nagging wife. Edward Trelawny's celebrated memoirs confirmed Holmes's portrait while suggesting also that Mary was a relentless social climber, frantic to be accepted on any terms. Why, I wondered, should Shelley have left his pretty young first wife and risked disgrace for such a woman? If he did have an affair with Mary's stepsister, well, why not? They lived in the same house; they all believed in free love; Claire Clairmont sounded amusing and attractive. If Mary spent her widowhood struggling to promote her husband's reputation and to elevate him to the status of a saint, she was no doubt compensating for having failed him during his life. This, I am embarrassed to remember, was how I presented Mary in my novel. I thought it was the truth.

Biographers are often drawn to a subject with whom they have made some form of identification. Living on my own in London and bringing up a young son on not very much money, I began to think about Mary again. She, after Shelley's death, was forced to bring her little boy back to England from Italy, the land she loved, in order to obtain an allowance – she had no money of her own and Shelley's will had been lost – from her disapproving father-in-law, Sir Timothy Shelley. Her own father, William Godwin, once highly regarded as the author of one of the boldest works of the late eighteenth century, *An Enquiry concerning Political Justice*, was by 1823 destitute and dependent on Mary's help for his own survival.

Despite Sir Timothy's grudging payments, all of which were expected to be returned to the estate, with interest, after his death, and his insistence that she should neither publish his son's works nor use his name, Mary managed to write successfully enough to keep them all. At the same time, although she was herself treated as a social outcast, she risked her reputation to help her friends. 'I have ever defended women when oppressed,' she wrote in the journal to which she confided her most private thoughts. When one friend was exiled from her husband's house because she had been having an affair, Mary unhesitatingly championed and cared for her; when another had an illegitimate child, Mary helped mastermind a daring plan to send her abroad on a forged passport as the 'wife' of a woman who had boldly decided to become a transvestite. This, I began to realize, was a woman of exceptional courage and determination. She had no need to reproach herself for not having, like her mother, written *A Vindication of the Rights of Woman*; she was a heroine in her own right.

The more I read, the more Mary intrigued me. Not only did she live in a period of radical social transition, commencing in the bitter aftermath of the French Revolution and ending in the age of commerce – she died in 1851, the year of the Great Exhibition – but in what a circle! Not only Coleridge, Byron, Scott, Trelawny, but Melbourne, Disraeli, Lady Blessington and Caroline Norton – Mary had known them all. Outcast though she felt herself to be, her friends had included the most fascinating and influential people of her times. It seemed a cruel irony that Sir Timothy Shelley, a wealthy provincial landowner whose world was circumscribed by the borders of his Sussex estate and who, it happens, was in no position to sit in judgment on the behaviour of his son's young widow, should have possessed the power to control and restrict the life of a woman far superior to himself.

Curiosity was further piqued by many mysteries and apparent contradictions in her story. Why did Mary give the name of her adored dead child to the little boy who is wantonly destroyed by Frankenstein's creature? Did she, shortly after eloping with Shelley, resist or obey his instructions to have an affair with the man he regarded as his closest friend? Why did she turn so violently against this friend a year or two later? How much did she really know about the mysterious child – some believe it to have been Claire Clairmont's – adopted by Shelley in Naples and registered by him as Mary's baby? Why, when she so adored her father that she wrote of 'my excessive and romantic attachment' to him, did she abandon her attempt to write his life, knowing how much posthumous fame had meant to William Godwin? Why, when she evidently enjoyed flirtation and was sought after by many men, did she never remarry? Why, when she treasured her imagination and used it to produce such a powerful work as *Frankenstein*, could she never again match its vivid intensity? Was it some secret knowledge or experience that made her strangely apprehensive about her son's sexual life? What were the 'calumnies' which caused her to be shunned by many after her return to England in 1823 and which were still being whispered when she died? Easily duped, as she often ruefully acknowledged, did she ever discover that she had been involved in a plan to smuggle a forged Titian into England for the new National Gallery? There were many questions to be asked and nowhere answers to be found.

This was not, however, for lack of material. Mary Shelley has, over

the last twenty years, become one of the most popular subjects for
students of the Romantic period, second only to Wordsworth. In
Japan, she is a literary cult. Examinations of her novels and of her
editing of her husband's poems could fill a bookcase. Emily Sunstein's
Mary Shelley: Romance and Reality (1984; 1989), the most recent biography, celebrates Mary as an erudite and independent woman and a
writer of significant merit in a period which, if we set aside Maria
Edgeworth and Jane Austen, is not rich in female authors of distinction. Betty T. Bennett's fine three-volume edition of her letters,
together with a splendid one-volume edition of her journals by Paula
Feldman and Diana Scott-Kilvert, have recently been augmented by
the magnificent edition of the Clairmont correspondence assembled
by Marion Kingston Stocking.

The academic reader is well served. The general reader is not so
fortunate. There are now accessible major biographies of every
important literary figure of the Romantic period with the exception
of Mary Shelley. Muriel Spark's lively and unsurprisingly shrewd
study of her, written in 1951, was updated in 1988, but this is an over-
view of her life and works rather than a comprehensive biography.
The enthusiasm which greeted Claire Tomalin's publication in 1998
of *Maurice*, a long-lost short story which Mary had written for a little
girl in Italy, demonstrated how much public interest in Mary Shelley
has grown. This was cheering news, for by 1998 I was already fully
committed to writing this book.

I am, in several respects, extremely lucky. This is the first time that
one of Mary Shelley's biographers has been able to make use of
authoritative printed editions, not only of all her correspondence and
that of the Clairmonts and Fanny Imlay, Mary's half-sister, but of her
short stories, her travel writings and five novels. The only major
work relating to Mary which remains unpublished is the daily journal
which her father kept until his death in 1836 and of which I have
made extensive use. Fortunate in having turned up several documents
and letters by and relating to Mary which have not been previously
published, I have been lucky above all in having had the time to
explore the wonderfully rich variety of locations in which Mary lived,
and in living at a time when so many of them survive.

Places, I have often found, are the key to understanding. The little
churchyard of St Pancras where Mary used to visit her mother's grave
as a child and where her love-affair with Shelley began is now
hemmed in by railway lines and roads, not footpaths and cornfields.
Sitting there at dusk, on a summer evening, however, the traffic begins
to fade and it is not, after all, hard to imagine a little girl in 1800,

learning to spell from the letters on Mary Wollstonecraft's gravestone.
Nor is it hard to conjure up the pale, excited girl with a cloud of red-
gold hair who, in the summer of 1814, was standing here when she
first told Shelley that she loved him. Climbing the steep twisting path
up to the Casa Bertini, the Shelleys' home at Bagni di Lucca, sneak-
ing, without permission, up to the dusty library of books on the top
floor of Byron's grand palace on the Lung'Arno at Pisa, roaming
through the abandoned gardens there behind the Shelleys' own old
home across the river, sitting, dazzled by light, on top of the little
castle of San Terenzo which looks down on the Villa Magni and the
bay where Shelley took Mary sailing the month before his death; all
this brings the past to life with a jump.

What began as curiosity becomes obsession when you find yourself walking the streets of London in a daze. There are no paving
stones beneath your feet, no cars, no office blocks. You hear the
clatter of iron wheels, smell the horsedung, see, in a sudden swish of
black silk and the glimpse of a shawl, Mary and Claire hurrying down
a narrow street towards the carriage where Shelley is waiting, in 1814,
to lead them to adventures such as these two impatient, headstrong
young women have only read about in novels.

PART I

A Motherless Child

CHAPTER ONE

THE AGE OF PROMETHEUS

1789 – 1800

> 'Twas in truth an hour
> Of universal ferment; mildest men
> Were agitated; and commotions, strife
> Of passions and opinions, filled the walls
> Of peaceful houses with unquiet sounds.
> The soil of common life, was, at that time,
> Too hot to tread upon . . .
>
> Wordsworth, *The Prelude* (1850), Book IX

ONLY SEVEN PRISONERS WERE AVAILABLE FOR RELEASE WHEN THE citizens of Paris marched on the Bastille, but numbers were irrelevant. A symbol of power had been demolished. Thomas Paine, an Englishman, arranged for the key of the old fortress to be delivered to President Washington in the United States as a token of the inspiration which American independence had offered to Europe. 'My country is the world, and my religion is to do good,' Paine declared two years later in *The Rights of Man*: this was the spirit in which liberal-minded Englishmen and women prepared to greet the new and honourable age of the republic in 1789. Among them, although they had not yet met, were Mary Shelley's parents, the philosopher William Godwin and Mary Wollstonecraft, the architect of modern feminism.

We talk of a Romantic period. To those who lived in it, these years marked a return to the civic virtues and high ideals of the Roman republic. The time had come, they believed, in which aristocrats and commoners could unite to make a new and better world. Louis XVI was praised in England for the readiness with which he accepted his country's need to reform. Life, for all who sought change, had never seemed more full of promise.

Everything modern, as the century entered its last decade, endorsed the mood of hope and expectation. Up and down the country, the inventions of chemists and electricians were being observed and discussed. The painting in which Joseph Wright showed a homely family watching the death of a bird in the vacuum created by an air pump, no novelty by 1789, caught the spirit of an age more accurately than the artists whose feathery landscapes depicted a countryside free of factories and smokestacks. The first electric chimes, producing mysterious music through an electric pulse from charged metal points, offered a popular climax to science lectures. Fulminating rods presented spectators with an entrancing display of light dancing in glass funnels when they were struck by charged rotating balls. The chemist Joseph Priestley had devised an electric machine capable of exploding a glass sphere.

Prometheus, so the story went, was a god, a Titan who took clay from the plain of Boeotia and from it, moulded man. The secret of creation seemed only a leap away from the grasp of chemists and physicists at the end of the eighteenth century when the Italian anatomist and physician Luigi Galvani deduced the existence of 'animal electricity' (as opposed to the 'natural' electricity generated by machines or lightning) from the contraction of a dead frog's moist muscles when placed in contact with two different metals. Galvani's conclusions were published in 1791 and were hotly defended, after his death in 1798, by his cousin Giovanni Aldini, whose speciality was the animation of corpses, both animal and human, by the application of electric currents.

Alessandro Volta, a Fellow of the Royal Society who generously coined the name 'galvanism' for his friend's 'beautiful and most surprising discoveries', challenged 'animal electricity' with his 'contact theory', leading to the invention of the voltaic 'pile', a primitive electric battery, described by Volta to Sir Joseph Banks, President of the Royal Society, in March 1800. Asked to referee Volta's paper for publication by the Society, William Godwin's close friends, the physicist William Nicholson and the distinguished chemist and surgeon Anthony Carlisle, were able – within weeks – to construct a pile and, by decomposing water into oxygen and hydrogen when an electric current was passed through water, to discover the principle of electrolysis.

If Volta was the father of the electric cell and the volt named after him, so Galvani's 'animal electricity' revealed, by a process of deduction, that nerves were not, as Descartes and his contemporaries had supposed, water pipes, but electrical conductors. The image of a being electrified or galvanized into life was born, some twenty years before Frankenstein's Creature, in the cabinets, laboratories and dissecting rooms where William Godwin's friends experimented, noted, and discussed their discoveries.

The dream of progress captured the imagination of the country. Novelists, poets and philosophers drew on James Watt's patented steam engine for their powerful images of wheels and chains. Travellers in the new mail coaches compared notes on the speed of their journeys and were ready to risk death from pneumonia for a night-ride on the roof above the heads of the pounding horses. Sea captains risked a more lingering death in the pack-ice of the Arctic seas as they searched for a passage which would link England to India. In 1781, William Herschel identified Uranus and connected England to the heavens by naming the planet for the king, Georgium Sidus, George's Star. Essayists of the 1790s invoked the name of Uranus' grandson, Prometheus, as a model, not a warning to overreachers. All, now, seemed possible.

The first suggestion that too much progress could be a dangerous thing was heard in November 1790, when Edmund Burke's *Reflections on the Revolution in France* offered a seductive defence of the king's right to sit in his palace and the lord in his enclosed park. This, Burke argued, was how society was meant to be; equality was a futile dream. His friends found it hard to fathom why the man who had championed the rights of American colonists should be so appalled by France's bold act of emulation, but Burke was haunted by the memory of bloody revolution in London, when a wave of anti-Catholic feeling led to the Gordon Riots of 1780, to the looting of houses and burning of chapels by an uncontrolled mob. Later, Burke would be seen as a prophet; in 1790, he seemed out of step, at least with advanced opinion. Mary Wollstonecraft, then aged thirty and having just settled her younger sisters as teachers in a Putney school, was one of the first to snatch up her pen and write an emotional response. *A Vindication of the Rights of Men* was published anonymously at the end of the year. The author's identity was not a well-kept secret.*

---

* Her timing was fortunate; when a second, signed edition was printed by her friend Joseph Johnson, in January 1791, its title swiftly connected her to that more famous revolutionary, Tom Paine, whose *The Rights of Man* was published shortly afterwards. Mary Wollstonecraft, admired but hitherto little known for a novel, *Mary* (1788), for a collection of children's tales, *Original Stories* (1788) and for her hastily compiled *Thoughts on the Education of Daughters* (1787), was now a name to be reckoned with.

In 1791, a nine-hundred-strong group of revolutionists felt confident enough to celebrate Bastille Day in London with a dinner and a song which united political change to the latest scientific discoveries.

Fill high the animating glass
And let the electric ruby pass
From hand to hand, from soul to soul:
Who shall the energy controul
Exalted, pure, refined,
The Health of Humankind![1]

The English revolutionaries of 1791 hailed science as a symbol of change. To the government and the less educated, it had become a threat. A similar dinner in Birmingham was broken up on the same day by an organized mob. The Meeting House of which Joseph Priestley was the minister was set alight; so, tragically, were the great scientist's library and his laboratory. Thomas Paine had just published the first part of *The Rights of Man* in opposition to Burke's warnings of the birth in France of a 'political monster' which would end by devouring its creators. Remembered as the man whose writings had helped to stir up revolution in America, Paine was now advised to leave England for his personal safety.

In 1792, the French abolished the monarchy and put their king on trial. Mary Wollstonecraft, established as a leader of the New Philosophy with her second political publication, *A Vindication of the Rights of Woman*, followed Paine to Paris in support of that feverishly brilliant group of revolution-minded orators, the Girondists.

Meanwhile in England in 1793, only a month after the execution of Louis XVI, and in a climate of increasing panic and the savage repression of all pro-revolutionary activity, William Godwin published one of the most influential books of the decade. *An Enquiry concerning the Nature of Political Justice* was a copious, orderly and determinedly rational argument for justice in a society of equals. Marriage, organized religion and centralized government were among the author's prime targets; his first edition gave implicit approval to events across the Channel by praising new political institutions if they taught men to cherish feelings of equality and independence.[2] As Mary Wollstonecraft's work established her as the mother of modern feminism, so William Godwin's *Political Justice* earned this peace-loving and unrevolutionary man his reputation as the father of anarchism. France had already declared war on England, but the thirty-seven-year-old author managed to place a copy of his brave book in the French ambassador's hands three days before the diplomat was ordered to leave the country.

Despite the fact that *Political Justice* urged Britain to follow the French example, Godwin escaped prosecution. Paine's work had cost an accessible sixpence. At £1 16s., Pitt's government doubted that Godwin's would find enough readers to threaten the constitution.[3] The government had misjudged the public's enthusiasm for change. The first edition of *Political Justice* sold over three thousand copies in quarto, the large size, alone. In radical circles, Godwin's book made him the philosopher king; Wordsworth spoke for many when he told a young lawyer to throw away his chemistry books and read Godwin on the doctrine of necessity.

Although Godwin was never prosecuted or imprisoned his friends were not so fortunate. In 1794, with the country committed to what was optimistically anticipated as a short war against France – in fact there would be no enduring peace for another twenty years – the government stepped up repressive measures by suspending habeas corpus. Imprisonment was now possible without trial. Godwin's remarkable novel about obsession, guilt and pursuit, *Things as They Are, or The Adventures of Caleb Williams*, was published that year, but without the Preface in which the author denounced the government's abuse of its powers; the publisher did not dare print it. In the autumn of 1794, Godwin published a pamphlet setting out the constitutional reasons why the government should not condemn thirteen of his friends and associates to death for demanding parliamentary reform. Bravely, he risked imprisonment by publicly linking himself to the accused, appearing every day at the infamous October 'Treason Trials' where Sir Thomas Lawrence one day sketched him in court, sitting shoulder to shoulder with one of the charged men, his friend the playwright Thomas Holcroft.[4] Writing to Joseph Gerrald, another victim of the government's new policies, on the eve of his trial in Edinburgh at the beginning of the year, Godwin urged the accused man to stand his ground with neither bitterness nor fear. With courage and calmness, he wrote, they could still 'shake the pillars of the vaults of heaven'. A steadfast attitude would, he was convinced, lead the court to an honourable verdict: 'The jury, the world will feel your value, if you show yourself such a man . . . You represent us all.'[5]

Godwin's cogently reasoned pamphlet secured acquittal or a dropping of charges against most of the defendants at the Treason

Trials, but Gerrald was not so lucky. Found guilty of sedition, he was transported to New South Wales the following year. Godwin, one of Gerrald's most regular visitors in his months at Newgate prison, did not reproach himself for having urged Gerrald to stand firm. Guilt formed no part of his philosophy. It was unlikely, in any case, that a not-guilty plea would have rescued Gerrald from conviction.

An attack on George III's carriage in the autumn of 1795 offered further proof to the government that the radical vipers in England's bosom must be strangled. Two emergency bills were introduced for the purpose of suppressing all political meetings and controversial publications. Godwin's response, an eighty-six-page anonymous pamphlet, defended freedom of speech, but not in a way that was likely to please his radical friends. Opposing the government's draconian measures, he also warned the debating societies that they were becoming dangerously close to the French Jacobins in their reckless language and incitations to violence. Reasoned discussion leading to gradual change was the course which Godwin proposed. He never veered from it.

The two 'Gagging Acts' of 1796 marked an end to free speech and a free press. There would be no revolution in England. But William Godwin had become a hero to everybody who shared his belief that conditions, and man himself, could be altered and improved by the unfettered exercise of reason, that prison sentences were worse than useless, that the government was a 'brute engine' designed to crush, not to enlighten and assist. 'No work in our time gave such a blow to the philosophical mind of the country as the celebrated *Enquiry concerning Political Justice*,' William Hazlitt wrote almost thirty years later in *The Spirit of the Age*. Compared to Godwin, he wrote, Paine had seemed a fool, Burke a 'flashy sophist'. The Hazlitt and Godwin families had been close Norfolk neighbours and friends, but there was no special pleading in the younger man's observation. 'Truth, moral truth' had been revealed in Godwin's work, he wrote; the eight books which comprised *Political Justice* were recognized as 'the oracles of thought'.[6]

Recognition had been slow to come, although Godwin had always been seen as a star in his own family circle. Born in 1756, he was the seventh child of thirteen born from a paternal line of dissenting ministers, Dissenters being that large group of Protestants whose refusal to conform to Church of England practices debarred them from civil rights and education at Oxford and Cambridge. He was a precocious boy, and an earnest one. At home, he delighted the family with sermons delivered from a kitchen chair in a borrowed wig; walking across the fields to his first school with a small friend, he decided one day to lock him in the Meeting House and to pray over him after terrifying the child with visions of damnation culled from the grim collection of Calvinist texts in John Godwin's study.

Death made Godwin a youthful stoic. At least four of his twelve siblings died in infancy or as young children.* One, in a horrifying incident which he never forgot, drowned in the horsepond at Guestwick in Norfolk where he lived from the age of four. Sent off from the crowded little house on long visits to a childless female cousin, William shared her bed and was lulled to sleep nightly with a warning to prepare himself for his end. 'This lesson made a long and deep impression on my mind,' Godwin wrote. Explaining his affection for the grim old lady, he inadvertently disclosed that it was a love born of desolation. 'There is nothing,' he observed, 'that the human heart more irresistibly seeks than an object to which to attach itself.'[7]

If Godwin's later views on education were unusually liberal and kindly, it was partly the result of his own unhappy experiences. He was only eleven years old when he was sent off to be the sole pupil of Norfolk's finest teacher. Samuel Newton was a Norwich minister who preached of the devil with enthusiasm and threatened the rod at every opportunity. The pleasure which he took in using it, Godwin recalled, was that of a butcher who, having retired, will still travel miles to savour the slaughter of an ox. Ordered to maintain silence about his chastisement, Godwin consoled himself with long hours in Mr Newton's library. Here, having had a dour home education based on the Bible and numerous edifying works on the pleasures of the grave, he devoured the novels of Richardson, Smollett and Fielding, and a series of tomes on ancient history which fired a lifelong passion

---

* The number of Godwin's siblings who outlived childhood is uncertain. Hull, the eldest brother, remained with his family on the Norfolk farm with their mother. Joseph, John, Nathaniel (Nattie or Nat), Hannah and Harriet are the names which appear in Godwin's (unpublished) journal. Harriet seems to have been the wife of Joseph rather than a full sister.

for the causes of liberty and public virtue. By the end of three years, he was well-read, well-whipped and, despite Newton's best endeavours, confident to the point of arrogance.

Mr Godwin Senior died in 1772. His widow, anxious to do what was best for her clever son, the one most likely to provide support to an indigent family, took him to London the following year to be educated at a dissenting academy. Rejected by Newton's old college of Homerton, the seventeen-year-old youth was accepted at Hoxton, where he spent the next five years. Here, for the first time, Godwin breathed the fresh air of liberalism. Hoxton was considered by many to be the best academic institution in England. Free inquiry was encouraged; pupils were urged to examine both sides of every question. Locke, whose works were still banned at Oxford, was revered at Hoxton; Godwin, brought up by his Calvinist father to believe in original sin, learned that a child is made by what it learns and how it learns. From his principal tutor, Andrew Kippis, he acquired the stimulating idea which lies at the heart of *Political Justice*: man is born free and has no obligation to submit to the will of a government unless he judges that will to be imposed for the good of all. 'We dissent,' Kippis wrote, 'because we deny the right of any body of men, whether civil or ecclesiastical, to impose human tests, creeds, or articles; and because we think it our duty, not to submit to any such authority, but to protest against it, as a violation of our essential liberty to judge and act for ourselves in matters of religion.'[8] This, to a young man who recognized the injustice of a system which refused Dissenters employment in any job which required the taking of an oath, while forcing them to establish their own academies, registers and burial grounds, was intoxicating stuff.

The study of history as a college subject stems from the dissenting academies. Encouraged by Kippis, Godwin formed an enduring interest in those periods when England had undergone a liberalizing change – the Reformation, the Commonwealth, and the 'Glorious Revolution' of 1688 to which all Dissenters looked back with nostalgia and pride. But Kippis also broadened his pupil's knowledge of philosophy and the classics. Excelling in Greek and Latin, Godwin acquired a good working knowledge of Italian, French, German and Hebrew. He did not meet Mary Wollstonecraft, although her family were living in Hoxton at that time, but the academy brought him together with James Marshall, a kind, gentle and, although he was almost always poor, invariably generous man who became his lifelong friend.

Mrs Godwin had hoped that her son would follow his father into the church as an independent minister. This, after leaving Hoxton, was the direction he took. But Godwin had become too widely read and too full of questions to please the congregations he briefly led in Suffolk and then Buckinghamshire from 1782 to 1783 before moving to London. One dissatisfied attendant remembered that the young man had preferred 'coursing' to giving sermons;[9] others at Stowmarket objected to his readiness to offer communion before being ordained. A more certain cause for trouble was the fact that Godwin had come to believe that biblical characters, and Jesus himself, were non-divine historical figures. Not yet an atheist, he was no longer a conventional believer, and too honest to pretend. By the summer of 1783, he had, perhaps under the influence of Andrew Kippis, decided that a teaching career was more congenial than the pulpit.

Godwin's project for a school never advanced beyond renting a potential home for it at Epsom and placing a single advertisement in an anonymously published pamphlet. The lack of response was not entirely surprising; enthusiasm for his system caused Godwin to overlook all practical details. There was no mention of length of terms, fees, meals or even of a proposed teacher and his qualifications. What the prospectus does reveal is that Godwin already knew the kind of father he wanted to be. Imagination was to be encouraged and developed. Teaching should be a gentle discipline directed to building sympathy between master and pupils. The chief and laudable object would be to form not a prodigy but 'a reasonable human being'.[10] It seems, with such humane ideals, a shame that the project never got beyond its initial stage.

The collapse of the school plan led Godwin to decide to make his living by writing. High-minded dreams were shelved. Lodging wherever he and his friend James Marshall could find cheap rooms in London, Godwin wrote eleven books and enough reviews to fill another dozen over the next eight years. There was nothing to which he would not turn his hand – bad romantic novels for the circulating libraries, plays, biographies and even, on commission, a handsome three-volume history of the peerage.

Despite Godwin's later reputation as a ruthless and persistent sponge, a perpetual drain on the pockets of his friends, family letters show him to have been both generous and patient. His own needs were simple; all earnings were channelled into helping friends and his less able siblings. Ann Godwin's letters, written from the Norfolk small-holding she shared with Hull, the eldest of her sons, show how much she depended on William to take care of the family and to deliver news of her other children.

They had not done well for themselves. Two brothers went to sea, where one got into such difficulties that Godwin had to write a letter on his behalf to the ship's captain, pleading for clemency and invoking the pitiful situation of a widowed mother. Another brother, John, was frequently reported to be on the point of starvation as a clerk in the Temple, although Godwin seems to have done all he could to help. Nathaniel ('Nattie') made an unsuccessful attempt to avoid being press-ganged into the navy and was obliged on his return to England to take up work as a journeyman. Joseph, the brother of whom Godwin saw the most, made an unhappy marriage before finding what Godwin reassured their mother was 'a comfortable place' as a servant.

Only Hannah, who wrote poetry and had established herself as a London dressmaker with a congenial circle of – in her mother's view – distressingly godless friends, was on an equal social footing with her brother, even to the degree of trying – unsuccessfully – to find him a wife. Godwin showed his respect, much to the annoyance of their mother, by giving Hannah the genteel title of 'Miss Godwin' and making no brotherly comments on her Sunday outings with James Marshall. (Sunday, for a respectable girl, was not a day to go dallying with unmarried gentlemen.) 'Why can't you call your sister Hannah, as well as you call me . . . Hon'd Mother,' old Ann Godwin demanded in a letter written in 1788, when her son was thirty-two; 'it would be full as agreeable.' But she softened later in the letter, thanking him for giving five shillings to one of his luckless brothers at a recent meeting.[11] Sometimes she repaid his generosity with a comforting gift of a basket of eggs or a goose, sent up to town with the Norfolk carrier.

The real worth of Godwin's kindness appears still more clearly in his relationship with Thomas Cooper, a cousin who had been left penniless after the death of his father in India. Godwin, in 1788, made up his mind that young Thomas must be properly educated, whatever the cost to himself in time and effort. (He had just been forced to find a cheaper lodging to save money.) Master Cooper was not at the time particularly grateful for having all of Shakespeare's plays read and explained to him. A furious memorandum has survived in which he wrote out all the insults he imagined Godwin offering behind his back.[12] These included the words 'brute' and 'viper' and, given that the novelist Amelia Alderson once scolded Godwin for calling her a bitch,[13] the terms are not beyond belief. It is hard to imagine what Cooper's feelings were on receiving back a calm explanation that his feelings were irrelevant to their relationship. If the young man became 'virtuous and respectable', his mentor would have achieved his purpose. 'I am contented you should hate me. I desire no gratitude, and no return of favours, I only wish to do you good.'[14]

Godwin kept his word, supporting Cooper both in his years as a pupil and in his early, unsuccessful attempts to become an actor. He could not escape gratitude. When Cooper eventually became a celebrated thespian, known for his mesmerizing performances in *The Iron Chest* (the dramatized and hugely popular version of *Caleb Williams*), he remembered his severe guardian with love, as 'one of the most pure and benevolent of men', somebody who had been 'much more than a common father . . . he has cherished and instructed me.'[15]

On Sunday, 13 November 1791, Godwin went to the crowded little room near St Paul's where the publisher Joseph Johnson held fortnightly dinners. He had come to meet a fellow guest, Thomas Paine. Hard at work on his own masterpiece, *Political Justice*, Godwin was eager to exchange views with the man whose book he had so profoundly admired. But the conversation around Johnson's table that day was dominated by a contentious auburn-haired woman, no longer young (she was thirty-one), whom the kindly publisher had taken under his wing after her brief career as a governess in Ireland in 1786–7.

Godwin had glanced at and thrown aside Mary Wollstonecraft's hastily written *A Vindication of the Rights of Men*. He may have been aware that she was in the throes of preparing a far more important book, one on which it is possible that Paine was advising her. He probably knew nothing at all about the hopeless attachment she had formed to Henry Fuseli, the dapper, irascible and fetishistic Swiss artist, small, white-haired, cat-eyed, who became Professor of Painting at the Royal Academy in 1801 and who had already produced one of the most erotic and influential paintings of the Romantic age, *The Nightmare*. The scorn which Mary expressed for the convention of marriage at this time may have been partly fuelled by the fact that the middle-aged Fuseli had recently married a seductive and strong-willed young woman blessed, like Mary, with a sumptuous mane of auburn hair. (Fuseli's paintings show a consistent and erotic fascination with women's hair.) He was, however, ready to allow Mary to play the role of muse to his genius. She had, in September, moved home to live nearer the Fuselis; observant friends noticed that she was, for the first time in her life, taking care with her appearance.

All Godwin noticed that Sunday was that Miss Wollstonecraft seemed opinionated, censorious and dully conventional in her religious views: Godwin himself was becoming increasingly attracted to atheism under the influence of his friend, Thomas Holcroft. He was in no state to feel romantic; work on his book was getting him down. He had been feverish the day before Johnson's dinner and he was 'costive' on the following one. In the memoir he later wrote of Mary's life, he uncomfortably recalled that she and he had been so vociferous in their disagreements at Johnson's dinner that poor Paine, never much of a talker, had been reduced to occasional interjections. Mary left no record of her own feelings, but the fact that she made no attempt to follow up the meeting is significant. Godwin's home in north London was only half an hour's walk from her own, and Mary was quite bold enough to call on a man who interested her. She made no call.

The first indication of interest comes in March 1792 when Godwin made a note in his diary: 'Story of Mrs Wolstonecraft.' No name appears by this entry to indicate the source, but the word 'story' suggests that it may have been an account of her life. Any one of Mary's friends might have given him a brief outline of her past; of a precarious, slipshod upbringing in Yorkshire with little schooling and, unlike himself, no religious indoctrination; of the family's return to Hoxton when she was fifteen and the acquiring of some basic religious tenets from a friendly clergyman; the beginning of an intensely affectionate relationship with a graceful older girl, Fanny Blood; of working as a lady companion in Bath before helping one younger sister, Eliza, escape from an unhappy marriage and coaxing another, Everina, to join them in starting a school at Newington Green, north of London. Here, among a network of Dissenter households, including that of Thomas Rogers (the father of Samuel, who would be Byron's and Mary Shelley's friend in later years), Mary Wollstonecraft had more success in finding friends than managing a school. Eliza and Everina progressed from teaching posts in Putney to working as governesses. Mary, having had the miserable experience of seeing her darling Fanny Blood, now a married lady, die in childbirth at Lisbon, went in 1786 as a governess-companion to the grand family of Lord Kingsborough of Mitchelstown in Ireland. She found a lasting admirer and apostle there in one of her pupils, young Margaret King, but the aristocratic mother infuriated her, a feeling which was not concealed and which helped lose her the post. In 1787, she returned to London and found a kind substitute for her feckless father in Joseph Johnson, who published her novel and children's stories the following year. Johnson failed, however, to prevent her impetuous attempt at a *ménage à trois* with Fuseli and his young wife.

Mary's life had, until this point, been hectic and muddled; response to the two *Vindications* promised a change for the better. By 1792, she was respected, admired and, by many of her circle, greatly loved. Godwin must have known and perhaps read *A Vindication of the Rights of Woman*, the book which, although its sales were not large, earned her a place among the most influential writers of the time on education and the role of women. His laconic journal entry, 'Story of Mrs Wolstonecraft', tells us only that he was interested enough to listen to some account. He still had time for nothing but the writing of his own book. At the end of 1792, determined to break an association which was bringing her nothing but unhappiness and which was distressing Fuseli's wife, Mary Wollstonecraft left England for France.

When Godwin next met Mary in London four years later she was in the last throes of another deeply humiliating and unhappy love-affair. While living in Paris, she had been introduced to an intelligent, easygoing American entrepreneur called Gilbert Imlay. They became lovers. When some four hundred English citizens living in Paris were peremptorily imprisoned in October 1793, Mary allowed Imlay to offer her the protection of his American citizenship by registering her as his wife. Legally, she remained a spinster; her letters show that she sincerely believed an emotional commitment of a lasting kind had been made by them both.

Strong, loving women have had their hearts broken by worthless men since the beginning of time; few have fought to keep them with such self-lacerating tenacity as Mary. She gave birth to a daughter, Frances, in May 1794; three months later, Imlay returned to England on what Mary assumed would be a brief trip to supervise various business matters.* Imlay did not come back. He did, eventually, write urging her to follow him. When Mary, together with her maid and baby, returned to England in the early spring of 1795, her lover had changed his mind. Instead of the family home she had been fondly imagining, furnished lodgings in Charlotte Street were recommended to which Imlay made occasional brief visits during the two months she lived there. For a woman who was still deeply in love it was an

---

* Imlay's trade was largely based around shipping iron, soap and coal into wartime France from neutral countries. He arranged to be paid in Bourbon silver which he would receive in Sweden. Joel Barlow, a fellow American living in Paris, joined the scheme for breaking the British blockade; their Franco-Swedish colleague was one Elias Backman. Imlay's part was to arrange shipping from Le Havre.

unbearable situation, made still more painful by the discovery that Imlay had replaced her with a young actress.

'Perhaps no human creature ever suffered greater misery, than dyed the whole year 1795, in the life of this incomparable woman . . .' Godwin later wrote in a state of forgivable indignation. 'Why did she thus obstinately cling to an ill-starred unhappy passion? Because it is the very essence of affection, to seek to perpetuate itself.'[16]

She tried to kill herself. Imlay, torn between guilt and impatience, decided to make use of her while offering her a change of scenery and, perhaps, mood. One of his most risky ventures had turned out badly. A ship, bought and secretly dispatched to Gothenburg with the equivalent of half a million pounds stowed in silver bars and plate, had disappeared en route. Imlay's only hope of compensation lay with the Scandinavian courts. Someone would have to undertake the journey; the apparent helplessness of a good-looking woman, travelling alone, might work to his advantage.

Mary, who took her baby daughter with her, returned from her dangerous four-month mission to Sweden and Norway at the end of September. It is not clear whether the registering of the missing boat at Gothenburg two weeks later, with no mention of its cargo, was the result of her efforts. If so, she had even more cause to feel desperate when she learnt, not from her lover but his servants, that Imlay had found yet another mistress and was planning to live with her. Leaving word of where she was going, Mary hired a boat to row her up the Thames to Putney where, after weighting her pockets with stones, she jumped off the wooden bridge. When Imlay's carriage arrived, her unconscious body had already been dragged from the water.

This second attempt at suicide frightened Imlay into agreeing that he would, as she wished, try to find a house where they could all, Mary, the baby and his mistress, live together. The house had not yet been chosen when he changed his mind and went on a three-month visit to Paris with his girlfriend. It was during this grim period that Mary, having regained the lyrical, tortured letters she had written to Imlay from Scandinavia, compiled from them the book which Joseph Johnson published as *A Short Residence in Sweden, Norway and Denmark*. She even, to her everlasting credit, began work on a play in which she tried to turn the tragic circumstances of her love-affair to comic use.[17]

Mary was still hoping for a reunion with Imlay in January 1796, when she and William Godwin met again at the home of their mutual friend, Mary Hays. Godwin had not been eager for the meeting. In his letter of acceptance to Miss Hays, he observed that he knew how often Mrs Wollstonecraft had given herself the pleasure of deprecating him in public, although he gave away no hint of what her comments had been. Mary, indeed, had a sharp tongue, and Godwin's tendency to dominate conversations and his dislike of being contradicted might have stuck in her mind from their first unfortunate meeting in 1791. The most he was now willing to promise Miss Hays was that he would treat this 'enemy' as fairly as he would a friend.[18]

Godwin turned forty in 1796. The red crayon drawing which Lawrence made of him and his friend Holcroft two years earlier shows a slight, elegant figure with unpowdered hair above a high forehead. The eyes are open, round and inquiring, the nose thin and long. He is not unattractive, but it comes as a surprise to learn that some of the cleverest and best-looking women of the time doted on him. Mary Hays, who was not among the second category, had become so demanding and verbose a correspondent that Godwin's only resource was to refuse to write back. *Memoirs of Emma Courtney* (1796), Mary Hays's novel, reflects this unhappy situation as calm, rational Mr Francis/Godwin advises Emma/Hays to examine the causes for her violent feelings. The playwright Elizabeth Inchbald, fondly remembered by Godwin as 'a piquante mixture between a lady and a milkmaid', let him edit her best-known novel, *A Simple Story* (1791). Godwin admired it and the witty author enough to read the book, and note the fact, five times. Amelia Alderson, a spirited young novelist, dramatist and actress from Norwich Quaker circles, had attended the Treason Trials with Godwin and her father and had a close enough relationship with him for Godwin to carry her slipper in his pocket. Dearest of all to Godwin, it seems, was Maria Reveley, the musical and, by all accounts, enchanting wife of an architect. Educated in Constantinople, where she learnt to ride sidesaddle, and in Rome, where she was taught painting by Angelica Kauffmann, Mrs Reveley had all the virtues of her circle except literary ability and Godwin was deeply attached to her. This relationship had, however, become less intense in recent months, possibly owing to the intervention of Maria's husband.[19]

Godwin was not, then, looking for romance when he went to Mary Hays's house on a cold afternoon early in 1796. He was not even looking forward to meeting the woman Miss Hays thought such a wonder. He returned home in a different, and troubled, state. Mary Hays thought Mrs Imlay had been unusually vivacious; Godwin reached a different conclusion. To him, it seemed painfully clear that the woman he had just met was in a state of considerable anguish. She bore only a faint resemblance to the obstreperous martinet of 1791. Perhaps Miss Hays had told him something of Imlay's behaviour;

certainly, Godwin went to the trouble of obtaining Mary's latest work. It had a profound effect on him. 'If ever there was a book calculated to make a man fall in love with its author,' he wrote later of *A Short Residence*, 'this appears to me to be the book.'[20]

In February, a few weeks after this meeting, Godwin paid a call at the house where Mary was staying; she was not at home. Presumably informed of his visit, Mary was still hoping Imlay might come back to her. By March, a final exchange of letters with her former lover had extinguished all hope. On 14 April, after spending a reviving month in the country with an old friend, Mrs Cotton, Mary was feeling enterprising enough to walk down the hill from her lodgings in Pentonville to the newly created estate of Somers Town, north of what has now become Euston Road, where Godwin had a home in Chalton Street. She knocked at his door, and was admitted. The following week, Godwin arranged a dinner for some close friends. His undisclosed purpose was to introduce them to Mary Wollstonecraft.

For a cautious man, Godwin was positively reckless in his courting. By June, he was ready to submit a love poem, to which Mary nervously responded that he had said nothing until now about his feelings for her. She wanted, she told him, 'a bird's-eye view of your heart'. Invitingly, she accompanied the letter with a volume of one of her favourite books, Rousseau's *Julie, ou La Nouvelle Héloïse*.[21] 'Shall I write a love letter?' Godwin asked her tenderly in July, when he was taking his annual holiday in the country:

> May Lucifer fly away with me, if I do! . . . Well then, what shall be my subject? Shall I send you an eulogium of your beauty, your talents & your virtues? Ah! that is an old subject: besides if I were to begin, instead of a sheet of paper, I should want a ream.[22]

Godwin ended the letter by promising that when he returned in a week, he would stay by her side, 'to depart no more'. He arrived home to find that Mary, who had been contemplating a life abroad, had decided instead to move into rooms conveniently close to Chalton Street.

A very private love-affair was consummated in the middle of August when Godwin's diary recorded, in endearingly transparent code, 'Chez moi, toute.' Letters were carried to and fro by Mary's maid and by her little daughter Fanny Imlay, who grew fond of the kind, shabby gentleman whom her mother scolded for stuffing her with cakes and biscuits. To Fanny as to Mary's friends, the handsome and recently divorced Cornish portrait-painter John Opie, a frequent caller, must have seemed a far more plausible candidate for the role of lover than sober, orderly Mr Godwin.* Even such close friends of Godwin's as Thomas Holcroft and the surgeon Anthony Carlisle had no clue from his behaviour of what was afoot: given the choice of a meal in with Mary or the opportunity to attend a lecture, he never hesitated. Outside his own door, he was still ready to play the confirmed bachelor, agreeable to all women, committed to none.

All of Godwin's natural cheerfulness was required to combat the terrors of a woman who had suffered so much humiliation at Imlay's hands. The ease of an equal, mutual love was alien to her; time and again, Mary withdrew with a forlorn declaration of her independence, protecting herself against rejection. 'Be happy. Resolve to be happy,' Godwin urged her on 17 August. 'You deserve to be so. Everything that interferes with it is weakness and wandering; and a woman like you, can, must, shall, shake it off.' But Mary's fears were deep-rooted and there was, as Godwin came to understand, an ineradicable tendency towards melancholy in her nature. Feelings of 'sublime tranquillity' were constantly overwhelmed by presentiments of misfortune against which her continuing religious faith provided an insufficient bulwark.

Marriage played no part in their plans. Godwin had written vigorously against it as an odious institution; Mary had both preached and practised the doctrine of free love. But her registered title of Mrs Imlay had allowed her to protect Fanny's illegitimacy. The discovery that she was pregnant again, five months after they had begun sleeping together, came as a shock to them both. Godwin, no expert in such matters, had relied on the rhythm method to protect them; Mary proudly assured him that she was ready to survive the consequences of her behaviour alone.

How was it possible for Godwin to let her do so? The women of his circle were progressive in conversation and theory; he was perfectly aware that few would put those theories into practice. If Mary gave birth to a child out of wedlock, she would instantly be robbed of both reputation and friends. Principles, in such circumstances, would have to be dropped. On 31 March 1797, accompanied only by Godwin's loyal friend James Marshall, the couple were married at the little local church of St Pancras. Terse as always in his journal, Godwin recorded the event in one word: 'Panc.'

The news, reluctantly released, was coolly received. Only old Ann

---

* Opie's feelings for Mary have never been quite clear, but the portrait he painted of her in 1797 is full of warmth and glowing colour. In 1798, he married Godwin's friend, Amelia Alderson of Norwich.

Godwin was delighted to think that her dear son had a wife at last. Several of Godwin's female friends, Elizabeth Inchbald and Sarah Siddons among them, professed outrage.* How, they wished to know, were they to rejoice at a marriage which revealed the fiction of Mary's status as 'Mrs Imlay'? These fairweather friends kept their distance; others, like Maria Reveley and the novelist Eliza Fenwick, offered congratulations and friendship to a woman they warmly admired.† Amelia Alderson, amused by the gap between sublime ideals and conventional expectations, borrowed some of the details of Godwin's marriage and a good deal of his views on the subject for her novel, *Adeline Mowbray* (1805). Having married John Opie herself in 1798, Amelia saw marriage as a social necessity and forced the spirited Adeline to die regretting her independence. The deathbed recantation is not wholly convincing; it was Godwin's lack of religious belief, not his unexpected marriage, which caused Amelia to keep him and his wife at a prudent distance as she herself became increasingly devout.

Godwin had already begun planning for the future. The evening before the marriage ceremony, he met Mr Leroux, the builder who had been responsible for developing most of the new Somers Town estate. Leroux, who controlled the leasing of its houses, many of them to the less wealthy members of French emigré society, offered him a house in the Polygon, a handsome sixteen-sided development standing on the edge of the low, flat fields which looked westwards to the remote bulk of Primrose Hill and, far away to the north, the high heathland of Hampstead and Highgate. The developer had a home in the Polygon himself; the house he recommended to Godwin, No. 29, could be rented from a Miss Leonora Knapp of Kentish Town at a reasonable price. Godwin took it. For work purposes, he kept a couple of rooms round the corner in Evesham Buildings. Sometimes, since theirs was to be a modern marriage, with proper respect for each other's needs and privacy, he expected to sleep there.

Independence was maintained by mutual consent. The couple continued to make and receive calls without always bothering to consult each other; sometimes, Mary signed her letters in sturdy republican style as 'Mary Wollstonecraft femme Godwin'. There had never been any doubt about the sex or name of their baby. It would be a boy, and they would name him William.

---

* Mrs Siddons's high-mindedness was particularly chilling, since Mary Wollstonecraft had become friendly with her family and often dined with her relations, the Twisses.
† Eliza Fenwick had published a forward-looking novel, *Secresy*, in 1795; her husband John was a friend of Godwin's.

CHAPTER TWO

A BIRTH AND A DEATH

1797 – 1798

'I firmly believe that there does not exist her equal in the world. I know from experience we were formed to make each other happy.'

William Godwin to Thomas Holcroft, 1797[1]

GODWIN'S FRIENDS RAISED THEIR EYEBROWS AT THE MARRIAGE. His mother sent her hearty congratulations together with a basket of eggs and the promise of a feather bed for a servant's bedroom. Her only worry was that her sensible William might make the same mistake as his brother Joseph.

> My dears, whatever you do, do not make invitations and entertainments, that was what hurt Jo. Live comfortable with one another. The Hart of her husband safely trusts in her. I cannot give you no better advise than out of Proverbs, the Prophets, and New Testament . . . Your eggs will spoil soon if you don't pack them up in sawdust, bran, or something of the kind and turn them often. 'Tis pitty to pay carriage for them if they don't keep.[2]

There must have been times when Godwin wished that his wife was as domesticated as his mother. Their arrangement was supposed to be one of equals, but he was old-fashioned enough to assume that, while he was peacefully writing in Evesham Buildings, Mary would be looking after the day-to-day affairs.

In this, Godwin had mistaken his woman. Mary meant to emulate the success of *Caleb Williams*, a book still popular with the circulating libraries fifty years later, with a novel of her own. Her first, *Mary*, had been dashed off; if *Maria, or The Wrongs of Woman* showed more feeling than art, it was not for lack of hard endeavour. With a book to write, she had no time to waste on housekeeping. She was, she told Godwin, no more fitted to the unpleasant business of daily dealings with 'trades-people' than he was himself; besides, 'my time appears to me, as valuable as that of any other persons accustomed to employ themselves.'[3] Neither would she accept instructions about her choice of social engagements. She was willing to sacrifice a country outing to meet Hannah, her new sister-in-law, but she was not prepared to be told whether or not she might dine alone with Godwin's playwright friend, Thomas Holcroft. 'I like to see new faces, as a study,' she defended herself, although Holcroft's face was perfectly familiar to her.[4]

There are many moments in the correspondence between this strong-willed couple to remind us of the passion with which they had disagreed at their first meeting. Godwin was forty-one; his wife was thirty-eight. They were too old to surrender the habits they had formed, and the sense of independence was strong on both sides. It seemed to Godwin, when he took a long jaunt out of town to the west Midlands in June, that he was behaving like the most dutiful of husbands. He had made himself amiable to Mary's sister Everina, a woman who turned out to have all his wife's spirit but little of her charm. (Everina was employed as a governess at the Staffordshire family home of Godwin's benefactor, young Tom Wedgwood.) He had chosen a pretty little Staffordshire mug for Fanny with her initial in a garland of flowers. He had written almost every day. Mary had no need to chide him, he thought, for extending his stay to catch a glimpse of Lady Godiva at Coventry Fair. It did not occur to him that gawping at a slender beauty in a 'close dress' was not the most tactful pleasure to share with a pregnant wife. A little delay, he wrote briskly, was 'not necessarily tragical'.[5]

All delays and absences were tragical to a woman who lived in terror of being deserted again. After icily acknowledging that it must indeed have been tempting to stay for such a fine show, Mary asked if he thought his wife as unfeeling as 'a stick or a stone'. For himself, he had clearly forgotten how to think or to feel; as for her, 'I am afraid to add what I feel. Good-night.'[6]

Mary had right on her side. Godwin was a kind man and a good man, but he lacked emotional intuition. He himself admitted that he had no tact. (In another letter dating from his journey to Staffordshire, he referred to a new female acquaintance as clever enough to outshine all the goddesses of the Pantheon; news of a young friend's marriage plans produced the thought that it was like hearing of a prison sentence to hard labour.) Godwin was baffled by his wife's distress when he indicated the flaws in her religious beliefs; he was puzzled by her anger over the siege laid to him that summer by a young lady to whom Mary had initially been kind. Shaw's Professor Higgins could not have been more perplexed than Godwin by his wife's inability to be reasonable, to behave like a man.

If Godwin and Mary sometimes sound like Katherine and Petruchio at war, the confessions of their mutual love have all the corresponding sweetness of an honest and robust relationship. 'Take care of yourself, my love, & take care of William. Do not you be drowned, whatever I am,' Godwin wrote just after setting off on his country jaunt that June with Basil Montagu, a clever young man who had temporarily thrown over his law studies to learn philosophy from the author of *Political Justice*. 'I remember at every moment all the accidents to which your condition subjects you . . .'[7] And Mary, missing her husband even before his letter had arrived, confessed that the first frisks of 'Master William' in her womb made her anticipate the baby's birth 'as a fresh twist to a knot, which I do not wish to untie'. Her love for him had grown, she added, even beyond 'when I promised to love you for ever . . . You are a tender, affectionate creature; and I feel it thrilling through my frame giving and promising pleasure.' Of course, as a thoroughly modern wife, she did not wish to have him 'always at my elbow', but then she grew wistful and added that 'at this moment I did not care if you were.'[8]

When, later, Godwin found himself trying to imagine the happy state in which Mary had spent her first months with Gilbert Imlay, he had his own experience to draw on. Like Imlay, he had watched her emerge from the shadow of a disappointed love into light and confidence. She was, he wrote, a female version of Goethe's Werther, one of those rare beings 'endowed with the most exquisite and delicious sensibility, whose minds seem almost of too fine a texture to encounter the vicissitudes of human affairs, to whom pleasure is transport, and disappointment is agony indescribable'. But under the spell of love, her whole nature was transformed. In unmistakably sexual imagery, he compared her to a serpent on a rock which had sloughed its old skin to display the brilliant sleekness of youth. Here, and in the description which follows, we are seeing not Imlay's Mary, but Godwin's.

She was playful, full of confidence, kindness and sympathy. Her eyes assumed new lustre, and her cheeks new colour and smoothness. Her voice became chearful; her temper overflowing with universal kindness; and that smile of bewitching tenderness from day to day illuminated her countenance, which all who knew her will so well recollect, and which won, both heart and soul, the affection of almost every one that beheld it.[9]

This is the Mary Wollstonecraft we see in the portrait which John Opie painted of her that summer, with the curve of a smile rounding her cheek, the softness of the famous auburn hair carelessly bound up behind, and the swell of her stomach frankly exposed to view by the new high-waisted style which allowed liberated – and pregnant – ladies to leave off their merciless stays. Here, and in Godwin's memorable description, is the matchless Mary he loved, even if he did not always understand her. That came later, in the painful months when he was collecting material for her life.

The greatest bond between them was their unborn child, referred to so often and so tenderly in their letters. They began to call each other 'mama' and 'papa' as they discussed the way their William would be brought up. Mary adored children. In her brief career as a governess in Ireland with the Kingsborough family, she had won the enduring devotion of little Margaret King who, as Lady Mountcashell, would later take pride in claiming that her ideas on education were based on the practical and kindly teachings of Mary Wollstonecraft. The letters Mary wrote to Imlay from Sweden are at their most moving in their references to Fanny, the 'frolicker' and 'cherub' over whose uncertain future she agonized. Her views on education altered as she matured, but they were linked by an enduring faith in love as the key to all. Sharing Godwin's memory of an unhappy and neglected childhood, she shared with him too a conviction that the recipe for success in life lay in a happy and secure upbringing. In a passage from *A Vindication of the Rights of Woman* which caught Mary Shelley's eye long before she wrote about Frankenstein's reviled monster-child, her mother observed that a 'great proportion of the misery that wanders, in hideous forms, around the world, is allowed to rise from the negligence of parents'.[10]

Female education had been a subject of primary importance to Mary long before she gave birth to a daughter. Much of *A Vindication* had been written as an attack on Rousseau's *Emilius* (*Emile*), a book which she disliked as strongly as she admired *La Nouvelle Héloïse*.

Angered by Rousseau's emphasis on women as the weak, dependent pupils of their husbands, formed to flatter, captivate and allure but never to think for themselves, Mary stressed the importance of equal opportunity. Girls, in her view, would benefit from sharing in the vigorous exercise permitted to their brothers. (She had painful childhood memories of being kept sitting in useless activity for hours at a time by a vicious father and a mother who never resisted his will.) Girls should be co-educated in day schools for all social classes and tutored, until the age of nine, in a wide range of subjects which would include anatomy, medicine and the art of debate. Sex education could be given from the self-evident examples of domestic pets. Neatness of appearance was unfailingly emphasized. (We get a nice sidelight on contemporary life in Wollstonecraft's reproaches to women too idle to take off their party dresses before crawling into bed.) Modesty, of the kind which Rousseau praised as a form of calculated titillation, was abhorrent to her. Education had achieved its ends if it produced self-respecting, reasoning women who saw no shame in earning their own keep.

Like Godwin, and Locke before him, Mary was vigorously opposed to the notion that children should be restrained and checked. Many of the most remarkable women, she noted, had been allowed liberty when young. It was a principle she had put into practice when she was in charge of Margaret King; under her care, Margaret had flourished.

Experience had softened some of Mary's views. Vanity, which she had seen as a dangerous vice in *A Vindication*, had come to seem no more than an 'enviable harmless' quality, producing a charming 'gai[e]té du coeur' in the young women she met in France.[11] Godwin had taught her to see that the reading of novels was not such a depraved activity as she had previously supposed. And, while she had once thought that 'women of sensibility', that is, women of feeling, were the least fitted to look after young girls, she now believed that stimulating a child's imagination was among the most important aspects of its upbringing.

The best guide to Godwin and Mary's thoughts on education is *The Enquirer*, the collection of essays which Godwin wrote while he and Mary were discussing the upbringing of their unborn child. It is a work which starts from and constantly reverts to a single thought, that 'The true object of education, like that of every other moral process, is the generation of happiness.'[12] A happy child, these liberated parents thought, would be inquiring, cheerful, affectionate and articulate. To help it become so, there should be no threats, no sense of force, censure or restriction. 'I cannot ardently love a person who is continually warning me not to enter his premises, who plants a hedge about my path, and thwarts me in the impulses of my heart,' Godwin wrote, remembering the harsh ways of his own early teacher, Samuel Newton of Norwich.[13] Don't condescend, he warned; remember that children are to be brought up, not the adult down. Reason with them. Encourage them to grow beyond you and to relish the modern world of science and discovery. Let them see what is wrong in the world as well as what is good. Above all, let them choose for themselves.

The Enquirer is a remarkable book, generous, hopeful, compassionate and wise. Reading it brings us close to the Godwins and their way of thinking; here, Mary's sensibility is perfectly matched to Godwin's dream of creating a wholly benevolent society.

In 1795, Mary had begun a child's primer called *Lessons*, intended as the first of a series of books for little Fanny, then one year old.[14] In 1797, she took it out and started making additions intended for the new baby. 'See how much taller you are than William,' she tells Fanny in Lesson X; in Lesson XI: 'I carry William, because he is too weak to walk.'

Another of these endearing short lessons invites Fanny to dry her tears after a fall and come out for a walk in the fields. Mary's letters give us other glimpses of such expeditions. Both Maria Reveley and Eliza Fenwick had toddlers of an age to romp with Fanny and, as the grass parched in a strange, turbulent summer of violent storms and excessive, suffocating heat, the children were often taken out into the flat fields lying on the north side of the Polygon, to play at haymaking with miniature rakes and pitchforks. Mary, no believer in languishing on a daybed during the months approaching childbirth, went on long walks with her husband, strolling under a parasol across Lamb's Conduit Fields, up to the inns and noisy staging posts of Holborn and on to the booksellers of Ludgate Hill where pleasant gossip was to be gleaned. Sometimes they walked out early, past the tea-gardens and the modest homes which workmen were beginning to build for themselves on the eastern fringes of Somers Town, to breakfast in the shady hamlet of Sadler's Wells. Mary's health was excellent, but she had to remind the inexperienced Godwin not to walk too fast. She was looking forward to liberation from the frisky burden of Master William.

Inclement weather often kept them indoors. The storm of 16 July was felt all over the country. In London, not even the oldest inhabitant could remember anything to equal it; a contributor to the *Gentleman's Magazine* recalled 'the fiery agitation of the firmament seeming momentarily to threaten the earth with universal conflagration . . . the consequences cannot be contemplated without horror.'[15] The storms continued with almost equal violence into the third week of August; a week earlier, the King's Assistant Astronomer, Caroline Herschel, was the first to sight a new comet in the sky. To the Godwins, it was an augury of hope. 'And thou, strange Star,' Mary Shelley wrote twenty-five years later:

> ascendant at my birth
> Which rained, they said, kind influence on the earth,
> So from great parents sprung I dared to boast
> Fortune my friend . . .[16]

On the evening of 29 August, Godwin and his wife sat cosily reading a favourite book, *The Sorrows of Young Werther*. 'En famille,' Godwin fondly wrote in his journal, relishing the prospect of his first child's arrival. 'I have no doubt of seeing the animal* today,' Mary reported to him the following morning; she allayed his anxiety with a calm request for a novel or a newspaper to while away the tedium of waiting.[17]

Ideally, Godwin would have liked his wife to be attended by a male doctor, probably his friend, the chemist and surgeon Anthony Carlisle. But Mary overruled him. A midwife was all she required. Fanny's birth had given her no trouble. She expected to be up for dinner the following day. Godwin was still working in his rooms that afternoon when a note from Mary arrived, telling him that Mrs Blenkinsop, an experienced midwife from the Westminster Lying-in Hospital, was in attendance and a safe delivery was confidently expected, 'but that I must have a little patience'.[18] Strangely, they were the words which her mother had spoken just before her death.

It took nine hours for the baby to be born. Godwin was summoned in shortly before midnight to see, not the expected William, but a healthy baby daughter, a new Mary. It was a joyful moment, lovingly recalled in several of his novels. A short time later, the midwife asked him to send for assistance. The afterbirth had not come away. It was

---

* Odd though it sounds to our ears, 'animal' was a word frequently applied to babies. In 1795, Wollstonecraft had reported to Imlay of Fanny that 'my animal is well' and was being weaned.

two in the morning, but Godwin was sufficiently alarmed by Mrs Blenkinsop's manner to take a carriage across London to the Westminster Hospital.* He brought back Dr Poignand, the only member of the Royal College of Physicians who also held a licence as a midwife.

Poignand shared Mrs Blenkinsop's concern. He went to work at once and continued for a period of hours until he believed all of the placenta had been pulled free. He probably worked with his bare hands. Mary told Godwin the next day that she had never known such pain.

Both Anthony Carlisle and George Fordyce, a doctor Mary had known and trusted for almost fifteen years, were reassuring when they visited the Polygon that day, a Thursday. All was going to be well. Fanny was dispatched for a short holiday with the Reveleys; Godwin felt easy enough to go back to his work room.

Sunday was the turning point. Godwin had invited his sister to dine at the Polygon with her friend, Louisa Jones, a young woman who was being considered for the post of nurse to Mary and Fanny. He came back from a visit across town to hear that his wife had been suffering from shivering fits. The guests were hastily put off. Mary asked Godwin to eat in the little ground-floor parlour instead of the dining-room on the first floor which was directly below her bedroom. Perhaps she wanted to avoid alarming him; her next shivering fit was so violent that the floorboards rattled.

The following day, Fordyce gave Mary the heartbreaking news that she must stop feeding her baby in case her milk poisoned it. She tried to join in the laughter when puppies were brought to drain her overflowing breasts. By now, a terrible play was in progress. Mary seemed to believe she would recover; Godwin had been quietly informed that there was little hope. On Wednesday, summoned by an anxious Basil Montagu at Godwin's request, Anthony Carlisle arrived to take charge of the frightened household. His sweetness and consideration had helped them all to endure, Godwin told him later; he was a hero among men.

Carlisle, later knighted for his services as Surgeon Extraordinary to the Prince Regent, was renowned for his kindness and for an uncommon faculty for making friends. He was not, however, regarded with

---

* The name is misleading: the hospital was, until 1834, no more than a large dispensary for the local area. Surgeons were, however, attached to it; Anthony Carlisle, who had been the principal surgeon there since 1783, did much to get the hospital enlarged and improved. The lying-in hospital was separately housed.

much respect by his fellow surgeons,* and Fordyce was notoriously erratic in his diagnoses. It does not follow that any other doctor could have done better. Puerperal fever was common enough to wipe out whole wards of women at a time, but by 1797 only one Scottish doctor, Alexander Gordon, witnessing an outbreak in Aberdeen, had made a tentative connection between the birth attendant and the rapid spread of infection. All poor Godwin could gather from the many doctors who attended his wife at the Polygon during the dreadful last ten days of her life was that the afterbirth had been insufficiently extracted. In fact, had it been left in place to expel itself naturally, Mary might have survived. The disease was introduced on the hands that endeavoured to save her.

Godwin was constantly in Mary's room during the last three days of her life. So were Mary Hays, Eliza Fenwick and Mary's devoted maid, Marguerite. Four male friends kept vigil in the ground-floor parlour, in case any messages could be run; Carlisle was in constant attendance. On Friday, 8 September, Godwin tried to discover his wife's wishes regarding the children without disclosing the hopelessness of her case. (Carlisle insisted that her hopes of recovery should be encouraged.) Godwin's diary for that day recorded a 'solemn communication', although his subsequent memoir of Wollstonecraft states that she had nothing to communicate. Mary did have one message to give. Shortly before her death, she whispered to Eliza Fenwick that Godwin was 'the kindest, best man in the world'.[21]

She died on the morning of 10 September. Godwin noted the time but not the fact in his journal. For a man who resolutely opposed the comforting notion of an afterlife, the loss was absolute. In *St Leon*, the novel which he wrote the following year and in which his friend Holcroft found a moving portrait of Mary in Marguerite de Damville, he relived the birth of his child, the death of his wife, and the void into which he knew she had gone.

---

* 'As a surgeon he was far inferior in every way to his colleagues Anthony White, James Guthrie and William Lynn,' wrote J.F. Clarke in *Recollections of the Medical Profession* (1874).[19] Carlisle must nevertheless have seemed the best man available. He was the leading surgeon at the Westminster Hospital, a position he retained until 1840; he had studied under the great John Hunter at the Windmill Street school; he was held indispensable by the Prince Regent; Carlisle took a lively interest in the advance of medical science. The explorer and surgeon Mungo Park rated him highly enough to bestow his own medical instruments on him; in 1834, he became a willing adviser and mentor to the anatomist and paleontologist Richard Owen in the year of Owen's influential lectures on generation to the Royal College of Surgeons.[20] Later in life, Carlisle acquired a reputation for being vain and crotchety; this was not true of the man on whom Godwin's household gratefully relied in 1797.

Great God of heaven! what is man? and of what are we made? Within that petty frame resided for years all that we worship, for there resided all that we know and can conceive of excellence. That heart is now still. Within the whole extent of that frame there exists no thought, no feeling, no virtue. It remains no longer, but to mock my sense and scoff at my sorrow, to rend my bosom with a woe, complicated, matchless and inexpressible . . . I never loved but once; I never loved but Marguerite.[22]

He could not bring himself to follow Holcroft's urging and deliver Mary's body up for useful dissection. A death mask was made. Tresses of her lovely hair were cut and preserved in the custom of the time, for himself and for the children. Opie either gave or sold him the life-like portrait to hang in the room which had been hers, and which Godwin now made his. The finality of death made it all the more important that her memory should be kept alive.

The funeral was held on 15 September at the little field-enclosed church of St Pancras where Godwin and Mary had married only a few months before. A grave was dug in the north-east corner of the churchyard.* None of the friends Godwin had urged to attend were believers, but only one, George Tuthill, refused to compromise himself by entering a church, even when Godwin begged him to abandon 'so cold a reflection'.[23]

Misery rather than principle kept Godwin himself loitering wretchedly in James Marshall's lodgings, where he tried to read a book about child education before writing a letter of gratitude to Anthony Carlisle. He could not trust himself to write about 'the dear deceased'; he hoped that Carlisle reciprocated the love he felt for a man who combined 'so clear and capacious an understanding, with so much goodness of heart and sweetness of manners'. Above the solace of friendship, Godwin asked his friend for the devastating candour which he himself offered only to those he loved: 'But, above all, be severely sincere. I ought to be acquainted with my own defects, and to trace their nature in the effects they produce.' Unusually, for a man of restrained expression, he signed the letter, 'with fervent admiration and regard'.[24] From any other man, it would have seemed an extraordinary letter to write during the funeral of his wife. It was entirely in keeping with the character of William Godwin.

The baby was brought home from Mrs Reveley's two days after the funeral. She was now the only Mary in Godwin's life. Hoping to

---

* This part of the churchyard was demolished to make way for the new railway line some sixty years later.

identify in her the qualities of his late wife, Godwin persuaded Carlisle's friend, the physicist William Nicholson, to undertake a phrenological examination on 18 September. Nicholson, no expert, did his best and sent his assessment on the same day. The baby had been squalling during the examination, and his chief concern had been to reassure the widower that there was no physical evidence of a difficult nature; 'resigned vexation', perhaps, but no indication of 'sullenness' or 'scorn'. The area encompassing the eyes and brows showed again that she was 'surely not given to rage'. The shape of the head suggested 'considerable memory and intelligence', but 'it would be silly to risk a character' on such a brief assessment.[25]

We do not know whether Godwin took comfort from this; we do know that he was eager to establish a firm distinction between the child of Gilbert Imlay and his own. He had always argued that children are born intellectually equal; in the first year of Mary's life, he recorded a change in his views. Education remained 'a powerful instrument, yet there exist differences of the highest importance between human beings from the period of their birth.'[26]

In October 1797, Mary Wollstonecraft was highly enough esteemed for so sedate a publication as the *Gentleman's Magazine* to publish the following tribute.

> Her manners were gentle, easy, and elegant, her conversation intelligent and amusing, without the least trait of literary pride, or the apparent consciousness of power above the level of her sex; and, for soundness of understanding, and sensibility of heart, she was, perhaps, never equalled. Her practical skill in education was even superior to her speculations upon that subject; nor is it possible to express the misfortune sustained, in that respect, by her children.[27]

This respectful attitude did not survive the publication, in January 1798, of Godwin's memoir of his wife.

Rousseau's *Confessions* pale beside the unflinching candour with which Godwin presented details which most of his readers would have preferred not to know, or to seem not to know. The *Memoirs of the author of 'The Rights of Woman'* did not allow for the luxury of hypocrisy. Fanny's illegitimacy was as frankly acknowledged as the fact that Godwin's own daughter had been conceived out of wedlock. Mary's suicide attempts, which had previously been the subject of rumour rather than certainty, were no longer left in doubt. Railing against the double standards of women like Elizabeth Inchbald, Godwin did more, in the short term, for her cause than his wife's. The last nail hammered into the coffin of Mary's reputation was his simultaneous publication of the letters she had written to Gilbert Imlay at the height of their affair.

The *Monthly Review*'s contributor, one of the mildest, waited until the autumn issue to wonder what on earth Mr Godwin could have been thinking of when he exhumed a history

> which we must read with pity and concern, but which we would have advised the author to bury in oblivion. Blushes would suffuse the cheeks of most husbands, if they were *forced* to relate those anecdotes of their wives which Mr Godwin voluntarily proclaims to the world.[28]

Others were less kind, notably the Tory journals who already viewed Godwin as a political outcast and his wife as a threat to womanly virtue. The new *Anti-Jacobin Review*'s index for 1798 noted under the heading 'Prostitution': 'See Mary Wollstonecraft.'[29] Hannah More, whose educational views were not radically different from Mary's own, opened her 1799 book on female education with an attack on 'The Female Werter, as she is described by her biographer' for daring to defend adultery.[30] Mary's friend, the philanthropist and biographer William Roscoe, pitied her the fate of being mourned by a husband 'with a heart of stone'.[31]

Scandal and hostile reviews had the predictable effect of making the *Memoirs* more discussed than read. By 1801, the anonymous author of 'The Vision of Liberty' was ready to believe that Godwin had told a story of 'brothel feats of wantonness':

> Being her spouse, he tells, with huge delight,
> How oft she cuckolded the silly clown
> And lent, O lovely piece, herself to half the town.[32]

The damage was enduring. *A Vindication* was not republished until the 1840s.[33]* References to it were hedged by warnings against the character of the author. As late as 1833, the author of a six-volume book on British painters jeered at the 'ridiculous advances' made by Mary to Fuseli, hailed here as 'the Shakespeare of canvas' for his celebrated engravings of Shakespeare's plays. Reviewing this, the *Quarterly* wondered if the author had been able to transcribe without

---

* Strangely, neither Godwin nor his daughter showed any interest in republishing Mary Wollstonecraft's most important work.

laughing Mr Godwin's account of a relationship based on '"refined sentiment, and the simple deduction of morality and reason." Refined Sentiment!' jeered the *Quarterly*. 'Morality and Reason!'[34]

The *Memoirs* cost Godwin several friendships and helped to identify him as a cold-blooded monster. The fault was not all his, and he probably knew it. Publications like the *Anti-Jacobin Review*, which had a secret subsidy from the government, were dedicated to ridiculing anyone whose ideas offered a threat to the establishment; *Political Justice*, with its proposals for a self-governing benevolent society of equals, made Godwin a prime target for the review's crude satire. He was known to be against marriage and official religion; he was (wrongly) believed to favour abortion, easy divorce and infanticide. The *Memoirs* enabled the government's supporters to tar Mary with the same sticky brush. From 1798 on, Godwin and his late wife were repeatedly singled out as wrong-headed, irresponsible enemies of public safety, the kind of loose-living idealists of whom honest Englishmen should beware.

Little Mary knew nothing of this. Her mother was spoken of with a love amounting to veneration by her father and by the women whose comforting arms embraced her. The mother she knew was the warm-eyed lady who smiled from the wall in her father's study, whose grave she was taken to visit when she was still too small to understand quite what death meant.

It is hard to be sure at what point and to what degree Mary felt that her own birth had robbed this beautiful, vital woman of her life – her mother was only thirty-eight when she died. Frankenstein's creation of a child he perceives as abhorrent may tell us something dark and troubling about Mary's view of herself. It reveals nothing of her feelings towards Mary Wollstonecraft. But it is worth noticing how closely the infamous creation scene is linked to one of Victor Frankenstein's most nightmarish fantasies. He has already seen the Creature move and open an eye when, retreating to his bedroom, he has a hideous vision of his beloved cousin, Elizabeth Lavenza.

> I thought I saw Elizabeth, in the bloom of health, walking in the streets of Ingolstadt. Delighted and surprised, I embraced her, but as I imprinted the first kiss on her lips, they became livid with the hue of death; her features appeared to change, and I thought that I held the corpse of my dead mother in my arms; a shroud enveloped her form, and I saw the grave-worms crawling in the folds of flannel.[35]

Waking, Frankenstein is confronted by his own and to his eyes, hateful creation as, smiling, it stretches a hand towards him. His response is to rush away from it. Does the clue to Frankenstein's hysterical aversion to his 'child' lie in the horrible train of connections its birth has mysteriously stimulated? His mother died, as we have already been informed, from a fever caught from Elizabeth. Mary may well have blamed herself for the puerperal fever of which Mary Wollstonecraft died. No doctor knew enough to lift that troubling conviction from her mind. Godwin, however privately, may have shared it.

One could fill a book – and many books have been filled – with such speculations.[36] But it is not always wise to see Mary Shelley's fictions as exactly reflecting the truth. 'He adored my mother,' she wrote in one of her short souvenir album stories; 'he mourned for her to the verge of insanity; but his grief was silent, devouring, and gloomy.'[37] It sounds just right; surely this is how William Godwin must have been after Mary's death? Godwin's distress was great and sincere, but by April 1798 he was looking for a new wife.

Mary did not open the *Memoirs* until she was past girlhood. Reading them in the full knowledge of her mother's fallen reputation, she understood for the first time the danger of absolute candour. The *Memoirs* offered her a lesson which, however contrary it was to her father's teaching, she took to heart: telling the truth does not require the whole truth to be told. 'You misunderstand me,' observes a lady in a tale Mary Shelley never completed:

> I do not demand that you should make any confessions, but merely relate those events that have taken place that have reference to yourselves – not telling all the truth if you have anything you wish to conceal (and who has not?), but promising not to falsify any thing.[38]

CHAPTER THREE

FATHER AND DAUGHTER

1798 – 1801

'Tell Mary I will not give her away, and she shall be nobody's little girl but papa's.'

William Godwin to James Marshall, 11 July 1800

STEPMOTHERS DO NOT APPEAR TO ADVANTAGE IN MARY'S fictions. In her later writings, however, the love between fathers and daughters is presented in terms of almost religious intensity. 'When a father is all that a father may be . . . the love of a daughter is one of the deepest and strongest, as it is the purest passion of which our natures are capable,' Mary wrote in 1830.[1] Five years later, in another story, 'The Elder Son', she described a father whose reserved manner and measured style of speech masked the strength of his feelings.

> He never caressed me; if ever he stroked my head or drew me on his knee, I felt a mingled alarm and delight difficult to describe. Yet, strange to say, my father loved me almost to idolatry; and I knew this and repaid his affection with enthusiastic fondness, notwithstanding his reserve and my awe. He was something greater, and wiser, and better, in my eyes, than any other being. I was the sole creature he loved; the object of all his thoughts by day and his dreams by night.[2]

This heightened feeling appears again in *Lodore*, published in 1835. In this novel, Mary isolated a father and his baby girl in a remote American settlement. As in 'The Elder Son', the eponymous hero is shown as a chilling figure whose chief object of devotion is his child; again, Mary offers a portrait of exclusive love, while emphasizing that it can only flourish when complete obedience has been enforced. It takes no more than a disapproving look from Lord Lodore to make his daughter Ethel 'turn as with a silken string, and bend at once to his will'. But the rewards are great.

> She grew into the image on which his eye doated, and for whose presence his heart perpetually yearned. Was he reading, or otherwise occupied, he was restless, if yet she were not in the room; and she would remain in silence for hours, occupied by some little feminine work, and all the while watching him, catching his first glance towards her, and obeying the expression of his countenance, before he could form his wish into words. When he left her for any of his longer excursions, her little heart would heave, and almost burst with sorrow.[3]

In fiction, Mary could recreate the past and see herself as the chief and adored companion of a lonely father. This is not quite how it had been. Godwin's journal shows that he briskly returned to his old way of life, working first on the *Memoirs* and then on a play, 'Alonzo' (later retitled *Antonio*). He resumed his regular visits to the theatre; he dined out, frequently, with friends. Concerned though he was for the welfare of his little girls, his work took precedence over their needs. Mary's fictional fathers subdue their children with disapproving looks; so had Godwin: 'the idea of his silent quiet disapprobation makes me weep as it did in the days of my childhood,' she would write to her husband in 1817, when she was twenty.[4]

One work suggests that there had been a softening in Godwin's nature from which Fanny and Mary might have benefited. The subject of *St Leon*, the novel he wrote in 1798–9, was the difficult and isolated position of the man who knows he is truth's oracle. Godwin's work had isolated him; St Leon's acquisition of the elixir vitae and the philosopher's stone attracts envy, hatred and, eventually, results in his being cut off from the human race. The character of Bethlem Gabor, a good man made into a misanthropic monster by the murder of his family, is the best thing in the lamentably confused fourth volume of this novel.* Of significance to Godwin's disciples and to his children was the retraction he made in the Preface. Alluding to the justice which he had pre-

---

* Mary did not read *St Leon* until her teens, when Gabor's combination of nobility and malevolence struck her sufficiently for her to draw on his nature and situation for Frankenstein's creature.

viously argued should be sternly impartial, he now acknowledged that justice was 'not incompatible' (Godwin loved his double negatives) with a 'culture of the heart'. Further than this, he recognized that 'domestic and private affections' were an inseparable part of man's nature. These were the retractions of a man warmed by the affection of an impulsive, warm-hearted woman, and Mary Wollstonecraft's influence is apparent throughout the novel in St Leon's Wordsworthian raptures over the beauty of nature and the solace it offers. The man who wrote in this spirit and with such evident sincerity cannot have been altogether stern as a parent. His daughter's fictional fathers veer strikingly between icy remoteness and passionate, demanding affection. This is probably an accurate reflection of Godwin's behaviour. He loved his child; he would not allow her emotional needs to take precedence over his customary habits.

It is unlikely that either Fanny or little Mary were aware of the determination with which Godwin set about finding a second wife after their mother's death. Rebuffed in the summer of 1798 by Harriet Lee, an authoress he had met on a brief visit to Bath, he proposed to the recently widowed Maria Reveley. But Maria had another suitor. Instead of Godwin, she married John Gisborne, a moderately successful merchant with cultivated tastes and an interesting family.* Maria and her new husband set off in 1800 to make a new life in Italy; Godwin set about looking elsewhere. His presentation of a copy of St Leon to Elizabeth Inchbald, together with a strong hint that he might call on her at home, suggests that his intentions were serious. Mrs Inchbald, who had not forgiven his scandalous relationship with an unmarried woman, or the way he had chosen to relate her sordid history, told him to stay away.

Marriage had given the virginal Godwin a taste for sensual pleasure; wooing the middle-aged Harriet Lee, he warned her against the atrophying effects of celibacy while he extolled the 'Promethean fire' sparked by affection and parental love.[5] But the children and the care of them were his main concerns. 'The poor children!' he wrote to Mary Wollstonecraft's old friend Mrs Cotton shortly after his wife's death. In theory, few men were better equipped to educate their daughters than Godwin; in practice, he mournfully acknowledged

---

* One sister married the musician and composer, Muzio Clementi; another married the astrologer and watercolourist, John Varley.

that he lacked the proper experience and understanding by which 'to direct the infant mind. I am the most unfit person for this office; she was the best qualified in the world. What a change.'[6]

Rejections did not discourage him from the search for a woman who would cherish and supervise the little girls. His need to find a wife was strengthened by a well-founded fear that Mary Wollstonecraft's sisters, disapproving of the *Memoirs* and terrified of the book's possible effect on the reputation of the school they had opened in Dublin, might hit back by staking a claim to Fanny and baby Mary. To lose his pets to a couple of grim and hostile aunts in Ireland was an intolerable prospect.

In the absence of a mother, Fanny and Mary were nevertheless surrounded by loving attention. Louisa Jones, with whose sisters Godwin stayed when he began courting Harriet Lee in Bath, presided over the Polygon as housekeeper and nurse for the first fifteen months of Mary's life. An awkwardness which arose when Miss Jones became involved with a protégé of Godwin's, John Arnot, was resolved by a new arrangement in which Miss Jones moved out and visited on a daily basis. Marguerite Fourneé, Mary Wollstonecraft's maid, who had cared for Fanny since babyhood, stayed on in the house and continued to help out after marrying a French neighbour at the close of 1799; Cooper, a cheerful nursemaid who doted on Mary, supervised their daily routine. Eliza Fenwick, a mother herself and one of Mary Wollstonecraft's staunchest admirers, kept a fond eye on the little girls.

Godwin's family, to whom he had always been so unstintingly kind, took a strong interest in the new baby. Mary saw her aunt Hannah every fortnight when she came to dine at the Polygon; uncles and young cousins dropped in to inspect her, while the number of visits made by Godwin's good-hearted but imprudent sister-in-law Harriet (Joseph's wife) suggests that she often helped out with nursing duties. Anthony Carlisle, refusing to take any payment for his calls, was able to advise when the children were ill and when, alarmingly, Mary suffered a dangerous fall in the first four months of her life.

The excitement of a new grandchild could not tempt old Mrs Godwin away from the Norfolk farm where wartime conditions had reduced them to a diet of meal, bread and pancakes, but Mary provided a diversion from her continuing worries about Hannah's lack of religion, Harriet's spendthrift ways and Natty's failure to find a wife or a steady job. Between thanking Godwin for getting a nephew into the Bluecoat School and fretting over the awful vision of penniless Godwins adrift in a city of vice and playgoing, Ann deluged the

Polygon with gifts and questions. Had Mary been weaned yet? Was she being properly fed? Had Godwin remembered his late wife's sensible views on the benefit to children of fresh air and exercise? She knitted socks and mittens; she sent material for making little dresses; she lavished gifts. A garnet set in enamel was followed by an amethyst set between two 'sparks' and a precious snuffbox, a family treasure, which Godwin put away for his daughter with the tresses of Mary Wollstonecraft's hair and a ring which had belonged to Fanny Blood, her mother's dearest friend.

Women naturally gathered where there were motherless babies to be cherished, but the tall house in the Polygon also attracted a number of men more interested in talking to Godwin than seeing his daughters. William Hazlitt, whose family had a long history of friendship with the Godwins, made frequent visits; so did an observant young lawyer, Henry Crabb Robinson, whose diaries still carry a faint aromatic whiff of pipe-smoke between their tightly packed pages. The year 1800 also marked the beginning of a close and enduring friendship between Godwin and Charles Lamb. A small, pale, nervous-mannered young man with a disproportionately large and noble head, Lamb earned his living as a clerk at East India House and with his elder sister Mary kept a home as oddly cheerful as any from a novel by Dickens. Gin, whist and smoking were Lamb's modest vices. Volatile and bright as a dragonfly in his rapid, charmingly inconsequential conversation, Lamb easily masked the sadness of living with a sister he adored but who, from time to time, reverted to madness – the madness which had, in 1796, led her to kill their mother, to whom she had been a devoted child. More than a little unbalanced himself, Lamb was intrigued and sometimes alarmed by Godwin's eccentric behaviour; he was unaware of how anxiously his host was recording the spates of 'deliquium' which often afflicted him after his wife's death. They added to Godwin's fears for the children. Carlisle sensibly advised him to take a rest from his work; Godwin was too poor and too conscientious to listen.

James Marshall was a regular presence in the Polygon as Godwin's secretary and general factotum; gentle and affectionate, he was regarded almost as a second father by the children. Characters like Collins the gardener are too shadowy to distinguish. But the visitor who took to them most strongly from the first was the Lambs' beloved friend, Samuel Coleridge. Red-lipped, large-eyed and so brilliant in his unstoppable loquacity that even Godwin, who liked to guide conversation, sat and listened, Coleridge erupted into their lives like a meteor in the winter of 1799. He came for meals and stayed for days.

The habit of daily prayer with the children at the end of each day, though it needed the atheistical Godwin's acquiescence, was probably Coleridge's introduction. His recital one evening of 'The Rime of the Ancient Mariner' left Mary, hiding behind a sofa when she should have been in bed, with an unforgettable memory of an ice-bound sea and a man haunted by the swift, unstoppable treading in his wake of 'a frightful fiend'. The image stuck; it haunts the story of *Frankenstein.*

A new father himself, Coleridge was overcome by the pathos of the little motherless Godwins, whose unchildlike silence appalled him when he first met them. 'Kisses for Mary and Fanny – God love them!' he wrote after his move to the Lake District in the spring of 1800.[7] When his second child was born – Godwin gently declined the role of godfather – Coleridge could think of no finer compliment than to see a resemblance in Derwent's charming plumpness to pretty little Mary.[8] Disappointed by Godwin's refusal to be tempted away from the city into cottage bliss at Keswick, Coleridge comforted himself with memories of their pleasant conversations in the book-lined study of the Polygon, with Mary Wollstonecraft's portrait staring serenely down on them. Godwin was kind, he wrote, to thank him for having softened his emotions, but credit was due elsewhere:

> as to your poetic and physiopathic feelings, I more than suspect that dear little Fanny and Mary have had more to do in that business than I. Hartley sends his love to Mary. 'What? & not to Fanny?' 'Yes – and to Fanny – but I'll *have* Mary.'[9]

Two months after Coleridge's departure, Godwin decided to leave the children and the redecorating of his house in James Marshall's care while he went to Dublin. Godwin's references to 'special' reasons for his first departure from English shores suggest that this was more than a pleasure trip. The Wollstonecraft sisters had finally raised the question he dreaded, of whether they should not take over the care of one or both of the children.

Godwin had no intention of handing either Fanny or Mary, let alone both, to the women who had, despite long histories of dependence on their late sister for help and encouragement – shown no enthusiasm for her achievements. The portrait he had painted of Mary Wollstonecraft in the *Memoirs* stood between them. Godwin was proud of his sincerity; Eliza and Everina regarded it as unforgivable. This difficult encounter was the only flaw in an enjoyable holiday. Godwin's letters to Marshall report with undisguised delight his pleasure in a new friendship with the barrister John Curran ('wild, ferocious, jocular, humorous, mimetic and kittenish; a true Irishman . . .') and in dining with 'three countesses'.[10] Godwin's cynical view of Burke's reverence for the aristocracy did not make him immune to the charms of a title.

One of the three noble ladies was the former Margaret King, the little girl his wife had loved enough to dream of adopting when she went to Mitchelstown as a governess. Margaret was now Lady Mountcashell, a married lady with a brood of children on whom to practise Wollstonecraft's educational methods. Godwin, once he had recovered from the shock of a six-foot countess who dressed from choice as drably as Eliza Fenwick did from necessity, and whose muscular arms were naked almost to the shoulders of her grey gown, was ready to admire her republican spirit as much as her educational methods. Coleridge belonged to the old school of thought which held that children were adorable and transferable playthings; Margaret Mountcashell was the first woman Godwin had met since his wife's death to reassure him that his own approach was absolutely right. 'In what you say concerning the propriety of treating children with mildness, kindness and respect, you express exactly the opinions I have long entertained,' she wrote shortly after his return to England.[11] Like Godwin, she believed in the need to teach children 'as early as possible to think for themselves . . . My greatest object is to make my children happy and virtuous . . .'[12] This aim was good enough as far as quiet, depressive Fanny was concerned; Godwin believed that his own daughter was destined for higher things.

Godwin may have relished the prospect of a break from parental care; he soon found himself missing the caressing company of his little girls. The letters he wrote to James Marshall disclose a tenderness and easy intimacy strikingly at odds with the severe fathers of some of Mary's later fictions. 'You do not tell me whether they have received or paid any visits,' he reproached Marshall, before urging him to tell Mary that 'papa will soon come back again and look out at the coach-window and see the Polygon across two fields from the trunks of the trees at Camden Town. Will Fanny and Mary come to meet me?' Fanny was promised six kisses if she would help Mr Collins in the garden and keep some strawberries and beans for him. 'But then Mary must have six too, because Fanny has six.'[13] He wanted them to know that he thought of them every day and that he had seen no children in Ireland half so lovable as his own.[14] Love could never entirely quell the educator; he also wanted to know how Fanny's reading was progressing (she was still on a spelling book at the age of six) and to have the children follow his route home on maps.

———————

Fanny and Mary lived in a country which was at war with France, but they were surrounded by the chatter of French voices every time they were taken out of the house. The churchyard where their mother was buried was full of French graves; in the two local hospices run by their kindly neighbour, Abbé Carron, old Frenchmen chanted their morning and evening prayers. When Mary followed Fanny to a nearby day-school at the age of four,* their playmates were the children of emigré parents, all, naturally, in favour of England's war against a regime which had forced them into exile. Carron called Somers Town 'little France'; to the less well-disposed, it was 'Botany Bay'.

Somers Town was well organized under the tireless care of Carron, but it never became fashionable. Only one conveyance a day linked it to London and it had the disadvantage of being unpleasantly close to the smoking brickfields which marked the city's slow western march towards Paddington village. But the area was full of life. Watchmakers, goldsmiths and engravers worked behind the windows at street-level; the local volunteer corps, smartly equipped with red, white and blue uniforms, paraded up and down banging drums, blowing whistles and, in their weekly target practice, firing muskets until they were disbanded for subversive behaviour in 1804. A crippled and half-witted muffin-seller, informally known as the Mayor of Garratt, trundled his cart around the square enclosing the Polygon's graceful circle of houses until the nightwatchman began his rounds.

Peeping from the nursery windows at the top of No. 29 The Polygon, Fanny and Mary could look down on the circle of tidily divided gardens behind the house to watch Mr Collins laying the strawberry nets or staking out a bean row. They could see across the fields of Twenty Acres and Fig's Mead to where the tall elms swayed their heads above Camden Town; north-west of them, the bald high dome of Primrose Hill jutted above the fields, looking ever so slightly like Mr Godwin's head. Sometimes, a flash of light and a soft explosion told them that a duel – rarely fatal on this site – was taking place

———

* This may have been the school briefly undertaken by Eliza Fenwick as one of her increasingly desperate ways to earn money. She only found six pupils and the project was rapidly abandoned.

outside Mother Red Cap's tavern at Chalk Farm, known better to Fanny and Mary as the place where they went to drink syllabubs or to see a cow being milked; once, a manned balloon came sailing across the sky from Vauxhall's pleasure gardens, to land in one of the fields just north of their home.

Visits to the city and its entertainments were rare events. Fanny, at the age of four, was taken to a children's play and, with Marshall in attendance, to admire the grotto made by Alexander Pope at Twickenham. Mary, too young for such treats, became familiar with the sandy footpath to St Pancras churchyard where, when she had spelled out the letters on the stone marking her mother's grave, she was free to explore.* As a small girl, she probably took most pleasure in peering through the churchyard fence at the clear, bubbling waters of the Fleet river, still sweet at Somers Town before it began its long inglorious plunge towards the Thames as the dirtiest open sewer in London.

These regular visits to the churchyard helped strengthen Mary's sense of the mother she only knew through Opie's portrait. The little book of 'Lessons' in which she featured as baby William was probably the first she read. Even before she could puzzle out the words of *Original Stories*, the collection of tales Mary Wollstonecraft had written for her pupil in Ireland, Mary could admire the delicately engraved illustrations which the publisher had commissioned for the second and more expensive edition from William Blake, then at the beginning of his artistic career. One showed a mother standing between two little girls, imaginably Fanny and herself. Another showed two dead children lying under the gaze of a tall, gaunt man, not quite human. Someone must have read Mary the accompanying story, of how the man ran away from civilization to live alone, dependent on the kindness of passing strangers. Was it here that the idea of *Frankenstein* was born?

It would seem absurd to be searching for the sources of an eighteen-year-old girl's novel in the impressions of a child if the child's life had been an ordinary one. But Mary's was not ordinary. Quicker and more impressionable than Fanny, she was shown off to

---

* Some confusion surrounds the grave-site. The willows supposedly planted beside it had disappeared or died by 1816; on 5 March 1834, Godwin noted in his journal that one N. Smith and his daughter's publisher Edward Moxon called on him with regard to 'monument, MWG'. Perhaps the earlier grave had been defaced during a period when Wollstonecraft's name was connected with scandal; this could have been a note for a substitute to be erected. It is also possible that Moxon was arranging the installation of the first public monument erected to Mary Wollstonecraft Godwin.

visitors as a Mary Wollstonecraft in the making and brought into the parlour to listen to the conversation of her father and his friends.

Science and physicianship were frequent topics of conversation in Godwin's home, especially when Anthony Carlisle, a staunch believer in medical experiments, was visiting. She was six years old when Carlisle came to the Polygon with a story which no search for *Frankenstein*'s origins can overlook.

It was customary for the bodies of murderers hanged at Newgate to be handed over to doctors for dissection at anatomy theatres. In February 1803, the *Annual Register* reported an experiment on one such victim by John (Giovanni) Aldini which had taken place in front of an assembly of 'professional gentlemen'. Nothing would have kept Carlisle from being there to observe an experiment by the man who was locked in combat with Volta over the question of whether the body contained an electrical 'vital' fluid. Aldini had already shown that he could make a decapitated mastiff kick its legs while the head clashed its jaws in audible rage; on this occasion, a vast machine comprising two hundred and forty metal plates was wired to the corpse's head. This was the result, a disconcerting one even for such a sceptic as Carlisle.

> On the first application of the process to the face, the jaw of the deceased criminal began to quiver, and the adjoining muscles were horribly contorted, and one eye actually opened. In the subsequent course of the experiment, the right hand was raised and clenched, and the legs and thighs were set in motion, and it appeared to all the bystanders that the wretched man was on the point of being restored to life.[15]

The experiment was hurriedly terminated. When repeated at a later date, the corpse jerked up an arm and struck one of the observers in the eye. To a man with Anthony Carlisle's interest in the advancement of medicine,[16] and to Godwin, whose most recent subject (in *St Leon*) had been the danger of seeking ways to prolong life, this offered rich matter for discussion. Electricity's power to animate seemed beyond doubt, but law restricted medical experiments of this kind to the corpses of felons. What if Aldini went further? What if he succeeded in restoring the body of such a villain – the man had been hanged for murdering his spouse – to life?

CHAPTER FOUR

A SHARED LIFE

1801 – 1807

'[Mrs Clairmont] became certainly towards him a meritorious wife; though towards others I doubt both her sincerity and her integrity.'

Henry Crabb Robinson[1]

THE GODWIN FAMILY ACQUIRED A NEW NEIGHBOUR IN THE Polygon in 1801. Writing Godwin's biography in the 1870s, Kegan Paul related that Mr Godwin often liked to sit on the balcony outside his window on pleasant evenings. He was startled but not displeased when the new tenant of No. 27 asked if she had the honour of beholding the immortal author of *Political Justice*. A later version of his first encounter with Mary Jane Clairmont added the detail that, on every subsequent occasion that Godwin walked into the garden of No. 29, Mrs Clairmont would hurry into the garden of No. 27, 'and walk up and down clasping her hands and saying to herself, "You great Being, how I adore you!"'[2]

However the connection came about, Godwin was quickly enslaved. 'Meet Mrs Clairmont,' he noted on 5 May 1801. Three weeks later, Fanny and Mary, now seven and almost four, were taken to make friends with the Clairmont children, five-year-old Charles and three-year-old Jane. On 6 July, the two families set off to Lambeth for a performance of *Puss in Boots* at Astley's Theatre. A week later, Godwin recorded the progress of his new relationship with an 'x' of uncharacteristic curvaceousness: 'x', in Godwin's journal, signified sexual activity. In December, trapped again by an unexpected pregnancy, Godwin went secretively to church in distant

Shoreditch for a second marriage; the baby, born the following June, did not survive.

Godwin already knew Mary Jane for a fibber when he agreed to undergo two marriage services in the same day. The first register presented her as she seemed to be, the widowed Mrs Clairmont; the second named her as a spinster, Mary Jane Vial. A third register entry, made after the birth of William Godwin in 1803, declared Mrs Godwin to have been born a Devereux.

Prodigious detective work has uncovered some of the elusive lady's tracks.[3] Born to Pierre de Vial and his first wife in Exeter, Mary Jane ran away to join her father's relations in France when still a child (possibly in rebellion against his second marriage). Her accounts to Godwin of this exploit – which he greatly admired – and of the elegance to which she became accustomed in France, were close to the truth. The story of her subsequent marriage to Mr Clairmont was a fantasy. There may never have been a Mr Clairmont in her life; there was certainly no husband. Charles, born in 1795, was the son of a Swiss merchant, Charles de Gaulis, who lived with her in Bristol and died in Silesia the following year. Jane was the daughter of a second relationship which appears also to have ended in desertion, followed by penury and incarceration in a debtors' prison.* By May 1801, however, the resilient 'Mrs Clairmont' had raised enough money, probably by translation work, to take a house in the Polygon.

Godwin had hidden his courtship from his friends; perhaps he sensed that they would disapprove. Tactless, gossip-loving and habitually untruthful, Mary Jane struck most of them as a poor substitute for Mary Wollstonecraft. Eliza Fenwick, lured into indiscretion, grew bitter when Godwin reprimanded her for scandalmongering. She had only done as his wife wished, she defended herself; her grovelling letter restored an uneasy peace.[4] Eliza disliked Mary Jane for making trouble; Lamb hated the woman who had robbed his friend of dignity. This 'widow with green spectacles' had made poor Godwin as foolish as Malvolio, all smiles, bows and wriggles, he noted with disgust in November 1801, a month before the marriage.[5] 'Mrs [Godwin] grows every day in disfavour with God and man,' he wrote to a friend eight years later. 'I will be buried with this inscription over me: – "Here lies C.L. the woman-hater" – I mean that hated *one woman*.'[6] He jeered at Mary Jane's big bottom, he mocked her as 'the bad baby' for her

---

* Jane, whose full name was Clara Mary Jane, is better known today as Claire, the name she chose for herself in the autumn of 1814.

tantrums and he cursed her as 'that d—d Mrs Godwin' and 'a damn'd infernal bitch' when, blissfully unaware of his feelings, she came unasked to his home and triggered one of his sister's bad spells by staying too late.[7] Mary Lamb shared his views, telling Hazlitt's wife on one occasion that Mrs Godwin reminded her of the spiteful sister in the fairy story, 'Toads and Diamonds'.[8]

These were not the only enemies Mary Jane made. Henry Crabb Robinson, conceding her merits as a wife, doubted 'her integrity and truthfulness towards others'.[9] (When he met the authoress Anna Jameson in the late 1830s, Robinson found it hard to trust her simply because her face reminded him of Mary Jane's.) James Marshall, evicted from his place at Godwin's fireside, took away shocking memories of a woman whose temper was both 'undisciplined and uncontrolled'; the businessman Francis Place bore this out with an allusion to 'the infernal devil to whom he [Godwin] was married'.[10]

Robinson had at least noted that Mary Jane was a good wife; other sources show a generous, warm-hearted woman. The American Aaron Burr, the disgraced former vice-president, found Mrs Godwin both 'pleasant and amiable' when he was living as an almost friendless fugitive in London in 1808, gratefully dependent on the Godwin family for hospitality and financial aid.[11] Percy Bysshe Shelley's young wife Harriet, although she later changed her mind, was positively enthusiastic. 'There is a very great sweetness marked in her countenance,' she noted after their first meeting in 1812; Mrs Godwin impressed her as 'a woman of very great magnanimity and independence of character'.[12] Old Ann Godwin, meeting her new daughter-in-law for the first time when the couple paid a visit to Norfolk in the autumn of 1803, was also pleasantly impressed by Mary Jane's 'many amiable qualities'. The couple seemed well-suited, 'in such helth and so happy in consulting to make each other so which is butiful in a married state'.[13]

Mary Jane was a troublemaker and a liar; she was not a fool. A skilled translator (her version of *The Swiss Family Robinson* was for many years the standard text), she was knowledgeable, amusing and well-read. Her book about Herne Bay, written late in life, is as full of humour as it is of apt quotations.[14] Her care of the children is borne out by Aaron Burr's comments on the neat and pleasing appearance of 'les goddesses', as he skittishly termed Fanny, Mary and Jane. We have a glimpse of her as a good housekeeper and affectionate wife in a letter written when Godwin was away from home in September 1805. This, she wrote, was how she dreamed of his return:

our bedroom nicely cleaned, the furniture put up, have fancied your arrival at seven, your stepping into more than half our bed, the kind embrace, the cup of coffee all ready, the refreshing slumber for an hour, the broken day, the fete of walking with you to town and idling all the day with you . . . My dearest love . . .[15]

There can be no doubt that Mary Jane often drove her studious husband to distraction. She would bounce out of the house in a rage, announcing her intention of never returning. She would grumble incessantly about the fact that they lived in London and not in the country where, she was convinced, she would find true happiness. She made much of the fact that she had been brought up to expect a ladylike existence. She nagged Godwin to see less of Lamb, Coleridge, Humphry Davy and Carlisle, and more of her own French emigré friends. She wanted control. Man 'has his wife to read him lectures, and rap his knuckles', Godwin noted after thirty years of marriage.[16] But he loved his voluptuous, energetic wife. In a touching letter written in 1812 and proudly cited by his stepdaughter as proof of his devotion, he praised Mary Jane's courage and cheerfulness, regretted the financial difficulties for which he held himself responsible and wondered if she had not deserved to become 'something much better than my wife'.[17]

There is an intriguing gap in the treasure-trove of family papers relating to Mary Godwin's early life. Until 1814 and her impetuous departure from home, not a scrap of a letter or note has survived either from or to her, a fact which becomes even more startling when we know that she was away for the best part of three years, during which Godwin's journal shows that he was in regular correspondence with his daughter. Something, plainly, has been hidden from us, but why and by whom? Did Mary or her nineteenth-century archivists want to obliterate a period in which she angered her father by refusing to show proper deference to his second wife?* Not knowing what the

---

* It is striking that, although letters to Mary's stepsister bear references to Mary's savage temper (see Chapter 21), there are no such indications in the correspondence which passed from Mary to her descendants, much of which was destroyed. It was important for Mary's posthumous reputation that she should seem calm and reasonable; this was only a partial truth. The few hints we have, from E.J. Trelawny, Leigh Hunt and his son Thornton, and to a degree from Godwin himself, leave no doubt that Mary had a fierce temper, but that she was unusually calm until aroused.

letters contained, we can only conjecture, but it is difficult to think of another reason why they should have disappeared.

In the autobiography Mary never wrote, she would certainly have drawn a sharp line across her childhood at the end of the year 1801, when Godwin's second marriage threatened what Mary later described as 'my excessive and romantic attachment to my father'.[18]

Many changes followed Mary Jane's arrival at No. 29. James Marshall, who had been living at the Polygon, was evicted to nearby lodgings; Louisa Jones, Marguerite Fournée and the nursemaid were replaced by a Miss Hooley, a young housemaid called Betsey, a governess, Maria Smith, and Mr Burton, a daily tutor. Fanny, grateful to be spared an attempt in 1805 by her Wollstonecraft aunts to have her sent away to boarding-school, adapted quietly to the new regime. Having begun life as such a rosy, romping child, she had pined since her mother's death. Charles Clairmont's comment that it would be sure to rain on Fanny's birthday gives us a taste of her sad nature; Jane, a bouncy little extrovert, found her gloominess oppressive. Mrs Godwin, doing her best to cheer the girl up, sometimes took her along on visits to friends in the country.

Fanny was docile; Mary, fiercely protective of her relationship with her father, was not. Jane, comically opposite in appearance with her dark curly hair and almost black eyes, remembered the awe she had felt of Mary's cleverness, of her pale skin, intense hazel eyes and – her crowning glory – a nimbus of red-gold hair, fine as a filigree web. Jane gave in to what Godwin disapprovingly called 'baby-sullenness' when she failed to achieve quick results in her lessons; Mary's quiet perseverance showed her up. A little annoyed that Mary should always be seen as the more talented child – both she and Fanny showed a precocious gift for drawing – Mrs Godwin had tutors employed to teach Jane how to sing and play the piano. Envious of the interest shown in Mary by visitors disposed to see her as an infant prodigy, the offspring of a remarkable union, Jane was encouraged to take pride in her Swiss connections and to believe that she was connected to the English peerage on her father's side. The spirit of rivalry was strong. Mary, invited to be on loving terms with her stepmother, kept as cool a distance as it is possible for a small proud girl to maintain.

In later years, Mrs Godwin lamented all the trouble she took to give the girls a ladylike education. Sunday services, attended at the local Anglican church in Somers Town and later at St Paul's, were followed by tests to make sure that the children had listened carefully to the sermons. (This was Godwin's province, although it is unlikely that he, as a non-believer, accompanied them to church.) Meals – nobody ever disputed the fact that Mrs Godwin was an excellent cook – were never discussed. Beds were hard – Mary could not bear to sleep on a soft mattress in later life – while clothing was plain and neat.

The paucity of references to outings in Godwin's diary does not mean there were none without him. There were picnics on Hampstead Heath, outings to tea-gardens, visits to the jolly entertainments which were a part of all London children's lives. (A circus at the Lyceum, for example, offered 'Tight-Rope Dancing by the Child of Promise and Signor Saxoni', 'Horsemanship Unrivalled by the Celebrated Little Devil' and 'The Egg Hornpipe, over twelve eggs, by Mr Robinson blindfolded'.) On Mary's eleventh birthday, she was taken to Westminster Abbey, to admire a bedraggled display of royal waxworks in Abbot Islip's Chapel, along with the abbot in his winding sheet. Madame Tussaud's two hundred effigies, agreeably combining the gory with the sedate, were on view in the Strand; travelling shows of the kind trundled around by Mrs Jarley in *The Old Curiosity Shop* were set up wherever there was space for a booth.

Visits to artists' studios, including Turner's in Harley Street, were Godwin's ruse for firing the children's imaginations; his daughter probably took more pleasure in visiting the Exeter Exchange where, for the huge price of half a crown, real lions and tigers could be stared at and, when prodded, made to roar. On rainy days, armed with brushes and pans of colour, Jane and Mary taught baby William – Godwin's only son was born in 1803 – to read by painting over the syllables in tiny paper-bound books of the kind typified by Eliza Fenwick's *Mary and Her Cat* (1804).

Livelier works than poor, hard-working Mrs Fenwick's had already begun to issue from the Godwin household. Publishing his first children's book in 1803 under the pseudonym of William Scolfield, Godwin made his preface into an attack on the 'modern improvers [who] have left out of their system that most essential branch of human nature the imagination'. Imagination, Godwin argued, 'is the ground-plot upon which the edifice of a sound morality must be erected'. How, he wished to know, could any child be expected to feel interest in stories which had no giants, or dragons or fairies, in which the young were always good and the old always demure and rational?[19]

The book in question was the first volume of *Bible Stories*, later renamed *Sacred Histories*. Written in the direct and appealing style which marked all Godwin's works for children, it presented the Old and New Testament as a series of historical tales. The illustrations (the first showed a maternal-looking angel hovering over the head of a forlorn young lady) must have greatly appealed to motherless Mary; her affection for the stories is borne out by one she later wrote herself, in which she described the boy-hero sobbing over just such tales.[20]

Encouraged by the book's success and by his children's enthusiasm, Godwin followed it in 1805 with a retelling of Aesop's fables. The Preface to *Fables, Ancient and Modern* (the author this time was one 'Edward Baldwin') argued once again that children learned best from lively, imaginative storytelling. Moral conclusions tacked on by earlier writers were replaced by affectionate hints to his own family. 'The Boys and the Frogs' was used as a warning to 'my dear Charles' to be kind to animals, while 'The Country Maid and her Milk Pail' gave a gentle reproach to his daughter. 'You are sometimes thoughtless now; but I am sure you will cure yourself soon, and when you are sixteen or twenty, will be the most considerate creature in the world.' Mary's fondness for the book is borne out by the many allusions in her novels to Godwin's reworking of the story of the two jars, in which the fragile china jar saves herself in a stormy sea by refusing help from her brass sister. Independence, Godwin taught her, is always admirable.

The *Fables* is a delightful work, still readable today. Ignorant of its true authorship, the *Anti-Jacobin* joined the *British Critic* in praising Baldwin's book as the best available version of Aesop.

Godwin was in tune with the times. Despite a vigorous rearguard action being fought by Mrs Sarah Trimmer and her cronies to defend children against the dangerous influence of imaginative writing, the first years of the nineteenth century marked an upsurge in nursery rhymes and fanciful tales. Both Mary Wollstonecraft's old friend William Roscoe and Catherine Dorset (whose novelist sister Charlotte Smith was a close friend of both the Godwins) were producing a mass of charming story-poems, with titles such as *The Butterfly's Ball*, *The Grasshopper's Feast* and *The Lion's Masquerade*. Their illustrator, young William Mulready, had become one of Godwin's protégés; their publisher was Benjamin Tabart, Mrs Godwin's most regular employer in her freelance writing career.

In other circumstances, Mary Jane might have followed Eliza Fenwick and a mass of other hard-up, well-educated women and tried to set up a school. With a husband who so evidently enjoyed writing for children and whose ambitious project to write a history of England as substantial as Hume's would never feed and clothe a growing family, Mrs Godwin persuaded him to consider starting a children's bookshop of their own. Children's books would provide a steady and much needed source of income; among other worries, they needed to find money for Charles's school bills at Charterhouse. (Christ's Hospital, where education was free and excellent, had turned him down.)

The frequency of Godwin's perplexing blackouts may have strengthened his readiness to turn to work which was less intellectually rigorous. The word 'deliquium' had been frequently noted in his diary since Mary Wollstonecraft's death; identifiable now as a form of narcolepsy, it had often amused friends who saw the philosopher falling asleep, apparently from boredom, at dinner-tables. In 1800, the fits had seldom lasted for longer than a minute; in July 1803, he was afflicted with severe attacks over three consecutive days. Godwin had eccentric friends by the score to offer faddish cures, including abstention from wine and meat-eating.* The most convincing diagnosis, given by Anthony Carlisle, was that the 'deliquium' was connected to mental stress.

Innocent of the pitfalls, Godwin willingly listened to Mary Jane's arguments for bookselling as a trade which would provide them with a good income while requiring, in her optimistic view, little mental exertion. Not many years earlier, he had reviled booksellers in one of the *Enquirer* essays as contemptible figures, servile, cringing; now, cheered by the friendliness of his reviews and spurred on by his wife's enthusiasm, he prepared to become one. His daughter would eventually form the view that this was one of the worst decisions he ever made; Godwin would always maintain that it was one of the best.

His own name was too notorious for use; their first enterprise, in a lane of grubby curio kiosks off the Tottenham Court Road, was begun in the name of Hodgkins, the man employed to run the shop. Among its first offerings, along with a handsome line in stationery, were two more books by Godwin, each showing children what results perseverance and intelligence could bring. *The Looking Glass: A True History of the Early Years of an Artist* (1805) used the life of William Mulready to fire lazy Charles with zeal for his schoolwork; *The Life of Lady Jane Grey* (1806) pointed to her uncommon intellectual achievements – they included a sound knowledge of eight languages before the age of twelve – as an inspiration to the girls. Godwin also

---

* The years of war with France, when meat became expensive and wine difficult to obtain, were marked by a rise in water-drinking vegetarianism.

used this short work to advocate religious tolerance, reminding his readers that not all Roman Catholics shared Queen Mary's enthusiasm for burning 'good bishops' and 'pious clergymen . . . merely on account of the sentiments they honestly entertained respecting God and religion'. Married to a Catholic who now supervised his household, Godwin used the final chapter to point out that Catholics too can be 'an ornament to human nature'. It was a point worth making in the unequal days before Catholic emancipation.

Kegan Paul, Godwin's first biographer, was assured by Mary's son and daughter-in-law that all the Godwins' income went on educating Charles and Jane, while poor Fanny and Mary learnt nothing but housework. Jane Clairmont's own recollection that every child in Godwin's household was expected to be a prodigy was equally fantastic. *Festina lente* was the often repeated motto of Godwin where his own family were concerned. Asked by an inquisitive lady correspondent, Mrs Fordham, whether he was using his late wife's educational system, he snapped that he and Mrs Godwin lacked time for novel methods.[21] His answer was misleading; everything we know about his daughter's early years suggests that she was being taught in a way of which her mother would have approved. Writing to another friend, a bookseller, Godwin expressed his dislike for any method which aimed to produce 'little monsters of curiosity'.

Armed with a governess, a daily tutor, a French-speaking stepmother and a father whose books were all tried out first at home on the children, Mary was neither pushed nor educationally deprived. In an unpublished extract from a letter to their friend Lady Mountcashell, Mary Jane Godwin assured her that the children had been educated in a most superior manner: 'Charles knows Latin Greek and French, mathematics and draws well. The girls have been taught by Mr Godwin Roman Greek and English history, French and Italian from masters. Frances and Mary draw very well.'[22]

Mary Jane's claims always have to be taken with a pinch of salt, but there is no doubt that all the children benefited from being trial readers of Godwin's *The Pantheon* (1806) and his histories of England (1806) and Rome (1809): 'Their remark was How easy this is! Why we learn it by heart, almost as fast as we read it!' he proudly informed readers of *The History of England*. *The Pantheon*, dedicated to Charles's headmaster at Charterhouse and boldly illustrated with pagan deities, two of them stark naked in the first edition, became part of Keats's travelling library; the little *History of England* introduced Mary to Oliver Cromwell as a hero, the man who had 'governed the nation with more vigour and glory than any king that ever sat upon the throne'. The *History* also fired her enduring interest in the enigmatic figure of Perkin Warbeck, the self-declared Duke of York who had long fascinated her father.[23]

Mr Burton and Maria Smith attended to the teaching of geography, mathematics and chemistry; excellent works for girls were being published during this period and, judging by the well-thumbed 1807 copy of *Conversations on Chemistry* in the present author's collection, they were much enjoyed.* But it was the books on the list of the Juvenile Library, as it was now called, which most stirred Mary's imagination. In Mary Lamb's *Mrs Leicester's School* (1808), she could identify with the orphaned child who learned her letters from reading the words on her mother's gravestone – and probably spotted a portrait of her stepmother in Charles Lamb's mischievous tale of the wicked witch aunt. Reading Lamb's version of *The Adventures of Ulysses*, she travelled to exotic places and absorbed the gruesome scenes which Lamb had refused to delete at Godwin's request.

Not all the Juvenile Library projects reached fruition. Coleridge's sea poem and his proposal for three volumes of historical lives based on Plutarch's model were abandoned and Wordsworth declined to contribute, but Hazlitt supplied a grammar, while Godwin wrote another and edited three anthologies of poetry.

Mary Wollstonecraft had convinced him that poetry was an important part of education. *The Poetical Class-Book*, published in 1810 and probably assembled by Godwin himself, although its preface was written by a London schoolmaster, W.F. Mylius, introduced Mary to excerpts from *Paradise Lost*, to Wordsworth's 'Nutting' and Coleridge's 'This Lime-Tree Bower My Prison'.[24] *The Junior Class Book*, published in 1809 under Mylius's name, seems also to have been Godwin's work, so closely do the chosen texts reflect his views on social equality, benevolence and the importance of sincerity. It would be rash to underestimate the degree to which Godwin, rather than Shelley, formed his daughter's social and political views.

The Library's most enduring production, with the exception of Mary Jane's 1814 version of *The Swiss Family Robinson*, was Mary Lamb's graceful retelling, with contributions from her brother, of Shakespeare's plays. The first to be published was *The Tempest*; its

---

* *Conversations on Chemistry* was the book which first sparked young Michael Faraday's interest in the subject which became his vocation.

presentation of Shakespeare's best-known monster anticipates the beautiful, hermaphroditic creature represented in the 1831 frontis-piece to *Frankenstein*. This is the Creature not as his maker perceives him, but as he is entitled by his uncorrupted state to appear:

'O father,' said Miranda, in a strange surprize, 'surely that is a spirit. Lord! how it looks about! Believe me, sir, it is a beautiful creature. Is it not a spirit?'
    'No, girl,' answered her father, 'it eats, and sleeps, and has senses such as we have.'[25]

Mary herself was thought at one time to have been the eleven-year-old author of another publication on the Library's list, a reworking of Charles Dibdin's genial 'Mounseer Nongtongpaw'. (The title puns on an Englishman's mishearing of 'n'entends pas'.) This was an error; her contribution has now been shown only to have extended to some spirited ideas for extra verses which Godwin proudly forwarded to the author he had employed.[26] Mary's hand has also been detected in *The Parent's Offering; or Tales for Children* (1813) and *The Prize: or, The Lace Makers of Missenden* (1817). Both books appeared with the Library as the works of Caroline Barnard; one reason for seeing her as an alias for Mary Godwin is that she published nothing else, or nothing under this name. But pseudonyms, if we exclude the case of Godwin himself, were not a feature of the Library list. There are references to a 'Barnard' in Godwin's diary and the fact that the Godwins were in 1813 and 1817 living in the same street as a publisher called John George Barnard who did not have a juvenile list suggests a simple explanation. Why should members of Mr Barnard's family not have been approached by the publisher who was their nearest neighbour?[27]

The first great change in Mary's early life was marked by the Clairmont family's invasion of her home. The second was presaged by a spring day in 1807 when Godwin visited a new and rather under-tenanted street on Snow Hill, in the heart of the city's bookselling area.
    A tall cornerhouse was available for £150 per year. Five storeys high with a front door separating two curving windows, ideal for the display of books, 41 Skinner Street was big enough to house both the family and the business.[28]* Already deep in debt and behind with his

---

* The street's name suggests, misleadingly, a connection to the meat market of nearby Smithfield. It had in fact been named after an Alderman Skinner who had encouraged the street's development.

rent, Godwin boldly decided to quit the Polygon, close up the Hanway Street shop and borrow again. Mrs Godwin and the girls moved in August; Godwin joined them in November. It is possible that they left in stages to avoid attracting the attention of the Polygon's unpaid landlady. Ominously, the move was attended by a savage return of Godwin's 'deliquium'.

For Mary, the departure from pleasant, semi-rural Somers Town, from the view of fields and the northern heights of Finchley, Hampstead, Barnet, from the tranquil churchyard where her mother seemed only to lie asleep under the tall grass, marked the end of childhood.

CHAPTER FIVE

TENSIONS

1807 – 1812

'I believe she has nothing of what is commonly called vices, and that she has considerable talent . . .'

William Godwin to William Thomas Baxter, 8 June 1812

THE HOUSE ON THE CORNER OF SKINNER STREET, UNINHABITED FOR six years, seemed as rickety and shabby when Mary arrived shortly before her tenth birthday as it would do seven years later to Thomas Jefferson Hogg, when he caught a brief glimpse there of the girl with whom his friend Shelley was in love. Staring across the deep valley of the Fleet river to Holborn Hill, 41 Skinner Street stood in earshot both of the Saracen's Head coaching inn, where Nicholas Nickleby came to be interviewed for a teaching post at Dotheboys Hall, and of the deep bell of St Sepulchre's which used to toll the condemned to Tyburn and which still, by tradition, rang out the curfew every evening at dusk. An uglier sound was the nightly screaming of animals being slaughtered in candlelit abattoirs under Smithfield. It is easy to imagine how horrified an impressionable child like Mary must have been as she learned to connect the sounds of the night to the bloody carcases hanging outside the double row of butchers' shops in their nearest shopping street, the old Fleet Market. Is this where we should look for the nightmarish image in *Frankenstein* of Victor torturing 'the living animal' as he gathered body parts from which to assemble his creature?

Holborn was crowded with butchers and booksellers, but it was above all the area of prisons. In 1806, Godwin had bailed his old friend, the physicist William Nicholson, out of the Fleet fifteen times; now, poor John Fenwick had taken up residence there while his wife worked all week for the Godwins and did hack-work on Sundays. At Bridewell, little had changed since Hogarth used it as a setting for *The Rake's Progress*; at Newgate, women prisoners were packed into spaces as narrow as paupers' graves. Public hangings, escalating to unprecedented numbers between 1800 and 1820, drew large, excited crowds; twenty-eight people were crushed to death while viewing a double execution at New Drop, just outside the Old Bailey, early in 1807; the coming and going of the crowds was audible to the girls at Skinner Street, poring over their lesson-books in the schoolroom on the second floor. Below, Godwin paced or wrote in his semicircular library, surrounded by one of the finest collections of books in the country* and overlooked by Opie's glowing portrait of his first wife while her successor kept shop with Mrs Fenwick on the ground floor. Only when the doors and windows were tightly shut was it almost possible to forget the sordid nature of the area in which they had chosen to live.

Jane Clairmont, forever recalling her early life in shining contrast to the hard and bitter struggle for survival which came later, bathed Skinner Street in a euphoric glow, blotting out the turbulence and insecurity of a life governed by Godwin's increasingly precarious financial juggling as he borrowed beyond his means to support the new business, and by Mrs Godwin's unpredictable moods and her violent temper. Jane and Charles were slapped or whipped when they crossed her; Mary did not forget how her stepmother had dragged her from under a parlour sofa in 1806 when she and Jane hid there to listen to Coleridge giving a spellbinding recital of 'The Rime of the Ancient Mariner'. These moments had faded from Jane's mind. Commenting in 1871 on a letter in which Shelley had described Skinner Street as a grim, melancholy place, she described it as the happiest of homes, a hive of enjoyable activity. Shelley was presented here as the serpent destroyer of a child's Eden (the italics are mine).

---

* Godwin was a passionate collector and reader of books all his life. A catalogue made by him of the Skinner Street library in 1817 offers instant contradiction to the notion that Mary, who would have been in and out of that library every day she was at home, was the untutored pupil of Shelley. On the contrary, Godwin's books would have ensured that Mary was at least as well read as he when they met, deficient only in the knowledge of Greek which she promptly set out to remedy. The books listed in Mary's journals from 1814 on are always treated as though this was her first reading of them, but Godwin's library contained many of these volumes and Godwin was a man who believed all books should be read at least twice.

Skinner Street was dull to him, but to all others it was a lively and
cheerful life that had been led there till *he* entered it. All the family
worked hard, learning and studying: we all took the liveliest interest
in the great questions of the day – common topics, gossiping, scandal,
found no entrance in our circle . . .[1]

Aaron Burr's journal bears out this account. Jefferson's former
vice-president, having narrowly escaped a charge of treason in 1807,
spent five years engaged in cloak-and-dagger schemes in Europe –
one of his wildest plans was for Napoleon to invade the United
States. In 1811, Burr had run out of money and friends; living in a
single room at a secret location, he was so poor that he had to sell his
watch to buy coals. The Godwins were almost the only people in
London who helped him at this grim time. To him, as to Amelia
Curran, the lively and sexually emancipated daughter of Godwin's
friend, the Irish barrister, 41 Skinner Street was a haven of kindness
and hospitality.*

In 1808, Burr noted only that Mary bore little resemblance to her
famous mother; by 1811, she had become one of 'les goddesses', the
three flirtatious nymphs who brightened his loneliness with invitations to take tea in their schoolroom at the top of the house and
teasingly reminded him of his age by calling him 'Gamp'. On one
occasion, when the girls were all in high excitement at going to a ball
– the occasion being celebrated was the wedding of Godwin's
protégé Thomas Turner to a girl of part-Creole background,
Cornelia de Boinville – Burr used his small reserves to buy them
elegant stockings. Too embarrassed to present such a personal gift in
front of Mrs Godwin, however, he went home with the hosiery still
in his pocket.

On another occasion, Burr, a practised orator, was asked to judge
the skills of the goddesses' eight-year-old brother William as he
addressed them from an improvised pulpit in the schoolroom.
William's subject was 'The Influence of Government on the
Character of the People'; Burr was not surprised to learn that clever
Mary had written it. Following the lecture and tea, Burr was treated
to a display of singing and dancing. In an entry which briskly encap-
sulates the three girls' characters, Burr noted that Mary wrote the
speech, Fanny made the tea, and Jane spoiled it by an overdose of tea-
leaves. The cameo is charming, and yet we can't help noticing the

---

* Burr's journal makes several references to Amelia's affair with a man called Lovett – 'son
ami Lovett' – and to the fact that Amelia and Lovett visited Skinner Street together.

absence of Godwin from an occasion so lovingly designed to please and impress. William's speech was, after all, a replication of Godwin's own precocious kitchen sermons, of which his daughter had evidently heard stories.

Burr's journal of those dark months in England is full of affectionate records of the time he spent at Skinner Street, and of the Godwins' kindness;[2] they not only fed him and refused to accept repayment of their loans, but secured his passage home. Through Burr's lonely eyes, we see Fanny, Mary and Jane as a spirited, confident trio, coaxing him to join them upstairs instead of playing whist with his hosts, begging him to escort them to an evening with the Hopwood girls, the artistic daughters of a self-taught engraver living in Somers Town. (Hannah Hopwood was Mary's closest friend at this period of her life.) Together, they went to the theatre, celebrated the Godwins' wedding anniversary, and the unexpected success of Eliza Fenwick's daughter as a Drury Lane actress. On one occasion, when Burr's spirits were especially low, Godwin took Mary and Jane on a surprise visit to his lonely room. 'That family really does love me,' Burr gratefully noted.

Engrossed by his own problems, Burr was nevertheless aware of the Godwins' precarious situation. Generous though they were, he understood that they were in difficulties. 'Some finance affair,' he noted vaguely. Mary's appearance worried him. She 'has not the air of strong health', he wrote on 21 December 1811.

Burr's concern was not misplaced. Mary Jane, more practical than her husband in many ways, insisted on taking the children and herself out of the city every summer when the nearby cattle-market buzzed with flies, breeding in the bloody gutters and spreading the danger of disease. Her own daughter went to Miss Pettman's (or Petman's) boarding-school at Ramsgate in the summer of 1808; the whole brood were packed off to join the Hopwoods in Somers Town in the summer of 1809.* These were protective measures, but Mary's health was sufficiently poor for her to be sent away for much longer periods, for half a year to Ramsgate in 1811 and then, between 1812 and 1814, for the better part of two years to Scotland.

Mary was thirteen when her hand and then the whole of one arm

* Godwin's diary entries in the summer of 1809 show that Mary also visited the pretty village of Nutting, or Notting, Hill, past its heyday as a spa and not yet established as a popular centre for girls' schools. Emily Sunstein believes that she became a weekly boarder with a couple called Corrie (most probably, Corrie Hudson),[3] but Godwin's diary records several weekday events with Mary during this period. It seems more likely that Mary joined the rest of the children at the Hopwoods' home, particularly since she was close to their daughter Hannah.

first erupted in an acute attack of eczema. (Scrofula, or tuberculosis, was mentioned, but only in a letter her stepmother wrote much later.)[4] Henry Cline, an eminent young surgeon – his father confusingly bore the same name and followed the same profession – whom Godwin consulted on the advice of Anthony Carlisle, recommended sea bathing and the application of several poultices each day. Mary was taken with eight-year-old William to Ramsgate by her stepmother in the summer of 1811 and examined by a local doctor. His report was reassuring, but Mary's condition was severe; Mrs Godwin wrote home to express her hope that 'our poor girl will escape the dreadful evil we apprehended'.[5]

Mary's condition did not improve after her six-month stay in Ramsgate, where she was an isolated and unhappy boarding-school lodger. It had vanished by the time she returned in 1814 from two long stays in Scotland, where she lived in an affectionate, uncritical household. It is difficult not to construe the illness as psychosomatic, particularly when we know that her father also suffered acutely from eczema in times of stress. Conjectures have to be made in the absence of letters, but it seems clear that the move to Skinner Street marked the beginning of what Mary called 'my girlish troubles' and that these manifested themselves in a physical condition. The phrase comes from a letter Mary wrote in her twenties. 'And I am threatened with a return of my girlish troubles,' she confided to a friend. 'If I go back to my father's house – I know the person I have to deal with; all at first will be velvet – then thorns will come up –'[6] The person in question was, of course, her stepmother.

Mary's resentment had been fierce from the start. Mary Jane had been the instigator behind their move into the city from a semi-rural home which the little girl had loved, not least for its link to the mother she revered. She had pushed Godwin into a business which was beginning, by 1810, to look financially disastrous. Inadmissible but probably contributing to Mary's feelings of aversion, was the sensuality which Godwin found so attractive in his wife. Mary preferred to see her stepmother as a source of distress. 'I detest Mrs Godwin. She plagues my father out of his life,' she told Shelley in 1814.[7] This was not a true report. Godwin's letters show that he often remonstrated with Mary Jane over her lack of self-control, but not that he felt plagued or harassed by her exuberant volatility. He, a middle-aged husband, could usually judge when his wife was acting up; her own children, although not fond, were familiar with their mother's moods. To Mary, always drawing a silent contrast between this noisy, demonstrative intruder and the lovely speaking looks of her own mother as Opie had painted her, everything about the second Mrs Godwin was odious. The fact that her feelings were neither rational nor well-founded – Mrs Godwin's letters show her as a hot-tempered but well-meaning stepmother – did not make them easier to bear.

The relationship between Mary and her father became increasingly tense after the move to Skinner Street, and her hostility to Mrs Godwin was probably a major reason for this. Trying to please, Mary was conscious of always falling short of his expectations. 'His strictness was undeviating . . .' she remembered painfully in her unfinished life of Godwin. 'He was too minute in his censures, too grave and severe.'[8] And indeed he was. Leaving home for Ramsgate, Mary was coldly informed, via her stepmother, that she still stood a chance of becoming a wise and even happy woman, 'in spite of unfavourable appearances'.[9] Increasingly, Godwin made harsh comparisons between gentle Fanny, who never caused any trouble with his wife, and stubborn, glowering Mary. She is 'singularly bold' and 'somewhat imperious', he told Mrs Fordham, the lady who wanted to know whether Mary Wollstonecraft's educational principles were being applied to his children.[10] He was, however, ready to acknowledge that Mary was a diligent student, 'almost invincible' in her determination to master every subject she encountered. A shrewder man would have recognized this intense application as an appeal for the approval he hurtfully withheld.

Godwin's remoteness was caused, in part, by factors of which Mary was only dimly aware. The move to Holborn had opened a new and unhappy period in his life. Old Ann Godwin died in 1808; Mary Jane was wistfully – and comically – invited to step into her place as his new 'mamma', a role which added to her authority in the household. The death of the playwright Thomas Holcroft, one of Godwin's closest friends despite some bitter quarrels, came next, followed, at the end of 1809, by that of the publisher Joseph Johnson. Johnson's heirs called in his loans, including some £800 which he had, at various times, given to Godwin. When the bankruptcy of another of Godwin's friendly creditors was followed by a demand for the immediate return of an outstanding £500 loan, he had no funds to meet it. The assistance of the radical businessman Francis Place in 1810 clarified the situation and pointed to a way forward, but Godwin remained mired in debt.

The new loan arranged by Place had still not been made when Mary went to Ramsgate. An essay on the importance of marking burial sites, followed by a grim autobiographical fragment on the uselessness of expecting anything more rewarding than a quiet death, suggests how depressed Godwin had become. In such a mood, Mary's difficult behaviour (of which we have evidence in his reference to its 'unfavourable appearances') was simply an additional irritation. When Henry Cline suggested sending her off to spend six months by the sea, Godwin saw a way of easing at least one source of tension in the household. It was Mary Jane, the supposedly cruel stepmother, who agonized over whether they were doing the right thing in abandoning a sickly thirteen-year-old for six months; Godwin showed no such concern. Cline had suggested six months, he reminded his anxious wife, and 'to this recommendation we both assented. It shall be *so, if it can.*'[11]

Defeated, Mary Jane had a few last anxious words with Miss Pettman, the good-natured mistress of the school in Ramsgate where Mary was to remain from late May to December 1811. The child must be taken seabathing as often as possible and inspected by doctors as often as needs be. The poultices on her arm must be applied and changed at regular intervals. If necessary, she was to be allowed to make use of her sling. Godwin was informed by his wife that Mary was now 'decisively better'; reference to the fact that she had been spotted making 'involuntary' movements of the affected arm raises the interesting possibility that Mary Jane suspected Mary of exaggerating her illness.[12]* Having settled her stepdaughter at the school, she went back to London and to a ferocious confrontation with her husband. The cause of the quarrel is not known, but it was sufficiently violent for Mary Jane to spend the rest of the summer staying with friends in Baker Street.

Mary's stepbrother, Charles, making a ten-day visit to Ramsgate in late May at the end of his summer term at Charterhouse, was delighted by the chance to stroll along the cliffs and through fields of waving barley after sitting in a stuffy schoolroom and before being sent out to work (Godwin apprenticed him to a Mr Tate in the publishing business as soon as he returned to London). Mary, left in the care of Miss Pettman when her stepmother took young William back to London in June, felt exiled and desolate. She made no friends; the

---

* Mary Jane's references to a sling add to the puzzle of what, precisely, Mary was suffering from. Eczema, however bad, does not require a sling, and what was the 'terrible evil' which the Godwins had apprehended? Was Mary thought to be suffering from a life-threatening illness or was it an amputation which was being considered?

sense that she was being punished was increased by her father's conspicuous detachment: she received just one letter a month, as noted in his journal.

Without records, we have no notion whether she went to the weekly tea-parties at the Ramsgate Assembly Room or whether it troubled her to know that she was at the town's least smart school. 'All the fashionable embellishments of the fair' were taught to pupils of Mrs Saffery's and Mrs Grant's select seminaries, as described in contemporary town guides; Mrs Pettman's poky establishment on the winding high street was not deemed worthy of mention. Among her many seaside trips in later life, Mary never returned to Ramsgate. To her, the pretty little town – it had been embellished and improved in the popular Nash style by a female architect, Mary Gosling – was associated with feelings of rejection and loneliness. Her health, despite Mrs Godwin's cheerful predictions, did not improve there; Burr's concerned note on Mary's fragile appearance was made shortly after her return to London at the end of 1811 in a winter so cold that the Thames had frozen over.

Even Godwin may have recognized that six months was a long term of banishment for a girl who had just turned fourteen. Charles Clairmont, looked on by Godwin as heir to the bookselling business, had been sent off to learn the trade at Constable's in Edinburgh during Mary's absence, but a treat was arranged for the rest of the family to celebrate her return, an outing to the theatre to see *The Winter's Tale*.

More serious educational treats followed. Godwin had been advertising his friend Coleridge's new course of lectures on Shakespeare at the speaker's request. In January, Mary and her best friend Hannah Hopwood were taken to the last four of the series, delivered at the Corporation Hall in Fetter Lane. Godwin was disappointed by Coleridge's rambling delivery; if the attention of Mary and Hannah strayed, the cause was forgivable. Lord Byron, already notorious for his excoriating poem, *English Bards and Scotch Reviewers* (1809), was present in the audience.* The young peer's mass of curly hair, strikingly pale face and noticeable limp secured the attention which he was so fond of pretending he disliked. *Childe Harold* launched him into the grandest literary drawing-rooms of London a few weeks later.

Scott, not Byron, was the poet of the moment; at fourteen, Mary and Hannah were just the age to swoon over *The Lady of the Lake* (1810) with its enthralling pages of notes on superstition and second

---

* Henry Crabb Robinson's diary noted that Byron was in the audience on 20 January 1812; he was present on at least one other occasion.

sight, and to chant noble Marmion's last words as he died for England on Flodden's field:

Last of my race, on battle plain
That shout shall ne'er be heard again.[13]

Mary remembered Marmion's dying words twelve years later when she decided that the last man would be a subject worthy of a novel.

If Charles was envied for being in Edinburgh, when Scotland was all the rage, Mary, Jane and Fanny, often accompanied by Hannah, had plenty to entertain them in London. The marriage of Godwin's protégé Thomas Turner to the strikingly beautiful Cornelia de Boinville had opened new doors. Godwin was already on friendly terms with Cornelia's uncle, John Frank Newton, a keen vegetarian who published a book on the subject in 1811, *The Return to Nature, or A Defence of the Vegetable Regimen*. Newton and his wife, Cornelia's namesake, favoured a modern regime for their own children, who were encouraged to wear only a light garment in summer months and no hats or stockings, a practice which the Godwin tribe may have been happy to adopt when they were away from home.*

Mrs Newton and Cornelia's mother enjoyed a comfortable lifestyle supported by their income from slave plantations in the West Indies. Wealthy though the women were, they were enthusiastic republicans. Cornelia's own mother, Harriet de Boinville, owner of a home in Pimlico and a country house at Bracknell, near Windsor, had married one of the Marquis de Lafayette's aides-de-camp when he was sent to England on a diplomatic mission in 1789; at the time Mary knew her, de Boinville and his young son were away from home in Napoleon's army. Perhaps Mary, Jane and Fanny rather envied Cornelia a glamorous mother who looked remarkably young, spoke French and Italian as easily as English and flaunted her views by tying a broad red sash around her slender waist. It must have been hard not to draw unfavourable comparisons with dumpy Mrs Godwin in her green-tinted spectacles and drab black velvet gown.

Visiting the Newtons and the de Boinvilles, Mary heard for the first

---

* Shelley's friend Thomas Jefferson Hogg in his biography of Shelley gave a memorable but typically exaggerated account of the Newton family as nudists who allowed their children to romp naked among strangers. This detail was corrected by Lady Shelley, Mary's daughter-in-law, in a handwritten note made in one of her copies of Hogg's book. Her information derived either from another friend of Shelley's, Thomas Love Peacock, who knew the de Boinvilles and Newtons quite well, or from Mary herself.

time about the happy, sexually uninhibited life of the mythical Nairs, lovingly described in an eccentric work by Mrs de Boinville's friend, James ('the Chevalier') Lawrence. The Nairs, Mrs de Boinville airily explained, acted according to the principles of Mary Wollstonecraft's most celebrated work; this was just how Mary's mother would have wished life to be. Mary, at fourteen, must have been wide-eyed with surprise at the news that people could behave in such a way and be praised for it, even if they were living in faraway India. The more lovers a lady took, the more powerful her sense of liberation, Mrs de Boinville explained. It is not clear whether she practised what she preached.

Outings to these progressive households provided relief from a sense of strain at home. Besieged by creditors, Godwin had nightmares of following John Fenwick into the debtors' prison, too close to Skinner Street for easy sleep, if he could not secure a new loan. He was not in the mood to reassure his wife that the fine ladies who visited the shop did not, as she angrily claimed, regard her as a common tradeswoman. If Mary Jane found the experience unpleasant, she could send one of the girls down to serve in her place. Mrs Godwin did so and Lady Mountcashell, who took a lively interest in the upbringing of the Godwin girls, was later informed that young Mary had discharged the business of the shop with the prudent steadiness of a man of forty.[14]

Mary was unhappy; Jane was restless; Fanny, as always, kept her thoughts to herself. Godwin, closeted in his study, was too obsessed by his financial problems to notice the storm which was brewing under his roof. So out of touch was he with the situation that he complimented himself on the satisfactory way in which his educational methods appeared to be bearing fruit. 'I have again and again been hopeless concerning the children . . .' he wrote complacently to a new friend in March 1812:

> Seeds of intellect and knowledge, seeds of moral judgment and conduct, I have sown, but the soil for a long time seemed 'ungrateful to the tiller's care'. It was not so. The happiest operations were going on quietly and unobserved, and at the moment when it was of the utmost importance, they unfolded themselves to the delight of every beholder.[15]

The friend to whom Godwin sent this glowing account in March was Percy Shelley and it was a wish to impress that caused him to boast of his success as an educator to this new disciple and potential provider of financial assistance. Shelley, aged nineteen, had eloped the previous August with Harriet Westbrook, the daughter of a prosperous and fashionable coffeehouse-owner,* five months after being sent down from University College, Oxford, for printing heresies in a pamphlet flamboyantly titled *The Necessity of Atheism*. His father, while none too happy about this, had been made much angrier when his expelled son announced that he was not interested in being the heir to a handsome estate in Sussex, a baronetcy, and the castle built by his grandfather, preferring to settle for an annual allowance with no strings attached. His contempt for Timothy Shelley dated back to 1807 when young Percy, then a schoolboy at Eton, heard reports of the corrupt electioneering methods which had helped his father to re-election as MP for East Shoreham.

The Shelley family's grandest friend and neighbour, the Duke of Norfolk, had invited the boy up to his Cumberland estate in December 1811, in the hope of making him see sense. A brief rapprochement ended when Shelley was found to have been posting secret communications to Hellen, one of his younger sisters, urging her to support him. He had already accused his mother of an adulterous relationship with a music-master; this was the last straw. Summarily banished from the family circle, Shelley was in need of a new father-figure. Visiting the poet Robert Southey after his short stay with the Duke of Norfolk, Shelley thought his wish had been granted. Southey told him that his recently discovered hero, William Godwin, author of *Political Justice*, was not, as he supposed, dead, but running a bookshop in London.

Shelley had already dispatched two letters to Godwin even before he rashly tried to enlist the sympathy of his little schoolgirl sister. In the first, written on 3 January, he presented himself as an ardent Godwinian, eager to learn and to be of use. Godwin had a long experience of confused, excitable young men who wanted to be his protégés; he asked for more clarification. The second letter, written on 10 January, was far more promising; here, Shelley presented himself not as a protégé but as a potential patron. Godwin's replies grew noticeably warmer. 'You cannot imagine how much all the females of my family, Mrs. G. and three daughters, are interested in your letters and your history,' he informed his still unseen friend on 14 March.[16] By July, he could tell Shelley that all the ladies thrilled to the

---

* Mr Westbrook also owned a tavern on Cheapside, a fact which was used by some Victorian biographers of Shelley to suggest that Harriet, as the daughter of an innkeeper, might have been overfond of alcohol.

sight of 'the well-known hand' on a letter and that they were 'on the tiptoe' to know his latest news.[17] If Shelley wanted a father-figure, Godwin was happy to play that role to a young man whose generosity might yet be the saving of the bookshop and his honour.

To Mary, Jane and Fanny, their father's new correspondent sounded like the hero of a romance. Everything they knew about him derived from Shelley's own letters and, in particular, from the long account he had provided on 10 January. Here, convincing himself as he wrote that what he said was nothing less than the truth, Shelley converted the life of an indulged and privileged youth into the stuff of fiction. Cruelly treated by his father, 'a man of fortune in Sussex', and at school, he had taken refuge in studying old books about chemistry and magic 'with an enthusiasm of wonder, almost amounting to belief'.[18] He had written two novels while still at Eton, and had been almost expelled for trying to act on the principles of *Political Justice*. (This was a Shelleyan exaggeration; he had only recently read the book for the first time.) He had, since his union to a woman of similar views, been threatened with the prospect of serving in a distant regiment and of seeing his entailed inheritance bestowed on his younger brother. Omitted from Shelley's account as tedious and unnecessary were the facts that his father, Timothy, had been perfectly tolerant and kindly in the period leading up to his son's expulsion from Oxford, that he had supported Shelley's first literary endeavours and that his response to the expulsion had been to suggest a tour of Greece. The only person opposed to Shelley's right to his inheritance was the Shelleys' lawyer, William Whitton, whose own interests are easily perceived when we learn that his daughter was involved with Timothy Shelley's older, illegitimate son.

The girls, like their father, knew only what Shelley chose to tell them. To Fanny, Mary and Jane, it was a tale of injustice and high courage. Their grumbles were forgotten; all they longed for was to meet this thrillingly intense young man. The romance was not diminished by the news that his recent marriage had been undertaken as a means of saving Miss Westbrook from 'domestic oppressions' (actually, the misery of boarding-school, from which the sixteen-year-old Harriet had begged Shelley to rescue her). They were all invited to come and stay, as soon as a house could be found, in the wilds of Wales, a location Shelley had chosen out of admiration for Godwin's novel, *Fleetwood* (1805).[19] In the meantime, however, the Shelleys were off to Ireland, where they intended to forward the cause of Catholic emancipation by whatever methods proved most effective.

The girls were enthralled; Godwin's own feelings about Shelley were mixed. It was gratifying to be heaped with terms of esteem and reverence at a time when his name attracted little but abuse. The mention of a handsome inheritance was of considerable interest to a man deep in debt. He was not, however, happy about Shelley's assumption that the first edition of *Political Justice* represented his present way of thinking. The book had been heavily revised since then and an author, in the early nineteenth century, was judged by whichever edition of his work had appeared most recently. But Shelley, as his excited letters revealed, had taken the first edition for his Bible. The Godwin he admired was the man who had welcomed revolution, opposed marriage, advocated a form of free love based on a system of equal rights. Godwin still believed – and this was of great significance to his relationship with Shelley – that money belonged to the man who had most need of it and that it should be taken with no sense of gratitude. In almost every other respect, he had modified his views. Having found a cause, however, Shelley was not inclined to hold fire. Whether Godwin liked it or not, he had found a champion.

Godwin wanted not a champion, but a financial patron. He had, for many years, been on the receiving end of the philanthropy of such wealthy benefactors as young Thomas Wedgwood. Wedgwood had believed, as did Godwin himself, that money belonged to those who could be of most benefit to the world and that it was the duty of the rich to provide for such men. But now Wedgwood was prematurely dead and the patience of Godwin's other patrons had reached its limit with a man who gave away their money as casually as he solicited it. Shelley had stated in his first letter that he wished to make himself 'useful' by a friendship with Godwin, in his second, that he was heir to a substantial fortune, and in his fourth, that he wanted to present the philosopher's family with a house when he was of age. (He was now nineteen.) 'Philanthropy,' he added airily, 'is confined to no spot. Adieu!'[20]

On 30 March, Godwin took the plunge and wrote that he was ready to look on Shelley 'as a lasting friend, who, according to the course of nature, may contribute to the comforts of my closing days'. He could not have stated his expectations more clearly; Shelley had been chosen as the man to save the Godwin family from financial disgrace. Unfortunately, the letter went astray until June, leaving Godwin on tenterhooks about the kind of commitment his disciple might be prepared to make. Opening the letter at last, Shelley responded with a flourish which reminds us how disturbingly out of touch with reality he was at this time. There was a streak of lunacy in the family and Shelley, in the years between 1811 and 1815, behaved

with an irresponsibility and a carelessness of other people's feelings
that came close to madness. 'I should regard it as my greatest glory,
should I be judged worthy to solace your declining years,' he grandly
announced; 'it is a pleasure the realization of which I anticipate with
confident hopes and which it shall be my study to deserve.'[21]

It sounded magnificent. To Godwin, this profession amounted to
a contract. Shelley was now, as far as he was concerned, subject to a
lifelong agreement to underwrite his debts and provide for his security. This, in the world of *Political Justice*, was how things were meant
to be.

Godwin remained worried about his daughter. Her condition had not
improved since her return from Ramsgate; in March, the month in
which he described to Shelley the delight of a father in seeing the
unfolding of a child's talents, Godwin went to consult Henry Cline
about her progress. Cline recommended sending her away again,
preferably to another seaside resort.

Godwin had, since 1802, established a lively friendship with a
remarkable Scotsman called David Booth. A grammarian, brewer and
sometime schoolmaster living in Forfarshire, Booth could have had a
hand in arranging Charles Clairmont's position at Constable's publishing firm in Edinburgh; his young brother-in-law Robert Baxter
also worked for Constable. It may have been Booth who came up
with the proposal that Mary should visit the Baxter family near
Dundee, just across the Tay from his own home. Godwin already
knew Booth's father-in-law, William Thomas Baxter, although not
well; the two men had met in London in 1801. Baxter's response to
the suggestion was heart-warming; any daughter of William
Godwin's was welcome at his home for as long as she wished. An
initial visit of five months was agreed on, although Godwin insisted
that the first two or three weeks should be considered as a trial. If the
scheme worked, he offered to house the eldest of the Baxter daughters at Skinner Street for a similar period when Mary returned.

One thing which Godwin did know about both Baxter and Booth
concerned their religious beliefs. These are of some significance.
Godwin had spent the unhappiest part of his early life in the Norwich
home of Samuel Newton. Newton was a member of the small sect
known as Sandemanians after Robert Sandeman, their founder.
Sandeman, a Scot, based his beliefs around the teachings of his father-
in-law, John Glas; both Baxter and Booth were Glassites. It would be

shocking to suppose that Godwin actively wished Mary to experience some of the misery he had known; more reasonably, we can note that dissenting families maintained very tight links in the early nineteenth century, when they were still debarred from the educational and civil rights open to conventional worshippers.* The Glassites, like the Sandemanians, practised community of goods and opposed the accumulation of wealth by individuals; Newton's beliefs had formed the cornerstone of Godwin's own philosophy. He may have chosen the Baxter family for Mary out of a wish to see her follow in his footsteps.

This explains his choice of the Baxters, but not the fact that he was so willing to part with his only daughter so soon after having sent her away to Ramsgate for six months. His reasons have to remain a matter of speculation. Perhaps, he was concerned only for her health (he sought a second opinion on his daughter from a brilliant young doctor called William Lawrence, then at the start of his medical career); perhaps, he disliked the way she was being turned into a shopgirl; perhaps, we may dimly surmise, Mary Jane was eager to see the back of her strong-willed and aggressive stepdaughter, if she was properly cared for. It is even possible, at a time when Godwin's own future was uncertain, that he wanted to settle Mary where she might be able to make an alternative life for herself. She would be near to Charles; she would be in the landscape of Burns and Scott, which would please her; she would have all the sea air she could wish for, and she would have Baxter's brood of daughters for company.

On 7 June, Fanny, Jane and Godwin – but not his wife – accompanied a wan and apprehensive Mary down to the docks and on to the *Osnaburgh*. The boat journey to and from Ramsgate had taught her that she was a poor sailor; the voyage to Dundee usually took six days. Cline had, however, insisted that the sea air would do her good. Godwin hovered for an hour. He mentioned Baxter's name to the captain in the hope of securing a little special attention for his daughter; searching the passengers for a friendly face, he singled out a pleasant-looking lady who, a mother herself, was happy to act as chaperone. Out of sight of the docks, the lady left Mary to fend for herself. Miserable, seasick and terrified of being robbed, she tucked the notes she had been given for her support carefully inside her stays.

---

* This may also be the explanation for the Godwins' choice of the obscure Mrs Pettman at Ramsgate. It is possible that the better-known schools at Ramsgate were not open to Jane Clairmont or to Mary Godwin, as members of a dissenting household. It may also have been the case that their fees were too high for the impoverished Godwins.

This presented no obstacle to the pickpockets on board the boat; 'the first money I ever had, was so carried, and *lost*,' Mary remembered years later, when urged to bring money into France by the same method.[22] She arrived in Dundee peagreen and without a penny to her name, a humiliating experience for a proud young girl.

Back at Skinner Street, Godwin solaced himself by writing a long letter to Baxter, an explanation of his daughter's character and the way he wished her to be treated. He began by admitting to 'a thousand anxieties' at having consigned a sickly fourteen-year-old girl to a shipful of strangers. He was rightly afraid she would arrive in Scotland 'more dead than alive'.

Godwin had remained a fervent believer in sincerity; he frankly admitted that he did not fully understand his daughter's nature. She, like him, suffered from the fault of excessive reserve. He knew she was talented; he was sure she had no vices and little taste for frivolity. She would be happier enjoying the Scottish landscape than social engagements. Her once 'invincible' perseverance had slackened of late; Baxter was warned that she would need to be 'excited to industry'. He was especially anxious that her 'habits and conceptions' should not be indulged:

> When I say all this, I hope you will be aware that I do not desire that she should be treated with extraordinary attention, or that any one of your family should put themselves in the smallest degree out of their way on her account. I am anxious that she should be brought up (in this respect) like a philosopher, even like a cynic. It will add greatly to the strength and worth of her character.[23]

It is, despite the affectionate opening, a letter of frightening detachment. Reading it, good-natured William Baxter must have wondered whether Godwin was thinking of his daughter or planning a new essay on educational methods.

CHAPTER SIX

A GLASSITE HOUSEHOLD

1812 – 1814

> Talk with me
> Of that our land, whose wilds and floods,
> Barren and dark although they be,
> Were dearer than these chestnut woods:
> Those heathy paths, that inland stream,
> And the blue mountains, shapes which seem
> Like wrecks of childhood's sunny dream . . .
>
> Shelley, *Rosalind and Helen* (1819)

SHELLEY'S POEM, WRITTEN TO PLEASE MARY, LOOKED BACK TO Scotland through the eyes of two young women exiled to Italy. Not among his best, it captures Mary's wistful memory of a landscape she had loved, although she never again travelled north of London, preferring the gentler climate of southern England. Looking back on her life at Dundee in 1831, when she was describing her formative years as a writer in the Preface to her revised edition of *Frankenstein*, Mary remembered this as the time when her imagination began to flourish. Others, she wrote, might look at the northern shores of the Tay and think them dreary and blank:

> they were not so to me then. They were the eyry of freedom, and the pleasant region where unheeded I could commune with the creatures of my fancy . . . It was beneath the trees of the grounds belonging to our house, or on the bleak sides of the woodless mountains near, that my true compositions, the airy flights of my imagination, were born and fostered.[1]

Baxter is a celebrated name in Dundee. The main branch of the family made its money in jute and linen, winning the lucrative contract to supply sailcloth to the navy during the Napoleonic wars: Nelson's *Victory* was equipped with Baxter cloth. William Thomas Baxter, descending from the family's junior line, was not among these commercial giants. He prided himself on having given his girls what he thought of as a good European education, but Mary had difficulty later in persuading him that she did not see herself as their social superior.[2]

The house into which they welcomed her was comfortable rather than elegant. Misleadingly named 'The Cottage', it stood four miles east of the grey, densely steepled city of Dundee at Broughty Ferry, a long, low stretch of land looking out past a tall fifteenth-century castle keep and three rocks called 'The Graces' to the shining breadth of the Tay. Dimly visible on the other side was the little alehouse-crammed town of Newburgh, the home of David Booth and his wife Margaret, Baxter's eldest daughter.

Among several factors which persuaded Godwin to send Mary to Dundee was a wish to stimulate her interest in politics. He took no active political role himself after writing his great revolutionary work of the 1790s, but a careful reading of his books for children shows that he never missed an opportunity to enlist the radical sympathies of his young readers. Dundee had become famous as a nerve-centre for radicals and revolutionary discussion during the 1790s; in 1812, both Booth and Baxter were still stout Jacobins. Isabella, the daughter who rapidly became Mary's favourite in the family of four girls and two sons, knew the events of the French Revolution so well that she almost seemed to inhabit the past. Fervent in her loathing of Marat and Robespierre, she worshipped Charlotte Corday and Madame Manon Roland, who lost her life for her stubborn commitment to the distinction between anarchy and republicanism.

'She is certainly clever,' Godwin wrote a little grudgingly to Mary in 1821, after meeting her friend.[3] Intelligent, beautiful and imaginative, dark-eyed Isabella seemed born to be admired, but the fact that Mary was the daughter of one of the women she most revered put the younger girl on an equal footing. Isabella's own mother had died in July the previous year; newly bereaved herself, she could dimly guess at the burden of supposing yourself responsible for your mother's death. Inseparable allies, the two girls shared a love of reading poetry aloud, of the ghostly stories in which Dundee folklore abounded, and of imagining themselves as the characters about whom they read. Interestingly, the only known portrait of Isabella, painted when she was twenty-three, is in fancy dress as Lady Jane Grey, the intellectual prodigy Godwin had wished his daughter to emulate. The portrait also suggests that Isabella bore a startling resemblance to Percy Shelley.[4]

Dundee, sacked and plundered during the Civil War, had grown churchified and quietly prosperous in the eighteenth century. The Glassite church, an airy octagonal building dutifully attended by David Booth and the Baxter family, enforced weekly communion, 'contributions' or almsgiving and a modest way of life; the exotic-sounding 'love-feasts' which broke up long days of biblical readings and discussion consisted of hearty bowls of cabbage soup. Glassites kept themselves apart from other congregations and preserved unanimity by expelling any member who broke their rules, which embraced a mild form of vegetarianism and abstention from any form of gambling.

It is unlikely that Mary much relished her dutiful hours of attendance at the church or the forced exchange of 'the kiss of love' with Glassite elders, but the town itself was full of intriguing twisted alleys, cluttered bookshops and historic sites. Given Isabella's taste for macabre stories, Mary would have been shown the high mound at the end of Guthrie Street, where women accused of witchcraft had been burned in their scores, and the house in Calendar Close where a notorious witch, Grissell Jaffray, had resided. She would have climbed the Law, the tall cone-shaped hill behind Dundee on which, traditionally, young girls dabbed their cheeks with dew and made romantic wishes for themselves. The squalor of Holborn and the perpetual financial worries of Skinner Street seemed far away as she looked out over the great deforested flanks and bald escarpments of the northern mountains of Forfarshire: the navy's need for timber in the war years had stripped this area of Scotland almost bare.

Scottish references in Mary's novels bear out the claims made later by Christina ('Christy' or 'Kirsty') Baxter that the family provided Mary with the regular air and exercise her doctors had recommended by taking her on extensive tours of the country. In *The Last Man*, Mary's description of Dunkeld includes knowledgeable references to the larch forests which were a new feature of the area in 1812. In *Frankenstein*, her allusions to the country around Edinburgh, and her decision to send Victor on his journey north via Cupar, St Andrews and the Tay shore, echo at least one long expedition she made with Charles Clairmont, affectionately remembered by him in later life. ('Do you remember the walk we once took together from [Newburgh?] to St Andrews, & the divine sun-set we saw on the road? . . . I never see a fine sun-set without my mind's adverting to it.'⁵) Mary would certainly have become familiar with the 'Deil's Head' on the wild coast of Arbroath where Scott set some dramatic chapters of *The Antiquary*. She probably visited handsome Montrose, known then as Scotland's Venice. It is less likely that Victor Frankenstein's journey up to the Orkneys reflects personal experience. Such a lengthy expedition would have been a rash one for the Baxters to undertake with a young girl whose health was still unsound. Given that Isabella detested the Highlands and that Mary's account of the Orkney islands is an unconvincing one, the grounds for imagining Victor's journey to be based on first-hand knowledge seem slight.

Among the regular pleasures of Mary's stay were the visits across the Tay to Newburgh. Barns o' Woodside, rented by Booth from a relative of the house's owners, stood in a terraced garden sloping steeply down towards the row of white alehouses which dominated the little shoreside town. Standing at one side of the house was a turreted tower, converted by Booth into a grain store for his brewery venture.

Mary stayed three times at Newburgh and left a record of her devotion to Isabella on a pane of glass in the shadowy gallery at the back of the house, where the two young girls scratched their initials with a diamond ring. The pane was stolen in the 1970s, but the house, long, grey and full of eccentric features, is as secretive and oddly charming as ever. Isabella was fascinated by her small, sharp-eyed brother-in-law; Booth had a fiercely rational mind, and Mary already knew that he was the only man her father regarded as cleverer than himself. Perhaps Margaret Baxter, an invalid, seemed unworthy of such a brilliant husband; we might wonder what dreams were in the young girls' minds when they painstakingly set their own names on the house.

Superstitious locals nicknamed David Booth 'the devil' on account of his prodigious and self-acquired learning; to the visitors, he was a kind but capricious host. On one occasion, so Isabella told her grandson, he promised them a view of paradise and then took them down into the bowels of a coalmine, after thoughtfully providing oilskin hats to keep the water from dripping down their necks. 'For some reason, both Miss Godwin and my grandmother were very irate,' James Stuart added.⁶

Dundee legend claims that Mary began writing *Frankenstein* when she was living with the Baxters, a story pleasantly enhanced by the fact that Dundonians first saw Boris Karloff's shambling, hollow-eyed monster at the Royalty Cinema, built on the site of the Baxters' garden. Mary herself drew a firm line between the writing 'in a most commonplace style' which she had attempted before her visit to Scotland, and the inspiration she found in her new surroundings. 'I could not figure to myself that romantic woes or wonderful events would ever be my lot,' she wrote in the 1831 Preface to her novel, describing her time at Dundee, 'but I was not confined to my own identity, and I could people the hours with creations far more interesting to me at that age than my own sensations.'[7] She did not have far to seek for inspiration.

The Baxters' house looked directly out on the harbour from which the ships bound for the northern seal fisheries and the Arctic sailed out every April from one of Britain's biggest whaling centres: whale oil was the cheapest effective lubricant available for the city's rapidly expanding jute industry as well as a major source of lamp fuel throughout Britain. All around the lost area where Mary lived – not even a plaque now marks the site – names like Baffin Street and Whale Lane recall the importance of the trade. Everybody in town came to the shores of Broughty Ferry to see the vessels off. Many, trapped in the treacherous pack-ice which, in Mary's novel, pinions Walton's vessel for seven long weeks, never returned; the *Rodney*, frozen up and lost in 1810, was still being talked about when Mary arrived in Dundee. The ships which reached home, heralded by the stench of blubber, brought with them terrible stories of desolation, and icy mountains, and hunger, and shipboard mutinies, to fire Mary's imagination and revive her haunted early vision of Coleridge's death-attended mariner and his journey to 'the land of mist and snow', a quotation she put into the mouth of her own adventurous sailor.

The tale of Frankenstein's attempt to produce a living creature is enclosed by another story of a man and his promethean ambitions. Robert Walton, steeped in the histories of voyages he has devoured in his uncle's library, has already made expeditions on Greenland whalers when he decides to go in search of a mythical land beyond the North Pole, 'a land surpassing in wonders and beauty every region hitherto discovered on the habitable globe'. Beyond this, and connecting Walton's ambitions to those of Frankenstein's galvanic experiments, is his hope of discovering a natural source of electricity, 'the wondrous power which attracts the needle . . . the secret of the magnet'. When Walton looks for men to join his expedition, he takes for his lieutenant a man 'madly desirous of glory' who has served with him on one of the whaling ships; the fact that this intriguing figure never reappears suggests that he may, with Walton, have belonged to an earlier story.

The character of Walton, the driving ambition of his quest and the sense of isolation with which it has burdened him, belong to the later development of the novel. But it seems likely that an early version of *Frankenstein*'s enclosing story began here in Dundee, in the days when Mary remembered sitting under the trees in the garden or on the bleak slopes – probably of the Law – as she spun her thoughts into 'a succession of imaginary incidents . . . more fantastic and agreeable than my writings'.[8] She may never have written a word about Walton's expedition down. A powerful story does not need written form to germinate and flourish in the imagination. It is likely that the tale of a journey to the Arctic wastes had already taken shape when, in 1816, her thoughts began to revolve around a novel.

Letters from Skinner Street kept Mary informed about their new and still unseen friends, the Shelleys. She left for Dundee just before Shelley imprudently declared that it would be his 'greatest glory' to solace Godwin's declining years. A month later, on 14 July, Elizabeth Hitchener, a former schoolmistress with progressive ideas, was invited to stay for a night at Skinner Street on her way to join the Shelleys at Lynmouth in Devon. The invitation, proposed by Shelley himself, had been issued by the Godwins in the hope that their visitor would provide more information about the young couple.

Tall, bony and black-haired, Miss Hitchener was a Sussex teacher whose radical views had won Shelley's friendship and admiration. Claimed by him as the 'sister of my soul', she had become one of his closest allies since his estrangement from his family. Now, she was boldly risking her own reputation as she set off to live with him and Harriet. It was not at all clear to the Godwins whether their ménage was to be platonic, and Miss Hitchener's offer to take Fanny along with her on a visit to Lynmouth was rejected. The sense of disapproval, once felt, was matched. Godwin, Miss Hitchener informed the Shelleys, cut a poor figure as a family man, shutting himself up in his study and seeing his son and stepdaughters only at 'stated hours'.[9]

In September, Godwin extended his routine summer holiday to inspect the household himself, only to find that the Shelleys had abruptly left their rose-shrouded hillside cottage for an undisclosed destination. Shelley's allegedly subversive activities – which included sending rousing messages out to sea in wine bottles and distributing a pamphlet entitled *Declaration of Rights* in the local town – had been reported by suspicious government agents in the Lynmouth area.

Godwin, unaware of this reason for flight, knew only that he had made a long and arduous journey for nothing.

The hunger for benevolent activity which raged in Shelley like a fever took him from the west of England to the north coast of Wales. Here, at Tremadoc, the new town which a wealthy philanthropist had created and named after himself, an ambitious project to salvage some four thousand acres from the sea and to safeguard it and the town by a gigantic embankment was endangered by engineering mishaps and lack of financial support; Shelley, loyally supported by Eliza Hitchener and by his pretty, easily influenced young wife, threw himself into raising both money – he gave £100 himself, although he was desperately short of money – and a local labour force to rebuild the embankment. It was the hope of raising funds for the Welsh land scheme, together with the wish to meet Godwin, which finally brought the Shelleys and Eliza Hitchener back to London in October 1812, the month before Mary's first return from Dundee.

Harriet and Shelley had been puzzled by Miss Hitchener's cool accounts of their elderly hero. By October, however, they had lost respect for her views and on 8 November she was sent packing, with the promise of £100 a year to comfort her for having been insufficiently republican and excessively affectionate towards Shelley. Their beloved 'Portia' was now recast, in one of Shelley's frighteningly sudden changes of mood, as 'the brown demon'.

Now, writing to a friend she had made on their visit to Ireland, Harriet offered Catherine Nugent an ecstatic account of the household at Skinner Street. Miss Hitchener had described Godwin as cold. Harriet, on the contrary, found his manner 'so soft and pleasing that I defy even an enemy to be displeased with him. We have the pleasure of seeing him daily, and upon his account we determine to settle near London.' Eliza's judgment had been too hastily formed; Mr Godwin was 'quite a family man'. William seemed an 'extremely clever' little boy, while nineteen-year-old Fanny was granted a beauty of mind which 'fully overbalances the plainness of her countenance'. (We have touching evidence in this remark of the vanity and superficial judgment of Harriet, a simple but extremely pretty girl.) Jane Clairmont was reported to be living at a French boarding-school on the other side of London. They had admired John Opie's portrait of Mary Wollstonecraft and were intrigued to be told that Mary Godwin was 'very much like her mother'. Mrs Godwin, too, running the bookshop entirely by herself, impressed Harriet as a woman of admirable courage and independence. 'Oh, if you could see them all tomorrow,' she exclaimed. 'I am going to stay all day with them.

G[odwin] . . . has given up everything for the sake of our society. It gives me so much pleasure to sit and look at him.' He was, she enthused, just like a bust of Socrates.[10]

At fifty-seven, Godwin looked less like Socrates than one of the old-fashioned line of Dissenters from which both he and William Hazlitt descended. Short, thickset and solemn-faced, with a fair skin and a generous expanse of bald forehead above the thin, unusually long nose which his daughter inherited, he certainly bore no resemblance to the fiery apostle of Shelley's imaginings. But Shelley was as delighted as Harriet by the philosopher and his family, by their indulgent attitude, and by their friends. They had a brief encounter with Mary Wollstonecraft's former pupil, Lady Mountcashell, for whom Shelley formed a warm admiration.* An expedition for the purpose of exploding fireworks on Guy Fawkes night with William Junior and a small friend, introduced him to the congenial household of John Newton, a vegetarian Zoroastrian, and to Newton's clever and elegant sister-in-law, Harriet de Boinville.

Shelley's quarrel was with his father, Timothy. At twenty, he was still young enough to miss the agreeable company of his mother, Elizabeth Pilfold, a woman whose lively, spirited letters suggest that it was from her Shelley had inherited the playful and most charming side of his nature. Mrs Newton and Harriet de Boinville were old enough to become substitute maternal figures and, with their attractive combination of languor and republican zeal, to exert a potent influence. Comparing his sweet but simple wife to Cornelia Turner, Harriet's good-looking and well-educated daughter, now married to Godwin's protégé, Shelley felt the first twinge of uncertainty about his impulsive elopement. Harriet shone in the provincial society of Lynmouth and Tremadoc; she seemed merely young and a little foolish when placed in more sophisticated company.

Harriet was more at ease in Skinner Street. A cynic might wonder at Godwin's sudden addiction to the company of a cheerful and frank but unremarkable girl, and to a young man whose poetic taste seemed as troublingly immature as his plans to reform the world. (When, in December 1812, he first read the privately printed *Queen Mab*, in

---

* Estranged from her husband since 1805, Margaret Mountcashell had left him and her children to live with her compatriot, George Tighe, father of her three-year-old daughter, Laurette. She visited Skinner Street in 1812 to collect a young female servant, Elizabeth ('Betsy') Parker, whom she took to Pisa in 1814. In the light of what is to happen to Mary, it is worth noting how kindly disposed the Godwins were towards anybody else whose behaviour flouted the conventions: Aaron Burr, Lady Mountcashell and Amelia Curran were all well received.

which Shelley laid into the government, marriage and Christianity with breathtaking ferocity, Godwin was unimpressed.) His kindness was spurred by an increasingly urgent need for the money he had been promised. Godwin's financial position had worsened as the year went on. In November, Francis Place bluntly told him that, unless he succeeded in obtaining a 'very large sum' from his wealthy young friend, 'all would be lost'.[11]

The Shelleys were dining at Skinner Street on 11 November, the day after Mary arrived from Dundee with Christy, the eldest of Baxter's unmarried daughters. William Lawrence, the surgeon who had examined Mary just before she left for Scotland, was also present, probably to assess her progress. Christy, many years later, remembered that Shelley had been very attentive to a young wife with a beautiful pink-and-white complexion. She herself had been much struck by Mrs Shelley's purple satin dress. Thomas Love Peacock later insisted that Harriet had always been '*simplex munditiis*' (elegant in simplicity), but her clothes created quite a stir among the plainly dressed Godwins; Fanny enraged Shelley a few days later by innocently commenting that his wife seemed 'a fine lady'.[12]

The dinner at Skinner Street is usually thought to have been the occasion of Mary's first meeting with Shelley; if so, it is strange that neither of them ever alluded to it. It is likely that Mary stayed upstairs, recovering from the long sea-journey. Christy, a sharp-eyed observer, was on hand to tell her about their dinner-guest, a stooping, carelessly dressed young man with a high white forehead, a mop of brown curls and eyes which were blue, intense and startlingly prominent. Imaginative Jane, newly returned from her boarding-school on the other side of London, might have produced a description closer to one offered for that year by Shelley's friend, Thomas Jefferson Hogg:

> Bysshe* looked, as he always looked, wild, intellectual, unearthly; like a spirit that has just descended from the sky; like a demon risen at that moment out of the ground.[13]

In volatility of temperament, if not in brains, Harriet and her husband were well-matched. Two days after dining at Skinner Street, they rushed back to Wales without a word of farewell. Here, Shelley dutifully followed Godwin's suggestions for reading history, a subject he considered a waste of time, but he ceased to answer letters and

---

* Named Percy Bysshe Shelley after his grandfather, the first baronet (Sir Bysshe bought his title in 1806, when his grandson was thirteen), the poet was known as Bysshe only to his family and, seemingly, Hogg. Others called him 'Percy' or 'Shelley'.

avoided Godwin's company on his occasional visits to London. Harriet, confiding in her Irish friend Miss Nugent in January 1813, now expressed violent dislike for Mrs Godwin, scorn for their friend Amelia Curran ('a coquette, the most abominable thing in the world'), and anger at Godwin both for trying to persuade Shelley to join the politically languid Whigs, and for expecting 'such universal homage from all persons younger than himself, that it is very disagreeable to be in company with him on that account'.[14]

The reasons for this sudden change of attitude are unclear. Godwin may have become too pressing in his demands for the money which Shelley now wanted to use to benefit the people of Tremadoc. The acquaintanceship was not resumed until a fortnight before the birth of Shelley and Harriet's daughter Ianthe, at the end of June 1813; by then, Mary had returned to Dundee.

Duty, not choice, had dictated that Christy should accompany Mary to London; Mary's lack of affection for Isabella's dour elder sister can be gauged by a slightly unkind trick which she played on her shortly after their arrival. On 8 December 1812, the entire family went to supper with Charles and Mary Lamb. Charles, Mary warned, was very forward with ladies; Christy must watch out, for he would be sure to kiss her when they first met. Instead, to Christy's mortification, she received scarcely a nod of acknowledgment from a man who, as Mary knew, was ill-at-ease with female strangers.[15]

Godwin's terse diary entries and Christy's vague recollections as a very old lady are all the account we have of Mary's seven-month stay in London. Christy remembered that she shared a room with Mary and that Jane had been extremely pretty, with a round face, small features and curly hair. The girls had plenty of liberty, breakfasting on their own and supping when they pleased. Mrs Godwin was kind but not always truthful; Mr Godwin had made a special favourite of their guest. (There is something a little sad in Christy's wistful recollections; she so wanted to believe that Godwin and Lamb had been enchanted by her and that Mary had preferred her to Isabella.) Debate had always been encouraged at Skinner Street; Christy remembered how, on one occasion, she and Fanny had defended the right of women to be purely domestic against Mary's and Jane's Wollstonecraft-based argument that they should have outside interests and activities.[16] Less convincingly, she remembered that Fanny, at nineteen, still believed herself to be Godwin's daughter. A note Godwin himself made of an 'explanation' given to Fanny in 1806 when she was nearly twelve contradicts Christy's statement. The fact that Fanny's birth was not discussed with an inquisitive guest need not mean that the truth was unknown to her.

Despite the overshadowing worry of Godwin's finances and the misfortune of a fire in the bookshop shortly after Mary and Christy's arrival, there were plenty of expeditions and social engagements to entertain a shy Scottish girl. At home, they were called on by fiery, witty John Curran (whose imagined incivility had once caused Mary Jane to threaten a separation), by gentle James Marshall and by Charles Lamb (whose private opinion of Mary Jane had not softened); affection for Godwin had evidently caused some truces to be called with his wife. Writing home, Christy could boast that she had been taken to the first night of a fine play with all the grand literary folk of the city in the audience* and that she had been introduced to the Irish poet Thomas Moore and the essayist William Hazlitt. The great Scottish artist David Wilkie had gone with them to view paintings by Sir Joshua Reynolds.

Jealous of the respectful interest which adults always showed in Mary, Christy must have been considerably piqued when they visited Reynolds's former pupil, irreligious, gossip-loving old James Northcote, who painted the finest picture we have of William Godwin, and who in his conversations with Hazlitt spoke tenderly of Mary as 'Beauty's daughter'.[17] Mary, Christy was forced to realize, was regarded with something like reverence down in London. She seemed to accept it as her right when, admired for her beautiful complexion and finespun cloud of hair, she was told that she had been born under a lucky star, that comet which blazed so auspiciously just before her birth.

The most interesting of the many visitors to Skinner Street during this period, and one whom both Mary and Christy met on several occasions, was Robert Owen. A grave, strong-featured man in his early forties, Owen came to seek Godwin's views at a time when, having ably combined commercial success with social reform at his wife's family factory at Lanark, near Glasgow, he was planning a new partnership with the old legal reformer, Jeremy Bentham, and the Quaker William Allen. Bentham and Allen had agreed to buy out his former partners and to seek only five per cent return on their capital investment, in order to give Owen a freer hand with his experiment in perfectibility.

---

* This was Coleridge's unexpected success, *Remorse*; the entire Godwin family attended the première at Drury Lane and thrilled to the great sorcery scene in Act 3.

Owen and Godwin had much to debate. Godwin still believed that men are capable of improving themselves by acting as individuals in co-operation for the general good; Owen took the more authoritarian view that men can be improved by the circumstances in which they are placed. By giving his workforce of semi-destitute people proper schooling, housing and rules of behaviour, they had been led, he argued, to a better understanding of citizenship. Owen was often at Skinner Street during Mary's six months in London. She must have taken pride in seeing her father, not as a despised and needy bookseller, borrowing wherever he could smell money, but as a revered adviser, standing at the centre of a world which looked to a better future for mankind. Years later, she became a close friend of Owen's son.

Mary had eagerly resumed her old friendship with the Hopwood family; when she went back to Dundee in the summer of 1813, she persuaded Godwin to let Hannah go with her. All the Baxter girls were enthusiastic amateur painters; Hannah, Mary must have successfully argued, could pay for her keep by giving lessons. Mary's love of Scotland, apparent in her nostalgic 1831 Preface to *Frankenstein* and her enduring passion for mountain landscapes, is also borne out by the fact that she begged to be allowed to extend her stay there this time to ten months. A more personal reason was her deep attachment to Isabella, whose life was undergoing a surprising change.

David Booth came south to London in January 1814 for what would seem, from the regularity of his appearance in Godwin's diary, to have been the express purpose of seeing Mary's father. Lack of records has made it impossible to establish the precise date on which Booth's wife Margaret, a long-term invalid, died; did he come to London to ask Godwin for his daughter's hand? We know that she and Isabella had been frequent visitors to his home, that he relished their company, and that both were spirited and intelligent enough to attract this brilliant and demanding man.

If this was the case, Booth timed his visit badly. Godwin, in the early winter of 1814, was almost out of his mind with anxiety about the money which Shelley seemed ready to bestow on Tremadoc and on Leigh Hunt, the radical editor imprisoned in 1813 on a charge of insulting the Prince Regent in his paper, the *Examiner*, but never on his chosen mentor. If a proposal was indeed Booth's mission, and it is hard to guess what else could have brought him down from Fife for two weeks in the middle of a viciously cold winter, it was an unrewarding one.

If Booth did raise the suggestion, perhaps without Mary's knowledge, it was rejected. Returning to Scotland, he proposed to his late wife's youngest sister, Isabella – and was accepted. Socially, both he and the Baxters paid a high price for the match. The Glassite Church, unable to tolerate marriage to a wife's sister, pronounced the sentence of excommunication on both Baxter and the man who now became his son-in-law for the second time.* To be excommunicated was to be exiled; none of their fellow Glassites were permitted to maintain more than the barest contact with them after this.

William Thomas Baxter was not rich enough to support the popular notion that Booth married his daughters for their fortunes. There is little doubt that he was in awe of his brilliant son-in-law. Booth was a man who appeared always to achieve his ambitions; Baxter, kind, weak and thoroughly decent, adored by his children, complied with his wishes. Isabella would become the mistress of a fine house, and the wife of a man who would never crush her own bright intelligence; standing together, Baxter imagined they could survive the disgrace of public humiliation.

To Mary, such a bold flouting of convention became a definition of love; if Isabella, the girl she most admired and wished to emulate, could break the rules, then so could she. Reading *Maria*, the novel on which Mary Wollstonecraft had been working at the time of her death, she read what sounded like an appeal to stretch her own wings:

> Death may snatch me from you, before you can weigh my advice, or enter into my reasoning: I would then, with fond anxiety, lead you very early in life to form your grand principle of action, to save you from the vain regret of having, through irresolution, let the spring-tide of existence pass away, unimproved, unenjoyed. Gain experience – ah! gain it – while experience is worth having, and acquire sufficient fortitude to pursue your own happiness; it includes your utility, by a different path.[18]

An opportunity to gain experience was close at hand. Mary, a blooming sixteen-year-old no longer troubled by her afflicted arm, was remembered by her Scottish friends for her clear bright skin, her large hazel eyes and the crowning glory of her astonishing hair. Robert Baxter, a shy seventeen-year-old visiting home from the Edinburgh firm where he worked with Charles Clairmont, fell in love with her serene smile and the slanting sideways glances which fascinated all Mary's male admirers. It became part of the Baxter family's

---

* The marriage would also have been deemed illegal by Anglicans, but not an excommunicable offence.

unhappy history that Robert wanted to make Mary his wife and followed her back to London with that intention. Mary, unfortunately
for him, met someone else.

On 15 and 16 March, unusually, Godwin recorded having written
both to Baxter and to his daughter; the fact that Mary travelled home
four days later suggests that her father had ordered her return. Almost
two years after she first set foot in Scotland, she said goodbye to the
family who had made her one of themselves. Among the sensible
wool gowns and shawls needed to keep out the bitter cold of a
Scottish winter on the East Coast, she took back to London a brightly
checked tartan dress, of the kind that a Walter Scott heroine would
be proud to wear.

> *Sunday March 20 1814.* I went out to the Cottage in the forenoon [the
> diarist was a distant Baxter relative] to see Mary Godwin shipped for
> London – I understood she would be away by twelve, but the vessel
> did not sail [until?] two. The day cleared and we wandered about all
> the adjoining grounds. The vessel (old Wishart) at length came out,
> and about three o'clock the boat came ashore and took her on board
> from the Bottle Works.

Looking back to a row of figures waving from the shore, to a white
house lying between bare mountains and an ever-widening expanse
of water, cold silver in the low March sunlight, Mary held the images
in her mind. They had all, as the friendly diarist cousin noted, been
'very sorry-like to part'.[19] And now she could hardly see them. It
would be surprising if she did not shed a few tears. The kindly and
unassuming Baxter household had become closer to her idea of a real
home than her father's house of trade, oozing with the scent of lost
opportunities, haunted by the threatening presence of creditors at the
door. And what, she must have wondered, was her future there to be?
A day job at the counter and nights spent writing whatever her father
supposed would sell best on his list? The prospect was not cheerful for
a girl of sixteen. Perhaps she took some comfort from Robert Baxter's
hints of a marriage proposal to come.

CHAPTER SEVEN

LOVE AND CONFUSION

1814

1814. March 31: The Allied Armies, with the Emperors of Russia and Austria, together with the king of Prussia at their head, enter Paris – dethrone Bonaparte – liberate the Pope – proclaim the restoration of the Bourbons, in unison with the French people – avow civil and religious freedom – and announce peace and harmony to the whole world. *June 30:* Peace proclaimed at London with its usual formalities amidst the acclamations of an immense multitude.

Contemporary diarist, quoted in Edmund Blunden, Shelley[1]

THESE WERE THE GREAT EVENTS OF THE SUMMER OF 1814. A DISTANT relation of Percy Shelley's with rather different political views joyfully recorded the fêting of the new French king on his visit to London. Subsequent festivities were held in honour of the Emperor of Russia and the King of Prussia. The good old days of despotism were back, it seemed, with a vengeance. With peace established, a nation starved of continental travel took to the roads in a rush for the ports and boats to France where the innkeepers, prudently trebling their rates, awaited them with open arms. Booksellers, over the next few years, did a roaring trade in travel books.

Mary, exhausted from her week-long sea journey, reached London the night before Paris surrendered to the allies and two days before the formal deposing of Napoleon. The Godwins went out with the rest of the city to see it grandly illuminated to honour the return to Europe of legitimate rule, but there were no private celebrations at Skinner Street. While less extravagantly despondent than Byron and

Hazlitt, Godwin had shared their high hopes of Napoleon's reform plans for Europe. As a staunch anti-monarchist, he anticipated a return to the bad old ways with Bourbon rulers being supported and manipulated by venal churchmen.

The city was in a state of euphoria; 41 Skinner Street was, by contrast, as gloomy as a sepulchre. It took only a few days for Mary to discover the reason: Shelley, she gathered, stood alone between her family and the debtors' prison down the street.

Shelley, since he first wrote to Godwin in the spring of 1812, had been obtaining loans in a way seemingly devised to cause the maximum of damage to the Sussex estate which his family saw as a sacred heritage and which Shelley himself saw only as a source of funding for philanthropic activities. By taking out post-obit (post-death) loans, he had found a way to obtain large interest-free sums of money. Creditors were happy to provide the money he wanted if he would promise to return up to four times the amount of the loan after the deaths of Sir Bysshe, his grandfather, and of his father Timothy. Timothy was sixty-one in 1814 and Sir Bysshe was eighty-three; the creditors, never suspecting what old bones Shelley's father would make, were delighted with the bargains they had struck. Poor Mary, in the long-distant future, would be threatened with ruin by Shelley's impractical transactions in these early years.

The level of Shelley's borrowing had escalated rapidly after the summer of 1813 when he turned twenty-one, but none of the money had yet found its way to Skinner Street, to Godwin's considerable gloom. In March, however, a post-obit bond for £8,000 had been auctioned to obtain a credit of £2,500. This, so Godwin understood from his young friend, would be a gift to himself. The moneylenders, however, refused to hand over a penny until everything was legally underwritten. What, for example, if Shelley predeceased his children? He had married Harriet in Scotland. Was it certain that his offspring would have legitimate status under English law? As bastards, they would have no responsibility for their father's debts. This, from the lenders' point of view, was far from satisfactory.

The moneylenders' conditions, rather than a renewed passion for his wife, forced Shelley to obtain a marriage licence on 22 March 1814. Godwin, who had already been helpfully investigating ways to insure Shelley's life – in case he predeceased his father – was there to see that all was in order. The following day, the Shelleys were married for a second time in a Church of England ceremony. Perhaps Harriet, pregnant with their second child, saw this as a cementing of their love; it seems unlikely. A month later, Mrs de Boinville casually informed a friend that Shelley was 'again a widower'. This suggests that the couple were already leading separate lives.[2]

Shelley was still unknown to Mary, unless they had briefly met at the dinner in 1812; everything she knew was gleaned from the letters which Godwin had read out in the early days, and from accounts supplied by the rest of the family. Shelley was rumoured to be spending most of his time at Mrs de Boinville's home near Windsor and to be studying Italian with her daughter, Thomas Turner's wife. Cornelia was emancipated, intelligent and attractive. Turner was often away. The Godwin girls must have wondered if there was something in it. Perhaps they felt sorry for Shelley. He was so kind, so impulsive, so good-hearted; it was sad that Harriet should be spending such a lot of time with her elder sister, Eliza Westbrook, when she knew that her husband found Eliza's company detestable. If he was looking elsewhere, the blame surely lay with his wife.

The most careful sifting of the available evidence cannot bring us close to what was going on in Shelley's mind during the early months of 1814, but there is little doubt that his thoughts were confused. Harriet had already disappointed him by refusing to fall in love with Hogg as his poem, 'Thy look of love' had urged her to do the previous year. Fanny felt that he was attracted to her and became so moody and disturbed that Mrs Godwin packed her off for a long holiday in Wales on 23 May; impressionable Jane must have felt something more than sisterly affection for a young man who took the trouble to visit her boarding-school at Walham Green and who sought her company for long evening walks, even if he only did so because he was afraid to walk alone. (Shelley suffered from an enduring belief – we could call it a persecution complex – that he was being pursued by malevolent strangers, ready to spring out of the darkness and set about him.)

Everything points away from a happy marriage and yet, in June, Shelley was still planning to return with Harriet to the house in Wales. Unless we accept, first, that Shelley, after reading Godwin, had lost any belief that marriage entailed a mutually exclusive relationship,* and, secondly, that he was nearer to the edge of insanity than he had ever been before in his volatile career, nothing makes sense. Shelley, in 1814, was reinventing himself every month as a different character.

---

* Shelley remained strongly influenced by *Political Justice*, in which, in the 1793 edition, Godwin had written: 'Marriage, as now understood, is a monopoly, and the worst of monopolies. So long as two human beings are forbidden, by positive institution, to follow the dictates of their own mind, prejudice will be alive and vigorous.'[3]

The people he knew had also to be reinvented, to accommodate each new perception of events. His emotions were like a tinderbox, waiting for the match. Cornelia started a flame; Mary Godwin set the box on fire.

The first recorded meeting between Shelley and Mary was on 5 May. Godwin's journal shows that Shelley visited Skinner Street at least seven times before the end of the month. Since Mary often worked downstairs in the shop, there was ample opportunity for them to get to know each other. On 8 June – Thomas Jefferson Hogg, a barrister, was able to establish the precise date from a case which he had been attending – the two young men called at Skinner Street in search of Godwin. The philosopher was not at home; Hogg's account conveys the overwrought state of Shelley's mind when he tells us that Shelley repeatedly asked him where Godwin was, although Hogg can have had no idea.

> I did not know, and, to say the truth, I did not care. He continued his uneasy promenade; and I stood reading the names of old English authors on the backs of the venerable volumes [they were waiting in Godwin's study], when the door was partially and softly opened. A thrilling voice called, 'Shelley!' A thrilling voice answered, 'Mary!' and he darted out of the room.

But not before Hogg had caught a glimpse of a tartan-frocked and very young lady, 'fair and fair-haired, pale indeed, and with a piercing look'.

Shelley left the room to talk to her for a moment and then announced that there was no point in waiting. Godwin was out. Questioned as to who she was – a daughter of William Godwin? – Shelley gave the secret of his excitement away with the answer. Not only of Godwin, he told Hogg: 'The daughter of Godwin and Mary.'[4] The awed tone, if we can trust Hogg's memory, and the nervousness of Shelley's manner, combine to suggest that he was already deeply smitten, as much by the thought of Mary's glorious parentage as by the girl herself. An additional reason for his nervousness that day can be surmised from the fact that young Robert Baxter had just arrived in London. Baxter spent three days at Skinner Street, during which it seems likely that he proposed and was dismissed.

The frequency of Shelley's visits to Skinner Street in June must have been occasioned by his growing interest in Mary. Godwin, enmeshed in his financial concerns, was oblivious to what was going on. Jane, who later represented herself as a passive and credulous girl, a little in awe of her quiet, strong-willed stepsister, was enrolled as a useful ally as the romance developed. When Shelley and Mary walked out together, they took care to invite Jane to join them. Sometimes, as the summer heat grew, the three of them waited for the evenings to bring a little cool before they strolled down the street and into Charterhouse Square where, an observant gardener subsequently told Mrs Godwin, her daughter had walked alone up and down the paths while 'the fair young lady' and the young gentleman sat whispering in an arbour. Shelley took lodgings in Hatton Garden, just round the corner from Skinner Street. His only London friends were Hogg and young Thomas Hookham of the publishing and library firm, fashion-ably established in Bond Street.* Nothing could have seemed more natural, especially as a near neighbour, than that he should treat the Godwins' home as his own.

Writing a long explanatory letter to Hogg on 4 October, Shelley later tried to create a logical chain of events and to put his behaviour in the best light. It was when he was staying at Bracknell with the de Boinvilles, he explained, that he had realized that there was more to life than the 'cultivating' of Harriet. The more civilized company of Cornelia Turner had opened his eyes; he had felt something like love. Instantly, his feelings for Harriet had turned to physical disgust. He felt 'as if a dead & living body had been linked together in loathsome & horrible communion'. No mention was made of Harriet's having been unfaithful, although this would later become Shelley's chief defence against charges of deserting his pregnant wife. Walking almost forty miles from Bracknell to make a secret call on his mother at Field Place while his father was away, he thought himself into such an excited mood that he almost believed Cornelia was already his.† But Cornelia was unavailable.⁵

Shelley's letter then proceeded to the subject of Mary, and to explaining her effect on him. As a lover's portrait, it is rather odd. He had, Shelley said, been unable to resist Mary's persuasive and sometimes pathetic smile, or the 'wildness and sublimity of her feel-ings', revealed only in gestures and looks. She was 'not incapable of ardent indignation and hatred', as he must have discovered as soon

---

* The firm was sufficiently well-known for Hannah More in *Florio* (1786) to write of a young man: 'For he, to keep him from the vapours, / Subscribed at Hookham's, saw the papers.'
† Frederick L. Jones, in his edition of Shelley's letters, inserted the name of Mary here as the female in his mind; since Shelley's next paragraph describes the beginning of his rela-tionship with Mary and dates it to June, after the Field Place walk, the woman seems likely to have been Cornelia, rather than an anticipated Mary.

as he mentioned her stepmother. It was her intellect which had most attracted him, he told Hogg, and which left him dazzled, 'far surpassed [by her] in originality, in genuine elevation & magnificence . . .' But a despicable superstitious ritual kept him chained to the wife he no longer loved.

It was, in Shelley's account, Mary who took the initiative. Mary's own version suggests that his behaviour prepared the ground. On the evening of 26 June, Jane and she accompanied him to Mary Wollstonecraft's grave at St Pancras. Jane made a tactful retreat. It was then, Mary remembered, that Shelley 'oppened, at first with the confidence of friendship, & then with the ardour of love, his whole heart to me'.[6] Encouraged by her sympathetic manner, Shelley let his imagination loose on the past. Mary was given a vivid account of his unhappy Eton schooldays and of how Timothy Shelley, troubled by his son's increasingly erratic behaviour, had taken advice about having him dispatched to a private madhouse. (Shelley had a habit of converting his father's threats into acts; it seems unlikely that Sir Timothy would have taken such drastic measures.) He told her of his early obsession with magic, with death and with chemical experiments, material which would find its way into her creation of Victor Frankenstein.

Questioned by Mary about his marriage, Shelley hinted that Harriet had been unfaithful and even that the new baby might not be his. There is no reason to suppose that he had any reason to suspect Harriet; the first written mention of her supposed unfaithfulness appears over a year later and the source of the allegation was not Shelley but a gossipy friend of Godwin's. But Shelley, when excited, was capable of saying whatever came into his head. It is quite possible that he told Mary any lies necessary to win her sympathy. What matters is that Mary believed him. Godwin had brought her up to suppose that honourable men always told the truth.

Mary, by the age of sixteen, had absorbed the most inspiringly progressive aspects of her parents' beliefs, while discounting the revisions Godwin had made in his later writings. Like Shelley, she thrilled to the boldness of her father's role as a challenger of convention. Like him, she preferred to forget that Godwin's 1805 Preface to *Fleetwood* had painstakingly rejected the idea that he wanted man to 'supersede and trample upon the institutions of the country in which he lives'. The chief institution he had in mind was marriage. To his daughter, Shelley's marriage offered a challenge to act boldly in the name of love and *Political Justice*. She wanted to fulfil her destiny, to show herself as the true heir to her parents. Isabella had defied the Church to marry the man she loved; she would be bolder still. Shelley seemed hesitant; compared to him, Mary glowed like a young priestess, aflame and certain in her grasp of the situation. Her understanding, Shelley told Hogg,

> was made clear by a spirit that sees into the truth of things, & affections preserved pure & sacred from the corrupting contamination of vulgar superstitions. No expressions can convey the remotest conception of the *manner* in which she dispelled my delusions. The sublime & rapturous moment when she confessed herself mine, who had so long been her's in secret cannot be painted to mortal imaginations . . .[7]

Subsequent references by Shelley to the following day, 27 June, as having been his true birthday (he was born on 4 August), suggest that this was the day on which he and Mary first made love. The discreet north-eastern corner of St Pancras churchyard would have seemed an appropriate setting, as if Mary Wollstonecraft were presiding over their union. Her grave was conveniently shaded by willows.

The danger of allocating responsibility too confidently can be shown by quoting from three separate accounts of this celebrated episode in literary history. Harriet, writing a bitter letter to her Irish friend Catherine Nugent in November 1814, had no doubts:

> Mary was determined to seduce him. She is to blame. She heated his imagination by talking of her mother and going to her grave with him every day, till at last she told him she was dying of love for him.[8]

Jane Shelley, telling the story almost as she had heard it in the 1840s from Mary, her mother-in-law, made it seem impossible for any woman to have resisted Shelley's anguished appeal. Her account, published in 1859, added a twist of its own by killing off Harriet in order to present Mary, at their first meeting, as the angelic comforter of an unhappy widower. Mary, in this version, did nothing more than agree to become Shelley's second wife.

> Bysshe, in burning words, poured forth the tale of his wild past – how he had suffered, how he had been misled, and how, if supported by her love, he hoped in future years to enroll his name with the wise and good who had done battle for their fellow-men, and been true through all adverse storms to the cause of humanity. Unhesitatingly she placed her hand in his, and linked her fortune with his own.[9]

Finally, for the purpose of contrast, we have an account given by William Michael Rossetti, a poetry-loving Victorian who rightly suspected Jane Shelley of a cover-up. Rossetti restored Harriet to life and showed Mary acting as she had been taught to do by her parents' writings and example. To a man living at the heart of the Pre-Raphaelite circle, there was no shame in love without wedding rings.

> [T]here is no evidence at all that Mary did anything reprehensible with a view to supplanting Harriett, and securing Shelley to herself. When he sought her love, she freely and warmly gave it; and in so doing, she again acted strictly within the scope of her own code of right.[10]

This was not Godwin's view. On 6 July, having been coolly informed that he could expect only half the £2,500 which he regarded as already his, he learned that the rest of the money would be required to support Shelley in the new life he intended to live abroad with Mary. If Shelley tried to enlist his sympathy by pointing out that the hero of *Fleetwood* had eloped with a sixteen-year-old girl, Godwin probably responded by drawing his attention to the words of the Preface. Whatever he might have said once in *Political Justice*, he did not, in 1816, regard marriage as an evil monopoly: had he not married twice himself? Shelley refused to listen. Coolly invited to give support and even to provide a list of travel-contacts, Godwin refused to comply. It took him two days to summon up the energy to discuss the matter with his daughter, an event bleakly recorded as 'Talk' in his diary.

Harriet, already alarmed by what struck her as an unusually long silence – four days – from her husband, was summoned to a meeting in London the following week and informed of recent developments. She must have behaved with considerable dignity; on 14 July, Shelley thanked her for her understanding, assured her of his enduring brotherly friendship and hoped that she might come to appreciate Mary's sufferings, and 'the tyranny which is exercised upon her'.[11] The tyranny was, presumably, Mrs Godwin's wish to use her as a shop-assistant. Harriet cannot have forgotten that it was just this knightly sense of mission which had led Shelley, in the summer of 1811, to rescue her from the oppression of boarding-school. At the time of their elopement she had been the age Mary was now. At nineteen, poor Harriet was ready to admit to Catherine Nugent that she felt thoroughly over the hill, worn out by the never-ending drama of life with Shelley.[12] But she had no wish to be deserted. Having made a show of accepting defeat with grace, she struck back.

The next two days were taken up with a flurry of visits between the Godwins and the Shelleys. Harriet and Shelley called at Skinner Street together on 15 July. They were coldly informed that Godwin was not at home, but he paid a call on Harriet later the same day. It seems that Godwin promised to do his best for her; his intentions were reinforced the following day, when Cornelia Turner arrived at Skinner Street to talk about her own friendship with Shelley. A visit from Cornelia's mother on 18 July led Godwin to advise Thomas Turner to remove his wife from harm's way. She was sent to join her husband in Devon the following month and never saw Shelley again. Later accounts by Mrs Godwin and Jane Clairmont indicate that Mary was given a stern dressing-down, after which she promised Harriet not to interfere with her marriage. Shelley agreed to stay out of Skinner Street; reassured, Godwin wrote letters to Lady Mountcashell, who was about to leave London for Italy, and to the author Helen Maria Williams, a warm friend and admirer of Mary Wollstonecraft's who had lived in France for many years. It is just possible that, knowing Shelley planned to travel abroad, Godwin was writing letters of introduction. It is more likely that he was making arrangements to place his daughter in homes where she could be protected from an ardent suitor. Both Miss Williams and Lady Mountcashell were forceful characters; both would gladly have done Godwin a favour.

Godwin's record shows a tranquil third week of July. Somewhat astonishingly, he and Shelley saw each other almost every day, pre-sumably to discuss their financial arrangements, while Mary took up residence in the schoolroom at the top of the house. Godwin supposed that all was under control. He was unaware that Jane Clairmont was helping to smuggle love letters in and out of Skinner Street. Among the packets which were surreptitiously conveyed to the schoolroom were two books. One was of particular significance.

Shelley's brief 'A Refutation of Deism', which was published anonymously earlier in the year, arrived with Mary's name hand-somely printed on its calf binding.[13] The second book, inscribed to 'Mary Wollstonecraft Godwin', was a copy of *Queen Mab*. The poem had been dedicated to Harriet; Shelley undid the tribute with a few suggestive lines which alluded to a woman who deserted her beloved in a time of need. Mary did not find it difficult to interpret their meaning. She was being asked to honour their oath of love. And so she would.

Tiny printed hands – these appear in all early editions of the book – highlighted the notes to *Queen Mab* in which Shelley presented the propositions to which he attached most importance. Following them carefully, and registering that these notes included long quotations from, among others, the writings of her father, Mary could see her lover as Godwin's intellectual heir. But Shelley was more extreme than Godwin had ever wished to be. Monarchy, here, was yoked to gold and murder as one of the 'hateful sons of Heaven', while religion was presented as a cheat, the daughter of Falsehood. Christ's return from death was made to sound as unremarkable as that of the drowned persons who were often successfully resuscitated by the Royal Humane Society. The only difference, in Shelley's view, was that the RHS did their work without passing it off as a miracle.

The hand-signalled note which Mary examined most carefully concerned love, sex and marriage. Here again, she found Shelley carrying on the work her parents had begun before she was born. Marriage, he wrote, should continue only so long as there was mutual love; so much for Harriet. Ideally, marriage would be abolished and, along with it, the notion of enduring relationships. 'Love is free,' he wrote: 'to promise for ever to love the same woman is not less absurd than to promise to believe the same creed.'

Mary's own copy of *Queen Mab* offers the first clear evidence we have of her passionate and intense nature. She read it when their love seemed doomed; on the endpapers, she let another poet express her feelings of despair. 'To Thyrza' had been Lord Byron's lament for the loss of someone dear to him. 'Ours too,' Mary noted enthusiastically after copying Byron's reference to 'The glance that none saw beside'. Byron's poem alluded to a sacred pledge; the words which Mary added here echoed both the sense of loss and of commitment:

> . . . what shall I write that I love the author beyond all powers of expression and that I am parted from him.
> Dearest and only love by that love we have promised to each other although I may not be your[s] I can never be another[s] But I am thine exclusively thine – by the kiss of love . . . I have pledged myself to thee and sacred is the gift –[14]

The word 'sacred' recurs three times in Mary's entry on the endpapers; the last presents her lover as the 'sacred vision' to whom she was willing to dedicate herself. Confined to her lonely schoolroom with only Jane to solace her, Mary contemplated a future of solitary devotion.

Mrs Godwin related the next episode of the drama in retrospect to Lady Mountcashell. Showing her usual blithe disregard for the facts and eager to emphasize her own creditable role, she enlarged the time scheme, spreading what may have taken place in two or three days to cover two weeks.

On an unspecified date after Mary's interview with her father, Shelley dashed into Skinner Street with a wild look. Followed by Mrs Godwin (her husband was out of the house), he rushed upstairs to the schoolroom; she ran after him. Having been pushed aside 'with extreme violence', or so she claimed, Mrs Godwin burst in to find Shelley urging his beloved to swallow a bottle of laudanum before he shot himself – he produced a small pistol – and so ensured that they were united in death. Jane burst into screams, Mary turned 'pale as a ghost' and James Marshall, who had been waiting downstairs to dine with Godwin, hurried in to plead for calm. Mary, 'tears streaming down her cheeks', begged Shelley to go home and promised eternal fidelity if he would only be reasonable. Shelley did as asked, but left the laudanum behind. (This, at a time when laudanum was easily available over the counter, need not mean that he intended Mary to take it.)[15]

Shortly afterwards, almost certainly less than the week given in Mrs Godwin's account, the Skinner Street household was woken by a midnight visit from Shelley's landlord, bringing the news that his lodger had taken an overdose of laudanum. Hurrying around the corner to the Hatton Garden lodging, they found the patient already in the care of a local doctor.* Mrs Godwin stayed with him all the following day, after which they called in Mrs de Boinville, who slowly nursed him back to health. It was during this period, in Jane's recollection, that the bookshop porter became engaged as a carrier of love notes.

Certain details can be slotted into this sensational episode. Godwin's journal, which records no substantial break in his conversations and meetings with Shelley, shows that he had a talk with Jane on 22 July. Since the word 'talk' always meant serious discussion in Godwin's diary, it may mark the point at which his stepdaughter, sternly reprimanded, stopped carrying messages.

On 25 July, Godwin wrote a letter of earnest appeal to Shelley. 'You entered my home on 19 June,' he wrote, conferring an importance on this date that remains puzzling, for Shelley had been in and out of Skinner Street all that month, and said nothing about Mary to her father until 6 July. Godwin acknowledged that the next week of

---

* The use of laudanum and the mention of a doctor who lived in Hatton Garden suggest that Shelley had been attended by Joseph Adams, the Hatton Garden physician who supplied Coleridge with laudanum and who, in 1816, recommended him to the care of the Gillmans.

visits had been irreproachable. 'I trusted to your principles.' Shelley's feelings for Mary were derided as 'caprice and a momentary impulse over every impulse that is dear to the honest heart'. He went on to praise Harriet as 'an innocent and meritorious wife' before begging Shelley to spare 'the fair and spotless fame of my young child . . . I could not believe that you wd. enter my house under the name of benefactor, to leave behind an endless poison to corrode my soul. I would as soon have credited that the stars would fall from Heav'n for my destruction . . .'[16] Moving though Godwin's words were, it is hard for us – and was no doubt hard for Shelley – to forget that he was at the same time hotly pursuing his young 'benefactor' for the sum of approximately £2,500 which he believed he had been promised.

No record exists of the final days of secret planning. It is not clear whether it was Shelley, or Mary, or even Jane who proposed that they start a new life abroad. Jane's involvement is made probable by the fact that they intended to cross France, now open again to foreign travellers, and to settle at Uri in Switzerland, which Jane looked on as the home of the Clairmonts, and therefore herself. Much has been made of the fact that she was taken along for her skill in speaking French, but Shelley already knew the language well enough to have quoted extensively from Holbach's *Système de la Nature*, in the original, in the notes to *Queen Mab*. A double rescue from the supposedly tyrannous supervision of Mrs Godwin, together with his taste for forming communes, was reason enough for Jane's inclusion in the plan. Mary, heavily in her stepsister's debt for her work as chaperone, letter-carrier and general accomplice, is unlikely to have raised objections. She may not have known that Shelley intended his pregnant wife to join them as a sister of the commune at a slightly later date.[17]

Mary had already packed a small box with her first writings, her letters from Shelley, her father and her closest friends. She also, strangely, packed a letter from Harriet, asking Mary to persuade Shelley to come back to her. Shortly after four in the morning on 28 July, Shelley sent word that the chaise was waiting for them at the end of his street. Mary, at the last moment, became uncertain. She went to his rooms, then ran back to Skinner Street. A letter of farewell was written and propped on Godwin's dressing-table. At just after five, unobtrusively dressed in black silk gowns, the two young girls tiptoed down the stairs and out along the silent street to the corner of Hatton Garden: 'she was in my arms – we were safe,' Shelley wrote with his usual sense of drama.[18]

The strain and – possibly – the first stages of pregnancy made a poor traveller of Mary. Stops had to be made at every stage on the road to Dover so that she could rest. Shelley, convinced that they were being pursued, hired four horses at Dartford to increase their speed; the journey, nevertheless, took almost twelve hours.

They left Dover shortly before dusk in a hired fisherman's boat manned by two sailors. Just before dawn, a thunder squall struck the boat and a heavy, rolling sea swept in, almost capsizing them. Shelley prepared himself to die while Mary, mute with terror, leaned against his shaking knees. The squall subsided, however, and she even managed to sleep a little as a steady wind blew them towards the Calais shore. To Shelley, wide-eyed and watchful, a bright omen for their future seemed to appear as the sun rose slowly up, streaking the sky above the wide wet sands with light.

The news of their flight was, to the Godwins, devastating. In one impulsive moment, Mary and Jane had undone all the careful years of securing their good reputations and preparing them for respectable marriages. Writing to Lady Mountcashell in November, Mrs Godwin lamented having tried to make ladies of such an ungrateful pair. Better, she now felt, to have brought them up 'on an inferior footing as befitted our poverty they would never have attracted Mr S's attention and they might now be safe at home . . .'[19]

She had no hope of influencing Mary, but Jane might still be persuaded to listen to the voice of common sense. If she, at least, could be brought back from Calais, all was not lost. Travelling all night and crossing the Channel by day, an exhausted Mrs Godwin reached France on the evening after the runaways. Shelley and his companions, resting in the best rooms Dessein's celebrated hotel at Calais could offer, were informed that a fat lady had arrived and was calling for her daughter. Jane spent that night in her mother's room and probably swore that she had been abducted against her will; this was how Mrs Godwin would always tell the story. By the morning, Jane was ready to go home. It says much for Shelley's powers of persuasion that it took him only one brief discussion to change her mind. Strolling along the harbour front later that day, Shelley had the satisfaction of seeing their persecutor making her way heavily down to the Dover boat. Tyranny had been vanquished!

Charles Clairmont was given the task of passing the news on to Fanny and summoning her home from Wales. Godwin was offered a grim distraction. Another of his young disciples, one Procter Patrickson, a Cambridge student, had been showing worrying signs of depression. Godwin had sent him a little money, promising more, with a recommendation to read Seneca. Patrickson had then spent a weekend at Skinner Street and was told that no more money could be given to him for the time being. On 8 August Patrickson went back to Cambridge and shot himself. On the same day, ten-year-old William Godwin, unable to bear the gloomy house and its domestic traumas any longer, ran away from home. The fact that he was found two days later, unharmed, did not lessen the anguish of the two days during which Godwin and his wife appeared to have lost three of their family at a stroke.

Shelley, who had burst into their lives like a comet, had presided over the devastation of all their hopes. He had given far less financial help than he had promised. He had wrecked the reputations, the 'spotless fame' of their daughters. Harriet, whom they did their best to reassure, passed on the wounding gossip that Godwin had finally raised money for his business by selling two children to Shelley for £1,500.

PART II

Freedom

CHAPTER EIGHT

SIX WEEKS IN EUROPE

1814

'How much is lost by those who pass their lives in cities – They are never visited by those sweet feelings which to recollect alone is heaven . . . how boundless & terrific would be their surprize if they could suddenly become philosophers & view things in their true & beautiful point of view.'

The Journals of Claire Clairmont, 17 August 1814[1]

NOVELTY SHED GLAMOUR OVER EVERYTHING THEY SAW. Looking back over a distance of twelve years as she sat down to review a clutch of travel books, Mary still had a vivid memory of the thrill of her first days in France. The narrow streets of Calais were as thick with English visitors as if they were holidaying at Brighton, but to the young travellers, staring at the ladies of conscious fashion, hair scraped into precarious domes twice the height of their heads, skimpy dresses fluttering from waists which seemed to have taken refuge in their owners' armpits, much seemed wonderfully and comically foreign.

[W]e saw with extasy the strange costume of the French women, read with delight our own descriptions in the passport,* looked with curiosity on every *plât*, fancying that the fried leaves of artichokes were frogs; we saw shepherds in opera-hats, and post-boys in

---

* Their amusement probably derived from the fact that the passports, obtained at the Calais Custom House, offered a Frenchman's view of their character and appearance.

jack-boots; and (*pour comble de merveille*) heard little boys and girls talk French; it was acting a novel, being an incarnate romance.[2]

Memory made everything delightful. Mary had forgotten the heat, baking her until she was ready to faint as their quaint two-wheeled carriage rattled towards the capital across a landscape of broad, shadowless cornfields. Unpacking her few possessions in the gloomy rooms of the Hôtel de Vienne, she had a sudden pang of homesickness. Shelley was called in to peruse and admire the little box of her own writings, of letters from her father and her dear Isabella which she had carried away from Skinner Street. Later, they set out to explore the city; this, after all, was Paris and they were, after a fashion, on their honeymoon.

That night, Shelley noted in the journal that he and Mary had been 'too happy to sleep'.[3] Making love, discussing poetry, forgetting to eat, they discussed the letter in which – Mary had produced it from her box of writings – poor Harriet had suggested certain phrases which she might use to cool Shelley's passion. If Mary felt any pity for Shelley's wife, she chose not to acknowledge it in the journal of which Shelley was, at the beginning, the chief keeper. Perhaps she felt none; she knew, after all, very little of Harriet beyond the accounts which Shelley had given her, and these had not been kind. The fact that Mary had promised to stay away from Shelley did not mean she had to like the angry, tearful young woman to whom she had reluctantly given her word.

Reverently, Shelley noted down the wisdom of Mary's observations and the engrossing nature of their conversations. He was still a little in awe of his brilliant prize. 'I was not before so clearly aware how much of the colouring our own feelings throw upon the liveliest delineations of other minds,' he noted on 3 August, after Mary had read and offered her own interpretation of 'some passages from Ld Byron's poems'. These probably included 'To Thyrza', which she had written into the back of the copy of *Queen Mab* that Shelley had sent her in July.

Paris disappointed a couple whose imaginations had painted it in revolutionary colours. Frances Shelley, a distant relation by marriage of Shelley's who visited the French capital the following year, was entranced by the Tuileries gardens, where the orange trees were in blossom and the fountains were a reproach to London's arid parks; Shelley and Mary thought them formal and dull. Notre Dame was less impressive than they had expected; they had trouble in finding a painting to admire – it seems to have been Nicholas Poussin's *Winter*

– among the splendid loot Napoleon had assembled at the Louvre. Only the handsome outer ring of boulevards, where chattering crowds and tall trees hung with lamps reminded Frances Shelley of Vauxhall Gardens, were found to be quite elegant and pleasant.

It was easier for Frances, smart, wealthy and wholly in favour of the restored monarchy, to enjoy the city. She and her husband, like all prudent travellers, had come armed with letters of recommendation to French bankers. Shelley, leaving England in haste, had brought none. Instead of the money which his wealthy radical publishing friend Thomas Hookham had promised to send out, he received a letter reproaching him for irresponsible behaviour. On 4 August, his birthday – 'I thought it had been the 27th of June,' he romantically noted, remembering a moonlit evening at St Pancras churchyard – Shelley was forced to go looking for anyone who would pay a few francs for his watch and chain.

Trailing around the streets of a city where the absence of pavements obliged them to pick their way among the constant press of carriages, beggars and hawkers, and where the primly dressed and bonneted English girls felt embarrassed and out of place among the revealing, clinging gowns of Parisian ladies, they could not be blamed for disliking the city. It was heightened by their sense of isolation. Helen Maria Williams, the republican poetess from whom they had hoped for glorious stories of Mary Wollstonecraft's life in Paris, was out of town; a pompous Frenchman who bored them to tears with boasts of his patriotic acts, promised them everything and ended by producing nothing but stories. The best Shelley could do was to accept a reluctant loan of £60 from a banker to whom Hookham sent a grudging introduction. (Hookham's reluctance can be easily understood; not only was he a friend of Godwin's, but Shelley had coolly instructed him and his brother to look after hapless, abandoned Harriet.)

Sixty pounds was not a fortune, but Shelley calculated that they could, with care, cover the journey to Switzerland, if they travelled on foot. Early on the morning of 8 August, he and Jane went to market and came back with the ideal travelling companion, a donkey to carry their cases and books. Typically, they forgot to load it with their greatest treasure. The box containing Mary's manuscripts and letters, including all those that Shelley had written to her that summer, was left behind at the hotel and never recovered. This may be the simple explanation for the puzzling absence of Godwin's many letters to his daughter in the first sixteen years of her life. It does not explain the disappearance of her replies.

Shelley and Jane had been fleeced; they were only a few miles out
of Paris when the donkey sank down on its knees. Half carrying, half
dragging the poor beast to the next village, they traded it in for a mule.
The seller drove a hard bargain; travellers, as they had ruefully begun
to understand, were a prime target for sharp dealing in a hungry
country.

Slowly, and in increasingly low spirits, they made their way south-
east towards Troyes. The heat was relentless; the sun beat down on a
grim post-war landscape of burnt-out villages and blank, uncultivated
fields. Each long day ended with dread of what kind of night they
would pass. Milk and sour bread were sometimes all that was available
to eat; at one inn, Jane's pathetic account of rats scampering over her
face and her terror of their lecherous host obliged Shelley and Mary
to take her into their bed. Shelley, usually a vigorous and enthusiastic
walker, managed to sprain his ankle, forcing him to ride on the mule
while the girls, fanning the flies from their black silk travelling dresses,
plodded behind him along the dusty, interminable lanes. A week into
their pilgrimage, on 13 August, they decided to give up walking; the
mule was traded in part exchange for a carriage.

This was the first day on which Shelley found time to send Harriet
an account of the journey. Any guilt he may have felt was absolved
by a generous suggestion that she should make her way to Geneva and
join them at 'some sweet retreat' in the Swiss mountains. Hookham's
friend, Thomas Love Peacock, a coolly witty and erudite classicist
who had spent time with them in Wales and had grown very fond of
Shelley's young wife, would advise her on travelling expenses. She was
urged not to forget the necessity of bringing various legal documents
which he would require.[4]

Shelley's letter was tactless, bizarre and entirely characteristic.
There was no thought for Harriet's feelings at being deserted, or for
the fact that she was being invited to travel abroad for the first time,
and alone, when she was five months pregnant. Shelley, we may be
sure, believed he had Harriet's own happiness at heart. She would be
away from Eliza Westbrook, the sister he had come to regard – for no
good reason – as Harriet's evil genius; his wife in name only, she
would be a part of the happy, high-minded group guided by his
beloved Mary's noble mind. Mary was probably shrewd enough to
guess that Harriet would never take up such an unappealing offer –
and indeed Harriet did not. Shelley asked his wife to address her
answer to Neufchatel, but he had no response.

Flat fields gave way at last to wooded slopes and bubbling streams;
Jane, inspired by the approach to Switzerland – her homeland, in her

own romantic view – decided that she too would like to keep a diary. Mary had none to lend her. Shelley produced a red leather notebook into which he had already written some Latin and Italian passages, probably while taking language lessons from Cornelia Turner. It is impossible to suppose that Jane, admiring Shelley as she did, ignored his entries; no great linguistic skill was needed to discover their passionate nature. One read as follows:

Lecto me brachiis tenebat, delicio voluptatis pene deliquo cecidi. Basies mutes vitae reclamabant delecta labia! Timores quiescebat.[5]

(He was holding me in his arms in the bed. I almost died of madness and delight. Beloved lips were again seeking mutual kisses of life. He calmed my fears.) Even if Jane had not viewed Shelley in a sexual light until then, a sixteen-year-old girl must have been troubled and excited by words which sounded so seductive. Did they carry some secret message for her? Why had he not torn the pages out?

Two days after Jane received this ambiguous gift, the girls both took note of an encounter with a lovely child, Marguerite Pascal. Shelley was enchanted by her; only the reluctance of the girl's father had prevented him from adopting her on the spot. The nonchalance with which the impulse was recorded is disconcerting, but it was not out of keeping with Shelley's impulsive nature. His sister Hellen remembered how, during a school holiday, Shelley once tried to adopt a pretty little travelling acrobat; in 1811, he had investigated the possibility of obtaining and educating two young girls.[6] One of his first projects on their return to England would be to kidnap his sisters from school. Mary did not disapprove; her own mother had fostered a little orphan girl for a brief period and Godwin had acted as the father-figure to a whole row of young men. Firmly believing that a child's mind was the product of its environment rather than its parentage, she was as willing as Shelley to become a social tutor.

Marguerite Pascal was not available for the interesting experiment, and the travellers continued on their way, their spirits rising as the Alps began to show white heads on the horizon. Mesdames de Staël and Récamier, making their own pilgrimage to the Alps, had turned back with a sniff at such overrated crags – and because the sun had started to burn their daringly exposed bosoms. Mary and Jane, in their sensible high-necked dresses and with Wordsworth's raptures all ready for quotation, were appropriately enthralled. 'Their immensity staggers the imagination,' Shelley noted on their behalf on 19 August, when the Alps were still some hundred miles away in the distance, '& so far

surpasses all conception that it requires an effort of the understanding
to believe that they are indeed mountains.'

Three is an uncomfortable number for a honeymoon; hints of
irritation and resentment had begun to surface.[7] They were near the
Swiss frontier when Mary, looking very sad, raised the subject with
her companions of the difficulties always caused by men's behaviour.
Shelley quickly interpreted this as a reproach to him for separating her
from her father. Mary denied it and no more was said; Jane noted that
Mary had not been entirely truthful. A little further along, Jane made
another spiky comment. Shelley had suggested that Mary should
bathe naked in a stream – it was screened from view by overhanging
bushes – and let him gather leaves to dry her. Mary, according to Jane's
record, grew indignant at the idea of doing anything so improper.
The sense that Jane herself would have stripped off and plunged in
without a qualm is unmissable. Increasingly confident and obstreperous in her opinions, Jane earned herself a mild rebuke from Shelley.
His comments on her character did not please; she noted them down,
then mutinously ripped the page out of her diary.

The Alps did not disappoint; Switzerland did. Shelley's ardent and
frequent readings of *Fleetwood* had been their chief preparation for the
scenery. Although Godwin had never left Britain, careful research
enabled him to provide a strikingly vivid and exact account of Lake
Uri, the location they had chosen for their future home.

> It was a deep and narrow water, about nine miles in length, and skirted
> on both sides with rocks uncommonly wild and romantic, some per-
> pendicular, some stretching over our heads, and intercepting the view
> of the upper sky, and clothed for the most part with forests of beech
> and pine, that extended themselves down to the very edge of the
> water. The lake was as smooth as crystal, and the arching precipices
> that inclosed it gave a peculiar solemnity to the gloom . . . I thought
> of William Tell, and the glorious founders of the Swiss liberty; I
> thought of the simple manners which still prevail in the primitive
> cantons; I felt as if I were in the wildest and most uninhabited islands
> of the South Sea.[8]

Fed on this and the exotic setting of the Chevalier Lawrence's
accounts of free love among the Indian community of the Nairs,
Shelley had felt free to dream, and the girls with him. This was where
they would settle to live in communal affection and, if she so wished,
permit Harriet to join them for enlightening discussions.

The reality fell somewhat short. The Swiss, stolid and smiling,
showed none of William Tell's fire; the weather was too bad to allow

them to cross the lake; no cottages were available. Instead, they had to make do with some rooms in a large ugly house at Brunnen on Lake Lucerne, from which they could dimly see, through a mist of wind and water, the chapel where Tell had leapt ashore and regained his liberty. Mary and Shelley sat out by the dark water, reading Tacitus and discussing the opening for a novel Shelley wanted to write.[9] Jane, sent off to read by herself elsewhere, glowered up at the little mountainside chalets for spoiling the view. Too many people, and too much money, she decided; all were 'rich contented & happy. A poor beggar is never seen – The people are uninteresting for they are most immoderately stupid & almost ugly to deformity.'[10] Having expressed her views to her satisfaction, she retired early to bed.

After dictating the opening pages of his novel to Mary the following day, Shelley gave her some worrying news. Their sixty pounds had shrunk to less than thirty. If they travelled up the Rhine and through Holland, it was just enough to get them home to England. Jane was too hysterical to be entrusted with the truth. If they had to find reasons, the atrocious heating arrangements in their rooms could be blamed; the lodgings were heated with an enormous old-fashioned stove which, when it worked, almost suffocated them.

Jane seemed to accept this improbable explanation; tired of playing gooseberry, she even expressed pleasure at the prospect of going home. She waited for the first stop on the return journey to throw a fit of what Mary would name 'Janes horrors'. The horror had been brought on by reading *King Lear*, and Mary suspected her stepsister of trying to impress Shelley with her sensitivity. She was not wrong; later attacks of 'horrors' were unmistakably aimed at obtaining Shelley's attention. But the feelings expressed in Jane's diary sound heartfelt enough. She was, or thought she was, in love; the play seemed to offer a mirror to her own confused feelings. 'I think Lear treats Cordelia very ill – "What shall poor Cordelia do – Love & be silent",' she wrote that night. 'Oh [th]is is true – Real Love will never [sh]ew itelf to the eye of broad day – [i]t courts the secret glades.'[11]

Exclusion was a painful experience: entries in the lovers' joint journal show Shelley entirely wrapped up in his love for Mary, aware of their companion only as an intrusive third party. Noting Mary's seventeenth birthday at Basle, he doubted that they would ever be happier; they passed the following day reading *A Short Residence* aloud and comparing their own water trip to Mary Wollstonecraft's lonely journey. Reading also provided a welcome distraction from the company of their fellow travellers, a subject on which Mary and Jane were at one in their disgust. '[O]ur only wish was to absolutely annihilate such uncleansable animals,' Mary wrote after their first day on the Rhine; a week later, Jane noted that the men actually kissed each other, and that her soul had shrunk back from 'countenances begrimmed with mental & bodily depravity'.[12] Prejudiced though these remarks sound, they were echoed by many contemporary diarists. The German peasant class was insufficiently picturesque in costume or in manner to find favour abroad.

The 2nd of September was one of the rare days on which Shelley and Mary managed to have some time to themselves. Leaving the boat a few miles north of Mannheim, they were away from Jane for three hours, long enough to explore the surrounding foothills and, very possibly, to learn some of the folk tales and legends of the area.*

Frankenstein is a striking and unusual name. It has no resonance in Geneva, where Mary conceived her novel in 1816. It has strong links to this region of the Rhine. Castle Frankenstein was not among the popular hilltop castles competently sketched and painted by English visitors; it was, despite its towers and moat, hardly a castle at all, and well beyond a three-hour round journey on foot. But the outline was clearly visible from Gernsheim, where their boat was moored; any local hoping to earn a few coins with a good story would have told the young travellers about Konrad Dippel.[13]

A pastor's son, Dippel was born at the castle in 1673, when it was being used as a military hospital. After studying alchemy at university, he became a fashionable physician whose dream was always to buy and live in his birthplace. (He liked to sign himself as Dippel Frankensteina, Dippel of Frankenstein.) Chased out of Strasbourg after allegations that he had been robbing graveyards for his anatomical experiments, Dippel was convinced that he could bring a body back to life by injecting it with a concoction of blood and bone, often made from both mammal and human corpses. In Mary's novel, Victor Frankenstein would use animal bones to help manufacture his monstrous creature.

Like other alchemists of the period – their ambitious dreams gave Mary's father the subject for *St Leon*, the novel Byron thought his finest – Dippel experimented with the creation of gold and with an elixir of life. By selling the results to the nobility, he hoped to raise money to buy the castle. Instead, it went to a wealthy widow; poor Dippel, who boasted that he had found a way to live to the age of 135,

---

* Lack of German, a language which most English travellers found exasperatingly difficult, need not have stopped them from hearing such stories; the journals offer evidence of plenty of conversations having taken place, presumably in English or French.

died the next year, aged 61. Storytellers hinted at a pact with the devil, which Dippel had failed to keep. The intervening years had turned him into a favourite local legend, to be added to gruesome tales of a cannibal monster who, in times long past, used the grim little castle as his headquarters.

Sitting on the shores of Lake Lucerne, Mary had been introduced to one of Shelley's favourite books, the Abbé Barruel's *Memoirs, Illustrating the History of Jacobinism* (1797–8).* Here, Barruel traced the birth of 'the monster called Jacobin' to the secret society of the Illuminati at Ingolstadt. Ingolstadt is where Mary decided to send Victor Frankenstein to university; Ingolstadt is where he animates his creature, in circumstances and with methods similar to those used by Dippel. Journeying from Lucerne along the Rhine, Mary's disgusted comments on their fellow travellers had included this comment: 'Twere easier for god *to make entirely new men* than attempt to purify such monsters as these . . . loathsome creepers' (my italics).[14] God here, with the lower-case 'g' , is demoted to the level of a man who assumes godlike powers, a promethean overreacher.

And so, following closely on each other, we have a setting for Frankenstein's experiment, the hint of a newly created man of human manufacture, and the tale of Konrad Dippel's attempts to bring the dead to life. The idea for a novel about a whaling voyage had already taken shape at Dundee and may have been among the manuscripts that were carelessly left behind in Paris; the 1814 tour offered rich material on which to draw for the central subject of *Frankenstein*.

The beauty of the Rhine landscape captivated them all. Jane was convinced that she would never again care for a view which lacked a ruined castle; Mary, returning to the Rhine in her forties, longed to spend a full summer there, 'to penetrate the ravines, to scale the heights, to linger among the ruins, to hear *still more*' (my italics) 'of its legends, and visit every romantic spot'.[15] In the late summer of 1814, sitting in discomfort on deck to escape the low crowd who smoked and sang beneath them in the cabin, her only cause of complaint was the extreme slowness of the boat.

---

* Mary could already have been acquainted with Barruel's work through her home reading. Godwin drew on Barruel's account of the Illuminati for *St Leon*, in which the eponymous hero's pledge of secrecy and his setting aside of family ties to pursue his experiments with alchemy reflect the undercover activities of the society described by Barruel.

When they reached Holland, Mary, exhausted by the journey and no doubt suffering some physical discomfort in the early months of pregnancy, could find nothing to admire except the hedges; Jane, whose spirits invariably gravitated in the opposite direction, was in ecstasies. The willow-shaded canals! The green-shuttered country houses! The shining brick pavements of Utrecht! While Mary and Shelley prepared themselves for the crossing to Gravesend and talked earnestly 'of many thing[s] past, present & to come', Jane buried her nose in *Emile* and worked herself up into a state of fine indignation over the way Rousseau judged women by his fictional Sophie, one of the 'most finished and [deleted] of Coquettes . . . It is indeed partial to judge the whole sex by the conduct of one whose very education tended to fit her more for a Seraglio than the friend & equal of Man.'[16] It should not surprise us to find a strong echo of Mary Wollstonecraft in this energetic language; her books had accompanied the travellers on their journey. Jane shared with Mary and Shelley a happy conviction that they were behaving just as she, their presiding spirit, would have wished.

Bad weather hindered their return. Stranded at Maarluis, with a high west wind blowing out to sea and keeping them all in their rooms, Mary won admiring comments from Shelley for starting work on a story, since lost. She called it 'Hate', an intriguing title. Was the tale directed at those German passengers she so despised, or was she, as they drew nearer to England, warming to the theme of her hated stepmother? Least likely seems the notion that she would have written a story which focused on her hostility to Jane. Shelley might have sometimes wished Jane out of the way, but he was full of concern and affection for her. Mary would have had to be uncommonly brash to choose a hateful stepsister for her subject.

Always competitive and conscious of Mary's enviable intellectual superiority, Jane began writing a story of her own on the same day. She called it 'The Ideot' and planned it as a Wollstonecraftian tale of a sweet and noble girl who follows her own impulses rather than society's laws.[17] The theme suggests that Jane had been reading *Adeline Mowbray*, a novel on precisely that subject which was published in 1805 by Godwin's Norfolk friend, Amelia Alderson, who married John Opie. Neither this unfinished project nor Jane's comments on *Emile* suggest that she had any intention of returning to the Skinner Street fold.

The crossing was terrible. The captain sailed in defiance of warnings that they would all be drowned; if Jane's diary is to be believed, they almost were. 'The face of the captain was all anxiety – We asked him some trifling question but he said at present we must not plague him.' The breakers were beyond her wildest imaginings, vast ridges of white foam racing towards them across the sea and threatening to dash the boat to pieces. 'Poor Mary was sick as death & was obliged to go to bed,' she wrote with smug compassion, but 'Shelley and I sat upon deck & the waves which had become terribly high broke over us.' Later, even Shelley had surrendered: 'Every one of the Passengers were sick except myself.'[18] Mary, however, recovered enough on the second day at sea to conduct a fierce argument with a man who began defending the slave trade, and to note the fact in her journal.

Shelley's financial calculations proved frighteningly exact; the trio arrived back in England without having been able to pay the cost of their crossing. The captain was prepared to wait until money could be obtained; a boatman was found to row them slowly up the broad mouth of the Thames – and to keep them in sight. He was still with them when they caught the City stage, jostling grimly back to reality through streets crowded with carts and coaches, back into a dirty, smoke-hazed city, littered with derelict building sites. Paris had the excuse of being suspended in the middle of Napoleon's grand plans for its future; London, on a dull September day, seemed trapped in the past.

It was the beginning of an experience which was to become wretchedly familiar to them all, of a desperate hunt for money on this occasion, or a frantic flight from creditors on another. They went, accompanied by the unbudgeable boatman, from Shelley's bank to the Hookhams and on to the Voyseys, a family who had known Mary and Jane since they were children. The girls had often stayed in their London house; the Voysey children had been their playmates. Today, Mrs Voysey did not even want them in the house, let alone to lend them money. Her son was more sympathetic. Henry Voysey agreed to keep Shelley company as he set off to see if he could borrow from – of all people – his wife. For two long hours, while the sky grew dark, Mary and Jane sat in their hackney outside the closed door of Mr Westbrook's handsome house in Chapel Street, just off Grosvenor Square. The boatman did his best to keep the weary young ladies in good spirits; he had, Jane gratefully noted, been most kind. Eventually, Shelley emerged with the necessary sum and the three travellers settled themselves into a quiet hotel on Oxford Street, then a residential area.

The following day, they moved to lodgings at Margaret Street, off Cavendish Square and conveniently close to Chapel Street for Shelley's dealings with his wife. For Mary, it marked the beginning of a wandering life of which she later wistfully wrote: 'it seems as if I were never to be stationary – I who long so for a home.'[19]

CHAPTER NINE

EXPERIMENTS IN LIVING

1814 – 1815

'. . . good creature press me to you and hug your own Mary to your heart perhaps she will one day have a father till then be everything to me love – & indeed I will be a good girl and never vex you more . . .'

Mary Wollstonecraft Godwin to Percy Bysshe Shelley, 28 October 1814

MRS GODWIN HAD RETURNED TO SKINNER STREET FROM CALAIS ON 31 July with the news that her mission to rescue Jane had failed. Perhaps they still hoped that the runaways would make a speedy return: nothing seems to have been said on 7 August when Lady Mountcashell came to bid the Godwins farewell before she left England with her lover, George Tighe, and their small daughter, Laurette. A week later, Mrs Godwin decided to take their aristocratic friend into her confidence. The event was presented as if it had only just taken place. 'O my dear lovely child is gone,' she wrote in the first of a stream of letters which now exist only in her daughter's heavily revised copies.[1] In her mother's version, Jane was the innocent victim, abducted by a selfish and heartless young couple in need of an interpreter.

Godwin was still unable to believe that Mary intended more than a high-spirited escapade. He was ready at this point to take her back. A month after the dawn flit from Skinner Street, he readied himself for 'the hour of distress (which I believe, is not far distant) when these unworthy children shall again seek the protection and aid of their father'.[2]

Godwin underrated their determination. They had gone together; they would stay together. If they needed schooling, then Shelley would supply it. If they starved, so be it. There was to be no going back. Mary, as they now knew, was pregnant and it would only be a matter of time before her condition began to show; Jane, in her determination to stay with them, tarred herself with the same brush. The world, from now on, would disapprove and keep a shocked distance. But Mary Wollstonecraft's example flamed before them, bright as a lighthouse beacon over a stormy sea. She, too, had endeavoured to bring her warm understanding and reviving influence to a married couple, the Fuselis; it was not their fault that Harriet, like Mrs Fuseli, had declined their liberating proposal to live a communal life. Mary Wollstonecraft, too, had boldly bred and raised her lover's child. They could, in fact, fairly glow with the rightness of their behaviour and the feeble blinkered condition of those who questioned it.

It is hard not to pity the Godwins. Ostracized by many friends for their supposed complicity in the plot, appealed to by Harriet for support and still wretchedly dependent on Shelley, of all people, for the money to bail them out of debt, they were in an unenviable position. Reluctantly, for they were not unloving parents, they took the hard course of disapproval. Mary was forbidden to come anywhere near them; Jane was given the option of return, but only if she broke contact with Shelley and her stepsister. Fanny and Charles were told that, officially at least, they must support the Godwins in their stand.

Fanny's own position was singularly delicate. Neither a Clairmont nor a Godwin, she was being viewed by her Wollstonecraft aunts, Everina and Eliza, as a potential successor for the small school which they were running in Ireland. It was not a bad prospect for a plain, shy, penniless girl but the aunts, having already suffered from Godwin's candid memoir of their sister, were terrified by the prospect of another scandal; the Godwins were warned to keep Fanny away from Shelley's dangerous company. The few timid visits Fanny made to see Mary and Jane in London were acts of great courage; she got little thanks for them. Fanny, to the Shelley household, seemed pathetic in her submission. They laughed at her little squeaks of fear when, on one occasion, Shelley and Jane chased her through the dark and made a play of kidnapping her. It was no game to Fanny; her whole future was at stake.

Harriet's hopeful fancies of a penitent husband's return to the fold were briskly shattered. Shelley may have seemed subdued on 13

September when he needed money to pay for their crossing, food and lodgings; having obtained it, he was quick to remind her that he had formed 'a violent and lasting passion for another'. Harriet was invited to admire Mary's courage: 'she has resigned all for me.'[3] On 3 October, as Harriet's confinement drew near, her husband wished her well, asked for his stockings and handkerchiefs to be forwarded and told her to be realistic. 'I am united to another,' he informed her with the flourish of an eastern potentate; 'you are no longer my wife.'[4] Two days later, he coolly regretted the circumstances which had led to 'your estrangement from Mary & myself'.[5] The separation, Harriet was given to understand, was all of her own making.

Mary saw, not a deserted, pregnant wife, but a woman who was living in comfortable security while they starved. Harriet had a sympathetic older sister in Eliza, a comfortable home with her parents at Chapel Street, the commiseration of all. Mary had none of these. She grew cross and uneasy when Shelley showed pleasure at the news that Harriet had given birth to a son, Charles. So Harriet had produced an heir, Mary noted in her journal on 30 November: 'S[helley] writes a number of circular letters on an event which ought to be ushered in with ringing of bells &c. for it is the son of his *wife*.'[6] What right did Harriet have to write letters signed 'a deserted wife'? What did she know about feeling deserted?

Mary was feeling painfully isolated; she had not expected to be so punished for following her great mother's example. Sitting in the dingy lodgings at Church Terrace, St Pancras, into which they had moved at the beginning of October, she waited for visits from old neighbours and friends, from her dear Hannah Hopwood, from kindly Mrs Knapp, the landlady of their home at the Polygon, from anybody. Nobody came. Mrs de Boinville had the excuse that she had only just learned of her husband's death and was in mourning; Margaret and Louisa Jones, who had kept up with Mary ever since the years when they had nursed her at the Polygon, had none. Even Mary's former governess, Maria Smith, waited until the spring of 1815 to make a brief visit. Most hurtful of all was the silence from 'Izy', her beloved Isabella. Mary's letter to her was answered by a scathing rebuke from David Booth; Isabella's sister, Christy, rubbed salt into her wounds by sending expressions of regret at Mary's reckless behaviour.

Deprived of family and friends, Mary was reduced to the company of petulant Jane and the one young man who was prepared to risk being seen in Shelley's company. (Hogg kept a disapproving distance in the autumn; the Hookhams met Shelley on a strictly business basis.)

Thomas Love Peacock, more inclined in 1814 to become a poet than a novelist, was a narrow-shouldered, heavy-eyed young man with black hair and, when he dropped his reserved manner, a sharp sense of humour. Peacock was as capricious and ardent in his love-affairs as Shelley himself. Marianne de St Croix, a lady about whom little is known (Mary found her rather tiring and dreaded her occasional visits), was his current love; in January 1815, an expensive entanglement with a lady known to us only as 'Charlotte' landed Peacock in the debtors' prison for a few days. Sympathetic towards Harriet, whose good name and amiable character he always defended, Peacock understood Shelley's need for a more intellectual companion. The fact that Mary had been learning Greek and Latin since her return to England must have impressed a man who was himself a brilliant and self-taught classical scholar.

Peacock, like Shelley, had a streak of endearing simplicity; some of the happiest days in these early months in England were spent walking north from St Pancras to one of the many little ponds beyond Primrose Hill, where Shelley, aided by Peacock, launched tiny fleets of paper boats. Strolling on, they laid leisurely plots with Mary and Jane to kidnap Shelley's young sisters from school and carry them off to be re-educated, together with Peacock's Marianne, in some pleasant refuge – Wales, perhaps, or the west of Ireland. Listening to the discussions, to Mary's calm voice douching Shelley's gleeful schemes, Peacock began to see how his friends might be shaped into the characters of the beautiful Cephalis Cranium (brainhead) and Mr Escot, the vegetarian deteriorationist who blames man's downfall since the Golden Age on his carnivorous diet. (Shelley, unlike Peacock, was an ardent vegetarian.) He began work on *Headlong Hall*, his first conversation-novel, the following year.

Peacock had a chance to demonstrate his friendship when the threat of imprisonment for debt forced Shelley into hiding towards the end of October. Mary and Jane stayed on at their drab lodgings in Church Terrace, while Peacock sheltered his friend from the bailiffs at the home in Southampton Buildings which he shared with his elderly mother. Hogg dropped in to crack tactless jokes about men who kept two 'wives'.

Writing her novel *Lodore* some thirty years later, Mary must have been grimly amused by the fact that the chapters which won the most praise were those which were the least imaginative.[7] The realism so admired by reviewers was founded on her own vivid memory of life on the run in the autumn of 1814 and in particular of the miserable fortnight when Shelley and she had been forced into separation. It had been a time of intense anxiety, of hurried meetings in dark alleys and desolate squares, of plotting the secret delivery of letters, of endless fright that the bailiffs would somehow catch up with them. Lonely, apprehensive and so poor that she sometimes had only a piece of bread or a few biscuits for her day's rations, Mary counted the slow hours until midnight on Saturday evening when, for a whole day, the law forbade arrests.

The wait was sometimes unbearable. 'About six Mary proposes that we should go for Shelley in a Coach,' Jane noted on Saturday, 5 November. 'We do so – He won't come – Return home.' She passed the time by writing a 'very shocking' scene for a never-completed play while Mary dozed on the sofa until past midnight, when Shelley finally knocked on the door. Jane was amazed that the two of them could choose to spend all their time in bed: 'To sleep & talk – why this is merely vegetating.' But Mary was happy: 'Love in idleness' was how she contentedly recorded their day together. She remembered it when she was writing *Lodore*.

> The dusky room showed them but half to each other, and the looks of each, beaming with tenderness, drank life from one another's gaze. The soft shadows thrown on their countenances, gave a lamp-like lustre to their eyes, in which the purest spirit of affection sat, weaving such unity of sentiment, such strong bonds of attachment, as made all life dwindle to a point, and freighted the passing minute with the hopes and fears of their entire existence.[8]

The scene records a rare moment of content in a period of which Mary's memories were dark. In *Lodore*'s young Ethel Villiers, pleading with her high-principled husband to borrow from those who have the money to give, we catch an echo of Mary herself, begging Shelley to swallow his pride and seek help from his rich relations. Shelley did finally make such an appeal – it was rejected – to his great-uncle; in the novel, however, Ethel's husband angrily refuses to ask for aid. Edward Villiers represents Shelley at his most extreme, carrying Godwin's mistrust of gratitude to the point where it takes precedence over his wife's hunger and poverty. 'Ever since I knew what pecuniary obligations were,' he tells Ethel, 'I resolved to lay under such to no man, and this resolve was greater than my love for you; judge therefore of its force, and the violence you do me, when you would oblige me to act against it.'[9] This was a difficulty with which Mary became wearily familiar; she had chosen a man who, like her father, put beliefs before relationships. Neither Shelley nor Godwin were easy men to live with in this respect.

———

Reading the journals and letters from this period of Mary's life is a little like entering the traditional closing scene to the act of an opera buffa, when all the characters burst into song at once, converging, separating, contradicting, unifying. Godwin was, as always, keeping his laconic daily journal, compressing his own financial tribulations into a stiff list of names of possible benefactors, persistent creditors, never once mentioning his lost daughter; his wife was still keeping up a slanted account of recent events for the benefit of 'Mrs Mason', the name under which Lady Mountcashell had decided to start a new life abroad. (She took it from the kindly teacher in the stories which Mary Wollstonecraft had once written for her.) Mrs Godwin's reports were inaccurate but persuasive; Mrs Mason wrote back to say that, while Jane was evidently in no way responsible, Mary had behaved with predictable selfishness.*

In another corner of the stage stands Shelley, who in one revealing note described himself as 'an harp responsive to every wind'.[10] He was allowing his harpstrings to be vigorously plucked by Jane as she raised the pitch of her 'horrors' to full-blown theatrical performances, threw tantrums when she was excluded, and demanded all the attention, and more, that she had been accustomed to receiving at home.

Mary, at just seventeen, was precociously mature; Jane, only a few months younger, was still a child. It was this which made her so attractive and disarming to a man who loved to see himself in a teacher's role. When he was not being thoughtful, patient, considerate – and there are many entries in the journal to show that he was often so with Jane – Shelley was intrigued by the way he could manipulate her. Like his younger sisters, Jane could be frightened half to death with a little skilful guidance. Fear was an emotion which fascinated Shelley. His skill at promoting it in such a susceptible mind sometimes had alarming results.

Their conversation on the night of 7 October began with Shelley's ghoulish description of how soldiers were punished by having squares

———

* Mrs Godwin did lasting damage to Mary in this quarter; Mrs Mason always showed a marked preference for Jane, who was first presented to her as the innocent victim of Shelley's plans.

of skin cut from their backs; a little later, he reminded Jane that they had reached 'the witching hour' of night; could she feel terror in the silence? She could; shortly after two, she found the look on his face so disturbing that she ran off to her room upstairs. Shelley had gone to his own room with a book and was bending down to kiss Mary goodnight when he heard footsteps in the passage.

'Jane was there . . .' Her face, Shelley noted excitedly, had been ashy, lined with terror, eyes bulging from the sockets; she had begged him to come to her room. Surely he had touched her pillow? It had moved, seemingly by itself, from the bed to a chair. Unable to resist such clear evidence of witchcraft, Shelley left his book for a further session of horrors in the parlour. He was well rewarded.

> Just as the dawn was struggling with moon light Jane remarked in me that unutterable expression which had affected her with so much horror before. She described it as expressing a mixture of deep sadness & conscious power over her . . . her horror & agony increased even to the most dreadful convulsions. She shr[i]eked & writhed on the floor.[11]

This was rather more than he had bargained for. Mary was called in; it is worth noting that Jane's convulsions promptly ceased. A week later, on 14 October, Shelley reproached Jane for her 'insensibility & incapacity for the slightest degree of friendship'. By that evening, she was in tears; Shelley had to give up his place in Mary's bed to her. Wonderful to relate, he noted the following morning – his tone was decidedly sceptical – 'the chimney board in Janes room is found to have walked leisurely into the middle of the room, accompanied by the pillow; who being very sleepy tried to get back into bed again but fell down on his back.'[12]

'How hateful it is to quarrel – to say a thousand unkind things – meaning none – things produced by the bitterness of disappointment,' Jane wrote in her journal on the day of the chimneyboard's mysterious stroll. An apology from Shelley for having said anything to upset her had given some comfort; 'how I like good explaining people.' Her spirits had sunk again by the evening: '(can't think what the deuce is the matter with me – "I weep yet never know why – I sigh yet feel no pain.")'[13] But, if she really didn't know what was the matter with her, why did she try so hard to scratch this entry out? It is hard not to see the chimneyboard's outing as another attempt by Jane to attract the attention of a man who, as she knew, loved stories of ghostly happenings.

Everything points towards the fact that Jane was in love with

Shelley; did she sleep with him during this time? The possibility cannot be excluded, although her role was closer to that of a demanding younger sister. Shelley often found her infuriating and said so; he remained enchanted by her vivid imagination, her enthusiasm for his own beliefs, and her courage. He was furious when a (false) report that Mrs Godwin was dying lured her back to Skinner Street for a couple of nights. He was sympathetic when she announced that she would in future be known only by her first name, Clara (later changed to Clare, or Claire). He defended her against Mary's charge of a lack of sisterly feelings. 'I think that she has a sincere affection for you,' he told Mary the day after Claire had crept into her bed.[14] Mary's response was indirect. And 'I', she told him, mocking his words, 'have a very sincere affection for my own Shelley.'[15]

The point was not taken up again.

'Natalie [Kaisaroff] has all my pity no situation can be so terrible so agonizing as hers – between a lover & a parent –' Mary wrote to Claire about a young Russian girl in 1845. 'Running away is a thing people may do – *but* no one can ever advise it.'[16]

She knew what she was talking about. Claire, in the autumn of 1814, could rant about news of plots to have her locked up in a convent, or sent out as a lady companion, but she always had the option of returning home to Skinner Street, if she chose. Mary had been exiled. When Fanny paid the runaways a visit on 13 November, she told them that she did not dare talk to Mary; the letter of explanation which she had sent to Skinner Street had been rejected as 'cold and indelicate'; 'Papa' had warned Fanny that if she saw Mary he would never speak to her again. When Mary called with Shelley at Skinner Street, the door was shut; if they met Godwin in the street, he walked past without a glance. Again and again, Mary read her way through her parents' books, trying to understand why she was being punished for acting on their principles.

She could not bear to see her father as her enemy. The decision to exclude her from the family was – it must be – the fault of her stepmother. Mrs Godwin 'is a woman I shudder to think of –' she wrote in her journal on 28 October, when Shelley was living with Peacock, 'my poor father – if – but it will not do – read I dont know what – write to my love.'[17] In a distraught letter to Shelley, she conjured up the image of a loving Godwin kept from them by a heartless wife.

I detest Mrs Godwin she plagues my father out of his life & then –
well no matter – why will not Godwin follow the obvious bent of his
affections & be reconciled to us – no his prejudices the world & she –
do you not hate her my love – all these forbid it – what am I to do
trust to time of course – for what else can I do[?]^{18}

The autumn passed with no sign that Godwin was going to give in
to his affections; Mary continued to fret over the misery, not of her
own situation, but his. She only grumbled once about the gloomy
little lodgings at Church Terrace, when a blacksmith's son in the attic
above her bedroom celebrated his birthday by banging a tin kettle all
night. She learnt to make her own dresses, ate little, spent nothing.
But it tortured her to think of Godwin in poverty, of the bookshop
stocks being sold to pay off a fat banker. This was the news which was
filtering through to Church Terrace from Fanny and Charles
Clairmont; Mary, better than Shelley, knew how much her father's
business meant to him. She could not hide her unhappiness.

On 22 November, almost certainly at Mary's request, Shelley
visited Skinner Street, where he was encouraged to arrange a new
post-obit deal against the estate which would raise money for
Godwin's fiercest creditor. The transaction was accepted; by
Christmas, Shelley had disposed of a further £2,000 of his future
inheritance to raise £700 for Godwin. Mary Jane thanked him;
Godwin did not. Gratitude was not, he believed, appropriate, certainly not in the case of the man who had stolen away two of his
daughters. Shelley had promised to maintain him for the rest of his
days; Godwin intended to see that he kept his word.^{19} He saw nothing
wrong with accepting money from the man he continued to view as
the seducer of his daughter and was prepared to cut in the street.
Neither, although he sometimes found Godwin's demands unrealistic,
did Shelley question that he had a duty to maintain the older man, as
he had promised.

Four letters and a fragment survive of Mary's communications with
Shelley during the two weeks when he was in hiding from his creditors. All were written from Church Terrace, in sight of the churchyard where Mary often went to sit and read by her mother's grave.
Love, and the misery of having to live apart, is of course the main
topic of her letters; she knows Shelley will not sleep so well at
Southampton Buildings as he would if he was wrapped in her arms;
she laughs at the thought of him philosophizing with Peacock about
love when it would be so easy for her to demonstrate it; she longs to
be alone with him in the lovely Welsh cottage he has told her about,

'at a home you know love – with your own Mary nothing to disturb you . . .'[20] (This may have been a little dig at Claire and her unwelcome intrusions; it certainly shows no desire for communal life.)

More striking is the evidence, in Mary's letter of 28 October, of her feelings of deprivation and fear. The lovers had been living apart for five days. Here, after begging Shelley to join in her feelings of hatred for Mrs Godwin, she asks him to take the place of her lost father and writes as a scolded, penitent child:

> indeed I will be a good girl & never vex you any more I will learn Greek and – but when shall we meet when I may tell you all this & you will so sweetly reward me – oh we must meet soon for this is a dreary life I am weary of it – a poor widowed deserted thing no one cares for her . . .[21]

She had reached a low point. Shelley, although warm in his praises of Mary's intelligence, her disciplined mind, her stimulating influence – 'among women there is no mind equal to yours – and I possess this treasure'[22] – had written to her in haste, while finding ample time for a long letter to her stepsister, addressed, as he explained to Mary, 'in a feigned hand to surprise her'. Did Mary sometimes wonder if Shelley's love for her was neither that of a lover nor a father, but of the possessor of a trophy, of Mary Wollstonecraft reborn? Did she compare his tenderness to Claire to the remote, tutorial tone he sometimes adopted with her? How, sitting alone at Church Terrace, did she feel when she read his comments on the letter to Skinner Street in which she had defended their relationship? 'The simple & impressive language in which you clothed your argument – the full weight you gave to every part, the complete picture you exhibited of what you intended to describe – was more than I expected . . .' He went on to pay tribute to her subtle and 'exquisitely fashioned' intelligence. 'Yes!' he concluded. 'I am encouraged.'[23] True, he also wrote most tenderly of 'such sweet moments as we experienced last night'. He told her that, when she was away from him, his mind was dark as the river when the moon was down. He called her his beloved, his sweet Mary, his only love. And yet, lingering through the letters Shelley wrote during their separation is the sense of her value, not as a lover, but as a prize.

The journal shows another side of Mary's nature, tart, sharp-tongued, impatient. '[T]alk about going away & as usual settle nothing,' she noted on 15 October; three days later, Shelley and Claire sit up and 'for a wonder do not frighten themselves'. Hookham calls on 20 October: 'that man comes strictly under the appellation of a prig.' Shelley's wife is suspected of causing trouble at Skinner Street on 27 October: 'she is a detestable woman.' On 9 November, when

they moved to new lodgings in Nelson Square, down on the damp
flats south of the Thames and in sight of the reedy wastes of Lambeth
Marsh, Mary noted that Claire had become gloomy: 'she is very
sullen with Shelley – well never mind my love we are happy.'

The increasing number of irritable entries after this date could be
ascribed to pregnancy and ill health; the Claire factor should not be
overlooked. There had been a moment, shortly after the move to
Nelson Square, when it seemed as if they might be rid of her; she came
back after just two days at Skinner Street; since then, Shelley had
attached her to him as closely as a pet dog. Mary could not express her
thoughts about Claire too openly in a shared diary; her anger vented
itself in more general observations. Hookham was now a 'nasty little
man'. The extravagantly imaginative novels by Charles Brockden
Brown in which Shelley delighted were 'very stupid'. Fanny was being
'slavish' in her obedience to the Skinner Street rules. She had been
obliged to endure Claire's 'nonsense' about Hogg who, having come
to terms with Shelley's new lifestyle, was becoming quite a regular
visitor to Nelson Square. This was the time when, having failed to
recruit Harriet, Shelley began planning an alternative commune, in
which sexual freedom would be practised. The members were to be
Mary and Hogg, Claire and himself. Mary would demonstrate her
liberated spirit by dividing her favours between the two young men.

Hogg and Shelley had been friends since Oxford, where Hogg had
been fascinated by Shelley's oddity, his avid, perpetual consumption
of books, his passion for chemical experiments, his violent hatred of
convention and, above all, of religious convention. They had been
jointly expelled from the university, not for their collaboration on *The
Necessity of Atheism*, but for their stubborn refusal to deny their
authorship when offered this alternative by the Master and Fellows of
University College.

Superficially, the young men made an unlikely couple. Shelley,
gangling and elegantly dishevelled (he seldom wore a hat, left his shirt
unbuttoned and washed his shock of curls by dousing his head in a
bucket of cold water), came from a prosperous and public-spirited
family which could trace its lineage back beyond Sir Philip Sidney to
John Shelley of Michelgrove, who died in 1526. Hogg, noisy,
awkward and heavy-featured, came from a solid legal family in the
north. His own career at the bar was well chosen by a man who told
Peacock in 1817 that his chief ambition was to know 'all cases in Law
& all words and authors in Greek . . .'[24] Aggressive, excitable and
physically unattractive – Mary herself commented in 1836 on his
unfortunate appearance – Hogg was also capable of the reticence of

a prodded mollusc; even Shelley, trying to describe him to Maria
Gisborne, admitted that he was a hard man to know.

> I cannot express
> His virtues, – though I know that they are great,
> Because he locks, then barricades the gate
> Within which they inhabit; –[25]

Richard Holmes, in his biography of Shelley, speculated a homosexual aspect to the relationship between the two young men. This is
hard to substantiate; it is more helpful to see a form of emulation in
Hogg's sexual advances first to Elizabeth Shelley, the sister who most
resembled her brother, and then, when he was sharing lodgings in
York in the autumn of 1811 with the Shelleys, to Harriet. Shelley,
while insisting that he was not jealous, had defended his wife's right
to say no. Hogg's gauche persistence led to a stand-off; a widening rift
in the two young men's political views continued to keep them apart.

In the weeks after their return from Europe, shortly after a second
examination of James Lawrence's account of free love among the
Nairs, Mary and Shelley read Hogg's slight work of fiction, *Memoirs
of Prince Alexy Haimatoff*, published under a pseudonym by the
Hookhams the previous year. Alexy, tall, thin and with an unusually
small round head, shared more than his looks with Shelley. More surprising, given that Hogg had written the book long before he set eyes
on Mary Godwin, was the pleasing description of the girl, also called
Mary, with whom the dashing prince eventually falls in love. Alexy's
Mary is under average height, simply dressed and auburn-haired. She
has a forehead 'high and arched, of a degree of whiteness unparal-
leled'.[26] Mary Godwin was small, plainly dressed and her hair was
reddish-gold. Everybody who saw her commented on the unusual
pallor of her complexion and on her high, intellectual forehead. Did
Hogg, they wondered, have the gift of foresight?

They enjoyed the book; Shelley, praising it in an unsigned review
at the end of the year, drew flattering comparisons with the work of
the celebrated eighteenth-century dramatist, Vittorio Alfieri, whose
memoirs they had just read and admired.[27] On 4 October, Shelley sent
Hogg the long letter already mentioned, in which he justified his
desertion of Harriet and described his new-found happiness. On 14
November, Hogg was invited to call at Nelson Square. He was noted
by Shelley to have been 'pleased' with Mary. The two of them had
talked 'on very interesting subjects'.

Claire returned from her short stay at Skinner Street the following
day; on 16 November, while she and Shelley went 'hopping about the

town', Hogg visited Mary alone. Four days later, he earned her scorn by making 'a sad bungle' of a debate on the subject of virtue.

Harriet, as even her most loyal supporters acknowledged, was no intellectual; with Mary, Hogg confronted a mind well trained to match him in debate. His interest showed in the regularity of his visits; Mary began to apply herself seriously to the task of making Hogg a worthy companion for them. It was hard work. On 27 November, she was infuriated by his conventional attitude, noting that 'he is sadly perverted and I begin to lose hope'; two days later, she defeated him in a debate on free will and necessity: 'he quite wrong but quite puzzled – his arguments are very weak.' On 4 December, she felt she liked him better but still regarded him as 'un enfant perdu'; on 8 December, he was 'more sincere'. She had 'odd' dreams about him that night. 'I like him better each time,' she wrote on 24 December. Slow in mind though he sometimes seemed, Hogg's heavy, combative style may have reminded her of similar discussions with her father in happier days; Shelley, by contrast, was like a dragonfly, dazzling in movement, erratic in flight.

Mary's comments on Hogg were made in the journal which she and Shelley shared. She was writing not only to record her own feelings but to show Shelley that she was taking the friendship seriously. Shelley showed his approval by the tenderness of his own entries. He wrote of 'delightful' talks with her. She was 'the sweet Maie', when she slept, and 'the poor Maie' when she became sufficiently ill for William Lawrence, the surgeon, to be called to Nelson Square. He had opposed Hogg's attempt to have a sexual relationship with Harriet because Harriet herself had been distressed. Mary was ready to share his enlightened views. Shelley probably egged her on by telling her how much less liberated Harriet had been. 'I like him [Hogg] better each time,' suggests more resolve than enthusiasm, but she was clearly trying hard.

On New Year's Day, Hogg wrote a love letter to Mary and enclosed with it a gift, approvingly noted in the journal by Shelley. Hogg's side of the correspondence has disappeared, but Mary's reply suggests that she was thrown by this sudden development. 'You love me you say,' she wrote back;

> I wish I could return it with the passion you deserve . . . But you know Hogg that we have known each other for so short a time and I did not think about love – so that I think that *that* also will come in time & then we shall be happier I do think than the angels who sing for ever or even the lovers of Janes world of perfection.[28]

Claire Clairmont, years later, remembered that Mary had been a hapless pawn, trapped between Shelley's vision and Hogg's desire; Mary, she recalled, had wept bitterly over the prospect of having to sleep with Hogg, as Harriet had wept before her. But Mary does not sound like a victim and she was not writing to crush Hogg's hopes, only to postpone things. Her next letter, written three days later, struck a flirtatious note; he must be sure to come when she was alone: 'still I do not wish to persuade you to do that which you ought not.'

She wrote to him as 'Alexy'; she sent, at his request, a ringletted lock of hair; she coaxed him to go with her again and again to gaze at the statue of a beautiful female philosopher, Theoclea or Themistoclea, on exhibition among a display of military memorials. This was coquettish behaviour. Her letters were still telling Hogg that she could not contemplate a sexual relationship, not even with Shelley, until after the baby was born. Writing to him on 24 January, she took care to remain ambiguous about what she might choose to permit when she was a mother. Hogg would have needed all his legal skills to unravel just what he was being promised. All that was clear from Mary's letter was that everything was to be done out of their shared devotion to Shelley.

> I who love him so tenderly & entirely whose life hangs on the beam of his eye and whose whole soul is entirely wrapt up in him – you who have so sincere a friendship for him to make him happy – no we need not try to do that for every thing we do will make him that without exertion . . .[29]

Mary was going to great pains to spell out the fact that Shelley would always have first place in her heart, but it is hard not to conclude that she was discussing a sexual relationship with Hogg. Her letter ended with an assurance that she was writing 'to one, one loves' and wished 'Good dreams to my Alexy'. She may have cried in private, as Claire claimed; she did, nevertheless, share Shelley's views on free love. They had read about the Nair kingdom together; they admired Godwin's original attack on mutually exclusive relationships. Mary may not, in the end, have slept with Hogg; that does not mean she lacked the will, if not the wish, to do so.

Shelley's dissolute old grandfather, Sir Bysshe, died early in the New Year of 1815. Hurrying down to Field Place to learn the terms of the will, Shelley decided to make his visit the occasion of an outing for

Claire. This was seen as an act of gross impertinence; Sir Timothy refused to let him into the house. Shelley, as Mary gleefully recorded in the journal, responded by sitting on the doorstep with her copy of Milton's *Comus* ostentatiously opened to show her name on the flyleaf. She also noted that Shelley would receive the income from £100,000 on his father's death if he agreed to the provisions of the entail.

Claire and Shelley spent at least one night together at an inn before returning to lodgings with Mary in the bright new suburb of Hans Town (modern Knightsbridge), on the western fringes of London. The landlady was made suspicious by their erratic comings and goings and by Hogg's habit of staying overnight; on 8 February, Shelley and Claire found alternative rooms down the street. Mary gratefully noted that Hogg had used his holiday, an Ash Wednesday, to help her pack up for the move. They had a long talk, perhaps about Shelley's decision to gain instant credit and an annual allowance by selling his father a part of the legacy which had been omitted from the tightly controlled entail.* Godwin, who still viewed his own future as dependent on the Shelley estate, had been anxious to offer advice. They received what Shelley described as an 'equivocal but kind' letter from him the day before the move. Mary could easily perceive the reason for his sudden wish to be agreeable. It had nothing to do with the fact that she was now heavily pregnant and that she had not spoken to her father for almost six months.

The 1815 journal is full of intriguing deletions and gaps. Just enough remains of the next fortnight to show that, while up to the thrill of reading the newly married Lord Byron's romantic *Lara* – 'the finest of Lord B's poems,' Shelley noted – they were all in poor health. His insistence on a vegetarian diet may have been a contributing factor; turnips, potatoes, cabbage and carrots were the only vegetables easily available during the winter months. Mary's baby, expected in late April, was born prematurely on 22 February. The doctor who arrived just too late for the delivery granted the infant little chance of survival. Shelley urged Fanny to visit and try to console Mary. It tells us much about the complicated way in which life was being conducted that the Godwins chose that night to sleep

---

* Sir Bysshe's will had been designed to keep the estate intact for future generations. Strangely, he and the lawyers had overlooked his own inheritance from his brother Sir John Shelley and it was his own interest in this part of the legacy which Shelley wanted to sell his father in exchange for instant cash and an allowance. A settlement was agreed in April 1815; the possibility of a further disposition of the estate was examined in a separate Chancery case the following year.

away from Skinner Street, enabling Fanny to do the same without their official knowledge. When Charles Clairmont also arrived to offer Mary his congratulations, he brought along a gift of baby linen from his mother to Mary. Godwin's journal noted the young people's absence. All was known; nothing was said.

On 2 March, Claire, Shelley, Mary and the baby moved across London again, to Arabella Row, close to where John Nash was laying out plans for a king's palace on the site of old Buckingham House. This was a cheerful area and the rooms were more spacious, large enough, if they could afford to buy one, to accommodate the piano with which Claire, a gifted singer and player, could entertain them in the evenings when they tired of reading. Here, as Hogg's legal holidays approached, they planned to put their communal life into practice and defeat the absurdity of social conventions. 'We shall see you tonight and soon always – which is a very happy thing,' Mary told Hogg on the eve of the move.[30]

Four days later, she wrote again. It was a short letter.

> My dearest Hogg my baby is dead – will you come to me as soon as you can – I wish to see you – It was perfectly well when I went to bed – I awoke in the night to give it suck it appeared to be *sleeping* so quietly that I would not awake it – it was dead then but we did not find *that* out till morning – from its appearance it evedently died of convulsions –
>
> Will you come – you are so calm a creature & Shelley is afraid of a fever from the milk – for I am no longer a mother now.[31]

Mary suffered acutely from the loss of her child. Claire was frightened enough by her mood to send for Fanny. But Fanny did not come and Claire took the full brunt of her stepsister's untargeted misery. Any idea of a commune which included Claire was abruptly dropped. On 11 March, Mary bitterly noted that their situation was hopeless because Claire would not go and live at Skinner Street: 'then our house is the only remaining place – I see plainly – what is to be done –' The next day, a Sunday, she recorded a quiet morning, '& happy for Clary does not get up till 4'. Two days later, she talked to Shelley about the need to get Claire out of their home: 'the prospect appears to me more dismall than ever – not the least hope – this is indeed hard to bear.'

Hogg did his best to divert her in his clumsy way. Mary was taken to the menagerie at Exeter Change in the Strand which she had visited as a child and where she now saw a lynx, a panther, a hyena and a lion whose roar could be heard as far away as Holborn. Her feelings were often revealed by notes on an apparently unconnected subject: the sadness she expressed when the lion died two months later sprang directly from her own bereavement.

Infant mortality was tragically high in the nineteenth century; social historians invite us to suppose that parents felt their losses to a lesser degree then than we would today. But Mary felt deeply, and with reason. She had grown up believing that her own birth had killed a woman brimming with vitality; to bear and rear a child was the best recompense she could offer to herself and to the Fates to whom her journal sometimes darkly alluded. Instead, she now bore the sense of a double murder; not only had she killed her mother but she had allowed her own baby girl to die. The fault, in both cases, was felt to be hers.

The journal shows that Mary was haunted by the sense that her baby's death could somehow have been prevented. Perhaps she had been reading the curious account published in the 1814 *Edinburgh Review* of how Henry Cline, the doctor who had first attended her, had miraculously restored life to a sailor who had lain in a coma for seven months.[32]* On 19 March, Mary thought that her own seven-month baby had come to life again, 'that it had only been cold & that we rubbed it by the fire & it lived . . .' The following night, she had the same agonizing experience, of the dream which delusively fulfils a secret wish.

In this miserable state of mind, and with Shelley suffering from an illness which would later in 1815 be diagnosed (wrongly) as a rapid consumption, it is not surprising that Mary lost her enthusiasm – it may never have been so great as Shelley's – for carrying on their experiment in modern living. The journal becomes bleak and critical, although never of Hogg. Even the important news of Shelley's victory in the Chancery suit was merely noted on 20 April as 'L[ord]. C[hancellor] decides in S's favour', as an afternote to the fact that she had gone to sleep early.

Given her black mood, it was a happy thing for Mary when Shelley decided on 25 April to carry her off for a few days to the Windmill Inn at Salt Hill, near – and now encompassed by – Slough. His reasons were not particularly romantic – the creditors were still pursuing him – but Salt Hill was a famously pretty spot, adored by travellers; the

---

* The doctor had made an incision into the patient's skull with a trepan, a small circular saw.

letters which Mary wrote from there to Hogg are almost feather-brained with glee. They bear no relation to the sad, terse entries she had been making in the journal. Apologizing in decidedly saucy tones for having deprived Hogg of her company, Mary babbled like a brook about the prettiness of the inn, the greenness of the fields, the joy of an escape from London. Alone with Shelley for the first time since their elopement, and at a reassuring distance from her unlovely admirer, Mary was ready to flirt with the best of them. Hogg must have imagined that he was about to be granted the favours which were always held temptingly just out of his reach:

> Now notwithstanding your ill humour which would not allow you to write to me yesterday night – I expect a very long letter tomorrow & a very kind forgiving one too or I will never speak to you again.
> Well Jefferson take care of yourself and be good – the Pecksie will soon be back all the better for her Dormouseish jaunt & remember nothing take away from my Maiëishness.

> For Maië girls are Maië girls
> Wherever they're found
> In Air or in Water
> or In the ground.[33]

Mary signed herself off as his affectionate Dormouse, this being one of the pet names chosen by Shelley to represent her various aspects. (Pecksie, a virtuous chick in *The Robins*, a children's story by Mrs Trimmer, was good and dutiful; Maië was wild and free; the Dormouse, naturally, loved to sleep and live in the country.)

Mary's happiness – it was probably during this visit that William, born the following January, was conceived – did not survive the return to London. Four pages torn out of the joint diary cover a dark period during which she, Shelley and Claire stayed together at lodgings in Marchmont Street, off Brunswick Square. 'Remember the first Spring at Mrs Harbottles,' Mary reminded Claire five years later in a letter intended to prove that spring had always been a bad time for them: Mrs Harbottle had been their landlady at Marchmont Street.[34] Shelley, returning alone to 'my antient lodgings' in 1816, told a correspondent that the Marchmont Street rooms were haunted by 'the ghosts of old remembrances, all of whom contrive to make some reproach to which there is no reply'.[35]

Who were these reproachful ghosts? Is it possible that Shelley's relationship with Claire had become sexual on their visit to Sussex, and that an unwelcome pregnancy was disclosed at Marchmont Buildings?

Was Mr Godwin in the right when, after seeing Mary and Shelley together in the Strand one day in March, he told Charles Clairmont that it was a pity such a beautiful young man could be so wicked?[36]

If this was the case, and at least one relationship in the free-loving commune had thus gone beyond the stage of theorizing, a few jigsaw pieces fall into place. Mary's feelings of hostility towards Claire became increasingly strident, while Shelley took refuge in the Stoics, reading Seneca 'every day & all day'. On 10 May, two days after Mrs Knapp, the Godwins' former landlady, had rejected an appeal by both Shelley and Mary to take Claire in as her lodger, Mary went and had a long talk with James Marshall, the friend she looked on almost as a father.

On 12 May, Mary's journal entries approached a climax of barely repressed anger. Now, it was beyond her even to write her stepsister's name. Shelley had gone out with 'his friend' in the morning, and with 'the lady' in the afternoon. In the evening, he had the chance to 'indulge in' – a phrase which she then crossed out – a last talk with 'his friend'. The first thing Mary noted for the next day was: 'Claire goes.'

She went, and early, but Shelley went with her. When he left the house again after breakfast, together with Charles Clairmont, Mary began to suspect that they had cooked up a plan to join Claire and abandon her. Shelley was still absent when Hogg called late in the afternoon. She went to look for him in the nearby streets. She came back anxious, and alone. At half-past six, Shelley returned: 'the business is finished,' Mary wrote thankfully. Her next undated entry announced the start of a new journal 'with our regeneration'. The observation could be construed as referring to a life free of money worries. More plausibly, it celebrated the advent of a life without Claire.

Claire's departure from London coincided precisely with the end of the first stage of negotiations between Shelley and his father, via their respective solicitors. Sir Timothy agreed to pay off his son's debts, to buy back the post-obit bonds, and to provide him with a handsome allowance of £1,000 a year. Harriet was granted £200 against past expenses and promised a further £200 a year, payable quarterly from Shelley's own annuity. (Having once told Harriet that he, Mary and Claire were able to survive on four pounds a week, Shelley thought this very handsome.) Godwin was still waiting for the balance of the money promised to him in 1814. A little dishonestly, Shelley told his father that Godwin was owed £1,200 and then kept back £200 for his own use. Since Godwin happened to be facing a lawsuit for just £200, he felt greatly injured by this. Mary Jane, writing to Mrs Mason on 28 July, told her that Godwin had thanked his benefactor, but in terms of 'freezing coldness'. He continued, in accordance with their informal agreement, to demand the unpaid sum as his right. It is necessary, although hard, to keep reminding ourselves that Shelley had promised the older man – Godwin was now fifty-nine – his unreserved support. Godwin knew the details of the will. He could see for himself the wealth to which he believed Shelley had access.

A part of the sum which Shelley kept back was used to pay the cost of transporting Claire to Lynmouth, the remote and pretty north Devon village where Shelley and Harriet had once lived, and of covering her needs. A young and possibly pregnant Londoner would not have been expected to settle into absolute solitude, so far from home, for an unspecified length of time. If Claire was, like Shelley and Harriet, being lodged at Mrs Blackmore's cottage, she would need to pay for her board and food, and to be provided with a maid.* If she was pregnant, there would be additional costs.

Mary's relief at being rid of her stepsister was matched by Claire's joy at having escaped. Writing to Fanny after a fortnight in Devon, Claire told her that she was thankful to be living quietly after 'so much discontent, such violent scenes, such a turmoil of passion & hatred . . .'[37] This is usually read as an allusion to Skinner Street. It is much more likely that Claire was referring to the household from which she had recently been ejected and to which Mary sincerely hoped she would never return.

---

* Mrs Godwin claimed that Claire was sent to a Mrs Bicknell, a widow at Lynmouth. Shelley's former home there has two possible locations; a Mrs Blackmore still owned land there in the 1840s. The rate books for earlier years were unfortunately destroyed in 1980. (I am grateful to Mr John Travis of Lynmouth for his information on these points.)

CHAPTER TEN

RETREAT FROM LONDON

1815 – 1816

'We ought not to be absent any longer indeed we ought not – I am not happy at it . . . in fine either you must come back, or I must come to you directly . . .'

Mary Wollstonecraft Godwin to Percy Bysshe Shelley, 27 July 1815

LITTLE CORRESPONDENCE SURVIVES FROM THE MONTHS AFTER Claire's abrupt transportation to north Devon. Mary's second journal, covering the period between May 1815 and July of the following summer, has also been lost. If Claire believed herself to be pregnant by Shelley, these disappearances may not be accidental.

We do, however, have the booklist which Mary maintained with methodical care. She read voraciously and over a wide range; gothic novels are noted alongside travel books, philosophy, history, the classics and, as always, the books written by her father and mother. Many of these books were read with Shelley; just before Claire's departure, they had been studying *The Faerie Queene*, where they found a name which suited Shelley's necessarily elusive life remarkably well. She was his Maïë-girl, his dutiful Pecksie, his home-loving Dormouse. He in turn now became Mary's 'sweet Elf': one of the last random entries in the 1814–15 journal in Shelley's hand reads: 'The Maie & her Elfin Knight.' *The Faerie Queene* may also have helped to sow one of the seeds for *Frankenstein*: in Book II (canto x, Stanza 70) of Spenser's poem, Mary read that 'Prometheus did create / A man, of many parts from beasts derived'. Frankenstein 'tortured the living animal' to assemble the limbs for his Creature.

Distance failed to keep Claire out of their lives. She was, at first, grateful to have been found such a charming retreat. Popular with artists and poets in the years of war with France when British cliffs and gorges had to satisfy their thirst for the grandeur of the Alps, Lynmouth was unusually picturesque. Fanny was sent a rapturous account of Claire's pretty cottage, of plunging waterfalls and awe-inspiring mountains. Soon, however, she grew lonely. Shelley, besieged with letters, began laying plans for a visit.

Devon's remoteness made it attractive to a scandal-haunted couple expecting their second child. Mary was becoming increasingly miserable at her father's refusal to see or even to communicate with her. Hogg was busy at the bar; Peacock was planning to move with his mother back to their old home near Egham in Surrey. It would, they thought, be pleasant to settle near Peacock one day; in the meantime, they settled for a holiday at Torquay. Lynmouth, situated on Devon's north coast, was often misty and damp, not a good climate for a man who believed he might die of consumption. But Torquay lay on the sunny southern side of the county. Contemporary guidebooks extolled the little town's health-giving air, only equalled, so they claimed, by the reviving breezes of Clifton. The fact that Clifton was the Shelleys' next stop suggests that health concerns were helping to dictate their movements. Mary, terrified of losing her second child, was anxious to take good care of herself; Shelley, more than she, may have been attracted by the thought that they would be only a day's drive from Claire, although there is no evidence that any visits were made to her. They left London for Devon sometime before June.

Torquay in 1815 was a modest bathing resort which, like many such places, had been arrested in a semi-developed state by the Napoleonic wars. John Rennie's stone quays had been built; the local abbey of Torre had been gentrified for comfortable occupation by an old local family, the Carys. A half-finished terrace of white stucco houses hinted at a prosperous future, but grass sprouted between the paving stones outside the front doors. Members of the public were invited to climb a winding path to view Woodbine Cottage, the picturesque retreat of a Mrs Johnes of Herefordshire. Mary and Shelley probably lodged in the terrace below it, overlooking the broad blue crescent of Torbay.

Torquay was in the news that summer, but not because a runaway couple had taken up residence there. Captain Maitland of the *Bellerophon*, one of the warhorses of Nelson's fleet, sailed back from France to Torbay with Napoleon as his voluntary passenger; the fallen emperor had decided to entrust himself to the British government as likely to be the most merciful of his enemies. The Devon locals, and the crew, were charmed by him, by his compliments on the view – quite like Porto Ferrajo at Elba, he was heard to remark – and his willingness to display himself on deck. Strong sympathy was felt when he was taken off to Plymouth in preparation for his exile to St Helena.*

Mary chose Torquay for the setting of a simple children's story, *Maurice, or The Fisher's Cot*, written five years later when she was living in Italy. Describing the cottage where Maurice finds a home, Mary lovingly placed it under a bower of trees, at the foot of one of the red cliffs which buttress this part of the coast. A flowery bank rises by the cottage walls; a daisy-scattered green spreads beyond the door. The picture is sweetly conventional, but the loving precision of detail suggests that Mary's memories were happy ones. As at Salt Hill, she could revel in having Shelley to herself; together, they again read *Fleetwood*, their favourite among Godwin's novels. (Shortly before leaving London, they had read his most recent work, a study of Milton's nephews in which Godwin aired his unchanged republican views. No longer seen as a dangerous influence, he won some friendly notices.)

Fleetwood had led them to Lucerne and Lake Uri; now it seemed to point them towards North Wales, and the wild landscape in which Godwin had set the opening chapters. On 22 June, Shelley wrote to his old friend John Williams at Tremadoc, to ask if he knew of a house near the Caernarvon coast which they could take as tenants. Williams was well used to Shelley's vacillations; the following week, he heard that they were planning to rent a house near Windsor, located for them by Peacock.

What happened next is a mystery. On 30 June, Shelley told Williams that he was leaving Torquay the following day to look at the Windsor house. Four weeks later, Mary, writing from Clifton, on the Avon Gorge, addressed an agitated letter to his London lodgings in Marchmont Street: 'We have been now a long time separated,' she reminded him. He had not found a house. Even if he did not wish her to join him, she intended to do so, 'for I am quite sick of passing day after day in this hopeless way'.[1]

The cause of her worry became apparent in the next paragraph. She had written to Claire at Lynmouth several times and had no

---

* Napoleon arrived at Torbay in July 1815. Mary may still have been there, although Shelley had left.

answer – was Claire, perhaps, with him in London? Not daring to accuse, she suggested that Claire might have learned his whereabouts and decided to join him of her own accord: 'it would not in the least surprise me . . . that she should have taken some such freak – '

Pregnant and without friends in a town she had never visited, always conscious of the ease with which Shelley had abandoned Harriet the previous year, Mary was frantic. All her self-control was gone. She veered from scolding – how could he forget that the next day was the anniversary of their elopement, and not wish her to join him for his birthday on 4 August? – to wistful hints of how wild and Maiëish she planned to be when they next met. All their pet nick-names were invoked to coax him into a response. Finally, she became abject: 'do not be angry dear love – Your Pecksie is a good girl & is quite well now again – except a headache when she waits so anxiously for her loves letters – dearest best Shelley pray come to me – pray pray do not stay away from me.'[2]

Her mother, in her painful correspondence with Gilbert Imlay, had never written a more heart-rending letter. It was effective; Mary and Shelley were reunited and settled in their new home at Bishopsgate on the edge of Windsor Park by the end of that week.

In London, having settled Mary at Clifton, Shelley had been visiting William Lawrence, the eminent surgeon who had advised Mary on her health since 1812. Lawrence, a handsome ambitious man then in his mid-thirties, was of a different cast of mind to his young patients. He considered, for example, that it was entirely rational to derive Africans from monkeys, and to see them as something less than human, showing 'an almost entire want of . . . elevated sentiments, manly virtues, and moral feelings'.[3] The linking of Africans to monkeys was not unusual at that time; Lawrence was a man of his times in deducing that Africans were morally deficient. He showed more sense as a physician; Shelley was told to forget all about consumption and his imminent death. Two months later, Shelley told Hogg that, thanks to Lawrence, he had never felt better.

The alienated condition of black people must have preyed on Mary's mind during her lonely weeks at Clifton, forming a significant contribution to the social intention behind the celebrated Creature she brought to life in *Frankenstein* the following year. Made fashionable in the years when its neighbour, Bristol, had thrived on the slave trade, Clifton had fallen on hard times through the failure of its hot

well to draw customers away from Bath, through the national collapse of development plans at the beginning of the century, through
the falling price of sugar and through the official end to traffic in
slaves after the Abolition Act of 1807.* But abolition did not mean
that slavery in England had been wholly eradicated; a slave was
identified as part of the estate of one Thomas Armstrong of Dalston
in 1822 and the use of slaves in the domestic environment lasted well
into the nineteenth century. Individual slaves were being rescued from
such situations as late as 1843, although slavery had reached a formal
end with the Emancipation Act of 1833. Walking, as all Clifton ladies
did when they went shopping or promenading, down the shabby hill
of unfinished terraces and half-built crescents into elegant, slightly
raffish Bristol, Mary found herself in a world where it would have
been impossible to ignore the presence of a black population with
recent and bitter memories.

Her interest in their situation cannot be doubted. One of Godwin's
closest friends, John Thelwall, had been among the London
Corresponding Society members who spoke out against slavery in the
1790s when Manhood Suffrage and the Freedom of Slaves were the
twin planks on which the Society stood; Godwin had devoted a
whole section to the subject in his first draft of *Political Justice*. Shelley
and Mary shared Godwin's views. They refused to eat sugar because
it came from West Indian plantations, a principled decision at which
Peacock poked kindly fun in *Melincourt*, his second novel.

In October 1814, at a time when French slavers were seeking to
renew their trading rights – 806 petitions of protest were delivered to
the House of Commons – Shelley had drawn Mary's attention to a
long letter in *The Times* on the terrible conditions of the slaver cara-
vans in Africa. He knew she would share his feelings: 'See where I
have marked with ink,' he wrote, 'and stifle your horror and indignation until we meet.'[4] Two months later, they read Mungo Park's
account of his travels in Africa in 1795–7.[5] This work, published in
1799, had shocked the nation at the time; Mary was disgusted by
Park's argument that European traders were doing nothing discreditable, since a third of the country had been enslaved before their
arrival. 'Read and finish Mungo Park's travels,' Mary noted: 'they are
very interesting & if the man was not so prejudiced they would be a
thousand times more so.'[6] Two months later, she read a study of the
West Indian slave trade by Bryan Edwards.

---

* Unofficially, more Africans were carried across the Atlantic after 1807, to serve the coffee
and tobacco trade of Cuba and Brazil, than in the whole of the previous century.

Edwards was a reasonably liberal man, but here, as with William Lawrence, Mary encountered the view of a non-white as inferior, belonging to a different species: the African, in particular, was connected to monkeys by both descent and behaviour. Turning from Edwards's book, Mary could see black men being worked on Bristol Quay; she could hear the callously pragmatic views of those who had owned and now technically employed them. Surrounded by troubling evidence that abolition had brought little change of attitude to this part of England, Mary was provided with a new element of the story she began to write the following summer. In the nameless Creature, whose yellow skin, black hair and giant limbs allowed her to combine contemporary perceptions of the Eastern 'lascars' with the African and West Indian, she examined the plight of a seemingly non-human being, judged by his looks to be incapable of moral feelings or elevated sentiments. This was surgeon Lawrence's view; it was shared by many of the good people of Clifton and Bristol and, indeed, by many churchmen and politicians of the time.

If Mary's guess about her stepsister's presence in London was correct, her visit had been brief; she was at Lynmouth on 4 August, Shelley's birthday, when Mary rejoined him. This was probably the period Claire remembered most poignantly in 1835, when she described her stay in Devon as a time of exile and wretched loneliness.[7] Her spirits were not improved by a September letter from her charming and good-hearted brother Charles, in which he described the enjoyable time he was having staying at Shelley and Mary's new home near Windsor. The possibility of Claire's joining them was never raised; in October, she went to Ireland with her brother for a short time, when he was expecting to help open a distillery in Wexford. By the end of the year, however, both the Clairmonts were jobless and back in London.

A house without Claire in it was always a happier one for Mary. What they lost in musical entertainment, without Claire to play the piano and sing to them, they gained in peace. At Bishopsgate, living in a two-storey house of red brick, Mary had a garden for the first time since childhood days at the Polygon, a small staff to perform the domestic tasks which she never relished, and splendid views. Surrounded by abbeys, or their attractive ruins, they were next to the celebrated Cooper's Hill, one of the most admired prospect points in southern England. Beyond the house windows, a view across wild

Bishopsgate Heath stretched all the way to the shadowy paths of
Chapel Wood and the great artificial lake of Virginia Water. Old
Windsor was a mile away across the meadows. This was where, as Mary
must have known, her father had come in 1801 to attend the funeral
of a lady for whom he had considerable affection and some respect,
Mary 'Perdita' Robinson, the poet, novelist and actress who had saved
herself from prison for debt by becoming mistress to the Prince of
Wales, until he dropped her. Following her death, Mrs Robinson's
cottage and tomb had become quite popular with tourists.

Mary Wollstonecraft, visiting the area in 1780 when she was
employed as a widow's companion, had been entranced by it; so now
was her daughter. In her novel *The Last Man* (1826), Mary borrowed
the name 'Perdita' for one of her characters and recreated the setting
with great tenderness. Perdita's cottage, 'a humble dwelling', has often
been taken for a description of her own home.*

Shelley and Mary saw little, if anything, of their neighbours in the
large, prosperous hillside houses which, encircling Englefield Heath,
presided over the landscape; their companions were Hogg, when he
could escape from his legal work, Charles Clairmont, guiltily abandoning his adored stepfather to the volatile moods of Mrs Godwin,
and Peacock. Tactfully, perhaps, Peacock took Charles off on the all-
day walks which were his own favourite summer pastime, while Mary
studied or gardened and Shelley began work on *Alastor*, his first long
poem since *Queen Mab*. Gathered together at the Bishopsgate house
in the evenings, they discussed the return of the French monarchy,
quarrelled about vegetarianism, with which Peacock had no sympathy, and agreed on the pernicious nature of the government. They
decided, one lovely August night, to take inspiration from one of
Peacock's poems, 'The Genius of the Thames', and row a boat up to
the river's source. They set off the following day.

For Mary, loving the lap of water but dreading the violence of the
sea, this must have been an idyllic trip. Sadly, we have no letters or
journal notes to turn to for her sensations; imagination must fill the
gap. Carefully bonneted and with a travelling case under her seat, she
left the rowing and manoeuvres through an endless chain of locks to
her companions, while she gazed across the smoothness of the river's
breadth to pretty old houses buried behind high banks of purple
loosestrife and golden water-irises, to church towers and meadows,
the fast flicker of a current pulling towards a watermill, tiny heron-

---

* Mary was also alluding to the rustic home of Perdita in *The Winter's Tale*, a play which she
had always loved, and which she first saw with her father when she was fifteen years old.

guarded islets, clumps of flowering rushes, patient fishermen, slow barges, England at peace.

At Oxford, they left the boat to visit Shelley's former rooms and to look at the college quads and the suite of venerable rooms which housed the Bodleian Library. (Charles, describing it all to Claire, grew very Shelleyan and disdainful about the folly and corruption of a university which expelled those who dared to tell the truth.) Wandering at twilight through the high grass of Lechlade church-yard, Shelley found the setting for one of his gentlest early poems. 'Thus solemnized and softened, death is mild / And terrorless as this serenest night . . .' he wrote in 'A Summer Evening Churchyard'.

Elated by a sense of following the movements of the mind itself in the turns and twists of the river, Shelley wanted the journey to go on for ever. Why stop at the source of the Thames? Why not go on, by means of the canals, for a two-thousand-mile tour of Britain? Even Charles was a little shaken by this proposal, which was defeated by increasingly shallow water and by a thirsty herd of cattle which blocked their progress at Cricklade. Worn out – all four of them were obliged to get out and drag the boat through a mire of rushes at one point – they turned towards home. Peacock, who relived the trip in a couple of nostalgic chapters of *Crotchet Castle*, was especially pleased with himself for having bullied Shelley into eating three whole chops on the journey. Ten days of physical exercise rather than a single carnivorous lapse brought striking results. 'We have all felt the good effects of this jaunt,' Charles told Claire, 'but in Shelley the change is quite remarkable; he has now the ruddy healthy complexion of the Autumn upon his countenance, & he is twice as fat as he used to be.'[8]

Peacock's novels, most of which were written between the Bishopsgate summer and his engagement in 1819 as a clerk at the East India House, perfectly capture the balance in Shelley and Mary's household between unconscious comedy and high earnestness. *The Misfortunes of Elphin* includes, in a chapter on 'The Education of Taliesin', a sardonic account of life on post-obits which makes one wish that the author had tried harder to restrain Shelley's financial dealings; *Melincourt*, the novel which Shelley, Mary and Byron all thought his best, reminds us again of how deeply committed they were to opposing the slave trade. Best known for Lord Haut-Ton, a chivalrous orang-outang in whom Peacock poked fun at Lord Monboddo's belief in a lost simian civilization and at an orang-outang's favourable prospects as a parliamentary candidate, *Melincourt* offers us a taste of the principled discussions held around the Bishopsgate dining-table.

Mr Forester proceeded: 'If every individual in this kingdom, who is truly and conscientiously an enemy to the slave-trade, would subject himself to so very trivial a privation as abstinence from colonial produce, I consider that a mortal blow would be immediately struck at the roots of that iniquitous system.'[9]

Contradicted, Mr Forester makes a passionate and Shelleyan argument for the importance of individual example. Mr Forester is Peacock's most unequivocal presentation of the Shelleyan attitude. He was not always able to keep a straight face about Shelley's fancies: Peacock's later memoirs include stories of Shelley jumping into a ditch to hide from invisible bailiffs, and announcing that Mr Williams of Tremadoc had brought news to Bishopsgate of a fiendish new plot by Sir Timothy to have him placed in an asylum. In 1814, however, Mr Forester's attitude was one which Peacock endorsed.

The atmosphere of intellectual debate was one in which Mary had thrived under her father's roof and she was an active participant in the discussions. As classicists, however, the men outranked her. Naturally studious, she worked at remedying the deficiency. While Shelley, lying out under the great oaks of Windsor, began work on *Alastor*, Mary applied herself to Latin exercises. Writing to Hogg at the end of September, Shelley told him that her progress was 'such as to satisfy my best expectations'.[10] The tone is that of a tutor: was he consciously taking over the role of Godwin in her life? A month later, he wrote to offer personal liability to one of Godwin's most persistent creditors, for a sum of £200 or £250. Since this was approximately the sum which had been withheld from his payment to Godwin earlier in the summer, Shelley may have hoped that his obligations, fiscal and educational, had now been met.

Mary took great pride in *Alastor*, the first poem of any length which Shelley had written since meeting her. Reverence and gratitude, not lust and dreams of escape, were at the heart of the poem according to her interpretation. Here, she would tell readers of the first collected edition of Shelley's poems in 1839, they would find 'the outpouring of his own emotions . . . softened by the recent anticipation of death'.[11] It was all most characteristic; descriptions of the forest scenery and of the majesty of nature were peculiarly fine.

The enthusiasm Mary showed for the first major poem written since Shelley and she had been together is understandable. It becomes heroic when we look more closely at the poem. Hearing that a writer for the *Eclectic Review* had objected to one passage in the poem as profane, she declared that 'the world must be going mad', or so an equally indignant Claire Clairmont reported to a friend.[12] The reviewer had taken offence at a startlingly bold presentation of sexual climax. It represented the poet's surrender to his muse.

> He reared his shuddering limbs and quelled
> His gasping breath, and spread his arms to meet
> Her panting bosom: . . . she drew back a while,
> Then, yielding to the irresistible joy,
> With frantic gesture and short breathless cry
> Folded his frame in her dissolving arms.
> Now blackness veiled his dizzy eyes, and night
> Involved and swallowed up the vision . . .[13]

Mary was no prude. She praised the poem and defended the passage. She chose not to comment on the fact that the river voyage of the poem represents a restless, driven flight. (The word 'fled' recurs five times between lines 345 and 365.) Privately, as a faithful copyist and devoted reader, she must have wondered what *Alastor* was telling her about the domestic plans of her elfin knight, however contented he might appear.

Mary's second child was born on 24 January 1816. They called him William, after his grandfather. Shelley, writing to Godwin the following day, conveyed the news with the pointed comment that it would no doubt please Fanny and Mrs Godwin to know that the confinement had been favourable, and that the baby was well. Somebody else – Mary? – told him the baby's name: 'William, nepos,' Godwin noted in his diary, in an entry that defies any attempt to interpret his feelings.

The relationship between the two households had not improved; money, as before, was the primary reason, cloaking the fathomless bitterness of Godwin's sense that Shelley had knowingly and wilfully destroyed his daughter's good reputation. In July, when Mary was at Clifton, Godwin had been relatively cheerful, urging Fanny and Mrs Godwin, who were holidaying outside London, to share his relief that the burden of debt was about to be lifted. The autumn, however, had heralded a new wave of hungry creditors and he looked to Shelley to keep them off.

Shelley, as he wearily and repeatedly explained, was in no position to help. By March 1816, a test legal case had shown that the terms of Sir Bysshe's will could not be tampered with in the way that both he and his father had hoped. Sir Timothy had agreed to pay some more, but not all, of his debts and to continue his annuity of £1,000 a year, of which £200 would, as promised, be used for annual payments to Harriet.* Neither Godwin nor his chosen go-between, the agreeable but somewhat inept Thomas Turner, were able to grasp the fact that Shelley was no longer in a position to act as his benefactor or even to fulfil any past promises which Godwin might now regard as debts. The most he could do was to offer an untruthful assurance that he would not leave the country, despite his wish to hide Mary and himself 'from that contempt which we so unjustly endure'.[14]

Shelley's letters of explanation had been models of courtesy until now, especially given the cold rudeness of Godwin's responses. On 6 March, however, Godwin went too far. He indicated that he was at last ready, not to condone, but to forgive. Forgiveness, in this case, was not good enough. Shelley, tried beyond his limits by Godwin's pompous phrases, sent an explosive reply. Could Godwin not see how his own behaviour had helped to destroy the reputation of 'a young family, innocent and benevolent and united' and who, thanks partly to Godwin's ostentatious disapproval, were now ranked with 'prostitutes and seducers'? Why, if Godwin was so high-minded, was he still ready to communicate with a man he apparently abhorred, for the sake of obtaining money? 'Do not talk of *forgiveness* again to me,' Shelley wrote, 'for my blood boils in my veins, and my gall rises against all that bears the human form, when I think of what I, their benefactor and ardent lover, have endured of enmity and contempt from you and from all mankind.'[15] There was little use in taking the high ground against a man who knew that he was in the right: 'torture cannot wring from me an approbation of the act that separated us,' Godwin wrote back in language worthy of one of his fictional heroes.[16]

Fanny dutifully copied this letter out for her father; Mary was doubtless shown it by her angry lover. The pain which Shelley and Godwin wreaked on these two girls in seeking each to establish moral superiority is easily imagined.

By May, Godwin's worst fears had been confirmed; his golden goose was about to fly away. Rashly, Shelley endeavoured to pacify him with the promise that he would receive £300 during the course of the summer. In the meantime, he announced from Dover, Mary and he were about to leave England, perhaps for ever, travelling first

---

* The £800 a year on which Shelley expected to live with difficulty or at least without contemplating any further payments to Godwin amounted to £25,600 in real money today.

to Geneva. No reason was given for their chosen destination. Neither, oddly, was there any mention of the fact that Claire was to accompany them, although gossip quickly brought news to Skinner Street that Shelley was repeating his exploit of 1814 and running off to the Continent with, not one young lady, but two.

The reason Shelley gave for his departure was that he and Mary wished to escape the painful humiliation of being regarded as immoral. This laid the blame at Godwin's door; Shelley softened the implicit accusation with a qualified apology.

> But I have been too indignant, I have been unjust to you – forgive me – burn those letters which contain the records of my violence, & believe that however what you erroneously call fame & honour separate us, I shall always feel towards you as the most affectionate of friends.[17]

This tribute may have given a little pleasure to Mary, wondering if she would ever see her father again. The comfort for Godwin cannot have been great. Shelley, his one hope of financial support, had vanished, taking the girls with him. And they were bound for the most fashionable of Swiss resorts, where the stories likely to be woven around a blasphemous poet, a baby, and two ladyfriends, sisters to boot, were too awful to contemplate.

Godwin did not have long to wait before the stories began. His former friend Elizabeth Inchbald spoke for many when she tenderly inquired whether the philosopher had a daughter, or perhaps an adopted daughter, holidaying in Switzerland? She added a cruel hint that gossip was already beginning to circulate: 'But perhaps before you could have time to inform me, my thirst for the information might possibly be allay'd.'[18]

CHAPTER ELEVEN

STORMS ON THE LAKE

1816

'"We will each write a ghost story," said Lord Byron, and his proposition was acceded to.'

Mary Shelley, Preface to *Frankenstein* (1831)

THE HINT TO GODWIN OF PERMANENT EXILE WAS MISLEADING, and perhaps deliberately so. Peacock, given a retainer to manage their affairs while they were away, was asked to try to obtain the Bishopsgate house for their return. They might, Shelley told him, be away for a year, travelling eastward from Geneva. Still relishing the memory of their journey up the Thames, he intended to voyage by boat, accompanied by Mary and the baby. Mary Wollstonecraft had taken her little daughter Fanny to Sweden, a far more perilous journey, with no ill effect.

But why had they gone so suddenly, and why were they so set on going to Geneva? Shelley and his party would, of course, have been attracted by Lake Geneva's reputation as the refuge of the English enlightenment in exile, as the chosen home of Gibbon, Voltaire and Madame de Staël, and as the legendary home of liberty. This was not, however, the explanation for their journey.

In September 1815, Claire had made a brief visit from Lynmouth to Enniscorthy in Ireland. Here Charles Clairmont, with some financial assistance from Shelley, was planning to join a new distillery firm as one of three partners. Shelley, early in 1816, was still promis-

ing Charles the necessary capital but, perhaps after receiving a discouraging response from the businessman Francis Place to whom
Charles appealed for advice and help in obtaining temporary
employment while awaiting the outcome of the Chancery case on
the Shelley estate, the distillery scheme was dropped. Charles, whose
reluctance to be involved in his stepfather's bookselling trade had
greatly disappointed Godwin, made his way to France and a life free
of family responsibilities. Claire, who may at first have returned
from Ireland to Lynmouth, was alone in London by January 1816
and paying occasional visits to Skinner Street.* After spending some
time in lodgings at Foley Street, Marylebone, she decided to return
to the pleasant house in Arabella Row where Mary had lost her
baby daughter the previous spring. She made this move at some
point in March or, at latest, early April. She told nobody of her
whereabouts.

Vivacious, good-looking and with, as she remembered, a 'bright
colour', Claire was now almost eighteen. Mary had found love with
a poet who, much though Mary and Claire admired him, was far from
being a household name. (Shelley, in the spring of 1816, was better
known for the scandals he had caused than for the privately printed
Queen Mab and the as yet unpublished *Alastor*.) Byron, famous
enough already to think of himself as literature's Napoleon, was in
London and alone, after a stormy estrangement from Annabella
Milbanke, his wife of a year; he was rumoured to be living in
unconventional intimacy with his married half-sister, Augusta Leigh.
Each time Claire walked along Piccadilly, she saw people waiting
outside the curtained windows of 13 Piccadilly Terrace for a glimpse
of Byron; scandal only added to the fascination.

Byron also happened to have an influential position on the committee of London's principal theatre, Drury Lane; Claire, who had
already tried her hand at writing a play, decided to approach him. If
he could help her to become an actress or a playwright, well and

---

* Edward Augustus Silsbee, the Shelley admirer whose pursuit of manuscripts held by Claire
Clairmont gave Henry James the idea for *The Aspern Papers*, noted, after a conversation with
Claire in 1876, that 'while living in Devonshire? Mrs S approaching her confinement sent
for her while they were at Windsor. There she shortly ran off.'[1] The queried allusion to
Devonshire may have been Silsbee's own tentative attempt to create a time-scheme. Godwin's
diary shows Claire spending three nights at Skinner Street from 5 to 8 January 1816; she stayed
for one night on 16 February. Mary's baby William Godwin Shelley was born on 24 January.
It seems probable that Claire returned from Enniscorthy to Lynmouth for the rest of the
autumn of 1815, and then came to London. Godwin's meticulous journal records no visit
from her before January 1816.

good; if he could be persuaded to take a more personal interest in her, so much the better.

Later on in life, Claire liked to remember that she had been a timid girl; there was nothing shy about her assault on Byron. Reminiscing in old age to her attentive American visitor, Edward Augustus Silsbee, she claimed that her landlady's sister had given them a very proper and formal introduction. The letters tell a different story. Using assumed names and giving herself a hint of the noblewoman by stamping her letters with a pretty seal both Mary and she had been given by Shelley, Claire laid siege until she gained her wish, permission to visit Byron alone at his house some time late in March.[2] Conventional interviews were almost as formal as a royal audience, but Claire had the boldness to break away from accepted behaviour, and the confidence to get away with it. Perhaps, as an accomplished pianist with a good voice, she sang some of the haunting lyrics which Byron had recently written to accompany the musician and composer Isaac Nathan's *Hebrew Melodies*. However she set about it, the seduction worked; Byron was, briefly, charmed. He read her novella, offered an introduction to the Drury Lane committee and managed to forgive her for sharing the surname of Lady Byron's former governess, regarded by Byron as a dangerous, troublemaking spy.

Byron was amusing himself in the brief space of time before he left England for Geneva. Claire, however, was besotted. She told Byron that she had loved him in secret for a year. (She, Shelley and Mary had read *Lara* the previous spring and they were well-acquainted with the opening cantos of *Childe Harold's Pilgrimage*, the poem which, already published as if it were a complete work, had made Byron's name.) She was pitifully aware, as her clamorous, beseeching letters show, that her only chance of retaining his interest was her connection to two people who interested him far more than herself, Shelley and Mary Godwin. Shelley had sent Byron one of the first privately printed copies of *Queen Mab*; Mary was familiar by her name. Few in Byron's circles would have been unaware of her existence; gossip had spread reports of her scandalous cohabitation with a married man. The couple's arrival in London at Shelley's old lodgings in Marchmont Buildings, where they discussed the possibility of making a second trip to the Continent, gave Claire a flash of inspiration. Byron was determined not to let her follow him and his retinue out to Geneva alone; what if she produced Mary and Shelley as her chaperones? First, however, she had to prepare the ground.

Claire already knew that Byron admired Godwin and had twice

offered him help, giving him an introduction to the publisher John Murray in 1814 and trying, in early 1816, to divert a publisher's payment to himself into the emptier pockets of Godwin, Coleridge and the Irish playwright and cleric, Charles Maturin, later author of *Melmoth the Wanderer*.[3] Mary's background rendered her almost as interesting to Byron as he to her: for the past two years she had been devouring his poems. With careful deviousness, Claire set up a meeting. Mary was told only that Lord Byron was being very kind and helpful; Byron was bossily warned to keep quiet about their connection and to see that Mary was received with appropriate respect. 'I say this,' Claire added plaintively, 'because on Thursday Evening I waited nearly a quarter of an hour in your hall, which though I may overlook the disagreeableness – she, who is not in love would not . . . She is very curious to see you.'[4]

Coleridge had visited Piccadilly Terrace a few days earlier.* 'If you had seen Lord Byron,' he wrote later, his gratitude for his host's kindness and encouragement undimmed, 'you could scarcely disbelieve him – so beautiful a countenance you scarcely ever saw – his teeth so many stationary smiles – his eyes the open portals of the sun – things of light, and for light – and his forehead so ample, and yet so flexible, passing from marble smoothness into a hundred wreathes and lines and dimples correspondent to the feelings and sentiments he is uttering . . .'[5]

Mary, small, composed, sedate, hid her feelings better than the gushing Coleridge had probably managed to do. She thanked Byron, we can suppose, for his kindness to her father; she smiled demurely when he praised *Queen Mab*, which Byron warmly admired. Perhaps, if she was feeling bold, she told him that she had inscribed some lines from 'To Thyrza' in her own precious copy, given to her just before she eloped with Shelley. (It is unclear whether Mary ever discovered that Byron's Thyrza had been a boy.) They might have talked about her father's friend, John Curran, the gregarious Irish barrister and raconteur for whom Byron's enthusiasm was far greater than Shelley's, or of the occasion in 1812 when they had both attended one of Coleridge's lectures on Shakespeare. To Byron, who was not enjoying being cold-shouldered by the grand ladies who had fawned on

---

* Byron had invited Coleridge to Piccadilly Terrace in the hope of persuading him to publish 'Christabel', a poem which he hugely admired, together with 'Kubla Khan' and 'The Pains of Sleep'. His urgings were successful; the poems were published by John Murray shortly after their meeting. Byron already knew 'Christabel' well enough to be able to recite it, or part of it, from memory during his stay at Geneva.

him a year earlier,* it was refreshing to meet a girl who bore her own disgrace with such apparent equanimity. Nobody, meeting Mary, could view her as a scarlet woman; she was as remarkable for her self-possession as for her keen, intelligent mind. Only someone who knew her well could guess at the dark imagination operating behind her serene smile and large-eyed gaze.

It was, for them both, a memorable occasion. 'Mary is delighted with you as I knew she would be,' Claire wrote to Byron from Shelley's lodgings. She went on to tell him – an endearingly transparent ruse – that Mary was continually begging for his address abroad. 'She perpetually exclaims, "How mild he is! how gentle! So different from what I expected."'[7]

Claire had begun her letter of 21 April by telling Byron that they were waiting for the final news about the disposal of the Shelley estate; of equal importance, in Claire's overheated mind, was the fact that 'tomorrow will inform me whether I should be able to offer you *that* which it has long been the passionate wish of my heart to offer you.'[8] Since the relationship had already become sexual – Claire would not otherwise have been so free in her professions of love or so anxious to disguise the nature of their friendship from Mary – '*that*' appears to have been a child. It was her last chance to cement a fragile alliance; Byron intended to leave England in four days' time, travelling to Switzerland via the field of Waterloo in a gigantic coach modelled on Napoleon's. By the time he left, Claire had been granted her wish. She did not know it, but she was pregnant, although not, perhaps, for the first time.†

----

* The change of feelings towards Byron is strikingly summed up in a letter from Thomas Babington Macaulay to his mother. Macaulay had been an eager reader of Byron, seeing in him a modern equivalent to his adored Tacitus. ('Rien n'est égal à Tacitus. Sa genie me paroît de ressembler beaucoup à celle de Lord-Byron,' he told his mother on 17 April 1815.) On 14 April 1816, two poems which Byron had printed privately were published by his enemy, Henry Brougham, in a Tory paper, the *Champion*. One was a vicious portrait of his wife's governess and confidante, the hated Mrs Clermont. The other and still more damaging was 'Fare Thee Well'. Addressed to his wife, the poem presented Byron as a broken-hearted husband and father, cast out but still loyal: 'Even though unforgiving, never / 'Gainst thee shall my heart rebel.' To Macaulay, a brilliant schoolboy of fifteen, his hero seemed to have behaved like a cad. On 21 April, he invited his mother to share his disgust at 'the abominable, unmanly, conduct of the Peer-poet to whom we once paid such admiration'. Macaulay, along with many readers of the *Champion*, assumed that Byron himself was responsible for the poems' publication.[6]
† If, that is, Shelley got Claire pregnant in 1815. It remains a possible explanation for her being sent to as remote a spot as could be found after a period of intimacy with Shelley and a sudden breakdown in her relationship with Mary. Against this speculation, it has to be acknowledged that no allusion was ever made to a miscarried or aborted child, or none that has survived. This was during the period of Mary's 'lost' journal.

Shelley's party crossed the Channel a week after Byron. Writing from Paris to Geneva in the expectation that Byron would arrive there long before them, Claire gaily announced the approach of '"the whole tribe of the Otaheite philosophers"' – Otaheite, or Tahiti, being the legendary home of free love. Assuming that Byron had called them this in a complimentary spirit, Claire brightly predicted the likelihood of his having an affair with Mary:

> you will I dare say fall in love with her; she is very handsome & very amiable & you will no doubt be blest in your attachment; nothing can afford me such pleasure as to see you happy in any of your attachments. If it should be so I will redouble my attentions to please her; I will do everything she tells me whether it be good or bad for I would not stand low in the affections of the person so beyond blest as to be beloved of you.[9]

Poor Claire. Her mistake was to have fallen in love with the devil's mask which hid a surprisingly old-fashioned Regency dandy. Byron had not intended to flatter them when he mentioned the Otaheites; the idea of living in a commune of free love would have horrified him. The very fact that he was ready to spend time at Geneva, one of the most conventional resorts in Europe, would have given anyone but a Clairmont a hint of Byron's conservative nature; to Claire, as to Charles, Geneva's dullness was obscured by the glamour of their own – possibly mythical – Swiss connections.

They had had a damp time of it on their visit to Switzerland in 1814; the summer of 1816 was proving to be the worst in living memory for England and Western Europe. Writing a rather formal letter to Fanny – she copied it and its successor out for herself with a view to eventual publication – Mary described lashing storms and a terrifying night journey through the mountains; ten men had been required to hold the carriage on course as it lurched and plunged through pelting snow.[10]

But Geneva, looking across an inland sea of transparent blue, was bathed in light. Posing as husband, wife and sister in order to obtain their rooms, they settled into the handsome lakeside Hôtel d'Angleterre efficiently run by Monsieur Dejean at Sécheron, a mile from the town. Byron, arriving late at night two weeks later, entered his age as a hundred years in the hotel register and collapsed into bed. He had barely risen from it before Claire began her assault with the unfortunate mixture of bullying and desperation which marked her pursuit. She had her way; it was, as Byron ungallantly confessed to his half-sister Augusta at the end of the summer, hard to refuse a girl who had travelled eight hundred miles for the pleasure of going to bed with him, especially when he was a little short of admirers.

Claire was feverish with desire and apprehension; Mary was in a daily trance of pleasure. The mountains which recalled her beloved Scotland were a distant view, domesticated by a foreground of elegant villas and lawns sloping down to 'the lovely lake, blue as the heavens which it reflects, and sparkling with golden beams'. Their days followed an agreeably regular pattern, with midday study sessions indoors followed by leisurely strolls in the hotel garden, 'looking at the rabbits, relieving fallen cockchaffers, and watching the motions of a myriad of lizards . . .' At dusk, they sailed across the lake with Mary often bursting out laughing at the pleasure of the journey, or leaning back to watch a pale moon, Shelley's favourite emblem for her, as they drifted shorewards, back to 'the delightful scent of flowers and new mown grass, and the chirp of the grasshoppers, and the song of the evening birds'. Little William, who had been showing worrying signs of ill health before they left England, was flourishing again. She had never been happier.[11]

Fanny could always be relied on to put a blight on things. Her letter, written on 29 May, informed Mary that she had caused her 'a great deal of pain' at their last meeting and that she had been most unjust to call Fanny either 'sordid or vulgar'. (Their quarrel had probably been over Mary's sense that Fanny disapproved of her cohabitation with Shelley.) She did not know why Mary so despised her: 'I understand from Mamma that I am your laughing stock – and the constant beacon of your { } satire.'[12] Mrs Godwin can be blamed for being unkindly inventive, but it is revealing that Fanny believed her. Mary could, when she was angry or scornful, be very wounding.

Mary's next letter to Fanny, written on 1 June, was sent from their new home south of the lake. The house they had chosen for themselves and Elise Duvillard, a good-looking young Swiss woman engaged to care for William – herself already mother of an illegitimate child – was Maison Chapuis at Montalègre, a chalet with a private harbour, close to the village of Cologny. Byron's pleasure in their company was rapidly confirmed by his decision to join them after a week of daily jaunts across the lake. He had already toyed with renting the expensive Villa Diodati, set high on the Belle Rive bank with a terraced garden sloping down to the lakeshore and a balcony offering a magnificent view of the distant violet ridge of the Jura mountains. The villa, grey, handsome and reasonably modern, was one of the loveliest around the lake; it was only a tangled vineyard away from the little house at Montalègre. Byron took it on 10 June:

Monsieur Dejean promptly installed a telescope for the use of visitors to his hotel. Spying across the lake, the hotel guests argued about whether it was Mrs Shelley's or her sister's nightdress they could see hanging out to dry on the Diodati balcony. (Byron could have disillusioned them, although Claire was not always copying poems when she visited the villa; the white drapes were his bed-sheets.)

An intriguing sidelight on this view across the lake is provided by a letter written by one 'J.S' from Geneva on 6 June. 'J.S' may have been the Cornish baronet, Sir John St Aubyn, who subsequently bought a handsome country house near Geneva. His letter, written during a period of convalescence, tells us that a large colony of English had settled at Geneva for the summer, and that most of them had, like Byron, taken villas by the lake. From a reference to the presence of the Earl of Euston and 'his friend Mary', J.S. turned to a more exciting topic. 'Our late great Arrival is Lord Byron, with the Actress and another family of very suspicious appearance. How many he has at his disposal out of the whole set I know not, but different houses have been taken for both establishments . . .' J.S. had not met Byron himself, but he was ready to pass on the view of those who had. Byron had visited the home of a neighbour, a M. Pictet; guests present on the occasion thought him 'insolent and repulsive, and his countenance is very much disliked.' Of Shelley and his companions, however, J.S. could give his correspondent no further information.[13]

Few periods in Mary's life have been so eagerly discussed as the summer during which *Frankenstein* was conceived. Unfortunately for us, her daily record of life at Geneva occupied the last pages of the lost journal of 1815–16. She must have drawn on these entries for the vivid account which she wrote in 1828 as her contribution to Thomas Moore's *The Life of Lord Byron, with his Letters & Journals* (1830–1). Tactfully presented by Moore as having been Shelley's wife in 1816, Mary's identity as his source of information was concealed. She was quoted, extensively, but only as 'a person' who had been among Byron's circle. Writing out her recollections for Moore, Mary shifted and compressed events for dramatic effect in the confident belief that nobody would contradict her version. Claire, for reasons which will become apparent, was by 1828 only concerned with being excised from Byron's history. Shelley and Byron were dead; John Polidori, the young doctor who accompanied Byron to Geneva, had killed himself with a massive dose of prussic acid at the age of twenty-one.

Mary may never have known that canny John Murray had invited John Polidori to keep a diary of his travels with Byron. Edited and then transcribed by the doctor's sister (she destroyed the original), the diary was eventually published in 1911 by Polidori's nephew, William Michael Rossetti. This, together with a few details which Polidori published with his gothic tale, *The Vampyre* (1819), provides a skeleton outline against which to set Mary's recollections. But Polidori also has to be treated with caution. He noted Shelley to be a twenty-six-year-old consumptive when he was actually twenty-three and had been cleared of the disease. He believed Mary and Claire to be full sisters. Polidori was, however, sufficiently in Byron's confidence to know on the day after they all first met that Claire was his mistress and that Mary was not entitled to be called Mrs Shelley.

Polidori was less of a fool than Mary made him sound in the account she gave Moore and in her 1831 Preface to *Frankenstein*. Exceptionally handsome – he did not object to being mistaken for Byron on occasion – he had been a brilliant student at Edinburgh, and had published a play and a discourse on the death penalty before the age of twenty. Both the play, *Ximines*, and the poems which Polidori wrote in the summer of 1816 show considerable talent; in retrospect, Byron had nothing harsher to say than that poor 'Polly' had been hot-headed and passionate, with an unfortunate ability to get himself into scrapes.

The doctor's diary suggests that he fell a little in love with Mary. He appointed himself her Italian teacher. 'Read Italian with Mrs S,' he noted on 31 May; 'went into a boat with Mrs S, and rowed all night till nine; tea'd together, chatted, etc.' Writing her account for Moore's use, Mary may have been playing a private game when she described the extreme embarrassment of Polidori after Byron, 'in the highest and most boyish of spirits . . . and in that utter incapacity of retention which was one of his foibles', had merrily threatened to tell her about a mysterious lady with whom the young doctor was madly in love.[14] Byron was certainly conscious enough of the doctor's infatuation to suggest, when Mary was climbing the steep path to Diodati one day, that Polidori should make an eight-foot leap from the balcony and offer her his arm. The doctor gallantly did so – and sprained his ankle. He was laid up for more than a week. Mary dealt briskly with his passion. Polidori glumly noted in his journal that Mrs Shelley had told him she looked on him as a younger brother.

Polidori had his tumble on 15 June. His friends consoled him by agreeing to hear a reading of his new play. Mary, remembering the occasion for Moore, described Byron's attempts to keep a straight face during a scene which included the unfortunate line, "'Tis thus the goiter'd idiot of the Alps'. Seeking to offer comfort, Byron told Polidori that worse playscripts were often submitted to Drury Lane. The doctor was not deceived: 'worth nothing,' he wrote in his diary.

Polidori made another entry in his diary for that day, one which is suggestive when we remember that Shelley, author of the first 1818 Preface to *Frankenstein*, noted there that the story's central idea had first cropped up in a 'casual conversation'. This central idea was for the manufacture of life in a being assembled from animal and human parts. The casual conversation may have occurred on 15 June, when Polidori noted that he and Shelley had talked about 'principles, – whether man was thought to be merely an instrument'.

There was good reason for this to be a hot topic. In March, only three months earlier, William Lawrence, the doctor who had treated both Mary and Shelley, gave two highly controversial lectures in his new position as Professor of Anatomy at the Royal College of Surgeons. Polidori, as an ambitious and clever young doctor newly arrived in London from Edinburgh, would certainly have gone along to listen; he would have remembered enough to give the gist of their content to Shelley and, perhaps, to Mary.

The lectures had caused a furore and considerable embarrassment to the college; for a time, Lawrence was viewed as a traitor to his profession. His crime was to attack the received view of life as an entity separate from, and superior to, the physical body. Creation, Lawrence argued, had nothing to do with God, providence or any tale presented in the Bible. Reviewing the published version of the lectures in 1819, the reviewer for the *Quarterly* expressed his horror at the implications of Lawrence's view. Did man have no soul? Was he to expect only decay after his death? Had Lawrence nothing better to do than ape 'modern French philosophy' and 'the free-thinking physiologists of Germany'?[15] The reviewer was not alone in expressing superstitious horror. It was one thing for surgeons to attach voltaic piles to the bodies of murderers and attempt to galvanize them into life; it was another entirely for a professional anatomist to suggest that his powers might in any way equal those of God.

Both Mary and Shelley enjoyed, at the least, a professional friendship with Lawrence; they may even have attended his lectures. They were not trained, as Polidori had been, to grasp all of their implications, but the subject was one which fascinated them. The lectures, or allied matters, were discussed at the homes of Byron and the Shelleys from 15 June on, throughout the summer.

Beyond the windows, nature seemed eerily attuned to their

conversations. The weather became increasingly wild; Geneva's famous storms, when lightning flashes from peak to peak and the surface of the lake shivers like a boiling cauldron, were never more violent and recurrent than in the summer of 1816. Shutters snapped open on stabbing lines of light, blanched clouds, a roar of wind. This, as Mary and Shelley knew if they had visited one of England's most successful electrical scientists during their weeks in Devon, was perfect weather for generating electric power.* They could have imagined they were living in God's workroom, had they believed in God.

Shelley, Claire and Mary visited Diodati the day after Polidori's tumble. Byron, who was in the habit of staying up until three in the morning, suggested they should amuse themselves by reading a French translation of some German fantasy tales. Of the several which provide possible influences on *Frankenstein* – one concerned the animating of a corpse's stolen head – Mary singled out two in her 1831 Preface to the novel. One told of a gigantic spectre doomed to kill the heirs of his house with a kiss: 'Je vis devant le lit de l'enfant l'effroyable figure . . . Je vis le spectre se pencher vers l'enfant, et lui baiser doucement le front. Il se pencha ensuite par dessus mon lit, et baisa le front de l'autre enfant.'[17] Just so, she wanted to suggest in 1831, had the creature of her dreams looked threatening while acting with perfect gentleness towards his creator: 'He sleeps; but he is awakened; he opens his eyes; behold, the horrid thing stands at his bedside, opening his curtains and looking on him with yellow, watery, but speculative eyes.'

'These tales,' Shelley wrote on Mary's behalf in the 1818 Preface to *Frankenstein*, 'excited in us a playful desire of imitation. Two other friends . . . and myself agreed to write each a story, founded on some supernatural occurrence.' Shelley's account makes it plain that the two other storywriters were Byron and himself, and that, on a subsequent journey among the Alps (there had been no such joint journey into the mountains, only a lake tour), they had forgotten their 'ghostly visions'. In Shelley's account only *Frankenstein* emerged from the storytelling evening. Mary, in 1828, was ready to confirm this, telling Moore that her novel sprang straight from the storytelling session.

---

* Mary and Shelley were sufficiently familiar with electrical demonstrations and experiments to have been conscious of this. It is possible although far from certain that their interest had drawn them to visit the electrical scientist Andrew Crosse when they were living near him in Devon in 1815. Crosse had by that time rigged up his Somerset ballroom at Fyne Court as a gigantic laboratory with conductors, saucers of crystals, fifty leyden jars and 1,800 feet of copper wire coming in through the windows. Crosse delighted in showing his laboratory to visitors.[16]

By 1831, when a third edition of *Frankenstein* was published, following a series of stage versions of the story, Mary had a new explanation. Now, she wanted to connect the laborious process of creating a novel to Frankenstein's slow assembly and animation of his creature. She wrote now that she had not begun or even thought of a tale until some time after the story session. Stressing the point, she recalled how all the others (she tactfully omitted any allusion to Claire) had started at once. Byron wrote the fragment which he later published with *Mazeppa*; Shelley began a tale based on his early life; Polidori 'had some terrible story about a skull-headed lady who was so punished for peeping through a keyhole . . .' Day after day, Mary remembered in 1831, she had been tormented with inquiries about her tale: ' "Have you thought of a story?" I was asked each morning, and each morning I was forced to reply with a mortifying negative.'[18]

This assertion is undone by Polidori's diary in which, writing at the time as Mary was not, he stated that they all, with the exception of himself, began writing at once. It is unlikely that he would have neglected to mention the consoling fact, had it been a fact, that his admired Mary was also short of an idea.

On the following day, 18 June, the party again assembled at Diodati. Byron decided to indulge in a spot of the terror-raising with which Claire and Shelley were familiar from their nights of story-telling together in London. At midnight, gathered around a blazing fire and with the shutters closed, they 'really began to talk ghostly'. Byron, who had been bewitched by the effect Coleridge made on him when reciting 'Kubla Khan' in the Devonshire House library, decided to see if he could do as well himself. The results, noted by Polidori, were unnerving.

> LB repeated some verses of Coleridge's Christabel, of the witch's breast; when silence ensued, & Shelley, shrieking and putting his hands to his head, ran out of the room with a candle. Threw water in his face and after gave him ether. He was looking at Mrs S, & suddenly thought of a woman he had heard of who had eyes instead of nipples, which, taking hold of his mind, horrified him.[19]

A local doctor was called in; Polidori undertook to sit up with Shelley while the others, frightened and exhausted, went to bed.

Shelley himself made no reference to the 'Christabel' evening in his Preface to the 1818 edition of *Frankenstein*; neither did Mary in 1831. She had a good reason for not wanting to mention it; there is, after all, a startling likeness between the way the story of *Frankenstein* was supposed to have come to her, in a waking dream, and the supposed origin of Coleridge's 'Kubla Khan'. The 1816 publication of this poem was the first in which Coleridge provided his famous account of its emergence, towering out of his imagination while he dozed over a book. If Mary made no allusion to the 'Christabel' evening, it may have been because she did not want to draw too much attention to her own act of cool appropriation. She wrote the 1831 Preface in order to help sell the book; telling the best possible story mattered more than the truth. Polidori was reduced to the sidelines and made to sound like a buffoon; Byron, the most famous of the Geneva group, was brought to the fore to discuss with Shelley how life could be generated. Mary, following Coleridge's vivid example, sank into a receptive trance after listening to their conversation.

> When I placed my head on my pillow, I did not sleep, nor could I be said to think. My imagination, unbidden, possessed and guided me, gifting the successive images that arose in my mind with a vividness far beyond the usual bounds of reverie. I saw – with shut eyes, but acute mental vision . . .

Sceptics might ask themselves why, if the occasion was as exciting to Mary as she makes it in the Preface ('On the morrow I announced that I had *thought of a story*'), Polidori never recorded any such declaration in his diary. He was devoted to Mary; such anticipation and relief would surely not have passed unobserved.

Shelley set off on a brief tour of the lake with Byron on 22 June, leaving Mary to be entertained by her disabled gallant, the young doctor. Converting the lake voyage into a tour of the Alps in the 1818 Preface, Shelley announced that this was the point at which the beauty of their surroundings drove their own story-ideas clean out of their heads. This was a graceful conflation of events. Shelley, accompanied by Claire and Mary, set off for the Alps on 21 July. They failed to persuade Byron to go with them. Instead, they took a new journal. Along the route, as Mary ruefully noted on 22 July, they purchased a trapped squirrel which promptly bit her finger. Shelley carried the little creature in his arms until, losing its charm, it was dumped on a roadside railing.

Avalanches, tumbling torrents and gigantic pines rising towards them from mist-drenched valleys provided all the excited sensations the travellers had hoped for. At Chamonix, their chosen destination, they were told that the gigantic glacier was advancing by a foot each day, threatening to engulf the entire valley. Staring across the vacant breadth of a vast river of ice enclosed by dark mountains which soared above them to sunlit white peaks, Mary remembered the accounts she had heard in Scotland of the Arctic whalers, of risks taken and lives lost. 'This is the most desolate place in the world,' she wrote on 25 July after excitedly underlining the fact that she had at last seen the '*mer de glace*'.

Danger was an added incentive to intrepid tourists. Every hotel and inn they stayed at was packed with English, French and German travellers, eager to impart their awed sense of a superior power and to thank God for so kindly preserving them. Shelley, Mary and Claire, while happy to fill their pockets with the usual alpine souvenirs of rock fragments, crystal seals and flower seeds, were disgusted by the pious entries in the visitors' books they found at every stop. Giggling at their own wickedness, they signed themselves in as atheists: 'Mr Percy Bysche Shelley, Madame son Epouse, Theossteique la soeur εκαστοι αθεοι,' they wrote in the rest-hut at Montanvers. Given the daring nature of an entry which proclaimed them all to be atheists, it is surprising that they were so keen to present Mary as Shelley's wife. The next visitor, also a classicist, added a dry sentence in Greek: 'If this is true they are fools and miserable revellers in their folly; if not true they are one and all liars.'[20] It may have been Byron, visiting Montenvers with Polidori a month later, who tried to spare Claire additional scandal by partly erasing her signature.

Mary's new journal shows that she had started work on a story by the time they reached the *mer de glace*: 'write my story,' she noted on the rainy day before they scrambled up the steep path to the top of the glacier. Over a month had gone by since the evening of reading ghost stories around the fire; perhaps, in these desolate surroundings, her mind returned to the tale which she may have started to contemplate, and even to write, when in Scotland. This was the narrative of Robert Walton's search for a new land beyond the North Pole; it encloses, and became integral to, the story of Frankenstein.

They returned to Geneva on 27 July. Mary had enjoyed her visit to 'a world of ice', but she was pleased to be back: 'I longed to see my pretty babe,' she confessed to her journal. 'This is the second anniversary since Shelley's & my union,' she noted the following day, recording the date on which she, Claire and Shelley had fled to France. Full of tenderness for him, she began work on a hand-stitched balloon for his birthday present, strong enough to be flown on the lake from the boat which Shelley had purchased at the beginning of the holiday. Another present which she knew would please him was a telescope; the two of them went into Geneva to choose one on 2 August.

Mary was still in ignorance of Claire's pregnancy. Shelley had known about it for at least a month; after his lake voyage with Byron, he had thoughtfully added a clause to his will, bequeathing a princely £6,000 to Claire, and the same sum again to an unnamed person of her choice. He may, as the editors of Mary's journal suggest, have discussed Claire's situation with Byron during the boat trip and concluded that, since Byron was unwilling to take any financial responsibility, he ought to do something himself.[21]

Claire's pregnancy was the likely subject of the 'talks' which Mary recorded taking place between Shelley and her stepsister the day after their return from the mountains. On 2 August, Shelley and Claire went up to Diodati. Mary would have liked to go with them, but 'Lord B[yron] did not seem to wish it', she wrote with evident perplexity. Shelley returned with a letter which had arrived from the lawyers. The news was not good; his father was prepared to keep a promise to increase his annual allowance by £500 and to lend him £2,000, but only if he returned to England. Grand schemes for a year of eastern travel would have to be dropped. Fanny, a week later, sent a letter so heartbreaking in its anxiety about Godwin's finances and so wistful in its pleas for stories of the great Lord Byron that Mary and Shelley decided to find some token of their esteem. Fanny, on the day she died, was still wearing the pretty little gold watch which they bought for her in Geneva.

On 21 August, Mary noted that she and Shelley had a long discussion about her story; a week later, Fanny fulfilled her promise of sending them, among other books, their own copy of Coleridge's three recently published dream poems. Remembering the violent effect it had worked on him, Shelley read 'Christabel' aloud to Mary before they went to bed. This, not the earlier occasion specified in the Preface, may have been the moment when Mary's imagination at last took flight, quickened by Shelley's reading and by her recent journey to a landscape of terrifying isolation and grandeur.

Mary's 1831 Preface, when read alongside her journal entries for that cold and rainy August, lends support to this idea. On eight days of the first two weeks of the month, she spent part of the evening at the Villa Diodati, together with Shelley and Byron; the conversations, to which she represented herself as a passive witness, often returned to their favourite subject that summer, the principle of life. A story was going the rounds that Erasmus Darwin had once made an experiment with a piece of vermicelli which, when sealed in a glass case, had 'by some extraordinary means [begun to move] with voluntary motion'.[22]* Mary, a 'devout but nearly silent listener', became increasingly fascinated by the idea of spontaneous generation. 'Perhaps a corpse could be reanimated; galvanism had given token of such things; perhaps the component parts of a creature might be manufactured, brought together, and endued with vital warmth.'[23]

The setting provided her own galvanic spark. Watching the lightning leap across the distant mountain tops, listening to passionate discussions about the limits to which man's ambition to outdo nature might lead him, thinking of Shelley's own early years of experiments with electricity, of the strange ghost stories they had read, and of her tale of Walton's ambitious voyage, she felt the elements coalesce. On 26 August, Shelley's reading of 'Christabel' sparked a vision to match his own of 18 June. Where he had hallucinated a woman with eyes for nipples, Mary now saw a creature both horrifying and pitiful. This was the monster her promethean scientist would endow with life. Her journal noted that she had been busily writing a story in the days before Shelley read 'Christabel' to her: 'Write,' she wrote on 24 and 25 August. The day after the 'Christabel' reading, she stopped. She did not return to her work until 16 September. Three weeks had given her time to rethink and reassemble her material.

Source-hunting is a slippery business where the evidence is so contradictory. It is, however, worth remembering that 1816 was also the summer during which Byron began planning, and perhaps talking about, his ideas for *Manfred*. Published two years later, the poem was described to John Murray as being about 'a kind of magician who is tormented by a species of remorse . . . in the 3rd act he is found by his attendants dying in a tower – where he studied his art.'[24]

Here, in the idea of a magician haunted by his own guilt, we seem to have something very close to the idea of Frankenstein, who is tormented by the thought of the horror he has, through a form of magic, knowingly unleashed. Here too, in *Manfred*'s famous incantatory poem, is the terror with which Frankenstein invests his abandoned creature, always seen by him as a spectral, menacing presence:

---

* Mary, in her 1831 Preface, was careful to say that she was alluding not to what Dr Darwin had really done, but to 'what was then spoken of as having been done by him'. Darwin had, in his first note to *The Temple of Nature*, described a paste of flour and water in which 'the animalcules called eels' increased and enlarged, even when placed in a sealed glass phial. He also noted that these 'vorticella' appeared to come to life after being dried. Mary rejected this as a direct source of inspiration: 'Not thus, after all, would life be given.'

> Though thou seest me not pass by,
> Thou shalt feel me with thine eye
> As a thing that, though unseen
> Must be near thee, and hath been . . .[25]*

Matthew Lewis, the gothic novelist whose most famous novel, *The Monk*, was published the year before Mary's birth, arrived on 14 August to spend a few days with Byron. Joining in the spirit of the party, Lewis produced some hair-raising ghost stories which Mary faithfully copied into her journal. They have less bearing on *Frankenstein* than the fact that their narrator was fresh from a visit to his two slave plantations in Jamaica and full of concern about the slaves for whom he had come to feel affectionate responsibility. The London *Times* had recently reported a native uprising in Sierra Leone, leading to the murder of many of the white inhabitants. A corrected report on the following day, 7 May, showed that a bloodless riot had been hurriedly crushed by the local militia. The readiness with which the initial report had been accepted was much discussed.†

At some point, possibly as a result of Lewis's heated discussions with Byron and Shelley about the slave trade and unenlightened attitudes to black people, Mary decided to use her story to illustrate how environment and circumstances could act on an essentially virtuous being and lead him, through mistreatment, from light into darkness, into becoming what he was wrongly perceived to be. Her creature, Frankenstein's electrically charged child, would remind her readers of the danger and wickedness of their attitude to the people whose unpaid labour sweetened their coffee. The 1814 Treaty of Paris secured French trading rights in slavery for a further five years; the main characters of Mary's novel are all of French origin. Only the Creature, assembled from wherever limbs can be got, is made as rootless as a transported slave. Judged, as William Lawrence judged the black man, by his appearance and not by his acts, the Creature becomes an unprincipled monster. The fault is firmly attributed not

---

* This was also the summer in which Byron wrote 'Darkness'. When, nine years later, Mary began work on *The Last Man*, a novel which conveys a terrifying impression of the end of the world, she may have been partly inspired by Byron's memorably powerful vision of emptiness, when 'The bright sun was extinguished and the stars / Did wander darkling in the eternal space, / Rayless, and pathless, and the icy earth / Swung blind and blackening in the moonless air'.[26]

† *Galignani's Messenger*, the newspaper for travellers abroad, carried summaries of the *Times* reports. This was the form in which the news reached readers at Geneva.

to him but to the supposedly civilized Frenchmen who refuse to acknowledge his humanity.

Some critics have interpreted the Creature as a symbol of the French mob at the height of revolutionary rage, believing that in the moment of his transformation, when he seizes kindling to raze the house of the de Laceys – the family he has looked on 'in an innocent, half painful self deceit' as his protectors – Mary offers a warning and an indictment of her own hypocritical times. In the Creature's simple faith in the de Laceys as his guardians, she presented the attitude of the virtuous slave towards his owner. In his fall from innocence, she took care to remind the reader that these protectors had betrayed his trust. Thus, the mistreated and misunderstood slave had right on his side when he rebelled against those who refused to accept him as an equal member of their own species.

> I reflected that they had spurned and deserted me, [and] anger returned, a rage of anger; and unable to injure anything human, turned my fury towards inanimate objects . . . I lighted the dry branch of a tree, and danced with fury around the devoted cottage . . . I waved my brand . . . with a loud scream, I fired the straw, and heath, and bushes, which I had collected. The wind fanned the fire, and the cottage was quickly enveloped by the flames . . . As soon as I was convinced that no assistance could save any part of the habitation, I quitted the scene, and sought for refuge in the woods.[27]

Arrangements for Claire and her unborn child were finalized during the last days at Geneva. Byron proposed that it should be brought up by his half-sister, Augusta Leigh. When Claire objected, a compromise was reached, with Byron agreeing that he would not, for the first seven years of its life, place his son or daughter in a stranger's care. Claire was graciously permitted to act in the role of her own child's aunt until the moment when Byron might choose to send for it. With this arrangement, hardly ideal, they had to be satisfied.

Early on the morning of 29 August, Shelley and his little party packed their bags and set off for England, taking with them Canto III of *Childe Harold* and *The Prisoner of Chillon* for delivery to Byron's publisher. It is unlikely that Claire's condition won her much sympathy from her stepsister. Mary's journal gives nothing away. Any pity she may have felt would have been extinguished if she had known that Claire's last pathetic letter to Byron from Geneva dismissed all friendships but his as meaningless, irrelevant. 'I shall love you to the end of my life & nobody else,' Claire scrawled as the trunks were carried out of the house.[28]

But Byron, while he had been delighted by Shelley and impressed by Mary, had already written the tiresomely persistent Miss Clairmont out of his life. The child was alleged to be his own. He would, in time, do what he could for it. But who could tell? Rumour – there had been a good deal of unpleasant gossip while they were at Geneva – suggested that Shelley did not care whether he slept with Mary Godwin, her step-sister or both. The child might as easily be Shelley's. Shelley had, after all, seemed perfectly happy to bring it up in his own home; he had wasted no time in making arrangements for Claire's unborn baby in his will. Perhaps – well, Shelley's ways were not his. In the circumstances, Byron thought he had behaved rather well.

Mary, whatever she may have thought of Byron's fickleness to Claire, showed no lessening of affection for him. She continued to read everything he wrote and to associate him with a period of unusual happiness. 'Dear Lake! I shall ever love thee,' she wrote in May 1817 after reading the stanzas of *Childe Harold* which brought it all back to her.

> How a powerful mind can sanctify past scenes and recollections – His is a powerful mind. One that fills me with melancholy yet mixed with pleasure as is always the case when intellectual energy is displayed. I think of our excursions on the lake. How we saw him when he came down to us or welcomed our arrival with a goodhumoured smile. How very vividly does each verse of his poem recall some scene of this kind to my memory.

A line later, Mary expressed her hope that they would see Byron 'again & again – enjoy his society'.[29] Cross though she was with Claire for her silliness, she could not blame her for falling in love with such a man.

Arriving in Geneva in 1818, Shelley's cousin Thomas Medwin paid a respectful visit to Montalègre. Still anchored in the little harbour below Byron's villa, he found the boat which Byron and Shelley had jointly purchased and in which, when the evenings were fine enough, their whole party had gone out on the lake. The boat was rotten, half-submerged in water; the villa rented by Shelley was already lost in a tangle of undergrowth and untamed trees. Diodati remains, meticulously preserved and emblazoned with a plaque recording Byron's residence there; Maison Chapuis is gone, buried in an unlocated site under the Genevan suburb of Cologny.

CHAPTER TWELVE

DISTRESSING EVENTS

1816

'Give me a garden & *absentia Clariae* and I will thank my love for many favours.'

Mary Wollstonecraft Godwin to Percy Bysshe Shelley, 5 December 1816

CLAIRE'S CONDITION WAS ALREADY BECOMING APPARENT WHEN the trio left Geneva at the beginning of September. Any idea of returning to Bishopsgate was ruled out by the distressing news that the bailiffs had swooped after they had left the house and sequestered the possessions they had casually left there, expecting Peacock to protect their interests. A decision was taken that, while Shelley went to London to obtain the money due to him from his father, and to give Byron's manuscripts to his publisher, the girls would find discreet lodgings in Bath. The Godwins must be kept in the dark; they were all agreed on that. Better and more prudent to tell them Claire was in poor health and that Bath had been recommended as a suitable place for recovery. Duplicity could, in such circumstances, be argued into a form of kindness.

Claire had already been dumped once, when she was unceremoniously dispatched to Lynmouth the previous year; even Mary reluctantly had to agree that she could not be abandoned now, when they had already committed themselves to caring for her and Byron's unborn child. It was hard to bear. For three months, Mary had known a state of perfect happiness, living in a landscape which enchanted her, among company which had been more stimulating and exciting than any she could remember. Now, she must put all this behind her and live in dull seclusion in a fashionable town where she knew nobody and nobody knew her. That, of course, was the precise reason for going there; but the cause, the lovesick, ungrateful and self-willed cause, was her stepsister.

There were times when Mary wished Claire to the other end of the earth. Find them a house near mountains and water, just like Geneva, she pleaded with Shelley as he searched for their next home; promise that Claire would not share it with them; was it so much to ask? Sadly for Mary, it was a wish Shelley had no inclination to grant. Claire had made herself his responsibility when she joined them on their honeymoon elopement. Rejected by Byron and with a child on the way, she was more his charge than ever before. Whatever Mary might feel, Shelley remained deeply attached to her stepsister, and she to him. With the sweet conciliatory manner which had in it no more flexibility than a rod of iron, Shelley listened and refused to budge. Claire would stay with them for as long as he, and she, wished. In the meantime, Mary had a duty to care for her which he expected her to fulfil.

The lodgings Mary found in Bath were at 5 Abbey Churchyard, next to the Pump Room. If it was not quite as grand as living in the great sweep of Royal Crescent, it was certainly not secluded; nor were the rooms a little higher up the hill on New Bond Street, to which Claire moved as her confinement approached. Here, they were in the thick of things, able to stroll on Milsom Street among the visiting families of admirals and baronets whose arrivals were regularly proclaimed in the *Bath Chronicle*.

With no chaperone to escort her to the Assembly Rooms, where prettily ribboned and flounced dresses, peach kid half-boots and elegant wreaths were *de rigueur* for young ladies of fashion, Mary occupied herself by taking drawing lessons and attending a course of scientific lectures being given at Bath's Literary and Philosophical Society Rooms. Perhaps she ventured to the Theatre Royal, where Sheridan, one of her father's closest friends, was being posthumously honoured by performances of *The Rivals* and *The School for Scandal*.

Neither drawing lessons, lectures nor work on her novel compensated for Shelley's absence. She had been in Bath for a week before he suggested that she should come to Peacock's family home near Marlow and help them in the search for a new house. Mary left on the next morning's coach, arriving at Maidenhead on 19 September. Claire, sullen at being left in charge of 'Itty Babe' William and his Swiss nurse Elise, comforted herself with bossy reminders; Mary must be sure to buy Shelley a greatcoat and not to overwalk him.

Her warnings were unnecessary. Shelley, despite his frail appearance, could walk all day without any sign of fatigue or feeling the cold; it was Mary who was hard-pressed to keep up as Peacock, who had lived in the Marlow area most of his life, rushed them around all his favourite beauty spots. Like Shelley, Mary was enchanted by the combination of monastic ruins, riverside woods and quiet villages. As rural as they could wish, Marlow was also less than a day's walk from London.

There was not much warmth of feeling yet between Mary and Thomas Peacock; she was too aware of his loyal affection for Harriet Shelley to feel comfortable with him. But it was a relief to be away from Claire and her endless harping on the subject of Byron and his reluctance to answer her letters. At Marlow, when old Mrs Peacock had retired to bed with her candle, the conversation was more intensely political, more alive.

There was much to discuss. At Bath, young ladies prattled about balls, bonnets and the best way to show off their bosoms; the rest of the country was seething with dissatisfaction. The Corn Laws, prohibiting the import of foreign corn until home-grown wheat reached 80 shillings a quarter, had provided the situation for an explosion with the first bad harvest. Now that it had come, following the dreadful summer of 1816, the price of corn and, consequently, bread, had soared. The poor, unable to buy the staple of their diet, starved. On one occasion that autumn, Mary noted, they met a family who stood, crying from hunger, in the street; Shelley, predictably, was quick to provide. The Spa Fields meeting in London, triggering an intensely repressive course of action from a frightened government, was only a few weeks away. In September and October, working men were already gathering into clubs which, guided by the energetic spirit of *Cobbett's Political Register* and his 'Twopenny Trash' pamphlets, would decide what course of action to take. Shelley, describing the situation in a long letter to Byron, believed that swift and radical reforms were the only solution, a view which Mary probably shared. To her, as much as to Shelley, it seemed that they were living in very ugly times. Peacock took refuge in mockery; his companions were incapable of such detachment.

Shelley went back to Bath with Mary on 25 September. His thoughts still on Marlow, he sent off a long and friendly letter to Byron, painting an alluring picture of their household as an exile's haven. They were, he wrote, 'well and content. Clare is writing to you at this instant. Mary is reading over the fire; our cat and kitten are sleeping under the sofa; and little Willy is just gone to sleep.' All that was missing, when they settled in their new home, was a visit from their noble friend.[1] But Byron, cutting a merry swathe across the Continent on his way to Venice, had no plans to come home and no inclination whatsoever to live under the same roof as the pregnant and ever-hopeful Miss Clairmont. The person who could really have benefited from such tender invitations, poor Fanny, received none. Later, too late, Mary was overcome with guilt.

Perhaps it was Fanny's innately melancholy nature which caused them all to overlook the evidence of her growing despair. On 26 September, answering a (lost) account from Mary of life in Bath (how wonderful to be so calm, so studious and so contented, Fanny wistfully wrote), she told them that Eliza Bishop and Everina Wollstonecraft, with whom she had been hoping to travel back to Dublin to work as a teacher or governess, had left without her. She mentioned, too, that the aunts had 'entirely lost their little income from Primrose Street'. These were a group of shabby tenanted houses in a run-down area of London which Godwin had become involved with handling after his first wife's death. The sisters may have felt that Godwin had mismanaged the rents or treated them inappropriately, but that was no reason to abandon Fanny. More probably, although Fanny did not say so, the fact that she had maintained close contact with Shelley and Mary had prejudiced Eliza and Everina against employing their niece in a school.

A week later, Fanny wrote again; 'stupid letter from F,' Mary irritably noted on 4 October. What annoyed her in particular was the firmness with which Fanny denied that she had ever, as Shelley reported, described Mrs Godwin as spreading scandal and pursuing them '"like a hound after foxes"'. This, Fanny wrote, was a 'glaring falsehood' and she would not allow herself to be made its author. If there was gossip about them, the fault lay with Harriet, who had been telling stories during her summer visit to Mrs de Boinville, and with Mary herself:

> You are very careless and are for ever leaving your letters about[.] English servants like nothing so much as scandal and gosip – but this you know as well as I – and this is the origin of the stories that are told – And this you chuse to fasten upon mamma . . .

Fanny followed this vigorous scolding with a reproach to Shelley for letting Godwin down. (Shelley had informed Godwin that, having received less than £300 himself after his debts against the family estate were cleared, he could neither lend a similar sum nor commit himself to negotiating future loans.) To Fanny, the situation was clear-cut; Shelley had promised to help and now he must do so or give more precise reasons for his refusal. To do anything less was to cause 'papa' unnecessary emotional distress. It was, she added with passionate underlinings, 'of the utmost consequence *for his own* and the *world's sake* that he [Godwin] should *finish his novel* and is it not your and Shelley's duty to consider these things?' Fanny shared Godwin's belief that the worthy have an absolute right to be supported by those who have the worth to give. Like Godwin, she found it hard to grasp how little was actually available.[2]

Mary, who did not like to be chided, sent a prompt reply (both this and Fanny's response of 8 October have been lost). But she was not, as yet, alarmed. Life at Bath, now that Shelley was sharing it with her, was proving quite congenial. They walked about the city together, admiring its honey-coloured stone and the glimpses of the enclosing hills which she was attempting to draw for her teacher, Mr West. In the evenings, as Shelley read her a translation of Cervantes, she was tenderly struck by the resemblance between her beloved and Don Quixote, that most romantic of idealists. Shelley in turn was amused and charmed when, aware of the plot of Lucian's *Golden Ass*, Mary playfully speculated that their cat's fondness for roses might metamorphose her into a feline lady.

Fanny's letter of 8 October was recorded in Mary's journal without comment. This was the day on which Fanny left Skinner Street and wrote to Godwin from Bristol that she planned to 'depart immediately to the spot from which I hope never to remove'. Horrified by the implication, Godwin took the next coach to Bristol. Finding no trace of Fanny, he went on to Bath and spent an anxious night there – he made no contact with his family – before returning, empty of news, to London. On 9 October, Mary also received a 'very alarming' letter from Fanny. Claire, many years later, remembered how quickly Shelley reacted: he 'jumped up thrust his hand in [his] hair – I must be off.'[3] The girls were still sitting up at two in the morning when he returned from Bristol. He, too, had found nothing.

A second day of hunting was equally unproductive; on 11 October, following a tip, Shelley took the coach from Bristol to Swansea, the local port for boats crossing to Dublin. On 12 October, he came back to the anxious girls at Bath. The news, which he probably gathered from a report in the *Cambrian* that day, was, as Mary miserably noted in her journal, the 'worst possible'. Fanny had taken great pains to disguise her identity, but the article left no room for doubt.

On 9 October, the day after writing to Mary, Fanny had reached Swansea and paid for a room at an inn called the Mackworth Arms. Before swallowing a bottle of laudanum, she had written a note to explain that she intended to close the existence 'of a being whose birth was unfortunate, and whose life has only been a series of pain to those persons who have hurt their health in endeavouring to promote her welfare'. The signature had been burnt off. The newspaper article mentioned that the dead young lady's stays were embroidered with the initials 'MW', and that her few possessions included a little gold Swiss watch. The stays were Mary Wollstonecraft's; the watch was the gift Mary and Shelley had found for Fanny in Geneva that summer.[4]

The precise reasons for Fanny's suicide have never been clear. Godwin, talking to his old friend Maria Gisborne about it in 1820, dated her unhappiness from the elopement. He appeared to think that Fanny had been in love with Shelley, and that it was only a sense of duty which kept her at Skinner Street.[5] This shifted the responsibility away from himself and his wife; it may not have been far short of the truth. A poem which Shelley wrote only a few months after Fanny's death points in the same direction. Published by Mary without comment, it has always been supposed to allude to his last meeting with her half-sister.

> Her voice did quiver as we parted,
>   Yet knew I not that heart was broken
> From which it came, and I departed
>   Heeding not the word then spoken.
>   Misery – O Misery,
>   This world is all too wide for thee.

It may be that Fanny, who had not been told the truth about Claire's situation, hoped to join the younger members of the family at Bath and that she put this idea to Shelley at their brief meeting in London. His prudent reluctance to agree (Fanny could not be trusted to keep Claire's pregnancy a secret from the Godwins) might have seemed a woundingly cold rejection to Fanny's sensitive nature, but an insufficient reason to kill herself. The simplest and saddest explanation is that Fanny felt, as her last note suggests, that she had become a burden to her family. Her aunts were newly impoverished; the Godwins were penniless; so, it seemed, was Shelley. Whom could she expect to care for her? What option, to a young woman who had inherited all of her mother's depressive tendencies and none of her spirit and drive, was open but an obscure death?

On 13 October, Godwin wrote Mary his first letter since her elopement. 'I cannot but thank you for your strong expression of sympathy,' he wrote. His chief concern was that she should do nothing to attract publicity. 'Go not to Swansea,' he warned; 'disturb not the silent dead; do nothing to destroy the obscurity she so much desired.'[6] The tone was cold; the thinking was wise. Suicide was a criminal act, but Fanny had not been identified in the newspaper article and was unlikely to be, so long as they all kept away from Swansea. Her body would lie in an unmarked grave, but any grave was better than a suicide's burial at a lonely crossroads. With discretion, her name and theirs could be preserved from any further scandal. Discretion was maintained: Charles Clairmont, ten months later, still did not know that Fanny was dead. Friends of the Godwins who asked about Fanny were told that she had died of a fever on the way to Dublin.

Claire, fretting over her own future and Byron's evident reluctance to play any part in it, shed no tears. She had never much cared for Fanny, and did not mind saying as much. Mary's journal was reticent as ever, owning only that the news had given her 'a miserable day' and that she had put on mourning clothes. Writing to Shelley from Bath on 17 December, however, at a time when a suitable new home near Marlow had finally been located, she regretted that poor Fanny could not have held on to life a little longer, 'for my house would then have been a proper assylum for her – Ah my best love,' she went on, 'to you do I owe every joy every perfection that I may enjoy or boast of – Love me, sweet, for ever – But I {do} not mean — I hardly know what I mean I am so much agitated.'

This sudden outburst sounds as though Mary recognized the same suicidal tendency in her own nature and saw Shelley as having rescued her from Fanny's fate. They were both Mary Wollstonecraft's daughters; it was easier for Mary than for Claire to understand the course Fanny had chosen, and to blame herself. She knew how deep Fanny's feelings were for Shelley. 'It is only poets that are eternal benefactors of their fellow creatures – & the real ones never fail of giving us the highest degree of pleasure we are capable of,' Fanny had written to her shortly before her death: 'they are in my oppinion nature & art united – & as such never failing.'[7] But Shelley and Mary had failed her. Claire, not Fanny, had been their chosen companion. As Mary brooded over the nature of her outcast creature, endowing him with the sensibilities of the loving but unloved outsider, Fanny was much in her thoughts.

The sense of their shared contribution to Fanny's death brought

Mary and Shelley very close to each other. Living quietly at Abbey Churchyard, with only Mary's drawing lessons and an occasional troubling visit from the bailiffs to disturb their routine, they concentrated on Mary's novel.

Frankenstein is a great work because we can read what we will from it. It has the resilience, the elasticity and the power of a myth. Writers and critics have, since Mary's death, uncovered more ways of interpreting it than the young author can ever have dreamed of; biographically, it is important to notice how close the Creature's plight was, not only to Fanny, but to Mary's perception of herself. Her life, with the exception of their happy summer at Geneva, had become cruelly solitary. Her friends behaved as though she was dead; it had taken Fanny's suicide to produce a letter, one of cold instruction, from her father. She, like her creature, was unfairly condemned, judged not for what she was, but for how appearances made her seem. The fact that she was not married to Shelley did not make her wicked, any more than the Creature's unnatural birth and bizarre appearance made him evil.

If Mary's outcast creature reflected her passionate indignation about prejudgments made of the moral and intellectual status of non-Europeans, in particular African and West Indian slaves, he is also her thoughtful response to Shelley's *Alastor*, in which the narrator had embarked on a dangerous quest in graveyards and charnel houses to discover the secret of life, 'of what we are'. Mary's creature warns of the dangers inherent in scientific experiment without due thought for the results. Both Mary and Shelley were avid and intelligent readers of her father's novels; Frankenstein's allusions to his 'unhallowed' pursuits refer back to *St Leon*, while Mary's presentation of the Creature as the alter ego of his pursuer is in the tradition of both *Caleb Williams* and *Fleetwood*.* In his desolation, the Creature also seems to look back to Mary Wollstonecraft's haunting image in her Scandinavian travel book of herself as misery incarnate, condemned to the homeless life of the wandering Jew. It was a book which her daughter knew almost by heart.

Collaboration on a project adds 'zest and vivacity', Mary wrote many years later.[8] She, in 1816, was the writer, putting down her daily composition in good plain language which Shelley later worked over to produce an imposing rhetorical flourish. Their readings and dis-

---

* This theme was also employed in *Mandeville*, the novel which Godwin was writing while she wrote *Frankenstein*; it is possible that Mary saw this work in manuscript before its publication late in 1817.

cussions were joint. Bath was well supplied with libraries, offering travel books to add authenticity to Robert Walton's voyage, and Humphry Davy's lucid accounts of chemical experiments for her to work into Victor Frankenstein's scientific education. (Mary did not feel entirely at ease in this field; one of the surprises of *Frankenstein* is its paucity of scientific detail.)

More importantly for the book's theme and narrative, Shelley began reading *Paradise Lost* to her. Mary was already familiar with Milton's great work; it was these readings that led her to connect the Creature to Lucifer, the fallen angel. The difference, in the Creature's case, is that his translation into a force of evil is directly influenced by his education. Instinctively benevolent, he learns from the history of mankind to murder and to be cunning in his crimes. Again and again, Mary reiterated the notion, one dear to her father's heart, that man is a social animal, civilized by the knowledge that he is part of a group which shares the same needs. Against it, she set her own belief that it is from this supposedly civilized body that the Creature discovers its potential for evil.

It is impossible to judge how much of Mary's sympathy for the rejected, excluded Creature was drawn from her undying rage against Mrs Godwin as the usurper who took her mother's place and exiled her from her father's affections. This is a tempting reading of the story, but it draws us away from the earnestness of her intentions. Mary was Godwin's admiring daughter. Like him, she used sensational material for serious ends.

Frankenstein can easily be turned into a biographer's sandpit, but Mary's story of promethean ambition, of rejection, the denial of love, and the danger of judging by appearances, was intended to carry the weight of a social message. What may have begun as an extension of the story of an Arctic explorer, or as a gothic tale for fireside thrills, was developed as a vehicle for ideas and social criticism. But when, in later life, she spoke of creature and book in one breath as 'my hideous progeny' and invited it to 'go forth and prosper', she was aware that dramatized versions had already drained its life-fluid while hugely increasing its fame. *Frankenstein*, as performed on stage, became a spooky comic melodrama while the Creature, seized on by political cartoonists, became a symbol of danger, subversiveness and menace. By 1831, when she wished her new edition commercial prosperity, her serious intentions had, like the Creature in the novel's closing words, been 'borne away . . . lost in darkness and distance'.

Shelley shared in Mary's pleasure at the discovery of her talent. He noted her progress in their jointly kept journal; he praised it in his letters. Now, with the shadow of Fanny's death on their shoulders, it was more important than ever that he should prove to Godwin how well Mary had chosen; how he, as much as her father, could bring her gift to fruition.

Mary's journal for the weeks following Fanny's death shows a quiet and intensely studious life, blighted only by money worries and by her increasing impatience with Claire. It is possible that the appearance of three crescent moon symbols in the journal at this time recorded disagreements with her stepsister; the moons appear beside references to the bailiff's visits, however, and these provide an equally plausible source for coded comment. Shelley, who was fond of Claire, was reading and writing in the journal; it seems unlikely that Mary would have made such an overt record of her own hostility when the two of them were working in close and happy collaboration on her book.

At the beginning of December, when Shelley was still searching for a suitable house near Marlow, they were thrown into great excitement by the news that Shelley's poetry had at last found a champion. His admirer was Leigh Hunt, the radical editor and theatre critic to whom Shelley had given financial help when he was still enduring his two-year prison sentence for having, with his brother John, libelled the Prince Regent in their jointly owned paper.

On 1 December, the *Examiner* drew attention to Shelley's newly published volume of poetry and proclaimed him 'a very striking and original thinker'. Shelley sent off his thanks eight days later with a description of himself as 'an outcast from human society' whose intentions had been misunderstood. Using a voice strikingly similar to that given to Mary's creature in *Frankenstein*, he told Hunt that, with a few benevolent exceptions, 'all else abhor & avoid me'. He, plainly, longed for friendship; Godwin would have been enraged to learn that Hunt, shortly after this, was enriched by a handsome anonymous donation. Shelley's letters hinted that more would be forthcoming, both from Shelley himself, and from Byron. It was the beginning of a lasting friendship which would be a heavy drain on the pockets of both Shelley and Mary over the years.

Mary, writing tenderly to her 'Sweet Elf . . . a winged Elf . . . my airy Elf' at the beginning of December, still dreamed of life in a lakeside home, surrounded by mountains, and with Claire at a good distance from it, when Shelley went home-hunting again with Peacock.[9] He was also trying to discover the whereabouts of Harriet who, after spending the summer quietly at home with her family, had disappeared from sight. The house in Marlow which he finally chose, and rented for twenty years, was a handsome and substantial one, big enough, if that was the thought stirring in his mind as he searched for his wife, to provide accommodation for Harriet and his older children as well as for Claire and her now imminent baby. Mary promptly began drawing up plans for the decoration. They expected to move in the spring, after boarding with the Peacocks while renovations were carried out.

Shelley was back at Bath on 14 December, after a meeting with Leigh Hunt. The following day, a letter came from his friend Thomas Hookham, whom he had asked to undertake a search for Harriet. The contents were shocking. A body, found in the Serpentine, had been identified as that of Harriet Smith. This, it appeared, was the name under which Harriet Shelley had been living since early September at lodgings near her family's home in Chapel Street. A newspaper report published in *The Times* on 12 December declared that Miss Smith had been missing for six weeks and that she had been 'far advanced in pregnancy'. Her husband was alleged to have been abroad; it was assumed that she had been seduced in his absence.

It is just possible that the unborn child was Shelley's. No record exists for the period when he was in London, prior to the journey to Geneva. Did he, seeking to comfort Harriet at a time when he was leaving the country for an undetermined period, make love to her? It is not much less likely than the generally accepted view, that Harriet had an affair with an officer and when he was called abroad, returned to live with her family until her condition became noticeable. Claire, in her old age, insisted that this had been the case, but her memory was unreliable and her source of information was probably Shelley himself. Henry Crabb Robinson, talking to Basil Montagu, the lawyer and friend of the Godwins who agreed to help Shelley in his fight to obtain custody of Harriet's children, made one careful note in his diary. Shelley, when giving Montagu all the available evidence, had never said that he was *not* the father of this last baby. Robinson told Montagu that Mrs Godwin had given him to understand that the baby was the result of an ill-judged affair. Montagu was as familiar as Robinson with Mrs Godwin's propensity for telling lies. Montagu 'thinks it improbable', Robinson drily noted.[10]

Even if this was, shockingly, the true case, Mary knew nothing of it. She was with Shelley when Hookham's letter arrived. Shelley left for London at once. On 16 December, he sent her a long, semi-hysterical letter, in which he laid the responsibility for Harriet's tragic end on her sister, Eliza Westbrook. Clinging to the fact that Harriet had taken the name 'Smith', he claimed that she had been

> driven from her father's house, & descended the steps of prostitution until she lived with a groom of the name of Smith, who deserting her, she killed herself. – There can be no question that the beastly viper her sister, unable to gain profit from her connexion with me – has secured to herself the fortune of the old man – who is now dying – by the murder of this poor creature.[11]

Why Eliza should have been responsible, if these were indeed the circumstances he believed to have led up to Harriet's suicide, it was beyond even Shelley to explain. Everyone, he told Mary, shared his view that the Westbrooks were 'detestable' and that he had been the model of uprightness and liberality in his treatment of his wife. Shelley badly needed to clear himself of blame. More specifically, he needed to throw as unfavourable a light as possible on Harriet's family, if he was to obtain custody of his children in a Chancery case.

The casualness of his reference to Ianthe and Charles Shelley ('The children I have not yet got') suggests that he and Mary must have already discussed their future. Almost equally casual was the proposal of marriage which followed. The lawyers said that a marriage would strengthen their case, he told her. It would, he did not wish to deny, be a great benefit if she would agree. He counted on her to be a 'dear and tender' mother to Charles and Ianthe, as she already was to their own baby William.

Mary's answer, written immediately, is a testimony to her essential kindness and trustfulness. Unable to understand the need for a Chancery suit, she wanted him to find the children, 'those darling treasures that are yours', and bring them to her at once. Only at the end of the letter, while pretending that she was quoting Claire, did she express a little apprehension about these 'dear children whom I love so tenderly'. Would William, as the youngest child, now cease to be the favourite? He will 'lose his pre-eminence and be helped third at table – as his aunt Claire is continually reminding him,' she wrote. She made no response to his allegations against the Westbrooks beyond agreeing that Eliza was indeed 'miserable and odious'; perhaps she knew Shelley's ways well enough to ignore them. As to the marriage, she insisted only that if it took place, 'it must be in London'. A Bath wedding might attract unwelcome local comment on their previously unmarried state; a marriage in London could more easily be attended by her father. This was an event which would, she knew, give him pleasure. 'I long to hear about Godwin,' she wrote at the end of her letter.[12]

1. William Godwin (*right*) and his friend Thomas Holcroft at the Treason Trials, 1794, from a courtroom sketch by Sir Thomas Lawrence

2. Mary Wollstonecraft Godwin, painted by her friend John Opie in 1797, several months before her daughter Mary's birth

3. Detail from 'The New Morality' (1798), by James Gillray, from the *Anti-Jacobin Review*. Holcroft is in leg irons; Godwin reads his work. Coleridge and Southey flank the Cornucopia of Ignorance from which tumble the works of Erasmus Darwin, Godwin and Wollstonecraft. Paine is the crocodile, while Fox bestrides Leviathan (the Duke of Bedford)

4. The Polygon, Somers Town, where Mary spent her first years

5. St Pancras Churchyard, 1815, with the river Fleet in the foreground and Mary Wollstonecraft's grave allegedly to the right of the church, between the trees

6. An illustration by William Blake to Mary Wollstonecraft's *Original Stories*, prefiguring the monster's appearance before his creator in her novel, *Frankenstein*

7. Skinner Street from Fleet Market; No. 41, the house taken by Godwin as his bookshop, is on the left

8. Ramsgate, where Mary Godwin spent six months at a boarding-school in 1811

9. Mary Shelley's Scottish friend Isabella Baxter Booth, as Lady Jane Grey, *c.* 1814–16

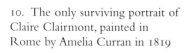

10. The only surviving portrait of
Claire Clairmont, painted in
Rome by Amelia Curran in 1819

11. Mary Shelley's stepbrother
Charles Clairmont, painted c.1835
when he was teaching in Vienna

12. (*above left*) This sketch, possibly of Mary Shelley but dated from the costume to *c.* 1825–30, was allegedly copied from a miniature painted at Geneva, and given by Trelawny to W.M. Rossetti

13. (*above*) Mary Shelley, by Reginald Easton; posthumously executed miniature, *c.*1857

14. (*left*) 'Clytie': this bust of a Roman lady, now at the British Museum, was, despite the low forehead, considered by her contemporaries to be very like Mary Shelley

15. (*above right*) A possible portrait of Mary Shelley, 1833–43, currently attributed to Richard Rothwell

16. (*above far right*) This may be the self-portrait from 1822 which Sir Percy and Lady Shelley were allowed to copy in 1863 when they were shown it at Lerici

17. (*right*) Mary Shelley, by Richard Rothwell, 1839–40

18. (*far left*) Elizabeth Pilfold, Percy Bysshe Shelley's mother, miniature from a painting done by Romney in 1794, when Shelley was two years old

19. (*left*) Timothy Shelley, his father, a Sussex squire and owner of Field Place, who inherited the baronetcy in 1815 on the death of his father, Sir Bysshe; miniature from a companion painting by Romney

20. (*below far left*) Amelia Curran, portrait of Shelley, 1819, reworked in 1822–3

21. (*below left*) The Curran portrait of Shelley. Photocopies show up the full, sensual mouth which Miss Curran tried to reduce and prettify in the reworked painting

22. (*above right*) As Shelley became increasingly etherealized, so his face became more improbably pixie-like. This is a typical interpretation of the Curran painting, first engraved by William Finden

23. (*below right*) Edward Ellerker Williams's watercolour of Shelley, *c.*1821–2, bears out Thornton Hunt's recollection that the poet had become quite corpulent by the time of his death

24. (*left*) Byron, drawn by
Count d'Orsay at Genoa in
1823. The sketch was evidently
executed after one of Byron's
periods of ferocious dieting

25. (*below*) The Villa Diodati,
rented by Byron in 1816: the
house where, famously, the idea
of writing ghost stories led to
the birth of *Frankenstein*

26. (*above right*) John Polidori,
Byron's clever young doctor, as
he was in 1816 when he met
Mary at Geneva. The portrait is
by F. G. Gainsford

27. (*below right*) The Auberge
at Sécheron in the early
nineteenth century

28. *The Mer de Glace*, by J.W.M. Turner. Visiting Chamonix and the Mer de Glace in 1816, Mary found one of *Frankenstein*'s most celebrated settings

29. The first page of volume 3 of *Frankenstein*, showing Mary Shelley's own hand

Day after day, week after week passed away on my return to Geneva and I had not the courage to commence my work. I feared the vengeance of the disappointed fiend yet I could not overcome my repugnance to the task. My health which had hitherto declined was now much restored; & my spirits when unchecked by the memory of my unhappy promises were proportionably. My father saw this with pleasure and he turned his thoughts towards the best method of eradicating the remains of my melancholy which every now and then would return by fits & with a devouring blackness over cast the approaching sunshine. At these moments I took refuge in the most perfect solitude. I spent whole days alone in a little boat watching the clouds & the rippling of the waves silent & listless. But the fresh air and bright sun seldom failed to restore me to some degree of composure & on my return I met the salutations of my friends with a readier smile, & more cheerful heart.

It was after my return from one of these rambles that my father calling me aside thus addressed one.

30. (*above left*) Mary and Shelley's first country home, the Bishopsgate cottage near Windsor which they took in the summer of 1815 and where Shelley wrote *Alastor*

31. (*below left*) Albion House, Marlow, where Mary, Claire and Shelley lived in 1817–18, showing the house after its later conversion to cottages

32. (*above*) Leigh Hunt, by Samuel Lawrence. Following their meeting in 1818 Mary Shelley became a lifelong friend of Hunt and his family

33. William Shelley, 'little Willmouse', painted by Amelia Curran shortly before his death at Rome in the summer of 1819

34. Allegra, Claire's daughter, called 'the little commodore' by Mary and much loved by Shelley, who left £6,000 for her care in a bequest to Claire

Shortly after this, Mary travelled up to London, staying with their new friend Leigh Hunt and his family. On 28 December, by which time the marriage plans had been settled, her father called on her; the following day, she and Shelley were invited to dine at Skinner Street. They were married in the city, in the presence of Mr and Mrs Godwin, at the handsome Wren church of St Mildred's, Bread Street, on 30 December. Mary, while indifferent enough to write the wrong date for the wedding in her diary, took sedate pleasure in signing herself 'Mary W. Shelley', with a charming little flourish to the final 'y', when she wrote to Byron on 13 January, to give him the news of baby Alba's safe birth.[13] (Alba was a pleasant pun on the name 'Albe' which they gave Byron from the 'LB' they called him in the journal; in Alba's dawn, Albe was born again.) Shelley, anxious to console Claire for the fact that she had been temporarily abandoned in Bath and that they were legitimizing their own union while she looked a lost reputation squarely in the face, mocked the marriage as insignificant. Seeking to amuse her, he reported on the ludicrous satisfaction of the Godwins. Mary's father, in particular, had been so 'studiously flattering', so polished in his attentions, so hospitable in his manner, that they were almost back in the devoted master-pupil relationship of earlier times.[14]

'A marriage takes place on the 29th,' was how Mary chose to record the wedding in her journal.* It must have given her some pleasure to be back in her adored father's favour. Harriet's death, while tragic, had served her well. The only clouds in sight hung over the future of Claire and her baby, the outcome for Shelley of the struggle to obtain custody of his older children, and the fate of her old friends the Baxters. One family in many to have been hit by the economic crisis, the Baxters, together with David and Isabella Booth, had been ruined.

Godwin, no longer the man who had championed the right of a woman not to marry, but a father who had suffered acutely from seeing his daughter act according to his long-rejected principles, was in a state as near to jubilation as a man of his sober habits could achieve. His brother Hull, who had sent a ham and a turkey for the wedding feast from the Norfolk farm, was grandly informed that Mary had married the eldest son of a baronet. She might even become rich – not that her father cared about that, of course; he

---

* The entry is confusing. Mary entered it as having been written on 16 December, the day after she recorded the news of Harriet's suicide. The 16th of December was the date on the letter in which Shelley urged her to consider marriage as a benefit to him.

could confidently predict that she would be 'respectable, virtuous and contented'. Godwin decided to spare his brother the knowledge that Mary had already lived with the baronet's son for two and a half years and that she had just become pregnant for the third time.[15]

It is easy to understand why Godwin should have wanted to gloss over the details of Mary's relationship. It is less easy to condone the active part which he and his wife took in spreading scandal about poor, dead Harriet Shelley in order to defend Mary's reputation now that she was herself a married woman with a fine future before her.

On 11 January 1817, a month after the identification of Harriet's body, an excited Shelley told Mary that the suit for his children had just been strengthened. Godwin had given him good news: 'he has evidence that Harriet was unfaithful to me *four months* before I left England with you.'[16]* Godwin's source was Thomas Hill, the loquacious editor of the *Monthly Mirror*. On the strength of further 'evidence' from Hill in May, Godwin fired off a letter to W.T. Baxter, telling him that Harriet 'had proved herself unfaithful to her husband before their separation' and that his source was an 'unquestionable authority wholly unconnected with Shelley'. Tommy Hill now claimed that Harriet had been 'guilty of repeated acts of levity'; he described her as having 'lately lived in open connection with a Colonel Maxwell. Peace be to her shade,' Godwin piously added before telling Baxter that Fanny had recently died of 'an inflammatory fever'.[17]

This was the letter which, when quoted to Jane Shelley in 1884, did most to confirm Mary's daughter-in-law in her view of Harriet as a promiscuous woman from whom Shelley had been fortunate to escape into Mary's consoling arms.[18] This was the view Jane Shelley had long dedicated herself to promoting, for Mary's sake.

Would Mary have been grateful? Probably not. Writing her journal on 12 February 1839, at a time when Hogg had reproached her for omitting Shelley's dedication of *Queen Mab* to Harriet in her edition of his works, Mary was overwhelmed with guilt about the past. 'Poor Harriet,' she wrote, 'to whose sad fate I attribute so many of my own heavy sorrows, as the atonement claimed by fate for her death.'

Jane Shelley, reading Mary's journal as she prepared her mother-in-law's papers for controlled publication in the 1880s, paused over this passage, decided it would do Mary's reputation more harm than good, and promptly cancelled it.[19]

---

* Godwin had altered his views on free love, but Shelley's eagerness to discover evidence of infidelity is strikingly out of keeping with the beliefs he had advocated and followed until this date.

CHAPTER THIRTEEN

AT ALBION HOUSE

1817–1818

'Adieu – Be not angry with us for being such new friends – for I like you too
well to wish you to forget me – or to be other than I am.
                                        Affectionately Yours   Marina'

Mary Shelley to Leigh and Marianne Hunt, 5 March 1817

THE GODWINS STILL BELIEVED – OR PRETENDED TO BELIEVE – THAT
Claire was in Bath for health reasons. It was in everyone's interests
that this fiction should be maintained. On 1 January 1817, the newly
married Shelleys returned to comfort and reassure the nervous expect-
ant mother as the time of her confinement approached. Alba was
born twelve days later; Shelley, his thoughts wholly occupied by the
struggle to obtain his older children, had already hurried back to
London to hear the Lord Chancellor's decision.

Mary, after living with Shelley for over two years, was becoming
adept at shuttling between her own studies and looking after her
vague, excitable husband. Besides reading *The Statesman's Manual*
(Coleridge's recently published religious meditations), Milton's
Comus and Smollett's *Roderick Random*, she found time in January to
work on her novel and study Latin. She even remembered to ask
Leigh Hunt's wife Marianne if she could kindly obtain Mr Shelley's
washing from him and have it laundered: 'Mr Shelley's thoughtless-
ness must be my excuse.'[1]

To Shelley, less concerned with dirty shirts than by the troubling
news that Harriet's father and sister were submitting religious

objections to his claim on little Ianthe and Charles, Mary sent a long
and loving letter on 17 January. He had been gone a week. 'Never
before have you been so long away,' she forgetfully lamented; '– it is
very melancholy.' He must be sure not to sit up too late, 'especially
when you are so fagged all day'. He must be very careful about how
he answered a letter which Claire had just written. 'Be kind but make
no promises & above all do not say a word that may imply any responsibility on your part for her future actions.' She was worried about
this, 'for you are warmhearted [   ] & indeed sweetest very indiscreet.'
She sent reports of William, their 'Blue Eyes [who] gets dearer &
sweeter every day – he jumps about like a little squirrel – and stares at
the baby with his great eyes.'

Perhaps Shelley had already admitted his greatest terror, that the
Lord Chancellor might not stop at depriving him of the custody of his
older children. Certainly, their own little boy was much in Mary's
thoughts. 'My William's birthday,' she noted on 24 January, the day
that Shelley's case was to be heard in London. 'How many chances
have occurred during his little years – May the ensueing one be more
peaceful and my William's star be a fortunate one to rule the decision
of this day – alas! I fear it will be put off – and the influence of the
star pass away.' She ended the entry by noting that she had gone out
for a walk with 'my sweet babe'.

The case was not an easy one to decide. The Westbrooks had made
it clear that they wished to retain guardianship of the children. They
strongly opposed their being placed in the care of an atheist who until
now had shown little interest in them and had 'unlawfully' cohabited
with a woman who was not his wife. Eliza, Harriet's sister, produced
a letter in which Shelley recklessly alluded to Mary as 'the lady whose
union with me you may excusably regard as the cause of your sister's
ruin'.[2] The case was, disappointingly, adjourned until 27 March. 'An
unhappy day,' Mary wrote on 25 January, the day after the postpone-
ment was announced. 'I receive bad news & determine to go up to
London.' She still found time to read parts of Sidney's *Arcadia* and of
Southey's translation of *Amadis of Gaul* that morning, before leaving
William to the care of their Swiss nanny, Elise. 'I wish Blue Eyes was
with me,' she wrote wistfully four days later, but William remained at
Bath until Claire was judged well enough to bring him to London.

It was almost two years since Mary had spent any length of time in
the city. Holborn, never uplifting, seemed grimmer and sadder than
ever after the war, awash with begging children and disabled soldiers.
Muddy-wheeled carriages clattered their iron wheels along the
narrow streets; poorly dressed crowds shuffled and staggered around

the local gin-shops. All that was missing was a recorder, but Hogarth had been dead for fifty years and Dickens was only five years old. The house at Skinner Street seemed always to be full of Mrs Godwin's relations.

Shelley, anxiously preparing evidence for the March case, spent most of his days and several nights with his new ally, Leigh Hunt.* Mary, after a 'disagreeable' conversation with her stepmother on 2 February, decided that it would be better for all concerned if they both stayed with the Hunts at their crowded household in the Vale of Health, seeing the Godwins only for meals. 'Sup with G[odwin] & have a pleasant conversation with him,' she noted before moving out on 7 February.

Named to disguise its earlier history as a malarial marsh, the Vale of Health lay below the steep hills of Hampstead and Highgate, a mile or so north of Mary's childhood home at the Polygon. Claire, judged fit to travel by 19 February, took rooms nearby with her baby while William and his nurse joined the Hunts. A plot was being hatched regarding Claire; the kindly Hunts had agreed to take Alba into their own house in due course and pass her off as a cousin's child. Later in the year, when they made a visit to the house Shelley had taken at Marlow, Alba could be brought along and unobtrusively 'adopted' by the Shelleys and Claire. The Godwins, who were still unaware that a child had been born, could continue to be deceived and awkward questions about Alba's parentage might be avoided.

Shelley and Mary were delighted by their hospitable hosts. Age – Hunt was thirteen years older than Mary – was no barrier. Marianne was a large, warm-hearted sculptress and painter whose way of keeping her children in order was to pop them on high stools as her models; the star of the house, glorious in his silken dressing-gown, was her olive-skinned, dark-haired husband. Dickens's Harold Skimpole, created in the early 1850s, did cruel justice to Hunt's shiftless charm in later years, but none to the handsome lover of culture, justice and beauty to whom Mary felt so drawn in 1817. The first to publish and call attention to young John Keats and one of the few to recognize Shelley's genius in his lifetime, Hunt would, before the year

---

* Hunt drew attention to the custody suit in the *Examiner*, alluding to a Chancery case which 'threatens to exhibit a most impolitic distinction between the Prince and the subject' if regard was not given to 'the most tolerant and best affections of humanity'. This, put in plainer language than Hunt dared use, was a declaration of the father's right to be awarded custody of his children. The piece was published three days after the adjournment was announced.

was out, be ridiculed by sections of the press as a leader of 'the Cockney school', supposedly composed of poets too badly bred and educated to understand the words they used – or so the privileged gentlemen who reviewed their work for the periodicals liked to claim.

Hunt, however arch and sentimental in his poetry, was better read than most of his critics. Byron thought his poems dreadful; Mary, sharing her husband's admiration of Hunt's bold treatment of an incestuous theme in *The Story of Rimini* (1816), showed less discrimination when, on 1 February, she reverently copied out the mawkish lines Hunt had written a year earlier, when his eldest son Thornton was dangerously ill.

> Ah! first-born of thy mother,
> When life & hope were new,
> Kind playmate of thy brother,
> Thy sister, father too;[3]

and so on. Perhaps Mary's enthusiasm sprang from sympathy, as she remembered her own lost Clara. Happily, Thornton survived. A bright, observant child, he was less taken by Mary than by her husband, whose gift for telling fantastic stories, playing games and behaving, in short, as though he and little Thornton were just of an age, made him easier to love. Mary, while more reserved, found it hard to resist his father's light-hearted manner. '[Y]ou shall never be serious when you wish to be merry', she promised Hunt on 5 March and added a confession: 'to tell a little truth I do not like Peacock a millionth part so well as I do you.' She ended by asking him not to hold it against them that they were 'such new friends – for I like you too well to wish you to forget me'. The letter was signed 'Marina', punning on the similarity between her own name and that of Hunt's wife. They had already exchanged locks of hair.

Godwin, an enthusiastic theatregoer, had never much cared for music. One of the most valuable services which Hunt, a fine singer himself, performed for Mary was to introduce her to the music of Mozart. 'H Mrs H & I go to the opera – Figaro – I am very much pleased,' Mary wrote in her journal for 1 February; for 'very much pleased', we should read 'enthralled'. Mozart became an enduring passion; music, during the darkest periods of her life, offered unfailing consolation.

There were many musical outings and evenings of song in the Hunts' parlour to while away a damp February. Sometimes, they made up parties for bracing walks across the frosty fields to Caen Wood, and up to Highgate where Coleridge, under supervision as a housemate in Dr Gillman's quiet, well-ordered home, was ready to talk for as long – and longer – than any guests could wish, on the firm understanding that there were to be absolutely no interruptions to the flow. On days too rainy for excursions, they sat around Hunt's study fire and talked politics. Godwin, greatly though Shelley still revered his work, was a figure of the past; Hunt and his *Examiner* offered a vigorous challenge to the present. Recharged by his friend's faith in political campaigning, Shelley began preparing a plea for parliamentary reform.

Pregnant for the third time – her second daughter would be born at the end of the summer – Mary looked on this ebullient, child-filled home as paradise. Nobody here treated her as a pariah; the Hunts' friends were as easy and welcoming as themselves. A touch of snobbery rather than poetic rivalry may have coloured the lukewarm courtesies Shelley and she extended to young John Keats, but Mary was delighted to meet the *Globe*'s Cornish editor, Walter Coulson, a man who combined encyclopaedic knowledge with a gift for deadpan mimicry. She was disconcerted to be introduced to the stockbroker-poet Horace Smith who, four years earlier, had merrily and publicly consigned her father to the whirlpool of Lethe in *Horace in London*, his second popular collection of satirical verse.* She could not be cross with him. A passionate radical with a sweet smile and an unfailingly open purse for needy friends, Smith rapidly became one of the Shelleys' most trusted confidants and supporters. Sitting with these new friends at Hunt's fireside while Marianne worked on painting silhouettes and the children clamoured for stories, Mary was, for the first time since her visit to the Baxters in Scotland, given a taste of happy family life. Only an occasional tiff when Hunt grew over-attentive to Bessy Kent, his snappish, good-looking sister-in-law, gave her pause for reflection. Poor Marianne; Mary knew how she must feel. Was this not just the delicate situation between Shelley, herself and Claire?

Mary left for Marlow at the beginning of March. The renovation of Albion House was supervised, as they had planned, from Thomas Peacock's home nearby. This was to be her first proper home and

---

* The first and better known collection was *Rejected Addresses* (1812); *Horace in London* was published the following year.

Shelley pandered to his wife's wish for an elegance she had never known. Too poor to resolve Godwin's unending financial problems, he still managed to spend – on credit – well over a thousand pounds on upholstery, curtains and furnishings.

Their new home stood on West Street, away from the village and close to the rickety old wooden bridge which linked Great Marlow to the wooded Berkshire hills. Only faintly resembling the low-roomed and rather poky cottages which occupy the site today, Albion House was a handsome building, its long Georgian sash windows looking back on to a garden shaded by firs and cedars and out to a broad swathe of more open land beyond. There were five big bedrooms and, towards the river, a stable; the main feature was a splendid library, big enough for a ballroom and, Mary boasted to the Hunts, 'very fit for the luxurious literati'.[4] Lord Elgin's removals from the Parthenon, which were on the point of being put on display as a national treasure at the British Museum, had fired the country with a new enthusiasm for the art of the ancient world. Two full-sized statues, of Venus and Apollo, were purchased and installed as the library's guardians. Love and poetry would be Shelley and Mary's household gods.

Playful though the tone of Mary's letters was as she boasted of their new-found grandeur to the Hunts, an occasional patch of darkness reminds us that she was still at work on the last chapters of *Frankenstein* when she went to Marlow. Writing to Hunt on the anniversary of her first child's death, she confessed that she had just been troubled by a strange dream, 'of the dead being alive'. Perhaps, in the month when Shelley's custody case was being decided,* she dreamed of Harriet rising from the river bed to reproach the living.[5] Perhaps, nearing completion of her intensely imaginative work, she was living more in than out of it, seeing the Creature as he returns, seemingly from the dead, to brood over his creator's corpse. Certainly, in those last few weeks of sustained endeavour, it must have become almost impossible for her to distinguish between the worlds of dream and daylight.

---

* By a judgment given on 27 March, neither the Westbrooks nor Shelley were to have custody; instead, they were each to submit nominees for the children's guardianship, and to present plans for their future education which would be duly examined by a Master in Chancery. The children were, effectively, to be orphaned to protect them from being brought up by a father whose religious views were judged likely to damage them. It was almost unheard of at that time for a father not to be awarded custody, whatever his reputation. Shelley's outrage and bitterness seem less excessive in this context. He did not, however, make any attempt to exercise the visiting rights which he was granted and he had shown no wish to be in touch with the children in the period between Charles's birth in the autumn of 1814 and Harriet's death two years later.

Claire, travelling alone, was the first to join them at Albion House. Godwin, following hard on her heels for a genial four days of boat trips, riverside strolls and carriage drives at the beginning of April, returned to Skinner Street just before the arrival of his stepdaughter's pretty, dark-haired baby at Marlow. Alba was, as arranged, artfully submerged in a rowdy tribe of little Hunts; nobody questioned her parentage.

If Mary had been in raptures over the pleasure of living with the Hunts, her new friends were happy to return the compliment – and to stay rather longer. They had just spent a blissful day, dining, talking, wining and walking, Hunt wrote to his friend the composer and organist Vincent Novello in mid-April while Marianne diligently scrubbed the grubby patina off Apollo and Venus. And now:

> I am writing this letter, seated on a turfy mound in my friend's garden, a little place with a rustic seat in it, shrouded and covered with trees, with a delightful field of sheep on one side, a white cottage among the leaves . . . and the haymakers mowing and singing in the fields behind me.[6]

Half a mile away, sitting in the riverside ruins of Medmenham Abbey, Shelley was painting a very different picture. His long conversations with Hunt that winter had fired his sense of the poet as the unlegislated champion of justice. 'Laon and Cythna', the poem he threw himself into finishing before the end of summer, was his attack on a ruthless government. Prudently though he had located the poem's events in a distant country, Shelley's attack on contemporary England was impossible to misread. So, to all who knew Godwin's reputation, was his significance as the sage, the hermit who urges young Laon to carry forward the teachings he himself had offered to an earlier age. Driving Shelley on was the sense of personal injustice; the government which oppressed a starving nation was a magnified version of the cold legal figures who had deprived him of two of his children.

Writing in the woods or in his boat, Shelley became familiar in Marlow as a slender, stooping figure who often wandered home with flowers trailing over his hair and a carpet of briars stuck to a long, shabby brown coat, a kindly distributor of shillings, blankets – and sometimes of his wife's clothes – to the local poor. Dinner did not wait for him: Mary had grown used to the eccentric ways of a man who seemed happy to live on whatever could be munched as he walked along, book in hand. Later, when the oil-lamps had been lit and the children were asleep, she watched him slip quietly through the open doors of the drawing-room where Claire was singing to her own accompaniment. (The new cabinet piano was Shelley's gift to her, a credit purchase made through the Hunts from a friend of the Novello family. The seventy-five guineas it cost had still not been paid off four years later.)

Shelley's haunting 'My thoughts arise and fade in solitude' was written to be sung as a duet to music from Mozart's *La Clemenza di Tito*; it was probably first performed by Hunt and Claire at Marlow. The more intimate lines of 'To Constantia, Singing' were anonymously published the following year. Shelley wrote it for Claire who, in her old age, chose to claim that Constantia was among her given names.

> I have no life, Constantia, now, but thee,
>   Whilst, like the world-surrounding air, thy song
> Flows on, and fills all things with melody. –
>   Now is thy voice a tempest swift and strong,
>   On which, like one in trance upborne,
>   Secure o'er rocks and waves I sweep,
>   Rejoicing like a cloud of morn.
>   Now 'tis the breath of summer night,
> Which when the starry waters sleep,
>   Round western isles, with incense-blossoms bright,
>   Lingering, suspends my soul in its voluptuous flight.[7]

A love poem? Claire certainly thought so. Read in its entirety, Shelley's lovely lyric sounds more like a powerfully emotional response to the effect of her voice on a man whose imagination turned reality to shadow. That view of matters was not necessarily of much solace to Mary.

Shelley, not his wife, was the main focus of interest for the visitors to Albion House in the summer of 1817. His friends wrote, as they would of a saint, of his good deeds among the wretchedly paid lacemakers whose fine and difficult work was the chief source of local employment. On one occasion, it was remembered, he gave his shoes away and walked home barefoot. The villagers, coming to Albion House on Saturdays for the regular allowance Mary and he had set aside for them, thought Mr Shelley a perfect gentleman. The local landowners kept their distance from a man mad enough to buy crawfish from the vendors who hawked them through the streets, only to ensure that these delicacies were carefully returned to the river. Word probably got around that Shelley's companion on these outings was not his wife, but 'a dear female friend', who must surely have been Claire.[8] Invitations were not extended to the Shelleys by the squires to whom the unfortunate poor of Marlow appeared only as potential fomenters of revolution.[9]

Everybody had memories of Shelley; Mary appears only in occasional sideways glimpses, like a figure turned half away from view in a Dutch interior. The Hunts' eldest boy Thornton remembered Mrs Shelley as untidy, distracted and cross during their summer at Albion House; others had reason to be struck by Mary's kindness. It is not clear whether it was she or Shelley or both who decided that they should take in a local child called Polly Rose. We hear of Shelley playing games with Polly, setting her on a table beside Claire and dashing its caster-wheels up and down the length of the room. Sent off to work for the Hunts in their new Marylebone home, Polly was given a memento, the flowered plate from which Shelley often ate his supper of bread and raisins. She kept the plate. But it was Mary, Polly remembered fifty years later, who always used to tuck her into bed at Albion House, who told her what they had been talking about downstairs and always asked what she thought about the subject.[10] When thoughtless Marianne Hunt left for London without giving a present to Milly Shields, a local girl who had been employed to help Elise Duvillard care for William and Alba, Mary was the one who worried about finding a nice gown to give to Milly and 'a little note with it from Marianne that it may appear to come from her'.[11] Elise was promised gifts of clothes for Aimée, the little illegitimate daughter she had chosen to leave behind in Switzerland in her family's care. Always tender towards children, Mary worried over the young Hunts in her letters: 'Adieu little babes,' she warned; '– take care not to loose one another in the streets for fear one of you should be kidnapped but take hold of one another's hands & walk pretty.'[12]

On 13 May, after a month of patient transcription, Mary noted that she had finished copying out her novel. Now five months pregnant, she might have felt ready to rest; instead, she promptly began the task of rewriting and correcting the entries in the journal she and Shelley had kept on their runaway trip in 1814. The 'unpresuming' small volume was bulked out by adding edited versions of the two long letters which she had written from Geneva to Fanny in 1816; Shelley contributed two of the 'travel letters' he had written to Peacock and – the unadvertised jewel of the volume – his poem, 'Mont Blanc'. *History of a Six Weeks' Tour* came out in November, jointly published by the Hookhams and by Hunt's friend, Charles Ollier, a man with a keen sympathy for the Shelleys' political views. Knowledgeable acquaintances praised the unnamed author; a patronizing review in

Blackwood's Magazine the following spring complimented her for 'prattling' with such charm. The book did not offer much competition to the forthright and exuberant Lady Morgan's *France*, published the same year;* in 1820, Ollier told Shelley that there were no profits from which to pay the printer. Ninety-two unbound copies were still in stock when Ollier went out of business in 1823. Shelley, in 1817, did his best to stir up sales by confessing their co-authorship to an inquisitive Thomas Moore. As a man who could always be counted on to spread gossip, Moore was also entrusted with the news that Mary had another little literary surprise coming along. It is more likely that Shelley was referring to *Frankenstein* than to the new baby which was due to arrive in late August.

Mary would have done well in modern times. The prospect of raising children while managing a career would not have daunted her. In 1817, between writing, helping to supervise little William and running a large new house crammed to bursting point with visitors, she put herself through a gruelling reading course in Roman history while she searched for her next subject. She was still only nineteen.

Leigh Hunt had only one complaint to make about Mary: she was too earnest for her own good. She was clever; he knew that. Hunt vastly preferred Mary when she suppressed her gleaming intelligence. He liked to see her listening, not talking ('yon nymph of the sideways looks');[13] he was delighted on a visit to the theatre when her gravity dissolved into sudden giggles at Launcelot Gobbo's slapstick humour. A family friend, the playwright James Kenney, had been struck by Mary's new-found beauty when he met her in February that year;[14] Hunt, however, could not quite rid himself of a feeling of chilly awe. The Mary he described sitting in a box at the opera as 'a sedate faced young lady . . . with her great tablet of a forehead, and her white shoulders unconscious of a crimson gown' sounds grimly intellectual.[15] Still, the tribute was gracefully intended, carrying a hint of slandered innocence in the striking contrast between white flesh and crimson gown.

The portrait Mary herself treasured from the happy summer at Marlow was drawn by Shelley in his dedication to 'Laon and Cythna', shortly to be retitled *The Revolt of Islam*. Here, tenderly addressing her as his queen, his friend, his twin, 'thou Child of love and light', he honoured her as the source of his inspiration, muse and prophetess.

---

* Lady Morgan (Sydney Owenson)'s success is confirmed by the fact that she was offered £1,200, a huge sum for a book at that time, for her next work, *Florence Macarthy*, published in 1818.

All the humiliation and loneliness Mary had endured became worth the pain when she read these lines.

> And what art thou? I know, but dare not speak:
> Time may interpret to his silent years.
> Yet in the paleness of thy thoughtful cheek,
> And in the light thine ample forehead wears,
> And in thy sweetest smiles, and in thy tears,
> And in thy gentle speech, a prophecy
> Is whispered, to subdue my fondest fears:
> And through thine eyes, even in thy soul I see
> A lamp of vestal fire burning internally.
>
> They say that thou wert lovely from thy birth,
> Of glorious parents, thou aspiring Child.
> I wonder not – for One then left this earth
> Whose life was like a setting planet mild,
> Which clothed thee in the radiance undefiled
> Of its departing glory; still her fame
> Shines on thee, through the tempests dark and wild
> Which shake these latter days; and thou canst claim
> The shelter, from thy Sire, of an immortal name.[16]

References to sweet smiles and gentle speech may jar on modern ears, but who could object to the admiring deference Shelley showed to Mary's intelligence, her wisdom, her right to inspire her own generation with the brave originality her parents had offered theirs? Mary, here, becomes the force of redeeming love, light in darkness. This, for the rest of her life, would be an image from which to draw strength and reassurance. It is curious that, praising the character of the young soothsayer in *Valperga*, Mary's next published novel, Shelley failed to see how close Beatrice was to his own celebration of his wife as muse and prophetess. In creating Beatrice, Mary made his image her own.

———

It was not until Mary was staying at Skinner Street at the end of May that she finally allowed her father to see the manuscript of *Frankenstein*. The dedication to himself – along with Shelley's Preface – was still missing. Even so, Godwin must have been struck by how forcefully and imaginatively Mary had clothed and reshaped his own ideas. 'Treat a person ill, and he will become wicked . . . divide him, a social being, from society, and you impose upon him the irresistible obligations – malevolence and selfishness.' The words are Shelley's, in a draft for an unsigned review with which he planned to draw attention to the published book.[17] The philosophy, promoted that year by his daughter and his son-in-law in two wholly different works, was Godwin's.

These were not good times for controversial works and the manufacture of a creature from human parts without divine assistance was highly controversial. John Murray expressed keen interest in the novel, cautiously presented by Shelley as his own work; he debated, and turned it down. Charles Ollier, Shelley's own new publisher, had either already rejected it or was still hesitating at the end of August when *Frankenstein* was finally taken on by the old firm of Lackingtons, which now dealt mainly in cheap books. Five hundred copies would be published in the late winter or early spring with a third of the net profits going to Mary, who retained the copyright. The author, by a convention of the time, would remain anonymous. This was unfortunate for Mary: with her husband writing the Preface, references to his 'friend' seemed a thin disguise for the fact that he had written the novel himself.

Five hundred was a small run, even for those times, and the offer was not handsome, but honour had been satisfied. Shelley had advised on and contributed to Mary's first mature work and he, not her father, had succeeded in selling it. He had replaced Godwin as her mentor. *Frankenstein* was their literary child.

Marianne Hunt's sister, Bessy Kent, together with her small tribe of nephews and nieces, followed the Hunts back to London in July. Little Alba remained, as planned, at Albion House but without any pretence being made that she was a member of the departed family. Instead, she was now exposed for the first time as Claire's fatherless child. Scandal was the inevitable consequence. The village of Marlow would probably have taken any oddity in the ménage in its stride. The problem lay with the local squirearchy and their circle, watchful and disapproving: 'country town friends are not very agreable,' Mary wrote with feeling that autumn.[18] Rather desperately, Shelley wrote to explain the difficulty to Byron. Should they farm the little girl out with two suitable ladies until he came to England? Could he understand that they had, although fond, become 'somewhat embarrassed' about her?[19]

Alba was an enchanting child. Mary, who nicknamed her 'the little commodore' for her lively stare and stocky stance, was sometimes haunted by the thought that this was how Fanny must have appeared to their mother at much the same age: 'I never see her [Alba] without

thinking of the expressions in my Mother's letters concerning Fanny,'
she admitted to Shelley. '– If a mother's eyes were not partial she
seemed like this Alba – she mentions her intelligent eyes & great
vivacity. But this is a melancholy subject.'[20] The embarrassment this
pretty little girl now caused the Shelleys was considerable. To anybody
who knew how intimately Claire had shared Shelley's life for the past
three years, there could be little doubt of Alba's paternity. Even
Godwin, when he and his wife were finally let into the secret, at once
assumed that Shelley was the father of pretty little 'Miss Auburn'.
(Godwin's private view of Shelley can be clearly seen in his absolute
lack of surprise that his son-in-law should have behaved in such a
way.) But Byron, while ready to acknowledge that he had a responsibility and even an inclination to play some role, was otherwise
engaged on a Venetian love-affair. He had no plans either to visit
England in the immediate future, or to offer help. The Shelleys were,
for the first time, made aware of their friend's ruthlessness. He was
neither grateful, interested nor conscience-stricken. If they wanted
him to take Alba into his home at this early stage in her life, they
would have to do the travelling themselves.

This, as a beautiful summer turned into a premature autumn,
became an increasingly attractive notion. Albion House, so cool and
shady on a hot June day, grew damp and cold. The books in the
magnificent new library sprouted mildew; Shelley, already exhausted
by the taxing work of producing a long and difficult poem in a relatively short period, was warned by William Lawrence that he needed
to stop work and give himself the benefit of a healthy climate. Italy
was recommended.

News came at the beginning of August that the Lord Chancellor
(Lord Eldon was described ten years later in the anonymously written
Biographical Keepsake as a man of 'mean and cruel intolerance') had
ruled decisively in favour of the Westbrooks; Ianthe and Charles were
to be placed with a clergyman nominated by Harriet's father.* Might
Lord Eldon go further and prosecute the author of *Queen Mab* under
the blasphemy laws, or seek to take away their beloved 'Willmouse'?
Even baby Clara, born at the beginning of September and named for
her aunt, might be at risk. Apprehensive before, Shelley now sensed
additional reason to place his remaining children beyond reach of the

---

* Shelley had been devastated by the news in March that he was to be denied custody of his
children. The August verdict confirmed this and went further, refusing guardianship to Mr
Longdill, the friendly lawyer who had been proposed by Shelley. His second choice, however,
Dr Thomas Hume, was approved on 28 April 1818 and confirmed on 25 July.

law; in Italy, they would be safer. Mary, frightened by Lawrence's diagnosis of Shelley's health and eager for any plan which would get the dear little 'Commodore' out of her home, was ready to assent. 'But are we rich enough to enjoy ourselves when there[?]' she wondered.[21]

William Baxter of Dundee, impoverished but kindly and cheerful as ever, was paying a visit to the Shelleys when Clara was born on 2 September. On another visit later in the month (Mr Baxter 'has taken a prodigious fancy to us', Mary reported to Shelley with transparent pleasure[22]), he mentioned that David Booth was proving an 'illtempered and *jealous*' husband to her dear Isabella. 'Mr B. thinks that she half repents her marriage – so she is to [be] another victim of that ceremony,' Mary announced to Shelley, who had fled to London with Claire, in an attempt to escape the duns who were again on his heels.[23] The lease on the Booths' fine house at Newburgh was being sold, Mary had heard; Christy, Isabella's elder sister, was living huggermugger with them; it all sounded very depressing.

Drawing encouragement from Mr Baxter's friendly manner, Mary began laying plans to coax her dear 'Izy' to liberate herself. It must be cautiously managed, or Mr Booth would grow jealous. First, she invited Christy Baxter to come on a visit, an invitation which was briskly declined. Shelley, told by his doctor to attempt nothing too strenuously imaginative, was coaxed by his wife into beginning *Rosalind and Helen*, a poem which – faintly – suggested Isabella in Rosalind and Mary in Helen, set against a dreamily evoked Scottish background recalled from Italy.

Shelley may have agreed to write a work in which he showed little interest – he went on with it, reluctantly, the following year – out of a sense that Mary was going through a particularly unhappy period. Part of her sadness stemmed from disappointment over Isabella. On 3 October, William Baxter had been ready to urge his daughter to challenge Mr Booth's hostility to Shelley, a man he had never met. It was time, he wrote, to recognize Mary's husband as a man who combined genius and amiability with 'truly republican frugality and plainness of manners'. Of course Isabella should come and join them: 'you could not do better . . .'[24] By the end of the year, however, Baxter had changed his mind. The Shelleys were suddenly informed that they were too grand for the company of any of the Baxter girls; they were equally baffled to learn that Shelley's 'freedom of thought and action' were now regarded as a threat to a married woman.[25]

Baxter was almost certainly acting under direction from his stronger-willed son-in-law. Booth had been in London at the end of November. Claire, as far as a shocked Booth could see, was not only in London but living with Shelley. Certainly, they were sharing a lodging, and not, he imagined, simply to save money. By January, Booth had seen and heard enough to reach severe conclusions. The Shelleys had 'strenuously resisted' the notion of marriage, he told his wife; 'Miss Auburn' [Alba] was Shelley's child; he and the mother brazenly lived in the same rooms in London while Mary stayed in the country. This was no company for a respectable woman.[26] So advised by her father and husband, Isabella was in no position to disobey.

This was a blow, but Mary had other reasons for depression. Clara's birth, attended by the local doctor, was followed by a long period of exhaustion. Mary fretted over her inability to produce enough milk to feed the baby which, following her mother's precepts, she was determined to do herself. She worried, as the mists gathered around Albion House, about Willmouse, for 'the poor little fellow is very susceptible of cold'.[27] She was made unhappy by 'an unamiable letter from Godwin about his wife's visits', noted in Mary's journal on 19 September. Mrs Godwin was, it seems, annoyed that her husband went to Marlow without her. Mary took rather childish revenge by telling Shelley to give Godwin her love but not his wife, for 'I do not love her', and by deciding that she would certainly not ask Mrs Godwin for the eight yards of stout Welsh flannel from which she intended to make warm winter underclothing for herself and little William.

Further evidence of Mary's low spirits appears in the way she now turned against their friends. The Hunts, Shelley heard from her letter of 24 September, had been thoroughly selfish, going off on a walk without warning when she, so long confined to the house by childbirth, had been eager to go with them. Perhaps the Hunts went to get away from a bad-tempered hostess. Peacock came in every day, Mary went on, 'uninvited to drink his bottle – I have not seen him – he morally disgusts me –' On the subject of Alba and the need to remove her, she became almost hysterical. Her departure 'ought not to be delayed', she told Shelley on 28 September and added, in case he had missed the point, that 'she should join her father with all possible speed.' Two days later, she reminded him that Alba's going 'must not be delayed'. On 2 October, infuriated by Shelley's silence on the subject, she wrote that she would have no peace 'until she is on her way to Italy – Yet you say nothing of all this – in fact your letter tells me nothing.' A fortnight later, Shelley was alerted to her terror that Byron might suddenly disappear: 'He may change his mind – or go to Greece – or to the devil and then what happens.' In the meantime, 'I think Alba's remaining here exceedingly dangerous.'[28]

If Mary sounds peevish, her situation makes her feelings wholly understandable. By the end of a single summer in their new house, they were mired in debt again. Doing a hasty round of potential creditors in London in September, Shelley was briefly arrested on the order of his own uncle. Mary, taught caution by her father's precarious business affairs, was terrified of what was to become of them and miserable at being abandoned. 'How happy shall I be – my own dear love to see You again – Your last was so *very* very short a visit . . .' she wrote on 5 October. 'Come teusday dearest and let us enjoy some of each others company come and see your sweet babes . . .' She ended by sending him 'a thousand kisses for you my own one'. By the 16th, she was growing frantic: 'So you do not come this night – Love – Nor any night – you are always away and this absence is long and becomes each day more dreary.' On 18 October, she wrote again. Godwin was about to make a visit. He was sure to ask questions about the future. They had already started arrangements to sell off the rest of their twenty-year lease on Albion House, but then, 'he will talk as if we meant to stay here and I must – must I? Tell fifty privarications or direct lies . . . Had you not better speak –' She would come to London, as Shelley kept suggesting, if only she dared. She reminded him of the occasion when all their possessions at Bishopsgate had been seized as soon as they left the house empty: 'here we have much more to loose & I must not leave this house untill such things as we do not dispose of are put in a place of safety.'

Shelley eased one of Mary's worries by accompanying Godwin to Marlow the following day; talk of their plans was skilfully avoided and the visitor went away full of good cheer. Claire was looking so neat, and so pretty, he told his wife, and it was all thanks to the good influence of Mary and Shelley. An inspection of the library had given him great satisfaction; Mary had evidently taken inspiration from his own methodical reordering of the Skinner Street books that summer, with new shelves being added and a proper catalogue made. All the indications were of security and permanence; and Shelley had again promised to underwrite his debts. One hardly knows whether to wonder more at Godwin's credulity or at his host's gift for deceiving him.

Mary let herself be persuaded to leave the house empty in November while she spent two weeks at new lodgings in London. Visits to the Hunts and to Skinner Street gave a lift to her spirits but she, like Shelley, was horrorstruck by the news that three men had, on 8 November, been executed as traitors in Derby. Their alleged crime, an attempt to stir up protest, had already been publicly connected to the undercover operations of a government spy. Shelley, outraged, immediately wrote a pamphlet on the death of British liberty; Mary approvingly recorded its completion. Whatever disagreements they might have had about Claire, or about the way Shelley kept recklessly borrowing against his future, they thought as one when it came to challenging injustice. This, they both believed, was his mission, to fight with his pen for free speech and a society ruled by love, not law. It was probably as well for Shelley's personal safety that his publisher, Charles Ollier, got cold feet after printing twenty copies. Boldly signed 'The Hermit of Marlow', it left little doubt about the author's identity.[29]

Literature dominated their lives at the end of the year. Godwin's *Mandeville* was published on 1 December. Mary took only a day and a half to devour a novel she thought almost equal to *Caleb Williams* in its power. After passing it over to Shelley, she decided to make amends to Peacock for her crossness that September by copying out his long poem, 'Rhododaphne', in her fine, easy-flowing hand. Shelley wanted her opinion of his own major work of that year; they had just finished discussing 'Laon and Cythna' when Shelley's nervous publisher announced that all printed copies would have to be recalled so that the brother–sister love theme could be modified, along with any passages which might be thought blasphemous and for which the printer risked prosecution. Even the title was to be altered. Aware of the difficulty of getting such a work published at all in the present political climate, Shelley submitted to Ollier's conditions. Mary must have thought herself lucky that nobody at Lackingtons had objected to Victor Frankenstein's passionate feelings for his first cousin. By 1831, when incest had become a still more unacceptable topic, she was ready to banish the blood connection and let Elizabeth become an adopted, but wholly unrelated, sister to Victor.

The fact that only five hundred copies of *Frankenstein* had been published did not mean that it went unnoticed on its appearance in January 1818. In her home circle, Mary was showered with praise for the extraordinary powers of her imagination and the boldness of her idea; the outside world, able only to note that the book was respectfully dedicated to William Godwin and that the tone of the Preface sounded masculine, credited Shelley with the authorship.

The homage which most pleased Mary came later, from her father. Writing to her in 1823, at a time when she was in desperate need of reassurance and comfort, Godwin told his daughter that it was, quite simply, 'the most wonderful work to have been written at twenty years of age [she was actually nineteen] that I have ever heard of'.[30]

The critics were less enthusiastic. One of the most hostile was the first to publish his opinion. Writing in the *Quarterly Review* in January, the rigidly right-wing critic John Wilson Croker (he was Secretary to the Admiralty throughout the long period of Tory rule) damned Mary's novel as 'a tissue of horrible and disgusting absurdity', written by one of the 'out-pensioners of Bedlam' who formed William Godwin's school. Croker's aggressiveness was probably increased by his evident belief that *Frankenstein*, which carried a dedication to Godwin, had been written by the blasphemous author of *Queen Mab*. Another reviewer, in *La Belle Assemblée* (March), thought the book audacious and impious, but likely to win popularity by its originality and good style. The episode of the Creature's vicarious education when living beside the de Laceys' cottage was, however, condemned as wretchedly implausible, an objection made by almost all the reviewers. The *Edinburgh Magazine* (March) conceded moments of beauty and a certain fascination in the subject; the *British Critic* (April) found the mixture of absurdity and horror strongly reminiscent of Godwin's *Mandeville*. The *Gentleman's Magazine* (April) was milder, praising the author's inventive talent and descriptive gifts. The *Monthly Review* (April) curtly dismissed an 'uncouth' work, void of any moral or philosophical conclusion, although leanings toward the doctrines of materialism would have merited scrutiny in a more serious novel. In June, the *Literary Panorama* dismissed *Frankenstein* as a weak imitation of Godwin's *St Leon*.

It is impossible to know how many of these reviews were read by Mary, given that she had left England before most of them appeared. We do know that she was delighted by the appreciation which her father's friend Sir Walter Scott wrote for the March 1818 issue of *Blackwood's Magazine*. Shelley had sent Scott a copy of the novel at the beginning of the year and Scott understandably took the book to be his own work; writing to thank him for his kindness, Mary proudly revealed the truth. She had, she explained in her letter of 14 June, only concealed her name 'from respect to those persons from whom I bear it'. This suggests that she was fully aware of the bold impiety of her invention, and of the implications of portraying man as creating man, aided only by science. The novel's dedication to her father was the nearest she dared come to exposing her connection to him and, consequently, doing him harm.

It would be a mistake to imagine that the fame of a book depends on the number of published copies. Mary Wollstonecraft's *Vindication* achieved its celebrity – and notoriety – by word of mouth and by privately circulated copies; this seems also to have been the case with

Mary's *Frankenstein*. In August 1818, Peacock wrote to tell Shelley that, on a visit to Egham racecourse, he had been pestered by 'a multitude of questions concerning "Frankenstein" and its author. It seems,' he added, 'to be universally known and read.'[31] While this does not mean that every household in the land was talking about Mary's book, it does suggest that the novel's reputation had already spread far beyond what might be supposed from the small number of copies printed. The fact that Peacock was singled out for interrogation by the racegoers indicates that there was a degree of certainty about the book's authorship. Peacock's role as the Shelleys' friend would have been well known at Egham, which was only a few miles from Marlow.

It is not clear what was behind the words 'Le rêve est fini' which Mary wrote and then crossed out in her journal for 22 December. Perhaps it was a reference to the end of their dream of a happy country existence at Albion House; a purchaser had been found to take on the remainder of their lease. January 1818 was the last bonechilling month they spent there. For Shelley, there was less reading than usual due to a painful eye infection caught while paying visits among the poor villagers over Christmas. Games of chess became a regular feature of Mary's diary; a lengthy visit from Hogg and the regular calls of Peacock offered welcome diversion. Neither Mary nor her husband seem to have been conscious that Peacock was falling in love with Claire. His suit was hopeless; Claire was still trying to accept that she had given her romantic, impulsive heart to a man who had merely, and briefly, enjoyed her body. She was in no mood for lovemaking.

Godwin, paying them a last quick visit in late January together with his thirteen-year-old son and namesake, went home feeling confident about his financial future. Mary was reading *Rob Roy* and packing up their possessions in the first week of February when the storm broke.* Shelley had obtained a new post-obit on 30 January, promising away £4,500 on his father's death to obtain £2,000 that day. Godwin, who had been anticipating a hefty share to relieve his own considerable debts, received a small percentage, perhaps as little as £150.[32] This was not acceptable at a time when Godwin knew that Leigh Hunt, a relatively new friend with no family connection, was being given well over a thousand pounds. Already cast down over the recent deaths of his sister Hannah and of his close friend the barrister John Curran, Godwin was moved to compose one of his most self-righteous letters.

---

* Despite Mary's anxious care for their possessions, a large quantity of letters were lost, destroyed, or possibly sold by their landlord in the years after they left Marlow.

He insisted on his right to an interview at which he proposed to explain the principles which Shelley had, in his view, betrayed. Shelley declined to answer. Mary, who loved them both, was in misery. Shelley seemed always able to borrow against his estate; her father had no such resource. What, when they had gone abroad, perhaps for ever, was to become of him?

There was, as a result of this unhappy situation, little intercourse with Skinner Street in the hectic weeks before the Shelleys and Claire left England. Staying at lodgings in Great Russell Street – Mary disliked them but could find no alternative – they plunged into every form of culture and entertainment the city could offer. Dinners with the Hunts and their witty, poetry-loving friend Horace Smith were interspersed by nights at the theatre or the opera. They admired the Elgin Marbles in their new home at the British Museum; they went with Peacock to see the great India Office library. (Peacock took up his appointment as a clerk at East India House shortly afterwards, following in the footsteps of Charles Lamb.) An exhibition of Salvator Rosa landscapes and a gigantic scenic view of Rome on display in the Strand whetted their appetite for the pleasures in store when they reached Italy; both Mary and Claire had already begun their background reading. Visiting the enticingly named 'Inventors' House' in St Martin's Lane, Mary listened to the Apollonicon, an astonishing painted organ with nineteen hundred pipes capable of imitating 'all the most admired wind instruments, with the effect of a full orchestra'.[33]

Isabella Booth came down from Scotland to visit her father in London. She told Mary of her plans. Six days before leaving England, Mary wrote to her, begging for a secret meeting and for a chance to introduce their young children to each other. It would be nice to think that Isabella defied her husband's wishes and took the risk. No record survives to tell us that she did.

It was probably Mary who decided that William, Clara and Alba should be baptized together before they left England. The service was performed on 9 March; Alba was renamed Clara Allegra, the second name having been chosen for her by Byron in memory, perhaps, of the Montalègre area in which the Shelleys had been living during their summer at Geneva.*

Mr and Mrs Godwin, still distressed by their son-in-law's refusal to

---

* Alba was baptized at Byron's request; the baptisms of William and Clara were undertaken to secure their legitimate status at a time when their parents were full of fears about the Lord Chancellor's seemingly malevolent attitude to Shelley's children.

produce the money they believed he had promised them, did not attend the triple christening, although Shelley called on them at Skinner Street that day, perhaps to request their presence. The departure was planned for 11 March. On the final evening, 10 March, Godwin's resolve weakened and he decided to visit their lodgings in Great Russell Street. The timing was unlucky.[34] Mary had just finished dining with the Hunts and Peacock, after a disappointing visit to the opera for *The Barber of Seville*, the first performance in England of Rossini's work. She was exhausted after a long day of packing; Shelley fell asleep even before the Hunts went home. Then Godwin came. 'Our adieus,' Mary noted with her usual reserve. If she cried a little at the thought of leaving behind the father she loved and worried for so much, she was not going to admit such weakness to her diary.

The party of eight, including the three babies, Claire, and two nurses, Elise Duvillard and young Milly Shields from Marlow, left for Dover at dawn the following day. Peacock and Horace Smith had been put in charge of their finances, a job which Peacock uneasily realized was going to involve placating a large number of angry creditors. (For a man who cared so much about public welfare, Shelley was extraordinarily indifferent to the hardship he imposed on the families from whom he freely took, for a piano, a carriage, a new set of curtains.) Two days later, after a brisk and unpleasantly choppy crossing, the travellers arrived in Calais for the third time.

Perhaps with a view to constructing a second travel book, Shelley and Mary resumed their old habit of keeping a joint journal. Advancing towards Italy, they began to regain the high spirits of the excited runaways of 1814. 'The sun shines bright and it is a kind of Paradise which we have arrived at . . .' Mary wrote happily to the Hunts from Lyons. 'Shelley's health is infinitely improved and I hope the fine climate we now enjoy and are proceeding to will quite restore him . . .'[35] Her letter bubbled with anecdotes and observations. Life offered itself again as a grand adventure, a leap into the unknown.

PART III

Italy

CHAPTER FOURTEEN

JOYS AND LOSSES

1818

On the beach of a northern sea
Which tempests shake eternally,
As once a wretch there lay to sleep,
Lies a solitary heap,
One white skull and seven dry bones . . .

Shelley, 'Lines written among the Euganean Hills' (1818)

SITTING ALONE AT MARLOW IN EARLY FEBRUARY WHILE THEIR possessions were stowed away in packing cases, Mary read not only Scott's *Rob Roy* but three of Byron's most wildly romantic works, *Lara*, *The Corsair* and *The Giaour*. It was not easy to imagine their author as a doting father: Mary, who had spent most of the autumn of 1817 urging Shelley to persuade Byron to undertake the care of his baby daughter, must have suffered at least a few moments of unease. Crossing the gloomily impressive mountain pass which separated France from Switzerland at the end of March 1818, the travellers stopped at Chambéry, where Elise Duvillard's family had come to meet them. Here, she found reassurance. Aimée, Elise's little illegitimate daughter, seemed a happy, thriving child, quite unaffected by the fact that she was being brought up without a mother's love.[1] It had, in any event, occurred to none of their party that Claire would be separated entirely from her little girl. They imagined that Byron might wish to spend the summer with them at some pleasant villa of their choice. After that, they supposed, Claire would be offered an arrangement by which the newly named Allegra would spend time with both her parents, if not under the same roof. It was, Mary reassured herself, all for the best.

The alpine ascent began on 28 March, the day after their meeting with Elise's family. Less pious than most travellers of the time, the Shelleys thanked Napoleon rather than God for the splendid road which took them over the top of Mont Cenis without mishap, despite the fact that the passes were thick with snow. Shelley, Claire noted, sang all the way up, while inviting them to see the snowy mountains as God's own troop of ballet-dancers. The Jungfrau's name and elegant line made it, he announced, the celestial equivalent to Mademoiselle Milanie, most charming of all the young dancers they had seen in London that winter.[2]

On 30 March, they left the domain of the King of Sardinia – crisply renamed 'King of the Anchovies' three years later in a best-selling guide to Italy by the fearlessly outspoken Lady Morgan – for that of the Emperor of Austria, ruler of Lombardy and Venetia. Italy, as Metternich commented in 1849, had become an empty title, a mere geographical expression. Following Napoleon's defeat in 1815, it had reverted to its old complexity, a patchwork of duchies, kingdoms and states, each of them tightly protected by border controls and each employing spies to maintain detailed notes on all foreign visitors and their political activities.

Having so far suffered only the minor irritation of a temporary confiscation of the works of Rousseau and Voltaire from Shelley's collection of books at the French border, the travellers had no political axes to grind. Safely arrived at Milan, Mary sat down to write an ecstatic letter to the Hunts. Everything, in comparison to 'wretched' France, was perfect. Even the peasants' carts were pulled by 'the most beautiful oxen I ever saw'. The inns were excellent, the bread 'the finest and whitest in the world'. Mary had, she admitted, been astonished by the way an opera audience at Turin had chattered from beginning to end of the performance; she was sadly disappointed by the drab bonnets and pelisses worn to the opera at La Scala, but then, the boxes were so elegant, the pit a bargain at eighteen pence a seat and the ballet of *Othello* 'infinitely magnificent', with dancing finer than they had ever seen in London. The children, 'the chicks', were all well, and Shelley's health 'infinitely improved'. 'I like this town,' she added; they were planning to spend the whole of the summer nearby, on Lake Como. She had not sounded so happy since the visit to Geneva.[3]

Anticipating Byron's arrival to collect his daughter and renew their friendship, Shelley and Mary went off alone together to Lake Como to seek a house beautiful enough to tempt him into a long visit. The three days they spent there – for the first time since leaving England, free of nurses, and children, and Claire – left Mary with an impression of almost unearthly serenity. Revisiting the lake more than twenty years later, she lost herself again in the beauty of the scenery and in a wistful certainty that this, if anywhere, was the spot to which Shelley's spirit might have returned. Writing her third novel, *The Last Man*, in 1824–5, she remembered the house with which they fell in love, standing above the lake on a hillside thick with sweet-scented myrtle and tall cypresses.

> Ten miles from Como . . . was a villa called the Pliniana . . . Two large halls, hung with splendid tapestry, and paved with marble, opened on each side of a court, of whose two other sides one overlooked the deep dark lake, and the other was bounded by a mountain, from whose stony side gushed, with roar and splash, the celebrated fountain . . . If some kind spirit had whispered forgetfulness to us, methinks we should have been happy here.[4]

There was a thunderstorm over the lake just before they left, reminding them of the nights of storytelling and scientific speculation with Byron at the Villa Diodati. The Pliniana would, they were sure, appeal as much to his imagination as to their own. After making inquiries about renting the villa, they returned to Milan, where Shelley wrote Byron a long friendly letter, urging him to come and spend part of the summer with them on the lake.

Shelley's first Italian letter never reached Byron; this one brought a chilling response. It seemed that he had no intention of coming to stay and no great wish to see them. A messenger was being sent to collect Allegra. Claire must understand that all contact with her child would then come to an end. (Byron's sudden proprietorial attitude to Allegra had been strengthened by learning that he had no chance of gaining custody of Ada, his only legitimate child.) On 22 April, the messenger, Mr Merriweather, an English shopkeeper working in Venice, arrived; panic-stricken, Claire announced that Allegra was ill and could not leave. Shelley, who had heard local talk of Byron's disreputable life in Venice, now saw nothing ahead but sadness for everybody. It would, he told Claire, be far better if they ignored their friend's commands and continued to look after the child as part of their own family.

This idea may have appealed to Claire; it horrified Mary. It was at this point that she intervened. Initially, they had agreed that Allegra should travel on to Venice with young Milly Shields; Mary now proposed to exchange Milly for Elise. Older (she was twenty-three),

better-educated and more capable, Elise would be a reliable correspondent on the little girl's welfare and a bulwark against whatever
depravities Venice had to offer. Allegra would be safe with her.

Claire, to Mary's relief, took the bait. On 26 April, the day before
her birthday, she wrote Byron a heartbroken letter in a pathetic
blotched scrawl, begging him to treat Allegra with all the affection of
which she felt him to be capable, introducing him to Elise as 'the most
eligible person we could procure . . . a mother herself', and begging
for sympathy in the sacrifice she was about to make.

> I love her with a passion that almost destroys my being she goes from
> me. My dear Lord Byron I most truly love my child. she never checked
> me – she loves me she stretches out her arms to me & cooes for joy
> when I take her . . . I assure you I have wept so much to night that
> now my eyes seem to drop hot & burning blood.[5]

On 28 April, Allegra, Elise and Mr Merriweather set off for Venice.

Perhaps it was as well that Byron had resisted their invitation; it
transpired that the lovely Villa Pliniana was not, after all, available.
With no fixed plans other than to visit the glorious cities – Florence,
Rome, Naples – of which they had heard the most, the Shelleys, Claire
and Milly Shields left Milan on 1 May and made a leisurely journey
down to Pisa. A pretty university town flanking the Arno, it had
recently fallen into economic decline. The population had dropped
from a hundred thousand to a mere sixteen thousand; the cobbled
streets were thick with grass. Mary dutifully clambered up the 224 steps
of the leaning tower to look down on the Piazza dei Miracoli, but she
could take no pleasure in a city which set chained gangs of prisoners
to the task of street-cleaning. Weeding out the grass was not in itself
taxing work; it was the chains and the inescapable analogy to slave
labour which were disturbing. Similar scenes in Rome would gradually immunize Mary's social conscience; newly arrived, she was overcome by disgust. Claire, however, took comfort from Elise's letter
reporting their safe arrival at Byron's Venetian home. Allegra had been
kindly received: 'they dress her in little trousers trimmed with lace &
treat her like a little princess,' Mary told the Hunts.[6] Byron, moreover,
had deigned to scribble a few lines at the bottom of Elise's letter.
Unhappy though she was, Claire was consoled by the thought that she
might, after all, be allowed to see her daughter before too long.

Instead of waiting at Pisa to call on Lady Mountcashell, who as Mrs
Mason now lived quietly on the edge of town with Mr Tighe and
their two daughters, the travellers moved on to Livorno, an hour's

drive down the coast. It was 'a stupid town', Mary noted on 9 May, unimpressed by the cosmopolitan port's broad streets and handsome piazzas. But they had not come here for culture. Armed with a letter from Godwin which skirted his daughter's scandalous history to describe her as a respectable married lady on her travels, Mary was hoping to receive a call from the woman who had been on hand to help care for her in the first weeks of her life and who had known both her parents.

She was not disappointed. Maria Gisborne, the former Mrs Reveley, called at their inn soon after receiving Godwin's letter and his daughter's covering note: 'she is reserved yet with easy manners,' Mary recorded in approving tones. They spent much of the following day with her; walking out along the sea-wall in the evening, Mary met Mrs Gisborne again and coaxed her into 'a long conversation about My Father and Mother'.

Shelley liked this quietly cultivated woman for being a democrat and an atheist; Mary admired the wide range of her accomplishments. A proficient linguist – she taught Shelley Spanish at a later date – and a sensitive and accomplished musician, Mrs Gisborne was also a skilled artist. Her greater attraction, in Mary's eyes, was her connection to the past. Here was a woman who would have made an ideal stepmother; it was hard to look graciously on John Gisborne, the man for whom William Godwin had been displaced.

Large nosed, thin lipped and with an unfortunately adenoidal voice, Maria's husband was slow to win the Shelleys' affection, although Mary acknowledged that there might be more to him than she had supposed when he let her borrow and copy his own transcription of the thrillingly horrifying history of Beatrice Cenci, the young girl who murdered her incestuous father and was executed for the crime in 1599. Both Mary and Shelley preferred the company of Henry Reveley, the mild thirty-year-old son of Mrs Gisborne's first marriage. One reason, of course, was that Henry belonged to the Eden of Mary's earliest years: he could still remember playing with Fanny in the hayfields behind the Polygon. Another was that, in contrast to the somewhat stuffy society of the Gisbornes' English friends – one, Mr Beilby, was pompously delighted to discover 'an anachronism in the allusion to the tea-tables of Petersfield' in Godwin's *Mandeville*[7] – Henry was a man of the future. Mr Gisborne's career as a merchant had not flourished; Henry hoped to make the family rich by his schemes for a steam engine which, he believed, could be used to power a boat. It was not an impossible dream; steamships had been plying between Liverpool and Glasgow since 1815. Henry Reveley had noticed the difficulty and slowness of transporting cargo along the coast from Livorno to Genoa; he dreamed of powering a boat big enough to carry goods between Italy and France. It was three weeks before he could be persuaded to show his engine off to the visitors; Shelley, a believer in the transforming benefits of science, was entranced. Mary, noting that Mrs Gisborne was a devoted but over-protective mother, hoped that success would bring Henry a little nec-essary independence. Sadly, investment in this potentially lucrative venture turned out to be one of Shelley's most expensive mistakes.

   Shortly before their visit to inspect Henry Reveley's engine, Shelley had found himself and his companions a more rural retreat. Two weeks later, on 10 June, they said their goodbyes to the Gisbornes, while begging them to visit their new home at Bagni di Lucca, a pretty little spa sixty miles to the north, closely wrapped in the wooded folds of a mountain landscape. Casa Bertini, the house which Shelley had rented for the summer of 1818, stood beside the oldest of the marble hot baths and the Grand Duke of Tuscany's disused chapel at the top of a steep and twisting cobbled street. Cool shadowed rooms, filled, to Mary's relief, with sturdy new furniture, opened behind on to a long rectangle of grass terminating in a dense hedge of laurels. The river Serchio, far below, was shut out of sight; visible from every window and filling the air with a scent rich as jasmine, were the sweet chestnut woods which climbed to the top of the surrounding hills.

   For the first two weeks they had the place almost to themselves; towards the end of June, the lower part of the town became a throng of fashionable English, queuing up to make the acquaintance of the Bagni's most illustrious visitor, Princess Pauline Bonaparte. Balls and elegant promenades became the order of the day; Shelley escorted Mary and Claire down to watch waltzes and quadrilles in the pretty old casino (the Italian equivalent of the English assembly room); to his disappointment, they grew shy and refused to take part. Mary, eager to practise her Italian, was scornful of the English colony's refusal or inability to speak any language but their own; she did, however, sympathize with their dislike for being carted about in sedan chairs, Italian style. Bagni di Lucca had a large and splendid riding-stable and the Shelleys made good use of it. Mrs Gisborne, who had no doubt formed a fairly clear view of Mary's affection for her step-sister, probably smiled when Mary informed her that poor Claire had taken a tumble from the saddle and hurt her knee, 'so as to knock her up for some time'.[8] When Shelley decided on an adventurous five-mile ride up into the Apennines, to the famously beautiful Prato

Fiorito, Mary rode alongside him while Claire crossly nursed her leg at the villa. Claire, as the journals show, was singularly tactless in her assumption that, wherever Mary and Shelley went, she, like Mary's unloved little lamb, must also go.

The household was easy to run. They had Milly Shields to supervise the children, a woman to wash clothes and scrub floors and, in Paolo Foggi, a helpful factotum who was also willing to cook and, Mary ruefully became aware, to cheat them at every possible opportunity.* Shelley wrote in the garden or wandered up into the woods to read beside a clear pool in which, with nobody around to complain, he bathed naked; Mary divided her time between an intensive reading schedule (it included Horace, Gibbon, Virgil, Livy, the plays of Ben Jonson and a second reading of Shelley's *The Revolt of Islam*) and long, delightful walks: 'I like nothing so much as to be surrounded by the foliage of trees only peeping now and then through the leafy screen on the scene about me,' she told Mrs Gisborne.[9] Unlike her husband, who was overwhelmed with homesickness when he read Peacock's accounts of evening strolls in the Marlow woods, Mary was wholly under the spell of her new surroundings.

Reports filtering through Peacock's letters to Shelley confirmed that *Frankenstein*, if not universally admired and praised, was certainly being discussed. Cheered by Scott's discerning review and encouraged by Shelley, Mary began casting about for a new subject. Her father, made fonder by absence, sent Shelley a friendly letter in which he outlined a project he thought perfect for his scholarly daughter, a collection of short histories of leaders of the Commonwealth established by Oliver Cromwell after the execution of Charles I. Background reading, he thoughtfully added, would not be hard; only a few reference books would be needed.[10] Godwin's suggestion showed a shrewd appreciation of where Mary's greatest skill lay; years later, some of her best work took the form of concise, well-informed biographical essays. Shelley, unfortunately, had other plans in mind. Twenty years later, Mary recalled that he had urged her to write a tragic drama; 'he conceived that I had some dramatic talent, and he was always most earnest and energetic in his exhortations that I should cultivate any talent I possessed, to the utmost.'[11] At the end of the summer, he was still pressing her to begin writing a play about Charles I; in 1821, he took over the project. Godwin, meanwhile, decided to write a History of the Commonwealth himself.

---

* Paolo Foggi was probably hired in Livorno, since Mary, writing to Mrs Gisborne on 15 June 1818, refers to him simply as 'Paolo', adding that he has been 'exceedingly useful'.

Shelley did his best to fire Mary's enthusiasm for the subject he had chosen with evening readings from Hume's *History of England*; sitting under a starry sky on a summer night, with fireflies flickering across the grass and music floating up the hillside from the ballroom of one of the aristocratic visitors, she found it impossible to think about life in Stuart England. She made no secret of the fact that she was happier copying out the translation of Plato's *Symposium* on which Shelley was working at Bagni di Lucca.

It was, Shelley told the Gisbornes on 10 July, just a diversion, an exercise, a way of giving Mary 'some idea of the manners & feelings of the Athenians'. He was being prudently nonchalant; the *Symposium*'s subject, homosexual love, had put it out of bounds for English readers who knew no Greek. Shelley, as Richard Holmes has pointed out, was 'the first major English writer to attempt an objective account of Platonic homosexuality' and to show, through his translation and the essay it inspired him to write, 'that Plato's conception of love has a universal application'.[12]

The copying was done during the day; the essay, or *Discourse*, emerged from the discussions which took place in the cool of the evenings, out in the narrow garden of the Casa Bertini. Here, talking with Mary and Claire, Shelley shaped his argument. In Plato, he found a reflection of his own enduring belief in the power of love to uplift and purify, to annihilate evil. This was his creed. This unquenchable faith in love as a universal panacea was what Mary loved most in him. Reading the *Discourse* at the end of this tranquil summer, Mary seemed to be looking down through clear water at her own reflection, Shelley's image of all she meant to him.

Degraded by an age which treated them as inferior beings, Shelley argued, women had been robbed of the power to inspire love.

> They were certainly devoid of that moral and intellectual loveliness with which the acquisition of knowledge and the cultivation of sentiment animates, as with another life of overpowering grace, the lineaments and the gestures of every form which it inhabits. Their eyes could not have been deep and intricate from the workings of the mind, and could have entangled no heart in soul-enwoven labyrinths.[13]

The act of love itself, Shelley wrote elsewhere in the *Discourse*, 'is nothing'; love, in its highest state, was identifiable in the moment of meeting someone, some 'frame, whose nerves like the chords of two exquisite lyres, strung to the accompaniment of one delightful voice, vibrate with the vibrations of our own'.[14] This state of intuitive empathy was what Shelley yearned for in all his relationships; in the summer of 1818, it still existed between himself and Mary. The deep and thoughtful eyes were hers; the 'one delightful voice' was, perhaps, a graceful allusion to Claire, their perpetual companion.

It was August and fiercely hot, even up here in the hills, when the spell broke. Mary was contentedly copying out the continuation of *Rosalind and Helen*, the poem about herself and Isabella Booth which Shelley had begun at Marlow, when two letters arrived from Elise in quick succession. The main news which they brought was that she and Allegra had been moved out of Byron's home and put in the care of Richard Hoppner, the British consul in Venice. Thomas Moore, collecting biographical information some years later, heard from Byron's mistress Teresa Guiccioli that Byron felt Elise was too young and inexperienced to have sole charge of Allegra, and thought it best to put her under Mrs Hoppner's supervision.[15] But Elise seems also to have hinted that Byron was preparing to debauch his daughter; the following year, Claire told him that she could foresee his becoming another Count Cenci: 'Allegra shall never be a Beatrice.'[16]

The idea of Byron's setting out to bring up a year-old child as his mistress was patently absurd, but Elise, no stickler for the truth, may have been ready to say anything which would bring her former employers to the rescue. 'Elise was a pretty woman. Byron was thought to be intimate with her by some,' Claire told E.A. Silsbee in the 1870s.[17] If Elise had become pregnant by Byron and was now living with strangers, she had every cause to send alarming messages in the hope of restoring herself to the safe care of the Shelleys before her condition became apparent. Mrs Hoppner, a fiercely conventional Swiss woman, would have had little sympathy for a nursemaid's predicament.

For whatever reason, and with whatever stories, Elise persuaded Claire that it was her duty to go instantly to Venice. It is not clear what Claire planned to do next; probably, she meant to make a direct appeal to Byron for the return of her daughter. Shelley, conscious that her sudden appearance in Venice was likely to enrage Byron and increase her own misery, decided to intercede on Claire's behalf. Elise's second letter arrived on 16 August. Shelley and Claire left Casa Bertini the following day. Mary, making brief mention of 'important business' which had taken them to Venice, wrote to invite the Gisbornes to come and lighten her solitude. She promised to read them Shelley's translation of the *Symposium*, adding a cautious warning that 'in many particulars it shocks our present manners, but no one can be a reader of the works of antiquity unless they can transport themselves from these to other times and judge not by our but by their morality.'[18] Shelley would have been proud of her.

The Gisbornes arrived eight days later. They found Mary pale and nervous. Little Clara was ill and she herself had been sick for two days. 'Well my dearest Mary are you very lonely? Tell me truth my sweetest do you ever cry?' Shelley had tactlessly written during a day's halt at Florence; he urged her to be cheerful and to please him by working on her play.[19] But Mary was too sad for work; even Mrs Gisborne could not drive away the terror she always felt when Shelley left. The memory of how easily he had abandoned Harriet was never far away.

Clara was still ill when Shelley's second letter reached Mary. It had taken five days to arrive and the contents required immediate action. Claire and he had met and liked the Hoppners. Acting on their advice, Shelley had pretended to Byron that Mary and the children had come with them and were now staying with Claire at Padua. Byron, full of friendship towards Shelley, had said, first, that Claire should have Allegra back for good, and then, that she should have her for a week. He had offered to lend them all his own summer home at Este, which was not far from Padua.

So far, so good; the offer had been accepted and acted on. But it would not do for Byron to discover that Claire and Shelley were living alone at his villa; the only solution Shelley could find was for Mary and the children to come immediately to Este. The rest of his letter was taken up with details about the quickest route. An order for £50 was enclosed to cover her costs. 'If you knew all that I had to do!' he exclaimed, before asking her to 'be well be happy come to me & confide in your own constant & affectionate PBS'.[20]

Shelley did not know how ill his baby daughter was; he would probably still have insisted on the journey. It was painful for Mary to compare the tender chivalry with which he had insisted on chaperoning Claire with his easy supposition that she, acting alone, could pack up the house at Bagni di Lucca and set off on a hot, arduous journey across Italy with a nine-month-old baby. Mrs Gisborne, whom she consulted, could see no alternative. Paolo Foggi, the invaluable factotum, was dispatched to make the necessary travelling arrangements at the nearby town of Lucca. On the next day, 30 August, Mary sadly noted: 'My birthday – 21 – packing.' This was not how she had planned to spend it; had all gone as intended, they would have been readying themselves for a sea voyage down to Naples for the winter months. 'O Mary dear, that you were here; / The Castle echo whis-

pers "Here!"' Shelley charmingly entreated her from Este in his poem
'To Mary': it was easier for him to imagine than for her to achieve.

Travelling towards Este over the next four days in the company of
Paolo, an inexperienced young English nursemaid and her own feverish child, now suffering acutely from dysentery, Mary must have been
rigid with resentment of Claire. If she had not been so determined
to have Byron's child; if she could only have consented to leave
Allegra in the Hoppners' care: it did not bear thinking about.

Clara was still dangerously ill when they reached Este; Shelley and
Claire might have been more concerned if they had not both been
struck down themselves, Claire with a mysterious ailment which had
been troubling her for most of the summer, Shelley from food-
poisoning. Neither of them took their illnesses lightly; occupied with
their own ailments, they were eager to reassure the anxious mother
that her child was only suffering from teething problems.

Mary, while resolutely refusing to leave Clara for a visit to Venice,
did her best to distract herself. She read Italian poetry and plays; with
her thoughts still on the strange incestuous history of Beatrice Cenci,
she started a translation of *Mirra*, a treatment of the forbidden love of
a father for his daughter by one of Italy's greatest modern playwrights,
Vittorio Alfieri. The frequency with which Mary herself made literary use of a relationship between father and daughter might cause
a modern reader to wonder if some hidden experience between
Godwin and his daughter was being exorcized on paper. This notion
should be dismissed. There are, undoubtedly, elements of autobiography in Mary's fictional works, but the theme of love between rela-
tives was not uncommon at that time. British publishers were often
discomforted by it and this was the probable reason why one of
Alfieri's finest works remained without a translator. It is, however,
true that Mary's own powerful attachment to Godwin gave her a
reason for being drawn to explorations of father–daughter relationships in her work and in that of other writers.

Shelley, beginning on the most technically dazzling and ambitious
of his works, *Prometheus Unbound*, was all encouragement. He liked
to feel that they were working in harmony; generously, he longed for
Mary's success as much as for the acknowledgment which continued
to elude him. Mary continued to regard *Mirra* as the noblest of
Alfieri's dramas, but she did not complete the translation.

Health apart, they felt they had landed in paradise. The house, I
Cappuccini (now the Villa de Künkler), was airy and light. Its
windows faced away from the plump wooded cones of the Euganean

hills, looking across a fruit-laden garden with a vine-trellised path leading to the summerhouse which Shelley promptly converted into a study, and out to the wide green plain of Lombardy. In the fore-ground, separated from the garden by a deep ravine, stood a gloomy fortress once owned by the Medici family, 'whose dark massive wall gave forth an echo', Mary wrote with evident relish for its gothic charm, 'and from whose ruined crevices, owls and bats flitted forth at night, as the crescent moon sunk behind the black and heavy battle-ments'.[21] Her affection for the place remained strong; writing in 1833 on Petrarch, whose last home had been nearby at Arqua, she found an excuse to praise 'the ancient and picturesque town of Este'.[22]

Little Clara's health did not improve. The doctor at Este was hope-lessly inadequate. Shelley, visiting Venice to request an extension of Allegra's visit, was told by Byron that his own doctor, Aglietti, was by far the best man to consult. Mary was instructed by her husband to chaperone Claire to a doctor's appointment at Padua, bringing the baby with her. Claire would then return to Este, while Shelley con-ducted his wife and Clara to Venice – and Aglietti.

They left Este well before dawn on 24 September, hoping to avoid the heat of the day. By the time they reached Padua, Clara's condition had deteriorated. Ahead of them lay the slow journey along the Brenta canal to Fusina where, to their dismay, it transpired that their passports had been left behind. Either the baby's convulsions or Shelley's fury persuaded the Austrian guards to break the rules.

'It is strange, but to any person who has suffered, a familiar circum-stance,' Mary wrote in Venice twenty-two years later, 'that those who are enduring mental or corporeal agony are strangely alive to imme-diate external objects . . . a relief afforded by nature to permit the nerves to endure pain . . . Thus the banks of the Brenta presented to me a moving scene; not a palace, not a tree of which I did not rec-ognise, as marked and recorded, at a moment when life and death hung upon our speedy arrival at Venice.'[23] She waited, holding Clara in her arms, in the hallway of an inn while Shelley rushed in search of Dr Aglietti. When he returned, Mary, white-faced and mute, was standing where he had left her, still holding the baby. Clara was dead.

'This is the Journal book of misfortunes,' Mary wrote bitterly in her diary that evening, seated at a desk in the Hoppners' house. Two days later, Clara's small body was buried on the lonely beach of the Lido, as desolate as the sea which stretched beyond it. No tablet marked her grave.

They returned to Este a few days later, taking with them Byron's *Ode to Venice* and *Mazeppa* which he had asked Mary to transcribe, probably with the kind intention of giving her an occupation. Frightening symptoms of ill health in little 'Willmouse' brought them hurrying back to Venice in search of better doctors on 11 October. Mary remained there until the end of the month, dining daily with the Hoppners and, since he seemed to wish it, offering Byron her view of his unpublished memoirs. On 24 October Shelley left her to collect Allegra from Claire at Este. Perhaps, despite the relief of almost daily rides with Byron and the long, enthralling conversations on which he based the poem *Julian and Maddalo* which was completed the following year, Shelley was anxious to distance himself from the reproach of Mary's sad face. He was certainly in no hurry to return; he remained at Este, alone with Claire and Allegra, for four full days.

Godwin's well-intended letter of consolation did not reach Mary until long after Clara's death. In it, he invited his daughter to consider this as the first hardship she had been asked to bear and to recollect that 'it is only persons of a very ordinary sort, and of a pusillanimous disposition, [that] sink long under a calamity of this nature. I assure you,' Godwin continued confidently, 'that such a recollection will be of great use to you. We seldom indulge long in depression and mourning, except when we think secretly that there is something very refined in it, and that it does us honour.'[24]

Harsh though Godwin's prescription sounds, it was given for reasons of affection and concern. Godwin had lived with Mary Wollstonecraft long enough to be aware of the strong streak of melancholy in her character. He knew of her attempts to kill herself; he recognized that his daughter had inherited her mother's nature. When he urged her to be cheerful and resolute, he was writing in fear that Mary's despair might become self-destructive.

Godwin's letter did not arrive until the winter. Mary had already done her best to keep her unhappiness to herself, but it was hard. Clara had deliberately been given the name of their first dead baby, as if to preserve and encompass her. Now, both were gone and, try as she would, Mary could not rid herself of the thought that it was the journey Shelley had forced her to make across Italy in the height of summer which had helped to cause their second child's death. Even if she never voiced the accusing thought, her feelings were apparent. 'One looks back with unspeakable regret and gnawing remorse to such periods,' she wrote in 1839 in her note to Shelley's poems of 1818. They included sections of *Julian and Maddalo*, 'Invocation to Misery' and 'Stanzas written in Dejection near Naples'. Kept from her sight at the time, these were the poems in which Shelley expressed his own sense of loss and estrangement. 'O Thou, my spirit's mate,' he wrote in *Julian and Maddalo*, in lines which seem to represent a personal situation:

> Who, for thou art compassionate and wise,
> Wouldst pity me from thy most gentle eyes
> If this sad writing thou shouldst ever see –
> My secret groans must be unheard by thee,
> Thou wouldst weep tears bitter as blood to know
> Thy lost friend's incommunicable woe.

It is possible that there were other factors at work which contributed to Shelley's own misery. His health was always a concern and it is even possible, as one critic has cogently argued, that his unhappiness stemmed from the knowledge that he was suffering from syphilis contracted during his brief period as an Oxford undergraduate – knowledge which he may not have shared with his wife.[25] This remains a matter of speculation; what is certain is that Mary was much affected by the loss of her second daughter and that she was not a woman who shared her deepest feelings with others when she was unhappy. She would not even allow herself the luxury of writing her thoughts in her journal, although this would be a solace in later years; the record of the period immediately after Clara's death is unusually terse. One day, she passed the time by writing the details of some ghost stories told by the Chevalier Angelo Mengaldo when he dined with the Hoppners. 'Thursday, 8th October: Read Vita di Alfieri & Livy – S[helley] reads Winter's Tale aloud to me', is a more typical entry.

A rare hint of what Mary was enduring is visible in an oblique description written more than twenty years later, when she was staying in Venice again.

> Evening has come, and the moon, so often friendly to me, now at its full, rises over the city. Often, when here before, I looked on this scene, at this hour, or later, for often I expected S's return from Palazzo Mocenigo, till two or three in the morning. I watched the glancing of the oars of the gondolas, and heard the far song, and saw the palaces sleeping in the light of the moon, which veils by its deep shadows all that grieved the eye and heart in the decaying palaces of Venice.[26]

On 5 November, after returning Allegra to the care of the Hoppners, the depleted party set out on the road again.

CHAPTER FIFTEEN

A MYSTERIOUS HISTORY

1818–1819

'Naples is, I can easily conceive, to most people, a delightful residence . . . Yet
we have been most dreadfully teized, and that has, in some degree, taken away
from our gusto for this place . . .'

Mary Shelley to Maria Gisborne, 22 January 1819

BYRON WAS NOT SURPRISED BY THE APPARENT CALMNESS WITH
which Mary had faced her loss. Mary, so Claire had written to him
early in 1818 from her lodgings in Bath, faced all troubles with the
serenity of a ship sailing 'under a gentle & favourable wind'. (This
suits well with Mrs Godwin's comment in 1814 that Mary, at sixteen,
showed the steadiness of a woman of forty.) Claire, with endearing
candour, went on to admit her envy to Byron. Oh, to have written
Mary's novel! –

> yet all yields when I consider that she is a woman & will prove in time
> an ornament to us & an argument in our favour. How I delight in a
> lovely woman of strong & cultivated intellect.[1]

Byron shared Claire's admiration of *Frankenstein*, and of its author.
Clever women intrigued him: one, Lady Melbourne, had been his
confidante and mentor; another, for a while, had been his wife. He
respected Mary's cool head enough to seek her advice, even at a time
when she was mourning the loss of her baby daughter, on whether
he should publish his memoirs. (Mary, according to her own recollections, saw nothing in them that was not publishable.[2])

As a mother, however, Byron thought Mary as much of a reckless fool as her husband. Of course, he had no idea of the circumstances which had led to Clara's death, or of Shelley's responsibility for dragging his wife and a sick baby across Italy to protect Claire and himself from scandal. Not all brigands on the road to Rome were murderers; not all foreign travellers were robbed; not all children died of malaria or dysentery. Nevertheless, the number of such incidents was disturbingly high and Byron thought his friends were tempting fate by setting off on a vagabond trip to the dangerous South with their remaining child, a pretty and delicate-looking little boy. He did not regret having removed Allegra from their charge.

Armed with the guidebooks written by the Reverend Chetwode Eustace, a Roman Catholic clergyman who had travelled extensively in Italy in 1801 and with whose conservative views they became increasingly impatient, Shelley kept his companions to a rigorous schedule of sightseeing as they travelled towards Rome along the Via Emilia. At Ferrara, they admired the paintings of Guido Reni ('the divine Guido'), visited the great library, saw the very chair in which the adored author of *Orlando Furioso* used to sit (in those times everybody who loved literature knew the plot and characters of Ariosto's epic, even if they hadn't read it) and the cell in which Tasso had been imprisoned. Goethe, who questioned everything, had mistrusted the cell's authenticity; Shelley took away a sliver from its wooden door as a keepsake for Peacock. At Bologna, Mary's eyes suddenly glazed; a glimpse of her misery coloured Shelley's description to his friend in England of a madonna's face, 'heavy . . . as if the spirit of a love almost insupportable from its intensity were brooding upon and weighing down the soul . . .'[3] They looked respectfully at triumphal arches, fell in love with Spoleto and struggled to find new ways to describe the celebrated cascade at Terni. It was, Mary thought, as beautiful as a painting – no, more so! 'The thunder – the abyss – the Spray – the graceful dash of water lost in the mist below – it put me in mind of Sapho leaping from a rock and her form vanishing as in the shape of a swan in the distance.'[4] Reaching Rome on 21 November, the Shelleys, together with Claire, Paolo Foggi and the two nurses, settled into 'a comfortable hotel', a relief after the weeks of staying at cold and often filthy inns. (One had been so bare of hospitality that Mary spent the night in her travelling dress and cloak.)

Rome, in the autumn of 1818, was in the throes of a massive excavation programme. Wandering over the tracts of open fields which reached even into the middle of the city, the visitors sometimes stumbled and hurriedly drew back as they found themselves peering down a hole in the ground at the crown of a Roman arch. Although they did not, like a startled Goethe, find the Sistine Chapel's altar being used as a picnic area, they grew rapidly accustomed to Rome's casual approach to its imperial past. Wandering through a maze of grassy lanes towards the Forum and scrambling over heaps of earth and rubble, they watched cattle grazing among the columns. Cabbages and artichokes sprouted in dishevelled gardens on the Palatine Hill; ladies in splendid, high-plaited headdresses squabbled over the price of fish among the ruins behind the Portico of Octavia. Pilgrims up from the South slumped in the sunlight with their eyes shut; a pious few knelt as a line of grimly hooded monks swept past. With competent ferocity, artists staked out the Colosseum with their easels; Mary, aching for Mrs Gisborne's skill as she trained her view-finder on appropriate subjects, sat among them while William, trotting at liberty, amused himself among the marble torsoes strewn about the ground, looking to his eyes like casually dismembered dolls.

'S. begins his tale of the Coliseum,' Mary noted on 25 November. Shelley never completed his conversational fragment in which, talking to a young stranger, an old man seems to hint at their own loss when he says 'with a deep and suffering voice, "that men have buried their children"'.[5] Further indications of the Shelleys' low spirits emerge from his account to Peacock of a visit one bright autumnal day to the Protestant cemetery on the outskirts of Rome. It was impossible not to think of Harriet, Fanny and their own two baby daughters, all gone to unrecorded graves, as they wandered among the monuments and tablets. The sky deepened to the dusty mauve of the Campagna plain; the dead seemed almost enviable, lying in such a quiet place. 'Such is the human mind,' Shelley mused, '& so it peoples with its wishes vacancy and oblivion.'[6]

The last part of their journey south through Italy was across notoriously dangerous territory. The Appian Way stretched west from Rome over the desolate malaria-haunted Pontine marshes before turning south on the coast at Terracina and dropping down through lonely hills to Naples. Shelley travelled on ahead with a terrified priest and a nervous merchant; a man was knifed to death almost at his feet in Capua. The experience was not unusual; the French poet and diplomat Alphonse Lamartine, travelling on the same route a few years earlier, passed a half-burned carriage with corpses lolling on the steps;[7] Marianna Starke, an intrepid travel-writer on whose accounts the Shelleys often relied, had been informed that this was the most dangerous road in Europe. Lady Blessington and Lady Morgan both undertook it with extreme nervousness; Shelley left Mary, Claire and the two nannies to brave it with only the untrustworthy Paolo Foggi for a guide.

'Cross the Pomptine Marshes,' Mary noted on 29 November. 'There are no houses or villages to be seen in the whole extent if you except 3 miserable post houses – the people you me[e]t have all a savage appearance – they appear to gain their livelihood by sporting or robbing when they dare – We meet many soldiers as patroles both on foot & on horseback.' She was, for once, quite glad to see them.

Anna Jameson, visiting the little coastal settlement of Terracina a few years later, gasped at 'beauty beyond what I ever beheld or imagined . . . an enchanted land, "a land of Faery"'.[8] Like Mary and Claire, she peered up the mountain above Terracina to glimpse the pillars of a vast temple to Jupiter and above it, a ruined fortress. Away to the north, rising from a perpetual wreath of mist, lay an island, in fact a promontory, which was said to have been the home of the enchantress, Circe; a very suitable place for such a sorceress to live, in the travellers' view. The sea air raised their spirits. Travelling on down to Gaeta and with the dreaded Pass of Fondi behind them, Mary and Claire thrilled to the – inaccurate – news that their inn stood on the grounds of Cicero's villa, and that his murdered body had been buried nearby. 'A poet could not have a more sacred burying place [than] in an olive grove on the shore of a beautiful bay,' Mary wrote in her journal. The next day, jolting through a landscape of hills that reared and curved like the waves of a frozen sea, they finally saw the distant smoke of Vesuvius spouting from the volcano's broken cone. Below it, the towers and palace roofs of Naples spread down the hillsides to the bay like a scene from *The Arabian Nights*. This was the landscape for which everything in Italy was mere preparation. Homer had been in Mary's mind as she stared across the sea to the headland of Montecircello; Naples, for romantic scholars, was the territory of Virgil, birthplace of Latin literature.

Shelley, left to his own devices and enjoying the benefit of the favourable exchange rates, had taken lodgings for them all at No. 250 Riviera di Chiaia. The most expensive street of villas in all Europe, the Chiaia justified its prices with a view which stretched from Vesuvius to the orange groves of Posilippo, of a bay flecked, by day, with as many white sails as a cloud of butterflies, and by night, with the pine torches of the fishermen. The gardens separating the villas from the sea were the favourite haunt for visitors; open to all, they were beset by the tireless sketchers who found it impossible not to paint one more charming child, costumed flowerseller or beribboned entertainer. Staying on the Chiaia, Lamartine exclaimed, was like living in the Garden of Eden.

Writing fifteen months later to a young relation of Shelley's who was then visiting Naples, Mary was full of nostalgia for its charms. 'I never found my spirits so good since I entered upon *care* as at Naples, looking out upon its delightful Bay,' she told Sophia Stacey. 'The sky, the shore, all its forms and the sensations it inspires, appear formed and modulated by the Spirit of Good alone unalloyed by any evil. Its temperature and fertility would, if men were free from evil, render it a faery habitation of delight – but as a Neapolitan said of it, "E' un Paradiso abitato dai diavoli." '9

And what, Miss Stacey must have wondered, was causing Mrs Shelley to harp so on the evil aspect of a city which she seemed to have loved? And, if she thought Naples so beautiful, why did her letter go on to compare it so unfavourably to Rome?

The answer lies in one of the most mysterious and baffling episodes in Mary's life, the story of Shelley's Neapolitan 'charge'. The charge was a little girl who was given the name of Elena Adelaide Shelley and who, left in the care of unknown persons at Naples when the Shelleys returned to Rome, died there in the summer of 1820. Who Elena Adelaide was is a mystery that has never been solved. She may have been a foundling, adopted by Shelley to comfort his wife for Clara's loss. She may have been his child by Claire, or by Elise Duvillard. She may have been Elise's child by Byron. She may, as Shelley's cousin Thomas Medwin first hinted in a book about Byron which he published in 1824, have been the daughter of a mysterious Englishwoman who had an affair with Shelley in London shortly before he left England, and who followed him to Naples. All that is known for certain is that she was not the daughter of Mary Shelley and that Mary, called on in 1821 by Shelley to answer a tale spread by their former employees, that Claire had given birth to his child while they were at Naples, passionately denied it. Mary was probably telling the truth, but that does not help us to guess how much of the story she knew, or whose the child was.

On 27 February 1819, the day before they left Naples for Rome, Shelley went to the local registry for the Chiaia district and presented a baby, untruthfully stated to have been born to himself and Mary precisely two months earlier, on 27 December, at 250 Riviera di Chiaia. The midwife was named; the two witnesses were a young local hairdresser and a cheesemonger, neither of whom are likely to have known anything of Shelley's private life. The baby was registered under the name Elena Adelaide Shelley.

Claire kept no diary at Naples; Mary's was brief. Shelley, although elaborately descriptive in his accounts to Peacock of their inspection of all the local sites, including the inevitable pilgrimage to the rim of the volcano, provided scant personal detail. Vignettes which litter the pages of contemporary travel journals, of the gambling which took place everywhere, even in the theatres, of back streets filled with 'idol' shops, of *lazzaroni* whose miraculous ability to do nothing at all with cheerful ease baffled and enraged all English visitors, of the pretty girls dancing tarantellas under trellised arbours; all these are strikingly absent from the Shelleys' accounts. We hear that Shelley became so ill on their journey up Vesuvius that they had to turn back, and that Claire's hysterical behaviour on the same expedition almost caused their guides to abandon her on the road. We know that Mary and Shelley read Winckelmann, extoller of stainless purity, on the art of ancient Greece and that Mary, still unsure of her next subject, was valiantly wading through a French edition of Sismondi's gigantic *History of the Medieval Italian Republics*. We know that on 27 December, the day on which Elena Adelaide was alleged by Shelley to have been born, Claire was sufficiently ill for Mary to make a note of the fact. We know that Shelley himself was confined to the house by illness for much of February, but that he grew well enough to make a long and difficult journey down to the temple at Paestum towards the end of the month. This illness was the explanation Mary later offered for the melancholy poems which Shelley wrote while they were at Naples. She was, at the time, unaware of their existence.

Mary was as terse with her correspondents as with her journal after their arrival at Naples in early December. Mrs Gisborne learnt only of their safe arrival and, nearly two months later, that they had been 'dreadfully teized', a word which then carried more meaning than the sense of slight vexation it conveys today. The teasing may have related to the behaviour of Paolo Foggi, whom they had recently dismissed. Mary, writing to Mrs Gisborne on 22 January, mentioned Paolo's dishonesty: 'he has made, I fancy, £100 – by us. lately he has cheated us through thick and thin.'[10] Shelley, writing to Peacock the following day, confirmed that Paolo had left them and added that Elise Duvillard had married him 'very much against our advice'.

Shelley's account fits neatly with Mary's statement to Marianne Hunt on 12 March, that Elise had been 'quite spoiled' by her stay in Venice and had gone to live in Florence after marrying their 'rogue of an Italian servant' at Naples and turning Catholic. Two years later, Mary's story had changed. In the letter of 1821 in which, writing at Shelley's request, she defended him from 'the foulest calumnies' (a charge made to the Hoppners by Elise that Claire had given birth to his child at Naples), Mary referred to 'an accident' which had led her to discover 'a connexion' between Elise and Paolo in Naples. A doctor had diagnosed 'danger of a miscarriage' and since 'I wd not turn the girl on the world without in some degree binding her to this man – we had them married at Sir W[illiam] A'Courts.'[11] (Sir William was British ambassador to the court of Naples.) So, we can choose between two versions of Elise's marriage; she undertook it against the Shelleys' advice (Shelley's account to Peacock), or she was dismissed after being forced by them to marry, because she was or had recently been pregnant (Mary's account to Mrs Hoppner).

The charge against which Mary was here defending herself had come to the Hoppners directly from Elise, or so they said. Claire, Elise had told them, was already pregnant when she came to Venice to see Allegra in the summer of 1818. She had taken medicines to cause an abortion; Shelley continued to supply these to her at Este and Rome, but with no success. Their child had eventually been born at the lodgings on the Chiaia in Naples. Shelley had bribed the doctor into silence and had taken the baby to a foundling hospital. Mary, according to Elise's extraordinary story, had known nothing, neither that Claire was pregnant, nor that a child had been born.[12]

This ugly tale seems to have reached the Hoppners during the summer of 1820 when Elise was once again living in Venice. The Hoppners were at this time irritated by the fact that Claire had been using them as a means of getting her messages through to Byron: 'Why indeed we have been selected by Clara [Claire] as the means of communicating with you I know not,' Hoppner wrote to Byron in May 1820. It must have been after this date that Elise told them her tale, for on 21 June Hoppner wrote again to Byron, sending love to Allegra and adding a gossipy hint: 'I am heartily glad, though I dare not tell you why, that you have not sent her to her mother.' Byron, replying on 20 July from Ravenna, where he was living with Teresa Guiccioli, his young mistress, made no allusion to this. On 6 September, Hoppner tried again to arouse his curiosity: 'I hope for his [Shelley's] sake that Clara and his atheism have driven him out of his wits, as I am loath to believe him so thoroughly depraved as I must consider him if he has not this justification.' This forced Byron to ask what it was they knew against Shelley; Hoppner's next letter, of 16 September, passed on Elise's story, one which he had evidently been hoping for an invitation to relate.[13]

Visiting Byron at Ravenna the following summer, Shelley was shown Hoppner's letter. His immediate reaction was to write and ask Mary to tell Mrs Hoppner whatever she herself believed to be the true facts. Mary was requested to send her letter to him, so that he could show it to Byron before they sent it on to the Hoppners. Mary did this. Her account was found, with its seal broken, among Byron's papers after his death. Quite possibly, Shelley gave it to him to forward to the Hoppners and Byron, after reading it, simply forgot. Equally possibly, Byron decided that a vindication of Claire might arouse the Hoppners' sympathy for her and enable her once again to use them as message-carriers.

'Claire had no child,' Mary wrote in this long and fluent letter, in which the handwriting never faltered, although she expressed horror and pain at the charges she was being asked to meet: 'Claire had no child the rest must be false.' But there had been a child, if not Claire's, and Mary already knew enough about it in April 1819 for Shelley to tell Mr and Mrs Gisborne that his wife was writing to explain why 'a combination of circumstances' would oblige them to return to Naples for six months at the end of May. This letter from Mary has not survived. It is the one which might have told us most about her own part in the plot.

Was Mary lying in her letter to Mrs Hoppner? Could Elena Adelaide have been Shelley and Claire's child? Baptized on the same day that her birth was registered, 27 February, she was alleged by Shelley to be precisely two months old. If Elena Adelaide was born on 27 December, the date on which Mary noted that Claire had been 'unwell', she could have been conceived on the journey to Italy. Claire had been unwell throughout the summer, but can we imagine that she managed to hide her pregnancy for all those months and that she was able to make an arduous journey up Mount Vesuvius a few days before secretly giving birth, and in rooms to which Mary assured Mrs Hoppner that she herself had access at all times? How secret can a birth without anaesthetic be? The one ringingly confident statement in Mary's letter to Mrs Hoppner was that denial: 'Claire had no child.' I think we should believe her.

A second and intriguing possibility is that Elise's story to the Hoppners derived from her own history, not Claire's. Mary's account of Elise's pregnancy never named Paolo as the father of her child. She told Mrs Hoppner that the two servants had only formed their 'connexion' at Rome in late October, just before they set out for Naples. This would certainly rule out the possibility that Elena Adelaide was their child, but not that Elise might have become pregnant by Shelley in the spring of 1818.* Perhaps, after bribing Paolo to marry Elise and leave their household in January 1819, Shelley decided to adopt his own daughter and register her as his legitimate child. Elise and Paolo certainly knew about something out of the ordinary which took place at Naples, enough for Shelley to lament to the Gisbornes on 7[?] July 1820 that 'Paolo has been taking advantage of my situation in Naples in December 1818.' Paolo, in 1820, was threatening to charge him 'with the most horrible crimes'.

It is, of course, possible that Paolo had decided to make trouble by conflating the rumour – of which Elise would surely have been aware – that Allegra was Shelley's child, not Byron's, with the adoption of a baby in Naples. It is certain that Paolo was attempting blackmail in the summer of 1820 and that he said enough to damage the Shelleys' both at Pisa and at Livorno. What he said is not known. But why should Elise, living apart from her husband by that time, have decided to carry gossip to the Hoppners? It is a point which has been over-looked by biographers: Elise had nothing to gain by slandering Shelley and Claire; she told the Hoppners only of a baby's being taken away from the lodgings on the Riviera di Chiaia. There is a slight but noticeable assonance between the name Elise (pronounced 'Eleessa') and Elena (pronounced 'Elaina').

Let us suppose, then, that the mysterious Elena Adelaide was Elise's baby by Shelley, that she was removed from the lodgings after her birth and that Mary then put up a fierce resistance to Shelley's scheme to register, baptize and adopt her as their own child. Did Mary compel him to leave the baby behind at Naples? This might connect to a brief visit paid by Elise to the Shelleys in the autumn of 1819, when they were staying in Florence. She could have been calling from courtesy; she could have been anxious to know about the child – her child's – welfare. A second child, alluded to in Elise's friendly letter to Mary of 17 July 1821, was probably Paolo's: 'j'ai fait une jolie petite fille . . . tre gaie . . .'[14]

The mystery baby died at Naples in June 1820. This was the month in which the Hoppners sent their first hint to Byron of a strange tale given to them by Elise. The young nurse's bitterness becomes wholly understandable if she had just heard of the death of a child she was forced to relinquish. She could hardly tell the Hoppners the truth; their own letters to Byron make it clear that the couple had a low opinion

---

* On 27 March, Mary had noted their brief meeting at Chambéry with Elise's parents and her illegitimate daughter. At a time which must have been emotionally distressing to Elise, we might wonder whether Shelley had offered her sexual comfort.

of Claire, regarding her as a bad mother and of loose morals. By trans-
ferring her own story to Claire, Elise had the release of unlocking her
unhappy secret and inflicting hurt on Shelley. Later, told by both Mary
and Claire of the damage she had done, Elise denied having ever said
anything. Mary, sending her own letter of denial to Mrs Hoppner via
Shelley, referred to Elise with unusual bitterness as 'this miserable girl'.
Claire, who may never have known how much her own name had
been slandered, remained on excellent terms with Elise, visiting and
being visited by her when they were both living in Florence in 1820–1.

There is a third possibility. Writing up his *Conversations of Lord
Byron* in 1824, Shelley's cousin Thomas Medwin has Byron alluding
to a lady who had fallen in love with Shelley after reading his poetry.
Perhaps Byron, who was fond of 'bamming', the practice of spinning
stories to credulous listeners, did tell Medwin some such tale for the
fun of it, but Medwin cited Shelley himself as a second source.[15]
Publishing his life of Shelley in 1847, Medwin claimed that he had
been told of a beautiful and aristocratic lady who was so overwhelmed
by the poet's high ideals and his belief in 'unfettered union between
the sexes' that she decided, after meeting him in London, to abandon
husband, family and friends to follow him throughout the world.
Medwin's proverbial inaccuracy placed the start of her pursuit in
1814; Shelley apparently told him that she had been spying on him
across the lake when he was at Geneva in 1816. In 1818, so the story
went, she followed him again; she had managed to stay in the same
hotel between Rome and Naples. She had arrived in Naples on the
same day; 'and at Naples – she died.'[16] This, Medwin decided,
explained the unhappy tone of the poetry Shelley wrote that winter.

Interest in Medwin's story as a possible solution has obscured the
fact that he never mentioned a baby. The editor of Claire's letters,
summarizing the available evidence regarding the mysterious Neapolitan adoption, speculates on the use of the name Adelaide. This was
a name which belonged neither to the Shelley nor the Godwin family
trees. Could the mother have been Adelaide Constance Campbell,
whose mother, Lady Charlotte Campbell, married her chaplain,
Edward Bury, while they were all travelling in Italy in 1818?* Should
we try to link her to the 'AB' of unidentified gender to whom Shelley

---

* According to another story told by Claire in old age to her most avid interlocutor, E.A.
Silsbee, there had been 'a Scrape' with a lady at Naples and both she and Mary had known
all about it. The fact that the lady – her nationality was not specified – was still alive made it
conveniently impossible for Claire to tell him more. 'She is under a promise of secresy,' noted
Silsbee, who seems to have been content to report any story that made a good yarn.[17]

instructed his London publisher to make two payments, of ten and twenty pounds, earlier in the year? But then Shelley also made a passing observation to Peacock on the thoughtful, heart-searching eyes of German ladies; should we start looking for a German Adelaide, or brood on the fact that 'Adelaide' means 'of noble birth'? Can anything be construed from the fact that two popular operas performed at the Teatro San Carlo in Naples in 1818 had the names Elena and Adelaide in their titles? We can, once we start to look, see potential mothers springing up everywhere; none offers more than the thin coincidence of a shared name.*

The least complicated answer of all strikes me as the most convincing. Shelley's letters to the Gisbornes consistently referred to the baby as his 'Neapolitan charge', as if the baby was of Neapolitan birth. It is possible that he knew the mother; it does not follow that he was the father. Shelley had, as we have already seen, a strong interest in adopting little girls; he could naively have assumed that Mary's anguish at losing Clara would be assuaged by the gift of a substitute.

History has lost sight of how commonly children were abandoned and adopted in Italy at that time. Polidori, visiting Pisa, had been shown the 'turning box of an establishment unknown in this country [England] . . . A miserable mother, hidden by her long veil, is often seen at midnight, to approach with a trembling hand, to stand a long time kissing and weeping over her infant, near this grate; a footstep is heard; she puts it into the box, turns it round; a bell rings the knell of separation, and she parts, perchance for ever, from her child.'[18] The novelist and travel-writer Marianna Starke, visiting Naples shortly before the Shelleys, was astonished to learn that her servants had recently adopted a foundling, although they had a family of their own: 'afterward, when we mentioned the circumstances to our Neapolitan friends, they informed us that such instances of charity were by no means rare among the common people.'[19] The Shelleys read Starke's book; this passage could even have alerted Shelley to how simple a process adoption was. His experiences with the Court of Chancery would have made him particularly anxious to legalize the process by a registration and baptism.

The absence of letters and the brevity of Mary's diary entries, when put together, suggest that she knew more than she ever acknowledged. Her own refusal to take charge of this substitute child, whatever its

---

* On 28 June and 12 July 1814, Godwin noted meeting an Adelaide in the company of the Kenneys, his wife and, on the second occasion, a couple called Mercier. The fact that 'Adelaide' has no surname suggests that she may have been a relation, probably of Mary Jane Clairmont.

relation to her husband, may explain her note of 'a most tremendous fuss' on the day of their departure from Naples, as Shelley rushed to make alternative arrangements for the baby's care. They made their peace with each other at lovely, wild Gaeta, where they spent a whole day strolling in woods and along the empty shore.[20] Here, Mary's fourth child was conceived. Five days later, the Shelleys and Claire were back in Rome.

———

They lodged at the Palazzo Verospi on the Corso, which was one of the smartest addresses in Rome. Shelley, despite his republican views, remained patrician in his habits: this was the street on which his father would have stayed, had he ever ventured so far as Italy. Perhaps Shelley was preparing Mary for her role as a baronet's wife; they had already begun to anticipate Sir Timothy's death. 'Il buon tempo verrà,' Shelley's new ring announced; Mary wanted to find him one with his family crest engraved as a seal.

Sir Timothy would have been impressed by the decorum of their Roman life. Mary and Claire took drawing lessons; Claire worked on her singing. They received calls from Lord Guilford, the son of George III's prime minister, and from Sir William Drummond, an authority on the excavation work being done at Herculaneum and Pompeii. They were presented to the Pope, a seemingly gentle old man who nevertheless left Mary feeling 'dreadfully tired'. Lord Guilford introduced them to the ancient and formidably erudite Marianna Dionigi, their near neighbour on the Corso. Attending the signora's evening conversaziones and relishing the chance to exercise their Italian, they felt most superior to the tongue-tied English guests who, as Claire maliciously noted, 'after having crossed their legs & said nothing the whole Evening, rose all up at once, made their bows & filed off'.[21]

Mary was more enthusiastic. 'How you would like to be here!' she wrote to Marianne Hunt on 12 March: '. . . my letter would never be at an end if I were to try [to] tell a millionth part of the delights of Rome – it has such an effect on me that my past life before I saw it appears a blank & now I begin to live – In the churches you hear the music of heaven & the singing of Angels –' A few weeks later, her secret hopes were confirmed; she was pregnant again. It seemed a happy coincidence that they should just have met Dr John Bell, a celebrated Scottish doctor who knew her father and who now became part of their own small circle of friends. Writing to Mrs Gisborne,

Mary told her that Bell's intended visit to Naples would be 'one reason' for their own return there. She was not yet prepared to disclose another, but she had already told Leigh Hunt that 'circumstances will keep us a long time' at Naples.[22] It seems that Shelley had persuaded her to reconcile herself to the adoption.

The Hunts and Maria Gisborne were thankful for signs that Mary had recovered from the loss of her daughter and was enjoying life in a city 'stuffed with the loveliest statues in the world'. There were still dark moments. It took only one cold day to drag Shelley's health down, Mary told Hunt; for herself, 'evil thoughts will hang about me – but this is only now and then –'[23]

She had several causes for despondency. The unresolved situation in Naples was worrying; Mrs Hoppner had sent them a cruelly tactless letter, hinting that Allegra was pale and pining and that Claire was a thoughtless mother not to take responsibility for her.[24] In England, Godwin was confronted by heavy demands for years of unpaid rent at Skinner Street, rent which he had happily assumed he was under no legal obligation to pay, having no single direct landlord. No letters between him and the Shelleys have survived from this period, but it would be surprising to discover that he had not communicated his distress to Mary.

The Emperor of Austria visited Rome for the Holy Week celebrations at the beginning of April. Mary's republican blood boiled at the sight of his officers pushing the meek crowds away with drawn swords. Enraged by the Roman people's inability to live up to the spirit of their glorious past, she wrote a short story in which she imagined the feelings of a Roman senator returning to the present. She called it 'Valerius, the Reanimated Roman', but her scientific interest in his return from death was minimal. What interested her was Valerius's response to the sight of his great city in ruins, the Forum become the Campo Vaccino, the Colosseum's arches broken and thick with weeds; at the Pantheon, she pictured his distress at finding the shrine of the old gods converted into a Roman Catholic church.

We can see hints of Mary's father in Valerius's 'placid and commanding' face. A direct allusion to Isabella Booth seems to be made when Valerius meets Lady Harley, a young woman of Scottish birth whose name is Isabell and whose husband, far older than herself, relishes the role of being her tutor. But 'Valerius' is also an affectionate record of Mary's own responses to her surroundings. She began her story at Naples; moving to Rome, she described all her favourite haunts, the Colosseum, Mount Palatine, the walks along the Tiber. 'This is of all others the place I delight most in Rome to visit,' she wrote after climbing with Valerius to the banks above the great ruined arches of Caracalla's Baths. This was where Mary herself often came to sketch and read, while Shelley, sitting nearby, worked on the last act of *Prometheus Unbound*. This, she wrote in her tale, is a place which 'joins the beauty and fragrance of Nature to the sublimest idea of human power; and when so united, they have an interest and feeling that sinks deep into my heart.'[25]

They had been in Rome for six weeks when Claire and Mary, driving through the Borghese Gardens, caught sight of a familiar face. Amelia Curran had been living in Rome for over two years; both she and her brother William, now in Paris, had remained on friendly terms with the Godwins. Still unmarried, although she was considerably older than Mary and Shelley, Amelia lived in a house filled with visiting artists, many of them Irish, in the Via Sistina at the top of the Spanish Steps. The narrow Corso in the midst of the city, she warned her friends, was no place for a small and delicate child as the dreaded season of malaria approached; convinced, the Shelleys hastily took new rooms in the house next to hers. The air on the Trinità dei Monti was, so everybody told them, the best in Rome; the views, stretching across the city, were magnificent.

Miss Curran earned her living by painting. She was not a particularly talented artist, but she probably hoped for more than the verbal thanks she received from Shelley for producing portraits of the entire family. Mary, who always regarded herself as an impossible subject for artists, was not much pleased by the result. '"You can have it,"' Edward Trelawny quoted her as saying years later, '"but it is unfinished, and she has made a great dowdy of me; I care nothing about it."'[26] She cared enough, however, to try to rescue the portrait from Trelawny's keeping in the last years of her life.

Young William Shelley began sitting for his portrait on 14 May. Like all who met him, Amelia Curran was enchanted by the little boy's pretty looks and high spirits; William was everybody's pet. More at ease by now in Italian than his own language, he chattered while he sat for her as a bohemian elf, a nightshirt pulled down from one shoulder, a rose clasped in his hand. A few days later, he sickened with a childish ailment, worms. Shelley returned from a day-trip to Albano on 23 May to find Mary worried and William no better; a week later, Mary wrote to Maria Gisborne that they had decided to follow Dr Bell's own change of summer plans and settle near Lucca or Florence. She could only feel confident about William if Dr Bell was in charge. Evidently uneasy, she added that he 'is so very delicate – and we must take the greatest possible care of him this summer'.[27]

William grew feverish and then comatose. On 2 June, Dr Bell called three times. On 5 June, Mary admitted to Mrs Gisborne that they were in despair, although the little boy had, by strenuous efforts, been revived from 'the convulsions of death' the previous day. 'The hopes of my life are bound up in him,' she wrote. Shelley spent sixty hours sitting by the bed and on at least one occasion broke down in tears. On 7 June, William died of malaria. The knowledge that he could have been spared if they had left Rome a month earlier, as originally planned, was almost unbearable. His parents buried him in the quiet Protestant cemetery at Rome where, a few months earlier, they had wandered as tourists. Attempts to locate the grave a few years later revealed that the little corpse had been moved and lost. Like his sisters, William lies in unmarked ground.

The Shelleys, Claire and the young English nanny, Milly Shields, left Rome as soon as William had been buried. They spent the next three months living near Livorno in a large stone villa, cool in summer, freezing as the autumn grew damp, out in the flat fields of the vineyards between the slopes of Montenero and the sea. By 1826, reviewing a collection of sketches of Italian life, Mary felt detached enough to write a charming and evocative account of life among the small farms, of fireflies flickering over the dark cornfields, the calls of the grape-pickers from tree to tree as they challenged each other at improvising rhymes. In retrospect, shivering in a damp London winter, it seemed to have been paradise.[28] In the summer of 1819, she could think of nothing but her loss. She had been a mother three times; each time, the child had been snatched from her. 'Oh, oh, oh fate, cruel giver of evil gifts, almighty shade of Oedipus, black Erinys, how overwhelming you are,' Shelley had written, quoting Aeschylus, at the end of her first journal. What sin, she wondered, could have merited such relentless punishment?

The old-fashioned concept of divine retribution was not one Mary had learnt either from Godwin or from Shelley; she began, nevertheless, to wonder if Harriet Shelley's death lay at her door and if this was the penalty that was being exacted. The thought would linger, and haunt her.

CHAPTER SIXTEEN

A LOSS AND A GAIN

1819–1820

Italy – Leghorn [Livorno]

Wednesday 4ᵗʰ [August 1819]
I begin my [third] journal on Shelley's birthday – We have now lived five years together & if all the events of the five years were blotted out I might be happy – but to have won & then cruelly have lost the associations of four years is not an accident to which the human mind can bend without much suffering

Since I left Rome I have read several books of Livy – Antenor [translation of an ancient travel diary found at Herculaneum] – Clarissa Harlowe – The Spectator – a few novels – & am now reading the Bible and Lucan's Pharsalia – & Dante[.] S is today twenty seven years of age –

Write – Read Lucan & the Bible – S writes the Cenci & reads Plutarch's Lives – the Gisbornes call in the evening – S reads Paradise Lost to me – Read 2 Cantos of the Purgatorio.

MARY HAD REASON TO BE MISERABLE, OF COURSE, BUT THE intensity of her grief was terrifying to the two people who shared the Villa Valsovano with her through the late summer of 1819. Her fourth child was due to be born in November; she dreaded the beginning of another cycle of hope, love and loss. 'I never know one moments ease from the wretchedness & despair that possesses me,' Mary told Marianne Hunt three weeks after William's death. She could not believe that he had been taken from her: 'William was so good so beautiful so entirely attached to me . . . Did you ever know a child with a fine[r] colour – wonderful spirits . . .'[1] Claire, truly frightened for the first time of what Mary might do, postponed a planned visit to Allegra, of whom they had heard nothing since April: 'I cannot imagine how she [Mary] could have been left alone,' she wrote to Byron a few months later.[2]

Shelley was equally unnerved. His gentle, reassuring wife had vanished, leaving behind only an image of her past self. 'My dearest M. wherefore hast thou gone / And left me in this dreary world alone,' he scribbled in his jotting book. 'Thy form is here indeed – a lovely one – / But thou art fled, gone down the dreary road, / That leads to Sorrow's most obscure abode . . .' A final, very faintly pencilled couplet revealed his determination not to be sucked into the same vortex of despair: 'For thine own sake I cannot follow thee / Do thou return for mine.'[3]

Heat, exercise and work offered Shelley his own defence against sadness. His study was a glazed room on the rooftop, typical of villas in the area, with a view across the vineyards to the sea. His exercise was a morning stroll to the shore with Claire, or to the Gisbornes. Maria, introducing him to Calderón's great intellectual dramas, may have pointed out the striking kinship between *Frankenstein* and *Life is a Dream* in which man, treated as a brute, becomes one. Peacock offered lighter solace with his newest work, *Nightmare Abbey*. Here was Mary as the grave and brilliant Miss Celinda Toobad; here was Shelley, as Scythrop Glowry, with a tower which could almost be seen as a prophecy of his life in a modern Italian turret; here, Godwin's novel *Mandeville* was mocked as 'Devilman'. But Peacock was at his sharpest in parodying the aura of romantic gloom in which Byron wrapped the part of his persona he reserved for public consumption.[4] Smiling at his friend's ability to offer criticism and yet never cause pain, Shelley went back to his own new play about the family of Beatrice Cenci, a verse-drama closer to Byron than Peacock in its style and subject-matter.

Plunged in grief, married to a man who refused to be drawn into sharing it, Mary kept to herself. She saw Shelley at meals, sometimes; they met every afternoon for a grim two-hour session translating Dante's *Purgatorio*, not a work designed to raise anybody's spirits. But Mary, as Shelley had recognized, was in that dangerous state of misery that feeds on itself. If he fled to the top of the house, it was because he could not bear to hear his wife accusing herself, and perhaps him, of having killed the children, while wishing, aloud and in her letters, that death would come and visit them again. 'I ought to have died on the 7th of June last,' she wrote to Leigh Hunt in September; the date of William's death was branded on her memory.[5]

She might, at such a time, have hoped for sympathy from her father. Godwin, in the summer of 1819, had more than the loss of a little-known grandson on his mind. Unable to pay the back rent on Skinner Street, he was threatened with eviction; a court case was being brought against him for £1,500 in arrears. Set for July, the case was finally heard and given against Godwin in October. Constables, the Edinburgh publishers, were pursuing him for a further £500. He had no one to support him. Charles Clairmont was abroad and penniless; young William Godwin had only survived three weeks of training as an engineer before being sent home with three fingertips missing.[6] When Godwin wrote to his daughter, he thought not of her loss, but of her husband's broken promises and the money which could still be sent to save the business and himself. Writing to Amelia Curran at the end of the summer, Mary wretchedly admitted that William's death had not lessened her father's demands and accusations: 'so I gain care every day.'[7] Shelley, meanwhile, had lost all patience with a father-in-law whose only interest in them seemed to be financial.

All letters but one from Godwin to his daughter during this period have disappeared; the sole survivor is often produced as evidence of his stony heart. It is certainly a tough letter, but it shows a genuine wish to rally Mary's spirits, to shake her out of despondency. A few harsh words – the lines were very lightly cancelled, remaining entirely legible to his reader – about Shelley's 'moral defects' conceded that 'they at least do not operate towards you'. Allegra, we should remember, was still assumed by the old Godwins to be Shelley's child.

There were, Godwin told Mary in this letter, written just three months after William's death, two classes of people in the world, the dependent and the supporters. Among this second group, a rare few were capable of changing and improving the human condition. Mary was one of these. She had a duty to society, if not to herself.

> You were formed by nature to belong to the best of these classes, but you seem to be shrinking away, and voluntarily enrolling yourself among the worst.
>
> Above all things, I intreat you, do not put the miserable delusion on yourself, to think there is something fine, and beautiful, and delicate, in giving yourself up, and agreeing to be nothing.
>
> Remember too that, though, at first, your nearest connections may pity you in this state, yet that when they see you fixed in selfishness and ill humour, and regardless of the happiness of every one else, they will finally cease to love you, and scarcely learn to endure you.[8]

Brutally candid, this was the honest counsel of a worried father. Mary, as Godwin frequently had cause to remind her, was heir to her mother's depressive nature. Mary Wollstonecraft had made two attempts to kill herself; poor Fanny had succeeded. Following the death of William Shelley, he saw the danger signs in his daughter's letters. 'Everything on earth has lost its interest to me,' Mary told Amelia Curran on 27 June. 'I am no[t] fit for any thing & therefore not fit to live,' she informed Marianne Hunt two days later. It is unlikely that the lost letters to her father struck a more cheerful note. Godwin refused to offer sympathy, believing that it could only deepen grief.

Brooding and withdrawn, Mary began work, not on the serious and scholarly novel she had planned to write, but on a fiction which would offer some release for her most unspeakable thoughts. The fact that she first called it 'The Fields of Fancy' shows that she was thinking about her mother in those late summer months: 'The Cave of Fancy' was an early attempt at a novel which Mary Wollstonecraft had abandoned, incomplete.

Rewritten as *Matilda*, Mary's novel is of interest chiefly as a work of self-revelation. It tells the story of a young girl (Mary herself was just twenty-two) whose mother dies giving birth to her. Matilda is subsequently exiled to Scotland while her heartbroken father travels abroad. She is sixteen and dressed in tartan – much as Hogg had remembered Mary when he saw her at Skinner Street in 1814 – when her father takes her back into his charge. Confused by Matilda's striking resemblance to her mother, he is forced by her questions to admit that his love for her is more ardent than it should be. He flees her presence. Called to a lonely cottage above a seashore, Matilda arrives too late; her remorseful father has already drowned himself. Shown the corpse, she is overwhelmed by the sense that the fault is hers and that payment must be made. Some of the guilt which surfaced here clearly related to Mary's concern that they were doing nothing to help Godwin at a time when his letters told her he stood on the brink of ruin.

It is not clear whether Mary showed Shelley the novel while she was writing it, or even if she intended to publish it. The candour of some of her revelations suggests that *Matilda* began, at least, as a private solace, a secret outlet. Courted by a young poet, Woodville, in the later chapters of the book, Matilda broods on her responsibility for the death of her father. It enrages her to see Woodville, just as it enraged Mary to see Shelley, gliding forward 'as an angel with winged feet might glide along the earth unimpeded by all those little obstacles over which we of earthly origin stumble'.[9] Mary, watching how Shelley drew on her misery for his portrait of Beatrice Cenci, allowed Matilda to express her own resentment. She feels 'like a character that he [Woodville] comes to see act . . . perhaps he is already planning a poem in which I am to figure.'[10] Pathetically, she showed her awareness of how Claire and Shelley must perceive her: 'I had become unfit for any intercourse . . . I had become captious and unreasonable: my temper was utterly spoilt.'[11]

It seems at first embarrassingly obvious why Godwin, to whom Maria Gisborne proudly showed Mary's manuscript when she visited London in 1820, should have disliked it. Mrs Gisborne herself thought the novel very fine; her journal recorded with surprise that Godwin, by contrast, considered it 'disgusting & detestable; and there ought to be, at least if [it] is ever published, a preface to prepare the minds of readers, & to prevent them from being tormented by the apprehension from moment to moment of the fall of the heroine.'[12] This, readers have usually supposed, shows that Godwin was alarmed by Mary's treatment of the father–daughter theme, and that he found it shocking. But incest was a feature of Romantic literature, indeed by 1820 almost a literary cliché; far from being shocked by it, Godwin was ready to praise *The Cenci* as one of his son-in-law's finest works.

The true source of Godwin's outrage becomes apparent when we look at the section of Mary's novel which follows the death of Matilda's father. In the letters she wrote from the Villa Valsovano Mary, agonized by the deaths of her children, had expressed a vehement desire for her own life to end; Godwin had given her good reasons why she should live. Instead, she sent him a novel which flaunted the idea of death the bridegroom, death the comforter, death the debt-collector. 'I go from this world where he [her father] is no longer and soon I shall meet him in another,' Matilda declares to her lover:

> Farewell, Woodville, the turf will soon be green on my grave; and the violets will bloom on it. *There* is my hope and expectation; your's are in this world; may they be fulfilled.[13]

It was the espousing of death, not Matilda's relationship with her father, which Godwin found so repellent. To a man for whom suicide befitted only the disgraced Roman who failed in his social duties, Matilda's attitude was weak, cowardly and unworthy of interest, let alone admiration. He could not contemplate offering such a work for publication. When Mary asked for the manuscript to be returned to her keeping, her father refused to comply.[14]

News reached the inhabitants of the Villa Valsovano of a massacre in Manchester on 16 August. Over five hundred people had been injured and some fifteen gored or trampled to death by sabre-wielding cavalry attempting to break up a peaceful reform meeting on open ground. Shelley was shocked into responding to 'Peterloo' by Hunt's lurid reports in the *Examiner* of the indiscriminate slaughter of thousands. *The Masque of Anarchy*, his rousing attack on the Tory oppressors, was as alive as *The Cenci*, the drama he dreamed of seeing performed at Covent Garden or Drury Lane, was dead. Hunt, seeing danger for himself as well as Shelley, refused to act as the publisher. One can see why.

> 'Men of England, heirs of Glory,
> Heroes of unwritten story,
> Nurslings of one mighty Mother,
> Hopes of her, and one another;
>
> 'Rise like Lions after slumber
> In unvanquishable number,
> Shake your chains to earth like dew
> Which in sleep had fallen on you –
> Ye are many – they are few.'[15]

Reading these lines makes it hard to understand why Mary, in 1839, felt able to claim in her notes to the poem that Shelley's revolutionary feelings 'had faded with early youth'.[16] He was, she tried to argue, merely urging the common sense of presenting a united front. It is unlikely that Sidmouth or Castlereagh, both attacked in the poem, would have agreed. Shelley's call to action could not have been more vehemently made – and it was twice repeated. The poem remained unpublished until after the passing of the Reform Bill in 1832.

The Villa Valsovano returned to life in early September. Shelley was ablaze again with a sense of poetic mission; Claire's brother Charles arrived on a visit from Spain, where he too had been making a reckless response to political events in England.[17] With two fiery Clairmonts to encourage him, Shelley embarked on a savage portrait of life under a corrupt government. 'Hell is a city much like London –' he wrote in *Peter Bell the Third* before yoking Castlereagh to Cobbett and Canning as 'caitiff corpses'. Mary was still exorcizing her loss in *Matilda*; Shelley had shaken off his sadness. They were, after all, about to become parents again.

'Pray how does Jhonny get on* & have you now another [child]?' Mary asked Leigh Hunt at the end of September. She envied them their brood. '. . . Marianne might well laugh if it were a laughing matter at the recollection of my preachments about having so large a

---

* John was one of Hunt's small sons.

familly when I now say that I wish I had a dozen – any thing but none – or one – a fearful risk on whom all one's hopes and joy is placed.'[18] The baby was due to be born in November and, since their friend Dr Bell, a doctor they trusted, was in Florence, Shelley went with Charles Clairmont on 23 September to look for lodgings. He returned to take Mary there by easy stages. After saying goodbye to the Gisbornes and promising Henry Reveley financial help with his steamboat project, they visited Mrs Mason's household at Pisa on 1 October before travelling inland to Florence. Mrs Mason, tall, cheerful and calm, was a reassuring figure. They promised to stay in touch.

'Well we are now tolerably settled in our lodgings,' Mary told Mrs Gisborne on 5 October in a letter which asked for a parcel of books and 'the very best green tea . . . at whatever price' to be sent to Mrs Mason as a present. 'We talk a great deal about you,' she wrote wistfully, and added, on Shelley's behalf, that they longed for news of the steam engine's progress.

The lodgings which Shelley had taken for six months were in the narrow Via Valfonde near Santa Maria Novella. Charles may have suggested them; their landlady was the wonderfully named Madame Merveilleux du Plantis, a friend of Mary Jane Godwin's who had visited Skinner Street earlier in the year.[19] Mary thought her featherbrained and bad-tempered; Charles fell promptly in love with her daughter Louisa, a chilly young beauty who thawed enough to go snowballing with Claire one January afternoon. The weather, so the Florentines said, had never been so bitter.

Pensions changed very little between the Shelleys' visit and E.M. Forster's memorable portrait of one in *A Room with a View* (1908). The Shelleys found themselves supping at a long table with the same agreeable mixture of clerics, painters and impoverished ladies who were making demure excursions to Fiesole when Henry James came there in 1870; when Percy Florence was born on 12 November, after only two hours of labour, Mary was visited and congratulated by the admiring wives of their fellow lodgers. Made miserable by the latest news of Godwin's lost case,[20] she drew comfort from seeing that pretty little Percy's most striking feature was a nose 'that promises to be as large as his grandfather's'. His body, she wrote in a moment of rare relief and merriment, was sure to be 'the quintessence of beauty, entracted [extracted?] from all the Apollos, Bacchus's, Loves and dawns of the Study [Studii] and the Vatican'.[21]

Scandal had dogged the footsteps of Shelley and his two companions ever since they had been spotted with Byron at Geneva by a group of bored tourists. Hints appeared regularly in their letters from Italy of awkward meetings, of turned backs, covert stares. However good the addresses Shelley chose for them, they were never encouraged to join the cliques which welcomed and even gushed over the Ladies Morgan, Blessington and Burghersh. Twenty-eight-year-old Sophia Stacey, the ward of Shelley's uncle, Frederick Parker, had a hard time persuading a lady companion that no harm could come from calling on her eccentric cousin Bysshe while they were in Florence. This was Miss Stacey's first journey abroad, and she wanted a little more adventure than Miss Parry-Jones seemed willing to provide. Before objections could be raised, Sophia had found rooms on the Via Valfonde. She intended to enjoy the company of her interesting relations; arriving two days before Percy's birth, she was in time to suggest his second name.

Sophia stayed for six weeks, visiting as often as they were willing to see her. It was impossible not to be melted by her eager friendliness. She was 'lively & unaffected' and very '*entousiasmée*' to see Shelley, Mary reported to Mrs Gisborne on 2 December, and added that she had a pretty singing voice – 'for an english delettanti'. Sophia, whose diary has survived only in extracts, was a little overawed by the seriousness of the Shelleys. He, she decided, was an 'uomo interessante' and very romantic. He and Mary were always reading. She even saw little writing-desks and lights prepared for a continuation of study when they retired to bed.[22] This did not, her tone suggests, comply with her own idea of a poet's marriage.

Visiting the Uffizi galleries with Sophia, Shelley made notes for himself on the statues. The Niobe, which he greatly admired, evoked poor Mary, tenderly nursing her new child while grieving for the ones she had lost. He turned away to eye the voluptuous Venus nearby. 'Her eyes seem heavy and swimming with pleasure,' he noted. '. . . The neck is full and swollen as with the respiration of delight . . .'[23] Shelley's sensual nature – Miss Curran had a hard job turning that soft and full-lipped mouth into a girlish bow when Mary asked for his portrait to be sent to her – was almost obliterated by the posthumous endeavours of a Victorian age. Here, we have a useful reminder of its existence. A man who could write with such relish of a woman's look of sexual pleasure was unlikely to be satisfied by taking second place to a baby and a reading desk.

Mary, after the birth of Percy, engrossed herself in his care and in study. Mrs Gisborne was begged to find books which would help her prepare the background for the historical novel she planned to write. She studied Greek. She fretted over her father's situation. Politically,

she remained close to Shelley, applauding the fiery poems he wrote
that autumn, following the news of revolutions in Naples and in Spain
with eager interest and sending Mrs Hunt a spirited diatribe against
Castlereagh which included the satirical proclamation: '"I believe in
all plots Cant feigns & creates & will use none but the language of
Cant unto my last day – amen!"'[24] Sexually, Mary withdrew.
Forgetting how recently she had told the Hunts that she longed for a
brood of children and envied theirs, she sternly reminded Marianne
that 'a woman is not a field to be continually employed either in
bringing forth or enlarging grain'.[25]

Her coldness made itself felt. Claire, one bleak February day, pointedly noted that a Greek author had written: 'A bad wife is like Winter
in a house.'[26] Shelley, as the Gisbornes began making plans for a long
visit to England, begged Maria to stay behind and keep Mary
company. Nine months after William's death, he confided, she
remained in a state of mind 'which if not cut off, cannot but conduct
to some fatal end'. He felt that he had lost all power to influence her.
She 'considers me a portion of herself', he told Mrs Gisborne in the
same unhappy letter, written in March 1820: she 'feels no more
remorse in torturing me than in torturing her own mind – Could she
know a person in every way my equal, and hold close and perpetual
communion with him, as a distinct being from herself; as a friend
instead of a husband, she would obtain empire over herself.'[27]

Mary did not want to exchange Shelley for a platonic companion,
as he was here suggesting; she wanted him to get rid of Claire.
Ironically, while Shelley begged Mrs Gisborne to stay and solace
Mary, Mary herself was begging Maria to stay as a buttress against her
stepsister. Tension had been there for some time, but it reached a crisis
early in 1820. Perhaps Claire tactlessly compared her own loss of
Allegra, about whose life they had heard nothing since the spring of
1819, to the death of Mary's children. Perhaps Shelley urged his wife
to show some of Claire's vigour and cheerfulness. It is more likely that
many minor irritations combined to make Claire's presence unendur-
able. Mary, reasonably enough, wanted her husband and child to
herself. Failing that, she wanted to ease the tension.

The person who did most to reduce it was Mrs Mason, their new
friend at Pisa. They had stayed in touch with her throughout the
autumn. Writing shortly before Percy's birth to thank Mary for a gift
of *Frankenstein*, Mrs Mason sent back her compliments and added
friendly messages from Laurette, the elder of her two small daughters
by George Tighe: 'she is delighted with you all & wanted to know
whether "that lady had yet made her child".'[28]

A highly competent mother with a vocational interest in the rearing of children, Margaret Mason was never afraid to offer advice. Mary's letters revealed her depression; she was warned that melancholy was not good for a nursing mother.[29] Shelley was told off for putting his faith in English doctors when he had one of the best in Europe, Andrea Vaccà Berlinghieri, on his doorstep at Pisa. Mrs Mason said that Vaccà prescribed the mild climate of his own town as the best cure for the ill health which continued to plague him. (Mary blamed its return on the sixty-hour vigil Shelley had kept by William's bedside in Rome the previous summer.) On 27 January 1820, the Shelleys and Claire moved dutifully down the Arno to Pisa. Milly Shields, the young nurse from Marlow, had already left and been replaced by a new Swiss nanny. Mrs Mason now briskly advised Mary to find an Italian girl instead.

Over the next two years, Shelley and Mary and, intermittently, Claire lived in a variety of handsome residences in Pisa. Starting on the north bank of the Lung'Arno, at the Tre Donzelle inn (it stood near to what is now the endearingly old-fashioned Victoria Hotel) then taking rooms on the mezzanine floor of Casa Frassi, they looked between the facing houses into almost uninhabited countryside, where a few Pisan streets trailed away into the flat green fields towards Livorno. Later, living on the south bank, they enjoyed a view across Pisa's red roofs to the cathedral's plump dome and the tower's rakish slant. Beyond them, a long lapping line of blue hills hid Carrara's marble quarries from view.

Their quarters were clean; the town seemed drab. Writing to Maria Gisborne in late February to ask about an 'upper servant' who might be prepared to iron and help their nurse to care for Percy, Mary begged for a visit in 'this most ugly town'. She was in bad spirits. Shelley was unwell, 'and we are all uncomfortable as usual'. Marianne Hunt received a scathing report on the ladies of the town, who dressed in dirty cotton gowns and soiled white satin shoes, their faces hidden by huge poke bonnets of pink silk with bows perched on the points of their chins. The men were 'fellows with bushy hair – large whiskers, canes in their hands, & a bit of dirty party coloured riband (a symbol of nobility) sticking in their buttonholes that mean to look like the lords of the rabble but who only look like their drivers – The Pisans,' Mary concluded with a sniff, 'I dislike more than any of the Italians & none of them are as yet favourites with me.' Dr Vaccà, 'a great republican & no Xtian', was, however, allowed to be 'very pleasant'.[30]

Their first rooms, until they were able to move up to the top floor of Casa Frassi, were uncomfortably crowded at a time when feelings between Mary and Claire were running high. Casa Silva, Mrs Mason's home on the Via Malagonnella, standing on the far southern side of the town, offered a welcome refuge. Both Mary and Claire became devoted to ten-year-old Laura (Laurette) and her five-year-old sister Nerina. Claire took the little girls out to the carnival masquerades; Mary surely had them in mind when she wrote two mythological dramas, 'Proserpine' and 'Midas'. The first, written in the late spring of 1820, shows her still dejected, brooding over the role of a 'child of light' who is condemned to live in darkness and who seems to mock Shelley's 1817 tribute to a 'child of love and light'. But 'Midas' is playful and even comic; it is nice to think of Mary helping the children rehearse it in the large, well-kept orchard behind their parents' home.

Mrs Mason welcomed new company. Her partnership with George Tighe, while courteous and respectful, had lost its fire; Mr Tighe, a reclusive man, spent much of his time out in the orchard experimenting with ways to improve a potato crop, earning himself the nickname 'Tatty'. Talking to her young visitors, Mrs Mason gave them her views on Irish politics, impressed them with accounts of having dressed as a man to get into medical lectures at an Italian university, and passed on a riveting account of England's about-to-be crowned Queen Caroline who, visiting Pisa during her six years in Europe, had been seen wearing a man's boots and even a man's top hat.

Mary's spirits rose a little as she gained some space with their move to the larger top floor of the Casa Frassi in March 1820. Claire began writing a travel book. Her journal never mentioned Mary. Instead, she noted a 'horrid' dream about Skinner Street and Godwin having one of his narcoleptic fits. Mary, with uncharacteristic rashness, wrote and begged her father to give up 'that load of evils', the bookselling business.[31] Godwin indignantly declined to do any such thing: 'I consider the day on which I entered this business as one of the fortunate days of my life,' he wrote back.[32]

The Gisbornes were off to England for the summer of 1820, partly out of concern for their investments there. Shortly before they left, Shelley visited them in Livorno and disclosed part or all of the story of Elena Adelaide, for whose care he urgently needed to transmit funds to Naples. Planning to keep Mary in the dark, Shelley asked the Gisbornes to correspond with him on this delicate subject under a false name. It cannot, however, have escaped Mary's attention that Shelley returned from Livorno looking grim; perhaps the Gisbornes had been unwilling to condone his behaviour or to help. His health, always a useful barometer of Shelley's mood, immediately declined.

So, with as much reason, did Claire's when, after a long and baffling silence, a letter arrived from Mrs Hoppner. It concerned Allegra, whom Claire had been hoping to visit at Ravenna, where the little girl was now living with Byron and his new love, Teresa Guiccioli.

Mrs Hoppner's letter was not nice. In it, with apparent noncha-lance, she passed on the fact that Byron was unwilling to let Allegra anywhere near the Shelleys. The reasons he gave were that the child would be underfed and without religious training.[33] But it was not Byron who provoked Mary's anger. The Hoppners, she told Maria Gisborne in England on 8 May, 'have behaved shamefully'.[34] Claire, meanwhile, sent a pleading letter to Byron, defending Shelley's char-acter and professing her own religious faith. Three days later, she drafted a second letter in which, intriguingly, she begged Byron not to listen to the gossip of a servant 'whom we corrected for his roguery & whom we wd not expose out of delicacy for you'.[35] She cancelled the passage and the letter was not sent; it does, however, raise the intriguing possibility that Byron might also have been at risk from Paolo Foggi's tales. The servant can only have been Paolo; what was this situation which they would not expose out of consideration for Byron?

The Hoppners' 'shameful' behaviour remains puzzling. Mary may have been referring to a proposal they had put to Claire in April 1819, that Allegra should be adopted by a rich childless widow, a Mrs Vavassour; Claire had turned the decision over to Byron, while reminding him that nobody could be more eager to care for Allegra than herself.[36] It is equally possible that Mary's indignation arose from the fact that the Hoppners had already started spreading rumours about the Naples baby. Elise was in Venice in 1820; her slanders could have begun at any point during this year.

Certainly, by mid-May, there was trouble afoot. Paolo Foggi had turned up. A letter from Mary to Mrs Gisborne, written on 18 June, told her that they had been forced to go to lawyers in Livorno because of 'an infamous conspiracy against us' and that Paolo had played a part in it. 'That same Paolo is a most superlative rascal,' she added: 'I hope we have done with him.' No evidence has been found of the nature of the conspiracy, but it seems likely that it related to Elena Adelaide. Foggi may not have known everything, but he knew enough to cause trouble and to ask for money; after his abrupt eviction from Livorno, Shelley, Mary and Claire took refuge from gossip in the absent Gisbornes' villa, Casa Ricci, on the outskirts of the town. 'Nay here we are we have taken possession' – Mary informed their friends with a touch of embarrassment at having moved into their home without invitation or warning. 'What do you say?'[37]

Two weeks later, Mrs Gisborne heard from Shelley that his mysterious little charge would be coming to live with them as soon as she recovered from a mild fever. Fortunately, perhaps, Mary was never put to this final test of her loyalty. The baby died in Naples on 10 June.

'Babe unwell – We are unhappy & discontented,' Mary noted a week later, on 17 June. She laid the blame for Percy's illness on her own milk, affected by the troubles Paolo had brought to their door. Shelley, enraged by yet another demand for money from his father-in-law, preferred to blame Godwin. On 7 August, he told Godwin that he had received Mary's permission to intercept any letters which might contain upsetting news. The tone is slightly uncomfortable; how freely, one wonders, had Mary given away the right to read her own mail? Had Shelley simply made a decision and decided to act upon it, without asking his wife? He was capable of such high-handed behaviour and Mary later expressed concern and puzzlement at the paucity of letters from her father.

The situation with Paolo Foggi, worries over Allegra and the continuing anxiety about her father all played their part in disturbing her. But the prime cause was in the house.

Among a series of terse entries in her journal, Mary had noted 8 June to be 'A better day than most days' for the reason that Claire went off on a trip. On 25 June, she wrote that she had been 'too much oppressed & too languid to do anything'. Her letters recorded savage squabbles among the servants in unusual, almost obsessive detail as she watched their quarrels reflect her own. 'Heigh ho the Clare & the Ma[ie] / Find something to fight about every day,' noted Claire on 4 July. Shelley, writing to Mrs Gisborne on 20 July as they prepared to move to a new summer house, enlisted her sympathy for Claire ('Poor thing! She is an excellent girl . . .'), while regretting that Mary had not the wisdom of a woman of forty-five, or even of her husband 'as misfortune has made me. She would then live on very good terms with Clare.'[38] Still unable to accept that it was high time for Claire to leave, he tried to sweeten Mary's mood and encourage her into good spirits: 'What Mary is when she a little smiles / I cannot even tell or call to mind, / It is a miracle so new, so rare,' he wrote in a graceful adaptation from Dante's *Vita Nuova*.

Mrs Mason had formed her own view of this uneasy triangle when the Shelleys were living in Pisa. Drawn to Claire, for whom she became the kind of mother-figure that Mrs Gisborne had already made herself to Mary, she found her own solution to their problem. In July, Claire was invited to visit Casa Silva by herself for a few days. She went there again on 21 August and, on Vaccà's advice, was lodged at Livorno to see if bathing would benefit a swollen thyroid gland which he had diagnosed as tubercular – and which she had airily dismissed, announcing that if she was scrofulous (tubercular), then he was ridiculous. Mrs Mason took advantage of Claire's absence to make arrangements for her to live as a paying guest in the Florentine home of Dr Antonio Boiti, physician to the amiable and enlightened Grand-Duke Ferdinand III of Lorena. Through Boiti and his German wife, Claire could acquire a new language while teaching English to their children; with German and French, she could become a governess and start a new life, independent of Shelley and her stepsister.

Neither Claire nor Shelley were happy about this arrangement, but the need for a change was recognized. By the end of the summer, Mary could dare to hope that she was free of her stepsister. After five years of a shared life, it was an agreeable prospect.

IN ABSENTIA CLARIAE

1820

Rain till one o'clock – at sunset the arch of cloud over the west clears away – a few black islands float in the serene – the moon rises – the clouds spot the sky – but the depth of heaven is clear – The nights are uncommonly warm

'My thoughts arise & fade in solitude
The verse that wd invest them melts away
Like moonlight in the heaven of spreading day
How beautiful they were – how firm they stood
Frekling the starry sky like woven pearl!'

Write – S reads Hyperion aloud – Greek[1]

Mary Shelley, Journal, 18 October 1820

A MILD CLIMATE, A CALM LIFE AND NO MEDICINE HAD BEEN ANDREA Vaccà's sensible prescription for Shelley's mysterious illness; with this advice in mind, Shelley, Mary and – until her departure for Livorno and Florence – Claire, moved at the beginning of August 1820 to a village four miles east of Pisa. Their house was most 'agreable', Mary reported to Amelia Curran on 17 August, '& with delightful scenery within a walk'. Percy was thriving, 'a great comfort', and the gentle climate was doing wonders for Shelley's health, 'which is to him a rare & substantial enjoyment'.

Small and sweetly sleepy, Bagni di San Giuliano lay beside an artificial canal linking the Serchio to the Arno. Above it, reared the mountain wall separating Pisa from its ancient enemies in the many-towered and stoutly barricaded city of Lucca. The Shelleys' new home, Casa Prini, stood in a broad crescent looking towards the spa casino and up to the steep wooded slopes of Monte di San Giuliano. Behind the house, a narrow garden led down to the canal on which, as soon as he had found a boat for sale, Shelley often rowed into the centre of Pisa or towards the neighbouring village of Pugnano. Less fashionable than Bagni di Lucca, San Giuliano had kept its village atmosphere; on one occasion when Mrs Mason was visiting them, Shelley's attempt to read out his latest poem, 'Ode to Liberty', was drowned by the snuffles and honks of a herd of pigs being sold under their windows.

Sitting in the garden at night under a sky thick with stars, they listened to prettier sounds, the soft whooping of owls, the leisurely slap of water as a boat slid past in the shadows. In the mornings, before the heat began to build, they walked along the canal's rough banks or up the winding mountain paths to peer into the mysterious little caves and grottoes in which, the superstitious locals said, fairies and witches lived.

Claire's long-awaited departure was the chief source of Mary's new contentment. On 17 August, she had confessed to Miss Curran that her stepsister's departure still seemed 'impossible'. On 31 August, however, Claire was dispatched to Livorno for a month, staying at the Gisbornes' empty house; her return on 1 October was sourly marked in Mary's journal with a drawing of the sun, a sign which reappeared on 20 October as Shelley escorted a sullen Claire to her new home in Florence with the Boiti family.*

Soothed by her new surroundings, Mary took time off from studying Greek to write a children's story for Laurette Mason. The fair copy, intended for publication, has not survived, but Laurette was made a present of the original manuscript. Affection or forgetfulness preserved it in her family papers, from which *Maurice, or The Fisher's Cot* was recovered and published for the first time in 1998.[2]

To a little girl who could scarcely remember England (Laurette was only five when her parents moved to Italy), Mary's simple story of a fishing village in the West Country was as full of wonder as a fairy tale; to modern readers, its interest lies in the element of the story which describes the loss to loving parents of a child. Mary cannot have intended her young reader to brood on the harsh laws which

---

* There is no known reason for Mary to have chosen to represent Claire by the sun, since sunshine was the very opposite of the emotional weather that prevailed when the two women shared a house. It may have been intended ironically, or to contrast with Shelley's fondness in his poetry for representing Mary by the moon.

separated Laurette's mother from the children of her marriage to Lord
Mountcashell; it is more likely that she was thinking of her own losses,
and of those close to her; of the three children they had buried, the
son and daughter Shelley had been forced to renounce, the little girl
who was now living at Ravenna with Byron and his young mistress.
Relieved though Mary had been to see Allegra go, she shared Claire's
concern for her life with a father who appeared to treat the child, at
best, as casually as the tribe of animals he took with him on his travels.

It was distressing and frustrating for Mary to see how, despite some
kindly attentions from the reviewers for *Blackwood's Magazine*, literary acknowledgment continued to elude Shelley, much of whose
poetry remained unpublished. Only bad luck, she felt, had kept *The
Cenci* from being accepted for performance in London; to her, the
play had marked a step towards the more popular work which would
bring him a wider audience. 'It was not only that I wished him to
acquire popularity as redounding to his fame,' she explained in 1839;
'but I believed that he would obtain a greater mastery of his own
powers, and greater happiness in his own mind, if public applause
crowned his endeavours.'[3] It was a reasonable assumption; most
writers thrive on having their work published. Mary was, however,
mistaken in thinking that she had any control over Shelley's creativ-
ity. When, back from a stiff day's climb up to the dizzy peak of Monte
San Pellegrino on 12 August, Shelley promptly responded with one
of his most fanciful and unearthly poems, she was dismayed. And she
said so.

Richard Holmes has suggested that it was Shelley's introduction of
the witch's beautiful bisexual angel child, Hermaphroditus, which
Mary found so discomforting. Mary was no prude; she was probably
telling the simple truth when she wrote, in 1839, that she had been
afraid of Shelley's 'discarding human interest and passion, to revel in
the fantastic ideas that his imagination suggested'. Beautiful though
the images were, Mary could not imagine them suiting 'the popular
taste': 'Even now,' she defiantly added, 'I believe that I was in the
right.'[4]

Criticizing poets is a dangerous business. Having told Shelley what
she thought, Mary was punished for her candour. The six tart stanzas
which preface *The Witch of Atlas* accuse her of being 'critic-bitten'
and for being ready to dismiss a poem just because its verses 'tell no
story, false or true!' Shelley's tone was playful; his message was as
pointed as a knife. Here was a complete and cutting reversal of the
tender homage he had offered in happier times, at the opening of *The
Revolt of Islam*.

To thy fair feet a winged Vision came,
  Whose date should have been longer than a day,
And o'er thy head did beat its wings for fame,
  And in thy sight its fading plumes display;
The watery bow burned in the evening flame,
  But the shower fell, the swift Sun went his way –
And that is dead. – O let me not believe
That anything of mine is fit to live![5]

The punishment for her presumption was taken a step further as Mary was requested to copy out the poem – and the introductory verses – for her husband on 14 August. 'Do,' she wrote tersely two days later: 'Finished.' The hurt was still apparent in 1824 when, publishing the poem for the first time, she omitted the six stanzas aimed at her. She did, however, print them in the 1839 edition of Shelley's works.

Mary was perplexed and a little hurt to learn, and at secondhand, that the Gisbornes had returned from England in early September without getting in touch. September came and went without any contact. Were they angry with the Shelleys for having borrowed the Casa Ricci without permission earlier in the summer? Had some new morsel of scandal reached them? Mary had often in the past scolded Maria affectionately for being a lazy correspondent, but this silence was too long. Taking matters into her own hands, on 16 October she made a surprise day trip to see them at Livorno. Mrs Gisborne seemed discomforted by her sudden appearance at Casa Ricci. She was not welcoming; all she would say was that she had sent a 'foolish' letter to San Giuliano which Mary would find when she reached home.

The distress which this letter caused suggests that it contained details relating to the Gisbornes' summer in London, where they had been staying with Mr Gisborne's sister Emma and her husband, the musician and composer Muzio Clementi. Mary had begged her friend to keep a daily journal of her visit, especially since she knew that the Gisbornes would be calling at Skinner Street. Maria kept the journal as requested but it was, by the end of her visit, embarrassingly clear that she would never be able to show it to Mary; the content was far too damaging. Now published, the journal makes it plain why the Gisbornes had been keeping Shelley and Mary at a distance since their return from England.

On 4 July, a month after the Gisbornes' first call at Skinner Street, Godwin had described Shelley to them as immoral, and 'a lover of falsehood'. Five days later, he told them that Fanny, Claire and Mary had been equally in love with Shelley; he was even ready to say that

Fanny had 'put an end to her existence owing to the preference given to her youngest sister'. Mrs Godwin, he added, blamed Mary entirely for the loss of Claire and looked on his daughter as 'the greatest enemy she [Mrs Godwin] has in the world'. On 3 August, the shocked Gisbornes were visited by their old friend, John Fenwick, Eliza's spendthrift husband. Fenwick had been given the awkward job of explaining that Mrs Godwin had issued an ultimatum; they could either stop praising Mary or stop seeing her stepmother. No paragon himself, Mr Fenwick also provided them with 'a very bad character' of Shelley. At their final meeting on 28 August, the Gisbornes were treated by Godwin to an extensive account of his financial dealings with Shelley; in case they missed the point, they were presented with a written list of the sums Godwin still believed himself to be owed. The Gisbornes did, however, manage to remove one of the old man's convictions: 'In the first conversation I had with Mr G[odwin] – about C[laire],' Mrs Gisborne wrote, 'he was still incredulous as to the real author of her misfortune.'[6] Much of Godwin's unappeasable scorn for Shelley derived from the belief that he was Allegra's father and that Mary had been expected to raise the child as her own; here, at least, Mrs Gisborne was able to soften his view.

The 'foolish' letter, which Shelley had already opened and scanned, was waiting for Mary when she reached Casa Prini late that evening. It filled her with indignation. Perhaps, knowing Mary's devotion to her father, Mrs Gisborne had preferred to suggest that Mary Jane was their source of information. Certainly, Mary now became convinced that her stepmother had wrecked one of her most treasured friendships. On 17 October, the day after visiting Casa Ricci, she wrote a stern letter, offering her friends the choice between coming to Casa Prini or being regarded as one of the enemy, united to 'that filthy woman', Mary Jane Godwin. 'Now is the time! join them, or us – the gulph is deep, the plank is going to be removed – set your foot on it if you will – and you will not lose the sincere affection of one who loved you tenderly.'

The challenge was not accepted; the Gisbornes kept their distance until the following spring. Maria's son Henry did not improve matters when he turned up to request the four hundred crowns needed to complete work on his steamboat. Shelley, who already suspected the Gisbornes of having gone cold on a scheme in which he had made heavy investments, refused. Writing to Claire on 29 October, Shelley described their former friends as 'the most filthy and odious animals with which I ever came in contact'. But Shelley's violent expressions should not be taken too seriously; he wrote to John Gisborne on the same day to ask, most affably, for advice on obtaining Arabic grammar-books.

One reason for Mary's eagerness to resume her friendship with the Gisbornes was never mentioned in her journals. The Gisbornes, during the Shelleys' unhappy summer at the Villa Valsovano, had offered them a welcome escape from each other with their easy, undemanding company. By the autumn of 1820, Mary was longing for her dear Maria, a motherly confidante with whom to share her feelings about Claire, to boast of little Percy's progress and, perhaps, to talk about her life with Shelley.

Their marriage, as Shelley's sharp prefatory verses to *The Witch of Atlas* suggest, was less loving than it had once been. Passion had waned, leaving behind a flavour of discontent. Mary felt that Shelley had put the deaths of their lost children behind him and that he resented the anxious care she lavished on their remaining child. She understood but regretted his decision to shut her father out of their lives and to deny his requests. He said it was for her own good; Godwin's letters invariably plunged her into despair. Shelley was right, she accepted that; it did not lessen her own sense of obligation and guilt.

If such feelings held them apart, the Shelleys remained staunch political allies. They had cause to celebrate as, eagerly following the news, they read of a sudden outbreak of revolutions across Europe, promising the downfall of kings and a welcome return of the republican ideals they cherished. An uprising in Spain had led to the declaration of a new constitution in March 1820; Naples had followed suit with a revolt led by a priest and a carbonari faction who promised a radical redistribution of land to the people. There was news of riots in Palermo and of another uprising to the north, in Piedmont. Mary, as she began to write *Valperga*, a story of the corrupting effects of power, was acutely conscious of the contemporary political situation and the parallels she could suggest. Still haunted by the thought of her father's imminent ruin and aware only of her stepmother's role in spreading vicious gossip to the Gisbornes, she planned to let Godwin sell the book for his own profit. If Shelley would not help him, she proudly decided, then she would do so herself. Shelley, still smarting at Mary's criticism of one of his most imaginative works, told Peacock in November that his wife was raking her new story out of fifty old books. He conceded, however, that the result would be 'wholly original'.[7]

The idea for *Valperga* was, so Mary remembered, born in 1817 at

Marlow; their summer at Bagni di Lucca in 1818 had led her to consider the medieval ruler of Lucca, Castruccio Castracani, as a possible central figure, the Napoleon of the fourteenth century. At Naples in January 1819, she had read more deeply about Castruccio's life in Sismondi's massive history of Italy and had been fired by the Swiss historian's enthusiasm for the democratically minded Guelph states of Tuscany and the idea of local, communal rule. 'This way of conducting oneself, to live in common, to make a part of one great whole, raises up human beings and makes them capable of the greatest things,' Sismondi had written.[8] This was a view which Mary shared and which she would use to contrast with Castruccio's thirst for acquisition and his faith in the power of the individual.

Mary had been unimpressed by Machiavelli's short and imaginative presentation of Castruccio as an ideal prince, a witty and ruthless tyrant not far removed in character from another Machiavelli hero, Cesare Borgia. Her Castruccio has none of the Machiavellian wit. But, unlike Machiavelli, Mary was not writing to celebrate a hero. Her story would be dominated by two powerful and very different women. The first, the bizarrely named Countess Euthanasia, is Castruccio's fictitious first love, the woman who shuns his proposal of marriage and seeks to defend the Guelph republics from the tyrant's acquisitive grasp. Euthanasia, perceived by Claire Clairmont as a portrait of Shelley, is an imaginative embodiment of the Shelleys' political ideals. Intelligent, pious and fearless, she owes much of her nature to the eleventh-century Grand Countess Matilde di Canossa, a woman who combined scholarship and beauty with uncommon courage. The fact that Matilde was the daughter of Princess Beatrice strengthens the likelihood that Mary had her in mind, since Beatrice was the name she chose for the second most important female character in the novel, Beatrice of Ferrara. A sixteen-year-old prophetess and heretic, Beatrice falls passionately in love with Castruccio and offers herself to him shortly after they meet. She pays for her boldness with a life of penitence and woe; perhaps Mary, who gave herself to Shelley when she was sixteen, was allowing Beatrice to play out her own feelings of anguished self-blame and regret.

By the time they moved to Casa Prini, Mary had found the background to her story; she had not yet decided on its precise location. On 12 August, while Shelley left San Giuliano to climb Monte San Pellegrino, Mary and Claire went off together on a cheerful and unusually sisterly expedition to Lucca. Claire copied out the inscriptions over Castruccio's tomb in the church of San Francesco; Mary energetically climbed the tower above the Palazzo Guinigi. It is, she told Leigh Hunt three years later: 'an old tower as ancient as those times – look towards the opening of the hills, on the road to the Baths of Lucca, & on the banks of the Serchio & you will see the site of Valperga . . .'[9] What Mary had actually seen was the bulk of the disused Convento del Angelo. This was the site she chose for the home of Castruccio's first love.

Originally named 'Castruccio, Prince of Lucca', Mary's novel only became *Valperga* in 1823, when William Godwin had the manuscript in his hands and was looking for a simple but striking title. It remains a puzzle why Mary should have given this name to Euthanasia's home. There is a Valperga in Italy, but it is in Piedmont, a long way north of Lucca. It is not even clear that Mary knew of its existence.* The most likely explanation is that she intended to make a connection to Walpurga, the missionary saint who travelled from England to Germany and whose body believed to exude a sacred fluid, a protection against the black arts which later became associated with Walpurgis Night. Mary had become fascinated by superstitious customs during her months at San Giuliano, taking careful note of local beliefs and visiting a mountain grotto said to be haunted by spirits. Witchcraft, in her novel, is the final undoing of poor Beatrice, whose attempts to regain Castruccio's love lead her to seek the help of Fior di Mandragola, a forest witch. Euthanasia, as Valperga's flawless custodian, is immune to the witch's powers; Beatrice dies, lovingly tended by Euthanasia, of the drugs with which Fior di Mandragola briefly bewitched her eyes.

Euthanasia's own death was, in Mary's view, one of the finest scenes in the novel. Imprisoning the Countess after her rash decision to join a plot to overthrow him, Castruccio realizes that he cannot stain his hands with the death of this saintly woman. Instead, he decides to send her into exile. Her death at sea, en route to banishment in Sicily, is related not as a tragedy but as the welcome release from life which her name implies. Too sceptical to canonize her, Mary succeeded, nevertheless, in creating a triumphantly appropriate ending for her secular saint.

---

* It is possible that Mary had heard or read something about the twelfth-century counts of Valperga, whose castle was at Mazze on the Lago di Candia in Piedmont. From 1100 onwards, the families of Valperga and San Martino were engaged in bitter dispute over the strategically valuable town of Pont, on which they both had claims. Valperga, in Mary's novel, is of strategic value to the tyrant lord of Lucca; when Euthanasia refuses to marry Castruccio, he becomes obsessed with gaining the fortress of Valperga from her.

Earth felt no change when she died; and men forgot her. Yet a lovelier spirit never ceased to breathe, nor was a lovelier form ever
destroyed amidst the many it brings forth. Endless tears might well
have been shed at her loss; yet for her none wept, save the piteous skies,
which deplored the mischief they had themselves committed: – none
moaned except the sea-birds that flapped their heavy wings above the
ocean-cave wherein she lay; – and the muttering thunder alone tolled
her passing bell, as she quitted a life, which for her had been replete
with change and sorrow.[10]

It is, as always with Mary Shelley's fiction, difficult not to read her
own continuing melancholy into her haunting meditations on the
transience of life. Into her elegy for Euthanasia, she put as much of
her present self as she had given of her past to the reckless, passionate
young Beatrice who offers her body to Castruccio and rejects the
existence of God.

Sending a brief letter to Godwin in August, Shelley had reported that
Mary now seemed wholly absorbed in caring for little Percy. The tart-
ness of the comment suggests resentment; Shelley found it hard to
understand how nervously Mary watched over their one remaining
child.

But Percy thrived and, with a novel in progress and Claire restricted
to paying occasional visits, Mary grew happier. Shelley was distant,
except when reading to her from a newly arrived volume of John
Keats's poems, or when they talked about political matters; the landscape was beautiful enough to offer consolation. Her journal entries,
always terse in periods of unease or unhappiness, began to expand.
Sitting out in the garden in October with her pen for a paintbrush,
she carefully recorded the slow gathering of evening clouds in the distance while Venus glittered above San Giuliano, 'and the trunks of the
trees are tinged with the silvery light of the rising moon'.[11]

A lyrical account of medieval farm life in the first chapters of
Valperga shows how closely Mary drew on her own surroundings. The
setting here is said to be Este; everything about it suggests the tranquil landscape around Pisa.

The hedges were of myrtle, whose aromatic perfume weighed upon
the sluggish air of noon, as the labourers reposed, sleeping under the
trees, lulled by the rippling of the brooks that watered their grounds.
In the evening they ate their meal under the open sky; the birds were

asleep, but the ground was alive with innumerable glow-worms, and the air with the lightning-like fire-flies, small, humming crickets, and heavy beetles; the west had quickly lost its splendour, but in the fading beams of sunset sailed the boat-like moon, while Venus, as another satellite to earth, beamed just above the crescent hardly brighter than itself, and the outline of the rugged Apennines was marked darkly below.[12]

Mary, peaceful, busy, doting on her pretty child, flourished in Claire's absence. Shelley, however, pined for her return. Claire's impetuousness, her warmth and her relish for adventure had become necessary to him; he did not see why he should have been obliged to exile her from his home. Late in October, news reached him that a rich acquaintance of his cousin Thomas Medwin was looking for companions to travel to the Middle East the following spring. Shelley's first thoughts were not of his wife but of Claire, pining at Dr Boiti's home in Florence. Claire, he knew, would jump at the chance of such a trip. 'This man has conceived a great admiration for my verses,' he wrote to tell her, 'and wishes above all things that I could be induced to join his expedition.'

> How far all this is practicable, considering the state of my finances I know not yet. I know that if it were it would give me the greatest pleasure, and the pleasure might be either doubled or divided by your presence or absence.
> All this will be explained and determined in time; meanwhile lay to your heart what I say, and do not mention it in your letter to Mary.[13]

Claire's reply has not survived; we will never know whether she was prepared to accept an invitation which offered her the chance to replace her stepsister as Shelley's companion. Perhaps she had lived with him long enough to treat such suggestions with scepticism; perhaps, as much as Mary, she understood that fantasy and reality walked side by side, often indistinguishably, in his mind. What Shelley wrote, in his correspondence as much as in his poetry, could never be relied on as evidence of his serious intentions or desires. Nevertheless, it was Claire, not Mary, who heard about the plan to travel abroad. It is possible and even probable that Shelley, in the autumn of 1820, was contemplating leaving his wife and child for his sister-in-law.

On 22 October a new and, from Mary's point of view, most unwelcome guest arrived at the Casa Prini. A portrait of Thomas Medwin, painted when he was about forty, shows the long face of a slightly dodgy vicar, not a vocation to which Shelley's second cousin ever felt the call. Four years older than Shelley, Medwin remembered him as a miserable little schoolboy at the Syon House Academy, as a budding writer of romantic novels and a sulky attendant at local dances in Sussex. They had lost touch when Medwin, bored with studying law in his father's offices at Horsham, went off to join the 24th Light Dragoons in Hindustan. A retired half-pay lieutenant who spent his spare hours hunting lions and tigers in the style of the day, Medwin preferred to use his nominal title of Captain; it sounded better and Medwin, a diligent courter of rich ladies and high society, had a care for such niceties.

Medwin was not a particularly attractive character, but he was not a fool. With Shelley's help and tactful editing, he published a collection of poems and essays about his experiences in India. He was already fluent in Spanish when he arrived at Bagni di San Giuliano; he was keen to work at Arabic with Shelley. He knew Latin well enough to translate Catullus in later life. He had a good memory and a lively imagination. He deserves some credit for renewing his friendship with his cousin at a time when Shelley's work was little-known and undervalued and when his connection with Byron, the most celebrated poet of the age, had become remote. Medwin's respect for Shelley's genius was heartfelt and this, coming from a cousin who had poetic ambitions of his own, was generous.

Mary couldn't stand him. 'He sits with us,' she wrote in a fury to Claire,

> & be one reading or writing he insists upon interrupting one every moment to read all the fine things he either writes or reads . . . He intends he says to translate all the fine passages of Dante . . . when he cannot make sense of the words that are [there] he puts in words of his own and calls it a misprint . . . S[helley] does nothing but conjugate the verb seccare & twist & turn Seccatura in all possible ways. He is Common Place personified.[14]

A *seccatore*, the word which even kind-hearted Shelley came to agree that his cousin deserved, was the name given to the Italian equivalent of the club bore. Lady Morgan, in her book on Italy, blamed the *seccatore*'s existence on the Italian habit of refusing to talk about serious subjects: 'men, thrown upon trifles, become tedious in their discussions.'[15] So it was with poor Medwin as – one can't help imagining – lifting a hand to stroke his military moustache, he invited the Shelleys to hear another reading from his Indian journal or a passage from his Dante translation. Mary was, however, impressed by his attempt to cure Shelley's illness with hypnotic skills learned in India. According to Medwin, she became skilled enough herself as a trance-inducer to cause Shelley to try and leave their bedroom by the window, 'fortunately barred'. Alarmed by her success, Mary made no further experiments.[16]

On 25 October, three days after Medwin's arrival at Casa Prini, the Serchio broke its banks. The narrow canal, lying at a level higher than the houses of San Giuliano, flooded down the back gardens of the little crescent and into the square in front, surrounding the buildings and finally bursting through the doors. Mary, calmly aware that neither the house nor its furniture were her concern, was entranced by a scene which could have been painted by her beloved Salvator Rosa.

> It was a picturesque sight at night to see the peasants driving the cattle from the plains below to the hills above the Baths. A fire was kept up to guide them across the ford; and the forms of the men and the animals showed in dark relief against the red glare of the flame, which was reflected again in the waters that filled the Square.[17]

Medwin had a delightful memory of them all scrambling into a boat from the upper windows of Casa Prini the following day. Mary's journal shows this to have been one of his many little fictions. The weather brightened, the flood receded; four days later, they went by carriage to Pisa and into new lodgings.

Casa Galletti, on the north bank of the Lung'Arno, stood next to the gloomily splendid marble palace of the Lanfreducci family; the builder, a former prisoner in the Crusades, had chosen to have a chain and the words 'Alla Giornata' carved over his door to remind himself of the value of hope. Shelley, conscious of a fretful and discontented Claire at Florence, sent off another of his treacherous notes. Mary, the baby and the Italian maids were ensconced on the lower floor, he told her; he and Medwin had managed to obtain rooms above: 'congratulate me on my seclusion'.[18] A revealing aside in his letter apologized for the fact that the last had been so dull; 'as it was taxed with a postscript by Mary, it contained nothing that I wished it to contain.' 'Taxed' is not an affectionate word; it underlines the growing coldness of Shelley's feelings towards his wife.

'☀ complaining of dullness,' Mary anxiously noted on 4 November. She was probably unaware of Shelley's plot to go adventuring in the East with her stepsister, a scheme which collapsed only because Medwin's rich friend failed to stay in touch; all Mary knew was that if Claire grew bored, Shelley would want to bring her back to join them. Still, in Pisa, Claire could always be dispatched to the house of Mrs Mason, who appeared to dote on her. A few days later, Mary learned that Claire would, indeed, be joining them for the four weeks leading up to Christmas. She did not record her thoughts.

CHAPTER EIGHTEEN

LIFE ON THE LUNG'ARNO

1821

'Mr Shelley is at present on a visit to Lord Byron at Ravenna and I received a
letter from him today containing accounts that make my hand tremble so much
that I can hardly hold the pen.'

Mary Shelley to Isabelle Hoppner, 10 August 1821

'ARE WE NOT WANDERERS ON THE FACE OF THE EARTH — HAVE PITY
on us,' Mary entreated the Hunts on 3 December 1820. Her tone to
the Hunts, her most regular correspondents, was often self-mocking;
far from feeling like a wanderer, she was hard at work on her novel
and, at the end of a month in Pisa, was beginning to feel that it was
not, after all, such a disagreeable town in which to live.

Pisa, with the exception of a second summer break at Bagni di San
Giuliano, became the Shelleys' headquarters until they left to live on
a windswept shore in the spring of 1822. It was, despite their initial
reservations, a city in which they soon felt at home. Magnificent lodgings could be obtained for a modest rent; the weather, even in the
depths of winter, was often almost springlike, with air scented by the
pine woods of the Cascine, separating the town from the sea. Tuscany,
under the rule of a benevolent grand-duke, was the most liberal state
in Italy, and Pisa, neglected and underinhabited though it had become
in the early nineteenth century, was full of charm. Lady Blessington,
arriving in 1827 with a yawn of dismay at the prospect of spending
six months in such a backwater, left her Lung'Arno home with real
regret; the poet Giacomo Leopardi, describing Pisa to his sister a few

years later, went into raptures over the cosmopolitan population, the ceaseless promenade of carriages and pedestrians along the riverside walks, the beauty of the architecture and of the language. In carnival season, which began a month after the Shelleys' arrival, tapestries draped from palace windows turned the town into a medieval paint-ing as ancient coaches gilded with family coats-of-arms rattled out of their dusty stables and over the cobbles of the grand Piazza dei Cavalieri, still shaped like the Roman theatre it had once been.[1] Dowdy though Pisa could seem in the sleepy months of summer, this, in winter, was the place to be. The presence of the grand-duke and his court always produced a glow of happiness in Pisan bosoms; it might be only for their agreeable climate that he had come, but it guaranteed that Pisa, not Florence, was for a short space of each year the centre of fashion, interest and culture.

Here, after a month-long Christmas visit from Claire, Mary grad-ually established what was for her a perfect balance between study and sociability. In England, she remained an object of scandal; in Pisa, free at last of the awkwardness of living in a *ménage à trois* with her hand-some stepsister, she could enter society.

There are few clues to Mary's appearance at this time. Shelley's poems often paid tribute to her serene expression and smile. Frequent requests to Peacock to send out combs suggest that she kept her waving red-gold hair pinned up, away from the high intellectual forehead she had inherited from Godwin. She prided herself on the small, white, unusually flexible hands which, to amuse a child, she could bend back like a contortionist; it startled and pleased her that people like Mrs Mason, who had not seen her since childhood, found her instantly recognizable. In the Marlow days, she had been a careless dresser; at twenty-three, she took more pride in her appear-ance. Medwin, who noticed his cousin's scruffy daily attire – Shelley was especially fond of a long grey coat like a dressing-gown – was impressed by the fact that he invariably 'made his toilette' for dinner with his wife. The fashion of the day was still for high waists and puffed sleeves; when Mary chose materials, they were usually in a pink stripe or a light pretty colour. Over her shoulders, she draped a lilac or blue chiffon shawl from Hadbib's famous store in Livorno. She may have grown a little plumper after bearing four children (increasing weight was a problem she combated with energetic walking and a light diet); grief had, she felt, robbed her face of its bloom.

Perhaps it was so, although she would be ready by the end of 1821 to tell Leigh Hunt that she felt physically and mentally rejuvenated.

But the interest which Mary's new friends took in her had more to do with her formidable erudition, her active interest in political events and her thirst for knowledge and experience.

Mrs Mason was in poor health in the winter of 1820–1; the couple who did most to introduce the Shelleys to a new circle in Pisa were the sociable, open-minded and cultivated Dr Vaccà and his wife. Sofia, 'la bella Vaccà', queen of the Pisan salons, knew everybody; their friends embraced members of the ducal court as easily as the teachers, writers and translators at the university where Vaccà's brilliance and goodness – he set three hours a day aside for work among the poor of the town – had earned him the reputation of a modern Hippocrates.

The first to make an impression, so much so that he became a nightly guest, was Francesco Pacchiani. On 3 December, Mary sent Leigh Hunt a rapturous account of this cadaverous black-eyed man, this 'profound genius' with 'an eloquence that transports', who delivered his ideas in language so beautiful that she could imagine him conversing with Boccaccio, one of her favourite writers, or Machiavelli. Perhaps it was under Pacchiani's spell that she decided for the first time to write Hunt a long letter entirely in Italian.

At fifty, the days of Pacchiani's high reputation as a brilliant logician and scientist – he held the Chair in Physics at Pisa in 1802 and impressed Volta by some of his experiments – were over; a good deal of his energy was spent in slandering the colleagues whose patience he had exhausted. By 1820, Pacchiani was shirking his university duties for the pleasures of literary society and womanizing. Known as 'the devil of Pisa', he revelled in his reputation, gleefully telling Thomas Medwin of the time when he had met questions about the kind of lady he was escorting by announcing that he was a republican, walking in a public street with a public woman.

Mary, like Shelley, loved and hated in fervent extremes. In December 1820, Pacchiani was wholly indispensable to them; by the end of January 1821, he stood revealed as a horror, foul-mouthed, obsessed with high society and wealth. His boasting was quite disgusting, Mary told Claire on 14–15 January. 'And then his innumerable host of great acquaintances! – he would make one believe that he attracts the great as a milk pail does flies on a summer morning.'

Pacchiani's disagreeable nature has caused him to be identified as a possible model for two of the unpleasantest characters in *Valperga*. The first, Benedetto Pepi, is the corrupt mentor of Castruccio in his early years. Pepi's sympathies with the anti-republican Ghibellines mark him out as a villain from the start (Euthanasia, the blameless

heroine, is a liberal-minded Guelph).* Pepi's belief that the world
should be governed by a few rich families certainly seems to echo
Pacchiani's obsessive interest in the social standing and finances of his
friends, but his operations as a corrupt usurer who hounds debtors
out of their estates also suggest that Mary was still haunted by her
father's troubled finances. Given that Mary had only just met
Pacchiani when she introduced the character of Pepi into her first
volume, it seems unlikely that she was drawing on him. More probably, Pepi was a mythical figure, inspired by the pack of wolves she
imagined snapping at the Skinner Street doors.

Pacchiani has a more convincing role in *Valperga*'s second volume
as Battista Tripalda, the evil canon of Perugia. Pacchiani had been
made a canon shortly before he entered Pisa university; his eccentricity – Medwin remembered with horror how he used to pick the
bones out of snipe with long skinny fingers – and his taste for obscene
jokes are mentioned as characteristic of Tripalda. Mary's own initial
enthusiasm and swift disillusion with Pacchiani seem clearly recorded
in the first account she gives of Tripalda. (He is, on this occasion,
acting as Castruccio's representative and trying to persuade Euthanasia
to abandon the stronghold of Valperga.)

> When he first appeared at Lucca, he was humble and mild, pretend-
> ing to nothing but uncorrupted and uncorruptible virtue . . . [But]
> . . . when he became familiar with his new friends, he cast off his
> modest disguise, and appeared vain, presumptuous and insolent,
> delivering his opinions as oracles, violent when opposed in argument,
> contemptuous even when agreed with . . . stories had been whispered
> concerning him, but they were believed by few; it was said that the
> flagrant wickedness of his actions had caused him to be banished from
> Perugia . . .[2]

Perhaps Mary had believed the stories whispered in Pisa about
Pacchiani; in the third volume, Tripalda is shown to have presided over

---

* Mary's own feelings about the Ghibellines and the Guelphs are made clear in the first
chapter of *Valperga*. 'The Ghibelines and the Bianchi were the friends of the emperor, asserting the supremacy and universality of his sway over all other dominion, ecclesiastical or civil;
the Guelphs and the Neri were the partizans of liberty.' Mary, in a year (1821) when the
emperors of Russia and Austria joined forces to suppress any changes of government due to
revolution and when King Ferdinand of Naples was compelled to 'invite' Austrian troops to
invade his territory and crush the carbonari rebels, had little sympathy for imperial rulers.
'We are also highly interested in the result of the Austrian counsels against Naples,' she had
told Mrs Gisborne, with whom she maintained a cool correspondence on practical matters,
on 13 December 1820. The Shelleys were evidently keeping close watch on events.

every depravity his creator could imagine. 'But I have said enough,' his beautiful victim tells Euthanasia, 'nor will I tell that which would chill your warm blood with horror.' All we and Euthanasia are allowed to know is that he had been guilty of crimes 'which it would seem that fiends alone could contrive . . . It was the carnival of devils, when we miserable victims were dragged out to –' There, frustratingly, the account is terminated.[3] Mary was no Marquis de Sade.

Pacchiani may have been an unpleasant man, but he was an invaluable source of introductions. One of the earliest was to Tommaso Sgricci, a thirty-three-year-old ex-law student who, by 1820, had made his name as a gifted improvisatore. His art, close to poetry, consisted of elaborating verse monologues on a given subject, often one picked by a member of the audience.*

Not everybody admired the elegant, slender little actor. Polidori, seeing him perform at Milan in 1816, thought him a bit of a charlatan; Sgricci's unconcealed homosexuality and a weakness for noble families did not always find favour. Mary, who first met him on 1 December, was as pleased by his eloquence as by his warm espousing of the carbonarist cause in Naples, a subject which was dear to her heart. The actor was invited to dine with them twice that week. On 21 December, she and Shelley went to hear him perform. 'Conceive of a poem as long as a Greek Tragedy, interspersed with choruses, the whole plan conceived in an instant,' she wrote ecstatically to Hunt eight days later: '. . . it was one impulse that filled him; an unchanged deity who spoke within him, and his voice surpassed in its modulations the melody of music.'

Sgricci was to perform again at Lucca in January; nothing was going to prevent Mary from being in the audience. Shelley had boils; very well, she would go to Lucca with Pacchiani and take the baby with her. The performance was cancelled and Pacchiani was forced to go back to Pisa; Mary was prepared to accept a stranger's invitation and stay on alone. Seated at last in the box of the imposing Marchesa Bernardini (Pacchiani had reverently hinted that she was 'one of the first ladies of Lucca'), Mary settled down to enjoy herself. She had always loved the theatre; she had loved nothing more than these extraordinary outpourings of inspiration. It was, she thought, as if she were watching the very act of creation made manifest. One member of the audience declared that Sgricci had

---

* The poet as improviser also became something of a cult in England at this time; Thomas Lovell Beddoes's 'The Improvisatore' was the eponymous poem of his popular collection of 1821.

got the history of his subject, Inez de Castro, all wrong, and the Marchesa sniffed that it was 'una cosa mediocra: to me it appeared a miracle,' Mary confessed to Claire in a long excited account of the evening. The story had been obscure and complicated; what Claire must imagine was the genius of a single man who could fill the stage with characters: 'when Pietro unveiled the dead Ignez, when Sancho died in despair on her body, it seemed to me as if it were all there; so truly and passionately did his words depict the scene he wished to represent.'[4]

Mary's enthusiasm for Sgricci did not develop into a lasting friendship and the actor left Pisa to tour the country later in January; her feelings for another of Pacchiani's introductions, John Taaffe, were never more than tepid. Taaffe, scathingly referred to by Mary as 'the Poet Laureate of Pisa', was a slightly pathetic character, disinherited and sent abroad by his Irish father after he unwittingly married a lady who already had a husband. He had been living at Pisa since 1816 and was the father of two children by a second marriage of somewhat insecure status. (His first 'wife' refused to divorce him.) Not even the fact that he was writing a commentary on Dante, one of her favourite authors, could induce Mary to produce more than a yawn of resignation at the prospect of an evening with Taaffe. She felt very differently about Alexander Mavrocordato, to whom the Vaccàs introduced her.

Shortage of money and the need of a warm climate had, by 1821, helped to make cheap and balmy Pisa home to a closely-knit colony of Greek exiles, all of whom were related to John Caradja, the former Hospodar, or Prince, of Wallachia. Mavrocordato had worked for a time as Caradja's political secretary, but Caradja's own position, as a Greek in the employment of the Turkish sultan, had led to threats on his life by extremists. In 1818, together with his daughter, her husband and the twenty-seven-year-old Alexander, Caradja had fled from Bucharest to the safety of Italy. Mavrocordato had, since then, become a leading figure among the Greek patriots, both abroad and in Pisa where he and his family shared the Vaccàs' Lung'Arno home. The freedom of Greece from Turkish domination was his grand obsession.

'Pacchiani and a Greek Prince calls,' Mary noted on 2 December 1820. She had, it was true, met Sgricci the day before, but her journal in Pisa had until then been uncommonly glum. 'The whole population are such that it wd. sound strange to an English person if I attempted to express what I feel concerning them,' she had noted on Percy's birthday, 12 November, before adding a misremembered quotation from Byron: '"Crawling & crablike thro their sapping streets."' But here was a prince, breathing fire on the subject of liberty, and suddenly her mood had changed: 'delightful weather,' she added after Mavrocordato's call, leaving us to suppose that he had helped to lift the clouds. Claire, a little later, heard that the prince was 'much to my taste gentlemanly – gay learned and full of talent & enthusiasm for Greece – he gave me a greek lesson & staid until 8 o'clock . . .'[5]

Short and thickset with a mass of black hair, large glistening eyes and splendid moustaches, Mavrocordato struck most people who met him as admirable, ardent and intelligent. He did not normally strike them as a lively or cheerful man. Evidently, he liked Mary enough to lower his guard and relax and even, perhaps, to flirt a little. He must have noticed that Shelley led a somewhat separate life, closed up in his study at the top of the Casa Galletti; he must have wondered about a husband who seemed indifferent to the number of hours his wife spent studying Greek with a youngish and not unattractive bachelor.

Certainly, the prince found Mary a stimulating and intelligent companion, one who was ready to share his passion for the cause of Greek independence. Her hopes of a new republic in Naples were crushed by the 'invited' army of 11,000 Austrians who came to uphold King Ferdinand's regime in March 1821. In the same month, the Greeks of the Morea rose up in rebellion against the Turkish oppressors; Greece, after this time, became the focus of Mary's own political interest.

Shelley, as the author of *Hellas*, is usually perceived as a passionate espouser of the Greek fight for independence; Mary was far better informed and more closely involved with events there, through her close relationship with Mavrocordato, whom she saw almost every day during the first three months of 1821. It is tempting to wonder if the idea for *Hellas* was in fact hers, although the approach and execution were unquestionably not. 'We are all Greeks,' Shelley splendidly declared in his preface to the poem, written towards the end of 1821. But Greece, for him, was a symbol, representing all oppressed nations; his preface went on to allude to England, Russia, Italy and Germany. To Mary, fired by almost daily conversations with Mavrocordato, the Greek cause was no symbolic fight for freedom but a vivid reality.

Political events brought their meetings to an end in the spring of 1821. '*AM* calls with news about Greece,' Mary wrote in her journal on 1 April; – 'he is as gay as a caged eagle just free.' News had come from the prince's cousin, Prince Ypsilantis, that an army of 10,000 had been raised to serve the cause of Greek freedom. Their Greek lessons were suspended for more important work, but long letters written in French, their most fluent common language, allowed the prince to continue to share his ambitions for Greece with a sympathetic and admiring confidante. They are affectionate letters, but there is no hint of passion in them; they do not lead one to think that Mary's relationship ever went beyond a devoted platonic friendship.

What did Shelley think? Would Shelley have cared? Publicly, he dedicated *Hellas* to Mavrocordato 'as an imperfect token of the admiration, sympathy, and friendship of the author'. Privately, he may have shared the opinion of a French historian who noted towards the end of the century that Mavrocordato 'n'avait pas cette éloquence qui excite l'enthousiasme . . . il ne frappait pas l'imagination . . .'[6] Mary's enthusiasm for Mavrocordato puzzled him. A few days after the prince's departure, Shelley told Claire that he was 'a great loss to Mary, and *therefore* to me – but not otherwise'.[7]

Mary's friendship with the prince, continued in correspondence long after he left for Greece on 26 June 1821, needs to be considered in the context of the last of Pacchiani's introductions, a beautiful Italian girl called Teresa Viviani with whom Shelley became passionately involved during their time at Pisa. The Shelleys met her in early December 1820, in the same week that they were introduced to Mavrocordato. It is possible that Mary's immediate interest in Mavrocordato, an interest which Shelley did not share, helped to drive him – as a very willing victim – into Miss Viviani's receptive arms.

They renamed her Emilia. It sounded more appealing and Emilia Viviani seemed born to the part of a romantic heroine, with her clear white skin and thick black hair which she wore loosely coiled, Greek style, on the nape of her neck. Emilia was the daughter of the governor of Pisa and imaginative enough to claim that her expensive and privileged boarding-school, two hundred yards from her father's home, was a prison in which a heartless stepmother had condemned her to dwell until marriage. The Shelleys were horrified by her tale. They believed it all.

Emilia's school, adjoining the convent of Sant' Anna, is still partly visible among the classrooms of a university annexe on Via Carducci. So is the drab plot of kitchen garden which was Emilia's only view of the outside world from the grim little rooms in which she kept the two caged birds the Shelleys gave her, together with a painting of the madonna and a portrait of her favourite saint. She changed saints quite frequently, but Mary only noticed that later. Initially, she was as out- raged as Shelley to learn that an intelligent and sensitive young woman could be locked up until forced into marriage. She made daily visits to the school; Claire was urged to write consoling letters to their lovely young friend.

Satirizing Emilia later as Clorinda in one of her most beguiling stories, 'The Bride of Modern Italy', Mary showed her choosing a new saint for every new love-affair: 'tell me, sweet Clorinda, how many saints have been benefited by your piety?'[8] Mary had the measure of Miss Viviani by the time she wrote her elegant, mocking tale. In the early months of 1821, she was sufficiently moved by the pathos and beauty of their 'imprisoned' friend to draw on her for one of the most important characters in *Valperga*. It was after meeting Emilia that Mary introduced a second heroine, the young prophetess of Ferrara.*

Beatrice of Ferrara's rejection of God had nothing to do with Emilia. Neither did her gift for prophecy, which owed more to Mary's faith in her own mysterious power to apprehend future events. But Beatrice's looks, her raven black hair, her oval face, her dark eyes, show that Emilia Viviani also made a contribution. Beatrice prophesies from the convent of Sant' Anna in Ferrara, a name which echoes Emilia's convent school of Sant' Anna in Pisa too precisely to have been picked by chance. It is tempting to see poor Beatrice's miserable end as a lovingly chosen pun- ishment by a creator who had, by then, lost all sympathy with the young Pisan.

Shelley had always liked the idea of satellite sisterhoods; a few weeks after his first meeting with Emilia in December 1820, he began writing a new poem in celebration of this subject. Why, he asked, not for the first time, should exclusive love be regarded as a benefit to mankind?

> I never was attached to that great sect,
> Whose doctrine is, that each one should select
> Out of the crowd a mistress or a friend,
> And all the rest, though fair and wise, commend
> To cold oblivion . . .

---

* Beatrice is also called the 'Ancilla Dei', a name which suggests that Mary drew on Suora Ancilla, or Sister Betsy, a young woman who made several visits to the Shelleys in 1820–1. An English girl, who went out from the Godwins to stay with Margaret Mason in Pisa, she became a nun and a nurse at the hospital of Santa Chiara. Claire also referred to her as Elizabeth Parker or 'Betsy' Parker in her later correspondence.

There was nothing new here to distress Mary; what might have upset her more was *Epipsychidion*'s clear indication that she was no longer Shelley's muse. Emilia, in the opening stanzas of his poem, was given Mary's own former role as the moon, 'thou Beauty, and thou Terror! / Thou Harmony of Nature's art! Thou Mirror / In whom, as in the splendour of the Sun, / All shapes look glorious which thou gazest on!' When the moon reappears in the central section of the poem, it represents Mary, but in the cruellest form. Here, she has become the planet's winter face, trapping the poet

> Into a death of ice, immovable; –
> And then – what earthquakes made it gape and split,
> The white Moon smiling all the while on it,
> These words conceal: – If not, each word would be
> The key of staunchless tears. Weep not for me!

This is the state from which loving 'Emily' leads him back to warmth; Claire, represented by the comet, 'beautiful and fierce', is urged to return and to become 'Love's folding-star' while the Moon, as Mary, 'will veil her horn / In thy last smiles'. Finally, the poet dreams of perfect union with 'Emily' on 'an isle under Ionian skies, / Beautiful as a wreck of Paradise' where they will become, in one of Shelley's favourite poetic fantasies

> the same, we shall be one
> Spirit within two frames, oh! wherefore two?
> One passion in twin-hearts, which grows and grew,
> Till like two meteors of expanding flame,
> Those spheres instinct with it become the same,
> Touch, mingle, are transfigured . . .

Shelley prudently chose to keep his poem out of Mary's sight until the summer of 1821. She was familiar with and had for a time shared his faith in a more generous scheme of love than monogamy. But how can she have responded to a poem which robed her in ice and which celebrated the writer's fusion, ecstatic and all-consuming, with the young girl to whom *Epipsychidion* was explicitly addressed? There was no attempt at concealment: Shelley unambiguously dedicated his work 'to the noble and unfortunate lady, Emilia V—, now imprisoned in the convent of —.' True, he intended to publish it anonymously, claiming that the author had died in Florence; what comfort can that have been?[9]

Mary, at the beginning of 1821, was still unaware of the nature of the poem her husband was writing; there are, however, hints that she was already having difficulty keeping up with his enthusiasm for their new friend. Emilia, filling time with writing flowery letters, assured Shelley – 'my Percy' – of her undying love; mischievously, she confided her fears that 'the beautiful Mary' was growing less affectionate. 'Mary does not write to me. Is it possible that she loves me less than the others do?' she asked him ten days after their first meeting.[10] On 24 December 1820, after thanking Mary for a gift of a chain, 'the symbol of that which binds and will eternally bind our hearts', Emilia reproached her for being 'a little cold', before delivering a barbed tribute to 'Mia adorata Amica': 'I know that your husband said well when he said that your apparent coldness [freddezza] is *only the ash which covers an affectionate heart.*'

How far did Shelley go in his relationship with Emilia? Writing to Claire on 16 January 1821, he assured her that there was no mixture 'of that which you call love' in his feelings for their friend; nevertheless, there are some indications that he behaved recklessly. Claire later recalled that he tried to persuade Mrs Mason to disguise herself as a man in order to play the part of Emilia's suitor and rescue her from the school. To join him? He would hardly have wished to send her home to an angry father and an unloving stepmother. On 3 September 1821, on the eve of a more conventional alliance arranged by her parents, Emilia nervously requested Shelley to be 'very prudent' and to take care to write to her in a more distant way. Writing to Byron eleven days later, Shelley told him that a good deal of fuss was being made in Pisa about his 'intimacy' with the governor's daughter. 'Pray do not mention anything of what I told you,' he added, 'as the whole truth is not known and Mary might be very much annoyed at it.' He did not, however, say what the 'whole truth' was and Byron did not ask.

Mary already knew enough by mid-September 1821 to have been annoyed and distressed. She had been shown *Epipsychidion*,* and had been told that Shelley intended to publish it. She was also aware that Emilia, shortly before her marriage, had attempted to extract a large sum of money from Shelley, a form of blackmail to which she drily alluded in a letter to Mrs Gisborne the following year.[11] His relationship with Emilia had, she admitted in this letter, caused 'a good deal of discomfort', but she was carefully unspecific. The relationship was

---

* There is no doubt that Mary saw the poem; in letters which she wrote in 1822–3, following Shelley's death, she quoted phrases from it, and in particular the hurtful allusions to herself as 'cold moonshine'.

airily dismissed as 'Shelleys Italian platonics'. Emilia was said to be leading her husband and his mother 'a devil of a life'.[12] The Shelleys never saw or heard from her again.

Pacchiani had been generous with his introductions, but his friends had all, with the exception of the amiable, slightly dull John Taaffe, been foreign; the Shelleys, estranged from the Gisbornes, weary of Medwin and seeing little of Mrs Mason in a year when her health was bad, longed for English company. Learning that John Keats was intending to visit Italy for his health, Shelley had already urged him to join them at Pisa in the winter of 1820–1. His intentions were generous; after reading *Hyperion* with Mary during the previous autumn, he believed that Keats might yet become one of the great poets of their time. But Keats, sensing condescension and thinking, perhaps, that Pisa sounded a dull spot, opted for Rome, where he died in April 1821.

The Shelleys, by then, had found all the English company they required in the form of Tom Medwin's friends, Edward Williams and his unofficial wife, Jane. This handsome young couple became their close companions, and a welcome replacement for Tom as he set off through Italy in search of a rich wife. 'We see the Williamses constantly,' Shelley wrote to Claire on 9 June 1821; but his praises were surprisingly limp. They were, he told her, 'nice, good-natured people, very soft society after authors and pretenders to philosophy'. The Williamses were, it seemed, reaping the benefits only of comparison with Pacchiani and John Taaffe.

Mary was, initially, more enthusiastic. The Williamses arrived in Pisa on 19 January. By the first week of February, she had decided that she liked Edward enough to let him try his hand at drawing her while she drew him out about their history and what had brought them to Pisa. More limited in his education than either Medwin or Shelley, Williams had left Eton for the navy after less than a year's schooling. He went on to serve with Medwin in India and, like him, had retired on half-pay when the army was reformed after the Napoleonic wars. Mary had heard enough of lions and tiger-hunts from Medwin; she was more interested in hearing the romantic story of Edward's love for Jane.

A year younger than Mary, Jane Cleveland was of military stock, the sister of a general in the Madras army, the wife, at sixteen, of a bullying naval captain in the East India Company from whom, with her brother's approval, she had separated the following year. Shortly thereafter – the date was never quite clear – she fell in love with Edward Williams. As boldly as Mary herself, she had broken with convention and in 1819 left England as his wife, although no divorce had taken place. Like Mary again, she had lived at Geneva, where their son, Edward Medwin, was born in February 1820 and named for their closest friend. Now they were expecting their second child, due in March.

This was a tale to win Mary's sympathy. She had not, at first, been much impressed by Jane, a slight, clinging young woman with dark hair, huge eyes, a swanlike neck and a long, downturned nose. While admiring her skill at flower arranging, her graceful appearance when seated at the pedal harp and the skill with which she could convert herself into a dashing Indian sultana in turban and silk pantaloons, the Shelleys initially found her less congenial than Edward, who had ambitions to become a playwright and whose skill as an artist was enviably assured. Jane seemed to have no especial talent. Neither Shelley nor Mary were aware of the capacity for mischief-making which had already caused trouble at Geneva.[13]*

Mary, always tormented by the thought that her birth had killed Mary Wollstonecraft, gladly helped at the birth in March of Jane's Rosalind ('Dina'). Jane's old-fashioned indolence after the birth allowed Mary the treat of replacing her as Edward's daily walking companion in a wonderfully sunny and springlike April. With Alexander Mavrocordato wrapped up in his plans for Greece, she was pleased to have this new and agreeable friend. Knowing nothing of boats, she shared Shelley's admiration for Williams's naval chat; when, on a moonlit canal trip from Livorno to Pisa with Henry Reveley, the young men's light-bottomed craft tipped over, neither Mary nor Shelley had the practical skill to understand that their nautical friend Edward had been at fault for raising a full sail in a high wind.[14] The expedition marked the return of Shelley's passion for water. In the old days, he had been content with paper boats or rowing on a stream; now, with Williams to encourage him, he began to dream of open seas.

---

* When the Cornish baronet, Sir John St Aubyn, who had entertained Medwin, Trelawny and the Williamses at Geneva, confided in Mary Shelley about his love-life on 10 June 1826, he begged her to be discreet with Jane. 'There are subjects I entertain few people with,' he told her, 'and whatever regard I may have for Mrs Williams, she is not of the number I should choose.' Edward Trelawny also had strong reservations about Jane's trustworthiness from early on.

Williams had lost most of his money when a banking house in Calcutta suddenly failed; like the Shelleys, he was delighted to find that splendid homes could be rented for a pittance in the vicinity of Pisa. In March, the Shelleys had taken Casa Aulla, a Prini home which is now the Hotel Victoria; in May, while they rented another Prini house at San Giuliano, the Williamses settled nearby in the country house of Marchese Poschi, on the road towards Pugnano.

The Poschi house seemed to them all to have dropped straight from paradise. Its gardens were shaded by cypresses and sweet-smelling limes; its grand central staircase swept up to the third floor as though in expectation of – at least – a king's arrival. Here, from June to the end of summer, the two families romped and chatted and laughed. Basking in such easy, undemanding company, Mary felt her own girl-hood returning. In Pisa, unpleasant gossip was spreading about Shelley's involvement with Emilia Viviani; away from the city, in the airy, frescoed rooms of the Williamses' home, she could ignore it. Working on the last chapters of *Valperga*, 'a child of mighty slow growth',[15] she had little to worry her at home beyond a day's illness in little Percy and a baffling silence from Skinner Street. 'I have not heard from Papa this age,' she wrote anxiously to Mrs Gisborne, now somewhat but not entirely forgiven, on 28 May. 'Pray enquire if there are letters for us at the Leghorn Post Office.' She had, perhaps, for-gotten Shelley's decision to act as her censor. In retrospect, Mary remembered only the laughter in the garden, the languid ease of long summer days. 'Do you remember,' she wrote to Jane Williams on 15 October 1822, '. . . how we used, like children, to play in the great hall or your garden & then sit under the cypresses & hear him [Edward] read his play?' By then, she was anxious to bury any mem-ories of Shelley which could cause her pain.

Shelley's health was, as Mary's letters sadly noted, no better. The 'nervous irritation' she described him as suffering from was not only physical in its origin. Writing *Adonais*, his lament for Keats, had made him painfully conscious of his own lack of public recognition. When Mary gave him her corrected second draft of *Valperga* to read in July, his immediate thought was that she should not prejudice the book's chances by calling herself 'the author of Frankenstein'.[16] Better, he reasoned, to try for popularity than to link the new book to a work which had been viewed as mischievous and dangerous. This was caution bred of despondency.

Watching the simple affection of Jane and Edward Williams, Shelley was bitterly aware of the lack of ease between Mary and himself. Unfairly, he longed for the freshness of first love, the calmness of a Jane who never seemed to quarrel or to show the nervous, excessive devotion with which Mary fretted over their last remaining child. At home, she seemed always taken up with the baby or her studies, but he noticed that she also found time to write to her scholarly Greek prince. Shelley was not a man who ever looked for fault in himself; no sign in his letters appears of a conscience, an awareness that his own behaviour with both Claire and Emilia might have been hard for his wife to bear, especially in the summer when she first read *Epipsychidion*. She had no cause to be cold; a change was required. Not until 1839 was Mary able to admit in public that this was the summer in which, in a draft notebook, he addressed to her one of his cruellest poems. It was all the more hurtful for being couched in tones of sorrowful reproach. The fault, naturally, was all hers.

> We are not happy, sweet! our state
>   Is strange and full of doubt and fear:
> More need of words that ills abate;
>   Reserve or censure come not near
> Our sacred friendship, lest there be
> No solace left for thee and me.
>
> Gentle and good and mild thou art,
>   Nor can I live if thou appear
> Aught but thyself, or turn thine heart
>   Away from me, or stoop to wear
> The mask of scorn, although it be
> To hide the love thou feel'st for me.[17]

A form of reconciliation had been achieved with the Gisbornes since the estrangement of the previous year. On their way from Livorno to make a new life in England, they consented to make a short stay with the Shelleys. The day after they left, 29 July, Mary sat to Edward Williams once again for a miniature portrait; she planned to give it to Shelley for his birthday the following week. Events were against her; a letter from Byron in Ravenna brought the dramatic news that the brother and father of his young mistress, Teresa Guiccioli, had been expelled from their home for involvement with one of the score of secret societies which had sprung up at the time of the abortive revolution in Naples. Byron, while prepared to go with Teresa to share their exile, was anxious to dissuade her from choosing Geneva, where he was still regarded as a figure of scandal by the English colony.

Shelley decided to make a cross-country journey to Ravenna to discuss the future. Byron might be persuaded to change his plans and come to Pisa instead. Shelley was also anxious, as was Mary, to know what Byron's intentions were for poor little Allegra.

News had reached them in March that Byron had decided, with the support of Teresa Guiccioli and her family, to lodge his four-year-old daughter at the convent of Bagnacavallo. Mary, who regarded the decision as regrettable but practical, had taken it upon herself to explain the situation to Claire. She, as Allegra's mother, was less calm in her reaction. She had shared the Shelleys' indignation at the confinement of Emilia Viviani in a convent school; it was beyond her understanding why they did not feel the same horror at the thought of a little girl being banished to what amounted, in Claire's imagination, to heartless imprisonment. A letter of such hysterical distress was posted off to Byron at Ravenna that Shelley, warm though he usually was in support of Claire, felt obliged to write and apologize. Claire expressed herself as she did, he explained on 17 April, 'as the result of a misguided maternal affection'. The apology was accepted; Claire was comforted by promises that she might soon be able to return to Pisa and live at the home of Mrs Mason. Not even Shelley felt ready to suggest that she should again live with himself and Mary.

Shelley did not trouble Mary with the news that he would be taking a small detour on his journey to Ravenna in order to spend his birthday morning with Claire; she may have been shrewd enough to suspect it. Her journal entry for his birthday, 4 August, was heavy with foreboding. Certainly, she was not happy when she wrote it.

> W[illiams] finished my miniature – 7 years are now gone – what changes what a life – we now appear tranquil – yet who know[s] what wind – I will not prognosticate evil – We have had enough of it – When I came to Italy – I said all is well if it were permanent – it was more passing than an Italian twilight – I now say the same – May it be a polar day – Yet that too has an end –

Two days later, she decided to read Williams her saddest and most personal work, the unpublished manuscript of *Matilda*. It is hard to imagine what response such a straightforward young man could have made to its revelation of grief and despair. No doubt it unnerved him, and he would have felt angry with Mary for drawing him away from the light cheerful world of the Villa Poschi into the unrelieved darkness of her most secret self. Shelley had probably told him that Mary suffered from depressions; Williams was callow enough to prefer a woman to keep her chin up and a smile on. He liked Mary; he didn't want to know about her problems.

There were no more entries in Mary's journal after her reading of *Matilda* until the last day of August, when she crisply noted that Claire had visited her for ten days. (Shelley had insisted that an invitation should be issued; Mary had reluctantly assented.) There was usually good reason for a gap in the journal; the cause on this occasion was the frantic letter which Shelley had written to her on 7 August, the morning after his arrival at Byron's Ravenna home.

Eleven months had passed since the Hoppners, hot with Elise Foggi's tale of a child born secretly at Naples to Shelley and Claire, and farmed out by Shelley at the foundling hospital, had sent their spitefully detailed account to Byron. He, until now, had kept their gossip to himself, or so he said. Carefully expressing his own scepticism, Byron gave the letter to Shelley on the night he arrived at Ravenna. (To the Hoppners, Byron had commented that Elise was a dubious source, but that he saw no reason to question the principal details of her story.)

Shelley's letter to Mary made no allusion to the baby he had registered as having been born to her and himself at Naples. He reported without surprise the fact that Elise had described Claire as his mistress: 'all the world has heard so much & people may believe or not believe as they think good.' What horrified him was the allegation that he had tried to procure an abortion for Claire and, when that failed, had torn the child from its mother and packed it off for adoption. How, he asked Mary, could anybody imagine that a man of his nature would destroy or abandon his own child? He wanted her to send him a letter for delivery to the Hoppners. She should deny the charge made against him, 'in case you believe & know & can prove that it is false: stating the grounds & proof of your belief'. The phrasing was strange; if he was not sure that she believed the charge to be false, how did he expect her to prove it, except by a lie? In a letter written the following day, he apologized for upsetting her but urged her again to act, for the sake of 'our dear Percy'. This was a threat; if she did not discredit the charge, Percy's future with them was at risk.

Composing her reply to Mrs Hoppner, knowing that Shelley would be the first to read it, must have been one of the hardest acts of Mary's life. She carried it off with uncommon conviction and skill. Making no mention of the mysterious baby Shelley had wanted her to take into their home, she acknowledged that Paolo Foggi had threatened them with 'false accusations', while stating that Elise, 'this miserable girl', had never been party to her husband's plots.

And now I come to her accusations – and I must indeed summon all my courage while I transcribe them; for tears will force their way, and how can it be otherwise? You knew Shelley, you saw his face, & could you believe them? Believe them only on the testimony of a girl whom you despised? I had hopes that such a thing was impossible, and that although strangers might believe the calumnies that this man propagated that none who had ever seen my husband could for a moment credit them.

She says Claire was Shelley's mistress, that – Upon my word, I solemnly assure you that I cannot write the words, I send you a part of Shelleys letter that you may see what I am now about to refute – but I had rather die that [than] copy any thing so vilely so wickedly false, so beyond all imagination fiendish.

I am perfectly convinced, in my own mind that Shelley never had an improper connexion with Claire – At the time specified in Elise's letter . . . we lived in lodgings where I had momentary entrance into every room and such a thing could not have passed unknown to me . . .[18]

It was the best she could do. It was an answer which carefully omitted any reference to the child Shelley had named Elena Adelaide. It contained an oath which seemed to be directed to Shelley himself, in response to his hints about Percy's future. 'I swear by the life of my child, by my blessed & beloved child, that I know these accusations to be false,' she wrote. The covering letter with which she sent this long and passionate defence underlined her greatest fear: 'God preserve my child to me,' she wrote to Shelley, 'and our enemies shall not be too much for us.' She added that there had been 'cunning' in Elise's story. She begged him to think again about his plan to move them to a house near Claire in Florence: 'I love I own to face danger,' she told him, 'but I would not be imprudent.'

Shelley, in receipt of Mary's response, gave it to Byron who, after studying its contents, seems to have felt no need to pass it on to the Hoppners. He had already given them the impression that he shared their faith in the details Elise had provided. Curiosity, rather than a wish to salvage damaged reputations, had led him to discuss their allegations with Shelley. The letter which had cost Mary such pains to write was thrust into a pile of other correspondence, and dismissed from his mind.

Two clear benefits came to Mary from Shelley's ten-day visit to Ravenna. The first was the news that Byron had agreed to enter a scheme with Shelley and Leigh Hunt to start a new journal, the

Liberal. All that was required now was for the Hunts to pack their belongings and sail for Italy where, they learned, they would be lodged at the grand home in Pisa which Shelley was going to find and rent in anticipation of Byron's arrival. Mary, who remained devoted to the Hunt family, was delighted by the prospect of their company. Byron reached Pisa at the beginning of November; it took another eight months before the Hunts, delayed by ill health and bad weather, finally arrived at Genoa.

The second benefit also related to Byron's decision to come to Pisa. His presence, Mary supposed, would guarantee the absence of her stepsister. Claire's feelings of outrage about Allegra's banishment to the convent of Bagnacavallo had not altered by the end of August. It would, Mary was confident, be impossible for her to contemplate living in the same city as Allegra's father, particularly when he had his pretty young mistress in tow. Mary was right; the only thing she had not counted on was that Byron would take another two months to make up his mind to come. In the interim, since Teresa travelled to Pisa ahead of him, Mary faced the interesting task of juggling her life between Byron's past and present mistresses.

CHAPTER NINETEEN

DON JUAN AMONG THE LADIES

1821–1822

'I begin to long for the sparkling waves the olive covered hills & vine shaded
pergolas of Spezia . . . if April prove fine we shall fly with the swallows.'

Mary Shelley to Maria Gisborne, 9 February 1822

MARY WAS PERHAPS FEELING A LITTLE GUILTY BY THE SUMMER OF
1821 about the readiness with which she and Shelley had accepted
Byron's decision to place Allegra in a secluded country convent at the
tender age of four. She had no wish to share her home with Claire
again for any length of time, but a period of gentler relations between
the stepsisters followed the letter of 10 August to Mrs Hoppner.
There, Mary had defended Claire's reputation as much as her own,
and she had done so with warmth. Claire knew nothing of the charge
or of Mary's response; she did know that she had regained their sympathy on the subject of Allegra's banishment to Bagnacavallo.

On 8 September, Mary, Shelley and Claire travelled together up the
coast to La Spezia in search of a house by the sea for the following
summer. Shortly before or during this three-day excursion, the Shelleys
told Claire that they were doing all they could to reunite her with her
daughter. On 15 August, shortly after his return from Ravenna, Shelley
had written to ask Byron if the little girl could not be lodged with
friends at Pisa, perhaps with Mrs Mason, who had two young girls of
her own. At Margaret Mason's house, Claire would be able to see as
much of Allegra as she wished without the risk of meeting Byron.

Shelley's attempts were unsuccessful. 'Allegra is not coming,' Claire sadly noted in her journal on 3 October; she was forced to comfort herself with Shelley's assurances that the little girl had seemed in excellent spirits when he visited her on his way to Ravenna in August. The nuns were devoted to her. Pretty and lively, Allegra's main concern had been whether 'mamma' was going to send her a dress of gold silk.[1] There was no need for Claire to be told that 'mamma' was not herself, but Byron's pretty young mistress. It was Teresa who had persuaded Byron to place Allegra at the convent, just as Emilia Viviani's pretty young stepmother had banished her husband's daughter to a boarding-school. This – a hateful custom in the eyes of English visitors – was the way of things in old-fashioned Roman Catholic Italy. A convent education went a long way towards removing the stigma of illegitimacy; in time, Teresa argued, Allegra might make a good Catholic marriage. The more distance placed between her and the unconventional ménage of Mr Shelley, the better would be her chance of a respectable future. Byron, after reading the Hoppners' reports, had not needed much persuading. If a convent could turn his strong-willed child into a young lady with half his Teresa's charm, he would feel well satisfied.

Little Percy, fondly described by Mary as 'a fine boy – full of life, & very pretty',[2] offered Claire some outlet for her thwarted maternal feelings; this, too, helped to soften Mary's attitude to her. Claire won more good marks for helping find furniture, both for their own new lodgings in Pisa and for the rooms which the Hunts, when they reached Italy, were to occupy in the palazzo Shelley had found for Byron on the Lung'Arno. Claire's reward came two days after the disappointment about Allegra; Shelley arrived at her lodgings in Livorno with an invitation to rejoin them at the Bagni di San Giuliano for the rest of October. He stayed on alone with Claire for three days or so, trusting that Mary's new amiability towards her stepsister would not be affected. Liberal though Shelley may have been in his views, he was not so modern or so generous as to give Mary an equal say when her wishes conflicted with his own. He wished Claire to be with them; his wife's feelings were of no concern.

Joyfully accepted by Claire, the new arrangement required considerable dexterity on the part of the Shelleys. Teresa Guiccioli, together with her father and brother, had arrived at Pisa in late August. Mary made a point of calling on this plump, golden-ringletted little lady as soon as she arrived and of offering her friendship. Throughout September, she had been seeing Teresa, affectionately described to Mrs Gisborne as 'a nice pretty girl, without pretensions, good-hearted and amiable', almost every day.[3] Teresa, growing increasingly nervous that her lover might change his mind about following her, was in need of reassurance; an introduction to Claire would cause nothing but damage.

The villa which the Williamses were still renting from the Poschi family provided an answer; staying with them, Claire could visit or be visited with no risk of meeting the young woman who had serenely banished Allegra to a convent on the other side of Italy. (Bagnacavallo was twelve miles from Ravenna.) Mary, still busily copying out her novel, kept no diary in October, but Claire's journal records a period of leisured contentment, of teaching Italian to Edward Williams, reading German with Shelley and – despite almost daily downpours – enjoying her routine four-mile walk to San Giuliano and back. We can, again, make what we wish of an entry for 18 October when Mary went to spend the night with the Williamses while Shelley and her stepsister stayed alone at the house in San Giuliano; the signs are that the relationship between Claire and himself remained loverlike in its intensity. On 11 December, he told Claire that his love for her was still a source of 'disquietude' to him and that he was suffering, in her absence, from 'a solitude of the heart'.

Shelley's own plan had been for Claire to stay near them throughout the winter, living with the Williamses, or so he told her. Mary was set against this scheme; so, for different reasons was Mrs Mason, who passionately believed that Claire could only benefit from an independent, scandal-free life. The case which this eminently sensible woman made was hard for Shelley to reject. Winter was the social season in Pisa, with the Tuscan court arriving from Florence and a swarm of English visitors moving into the Lung'Arno palaces. Scandal would be inescapable – and Byron would be furious. Did Shelley really want to incur Byron's wrath?

He did not. Claire spent her last day in Pisa at Casa Silva with Mrs Mason, packing up her possessions and stopping to write a spiky note to Mary. She wanted money from Shelley but she didn't want him to bring it himself 'because he looks singular in the streets'. She wanted all her possessions sent over at once and 'if you could out of your great bounty give me a spunge I should be infinitely obliged to you.'[4] The following morning, 1 November, Claire returned to the Boitis in chilly Florence. Travelling away from Pisa's sunny towers, she saw Byron approach and pass her, rattling along the dusty road in his monstrous Napoleonic carriage at the head of a train of horses and the menagerie of monkeys, dogs and exotic birds acquired on his travels.

Shelley had done handsomely by his friend and the travelling zoo. The Palazzo Lanfranchi, looking south across the Arno towards the

Shelleys' own new winter residence, was a great stone fortress of a building with a magnificent marble staircase, frescoed walls and enough creaks and groaning doors to promise an army of spectres for company. The rooms were, if anything, too vast; he felt forlorn. Teresa was settled nearby with her family; the Hunts, while sending assurances that they would come by balloon if it could speed their arrival,[5] were still in England, forced back to port by storms. Wistfully, Byron urged Augusta Leigh to come and keep him company, bringing, if she must, her husband. The offer was not taken up; Teresa's brother Pietro Gamba and a gang of male cronies who included Shelley, Williams, the newly returned Tom Medwin and John Taaffe, became Byron's regular companions.

Across the yellow river, in a long suite of rooms looking away from the Lanfranchi and out over the magnificent gardens to the rear of the adjacent palace, the Shelleys had settled on an upper floor of the tall Tre Palazzi di Chiesa on 25 October. They were, for the first time in their Italian travels, surrounded by furniture found and paid for by themselves. The windowsills were bright with flowers bought by Mary in the local markets. The Williamses, after sharing their rooms for the first three weeks, moved into an apartment on a lower floor. The two families were constantly in and out of each other's rooms, dining together at the end of days so glorious, Mary wrote to Mrs Gisborne on 30 November, that 'the burning sun of winter drives us to seek the shade'. She hinted at other sources of pleasure, since 'Claire is returned to her usual residence, and our tranquillity is unbroken in upon'. She wrote with rapture of Byron's latest poem, *Cain*, as appearing 'almost a revelation from its power and beauty', and with enthusiasm of a new plan, to go with Shelley to Greece, when her heroic friend Mavrocordato had freed it from the Turks, to 'one of those beautiful islands where earth, ocean, and sky form the Paradise'. Pisa, she added for good measure, had become 'a little nest of singing birds' since the arrival of Byron and Teresa.

This sounds like happiness, but Mary's moods were as volatile as her husband's. The same letter is full of complaints about the neglectful behaviour of Charles Ollier, the publisher who was sending them no news either about Shelley's *Hellas*, completed that autumn, or about Mary's novel. 'Ollier treats us abominably,' she lamented. Shelley had, two months earlier, sent their English publisher a long, detailed and laudatory account of *Valperga*, on which Mary was still working. The response had been overwhelmingly disappointing. Ollier, perhaps because he had done so badly out of Shelley himself, refused to be tempted into making a commitment. One can hardly blame him; to take an unfinished book on a husband's recommendation, sight unseen, is not businesslike.

Mary's complaint of 30 November marked the beginning of a last anxious month of revisions to a work which she now feared might not only fail to raise the substantial sum she wanted to give to her father, but might never be published at all. She was proud of *Valperga*. She had looked forward for months to seeing it in print. Now, her spirits sank. 'Correct the novel – read a little Greek – not well,' she noted on 30 November. 'Read the Hist. of Shipwrecks – not well – correct the novel,' she wrote the following day. (She was growing anxious about the Hunts' sea journey to Italy in winter.) On 5 December, she read 'Milton on divorce'. Tacitus followed: 'a dismal day'. Shelley, writing to Claire on the last day of the year, reported that Mary 'has suffered terribly from rheumatism in her head, to such a degree as for some successive nights entirely to deprive her of sleep'. Laudanum and the disagreeable method of scalding to raise blisters on the skin provided little relief. In January 1822 she reluctantly decided to let Godwin take the manuscript and do the best he could for it himself.

This was her private life. Publicly, after Byron's arrival in Pisa, Mary showed every appearance of joining in and enjoying the daily rituals which now revolved around their famous neighbour. Both Byron and Shelley were excellent shots, who enjoyed competing. Emilia Viviani's father, in his capacity as governor of Pisa and because he felt no great warmth towards Shelley or his friends, forbade any such sport in the Lanfranchi garden; instead, the sportsmen went off on most afternoons to fire their weapons in the orchard of a handsome old farm at Cisanello, two miles east of Pisa. Byron, plump and pale at this stage in his life, had become so averse to being stared at that he had himself driven to the city gate in a closed carriage before climbing into the saddle of a skittish but broadbacked Flanders mare. Shelley, Taaffe, Medwin and Williams ambled beside him while Jane Williams and Mary rolled along behind in Teresa Guiccioli's carriage. Sometimes, if Mary felt well enough, the two Englishwomen dawdled at the rear of the procession, poking at any interesting flowers or grasses in the hedgerows with the points of their furled umbrellas. They discussed their relief that, even though Mary was suffering, both Williams and Shelley appeared to be thriving in the beneficial climate of Pisa. Shelley was 'not quite well but he is much better', Mary informed Mrs Gisborne on 21 December; the climate and the company were doing him good. She almost always mentioned his name in conjunction with that of Edward Williams now. The two of them had become engrossed by boat-building plans.

Shelley, Edward Williams had written shortly after his own arrival at Pisa, was a delightful companion, 'extraordinarily young, of manners mild and amiable, but withal full of life and fun'.[6] The person to whom he was sending this description in April 1821 was his Cornish friend Edward Trelawny, then living in Switzerland and passing his time on shooting and hunting expeditions. Trelawny heard from Williams again in early December; this time, his interest was caught by the news that Byron was at Pisa. Trelawny knew little or nothing about Shelley in 1821; everybody knew about Byron. He was already keen to visit; his perfect opportunity came when Williams wrote again on 26 December. The news now was that they were all planning to shift up the coast the following summer and do plenty of sailing. Boats were required. Byron, naturally, wanted something handsome; Williams and Shelley were hoping for something fast and sleek. Trelawny knew – or claimed to know – everything relating to ships; would he join their 'select committee' to help with the design? Might his naval friend Daniel Roberts in Genoa take on the commission to build either, or both, the craft?[7] Trelawny arrived at Pisa on 14 January 1822, three weeks after Williams's invitation.

Mary, brooding over stories of shipwrecks and remembering only that she felt ill whenever she went to sea, was not in love with the project. She was, however, instantly entranced by the man who was being invited to help in their yacht's design. She admired Trelawny's height and handsome Moorish looks; she liked his easy manner and good-natured smile; she thought, after listening to his stories, that he was one of the most interesting men she had ever met. Nobody could spin tales like Trelawny. 'He tells strange stories of himself,' she noted on 19 January:

> Horrific ones – so that they harrow one up, with his emphatic but unmodulated Voice – his simple yet strong language – he Portrays the most frightful situations – then all these adventures took place between the ages of 13 and 20 – I believe them now I see the man – & tired with the everyday sleepiness of human intercourse I am glad to meet with one who among other valuable qualities has the rare merit of interesting my imagination.[8]

Mary had been deep in Scott's novels again that winter. Trelawny's tales introduced her to another world, one she had supposed only to exist in the dark, dramatic poems such as Byron had produced a few years earlier, *Lara, The Corsair, Mazeppa*.

Trelawny shared Mary's taste for these works. He kept a copy of

The Corsair under his pillow, or so he claimed. By the time he arrived in Pisa, he had already persuaded himself that he was the living original on whom Byron had drawn for inspiration. Even the Williamses had only known their Cornish friend – he was actually born in London – since meeting him in Geneva in 1820 at the home of the Cornish baronet, John St Aubyn. They knew nothing of Trelawny's domestic history, of the humiliation of a well-publicized divorce case, or of parents who had no high opinion of a feckless, troublesome, scantily educated third son who was now struggling to survive on £300 a year. (The naval war had ended when Trelawny was too young to be made a lieutenant, and thus to benefit from a pension.) In Pisa, Trelawny had a captive audience of innocents for whom he could recreate himself as the hero he longed to be. Surrounded by admiring listeners and with only Byron's cynical grin to warn him against going too far (Byron alone seems to have had Trelawny's measure) the newcomer joyfully converted a pedestrian naval career into that of a swashbuckling privateer.*

Writing his recollections of three months at Pisa almost forty years later, Trelawny embellished the truth again, with the kindly intention of adding lustre to Shelley's name. Less laudable was the viciousness with which he punished Byron for having failed to be the brooding, melancholy hero he had expected to meet. Trelawny was, above all, horrified by Byron's refusal to take his own romantic heroes seriously. To jeer at *The Corsair* was, in a sense, to jeer at Trelawny himself, and Trelawny was not a man who took kindly to being ridiculed. Shelley, a poet whom he imagined sitting in a woodland glade and gazing into a pool for inspiration, was the real thing; Byron, who shut himself up in a gloomy little parlour behind a billiard room, and produced poetry as methodically as a dairymaid churning butter, was clearly a fraud. It did not take Trelawny long to convince himself that anything good Byron wrote must have been under Shelley's influence, a view which Edward Williams readily supported. Williams, ironically enough, had been led to this view during his long conversations with Mary about her husband's work. It is ironic because Mary, the supporter of Shelley's superior claims, was the woman whom Trelawny would one day accuse of never having appreciated either Shelley or his poetry.

At the time, however, Trelawny was much taken by Mary. His later

---

* Trelawny invented a privateering hero, de Ruyter, with whom his spectacular adventures took place. The name was probably an unconscious recollection of the story of Admiral de Ruyter, who led the Dutch fleet in a highly successful raid on the English fleet in the Medway in 1667. Trelawny could have heard the story as a schoolboy.

description of her as 'rather under the English standard of woman's height, very fair and light-haired, witty, social, and animated in the society of friends',[9] is only a glancing recollection of a young woman who was as strong-willed, as imaginative and – which rather amused him at the time – as hot-tempered as himself. If Mary did, as he later remembered, start their friendship off with a string of girlish questions about 'operas, and bonnets, marriages, murders and other marvels', it had been no hardship to provide answers.

Trelawny and Mary, as her journal entries and letters make plain, were quick to make friends. She listened to his romantic tales; he heard, we must imagine, with fascination her first-hand report of the escalating war in Greece. (She was still in close touch with Mavrocordato and receiving his long, detailed accounts of the situation.) When plans were made to put on a private performance of *Othello* at Byron's palace, with Byron as Iago, Mary volunteered to play Desdemona to Trelawny's Moor. He knew the part well enough to misquote Othello's lines in letters whenever he wanted to dramatize himself. He looked, Mary observed to Mrs Gisborne on 9 February, very Moorish, 'a kind of half arab Englishman'. She must have been quite excited by the prospect of acting with him; Teresa, unfortunately, decided to prohibit a drama which she could neither take part in nor follow.

Trelawny arrived in Pisa at a time when Mary, her health somewhat improved, was ready to enjoy herself. January and February were the months of the Carnival, of the opera and an endless round of balls. 'I had thought of being presented,' she confessed to Mrs Gisborne on 18 January, but Shelley had been against it and now the grand-duke and his court had returned to Florence.

A modest form of snobbery of this kind may explain why Mary had since mid-December been paying occasional attendance at the Sunday services held privately downstairs by another inhabitant of the Tre Palazzi di Chiesa.[10] Dr John Nott, Anthony Trollope's model for Dr Vesey Stanhope in *Barchester Towers*, was a worldly old gentleman with grand connections – he had been sub-preceptor to Princess Charlotte – and with a fashionable following among Pisa's Protestant community. He had obligingly christened the unmarried Williamses' second child, Rosalind, on 30 December with Mary standing as godmother. Expecting to be welcomed after this and perhaps to meet some of Nott's smart little coterie, Mary was dismayed when the clergyman used his sermon to launch a vehement attack on atheists, taking Shelley for his target. An apology was made, but the damage was done. Everybody had heard Nott's views and that Mary had written an angry letter. It had all, as she told Mrs Gisborne some weeks later, made 'a great noise' among the English;[11] the ladies in Nott's circle promptly let it be known that they wished to have nothing to do with her.

Mary's exclusion was made harder to bear by the fact that Mrs Beauclerk, one of the liveliest hostesses in Pisa, had known Shelley as a Sussex neighbour and was expressing a wish to see him. He, perhaps somewhat disgusted by Mrs Beauclerk's readiness to leave her husband Charles at home in England while she set off for Italy with seven daughters up for offer, refused to follow up the invitation. Medwin went to Mimi Beauclerk's gatherings as often as he was asked, but Medwin was unthinkable as an escort. He had not, besides, suggested that he wanted a companion. (Medwin, it later transpired, had been pursuing his hostess, a handsome woman of good background with enough money to give excellent parties.)

On 23 January, Trelawny decided to undertake the introduction himself: 'go with him to Mrs Beauclercs in the evening,' Mary noted. They were graciously received, more on account of Trelawny's splendid moustaches and caressing stares than of Mary's subdued politeness. A couple of weeks later, while Williams and Shelley went off again to look for summer houses at La Spezia, Trelawny escorted both Mary and Jane Williams to a ball at Mrs Beauclerk's. It was the first such occasion Mary had attended since Mrs de Boinville's ball for her daughter's wedding in 1812.

Waltzes were all the rage; dancing with Trelawny, Mary was caught up in the swirl of movement and laughter and candlelit heat; Shelley was away; she was shaken by the violence of her feelings. Among what remains of the long journal-entry she made after the ball (a page was removed), she wrote of being roused from 'my ordinary monotony' into a state of feverish excitement: 'I would tear the veil from this strange world & pierce with eagle eyes beyond the sun – when every idea strange & changeful is another step in the ladder by which I would climb the –'[12] Trelawny's attentions appear to have been quite a stimulant. 'His company is delightful,' she told Mrs Gisborne the following day, 'for he excites me to think[,] and if any evil shade the intercourse[,] that time will unveil.'[13]

Shelley and Williams returned two days later on 11 February, in time to be coaxed into attending the *veglioni*, the public masked balls which were the highlight of the carnival season. Mary, competing against Jane Williams in Indian costume, borrowed a dress from her friend to appear as a Turkish lady. They danced until three in the morning. But by 25 February, the day after a dinner visit to Mrs

Beauclerk, Mary's taste for social life had evaporated. It was all so shallow. Certainly, Mrs Beauclerk and her friends were very amusing and hospitable, but what did they really care about? What were their interests, beyond love-affairs and gossip and dressing themselves up? 'The most contemptible of all lives is where you live in the world & none of your passions or affections are called into action – I am convinced I could not live thus,' she confided to her journal that evening. She had just been rereading *A Short Residence in Sweden, Norway and Denmark*; her mother, she was sure, would never have kept company with a woman like Mimi Beauclerk.

Edward Trelawny was convinced in later life that Mary had been an unfeeling wife to Shelley: why? Part of the answer lies in the fact that Trelawny was, during this time in Pisa, often living with the Williamses. Edward was his closest friend; Edward was also the chosen confidant of Shelley at a time when Shelley was making dissatisfied comparisons between his own marriage and the easy, tender relationship which existed between Edward and Jane. The week after Trelawny's arrival at Pisa, Shelley sent Williams a letter and a poem, allegedly by another author, which he urged Edward to show to Jane ' – and yet on second thought I had rather you would not', he added, unconvincingly.[14]

The poem began with the ominous declaration that 'The Serpent is shut out from Paradise'. This was easy enough to interpret: Shelley was nicknamed 'the snake' for his bright eyes and rapid, soundless movements; 'Paradise' was evidently the happiness he saw represented by his friends' domestic bliss. In the fourth and final stanza, he compared this comforting friendship to the 'cold home' to which he must return. Nobody reading it could doubt that Shelley was unhappy. The verses were 'beautiful but too melancholy', Williams noted on 26 January, but he did not question the sad picture they presented. He had already made a note that Shelley suffered from lack of wifely encouragement and required 'gentle leading'.[15] The poem only confirmed what the Williamses already suspected, that Mary did not support her husband as much as she should. It is probable that they shared their views with Trelawny, their housemate and friend. It is unlikely that any of them troubled to ask Mary for her side of the story. Shelley chose to present himself as the victim; increasingly, his frail health and mournful, needy letters combined in the minds of his friends to form the image of a martyr, bound to a cross-patch of a wife.

A slight chill estranged the two households of poets on 15 February. Mary noted that Byron's mother-in-law, Lady Noel, was dead.

Williams, learning that Byron was going to benefit from this bereavement to the tune of £10,000 a year, added a memo to himself: 'See X'mas Day.' On 25 December, Shelley and Byron had promised that whichever of them inherited his fortune first would pay the other £1,000. But Byron, knowing that it would be several months before he received anything and with Shelley already heavily in his debt for the Hunts' travelling costs, decided to treat the wager as a joke. Whatever money he had to spare that winter was intended for the *Bolivar*, the boat he had ordered as a rival to Shelley's.

Any irritation the Shelleys may have felt about Byron's reluctance to keep the terms of their agreement was eclipsed by a new storm blowing towards them from Florence; here Claire and Elise Foggi had met each other on 7 February at the home of a Russian family, the Boutourlins. Elise had called on Claire three days later: a cancelled entry in Claire's journal for 10 February clearly contains the words 'Naples and me'. Elise, evidently, had confessed the gossip which she had spread to the Hoppners. Neither Elise nor Claire knew that the story had already reached the Shelleys through Byron. Claire recorded a week of 'wretched spirits' in her journal, during which she wrote to and received an answer from Shelley. Claire fiercely obliterated the entry which revealed her reaction to his response; all we know is that she was in a state of violent agitation. Two days later, on 18 February, she wrote to Mary, to Mrs Mason, to Byron and to Charles Clairmont. She was, she announced, going to leave Italy at once and for ever.

Always impulsive, Claire could usually be coaxed into a calmer mood by the rational arguments of Mary and Mrs Mason, for whom she had a great respect; a servant was hurriedly sent to bring her from Florence to Pisa, where one or both of the ladies could try to reason with her. Mary spent the morning of 22 February describing her own distress at Elise's gossip and suggesting the best way to deal with it. It was good that Elise had appeared. Claire had always been close to her; she, if anybody, could exert some influence, force Elise to retract her hideous accusations. The notion of going off to another country was absurd; how could Claire think of such a thing when Mrs Mason and Shelley had been put to such trouble and expense – Margaret Mason had provided the introductions, Shelley the financial support – to give her a new life in Florence?

The counselling sessions, which probably followed some such lines, were effective; Claire returned meekly to Florence on 25 February. All Mary knew of the sequel was that Elise Foggi had finally – on 18 April – produced two letters denying her role as a spreader of scandal.

One went to Mary, the other to Mrs Hoppner.[16] She did not know that Claire had, on 12 March, made a note in her journal that she had given 'the Naples commission' to Elise's husband. This entry was vigorously cancelled in the new ink with which Claire began the next day's entry.[17] Its precise significance is still impossible to guess.

Even without knowledge of the mysterious Naples commissions, Mary must often have felt bound to a wheel of fire by her stepsister's demands and dramas. The business with Elise was still being settled when Claire, towards the end of March, announced that she could bear the separation from her daughter no longer. '17 March: Copy – walk with Jane – write to Claire – dine at the W's. Very weary,' Mary wrote. Her letter had no effect. On 21 March, Claire fired off a new idea. Allegra must be abducted from Bagnacavallo and the Shelleys must help her. Not even Shelley was up to this romantic plan; Mary tartly pointed out that, even if Claire managed to escape abroad with her daughter, somebody would have to answer for the consequences – and that somebody was likely to be Shelley. Byron might even challenge him to a duel: 'I need not enter upon that topic,' she added darkly, 'your own imagination may fill up the picture.'[18] Shelley, while seconding Mary's prudent advice, had other things to say. Claire was urged to write to him on 'another subject respecting which, however, all is as you already know'.[19] Her letters were to be directed not to Hodgson – a name which they had evidently used before in secret correspondence – but to Joe James and sent, not to the Tre Palazzi, but to the Post Office.[20] This secret subject had, we must suppose, something to do with their private relationship and, perhaps, with the mysterious commission which Claire had recently given to Paolo Foggi.

Writing on 20 March to warn Claire not to try to abduct Allegra, Mary was reduced to frightening her with superstitious warnings of the kind to which they were both susceptible. Spring had always been a time of bad luck for them both, she wrote, beginning with their dreadful weeks at Marchmont Buildings in 1815, just before Claire left for Lynmouth, and ending with the awkwardness of the Emilia Viviani affair of spring 1821. She could have gone on, but did not. The spring of 1822 was now being marked by the ascendancy of Jane Williams. In April, having failed to obtain a harp, Shelley gave his new muse a beautifully inlaid guitar in a close-fitting box.[21]* The poem accompanying the gift took *The Tempest* for its theme; Edward and Jane were invited to see themselves as Ferdinand and Miranda, while

---

* The guitar, of Pisan make, is now at the Bodleian Library, Oxford.

Shelley presided over them as Ariel, their magical guardian, locked inside the instrument until Jane should choose to release him with song. It was possibly in response to this offering that Williams sent a jovial invitation to a duel: 'I feel that I must parade you at 10 paces if you go on thus – If you will call yourself or send your second we will point out the ground.'[22]

It was, in a sense, all a game; Williams was not excluded and was, indeed, rather flattered to see his dim but beautiful wife so admired. The victim of the game was Mary. Shelley could pretend that he was imprisoned in the hollow body of an instrument, ready to vibrate with song at a sympathetic touch. Mary, too proud to acknowledge such an ordinary woman as her rival and too apprehensive to press Shelley about the current nature of his feelings for Claire, was the real prisoner, trapped by her impossible, games-playing husband into the role of ice-queen. Given the way Shelley was flirting with Jane and conspiring with Claire, it is hard to imagine how Mary Shelley was expected to play the role of a loving wife.

She was heavy with foreboding and sadness as she felt, perhaps even saw, Shelley slipping away from her: 'a hateful day,' she noted on 31 March, the approximate date of discovering that she was pregnant. A little over a year later, she confessed to Jane Williams that she had never expected a 'natural conclusion [to her pregnancy] – I wished it – I tried to figure it to myself but all in vain'.[23]

Edward Williams's journal, prosaic and self-satisfied, is a revealing document. On 8 March, he solemnly recorded his shock when Byron interrupted Shelley's declamation of a stanza of *Childe Harold* to ask what 'infinite nonsense' he was repeating. Not to know his own poem! And to decry it! Williams lacked a sense of humour; it never occurred to him that Byron was joking. With the same pompous gravity, Williams recorded on 15 March that he had read the first act of his new play – he was very proud of it – to Mary and that she had suggested various 'alterations'. The word seemed somehow to suggest that she had improved on his work; chewing on his pen, Williams added, 'alterations which I consider as amendments'. He could not quite bring himself to acknowledge that Mary had a superior mind to his own.

This habit of misinterpretation showed up again on the dramatic evening of 24 March. The Williamses were waiting in the Shelleys' flat to dine with them when Trelawny burst in with news of an ugly incident with an Italian soldier, a dragoon, on the way back from their usual sport of shooting at half-crowns in the Cisanello orchard. Shelley had been knocked off his horse, another man had been wounded and one of Byron's servants had stabbed the dragoon in the stomach with a pitchfork. The soldier, now being tended by Vaccà in the hospital, was expected to die. 'Trelawny had finished his story,' Williams went on,

> when Lord B. came in – the Countess fainting on his arm – S[helley] sick from the blow – Lord B. and the young count [Gamba] foaming with rage – Mrs S[helley] looking philosophically upon this inter-esting scene – and Jane and I wondering what the devil was to come next – [24]

Here, as clearly as anywhere, we see the view the Williamses had of Mary. Unstirred by her husband's injuries, she stood there calmly, observing; would Jane, would any loving wife, have been so detached, so cold? It is completely at odds with the account given in Mary's letter to Mrs Gisborne of 6–10 April. From Mary, not Williams, we learn that she had been present at the incident: 'It happened that I, and the Countess Guiccioli were in a carriage close behind, and saw it all, and you may guess how frightened we were,' she wrote. They had not gone to the Williamses' home, but to the Palazzo Lanfranchi, where Teresa had become hysterical with alarm. Edward Williams used his journal to write himself and his wife into the centre of a drama which had scarcely impinged on his evening at the Tre Palazzi. Mary, far from being the cold observer presented by him, had been an active participant, and remained so.

The following day, when the uproar over the wounded man was so great that Trelawny was afraid to leave his rooms, Mary went alone to the hospital on the other side of town. 'Go to the hospital – a day of bustle & nothings,' she wrote with her usual restraint. What she had actually discovered was that Masi, the young dragoon, was expected to die of his wounds. Dr Vaccà made it clear that the English friends of Lord Byron were no longer welcome in a city where blood had been spilt.

Against expectation, Masi survived. Byron, with a clearer sense than the rest of the group of Mary's coolness in a crisis, gave her the long job of copying out the various statements which were taken. Matching his apparent nonchalance with her own, Mary carried out the commission while letting it be known that she would prefer the job of copying poems. 'Excuse this annoyance from *womankind* & allow me to hope that it will not be long before you employ me on my usual interesting task. Is there any hope of our ever getting a copy of the Vision of Judgement?'[25] Byron, already grateful for Mary's conscientious friendliness to his young mistress, must have been amused by such clearly stated priorities.

Hearing of the difficulty of obtaining houses near La Spezia, Byron decided to give up his plan for spending the rest of the summer there with his Pisan cronies; instead, he announced his intention of taking a house near Livorno. This opened the way for Claire to rejoin the Shelleys. Full of strange forebodings about Allegra's health, she arrived in Pisa on 15 April and was smuggled into Mrs Mason's house, out of sight of the Lanfranchi palace where Byron was still in residence. On 23 April, Claire left with the Williamses to make a further search for suitable homes near La Spezia. 'Evil news,' Mary wrote in her journal that evening. Claire's unease had been prophetic; Allegra was dead of typhus.

For once, Shelley and Mary were in absolute agreement. All that mattered now was to get Claire away from Byron, whom she would – and did – hold responsible for callously abandoning a five-year-old child and allowing her to die. On 26 April, after confiding the dreadful news to the Williamses, Mary and Trelawny took Claire back to La Spezia. Only one house was now available, a lonely building beside the sea which they had previously contemplated and rejected. Trelawny left them on 28 April, travelling north to join his friend Daniel Roberts in Genoa and supervise work on the boats. 'Heard from Mary at Sarzana that she had concluded for Casa Magni,' Edward Williams noted the following day, '– but for ourselves no hope.'

A separation at this tense stage of their lives was unthinkable. On 1 May, the Williamses, Claire and the Shelleys crowded into the four habitable rooms of the house on the beach which Mary had reluctantly decided to take. After a day's unpacking and sorting, they spent the evening 'talking over our folly and our troubles'.[26] Beyond the shuttered windows, a raging sea beat in on a rocky shore.

CHAPTER TWENTY

AT THE VILLA MAGNI

May–August 1822

'As only one house was to be found habitable in this gulph, the W[illiamses] have taken up their abode with us, and their servants and mine quarrel like cats and dogs . . . "Ma pazienza" . . .'

Mary Shelley to Maria Gisborne, 2 June 1822

MARY, AS MUCH AS SHELLEY HIMSELF, HAD ALWAYS LOVED BEING near water. The blue depths of Uri, the sparkling crescent at Torquay, the dazzling breadth of Lake Geneva, the lazy shaded Thames, the rushing Serchio, the yellow, beguiling Arno: she could almost have drawn a portrait of her marriage in lakes and rivers and seas. None could rival the beauty of the bay of Lerici, glittering under the noonday sun, drenched in the silver of moonlight, boiling and lashing like a nest of serpents on a day – and there were many such – of squalls. Shelley, indifferent to the discomfort of a crowded house and the grumbles from hot attics of their Tuscan servants, was ready to proclaim that this was paradise. Sailing in the bay, or listening to the nightingales which, according to one visitor, sang sweeter and louder in the woods behind Lerici than anywhere else in Italy,[1] he was as free as the Ariel Jane Williams was always willing to charm out of her guitar. The weather, capriciously shifting from black skies and torrential downpours to days of blind, baking heat, reflected his own quicksilver temperament. This was Shelley's rainbow's end, his perfect home.

Lerici was a little fishing town, overshadowed by an old grey fortress standing above the sea. Centuries earlier, this had been the site of a cult of Diana, goddess of the woods and the moon. Henry James caught the scent of its sinister aspect when he spent a long autumn afternoon visiting the bay in the 1870s and lingered long enough to see, with eyes quickened by the knowledge of what had happened here fifty years earlier, how intently the 'pale faced tragic villa stared up at the brightening moon'.[2] Above it, dark woods of chestnut and ilex cloaked the hills.

The Villa Magni, rented in desperation by Mary because nothing else was available, was as solitary as a house could be. Five white arches held its broad terrace above the surge of the sea. Behind the terrace, from the beginning of May, the Williamses and the Shelleys lived in inescapable intimacy, eating in the hall which held their bedrooms narrowly apart. (Meals were a daily headache; the nearest supplier of provisions lived more than three miles away, across a river which the summer storms often turned into an impassable torrent.) Walking on the terrace in the evening, they could see the lights of Lerici glimmering to the south under the craggy silhouette of its castle; their nearer neighbours at San Terenzo, the hamlet which has now spread round the bay to enclose the Villa Magni, were a few fishing families. There was no sign here of the picturesque costumes beloved of tourists; the women of San Terenzo went barefoot and kept their hair from their faces with squares of rough cloth. Their language was incomprehensible; their songs and dances struck Mary as being entertainment fit only for savages, and not very friendly ones. 'Had we been wrecked on an island of the South Seas, we could scarcely have felt ourselves further from civilization and comfort,' she wrote.[3]

The land offered no escape, beyond the rocky coastal path to Lerici and the tangled paths of the woods which climbed the hill behind the villa's neglected garden. Sick and fretful in the early months of pregnancy, Mary could not rid herself of nervousness. Her only hours of peace came when they were gliding across the bay, when she leant against Shelley's knees and gave herself up to the blue of the sky, the soft rush of wind against her face. On land again, she was overpowered by the terror of some impending horror. She could neither describe it nor explain it; all she knew was that she wanted, desperately, to get her last remaining child away from this desolate place.[4] It was Percy, not Shelley, for whom she feared. Apprehensive, she became hysterical. Frustration emerged in shrill, white-faced rage or unyielding silence. Too late, she reproached herself in a long and anguished poem, 'The Choice', written the following year.

Now fierce remorse and unreplying death
Waken a chord within my heart, whose breath,
Thrilling and keen, in accents audible,
A tale of unrequited love doth tell.
It was not anger – while thy earthly dress
Encompassed still thy soul's rare loveliness,
All anger was attoned by many a kind
Caress or tear that spoke the softened mind: –
It speaks of cold neglect, averted eyes
That blindly crushed thy heart's fond sacrifice: –
My heart was all thine own – but yet a shell
Closed in its core, which seemed impenetrable,
Till sharp:toothed Misery tore the husk in twain
Which gaping lies nor may unite again –
Forgive me![5]

By the time Mary wrote the work from which these lines come, she was painfully aware of the impression her outbursts at the Villa Magni had made on their friends. The Williamses, drawing complacent comparisons with their own sunny relationship and full of sympathy for a saintly, put-upon husband, were shocked and disapproving. The tearful apologies alluded to in the poem took place in private; Mary's public image, not helped by Shelley's readiness to discuss the unhappiness she was causing him, had become that of a nagging, undisciplined neurotic.

Looking back, as she was driven to do over and over again, Mary readily acknowledged the conflict between her own misery and Shelley's love-affair with the bay. Guilt, the feeling that she had been scolding, cold, unloving, drove her to intensify the contrast in their response to life at the Villa Magni. But had it been so absolute as she punished herself by supposing?

'I still inhabit this divine bay, reading Spanish dramas & sailing & listening to the most enchanting music . . . my only regret is that the summer must ever pass,' Shelley wrote to his financial adviser and occasional creditor Horace Smith on 29 June, while admitting that 'Mary has not the same predilection for this place that I have.' But there are many indications that Shelley, as much as his wife, was going through a period of crisis. His health had never been better, but he wrote to Trelawny to get prussic acid for him, as 'a golden key to that perpetual chamber of rest'.* His old habit of sleepwalking returned.

---

* Shelley told Trelawny that he had no immediate plans to use the prussic acid, but we should ask if he could possibly have said anything else.

So did the hallucinations which had, in the past, often been vivid enough for Shelley to mistake them for real events. One, towards the end of their first week at the villa, was of a naked child (Allegra? Elena Adelaide?) who rose out of the sea, smiling at him and clapping her hands. Others, to be described later, were more sinister.

Shelley's work also suggests that his accounts to friends of a summer of exquisite happiness reflected passing moods rather than a settled state of mind. The beautiful 'Lines in the Bay of Lerici' beginning 'She left me at the silent time' are full of sadness. *The Triumph of Life*, the ambitious poem on which he was working in the last weeks at the villa, has been well described by Claire Tomalin as suggesting 'a deep and terrible disillusionment with the world. Its image of the huge chariot of death travelling on like a juggernaut, surrounded by a boiling, insect-like crowd of humanity feverishly pursuing pleasure and ambition before being extinguished, is the most hideous he imagined.'[6] Its influences, Andrea Orcagna's sombre frescoes of *The Triumph of Death* for Pisa's Campo Santo and, perhaps, local stories of Lerici's ancient cult of Diana, help to identify the poem's images of life's transience, of youth plunging towards the grave. The disillusion can only be explained as Shelley's own.

> '. . . thus on the way
> Mask after mask fell from the countenance
> And form of all; and long before the day
>
> 'Was old, the joy which waked like heaven's glance
> The sleepers in the oblivious valley, died;
> And some grew weary of the ghastly dance,
>
> 'And fell, as I have fallen, by the wayside; –
> Those soonest from whose forms most shadows passed,
> And least of strength and beauty did abide.
>
> 'Then, what is life? I cried.' –

These are the last lines of the poem as Mary edited it, since she omitted the fragmentary four lines which follow, but which do not complete the work. Shelley's nightmarish visions and dreams, when put together with his final lines, suggest that he was, in the summer of 1822, in a state of intense emotional turmoil for which Mary had little or no responsibility.

Shelley had rushed them into isolation in the days following Allegra's death, 'like a torrent, hurrying every thing in it's course', Mary told Maria Gisborne.[7] The news had reached them on 23 April; a week later, they, Claire and the Williamses, together with three small children, were squeezed into the Villa Magni. And here, on 2 May according to Edward Williams's journal, Claire walked into Jane's room and found them all discussing how best to break the news to her.

Perhaps she had already guessed the truth; her resilience amazed them. One savage letter slipped through the net by which Shelley tried to protect Byron from her fury; unexpected meekness followed. Claire asked for – and was sent – Allegra's miniature and a lock of her hair. She did not go to Livorno to see the small coffin dispatched to England, on Byron's instructions, for burial in the nave of Harrow church.* She did, to ease their limited accommodation, return to Florence for two weeks. 'She is vivacious and talkative, and though she teases [vexes] me sometimes, I like her,' Shelley wrote to John Gisborne on 18 June, shortly after her return. Mary, he added, was 'not much discontented with her visit'.

Relations between Shelley and Mary had become so bad by 18 June, following Mary's miscarriage, that she may for once have welcomed Claire's company as relief. She was also anxious to know if Claire had gathered anything while staying with Mrs Mason about William Godwin's affairs.

Mrs Mason had been appointed by Shelley as reader and censor of all Godwin correspondence; this had had the inevitable effect of increasing Mary's worries. She knew that Godwin's final lawsuit in April had been lost. This, she told Mrs Gisborne on 2 June, had put the crown on a season of misfortunes; but what of her novel, and where was her father living, now that he had lost his home? She begged for news: 'any information I could get, through anyone, would be a great benefit to me.' Mrs Gisborne did not dare flout Shelley's orders to keep his wife in the dark about all financial matters concerning Godwin. Mary welcomed Claire back to the Villa Magni because she came directly from the house in Pisa where Godwin's letters were received, examined and edited. Claire could understand how powerless Mary felt; she could even disclose that Mrs Mason

---

* Byron's wish was frustrated by the Reverend John William Cunningham, the sanctimonious vicar of Harrow who also prevented a plaque from being installed, regarding it as likely to set a bad example to young Harrovians. Allegra's coffin was buried outside the church, with no memorial.

strongly disapproved of Shelley's policy and disliked the role he had imposed on her.*

Meanwhile, the boat designed by Trelawny and Captain Daniel Roberts had arrived on 12 May with a crew of three. Two were sent back; the third, an eighteen-year-old boy called Charles Vivian, was kept on.

For Williams and for Shelley, it was like embarking on a love-affair. Trim, light, shallow-bottomed enough to be dragged on shore, their pretty little craft 'sailed like a witch';[9] she was 'a perfect plaything for the summer'.[10] Her name was her only flaw; Shelley, who had decided to call her 'Ariel', was outraged that Trelawny's first name for her, the *Don Juan*, had been painted, on Byron's instructions, in vast letters on the mainsail. Perhaps it was one of Byron's jokes, with Shelley as the butt; Shelley had, after all, begged him not to tell Mary all that he had confided about his relationship with Emilia. Byron already believed Shelley had slept with Claire; he had seen the way he behaved with Jane Williams at Pisa. But 'Lord and poet as he is he could not be allowed to make a coal-barge of our boat,' Mary told Mrs Gisborne.[11] After rubbing and scrubbing proved ineffectual, the offending patch of material was cut out and replaced.

Shelley and Williams's delight in their elegant new toy was crushed a month later when Trelawny and Roberts arrived on Byron's own boat. Handsomely equipped with two cannons and with the Countess Guiccioli's pink silk flag fluttering from the mast, the *Bolivar* sailed into view on 13 June. She saluted; they thought she must be a man-of-war brig. Byron's boat was, Williams noted enviously, 'the most beautiful craft I ever saw'.[12] Full of rivalry, they set Roberts to work adding top-masts and sails – notoriously the hardest to lower – to their own boat in order to make it faster. There was talk of making an extended false stem and stern.[13] Williams, bursting with nautical pride, made scornful references in his journal to the ignorance of 'weatherwise landsmen' while revealing his own inexperience as he noted that there was usually an afternoon breeze offshore on a fine

---

* Emily Sunstein[8] believes that Shelley showed his wife all Godwin's letters that summer, at Mrs Mason's urging; Mary's letters suggest otherwise. Her letter to Mrs Gisborne of 2 June complains of Godwin's writing 'in so few words, and in such a manner'. Godwin wrote to his daughter on many occasions between March and July 1822. His letters were seldom short. All letters to Shelley went via the Mason household. Shelley may have been acting out of kindness in endeavouring to protect Mary from the news that her father was not yet offering *Valperga*. Godwin believed, probably correctly, that his own financial difficulties would lead to his being offered poor terms.

day.[14] The sailors who took feluccas up and down the Lerici coast would have smiled at the idea that this was a discovery worth noting.

Mary had been suffering acutely from her pregnancy throughout May, during which month she kept no journal and wrote no letters. On 9 June, she collapsed. Edward Williams, who was becoming steadily less sympathetic to her as the source of his friend Shelley's unhappiness, thought she was faking her symptoms. She had been 'perfectly well' at breakfast, 'alarmingly unwell' during the day and then 'strangely better'. The 'strangely' is the clue to his thoughts: he did not believe in her illness.

A week later, although Williams omitted to record it, Mary almost died of a haemorrhage, and lost her fifth child. For seven hours, Claire, Jane and Shelley struggled to keep her awake with brandy, vinegar, eau de Cologne and, when the doctor was held up, ice, to staunch the haemorrhaging. 'Claire & Jane were afraid of using it,' Mary remembered two months later, 'but Shelley overruled them & by an unsparing application of it I was restored. They all thought & so did I at one time that I was about to die.'[15] Her husband's practicality had saved her life; still, it is hard not to wince at the word 'unsparing'.*

The miscarriage occurred on 16 June; two days later, Shelley wrote to the Gisbornes in England. He gave a good report of his own initiative and, after acknowledging that Mary was still weak, put his faith in sea-baths to restore her to health. It was hardly the moment at which to air his dissatisfaction with Mary as a wife, but the habit had become strong; he could not resist telling the Gisbornes how he longed for the friendship of 'those who can feel, and understand me.

> Whether from proximity and the continuity of domestic intercourse, Mary does not. The necessity of concealing from her thoughts that would pain her, necessitates this, perhaps. It is the curse of Tantalus, that a person possessing such excellent powers and so pure a mind as hers, should not excite the sympathy indispensable to their application to domestic life.

The Williamses, he added, were 'very pleasing . . . But words are not the instrument of our intercourse.'[16]

A drawing has survived from this period which has been conjectured to be of Mary Shelley. She had trained with artists and was thought

---

* Shelley had acquired some basic medical knowledge from observation visits to the wards of St Bartholomew's Hospital, during the months between his expulsion from Oxford and his elopement with Harriet.

to have some talent; it is, just conceivably, a self-portrait.[17] The woman it shows looks both haunted and drained; her huge eyes and gaunt cheeks suggest someone who might feel that her life had become unbearable. It might very well represent Mary as she looked in the weeks following her miscarriage. 'I am ill most of this time. Ill & then convalescent,' was all she would say of herself in her journal.[18] It was during this period that Shelley's feelings towards her showed themselves most clearly, in the form of dreams. Recalling them for Mrs Gisborne in August, Mary thought that six days had passed between the miscarriage and the night when Shelley, asleep but screaming, burst into her bedroom: 'he continued to scream which inspired me with such a panic that I jumped out of bed & ran across the hall to Mrs W's room where I fell through weakness, though I was so frightened that I got up again immediately.'[19]

Shelley, when woken, told them that his nightmare had begun with an image of the Williamses, bloodstained and with their bones starting through their skins, coming to warn him that the sea was flooding into the house. Shelley had seemed to wake up and to see that this was so when his dream changed: 'he saw the figure of himself strangling me'. It was this that had brought him running into her room, Mary explained, and yet, 'fearful of frightening me he dared not approach the bed'. To her, it must have seemed as though she was hideously reliving her own vision of Frankenstein as he wakes to see his newly animated creature standing beside him, ready, as he fearfully supposes, to do him harm. All this, she told Mrs Gisborne, had been 'frightful enough, & talking it over the next morning he told me that he had had many visions lately – he had seen the figure of himself which met him as he walked on the terrace & said to him – "How long do you mean to be content?"' To her correspondent, Mary dismissed these words as lacking any great significance: 'certainly not prophetic of what has occurred'. At the time, surely, she must have understood their import clearly enough; what could they have meant to her other than that Shelley's dream-double was expressing his weariness, his disillusion?

On 20 June, the Hunts and their six children finally stepped on to Italian soil at the port of Genoa. Exhausted after the voyage, they were in no mood for news from Shelley of his wife's ailments; Marianne Hunt was 'very ill herself – much more so than you imagine . . .' Hunt wrote reproachfully; 'and as to myself, I have become, since you saw me, an elderly gentleman, with sunken cheeks . . .'[20] Shelley, overjoyed by the arrival of his friend in whatever condition of antiquity, was impatient for their reunion; so for different reasons, was Hunt. 'I have been so hard run that I was obliged to spend it in housekeeping,' Shelley shamefacedly admitted when asked about £30 which Byron had promised to provide to the Hunts as a loan.[21] On 24 June, Shelley and Williams rigged the sails of the *Don Juan*, stocked the cupboards with provisions and were about to set off for Genoa when Mary had a relapse. Her state of mind was probably a contributing factor; Shelley's nightmarish visions, her own weakness and the stupefying heat combined to create a state of feverish apprehension. The voyage was put off.

Hunt sent word that he was going to make his way down to Livorno on 28 June. He wanted to make himself known to Byron, in whose home at Pisa he had been promised rooms. Shelley decided to waste no more time. On 1 July, he set sail for Livorno himself, together with Williams, Captain Roberts and their boy-crew of one, Charles Vivian. 'I could not endure that he should go,' Mary wrote later to Mrs Gisborne, ' – I called him back two or three times, I told him that if I did not see him soon I would go to Pisa with the child – I cried bitterly when he went away.'[22] Her only comfort was that he had promised to look for a house at Pugnano where they could spend the rest of the summer.

She wrote to him twice. One letter, according to Edward Williams, was 'of the most gloomy kind';[23] its tone can be guessed from the near-hysterical letter which she sent via Shelley to Hunt, begging him to stay away from the Villa Magni ('it would be complete madness to come') and describing herself as a prisoner: 'I wish I cd break my chains & leave this dungeon.'[24]

On 4 July, a loving note to Jane ('my dearest friend') arrived at the villa from Shelley, together with a brisk and businesslike letter for Mary. She must have felt ready to weep when she read it. He had not looked for houses at Pugnano. He could not say when he would return. The rest of the letter was taken up with news of their friends. Dr Vaccà had pronounced Marianne Hunt's illness to be grave (she lived until 1857); Hunt himself was cheerful but penniless. Byron, while willing to make a handsome gift of the copyright of his latest poem, *The Vision of Judgment*, for the first number of their new magazine, was unlikely to be able to offer further support since he was preparing to follow Teresa's family into a second exile. (The Gambas had been ordered to leave Tuscany after the fracas with Sergeant-Major Masi.) Shelley ended by expressing his wish for the thing his wife most dreaded, a continued residence at the Villa Magni.[25]

Four days later, despite uncertain weather conditions, Shelley, Williams and their boy sailor set out for Lerici from Livorno, carrying fifty pounds which Shelley had borrowed from Byron. The conditions have been variously described, but it seems clear that the *Don Juan* sailed into one of the sudden summer squalls for which this part of the coast was notorious.* With no deck and sails which were difficult to bring down in a hurry, a sudden gust was all that was needed to swamp it. Reports came later that either one or two of the feluccas which regularly undertook the journey from Livorno to Genoa had seen the little boat struck by 'baffling winds';† shouts to bring down the sails had been disregarded; at their next glance, the *Don Juan* had been engulfed.

By 11 July, a Thursday, the three women at the Villa Magni were growing anxious; only continuing bad weather kept Jane from having herself rowed to Livorno the following day. Friday was the day on which the week's post was delivered; it brought them a letter for Shelley from Hunt. Opening it, Mary saw that Hunt was asking for news of the travellers' safe return, having heard that the boat had left Livorno in a storm. The date of departure, 8 July, was named. 'I trembled all over,' Mary wrote in the long and harrowing account of the tragedy she sent to Mrs Gisborne in August. '– Jane read it – "Then it is all over!" she said. "No my dear Jane," I cried, "it is not all over, but this suspense is dreadful . . ."'[28]

Although still so weak that she had not been out of the villa for over a fortnight, Mary agreed with Jane that they must leave at once; Claire remained. The two women reached Pisa at midnight; they

---

* Another visitor to the region at the time, Agnes M. Clarke, noted in her journal that, preparing to sail from Lerici on 11 July 1822 on 'a sea which was as clear & smooth as a looking glass', it happened that a 'providential delay' preserved her from 'a sudden hurricane wh. Must have been fatal if I had been out at sea. The captain of the felucca (a coastal craft) refused to go . . . I find these sudden hurricanes are very frequent at this season on this coast.'[26] This is of particular interest, being so close to the date of the *Don Juan's* going down.
† When the *Don Juan* was located, Daniel Roberts, the builder, bought the raised shell and carried out an investigation of the wreck's condition. 'Trelawny tells me that in his, Roberts & every other sailor's opinion she was *run down*,' Mary wrote to Jane on 15 October 1822; 'of course by that Fishing Boat – which confessed to have seen them.' Trelawny and Roberts both welcomed an explanation which shifted the responsibility from the boat's designer and builder. It is possible that the boat was considered fair prey. According to Williams's journal, he and Shelley had already attracted adverse notice on 6 June when they drew pistols on a guard who attempted to prevent them landing on a military beach.[27] Random voyages along a coast well manned by forts by two Englishmen known to have been involved in an alleged attack on a soldier at Pisa would certainly have been considered suspicious. The felucca crew could have deliberately rammed the boat, knowing that money had been taken in at Livorno, and that the incident was unlikely to be investigated too closely. It is also possible that the evidence of ramming dated only from the time when the boat was lifted and brought ashore. Damage of this kind might have occurred at this stage and gone unmentioned.

went straight to the Palazzo Lanfranchi. The Hunts were in bed and, much to her relief, Mary was shown up to Byron's floor. Byron and Teresa could only confirm that the *Don Juan* had sailed on the previous Monday, in bad weather: 'more they knew not.' Horrified by Mary's exhausted appearance ('I looked more like a ghost than a woman – light seemed to emanate from my features,' she reported them as having told her[29]), Teresa begged the travellers to stay and rest.

They could not rest until they knew what had happened. Making the two-hour journey on to Livorno by carriage, they dozed at an inn until the first sign of light, when they went in search of Trelawny and Roberts. Captain Roberts was reassuring; he swore he had seen the *Don Juan*'s top-sails being lowered some ten miles out. (Neither Mary nor Jane questioned how, even with the aid of a telescope, he had managed this miracle of vision when everybody agreed that there had been a storm haze over the sea. The added top-sails were weighing heavily on Roberts's conscience by this time.)

By nine on the same morning, the two women were on their way back to Lerici under Trelawny's escort. Mary, as the carriage rolled through the shallow water of the river Magra, had to struggle to hide her emotions from Jane: 'I thought I should have gone into convulsions . . . looking down the river I saw the two great lights burning at the *foce* – A voice from within me seemed to cry aloud that is his grave.' Five days later, on 18 July, Trelawny left to make further searches; Mary, astonishingly, was still hoping for good news: 'I was very ill but as evening came on I said to Jane – "If anything had been found on the coast Trelawny would have returned to let us know. He has not returned so I hope."'[30]

The bad news had already come, although Mary did not know it. Claire, instructed by Trelawny to open his post in his absence, had read a letter in which Daniel Roberts said that two bodies, not yet formally identified, had been found. Acting as messenger was beyond her; she wrote a pathetic note to Leigh Hunt on 19 July, asking for advice and ending, helplessly: 'I know not what further to add, except that their case is desperate in every respect, and Death would be the greatest kindness to us all.'

Claire was saved by Trelawny's return that evening. The corpses mentioned by Roberts had been those of Edward Ellerker Williams and Charles Vivian; Trelawny himself had been shown a third body. He was able to identify Shelley only by the copy of Keats's poems which was still in the pocket of his jacket. By his own account, Trelawny did not need to say a word; Mary, however, remembered that he had been wonderfully graceful in breaking the news: 'he launched forth into as it were an overflowing & eloquent praise of my divine Shelley – until I almost was happy that I was thus unhappy to be fed by the praise of him, and to dwell on the eulogy that his loss thus drew forth from his friend.'[31] In this almost ecstatic state, she found the strength to write to her father. 'I have some of his friends about me who worship him – they all agree that he was an elementary being and that death does not apply to him,' she wrote and hurried to forestall the sympathy Godwin might from pity feel obliged to profess. '. . . I am not however so desolate as you might think. He is ever with me, encouraging me to become wise and good, that I may be worthy to join him.'[32]

The following morning, the widows and Claire packed up their belongings and returned, with Trelawny accompanying them, to their former lodgings in Pisa. Tearfully, the arrangements for burial were discussed. Neither Mary nor Jane could contemplate leaving their husbands in the quicklime graves on the shore where the three bodies had been hastily buried to conform with the quarantine regulations. Jane wanted to take Edward's remains to England; Mary wanted Shelley to lie near their little son William in the Protestant cemetery at Rome.

This, in Mary's experience, was their friend's finest hour. At a time when she and Jane Williams were paralysed by their loss and by the horror of their situation, Trelawny took control. He ordered an iron rack on which to burn the bodies, gathered and laid the wood and thoughtfully produced frankincense to disguise the smell. Williams, identifiable only by a handkerchief and a boot, was dealt with on 15 August. The following day, Hunt and Byron drove down to the shore in a carriage to observe Shelley's last rites, in the company of officials and a fascinated group of young fishermen. The corpse, now putrid and stained blue by the lime, was dug up and placed on the iron grid while Trelawny improvised a suitably pagan prayer. Everybody agreed that the ceremony was entirely appropriate for a poet who had already begun to seem to them like one of the spirits of his poems, a transcendent, not quite human power. It was all of a piece with Shelley's transformation from bone to spirit that the flame ascending into a blue sky should have quivered with almost unearthly radiance. There were no chemists among the awed observers to tell Trelawny that quicklime, when heated to incandescence, produces a flame of exceptional luminosity.[33]

This was the moment at which Trelawny converted himself into a keeper of the shrine, an earnest defender of the man he had known for less than six months but towards whom he now felt a veneration which would in time rival and threaten Mary's own dedicated love. The fault was partly hers. How could Trelawny not feel that a special link had been forged between himself and her husband when she allowed him, after supervising the cremation, to arrange and even help to dig the final burial plot in Rome? Writing to her on 27 April 1823, Trelawny reported on the laurels and cypresses he had planted around the grave and on the fact that, beside it, he had dug another, on Shelley's left 'so that, when I die, there is only to lift up my coverlet and roll me into it'. Mary might, he told her, have a place on the other side, 'if you like'.

Nothing, to a romantic mind like Trelawny's, could have carried more significance than his being charged with the care of Shelley's remains. Placing himself beside his friend in the cemetery was an act of uncommon assertiveness. Mary, who had left all arrangements to him, was in no position to challenge it.

Godwin, while Mary Wollstonecraft was being buried, had sat in James Marshall's rooms, concentrating all his thoughts on a letter of thanks to his friend Anthony Carlisle. Mary, while Hunt, Byron and Trelawny burnt the bodies on a scrubby, desolate stretch of shoreland, wrote the justly celebrated letter to Maria Gisborne from which come many of her words in this chapter. 'They are now about this fearful office,' she wrote on 15 August, the day on which Williams was cremated, '– and I live.'[34] Staying away, she spared herself little. Trelawny's horribly detailed account of the fish-eaten body of Williams – 'dreadfully mutilated – both legs separating on our attempting to move it – the hands & one foot had been entirely eaten – with all the flesh of the face' – was copied into her journal; she could not, it seems, bring herself to write out Trelawny's description of the cremations.

Mary's torment had begun the moment she heard that Shelley's body had been found; nothing now could be undone. Contrition was useless; she was left to scald herself with the memory of every angry word she had said, every time she had turned away, every time she had expressed cynicism or doubt. What use was there in telling herself that she had been driven by her need to protect their child? Percy thrived; Shelley, who had grown healthy enough that summer to surprise young Thornton Hunt with his fleshy cheeks and increased girth, was dead. For comfort, she was forced to turn to the poem he had written in the summer of 1821. 'Adonais is not Keats's it is his

own elegy,' she told Mrs Gisborne; reading it again, she drew some
solace from the image of Shelley

> . . . made one with Nature: there is heard
> His voice in all her music, from the moan
> Of thunder, to the song of night's sweet bird;
> He is a presence to be felt and known
> In darkness and in light, from herb and stone,
> Spreading itself where'er that Power may move
> Which has withdrawn his being to its own;
> Which wields the world with never-wearied love,
> Sustains it from beneath, and kindles it above.[35]

As his bones shrivelled to ashes on the shore, Mary's relationship
with Shelley was already being judged. No precious relic was brought
back for her from the funeral pyre. This was the age in which,
without photographs to be fondly framed and cherished, fragments
of the dead were invested with the value of talismans. Byron's choice,
the skull, fell to pieces in the flames. Trelawny burned his hands in
seizing a fragment of jawbone; Hunt took another. The heart, or the
part of the remains which seemed most like a heart, had failed to
burn, while exuding a viscous liquid.[36] Trelawny snatched it out;
Hunt requested and received this rather special relic of his friend.
When Mary asked if she might have the heart herself, Hunt refused
to surrender it. At some point shortly after this, Mary remembered
them sitting together in a coach and quarrelling bitterly; it took a
reproachful letter from Jane Williams to Hunt to compel a surrender.
The heart was rediscovered after Mary Shelley's death. Wrapped in
silk between the pages of *Adonais*, it had lain inside her travelling-
desk for almost thirty years.

Mary followed her painful transcription of Trelawny's report of the
uncovering of one or both of the bodies – the account seems to run
them together or to repeat itself – with a few disjointed entries in her
journal. Among them are a couple which show how swiftly she was
reaching towards the idea of a life that was about to be repossessed
and transformed.

> He is a man which like sea weed, when in its element, unfolds itself
> & becomes a plant of rare beauty & grace, but taken from that it is a
> worthless & ugly weed, trodden under foot without remorse
>
> Yet that same sea weed, so that you raise it from the ground & tend on
> it dividing & nursing its delicate fil[?us] will preserve its beauty – I do
> not despair of him.[37]

The task of defending and enhancing her husband's reputation would be her great work for the future, her consolation for the remorse she now felt. No blame would be attached to Shelley for the unhappiness he had caused her, for the extent to which he had forced her to accommodate his wishes, for the readiness – although she was not fully aware of his betrayals – with which he had represented her to their friends as an unsympathetic partner. All blame, in Mary's view, lay with herself; the exaltation of his nature and his work would be her act of reparation.

PART IV

A Woman of Ill Repute

CHAPTER TWENTY-ONE

BITTER WATERS

1822–1823

'I bear at the bottom of my heart a fathomless well of bitter waters, the workings of which my philosophy is ever at work to repress . . .'

Mary Shelley, Journal, 5 October 1822

AND THOU, STRANGE STAR! ASCENDANT AT MY BIRTH
Which rained, they said, kind influence on the earth,
So from great parents sprung I dared to boast
Fortune my friend, till set, thy beams were lost!
And thou – Inscrutable! By whose decree
Has burst this hideous storm of misery!
Here let me cling, here to these solitudes,
These myrtle shaded streams and chestnut woods;
Tear me not hence here let me live & die,
In my adopted land, my country, Italy![1]

Mary's unhappiness is apparent on almost every page of the new
journal which she began to keep in October 1822, when she and the
Hunts were uneasily sharing a home near Byron's on the outskirts of
Genoa. It is not clear whether she ever intended to publish 'The
Choice', the long self-lacerating poem which she wrote out in its
pages, but it leaves no room to doubt her feelings. Her anguish, profound and unappeasable, was made more bitter by the recognition of
her own faults, her coldness, her egotism, her quick temper. Was it
her own complaining letter which had driven Shelley to risk his life
trying to return as quickly as possible to the Villa Magni on a stormy
day? She would never know; she would always wonder.

Mary was still only twenty-four when Shelley drowned. Unhappiness drew her thoughts back to Mary Wollstonecraft, whose wretchedness she knew so well from *A Short Residence* and from Godwin's
Memoirs with their account of the last stages of her relationship with
Gilbert Imlay. Her mother had died at thirty-seven; it was no punishment to imagine herself following the same route. Thirteen more
years; she reckoned them up and found them long enough. In
thirteen years she could see Percy through school, publish all the
manuscripts of Shelley which she could collect and, most important
of all, write the life of 'a Celestial Spirit', his integrity and 'sweetness
of disposition . . . unequalled by any human being that ever existed'.[2]
This was another thrust at herself; she knew very well that sweetness
of disposition was not an attribute anybody had praised her for in the
past few years.

Shelley appeared to her in dreams; in her letters, she spoke, as if to
reclaim him, of 'mine own'; allusions to 'Him', 'He' and 'His' suggest
that the dead man had achieved the status of a deity in her thoughts.
He had, she liked to fancy, become the presiding spirit of the woods
and lakes and mountains he had loved. This was the promise he had
held out to her in *Adonais*: 'He is a presence to be felt and known /
In darkness and in light, from herb and stone.'

Her grief, after the first terrible night of searching for news of the
boat, was private. She spent August with Claire and Jane Williams at
their old lodgings in the Tre Palazzi di Chiesa at Pisa. Trelawny visited,
flirted with Claire and helped with the arrangements for transporting
Shelley's remains to Rome. 'He is generous to a distressing degree,'
Mary told Mrs Gisborne on 27 August. His behaviour was painfully
contrasted to that of Mrs Mason whose coldness bewildered her.

Mary, meanwhile, made herself useful to Hunt's invalid wife and
tried to smooth ruffled feelings between Byron and the noisy, unwelcome tribe of Hunt children who romped and yelled under the little
back room on the first floor of the Palazzo Lanfranchi where, stoked
with gin-punch, he was writing *Don Juan*. She did her best to comfort
Jane Williams who, haggard and distraught – 'no woman had ever
more need of a protector,' Mary sympathetically wrote[3] – seemed all
that a widow conventionally should – and that she herself did not. Her
calm exterior was perceived as lack of feeling. 'No one seems to
understand or to sympathize with me. They all seem to look on me
as one without affections,' she wrote with astonishment in her journal
on 21 October. And again, on 17 November, after an unhappy conversation with Hunt: 'a cold heart! have I [a] cold heart? God knows!
but none need envy the icy region this heart encircles.'

This apparent indifference, the stoicism which Godwin had taught his daughter to see as the noblest of virtues, added weight to the unkind gossip about Mary's failings which Jane Williams spread before she went back to England in the autumn of 1822. Leigh Hunt was a ready listener, having had first-hand experience of Mary's anger when he tried to justify his right to – of all painfully symbolic objects – her husband's heart. Writing to his sister-in-law Bessy Kent in September, he commented on Mary's 'extreme and apparently unmitigated bad temper' and wondered that it had not been cured by the love she evidently felt for Shelley. 'She certainly must have terrible reflections at times,' he added.[4]

This was after he had talked with Jane. Initially, Hunt was awe-struck by Mary's restraint. Writing to Bessy shortly after the bodies had been discovered, he told her that Mrs Shelley was coping remarkably well, 'better than could have been imagined'. It was from being shown this letter by Miss Kent that William Godwin first learnt of Shelley's death; he knew his daughter well enough to guess at the pain she was hiding. Mary's own letter, when it reached him, pathetically assured him that Shelley was still with her, inspiring her to emulate his wisdom and goodness, 'that I may be worthy to join him'.[5] Godwin let the religious sentiments pass without comment on this occasion. 'She has great courage,' he told her aunt Everina Wollstonecraft, 'though it is easy to see she is dreadfully overwhelmed by this disastrous event.' The couple had, he added, been 'doatingly fond of each other . . .'[6]

It was sad that Godwin could not bring himself to say as much to his daughter; the best he could manage was to rejoice that Shelley would no longer be able to keep back his letters. Mary could look forward to sharing the family's troubles to the full. 'You are now fallen to my own level . . .' Godwin told her; 'whatever misfortune or ruin falls upon me, I shall not now scruple to lay it fully before you.' It sounds heartless; it was not meant to be so. At a time when he was still – when was this not the case? – desperately short of money, he urged Mary to request whatever small sum she might need; for the present, he wanted her to come home and be comforted by 'your earliest friend'.[7]

Godwin's letter arrived in August, when Mary was still undecided as to whether she should go or stay. She did not want to be a burden on her hard-pressed father; she did not, on the other hand, see how she was going to support herself in the immediate future if she stayed on in Italy. Shelley had not insured his life; she had to wait until the end of October to learn from Peacock, one of the two executors, that she could expect the £220 allowance due for the quarter year during which he died.[8] In October, she also received ninety-seven crowns (a little over £50), divided with Jane Williams, as their share of the money raised from selling off the contents of the salvaged boat.* Payments by the *Liberal* for contributions from Shelley and herself brought in a further £36 towards the end of the year. By November, Mary felt sufficiently secure to send a gift of £12 to Claire, who had left Italy at the end of the summer to seek employment as a companion or governess in Vienna, near her brother. Mary's generous impulse was applauded by Mrs Mason, for whom it made 'a striking contrast' to the behaviour of Byron who had disgusted her by refusing to send Claire a penny.[10]† Mrs Mason may not have known, and Byron probably did, that Claire, during her last weeks in Pisa, had become closely involved with Edward Trelawny; since Trelawny's pockets were always generously opened to his friends, Byron might have assumed that he was taking care of a woman to whom he had become attached.

Byron never showed a trace of guilt about his callousness towards Claire; he did, in the summer of 1822, feel a little conscience-stricken about his past treatment of the Shelleys. The Hoppners' gossip had been welcome at a time when he wanted to keep Allegra away from Shelley and Mary; he had been free with his view of them as careless parents. Anxious to redress the harm already done, Byron now assured his friends in England that Shelley had been 'the *best* and least selfish man I ever knew – I never knew a man who was not a beast in comparison.'[11] As one of Shelley's two executors he now felt a degree of responsibility for Mary's welfare.

The solution he found was to invite Mary to be his fair copyist, a task she had readily accepted at Geneva and in Venice during the bleak days after her baby daughter's death. More recently, she had copied statements taken after the incident with Sergeant-Major Masi at Pisa. Byron had made his own fair copies of the first five cantos of *Don Juan*; the work he offered now was charity disguised as necessity. There is no proof of financial dealings in either Mary's or Byron's cor-

---

* The boat's contents included clothing, books, Williams's journal – on which Mary was later to draw for her projected 'Life of Shelley' – and the 'ninety odd crowns' that Shelley had borrowed from Byron. Byron, as Shelley's second executor, tactfully neglected to mention that this sum was by rights his; it, too, went to Mary.[9]

† Mrs Mason had tried to induce Byron to send money to Claire; Byron initially agreed and then consented to provide it only in the form of a loan to Mary, who could forward it if she wished. Mary, irritated by this suggestion, refused the offer.

respondence, but a letter of 1830 in which she warmly confirmed her father's view of Byron as 'generous, openhanded and kind',[12] together with frequent allusions in her letters to Byron's offers of money, suggests that payment was certainly intended. 'I am quite of the *old school* with regard to gratitude,' she told him on 27 November, drawing the line between herself and William Godwin's belief in unthankful acceptance.

Grateful though Mary was, she cannot much have relished the task of transcribing canto VI, in which Juan, disguised as Juanna, engages with the delectable Dudù in a harem of luscious odalisques. This was less a distraction than an affront to the sensibilities of a young woman whose October journal shows her reshaping her dead husband into a sexless angel, 'a spirit caged, an elementary being . . .' But she had never lacked perseverance; lips pursed, she carried on. When a phrase disgusted her, she simply drew a line or left a blank. Occasionally, she misread or omitted a word. Noting that Shelley had been left out of Byron's list of the poets of the age in canto XI, she drew his attention to it with an endearingly unsubtle hint. He had made a reference in his list to a period of eight years, she told him; how remarkable that he should have mentioned the exact time of Shelley's relationship with her![13] But Byron, oddly enough, for he had included Coleridge and Keats, declined to oblige her. Copying canto XV she believed she had found a portrait of herself, a rather pleasing one, in Aurora Raby who, 'radiant and grave

> . . . look'd as if she sat by Eden's door,
> And griev'd for those who could return no more.[14]

Did Mary fall in love with Byron in the months after Shelley's death? She seems hardly to have known the answer herself. Bewildered by her feelings after talking alone with him for two hours in October, she tried to rationalize her excitement. His voice was like nobody else's; perhaps it affected her because she always expected to hear Shelley's giving the response? This, so she told herself, was the answer to the enigma, to why Byron 'has the power by his mere presence & voice of exciting such deep & shifting emotions within me'.[15]

Was that all there was to it? Was Byron no more than a voice, triggering her memories of Shelley? She asked for, and faithfully kept in her dressing case until her death, a lock of his hair.* She took note

---

* The only others she kept were of her children, her mother and Shelley.

of the fact that Teresa was jealous of her, although with wonder that anybody could be jealous 'of a living corpse such as I'.[16] She took care to disguise the level of their intimacy. 'I see very little of L.B. he does not come here,' she wrote to Jane Williams from Genoa on 7 March 1823; just two days earlier, she had asked Byron to come and visit her 'this evening at your usual hour'.[17] 'Can I forget his attentions & consolations to me during my deepest misery?' she asked herself the following year when she heard of Byron's death. 'Never.'[18] As a widow, she had committed herself to Shelley's memory. 'After loving him I could only love an angel like him,' she told Jane Williams on 18 September. Byron was no angel – he even coolly read the letters Mary had sent in 1817 'from me to mine own Shelley' when her old writing-desk from Marlow was mistakenly delivered to his door in September. Mary's only worry was whether these letters might have said anything to upset him. 'There were some things a *little* against him,' she remembered, and then brightened: '– and others in praise of his writings.'

To Mary, assiduously though she had begged for it to be sent out to her, the desk's contents gave as much pain as pleasure.* 'What a scene to recur to!' she wrote in her journal on 7 October. 'My William, Clara, Allegra are all talked of – They lived then . . . their hands were warm with blood & life when clasped in mine. Where are they all? This is too great an agony to be written about.'[20] Percy, happily, was in excellent health. Sometimes, in her blackest moments, she wished he was not: 'you are the only chain that links me to time,' she had noted two days earlier: 'but for you I should be free.' But this was a mood which passed.

Byron's kindness helped to influence Mary's decision, at the end of the summer, to join the Hunts, who were now entirely dependent on his financial support of the *Liberal* for their own survival as well as that of the magazine, and to follow their patron to Genoa. Teresa's young brother Pietro Gamba had found Byron a house there, the Casa Saluzzo, in the pleasant suburb of Albaro. Jane Williams, armed with a purseful of London introductions from her friend, returned to England from Genoa on 17 September. At least one letter had been

---

* The desk contained only a portion of the Marlow correspondence. Many of the letters were lost or, perhaps, sold after the Shelleys left Albion House in February 1818. Mary had asked Peacock to make the storage arrangements, but some of the packing cases fell into the hands of their landlord who may have sold letters to pay himself for arrears of rent.[19] Peacock, however, told Mary (on 15 April 1823) that many loose papers were burned by the landlord's servants before he himself gained access to Albion House.

sent ahead of her. Unaware of Jane's propensity to gossip, Mary urged Jefferson Hogg to be kind to her and to listen to the woman 'who more than any other person can describe to you the last actions & thoughts of your incomparable friend'.[21] Hogg did as she asked; he soaked up every word.

Jane left their Genoa inn at four in the morning. Waking from a dream of Pugnano and the beautiful Villa Poschi – 'its halls, its cypresses – the perfume of its mountains and the gaiety of our life beneath their shadow' – Mary went grimly out to find lodgings for herself and the Hunts. As she walked along, listening to the roar of the sea, she felt misery of a kind worse than she had yet experienced. 'I am not given to tears,' she told Mrs Gisborne that day. This was worse, a '*stringemento* which is quite convulsive & did I not struggle greatly would cause violent hysterics'. She suppressed it. She found the Casa Negroto at the bottom of Albaro's steep hill; forty rooms, two marble staircases and a garden, all for £40 a year. She knew the Hunts were woefully short of money. Generously, she decided to cover more than half the rental cost herself although she and Percy were two to the Hunts' party of eight.

———

Charles Dickens, visiting Genoa in 1853, spent three months in the suburb of Albaro over which the expanded city now sprawls. His presentation of the view from the hilltop village tells us how the area looked when Mary was at Casa Negroto.

> The noble bay of Genoa, with the deep blue Mediterranean, lies stretched out near at hand; monstrous desolate old houses and palaces are dotted all about; lofty hills, with their tops often hidden in the clouds, and with strong forts perched high up on their craggy sides, are close upon the left; and in front, stretching from the walls of the house, down to a ruined chapel which stands upon the bold and picturesque rocks on the sea-shore, are green vineyards, where you may wander all day long in partial shade, through interminable vistas of grapes, trained on a rough trellis-work across the narrow paths.[22]

The views were beautiful, but the Hunts, assured by Mary that they would be delighted with the Casa Negroto, were unimpressed. '[T]he number and size of the doors and windows make it look anything but *snug*,' grumbled Marianne, longing for her cosy London parlour.[23] Mary took comfort from the fact that they had enough space to lead separate lives. She did not know the spiteful tales Jane Williams had been telling of her marriage; she did know that Hunt had become strangely unfriendly. She supposed it was because she had made such a fuss about his attempt to keep Shelley's heart; the quarrel had been very unpleasant.

The autumn proved bitterly cold; a small and inefficient stove failed to lift the temperature of Mary's rooms on the upper floor and she was forced to take refuge downstairs. A fire was small compensation for the continued rudeness of Hunt's manner; Marianne, who had discovered that she was expecting a seventh child, was cross, unwell and miserable. There were many occasions when Mary wished Trelawny had not bullied her into sharing a house with these supposed friends; she was less aware than he of the gossip which had gone before her. In the eyes of the expatriate colony in Genoa, she was still the girl from a radical background who had run off with a married man, borne his children out of wedlock and then let Lord Byron have his way with her and her sister, all with her lover's consent. Stories of suicides, of children put in foundling hospitals, of households of free love, were probably also doing the rounds. Claire had been wise to leave. As for Mary: '[T]he English at Genoa will not receive her . . .'[24] She seemed blind to her situation. 'T[relawny] says that I am the person in the world most ignorant of it & its character,' she noted after talking to him on 5 October. 'It is true I seldom see, I only feel evil.' Had he, one wonders, been trying to open her eyes to Jane Williams's scandalmongering?

Mary saw no future in the love-affair which had briefly flared up between Trelawny and Claire in the aftermath of Shelley's death. In Genoa, as she was well aware, he was sleeping with Gabrielle Wright, the wife of one of his friends; at the same time, he shamelessly asked Mary, who had a good command of French, to write on his behalf to a former mistress in Paris. 'Say everything,' he instructed her; 'tell her what I have been doing, where I am, how unshaken in my attachment, how delighted with her constancy . . .'[25] Warning him that his affair with Mrs Wright might get him into trouble, Mary had the poor reward of losing his company herself. 'I have only seen him three times since his return here,' she lamented to Jane on 15 October; a month later, however, Trelawny had become a regular visitor, easing the tense atmosphere around the Hunts' fireside. Writing to Claire on 22 November, Trelawny praised Mary's new-found meekness: 'as both of us are overbearingly self-willed and bad-tempered, such forbearance and toleration on her part argues great and real friendship . . . I am very loth to leave her!'

An orderly life was her chosen defence against depression. She had a box of wooden letters sent from England and began teaching Percy to read and to speak his own tongue. Her father was asked for books with pictures of animals and for a copy of Mary Wollstonecraft's *Lessons*, from which Mary had learned her own first words. Percy was not yet 'my beloved boy' – her lost William occupied that role – but he was 'my dear boy' and, when the Hunt children complained of his shouting at them in Italian, 'poor little darling'.[26] She walked down the winding hill path to the shore, she sketched the views, she studied Greek. In the mornings, she copied out Shelley's manuscripts before turning to Byron's unstoppable Cantos. For the *Liberal*, she wrote a short story, 'A Tale of the Passions',* reworked an old essay on Giovanni Villani and wrote another, much livelier piece, about Rousseau's beloved Madame d'Houtetot. 'I have made my first probation in writing & it has done me great good, & I get more calm,' she recorded on 10 November. After transcribing parts of Edward Williams's salvaged journal, she began a more ambitious project, a life of Shelley. Notional chapter headings – 'France – Poverty – a few days of solitude & some uneasiness' – suggest that she had serious intentions, but the few surviving pages of the project show how emotionally unfit she was for the task. She had only got as far as his schooldays when her account drifted off into an agonized acknowledgment of her own position. 'I am one cut off in the prime of life from hope, enjoyment & prosperity . . . the rock on which I built my hopes has crumbled away,' she wrote on the last page.[27]

Godwin strongly supported his daughter's wish to make her living as an author. Writing to her in November 1822, when she was plotting a drama to be set in medieval Italy, he urged her to consider the increasingly fashionable field of travel-writing. Lady Morgan's strong views on politics had not stood between her and success; Mary, too, might make her name in this field. Independence was not a hopeless dream. 'Your talents are truly extraordinary,' he told her. 'Frankenstein is universally known . . . and respected.

> It is the most wonderful work to have been written at twenty years of age that I ever heard of. You are now five and twenty. And, most fortunately, you have pursued a course of reading, and cultivated your mind in a manner the most admirably adapted to make you a great and successful author. If you cannot be independent, who should be?[28]

---

* Mary drew on her historical research for *Valperga* and, in the character of Despina, gave voice to her own grief. Hunt praised the story, but the reviewer in the *Examiner* of 29 December 1822 thought – rightly – that the central catastrophe was awkwardly contrived.

Godwin had not neglected the life of Castruccio which Mary had sent him at the beginning of 1822. He had renamed it *Valperga*, probably to distinguish the book from Machiavelli's well-known study of Castruccio. The female characters, especially Beatrice, 'the jewel of the book', struck him as admirable. The novel's main problem lay in its length: 'it appears, in reading, that the first rule you prescribed yourself was, I will let it be long,' he scolded his daughter. 'It contains the quantity of four volumes of "Waverley".'[29] The long battle accounts were reduced or banished to bring it down to an acceptable three-volume length. An edition of 1,250 copies was published by the firm of Whittakers early in 1823. By May, Godwin could congratulate his daughter on having sold almost half the impression: 'You have realized talents which I but faintly and doubtfully anticipated,' he told her.[30] Mary had wanted to make him a gift of the profits; she did not take up a kind suggestion from her stepmother to Mrs Mason that the advance should be restored to her 'if ever you are in want of it'.[31]

The reviews were friendly, although none of the critics thought the new novel a worthy successor to *Frankenstein*. To Mary's disappointment, they declined to be horrified by Beatrice's blasphemy. 'I am surprised that none of these Literary Gazettes are shocked,' she told Mrs Gisborne.[32] Analogies between Castruccio and Bonaparte, which struck them as banal, and which Mary reportedly denied having intended to suggest, attracted more comment than the power to foresee which Mary felt was such a remarkable force in all her work. 'Is not the catastrophe [of Euthanasia's death at sea] strangely prophetic?' she asked Mrs Gisborne. 'But it seems to me that in what I have hitherto written I have done nothing but prophecy what has arrived to. Matilda foretells even many small circumstances most truly . . .'[33] She was very proud of her clairvoyance: 'And what art thou? I know, but dare not speak,' Shelley had asked in his introduction to *The Revolt of Islam*, addressed to her. He had, she sincerely believed, paid homage there to her prophetic gift. Every one of her presentiments had been followed by a tragedy. Nobody ever pointed out to Mary that, dreading everything, she was likely on occasion to be proved right.

By August 1823, when most of the reviews of *Valperga* had appeared, Mary was ready to pretend that she had no great opinion of the novel. It was, she told Hunt, 'merely a book of promise, another landing place on the staircase I am climbing', but it annoyed her that the Hunt brothers had given it only a few lines in the *Examiner*.[34] Publicly, she was insouciant; privately, she was irked.

Sixteen years later, she urged Richard Bentley to add the book to his popular standard series, with a preface written by herself. It deserved 'fair play; never being properly published', she wrote.[35] Perhaps Charles Ollier, through whom she sent this request, failed to pass it on; more probably, Bentley, a shrewd businessman, smelt a poor seller and decided to resist. *Valperga* remained out of print until the 1990s.

Comforting relics were assembled and sent out to Genoa by Thomas Love Peacock: a ring which had belonged to her mother, a little diamond cross which Shelley had once given her, various books, manuscripts and the writing-desk containing her own letters. But, in the unfortunate absence of a will made by her husband, what Mary needed most was money.

Byron, for whose name Shelley's conventional and unliterary father felt scant respect, had already approached Sir Timothy about Mary's financial position, anticipating only that they might need to negotiate the exact sum she should receive. The response came in February 1823. It was not friendly. Mary, Sir Timothy said, was the woman who chose to be his son's mistress when he was already married; she had 'in no small degree, as I suspect, estranged my son's mind from his family, and all his first duties in life'. There could be no question of making her an allowance or of further communication on such a distressing subject.[36] To his own lawyer, William Whitton, Sir Timothy conceded that his son's death was 'a melancholy event' and that his second marriage was probably legal: 'He was particular in that respect.'[37] Whitton, whose daughter had married his client's older, illegitimate son (whose existence in no way softened Sir Timothy's condemnation of others' transgressions), had his own family's interests at heart; they did not include offering help to Mary Shelley or recognizing her son's rights. With Mary and little Percy out of the picture, Whitton could hope that the Shelleys might favour his own son-in-law.[38]* One sop was offered to Mary, but it was not a generous or kindly one. Sir Timothy was willing to maintain his grandson, but only on condition that Percy was removed from his mother's care and fostered by a third party, to be chosen by the Shelleys.[39]

---

* Whitton's hopes were limited by the fact that Percy Shelley's elder son, Charles, had already been installed at Field Place and was being treated as heir to the estate.

Byron, cynically familiar with a world in which women had no rights over their children, thought this offer better than nothing; Mary was astonished that he could imagine her accepting 'a beggarly provision under the care of a stranger'. Besides, 'I should not live ten days separated from him [Percy],' she wrote to Byron on 25 February. She wondered why he could not see what her father understood so clearly, that by surrendering her son she was acknowledging her unsuitability to be his mother? There was also a practical aspect, as Godwin had been quick to perceive. By giving up Percy, she weakened her claim to Shelley's heavily encumbered estate: 'the advantage to them [the Shelley family] if the will came to be contested would be too immense –' she told Byron. It was a cruel shock; three months earlier, she had been making arrangements to have a seal engraved with the Shelley crest. Then, she had supposed that she would be recognized by Sir Timothy as a member of their family; now, she found herself rejected, disowned.

Seeking advice from everyone she knew, Mary found that no clear picture emerged. Byron urged her to leave Italy and give up her child; Mrs Gisborne and Trelawny advised her to stay in Italy; Mrs Mason and Godwin thought she should return to England, but keep charge of Percy. Hogg's response to a long appeal for legal counsel from Mary never reached her, but Jane Williams hinted that he shared her own view: Mary should let Percy go and keep out of the country. 'Indeed, you surprize me by saying that *wise heads* think that my presence might hurt my negociations with my father-in-law,' Mary sharply responded; just how did Jane imagine Percy was going to be bestowed on the Shelleys, if his mother stayed in Italy?[40]

Departure, by the time Mary wrote this letter to Jane in April, had become the only option. Byron had decided to donate the *Bolivar* to the Greek cause and to go out there himself, together with Pietro Gamba, 'half mad with joy at the very idea', and Trelawny, to whom Mary was asked to pass on an invitation to join them. 'I cannot continue to live under Hunt's roof,' Mary told Jane on 10 April; she planned to leave for England immediately after the birth of Marianne's child. Byron remained most generous in his offers, she added, and then undercut the tribute by supposing that the £2,000 bequeathed to him by Shelley for his executorship would help to keep him sweet.[41] We should not take too much notice of this acid aside; Mary's letters to Jane show that she was anxious to mask her affection for Byron. Only when writing to this correspondent did she consistently denigrate and mock him. Her prudence was well-advised.

Mary and Jane had, so far as she knew, lived like sisters in their first weeks of widowhood. Jane should have been delighted to hear of her return to England. If so, she made a remarkably good job of hiding her feelings. 'I am sure,' she wrote to Mary on 27 March, 'your return can bring nothing with it but misery to yourself & the knowledge of this will destroy the pleasure I should otherwise have in seeing you.'[42] Other letters followed, in a similar vein.

A less innocent woman than Mary might have wondered at the intensity of Jane Williams's campaign to keep her away from England, but Mary, as Claire tartly reminded her a quarter of a century later, was uncommonly good at not looking closely at things which might wound her.[43] The truth of the situation seems to have been that Jane's connection to Shelley, combined with the tragic circumstance of her 'widowhood', had given her an importance she had never previously enjoyed. Hogg, always fascinated by the women Shelley loved, heard enough of his friend's feelings for Jane – and from whom but Jane herself could he have learned them? – to be drawn into a new pursuit. He may not have encouraged Jane's storytelling – one letter, written in 1824, suggests that he was shocked by her relish for deception[44] – but he did not stop her. Unchecked, she recounted the stories of Shelley's unhappiness, his envy of her own marriage, his despair at being married to such a cold and unsympathetic wife. By August 1823 Hogg had been persuaded that Mary's sense of bereavement was only 'imaginary'.[45]

Hunt, at least, now knew that Jane was an unkind, untrustworthy witness. Throughout the winter of 1822, he was haunted by a brief visit he had paid in October to the deserted Villa Magni, and to 'those melancholy rooms' to which Shelley had been returning when he drowned.[46] Mrs Williams's stories of Shelley's unhappy marriage had been persuasively told; Mary's occasional outbursts added credibility to Jane's account. At some point in June 1823, however, Mary and Hunt had a long discussion during which he and she both spoke their minds and became reconciled. 'You know somewhat of what I suffered during the winter during his alienation from me,' Mary wrote to Jane, not knowing what coals of fire she was heaping on her friend's head; 'he was displeased with me for many just reasons, but he found me willing to expiate as far as I cd the evil I had done, so his heart was again warmed.'[47] Here, Mary was too harsh on herself; Hunt sent a stinging rebuke to Jane Williams. Writing to his friend Vincent Novello, he urged him to be kind to Mary when she reached London, and to ignore her deceptive air of reserve. He had by now come nearer to understanding the apparent contradiction in Mary's nature, the cool exterior concealing strong emotions:

She is a torrent of fire under a Hecla snow; but I believe, as Mr
Trelawny a friend of his [Shelley's] tells me *he* believed, even when
most uneasy with her, that she had excuses of suffering little known
to anybody but herself; these ought now to be more readily granted
her on account of the touching remorse she confesses for ever having
treated him with unkindness.[48]

Even here, it is plain that Mary, under whatever duress, remained discreet. Trelawny and Hunt could only guess at what these 'excuses of
suffering' had been. They might have been caused by her own ill
health or her worries about her family; they might have related to the
Naples baby, to Shelley's feelings for Claire, Jane Williams and Emilia
Viviani, or to the loss of her three children. She provided no details,
but both Trelawny and Hunt now knew that she had been given real
cause for unhappiness.

———————

Mary's last weeks at Albaro were clouded by what she later described
as Byron's 'unconquerable avarice'.[49] He had, the day after Marianne
Hunt's safe delivery of a child on 9 June, promised to arrange and pay
for Mary and her son to travel in comfort to England. Hunt, to whom
Mary now turned for advice, was largely responsible for disrupting
this arrangement.

On 28 June, Hunt reminded Byron of his promise. Such unwillingness was apparent on his side, or so Hunt told Mary, that Hunt decided
to mention the thousand pounds still owing from the wager with
Shelley on their respective inheritances. Byron, put in the wrong, took
umbrage. Instead of paying the wager, he promptly resigned his claim
on Shelley's estate to twice that sum for his duties as executor. He did,
however, continue to insist that he would pay Mary's travel costs. Mary
felt obliged to refuse his offer after being shown various notes and
letters Hunt had received from Byron. These, she told Jane Williams
on 2 July, were 'so full of contempt against me and my lost Shelley that
I could stand it no longer'.

Hurt may have caused Mary to exaggerate Byron's contempt; he
remained baffled by her sudden hostility. Anxious to do well by her,
he made a tactful arrangement for Hunt to collect the necessary sum
from his banker in Genoa and tell whatever story he liked to save
Mary's pride. Hunt took the money and, shockingly, kept it. John Cam
Hobhouse, visiting Genoa in 1828, was shown the signed receipt.[50]
Mary remained convinced that Byron had broken his promise. He did

not, after all, care even enough to help her to travel in comfort. She never knew that Hunt had been given money for this purpose.

It is a sad little story, made more so by evidence of Mary's own efforts to bridge the gulf opened by Hunt between herself and Byron. 'Di bueno! I don't know what to say to you, my dear, for I can't do anything,' Teresa wrote in response to the first of several appeals for help.[51] Distraught herself at the prospect of Byron's imminent departure, Teresa had little time for Mary's wounded feelings. She did pass on Mary's anxious request that Byron should forget whatever pain she had caused him. Sharp words had clearly been spoken. On 10 July, Teresa reported that Byron sent her greetings and wanted Mary to know that 'he had no feeling of enmity'.[52]

Trelawny, Teresa's brother and Byron embarked for Greece on 13 July, together with Byron's horses, dogs, doctor and enough medicine to cure the ailments of a battalion. (Storms kept them anchored in port for a further five days.) One of Byron's last actions was to ask Mary if she would visit the Casa Saluzzo directly after his departure and comfort his heartbroken mistress. This is not a request that a man with a bad conscience would have found easy to make. Byron believed he had behaved decently. Hunt had been provided with funds for his family's move to Florence and for Mary's journey to England. It was not until they were at sea that Trelawny, by his own account, revealed that he, not Byron, had paid Mary's fare. Byron insisted on repaying the sum and then, so Trelawny said, forgot the debt.[53]

Trelawny's version, as so often, was a half-truth. Mary had borrowed a little money from him; the deficiency had been supplied by Mrs Mason, who loaned it but asked for repayment 'should you ever grow rich'.[54] Perhaps she was easing her conscience; Margaret Mason had never disguised the fact that she preferred Claire to Mary, an injustice which had been fuelled by Mrs Godwin's spitefully inaccurate accounts of Mary's behaviour in the summer of 1814. Mary left Albaro on 25 July, burning with indignation at Byron's apparent meanness, and singing the praises of Trelawny's 'unalterable goodness'. The only kind thing she could find to say of Byron now was that he had kept her at Genoa long enough to restore her friendship with Hunt, 'one whom I am sure can never change – '[55]

Travelling without an escort, Mary was determined to make her way across France as quickly as possible, 'alone with my child', she reminded Jane Williams on 30 July. Perhaps her thoughts were of her mother's trip to Norway and Sweden with little Fanny at much the same age. Percy, now almost four, was a cheerful traveller: 'he has been very good & is no trouble to me at all,' Mary told the Hunts on the same day. Once, when she had to rebuke him for 'self-will', she was amused to be complimented by an impressed father of six: '"Madame – vous avez du caractere."' [56] The scenery and passers-by provided her with rich material for the lively, tender letters she sent the Hunts from every halt, filling them with affectionate messages to the unruly tribe of children who were now on their way to new lodgings in Florence. ('How is Thorny's temper, Johnny's verses – Mary's "Deuce takeits" – Swinburne's quiet looks . . . Percy's martyrdom – Henry's "Magnificent eyes" – & little Vincent's gentle smiles . . . Percy wants to send Sylvan a play thing . . .' [57])

Mont Blanc and the surrounding scenery gave her for the first time a happy sense of Shelley's continuing presence, watching this same landscape. Even so, it was a nightmarish trip. 'Although I would not risk another night & day's journey like the last, yet it is pleasant to look back & find that I have done a five day's work in 24 hours,' she told the Hunts on 7 August, after being insulted by 'a wretch' who had reduced her to tears and being taken 'really ill at 2 in the morning on a desert road . . .' Reaching the Hôtel Nelson in Paris on 13 August, she was presented with another of Jane Williams's frantic entreaties to her to stay out of England. There was more comfort in a visit the following day from the Hunts' friend, witty, merry Horace Smith, who invited her to come out to his family's little house at Versailles.

Mary may already have heard from her father that *Frankenstein* had been made into a play that summer, on the strength of which Godwin lightly revised his daughter's book for immediate republication in a new two-volume edition. Mary herself had given so little thought to the novel in recent months that she made a present of an abandoned early revision of her own to one of Trelawny's friends, a Mrs Thomas who, unusually among the disapproving English community in Genoa, had been prepared to call on her. [58] Now, to her amused surprise, she heard from Horace Smith that *Presumption; or, The Fate of Frankenstein*, a dramatization by Richard Brinsley Peake, had come on at the sensation-loving Lyceum.* T.P. Cooke, who had already played the lead at the Lyceum in 1820 in *The Vampire, or The Bride of the Isles* (based on Polidori's novella), was said to have been so terrifying as a blue-painted Creature 'as caused the ladies to faint away & a hubbub to ensue'. A few days later, Mary was disappointed to hear that the

---

* This, rather suitably, was where the first staging of Bram Stoker's *Dracula* took place later in the century

ladies had not been so very frightened, but that 'the first appearance of the Monster from F's laboratory down a staircase had a fine effect . . . the piece fell off afterwards – though it is having a run.'⁵⁹* Passing this news on to the Hunts, Mary could not resist telling them that *Don Juan's* shocking new Cantos were having a 'limited sale'; just for a moment, her own fame seemed to be outshining Byron's.

Mary's long letter to the Hunts during her visit to Versailles was the first since Shelley's death in which she sounds thoroughly happy and at home. The Smiths were near neighbours at Versailles of an old friend of her father's, James Kenney. Kenney had, many years ago, married the widow of Thomas Holcroft, another of the Godwin circle. Louisa, Holcroft's seventeen-year-old daughter, was at home to charm with her blushes and pretty manners. Kenney, a small, cheerful Irishman, was full of the success of his own most recent play at Drury Lane; the house at Versailles bubbled with London gossip, of Charles Lamb's having become reclusive, of Mary Lamb being the most faultless of ladies, of plays being censored if they had nine 'damns' in the performance, thanks to the prudish influence of Theodore Hooke's Tory-spirited *John Bull*. Mary heard of Hazlitt meeting his wife in the street just after their divorce and sitting down with her to have a nice slice of boiled pork. She also heard, with interest, that Horace Smith was paid £200 a year for occasional light contributions to the *New Monthly Magazine*.

Talking, laughing, discussing plays, Mary was reminded of the best of the old days at Skinner Street. But her spirits sank when the conversation turned to her own future. Godwin was reported to be in good heart and friends had rallied round to help pay the costs of his lawsuit and back rent. His new home was, while not grand, big enough for him to continue to operate as a bookseller, but as for her stepmother, 'well – pazienza! Kenny did not give a favourable account of William [William Godwin, Jr] either,' Mary reported to the Hunts: 'vedremo!'⁶⁰ She decided not to spend a day more than was necessary under her father's roof.

There was a moment at the Smiths' home when, hearing the opening chords on a harp of a song which Jane often sang when they were in Italy, she had to ask them to stop; it was hard to look cheerful

---

* Cooke's blue body, together with the Monster's striking first descent from the laboratory – his creation was never shown – became standard features of all subsequent productions. The title *Presumption* shows that the subject was being carefully presented as a moral tale of hubristic endeavour. This did not stop a few stalwarts from protesting – which did the play's success no harm at all.

and resolute when the Kenneys warned her that she would be miserable in England. But they were all so good to her, so kind and, knowing little of her life abroad with Shelley, so blessedly unreproachful.

One comment pleased her above all others during this cheerful interlude; she could not resist passing it on to the Hunts. 'Mrs K[enney] says that I am grown very like my Mother,' she told them proudly, 'especially in Manners – in my way of addressing people – this is the most flattering thing anyone cd say to me. I have tried to please them, & I have hopes that I have succeeded.'[61]

Setting out from the Kenneys' home for Calais, Mary took comfort from their assurances that they would be visiting England before too long. She felt the need of such friends as these as she looked towards the English shore, not as a homecomer, but with the apprehensive eyes of an exile.

FAME, OF A KIND

1823–1824

'Well – first I will tell you journalwise the history of my 16 days in London. I arrived monday the 25ᵗʰ of August – My father & William came for me to the Wharf. I had an excellent passage of 11½ hours . . . the smoke of our fire was wafted right aft & streamed out behind us [this was Mary's first steamboat journey] – but wind was of little consequence – the tide was with us – and though the Engine gave a 'short uneasy motion' to the vessel, the water was so smooth that no one on board was sick & Persino played about the deck in high glee. I had a very kind reception in the Strand [Godwin's new home] . . . the house, though rather dismal, is infinitely better than the Skinner St. one – I resolved not to think of certain things, to take all as a matter of course and thus contrived to keep myself out of the gulph of melancholy, on the edge of which I was & am continually peeping. –

But lo & behold! I found myself famous! . . .'

Mary Shelley to Leigh Hunt, 9–11 September 1823

ONLY THE DROPPING OF WAISTLINES AND DEEPENING OF BONNET brims appeared to have marked the five-year gap since Mary's last visit to Paris. Arriving in London at the end of August 1823, under skies washed white by a piercing east wind, she felt as though she had stepped into a city of the future. Even the accent had changed. The voice of the new London's streets was loud, flat and full of money.

George IV, together with his favourite architect, John Nash, had been building almost without pause for the past five years, building for his own glory in a style to prompt imperial comparisons, and building for commerce, with the aim of turning London into one of the world's leading industrial cities. By 1823, the Regent's Canal, spanned by forty bridges, had opened the way for cargo barges to slide into the heart of the city; Regent Street now cut a bold swathe from north Marylebone almost to the door of Carlton House; enticing shops under the soaring roof of Nash's Quadrant in Regent Street formed part of an ambitious thrust away from the old town's tightly laced Mayfair centre, forcing builders and consumers east, towards the City.

The smartest money in town was going into expansion and development. The Duke of Wellington had put money into Brunel's scheme to drive a tunnel under the Thames; Thomas Cubitt was laying the foundations for a series of elegant squares in the five fields of marshland separating Chelsea village from Westminster. In Regent's Park, Nash had almost completed his vision of an urban Arcadia for the wealthy. The tall chimneys of brick kilns spread their bitter clouds over the hayfields surrounding the villages of Mary's childhood, Notting Hill, Paddington, Kilburn, Kentish Town.

Nothing was as her memory had preserved it. Elegant Buckingham House was gone, torn down to give George IV a palace to match his bulk; nearby, a giant Achilles forged from dismantled cannons saluted England's hero, the Duke of Wellington, in another unfinished monster-home on the site of old Apsley House. Gaslight, as bright as if all London had taken to the stage, streamed down on the muddy streets where linkboys, a mere five years ago, had guided ladies to safety with flaming torches.

'I think I could find my way better on foot to the Coliseum at Rome than hence [her lodgings near Brunswick Square and Coram's Fields] to Grosvenor Square,' Mary lamented to young Louisa Holcroft at Versailles;[1] in her journal, she noted that she felt like an exile, the last relic of a beloved race returning to a country she no longer knew. The sense of being the sole survivor was melancholy and strong; Shelley and Williams were dead; Polidori had committed suicide; Trelawny and Byron were on their way to Greece and, perhaps, to their deaths on a battlefield. Only she was left.

Struggling to find her way through the crowded streets, she saw London through the eyes of a bewildered tourist. A silk-roped balloon sailed overhead; a hectic sunset turned the city into a panorama by her father's friend, John Martin. Newly popular – his lurid canvases of *The Destruction of Herculaneum* (1822) and *The Seventh Plague* (1823) appealed to the late Georgians' taste for sensation – Martin had done little more than dramatize the tumbled heaps of stone, the stucco shells and stranded pillars among which his admiring viewers now went about their daily lives.

The idea for a novel began to form, triggered by Mary's perception of herself as a stranger in the wreckage of a great city. Martin's 1823 title gave her an idea, an attractive one to a writer haunted by the sense of her isolation. *Frankenstein* had been set at the end of the eighteenth century; what if she moved into the future, to the end of time? What if the world's population had been devastated by a plague of the kind imagined by Martin? How would it be carried? How would people respond? These were the questions she began to examine and turn over during her first weeks in London as the idea for *The Last Man*, one of her most imaginative and ambitious works, took shape.*

A two-week residence at the new family home returned Mary firmly to the present. Neither Nash nor his royal master had troubled their minds with schemes for the shabby east end of the cobbled Strand, where Godwin's new house and business premises squatted in the shadow of St Clement Danes, Samuel Johnson's favourite local church, among chop houses, printers, engravers and purveyors of curiosities. The recently uncovered skeleton of a mammoth was on show nearby.

Here, surrounded by the theatrical and literary friends who lived and worked in this lively, crowded, hackney-clattering area, the Godwins were gallantly back at work as proprietors of the Juvenile Library. Their list, as Percy's mother could hardly fail to observe, included several new children's books and one older one, reprinted from 1819, by Mrs Caroline Barnard. Its title, *The Fisher Boy, or Worth in Humble Life*, enabled Mary to guess why Godwin had brusquely rejected *Maurice*, her own modest tale of a fisher-boy; the two stories even shared Weymouth for a setting.[2] With Mrs Barnard already on his list, Godwin would not have wanted another, paler treatment of an almost identical subject. Business came first.

Mrs Godwin, whose reproaches and intrusive questions Mary had been dreading, was unexpectedly amiable and sympathetic. Godwin, milder and slower than when she had last seen him, busied himself

---

* A rash of poems, novels and paintings on this subject, including John Martin's first 1826 sketch for *The Last Man* (1849), may also have been inspired by rumours that the plague of cholera which broke out in Bengal in 1817 was steadily advancing towards Europe. It reached Sunderland in the north of England in 1831 and London in January 1832. Most major cities in England were affected by a disease which thrived best in the poorest areas. The epidemic had shrunk to a handful of cases by the summer of 1832, partly as a result of fierce sanitary regulations. One of its last victims was Mary's half-brother William. It was as a consequence of the 1832 cholera epidemic that the massive task of reforming London's drainage system began.

with arranging entertainments, a visit to the Tower, a day's outing down the river to Richmond where Marianne Hunt's young brother Tom, a future star of Drury Lane, was treading the boards. Amelia Curran, making one of her long visits to London, was asked to dine; Charles and Mary Lamb came, bursting with pride in their pretty adopted daughter Emma Isola and a home of their own at last on the banks of New River in Islington. Life was being kinder to the Lambs than the Godwins; Mary had not needed confining for two years; Charles's regular contributions as Elia to the *London Magazine* had won him literary celebrity. Having known Mary Shelley since her childhood, they urged her to call as often as she could find time to make the journey. It is unlikely that they made much reference to her loss; Lamb, always capricious in his likes and dislikes, had never cared for Shelley.

Better placed than most to give Mary a clear account of her father's situation, Lamb was unable to be reassuring. Godwin had moved into his new premises at 195 The Strand on 26 June 1822, still hoping that Shelley would send financial help. On 23 December 1822, his former landlord at Skinner Street obtained another charge against him, for £373 6s. 8d. Only £220 had been raised from friendly supporters by July 1823, of which £100 had already been spent. Charles Lamb was among the signers of a new appeal which endeavoured to raise funds for Godwin by public subscription, arguing the importance of allowing him to continue work on his massive History of the Commonwealth unimpeded by financial worries. Other signatories included William Lamb, John Murray, Sir James Mackintosh, Henry Crabb Robinson and Lord Dudley. Godwin, while assuring his friends that no financial troubles would prevent him from continuing work on his book, was a very worried man at the time of his daughter's return to England. He was still being pursued for the arrears of his rent on Skinner Street and, for all the professed affection of aristocratic admirers like Lady Caroline Lamb (Lady Caroline sent scrawled invitations to her home at Brocket Hall and asked kindly for accounts of Mr Godwin's 'interesting and beautiful' daughter[3]), most were readier to pay tributes than open their purses.

Everybody now spoke warmly of Godwin; none could afford to indulge his continual need of financial support.* To Mary, who had learned something but not all of this from her father's letters, it was

---

* Read, the landlord at Skinner Street, came to an arrangement with Godwin in November 1823 which allowed him to settle, for the time being, with a part payment of the £430 he now owed.

clear that she would have to start finding ways to earn enough to keep him as well as herself. Who could tell? Perhaps Sir Timothy's attitude would soften when he saw the journey she had made. She and her father were to see his lawyer on 3 September: she remained hopeful.

Usually reserved, the sixty-seven-year-old Godwin made no secret of his delight in having Mary home again. She was, he told her fondly, the only member of the family he could depend on now; when he drew up a new will in 1827, he made sure that Mary, due to inherit both the Opie portrait of her mother and the Northcote painting of himself which had always hung opposite it, should also have control over his literary estate.[4] Mary, not his amiable, hare-brained son William, was to be the curator of his reputation. Mary would know what to keep and what to burn.

Mary's twenty-year-old half-brother had already won her sympathy when Godwin brusquely dismissed him in one of his letters as 'no smiler'; with an uncertain future, a volatile, exhausting mother and a father whose high expectations could never be satisfied, it was hard to imagine that William had much to laugh about. Since they had last met, she was pleased to discover, he had become interested in music and the theatre, and in writing. Having recently become a parliamentary reporter for the *Morning Chronicle*, he was hoping to review for the *Opera Glass*, a new venture by his American friend, the actor and playwright John Howard Payne.

While sharing her father's view of William's unsteadiness, Mary liked his warmth and laughed at his puppyish enthusiasm, the way he rushed at new projects and teased his father as 'the old gentleman', an expression which she also irreverently adopted behind Godwin's back. Others complained that young William was a noisy oaf; Mary found him responsive and kind. She often coaxed him to come with her on walks to the wooded slopes around Caen Wood and Highgate village where Coleridge sat sadly behind Dr Gillman's curtains, wondering what he had done to drive his son Hartley, Mary's old playmate, to refuse ever to see him again.* Perhaps they discussed Shelley's magnificent translations from *Faust*: Coleridge had been planning

---

* Hartley, a lost soul after being expelled in 1820 from his Fellowship at Oriel College, Oxford, had last seen his father in July 1822 when he borrowed some money and then failed to keep a second appointment with him. Coleridge later learned that he had gone back to Ambleside, where he became a lonely schoolmaster, received by nobody because of his drinking habits. Ironically, one of the causes of Hartley's despair had been the discovery that his own schemes for a great poem on the subject of Prometheus had already been realized by Shelley, a poet for whom he shared his father's deep admiration. Hartley abandoned his project after reading Shelley's poem, probably in late 1821.

such an undertaking since 1814, the year of Mary's elopement. Perhaps, having read and admired *Frankenstein, or The Modern Prometheus*, he talked with his visitor about his own plans for a lecture on the myth of Prometheus, which he gave to the newly formed Royal Society of Literature the following year. Mary must have been happy to see him again; her memories of Coleridge stretched back beyond the days when she and Claire had hidden under a sofa to hear him recite 'The Ancient Mariner'.

Mary's first London excursion, accompanied by William, her father and a distressingly haggard Jane Williams, was to see *Presumption; or, The Fate of Frankenstein*, now in its fourth week of performances at the Lyceum, just down the road from Godwin's new home. By late August *Presumption*, which lasted, with music, for approximately an hour, had been shifted from first to third place in the evening's entertainment, but Mary was still able to sense a 'breathless eagerness in the audience' as lightning flashes and thunder rolls announced that T.P. Cooke as the 'Creature' was ready to spring out on them from the concealed laboratory at the top of a narrow stage staircase.[5]* The cheap seats in the pit were only half-filled, but nobody left until the drama ended, a sure sign of success in the days when regular theatregoers seldom stayed for more than an act.

And so, when she had expected to be buried in oblivion, 'lo & behold! I found myself famous,' Mary told Hunt after watching this high-pitched travesty of her novel.[6] But this was a time when she would have preferred obscurity. The talk in London was still of her having run away with Shelley and her sister to live in an incestuous commune at Geneva with Lord Byron and Shelley sharing the young women's favours. The last thing Mary needed was the news that placard-bearers had been marching through London, urging playgoers not to attend 'the monstrous Drama, founded on the improper work called "Frankenstein"... This subject is pregnant with mischief.'[7]†

Appropriated for the stage, Mary's novel thrived. By the end of 1823, five versions of the story had appeared in London, often at rau-

---

* Cooke's offstage creation was originally a concession to religious spectators, who would not have tolerated a showing on stage of the work of God.
† This was probably a publicity stunt arranged by S.A. Arnold, who owned the Lyceum, also called the English Opera House, during this period.

cous theatres like the Royal Coburg (the Old Vic). There were two revivals in 1824. In 1826, T.P. Cooke crossed the Channel to play the Creature once again in a new French version. From then on, hardly a year passed without some adaptation of *Frankenstein*, usually farcical, never serious, being performed.[8] Mary made nothing from this pillaging of her work; playwrights were under no obligation to hand over money for their use of a book. The *Frankenstein* dramatizations scarcely acknowledged her existence as the original author; they guaranteed, nevertheless, an enduring connection between her small, ladylike personage and fiction's most celebrated monster. This, more than her treasured friendship with Byron, her life with Shelley, or her celebrated parentage, became the basis of her future fame.

Richard Brinsley Peake's stage production of 1823 marked the birth of a myth. That the monster and his maker had entered the popular imagination was clearly indicated the following year when George Canning, the Foreign Secretary, addressing the House of Commons on the question of emancipation, suggested that freeing rebel West Indian slaves 'would be to raise up a creature resembling the splendid fiction of a recent romance'.[9] Mary was pleased to have her book alluded to in Parliament by a politician she admired; Canning had, however, misread her intentions. She intended her creature to act as a warning against unsocial behaviour: do as you would be done by was the Godwinian message she meant to convey. Canning's allusion was part of an argument against freedom. Treat the slaves well, Canning argued, and see the horrors they will do. By 1830, the Creature was being referred to as Frankenstein; by 1840, it had evolved into a symbol for anything perceived as dangerous and out of control. A *Punch* cartoon of 1843 showed a ferocious apelike figure, clearly bent on damaging anything or anyone crossing its path. The caption was 'The Irish Frankenstein'.

Godwin's publication in July 1823 of a new edition of his daughter's novel, clearly identifying her for the first time as the author, was well-timed. Not only did the book reach a new audience, of playgoers, but it would provide her with a valuable byline, 'The author of Frankenstein', under which to write without contravening her father-in-law's ban on public use of his family name.* And writing, as Mary rapidly understood, was going to be crucial for her survival.

It was always in Sir Timothy's power to salvage Mary's reputation. By giving her a reasonable allowance, by publicly acknowledging her as

---

* Interestingly, Mary never considered the option of using her maiden name.

his daughter-in-law, by inviting her into his home, he could help her to be seen as the kind of lady on whom one's sister or daughter might call without fear of scandal.

Sir Timothy took the opposite course. Mary's fond supposition that little Percy would win the affection of his grandparents was misplaced; Percy was the child of a union which the Shelleys had condemned and continued to deplore. To show an interest in Percy was equivalent to expressing approval of his mother, the woman who, in their eyes, had lured Shelley away from his young and pregnant wife and, they did not doubt, encouraged him to pour his future inheritance into her father's open hands. Percy was of interest to his Shelley grandparents only if he could be separated from his mother.

Their attitude was not immediately apparent. On 3 September, Mary and Godwin went to call on William Whitton, the Shelleys' family lawyer. Presented with a sum of £100 for her immediate expenses and promised £100 a year on Percy's behalf, Mary's hopes rose. More, she imagined, would follow. Her sacrifice, in coming back to England from the sunny Italy she was already missing, was going to be recognized and rewarded. Whitton's response, she wrote cheerfully to Hunt, 'relieved me from a load of anxieties – I hesitated no longer to quit the Strand . . .'[10]

Shortly after moving into lodgings close to James Marshall's home overlooking Coram's Fields to the north of Holborn, she was brutally disillusioned. She did not know that Whitton had in fact urged Sir Timothy to grant her no personal allowance; she did, by the end of November, know that she was to receive a meagre £200 a year on which to live – £100 for herself, £100 for Percy, to be repaid, with interest, to the estate at the time of Sir Timothy's death. She would receive this allowance only if she remained in England and made no attempt to bring Shelley's name into the public eye. She was not to publish his work, nor was she to use his name in her own writings. There would be no family meetings, no correspondence, no pretence of affection. The allowance was ungenerous; the prohibitions were unkind. Cruellest of all, to a young woman whose long association with Shelley had, as Godwin once poignantly put it, deprived her of her 'spotless fame', was the Shelleys' decision to exclude her from their family, to treat her as a figure of disgrace.

Mary was already a social outcast. Mrs Gisborne, visiting London in 1820, had only dared to tell one member of her husband's family, the open-minded Emma Clementi, that she knew and even liked the Shelleys. In August 1823, the month Mary returned to England, Marianne Hunt's sister, Elizabeth Kent, was berated in the *Monthly*

Magazine (1 August 1823) for having dared to quote lines by Shelley in her book on the care of pot plants, *Flora Domestica*. The reproach was renewed in October by the *Eclectic Review*, with references to 'the atheist Shelley'. John Chalk Claris ('Arthur Brooke'), a poet who had been imprudent enough to write an elegy on Shelley's death, had been castigated by reviewers in the *Literary Gazette* (September 1822), the *Country Literary Chronicle* (October 1822), the *Monthly Review* (November 1822), the *Gentleman's Magazine* (December 1822) and the *Monthly Censor* (January 1823). Mary, as Shelley's widow, was assumed to share his deplorable views. The chilling behaviour of his parents did nothing to make her life easier.

Mary saw her mother-in-law as her principal enemy in the family. Her instinct may have been correct. Sir Timothy, when he did finally agree to meet his grandson in 1827, seemed genuinely affected by the sight of a small, shy, well-scrubbed boy who bore a marked resemblance to his father. Shaken, he continued to resist Mary's attempts to arrange a meeting for herself; perhaps, having heard from Whitton that she was a gentle, well-spoken young woman, he feared her effect on his feelings. He was not, by nature, a hard-hearted man. When his second daughter, another Mary, caused scandal in 1827 by leaving her husband and children to have a child with another – somewhat disreputable – man, Sir Timothy stood by her. So did his wife. But Mary Shelley was not of their blood. They had no interest in protecting her reputation. They owed her nothing but their anger.

Godwin, however short of money, had refused to waste time on writing articles and reviews since his early years as a hard-working journalist. Mary could see no alternative, although she longed to unrein her imagination on a novel and – Shelley's wish – a tragic drama. Godwin threw cold water on this second plan; shown the play she had written or sketched out in the months after her return to London, he was lethally candid. 'Your personages are mere abstractions, the lines & points of a mathematical diagram, & not men and women,' he told her. '. . . It is laziness, my dear Mary, that makes you wish to be a dramatist.'[11] She did not make a second attempt, nor did she forget Godwin's brutal words.

In October 1823, she had begun work on a piece about ghosts for the prestigious *London Magazine*, one of the few journals which had not published disparaging reviews of her husband's work. She drew on the spectral tales she had read at Geneva in 1816, and on others which she had heard from the Chevalier Mengaldo at Venice and which she had recorded in her journal during the terrible days following Clara Shelley's death there. On 13 December, Godwin wrote a discreet letter to the resourceful young publisher and magazine proprietor Henry Colburn, for whom he was writing his enormous History of the Commonwealth. Would Mr Colburn be interested in letting Mary 'try her powers' for him in the *New Monthly Magazine*, and at what rate? Did Mr Colburn have any particular subjects to suit her interests?[12] His approach was successful; Mary's submission of a piece on ancient and modern Rome the following month began a relationship which would eventually lead to Colburn's publication of *The Last Man* in 1826.[13]

Properly supported by the Shelleys, it is unlikely that Mary would ever have undertaken the short stories for ladies' annuals which she dutifully produced over the next sixteen years. Valuable to biographers and critics for their personal content, her contributions are for the most part wordy and pedestrian. Occasionally, like sun on steel, Mary's wit glints through. 'The Bride of Modern Italy', a story anonymously published in the *London Magazine* the year after her return, has the brio of a Peacock novella; here, tongue firmly in her cheek, Mary parodied her husband's predilection for rescuing pretty girls from their boarding-schools. Emilia Viviani, thinly disguised as 'Clorinda', is portrayed as a giddy flirt who teaches her suitors how to bribe her keeper with rum bottles and boasts of drugging the Mother Superior with opium cakes. Shelley, represented as an impressionable young English artist, is contriving a daring rescue mission to save his heroine from a planned marriage when a rival discloses that the wedding has already taken place, with no noticeable resistance from the bride.[14]

Here, and in a travel sketch, 'A Visit to Brighton', published two years later after a disappointing month in George IV's favourite resort, Mary demonstrated a gift for humorous writing which shrewder editors would have encouraged her to develop. What, she asked, were the beauties of Leman or Como when compared to the English seaside? 'Lovers of nature! Enthusiasts, who delight to drink deep joy from the various shapes and changes of earth and sky, behold me at Brighton! Was this the retreat of our pleasure-loving prince? the asylum of fashion? the resort of nobles? – this!' Mockingly, she went on to show herself in pursuit of Brighton's only park: 'twigs, meant for trees, stand about: as for a real tree, an inhabitant of Brighton is as ignorant of its shape and material, as a Venetian of that of a horse.'[15]

Mary's capacity for laughter, often gleamingly apparent in her letters, was one of her most attractive qualities. Leigh Hunt had never forgotten her breaking down in giggles at the slapstick scenes in *The Merchant of Venice*. Writing to Jane Williams in 1827, she looked back on summer evenings when they strolled home from expeditions to friends, laughing 'as if we were kittens in clover'.[16] Surrounded by friends, as she explained almost apologetically to Leigh Hunt, 'I easily forget myself – & at first carried away soon get beyond & carry with me the spirit of the company'.[17] She loved to enjoy herself; she was worried that if she did so people would consider her unfeeling. Alone with Jane, and perhaps with her jolly half-brother William, she was not afraid to be frivolous.

Mary's public persona remained severe and wan, that of a widow dedicated to the care of her father, her child and the posthumous reputation of her husband. This was the side of her which Henry Crabb Robinson, visiting Godwin's home one evening in November 1823, recorded in his journal. Mrs Shelley was noted to have looked elegant, sickly and young. (Mrs Godwin gushingly told her she looked no more than sixteen.) He could not believe such a fragile girl was the author of *Frankenstein*, a work which he still only knew by hearsay. Meeting her again the following year and still reeling from the poisonous gossip Mrs Hoppner had poured into his ears in Florence that summer, Robinson decided that Mrs Hoppner must be mistaken: Mrs Shelley still seemed withdrawn, but she was an interesting and charming woman.[18] He never saw the wicked, spicy side of Mary's nature; the curb was always on under her stepmother's roof.

Robinson's benign impressions were shared by two admirers of Shelley who approached Mary in the autumn of 1823. Bryan Waller Procter, a handsome invalid of thirty-six, was a poet and recently successful dramatist who wrote under the name 'Barry Cornwall'; Thomas Lovell Beddoes was the twenty-one-year-old son of the celebrated Dr Beddoes in whose Pneumatic Institute, long before, young Humphry Davy had introduced Coleridge to the delights of laughing gas. The published author of a play and a collection of poems, Thomas had a lurid imagination; his love of graveyard subjects reminded Mary of Shelley when they had first met.

Mary's visitors had a literary proposal to put to her. She, they knew, had been talking to Leigh Hunt's brother John about a scheme to publish Shelley's poetry, despite Sir Timothy's injunction. Hunt, although ready to act as the publisher, was in financial difficulties and facing a lawsuit. They would, Procter told Mary, be honoured if she would allow them, together with his brother Nicholas and an attorney, Thomas Kelsall, to underwrite the costs.

Shelley's name must be raised above the coarse derision of such magazines as the *Literary Gazette* and the *Eclectic Review*; most importantly, readers must see for themselves that his work was not all obscure or didactic, as the critics regularly implied. Mary could not have been more warm in her agreement. Collecting and transcribing Shelley's often almost illegible manuscripts had been her main occupation in the year following his death. Encouraged by Procter and Beddoes, she went back to her task.

Crabb Robinson described Procter as 'a man whom everybody loves'.[19] Mary was initially more reserved in her enthusiasm; she had heard both Byron and Shelley speak derisively of Procter's work. 'He is evidently vain, yet not pretending,' she wrote hesitantly to Leigh Hunt, 'and his ill health is for me an interesting circumstance; since I have been so accustomed to Poets whose frame has been shattered by the mind . . . Yet after all, except the Dramatic Scenes I do not like Procter's style.'[20] His head was, however, uncommonly handsome. He had a beautiful voice and a soft, sympathetic manner. Marianne Hunt had warned her that he was promised to Adeline Skepper, stepdaughter of her father's friend Basil Montagu, but Procter himself made no mention of being engaged.

Procter's visits to Mary's lodgings near Coram's Fields were rare, but they were long. 'I know some clever men in whose conversation I delight,' she owned to her journal on 18 January 1824, 'but this is rare like angels visits.' Even a few angelic visits had set her to dreaming of what it might be like to live with a man 'whose opinions I shd respect, whose qualities I should admire & whose person I should love'. Guilt-filled, she brushed the thought aside; her child was all she needed for company, or should be: 'you are clever, good, affectionate and beautiful – why does not your form fill my sense – your existence suffice for my content[?]' But she continued to be attracted to Procter; on 3 September 1824, she wrote of 'a Poet – who sought me first – Whose voice laden with sentiment, paused as Shelley's – & who read with the same deep feeling as he . . . who once or twice listened to my sad plaints & bent his dark blue eyes upon me . . .'

She had not seen Procter for four months when she wrote this; his marriage to Miss Skepper took place in October 1824. Perhaps he was finding his relationship with Mary a little too intense when he suddenly decided to stop visiting her: 'So much for my powers of attraction,' Mary noted.[21] There were no more meetings after his marriage; young wives seldom wanted a woman with Mrs Shelley's reputation in their homes. Everybody who had any contact with Godwin's circle knew that Shelley's first wife Harriet had been pregnant when Mary ran away with him; who was to say that she had changed her ways, or lost her passion for poets?

Mary had two suggestions to put to Leigh Hunt on 9–11 September 1823 in the letter which mentioned Procter's first call. One was that, if he cared about keeping the *Examiner* and its two affiliated papers afloat, he must stop borrowing so heavily from his brother John, who owned the larger share of the business and bore all the costs; the second was that he should write a preface to the edition of Shelley's poems which she was preparing. Hunt had, as she knew, already drafted an article on Shelley; such a professional journalist could easily supply the brief introduction she required.

Hunt, for reasons which have never been clear, was unwilling to oblige her. The *Examiner* continued to praise Shelley whenever an excuse arose, notably for his recently published translations from *Faust*. Hunt may have suggested or have written these anonymous tributes, but, besieged by reminders of an approaching deadline for his preface, he remained silent or made excuses. *Posthumous Poems*, which included those inspired by Claire, Emilia Viviani, Sophia Stacey and Jane Williams, their identities discreetly masked by asterisks and initials, was published in an edition of five hundred in June 1824. Mary wrote the Preface herself. Opening it with a mild rebuke to Hunt, she offered an ardent defence of Shelley's name. Praising him as a fearless crusader for 'the improvement of the moral and physical state of mankind', she gave this as 'the chief reason why he, like other illustrious reformers, was pursued by hatred and calumny'.

This was stirring stuff, but the collection showed little of Shelley's reforming passion: poems such as 'To the Lord Chancellor' and *The Masque of Anarchy* were neither included nor mentioned. The chief aim of the Preface was to defuse the image of Shelley the atheist, the troublemaker, the rebel. Mary's new Shelley was an altogether softer creature, 'the wise, the brave, the gentle . . . a bright vision', gone but 'not, I fondly hope, for ever: his unearthly and elevated nature is a pledge of the continuation of his being, although in an altered form.' In phrases such as these and with a collection which put the lyrical firmly above the political, Mary began the long, difficult task of transforming a poet known chiefly for a notorious private life and for his atheism into a sexless spirit, a saintlike celebrant of nature who had ascended from the beach at Viareggio as if to heaven in a quivering shaft of flame. Very possibly, she believed what she wrote; very certainly, she wanted others to believe it.

A few did. The Hunts' *Examiner* – naturally – praised her candour and looked forward both to her biography and the publication of her husband's prose. Hazlitt, in the influential *Edinburgh Review*, described the Preface, to Mary's annoyance, as 'imperfect but touching'; the *Literary Gazette*'s sceptical critic thought her praises 'too hyperbolic to be the effusion of genuine sorrow'.[22] But the book sold well; at least one poem, 'Stanzas written in Dejection near Naples', was, from then until the middle of the century, constantly reprinted in verse collections and copied into albums. Three hundred copies of *Posthumous Poems* had been sold when Sir Timothy, furious that his wishes had been disregarded, ordered the remainder of the edition to be withdrawn only two months after publication. Mary was warned that his payments would cease if she made further attempts to publicize Shelley's work. Such bullying behaviour only increased her determination but she took care, after this threat, to move behind the scenes.

It was unfortunate that, just as a few bold reviewers were starting to suggest that Shelley ought to be classed with Wordsworth and Byron, Thomas Medwin decided to publish his *Conversations of Lord Byron* and to include some personal details of Shelley's life. His book was published in November 1824; only a few references to Shelley's life were needed for the old stories to begin circulating again. In August, when *Posthumous Poems* was newly out, *Knight's Quarterly* had been ready to proclaim Shelley a great poet; by December, the critic of the *Universal Review* had read Medwin's work and was ready to dismiss him again as a 'miserable' one.

When Mary had first arrived back in England in the autumn of 1823, friendless and uncertain of her future, she had excited the interest of a gentle, eager playwright whose name she had heard mentioned a good deal by the Kenneys at Versailles. This was John Howard Payne, whose bad luck it is to be remembered only as the author of a sentimental song, 'Home, Sweet Home', and as the man Mary Shelley could never bring herself to love as much as he did her.

A spare, shy, chestnut-haired man with Shelley's large eyes and high forehead, Payne had made his name in America when, in order to rescue his widowed father from bankruptcy, he abandoned his education to become a celebrated boy-actor. Arriving in Europe in 1813, he moved between Paris and London, often for the purpose of avoiding creditors. Mary's father had known him since 1817,[23] but neither Godwin nor any of Payne's affectionate circle of friends could cure his unlucky habit of falling into debt.* His plays, including *Brutus* (1818) and two or three historical romps which he wrote with the anonymous assistance of his fellow expatriate Washington Irving, were not respected by the critics, but they were hugely successful with the public. 'Home, Sweet Home' was the song on everybody's lips when Mary arrived back in England; it was the hit of Payne's latest triumph, *Clari, or The Maid of Milan*. He had as usual made nothing from it; the profits had gone to Sir Henry Rowley Bishop, who composed the music.

Payne was already a great friend of Mary's half-brother when she first met him over a dinner at Godwin's home in the autumn of 1823. For the last three years, she was told, he had been supplying her father with free theatre passes. This, as Payne was quick to learn, was a sure way to earn smiles from a young woman who loved the theatre herself and preferred, if she could, to sit in good seats. She seemed to like him; on 4 December, he was invited to join Mary and her family to see her old favourite, *The Winter's Tale*. Soon, he would pluck up the courage to express his feelings, to hail her as 'a being so beyond all others, that, even though her qualities are certainly "images" of what is promised in "heaven above" I can kneel down & worship them without dreading the visitation upon idolatry'.[25] Mary was not yet ready for such adulation.

Pitifully short of friends in this hard and alien city, Mary may have been more grateful for Payne's timid friendship than she cared to show. Mrs Gisborne, however, was there and always comforting. 'She is my delight. her gentleness toleration & understanding, & not the least of her attractions, her affection for me, render her dear to me,' Mary wrote.[26] Hogg, to whom she confided this, had been prompt to pay her a visit, but his interest, as she could readily see, was to talk about her friend Jane Williams. Peacock, although a kind and conscientious executor, was too wrapped up in his new family, his job and his novels for more than the basic courtesies of friendship. Medwin found time for a quick dinner on a visit to London.

Godwin did his best. He had produced John Howard Payne. He invited Mary's old friend Isabella Booth to bring her little daughter for a visit on 3 September, a few days after Mary had first arrived from Paris. This, however, was not the happy occasion he had anticipated.

---

* The fault seems to have lain less with Payne than with the theatre-managers who exploited his financial naivety: 'the initials of the Little Theatre Royal Drury Lane have answers to the words Treachery, Roguery, Damnation and Liars,' he wrote to one of these affable villains who had done him out of £54.[24]

Isabella, her energy and strong intelligence ground down by an over-bearing husband and a continual shortage of money, had suffered a serious nervous breakdown; she was on her way to convalesce in Scotland with her father. 'Be kind to me Mary,' she wrote entreatingly on 1 November, but the old friendship could not be revived. 'The great affection she displays for me endears her to me & the memory of early days –' Mary wrote to Hunt a few days after their meeting, 'Else all is so changed for me that I should hardly feel pleasure in cultivating her society.'[27] Loyalty guaranteed that she would do what she could to help her unhappy friend; but all chances of intimacy had ended in the spring of 1818, when Isabella surrendered to her husband's wishes and refused to accompany Mary and Shelley to Italy.

What Mary wanted was not the friendships which kept her close to the Godwin household but a new life, away from it. She loved her father. She did not want to share everything with him, or to share in all his worries, day after day. 'My father's situation his cares and debts prevent my enjoying his society,' she wrote guiltily in her journal on 18 January 'of the second year after 1822'. She ached for new friends, but how was she to find them?

The man who did most to answer the needs of the two young widows* was Leigh Hunt. Shortly before Mary left Italy, he had written a warm letter recommending her to his musical friend Vincent Novello. Both Mary and Jane Williams, he explained, were badly in need of kindness; Mary would be a charming guest, so long as she was kept away from the subject of Shelley. Start her on that, Hunt warned, and she would become anguished and self-conscious, talking in the high-flown phrases of a novelist. Put her in a room with good music, however, and she would be as rapt and quiet as a Quaker.[28]

Novello and his large family had, for reasons of economy, recently moved out of London to a house on Shacklewell Green, lying between Hackney and Islington. Shacklewell today is a sorry huddle of unlovable streets at the foot of Hackney Downs and it was not much more charming then. Mary detested the area, 'that dreary flat – scented by brick kilns and adorned by carcases of houses'.[29] She saw nothing to admire in the Novellos' china and glass-crammed parlours, or in the dull little garden leading down to a damp arbour. The pleasure, for her, for Jane and for music-loving William, who often acted as their escort, was in the cheerful company.

---

* Jane Williams was always referred to as a widow by Mary and her friends. In fact, as she and Hogg, her suitor, were aware, her husband Mr Johnson was alive, undivorced, and in London.

Reading the accounts of Shacklewell evenings which Mary sent to the Hunts in Italy takes us into the chaotic, exuberant world of one of Dickens's theatrical families. Children tumbled everywhere. Charles Cowden Clarke (his father had been Keats's gentle schoolmaster) stood in one corner, crying 'charming' and 'beautiful', his face, 'like a bird's skull', glowing with feeling as he listened to a Novello family concert. In another corner was Keats's friend Edward Holmes, 'Werter the II – passionately fond of music & playing well'. Arthur Gliddon's pretty young wife was there, squabbling with her 'Caro Sposo' about the best way to boil a goose and bewailing the absence of the Hunts. Mrs Novello, known as the 'Wilful Woman' for her firm rule of a chaotic household, was pregnant for the eleventh time but smiling, 'ever smiling', while her beaming husband and his handsome brother Francesco led the evening's music, commencing with sacred songs from Mrs Blaine Hunt (nobody dreamed of referring to the fact that her brother-in-law had just been arrested as an accomplice in a grisly murder) and ending with Handel and Mozart, whose works Vincent Novello championed and helped to popularize. Sitting at a little distance, for Charles detested music, were the Lambs, Mary's square pale face wreathed in contentment, her brother's veiled in pipesmoke.[30]

This was a house in which Mary felt welcome and at her ease. She could joke with Mrs Novello about Godwin ('the O.G.' or 'old gentleman') and promise her 'twenty kisses such as woman may give to woman on your dear cheek'.[31] Safe in the knowledge that she was causing no jealousy, she could flirt with balding, plump little Vincent and call him 'Vincenzo'. 'Mr Novello is my prediletto,' she told Hunt. 'I like him better & better each time I see him . . . his kindness towards me & his playing have quite won my heart.'[32]

Novello had, since the age of sixteen, been the organist at the fashionable Portuguese chapel in South Street, Mayfair. Mary often went there to hear him play. He had converted her to instrumental music, she told Hunt, but he had also opened her ears to Haydn, whose oratorio, *The Creation*, would be revealed as 'the language of the immortals' in a moving scene set in the Alps towards the end of *The Last Man*.[33]

In later life, Mary, one of the Novello daughters, married Charles Cowden Clarke. Together, they published their recollections of a musical household. 'Very, very fair both ladies were,' Mrs Cowden Clarke wrote of the two young widows, but her more candid sister Clara remembered that the Novello children had not liked Jane Williams and dreaded invitations to visit her. (She did not say why.) For Mrs Shelley, however, the Novello daughters had nothing but admiration. Mary Cowden Clarke, still treasuring her gifts of an auto-graphed copy of *Frankenstein* and an Italian necklace of coral beads, spent a whole page describing the graceful angle of Mary's golden-haired head, her small, beautifully tapering fingers and the way her face flowered into life when she was speaking. Mary Shelley, she con-cluded, 'was the central figure of attraction to my young-girl sight; and I looked upon her with ceaseless admiration – for her personal graces, as well as for her literary distinction.'[34]

At ease among the Novellos and their friends, Mary described herself as playing 'the giddy schoolgirl'; she drank toasts, chattered in Italian and charmed everybody. It took an evening with Coleridge, in January 1824, to remind her of other, more glorious days: 'his beautiful descriptions, metaphysical talk & subtle distinctions reminded me of Shelley's conversation such was the intercourse I once dayly enjoyed,' she wrote in her journal the following day.[35] The Novellos would have been fine company, had she not been used to something finer still. 'I will go into the country & philosophize,' she added to her journal entry, and her thoughts drifted to Jane Williams, who was planning to move out of the smoke to the village of Kentish Town. With Jane, she would not feel the need for other companions, for they would share the company of the beloved dead. 'I love Jane more than any human being,' she wrote on the same meditative January evening: 'but I am pressed upon by the knowl-edge that she but slightly returns this affection.' Mary was not yet aware that Jane and Hogg had formed an intimate, possibly sexual relationship; she only knew that Jane seemed increasingly reluctant to spend time discussing their shared past.

Pining in the dark, damp English winter, Mary put on too much weight while she brooded over the quality of work she was being forced to write for money, and over Jane's lack of affection. She went to the theatre. She took long, vigorous walks: 'Ye Gods – how I walk,' she wrote to Marianne Hunt in March. She toured exhibitions, saw the Elgin marbles again, looked at prints, and climbed the muddy steps of the stagecoach to trundle out to Shacklewell for another musical evening.

Her spirits did not improve. 'I do not remember ever having been so completely miserable as I am tonight,' she wrote to herself on 14 May 1824. It had rained for weeks on end; Percy fretted at being kept indoors all day. She could not get on with her novel. She felt she had lost all her imaginative powers; without them, how was she to survive? The next day, she learned that Byron had died, not on a battlefield, but on a bed of fever and excessive bloodletting out in the sad malarial marsh town of Missolonghi. 'This then was the "coming event" that cast its shadow on my last night's miserable thoughts,' she wrote, astonished by her strange gift of presentiment: 'Albe – the dear capricious fascinating Albe has left this desart world.' Brooding on the deaths of all the people she had loved, she hated herself for surviving them: 'Why am I doomed to live on seeing all expire before me? God grant I may die young.' Byron's little meannesses were forgotten as she mourned the loss of 'that resplendent Spirit, whom I loved . . .' Looking at what she had just written, Mary hastily crossed out the words 'whom I loved'. She could only admit to having loved one man, even in the privacy of her journal: 'whose departure leaves the earth still darker as midnight,' she wrote instead.

A month later, the weather had changed. Walking out into the warm scented hayfields around Kentish Town and back to her lodgings near Coram's Fields in the shadows of dusk, she passed the neglected churchyard of St Pancras. 'Such, my loved Shelley now ten years ago – at this season – did we first meet – & these were the very scenes . . . My own love – we shall meet again,' she wrote on 8 June. Her spirits had lifted again; she had made a decision. She would put more distance between herself and her father's home. She would take herself away from the city in which she was constantly oppressed by her poverty and lack of friends. She would follow Jane's example and settle in quiet Kentish Town, among the fields and trees she loved. She would take care of Jane – and Jane would learn to return her love.

I shall again feel the enthusiastic glow of composition . . . feel the winged ideas arise, & enjoy the delight of expressing them – study & occupation will be a pleasure not a task – & this I shall owe to sight & companionship of trees & meadows flowers & sunshine –

England I charge thee dress thyself in smiles for my sake – I will celebrate thee, O England, and cast a glory on thy name . . .

LITERARY MATTERS

1824–1829

'Moore breakfasted with me on Sunday – we talked of past times – of Shelley & Ld Byron. He was very agreable – & I never felt myself so perfectly at my ease with anyone . . . He seems to understand & to like me. This is a new and unexpected pleasure.'

Mary Shelley, Journal, 2 July 1827

'THUS HAS PERISHED, IN THE FLOWER OF HIS AGE, IN THE NOBLEST of causes, one of the greatest poets England has ever produced,' the *Morning Chronicle* intoned in May 1824, reporting that Prince Mavrocordato had commanded funeral ceremonies to be conducted in all the churches of Greece.[1] Death came at a good moment for Byron; the image of martyr could be superimposed on that of libertine exile. It was of little consequence to obituary-makers that he had not died on a battlefield.

Trelawny was among the first into the gold mine thus opened to those who could claim even the slightest friendship with Byron. Writing to Mary on 30 April from Missolonghi, he unblushingly presented himself as Byron's daily companion of the past four years – he had been with Byron for just twenty months.[2] He wanted her help in getting his own account published by John Hunt in the *Examiner*. Modesty was not Trelawny's forte and he was eager to show that he, not Byron, had been the hero of the hour in Greece.

Mary knew her friend too well to take his claims seriously – a month earlier, she had teasingly informed him that his theatrical posturing reminded her of seeing Edmund Kean on stage, although

'Greek dress – pistols – Suliotes & woodcock shooting are more in your way'.[3] She let his assertions pass; Trelawny's account was published as he had wished, although in extract form. For the article she intended to write on Byron herself, Mary wanted a more reliable source. Commiserating with Teresa Guiccioli on a sorrow which – Mary warned her – time would only deepen, she asked for precise details. 'When was the last time that dear Byron wrote to you? Was he ill at that time? Be assured that anything that you send me, any copy of his letters, will be sacred to me; in asking for these monuments of his final moments I am moved by the true affection that I feel for him.'[4] She was still pressing Teresa for these 'monuments' a year later, although no longer on her own behalf.

Byron's remains reached London three months after the reports of his death. On 9 July, Mary visited the black-draped parlour of Sir Edward Knatchbull's home in Great George Street where four Greek vases containing Byron's remains kept guard over a coffin richly mantled in figured crimson velvet. His servants, Lega Zambelli and William Fletcher, were there to greet her; Fletcher offered the startling news that Byron's last words had been of Claire. (It is more likely that Byron was remembering his much loved friend, Lord Clare.) Three days later, standing at the front window of her new lodgings with Mrs Bartlett at 5 Bartholomew Place, Kentish Town, Mary watched Byron's hearse roll past at the beginning of its long journey north to Newstead. Deep in writing *The Last Man* (she was at the beginning of the second volume now and reading up background works on Constantinople for the setting), she was struck by the thought that this was 'his last journey to the *last* seat of his ancestors'.[5] The same grim correspondence between life and fiction had been in her mind on 16 May, when she wrote to Teresa of 'a new law of nature' condemning them all to an early death ('e moriremo tutti giovani').

A mile north of the last London stage at Battle Bridge (now King's Cross), Kentish Town stood among nursery gardens and hayfields at the side of a road only a little grander than a cart-track. Prettily situated below the woods and hills of Highgate, the village remained secluded. Jane Williams had fled there a few months earlier, in part because she needed a discreet location for her developing relationship with Hogg, in part for family reasons. 'Poor thing,' Mary had written indignantly to Leigh Hunt in September 1823: 'she is much persecuted by Edward's [step]Mother Who to save her own credit spreads false reports about her as much as she can. She even called on Mrs Godwin to warn her that I ought not to know her . . . England is no place for Jane.'[6] She still had no idea of Jane's attachment to Hogg; she saw only that Hogg was clumsily paying court.

Mary's own reasons for joining Jane were both honourable and selfish. She cast herself as the protector of a defenceless woman who was, like herself, reliant on a disapproving family to provide for her after Edward's death. This was her way of compensating for the past. Shelley had turned to Jane, as she now sadly recognized, because he lacked sympathy from her; by caring for Jane, she would be doing as Shelley would have wished. Selfishly, she relied on Jane's more cheerful nature to dispel her own sadness. 'You know my Janey's cheerful – gay & contented temper,' she wrote to Hunt on 12 August 1826: 'I cannot be sorrowful while with her . . . I cannot express to you the extreme gratitude I feel towards this darling girl, for the power she has over me of influencing me to happiness.'

Mary had other reasons for going to Kentish Town. Further away from the Godwins' home, it enabled her to cut her visits there down to a meal once a week. There was a good local school for little Percy and fields in which, as she happily noticed, he was ready to trot or fly his kite all day. And, by firmly declaring that she and Jane lived for each other, she could keep unwelcome suitors at a distance. John Howard Payne had become assiduous by the summer of 1824; John Chalk Claris, a recently widowed poet who wrote under the name of Arthur Brooke, was hinting an interest in matrimony. Mary liked Brooke for having written an impassioned elegy after Shelley's death, but had no wish to encourage his romantic hopes. His suggestion that she visit him at Dover was crushed: 'my bitterest enemy could hardly desire for me a greater punishment than a visit to the sea-side,' Mary told him on 13 July. She had already found comfort 'in the society of a beloved friend who lives near me'.

Jane was not quite the loving friend that Mary supposed her to be; what is remarkable is that she succeeded so well in masking her feelings of resentment. They were partly prompted by envy. Mary had written a book which had been turned into a play; she had a father who, however impecunious, seemed to know everybody of literary significance; she had the prospect, when Sir Timothy died, of becoming rich. In the summer of 1824, following Byron's death, she became important for another reason. She had been with him at Geneva, Venice and Pisa. She had read his memoirs; she had transcribed much of his work. Her husband had become one of Byron's intimate circle. No woman, with the exception of Teresa Guiccioli, was more necessary to Byron's would-be biographers than Mrs Shelley. Jane had scarcely known him.

Two applicants made their approaches within days of Byron's burial. The first, writing from Italy, was Thomas Medwin. Using the ingratiating tone which she remembered with mistrust, he paid tribute to Mary's superior knowledge of their dear late friend. What a tragedy that Byron's memoirs had been destroyed!* Now that these were gone, friends had begged him to set down his own records of the many intimate conversations he had enjoyed with Lord Byron. But of course, if Mary intended to produce a book herself, he would set his aside, forget the trouble he had taken, the money he had been promised. He could guarantee a glowing portrait of Shelley – and all the discretion a widow might require.[7]

Medwin's letter reached Bartholomew Place the morning after Thomas Moore, accompanied by their mutual friend James Kenney, had taken breakfast with Mary and requested her help with his own projected life of Byron. Deploying all of his considerable charm ('I never felt myself so perfectly at my ease with anyone,' Mary noted some time later[8]), Moore explained that there were parts of the book which could only be written if she helped him. The exchange was not to be one-sided. She wished to meet Washington Irving? Nothing could be more easily arranged. An excited Mary was escorted to the studio where the American author was posing for a portrait by his compatriot, John Gilbert Newton. She saw for herself the lean, attractive face, the deep-set eyes and noble forehead; he spoke, to her delight, of his admiration for Lord Byron. (Irving was sufficiently under Byron's spell to rent Newstead Abbey for a few weeks and to hunt down old retainers who had worked there in the past.) Mary was girlishly thrilled; here, she thought, was a man worth loving. Moore had granted her wish so easily; with the support he seemed so ready to give, she could enter the literary world which was currently keeping her at a distance. Shelley would approve of her helping this friendly, sociable man; had he not read a poem of Moore's to her at one of their first meetings?

The decision was made. Mary's response to Medwin has not survived but is unlikely to have been encouraging. Writing to Trelawny at the end of July, Mary firmly steered him away from writing a memoir himself. 'You have often said that you wished to keep up our friend's name in the world,' she wrote, '& if you still entertain the same feeling, no way is more obvious than to assist Moore.'[9]

---

* The memoirs had been thrown on the fire in John Murray's drawing-room on 17 May, supposedly at the behest of Byron's sister, Augusta Leigh, but more certainly on the instructions of John Cam Hobhouse, one of Byron's executors.

Medwin's book was published, however, in the autumn of that year. Hastily assembled anecdotes and five months of journal notes were artfully spun out to convey the impression of a life's worth of conversations; no uninformed reader would suspect that the author's knowledge had been gleaned over a few afternoon rides and leisurely evenings at Byron's billiard table. The potted biography of Shelley which Medwin tacked on as a long footnote was full of inaccuracies, among them the statement that Shelley had married 'his lovely and amiable wife' after Harriet's death, no mention being made of the fact that he had already been living with Mary Godwin for two years.

Knowing how much her early life with Shelley as his unmarried partner had helped to damage her name, Mary still refused to hide or lie about it during her first years back in England. Experience would teach her to become more guarded, but in 1824 Medwin's clumsy attempt at chivalry infuriated her. Publicly, she made little fuss about the book; privately, she told John Cam Hobhouse, who published a list of corrections in the new *Westminster Review*, that Medwin's account of Shelley and herself was 'one mass of mistakes' and that the entire book had been 'a source of great pain to me, & will be of more . . .'[10] *Conversations of Lord Byron* could not, in fact, have appeared at a worse time for Mary: in response to her publication of *Posthumous Poems*, Sir Timothy had angrily suspended her allowance. Now, she feared, he would read Medwin's long note on Shelley and assume she had chosen this artful means of subverting his wishes.

The book could not have come at a better time for Tom Moore. Medwin's book whetted appetites, while leaving the portrait frustratingly incomplete. Moore liked high society; the poignancy of Mary's situation was not sufficient to tempt him to make the long trip out to Kentish Town oftener than was necessary. By the summer of 1826, however, he had finished his life of Sheridan and was at the stage with Byron where he needed Mary's help. Of the group who had summered on the shore of Lake Geneva in 1816, only Mary and Claire Clairmont remained and Claire, now struggling to make a living for herself as a governess in Russia, wanted nothing more than to bury her disreputable past and, in particular, her connection with Byron. Claire would not talk.

But Mary would. She provided Moore with invaluable material; a greedier woman would have made sure she was well recompensed. Mary needed money, but her principles were clear. She would take money for an article, but not when it was based on the life of a famous friend: 'a new set of worms . . . grow fat upon the world's love of tittle tattle – I will not be numbered among them,' she told Marianne Hunt on 10 October 1824, alluding to Medwin's forthcoming book. She would take money for selling the copyright to Shelley's poems, if approached, but this was to protect his work from appearing in pirated editions and to maintain a degree of control. In the present case, however, she was neither the writer nor the relict.

Instead, in 1828, she dropped a hint that she would be glad to write for Moore's publisher, John Murray, and that she would accept an advance. This was awkward; Murray had already expressed an interest in publishing some of Shelley's poems, but, having declined *Valperga*, he had even less enthusiasm for her new project, a novel about Perkin Warbeck. *Frankenstein*'s success on stage had given her a name, but only as the author of that precocious work. Murray did, however, agree to make a loan of £100; Mary, regarding it as a commission, deluged him with suggestions for books. One was to have been a study of eminent women of the past, including Madame de Staël and Madame Roland. Murray refused to be enticed; Mary proudly insisted on repaying the money. She returned it on 12 November 1829: Murray would have none of it. A ledger entry for £100 on 23 December 1829 reads, quite firmly: 'Moore's Life of Byron: To cash paid Mrs Shelley (being on the relinquishing of a debt due from Mrs S from cash previously lent) for various contributions.'

The notebook Moore kept while writing Byron's life makes no reference to Mary's contribution;[11] his journals, however, note her loquacity. 'I can talk with more freedom to him than to anyone almost I ever knew,' Mary noted with wonder on 2 July 1827 after a long, delightful breakfast, during which she handed Moore her written account of Byron's memoirs, which she had read at Venice in 1818.* It seems likely that she helped him far more than he was willing to acknowledge. To take one small but striking example: Moore's life is our only source for Byron's declaration that he awoke one day and found himself famous. The comment is startlingly close to the exclamation Mary made to Leigh Hunt after viewing *Frankenstein* on stage in 1823: 'But lo & behold! I found myself famous!' Mary may have heard it from Byron himself and passed it on to Moore; she may even have put her own words into his mouth.

One person who had cause for grave anxiety about Mary's collaboration with Moore was Claire Clairmont. Claire did not trust Mary on the subject of Byron. Reading Mary's panegyrics of Lord

---

* Moore had never bothered to read the memoirs which Byron gave him when he visited Venice in the autumn of 1819. Mary had seen them a year earlier.

Raymond in her futuristic novel *The Last Man,* so clearly based on Byron, Claire must have been appalled. Byron was the man who had spurned her love, put her adored child in a convent and left her there to die. She had supposed that Mary shared this view. But Mary, far from exposing Byron as a monster, seemed intent on glorifying his name. When he showed up in her fifth novel, *Lodore,* Claire could stand it no longer. Hearing that yet another book was planned, she dared hope that it would not contain 'another Beautified Byron'. 'I stick to Frankenstein,' she wrote fiercely,

> merely because that vile spirit does not haunt its pages as it does in all your other novels, now as Castruccio, now as Raymond, now as Lodore. Good God, to think that a person of your genius, whose moral tact ought to be proportionately exalted, should think it a task befitting its powers to gild and embellish and pass off as beautiful what was the merest compound of Vanity, folly, and every miserable weakness that ever met together in one human Being.[12]

But this was in the future. In 1830, the year in which Moore's *Life* was published, Mary swore that there had been no collaboration, and her stepsister believed her. 'This is an erroneous supposition of Trelawneys,' Claire told Jane Williams in February 1830, after hearing of his belief that Mary had been secretly providing Moore with letters and recollections. Mary could not be so treacherous, or so untruthful. Trelawny was right, however. Almost the entire account of Byron's life at the Villa Diodati had come directly from Mary, the sole survivor now from that summer of 1816, apart from Claire herself. So had the vivid image of Byron crossing the lake singing the Tyrolese song of liberty (as does Lord Raymond in *The Last Man*).

One episode in particular stands out as Mary's work. It is the account of a storm which blew up when Shelley and Byron were sailing down the lake together. Shelley's own letter of the time described how, unable to swim, he felt humiliated by Byron's readiness to save him – and terrified by the prospect of death. An anonymous account of Byron at sea which had been rushed into print in the year of his death also drew on this episode, showing Shelley as a quaking atheist while Byron serenely confronted his fate. Mary, having read this account, appears to have coolly transferred the roles. In the Moore–Mary version, Shelley is heroically calm: 'seating himself quietly upon a locker, and grasping the rings at each end firmly in his hands, [he] declared his determination to go down in that position, without a struggle.' Here, we can see Mary reviewing

Shelley's death, imagining the frame of mind in which she longed to believe he had met those unknowable final moments when the *Don Juan* sank.

Curiosity as well as Moore's persuasive manner drove Mary to make prodigious attempts to coax Teresa into joining their alliance. Pietro Gamba had put a bundle of his sister's letters to Byron in Mary's safekeeping when he visited England in 1824. Condoling with Teresa on Pietro's premature death of typhoid in 1827, Mary took advantage of the occasion to ask if she might use these to provide Moore with 'a rough outline' of the relationship. Were there other letters from Byron? Could she have a copy of the love note he had written in English in Teresa's *Corinne*?* When Teresa failed to respond, she tried reproaches – 'povero Moore s'impazienza' – heavy-handed allusions to her own interest in Roman Catholicism (Teresa was a convent-bred Catholic); and, in desperation, threats.[13] Did Teresa know, Mary wondered, that Lady Blessington was preparing a book in which she intended to claim that Byron had been in love with her, not the Countess Guiccioli, when he was living at Genoa?[14] Such a claim could easily be disproved by a few devoted lines from Byron to Teresa for inclusion in Moore's book.

Teresa's girlish ringlets and dimpling smiles hid a shrewd and determined mind. She had no intention of parting with her most valuable possession. An assortment of documents duly arrived in London, but Mary had to wait until Teresa's visit to England in 1832 to be allowed a glimpse of the coveted Byron love letters, while returning those of Teresa's which she had cared for since 1824. This meeting marked the end of a friendship which had never been wholly sincere. Mary was always more intrigued by the spell this pretty but limited girl had cast over Byron than by her character; Teresa did not find Mary's social circle in London much to her taste. A furious exchange of letters with John Murray suggests that Teresa also believed that Mary had been copying the letters and poems entrusted to her by Pietro Gamba, and that she had been passing them on to the publisher. She 'had no right to make such a use of them', Teresa exploded in the autumn of 1832; she 'was also particularly requested by me of that'.[15] Moore's book, she commented in another indignant note, was so faulty as to be beyond correction.[16]

Moore's first impressions of Mary had been pleasing and it was no

---

* One wonders how Mary knew about this very private note. Had Teresa proudly revealed the inscription to Mary, or had Mary, perhaps, acted as her translator? Byron had written it in English, which Teresa did not speak.

hardship to him to be friendly while she was useful. They went to Holborn together to see his little son at Charterhouse school. They toured exhibitions and went on long walks during which Mary spoke freely about her friendship with Byron. They visited the studio of Sir Thomas Lawrence, who was painting Moore's portrait; occasionally they met at the home of a mutual friend, Joshua Robinson, in the village of Paddington. Knowing that a Tom Moore song, warbled out by the man himself, was always a treat for hostesses, Moore would later oblige at the parties which Mary began to give when she was able to move to a smarter, more central address near Portman Square at the close of 1827.[17]

Moore was charming but vain. He did not like adverse criticism. When Mary was rash enough in a letter, since lost, to offer some objections to the way Moore had treated the delicate subject of Shelley's atheism in the completed Life, he was furious. 'It is like a man being scolded by his wife at home besides being bullied abroad,' he wrote back; he went on to drop an unpleasant hint that she had better stop making trouble. He had found references to Allegra's upbringing in Byron's letters to the Hoppners 'which though important . . . I don't think you would like to appear'. Another threat followed, of a more obscure kind: 'Pray take care of yourself – keep clear of the law – don't wet your feet, and *don't* write criticisms.'[18]

Mary's work for Moore provided her with one useful literary introduction. John Bowring, Honorary Secretary of the Greek Committee in London and an admirer of Shelley's work, was willing to let her transcribe his correspondence with Byron for Moore's Life. A friendship sprang up; exchanges of news on their children suggest that Bowring was one of the few Londoners ready to make the dreary journey out to Kentish Town. As editor of the new *Westminster Review*, he was also able to offer Mary work. Articles and reviews were Mary's only means of eking out an allowance for which she was often forced to wait months, although reasons were seldom provided. Her heart was not in this kind of work, however. Some of the happiest entries in her journals are those in which she recorded the sense of imaginative release which came from writing novels. These were the works in which she felt able to 'pour forth my soul upon paper, feel the winged ideas arise . . .'

It is hard to think of another of her books, with the exception of *Frankenstein*, which demonstrates this sense of released, exultant imaginative power, so well as *The Last Man*. The novel embodies Mary's sense of herself isolated in a familiar but alien city, the last of a close-knit group. It also aggrandizes the figure of Byron as Lord Raymond. A more striking intention emerges when we look back to Shelley's last, unfinished poem, *The Triumph of Life*, written during the summer of 1822 at the Villa Magni.

Shelley's poem had opened with a magnificent but chilling image of Death as a feminine force, riding in her juggernaut over youth and old age, princes and peasants, levelling all. The plague appears in Shelley's poem, but as 'the plague of gold and blood' spread over the world by the greed of despotic rulers. Mary's novel can be read in part as a deliberate extension of Shelley's uncompleted work. She even signalled the fact in the sixth chapter of her third volume, putting the words into the mouth of Adrian, the character most closely based on Shelley. 'I have hung on the wheel of the chariot of plague,' Adrian exclaims, 'but she drags me along with it, while, like Jaggernaut, she proceeds crushing out the being of all who strew the high road of life.' Since Shelley's poem had used the image of the chariot, a female death-force and life as a highroad, there can be little argument about the connection between the two works. It was no accident; nor was the feverish intensity of the last and most powerful section of *The Last Man*, which again reflects the pace and follows the direction of Shelley's speeding chariot. 'Imperial Rome poured forth her living sea,' he had written; the novel, which begins at Bishopsgate, in the landscape where Shelley and Mary had made their first home, ends, in a scene of magnificent and terrible desolation, at Rome, where Mary's son had died, and where Shelley was now buried.

The characters of *The Last Man* are, as Muriel Spark has observed in a shrewd critical biography of Mary Shelley, little more than types. Raymond is the ultimate Don Juan; Adrian is the Don Quixote of idealists; Lionel Verney, the narrator who represents Mary herself, is the 'last man' whose final solitude reflects her own strongly felt identification with Coleridge's isolated Mariner. The most memorable scenes are those in which the characters become tiny, helpless players in a world governed by nature, in which their boats are lashed by storms, their deaths mocked by towering alpine scenes or by vast indifferent skies. But, thin though the characters seem to us, it is apparent that they were not so to Mary herself.

She wanted, plainly, to win admiration for Adrian. She gives him Shelley's beliefs, his looks, his habits. It is Adrian who stimulates Verney's passion for reading, who broadens his interest in politics and who inspires him to become an author. Try as she would, however,

Mary could not forget the nightmare side of life with Shelley, the ruthlessness of his irresponsibility: 'the sensitive and excellent Adrian, loving all, and beloved by all, yet seemed destined not to find the half of himself, which was to complete his happiness,'[19] she wrote, acknowledging that his search for happiness with Claire, with Emilia, with Jane, had merely been extensions of his response to her. It was a search which could never be completed, and which caused pain to everybody except the seeker himself. It is Adrian who insists, against Lionel/Mary's advice, that they must take young Clara, infant child of the heroine, out over a stormy sea to visit her parents' tombs. Clara and Adrian are drowned, in a scene which reminds us that Mary had never ceased to believe that Shelley was responsible for the death of her own Clara in 1818. Adrian is good, sensitive and high-minded; he is also shown to be selfish, irresponsible and neurotic. What we do not know is how much of this subversion of Adrian's noble exterior was unconsciously executed.

Examining all ideologies in her novel, Mary seems to have been most attracted to Burke's idea of an organic society which can be developed and improved only under enlightened guidance. This, at least, is the view she allows Lionel Verney to promote as he watches his small son go out on to the playing fields of Eton. But before casting Mary as a conservative, repudiating the ideas of both her father and her husband, we need to remind ourselves of the subject of *The Last Man*. Extinction is the vision Mary offers in her last scene; and here, following Shelley's last poem, she mocks man's aspirations. 'Neither hope nor joy are my pilots – restless despair and fierce desire of change lead me on,' Lionel Verney declares in the last chapter. From the novel's expansive opening vision of reform, Mary Shelley has narrowed the view to a single figure, whose wish for change is rendered meaningless by his lack of followers. Only the wish remains. Alone, Verney can achieve nothing. The conclusion is as bleak as the cry: 'Then what is life?' with which Shelley had ceased work on his last poem.

Settled at Kentish Town, Mary worked on the novel as steadily as her magazine writing would permit between the spring of 1824 and the summer of 1825. She veered – as most writers do – between flashes of ecstasy ('I feel my powers again – & this is of itself happiness'[20]) in the high summer of 1824, and blind despair ('all my many pages – future waste paper – surely I am a fool'[21]) at the beginning of 1825. There were times when the boldness of her subject and its range appalled her. She needed to wade through shelves of books on Constantinople and Greece to set the scene for Lord Raymond's battles and the pilgrimages of his friends; she needed, and persuaded

John Cam Hobhouse to obtain for her, permission to watch parliamentary debates to give authenticity to the English political scenes. She worried about the difficulties of describing the plague's slow spread; she resorted to plundering Trelawny's vivid letters for accounts of warfare.

Mary seldom discussed her writing in her letters; even in her journals, she would only occasionally allow herself to comment on an unusually high or low moment: 'write' was the usual terse record. Glimpses of Mary collecting material or finding inspiration come to us sideways. In 1824, she had been describing the scenery at Bishopsgate, but she wanted to provide a description of Windsor Castle and it had been made difficult because of the massive reconstruction of its silhouette which was then being undertaken; visits were prohibited. In 1825, Mary went back to confirm her details: she had hoped, she playfully told John Howard Payne, to have the additional treat of seeing George IV, 'my liege lord his sacred Majesty', strolling on the terrace:

> one old fat footman commiserated our fate mightily when we asked for the last time whether his Majesty was expected & told him that it was our last chance – 'I am quite sorry, ladies – I am sure his Majesty would have been glad to see you – he is always glad to see & be seen by ladies.'[22]

And if he had, she giggled on another occasion, she had every expectation that 'his most sacred Majesty would be en-netted . . . a coronation was the smallest thing in prospect.'[23]

Writing *The Last Man* was a welcome distraction, not only from her own financial worries, but from those of her father who, in the spring of 1825, was finally driven into bankruptcy and forced to give up bookselling. It had not, as she knew, been his fault; 1825 was a year of financial crisis, of which a major cause had been the recent surge in large bank loans, followed by the Bank of England's decision temporarily to suspend the discount facilities previously granted to substantial borrowers. Seventy banks went out of business; many of the grand plans for the rebuilding of London were temporarily abandoned, including those of Thomas Cubitt for Belgravia on the marshes. Not even Godwin could hope that friends would rescue him at such a time.

After several humiliating days of attendance at the Guildhall, he and his wife moved to a smaller, cheaper home, so badly maintained that the inside of the windows froze over in winter. It was in Gower Place, close to the newly cleared site for London's first university. Mary spent the first night with them, helping to arrange the furniture and unpack the crates of books. The business through which for the past twenty years Godwin had been quietly influencing the minds of the young, John Keats among them, was gone at last. 'That over, nothing will be left him but his pen & me,' Mary ruefully noted to Leigh Hunt on 8 April, but neither now nor in the future did she ever question or seem to resent her father's dependence on her. She would nevertheless remember this as the unhappiest year since her return to England.

The first chapters of *The Last Man* went off to the printer's in November 1825, while Mary was still completing her fair copy. On 1 January 1826, Godwin informed the publisher Henry Colburn that the final pages were in hand. Perhaps, he saw similarities to his own work in Mary's technique of interspersing lyrical domestic passages with scenes of extraordinary imaginative vigour. Perhaps, he knew that a good sale for Mary meant a little money for himself; certainly, Godwin made himself into the novel's most eager advocate. Colburn was urged to pay particular attention to the Introduction, in which Mary explained that the novel had been developed and enlarged from some mysterious pages recovered from the cave of the Sibyl at Naples in 1818. (The date pointed knowing readers towards the time of her own residence there, just as the mention of 2092 was meant to remind readers of the date of Shelley's birth.) The Introduction 'is in my opinion, if I am not partial,' wrote Godwin (who was), 'a chef d'oeuvre, explaining in the most fortuitous way how the work came to exist. I own I had no anticipation how it was to be done, & thought (like a blockhead) that this part must be a botch, instead of being, as it is, one of the great ornaments of the performance.'[24]

Subsequent letters fired off from Gower Place to the publisher received tepid replies. Colburn was uncomfortable with the book's futuristic setting; he feared that the theme and the title were already overworked. He referred to Mercier's *L'An 2440*, a remarkably prophetic work – it described revolution at Versailles and the downfall of a king – written in 1772; the book had been translated into English early in the nineteenth century. He must also have been tempted to mention the recently published poems by Thomas Campbell and by Mary's young friend Thomas Lovell Beddoes; both were entitled 'The Last Man'. Pressed by Godwin, he reluctantly offered £300. The average sum paid by John Murray to an established author of a three-volume novel in 1825–6 was £500; Colburn was paying as little to Mary as he could get away with.

His fears were borne out. The reviews were bad. Most of them pointed out that it was strange to find hackneys and postchaises being employed in an age of intercontinental air-travel; this was the mildest of their objections. 'The Last Man is an elaborate piece of gloomy folly – bad enough to read – horrible to write,' declared the *London Magazine*, to which Mary was a contributor;[25] the *Monthly Review* condemned 'the offspring of a diseased imagination and of a most polluted taste'.[26] An apparently flattering notice in the *Morning Chronicle*, claiming that Mrs Shelley had outdone all previous writers in her 'romance', was planted by Colburn himself.

'I do not wonder that Mrs Shelley did not succeed with her Last Man,' Hazlitt noted in an essay the following year, referring to the fact that her apocalyptic theme had seemed only to echo every other publication of the time.[27] This was kinder than some of Hazlitt's recent comments on Shelley; Mary bore no grudge against a man who now resembled one of the plague victims of her novel. 'I never was so shocked in all my life,' she told Marianne Hunt after meeting Hazlitt one day in the street: '. . . but for his voice & smile I shd not have known him – his smile brought tears into my eyes . . .'[28]

The critics' venom had not harmed the novel's sales so much as Hazlitt imagined, but their reception was hostile enough to make Mary hesitant about embarking on another major work. Instead, after reading newspaper reports of a two-hundred-year-old corpse which had been miraculously revived, she wrote a light-hearted account of the ancient gentleman's imagined response to modern times in a short story, 'Roger Dodsworth, the Reanimated Englishman'. It was a pleasant change from projecting herself into the future; the notion of animating a corpse had some appeal for the author of *Frankenstein*. Washington Irving's tale of Rip Van Winkle may have contributed something to the tale of a man lost in a modern age; the story's sly mockery of George IV was Mary's own contribution. The original Mr Dodsworth was said to have died in Charles I's reign; she decided to present his modern rescuer and interlocutor as an ardent Hanoverian. 'The king, God bless him,' Dodsworth's cheerful redeemer announces,

'spares immense sums from his privy purse for the relief of his subjects, and his example has been imitated by all the aristocracy and wealth of England.'
'The King!' emphatically ejaculates Mr Dodsworth.
'Yes, sir,' emphatically rejoins his preserver; 'the king, and I am happy to say that the prejudices that so unhappily and unwarrantably possessed the English people with regard to his Majesty are now, with

a few' (with added severity) 'and I may say contemptible exceptions, exchanged for dutiful love and such reverence as his talents, virtues, and paternal care deserve.'[29]

Mary sent her story off to Cyrus Redding, editor of the *New Monthly Magazine*, but he felt uneasy about publishing a piece which ridiculed the king's extravagance at a time when the country was in the grip of a financial crisis. By 1863, however, he felt safe enough. The story was published with Redding's explanation that he had 'lost' it shortly after Mary's submission.

Hostile reactions to *The Last Man* had an inevitable effect on a young woman too poor to ignore the requirements of fashion. Gothic fantasy, in which her novel had been rich, was on the wane; instead, she began researching the background for a more conventional work. The subject was the royal impostor, Perkin Warbeck, whose curious history she had first encountered in the child's *History of England* published by her father in 1809. Godwin, impressed by his daughter's scholarship and diligence, was full of encouragement and praise; the critics were respectful when the book appeared in 1830. (Colburn and his new partner, Richard Bentley, were the publishers.) Few people have read their way through *The Fortunes of Perkin Warbeck*; fewer still would argue that a long, laborious chronicle filled with unconvincing characters and turgid dialogue amounted to more than a waste of Mary's imaginative gift. The most interesting thing about it is that the author, directly after displaying the sparkle and wit of 'Roger Dodsworth', could have written a work so grimly lacking in humour.

———

Mary, as Peacock pointed out on her behalf to Sir Timothy and his representative, signed *The Last Man* as 'By the author of "Frankenstein"'. Reviewers had not been so scrupulous; Mary was punished with a further suspension of her allowance for, even if unwittingly, setting the Shelley name before the public. In the autumn of 1826, however, eleven-year-old Charles Shelley died of tuberculosis, causing Sir Timothy to review his plans for the estate. Percy, his only remaining grandson, was now his heir; Mary was graciously informed that she might have custody of her own son and a modest increase in her allowance to £250 a year. Sir Timothy then showed his usual concern for Mary's welfare by neglecting to pay her any maintenance at all until late the following year, by which time she had been reduced to begging what she could get from Jefferson Hogg and even, humiliatingly, from Claire's pittance as a governess.

Mary had never known Charles, born during the autumn of 1814. His death, while undoubtedly convenient, reminded her of the shattering blow dealt to Shelley in 1817 when Lord Eldon had denied him custody of Ianthe and Charles. 'I curse thee by a parent's outraged love, / By hopes long cherished and too lately lost,' Shelley had written in 'To the Lord Chancellor', a poem which she readily copied for friends, although she had not dared to publish it. Among the many Christmas annuals for which she began to write in the mid-twenties as a way of unobtrusively promoting Shelley's poetry while earning a living for herself, one was titled *The Biographical Keepsake*. The savagery of a contribution on Lord Eldon to this book so strikingly reflects Mary's – and Shelley's – attitude as to suggest that she was the anonymous author:

> many of England's most deserving people have suffered by his intolerable delays and doubts . . . we can never forget a thousand proofs of his mean and cruel intolerance . . . whenever it shall please the disposer of all events to remove him from the world, the nation will respire with still greater freedom.[30]

Sir Timothy's punitive attitude had by this time given Mary a terror of seeing her name in print; every time the words 'Mrs Shelley' appeared, she could be sure that her allowance would be withheld until she begged forgiveness. 'There is nothing I shrink from more fearfully than publicity,' she told Trelawny when he wrote to her in the spring of 1829, requesting her assistance with a life of Shelley. It was not just his book, she explained; it was the way the critics might write about it: 'each critique, each mention of your work, might drag me forward . . . Shelley's life must be written – I hope one day to do it myself, but it must not be published now.' Instead, seeking to mollify him, she suggested that he settle for some 'tribute of praise' in the autobiography which he was writing, a project of which she wholeheartedly approved.[31]

Trelawny, rightly convinced that Mary had been supplying Moore with letters and anecdotes, was enraged by her response. He would have been even angrier to learn that Mary was again providing just the kind of help he wanted to somebody else. Cyrus Redding, her friendly editor at the *New Monthly Magazine*, had undertaken to write a brief life of Shelley for a book to be published in France by Galignani in 1829 as *The Poetical Works of Coleridge, Shelley and Keats*.

Mary herself recognized the importance of an edition of the poems which would promote Shelley's name, and in such company. Her willingness to help with the memoir was, in part, a reaction against the latest account of her relationship with Shelley. Leigh Hunt, publishing his own recollections of Byron in 1828, had decided to follow Medwin's gloss on Shelley's second marriage. Once again, readers were led to assume that her relationship with Shelley had only begun after Harriet's death; no mention was made of the period during which she lost her first baby and gave birth to William. Mary, who had seen part of Hunt's book in 1825 and had begged him to give a truthful account of her first years with Shelley, was mortified.*

Redding, not Trelawny, was the beneficiary of her anger. Amelia Curran's portrait of Shelley, now back in Mary's possession, was loaned to him, allowing readers to see at last what the free-loving atheistical Mr Shelley had looked like. Mary made it clear that she wanted to write the memoir herself; denied the opportunity, she supervised and corrected Redding's manuscript. The style was not to her taste, but the words said what she wanted, which was a change: 'I see no positive assertion in it that was untrue,' she told Redding.[32] The date of her elopement was clearly established; no reader could misinterpret the indication that she and Shelley had lived together before marrying. This was as she, not others, wished it to be.

Given that the Redding memoir was published in 1829, at a time when Mary was still struggling hard to make friends, her determination to tell the truth was admirable. She wanted the world to know that she had lived in unwedded bliss. She wanted to publicize the fact that Shelley had left Harriet for her. She insisted that the marriage had not been their choice, but her father's. All of these statements were immensely damaging to a young woman who was trying to make a pleasant social life for herself. The Redding memoir makes it clear that, much though Mary wanted to be accepted, she wanted even more to be accepted on her own terms.

Equally striking is the fact that the Redding memoir presented Mary, at her own wish, neither as Shelley's wife nor as Godwin's

---

* This was a long article on Shelley which Hunt had sent John Bowring at the *Westminster Review* in 1825. Inaccurate in some details about Shelley and worrying in its allusions to Claire, the article had also distressed Mary by its slighting references to herself. This, from a man she had come to think of as one of her most loyal friends, was a shock: 'you have a feeling, I had almost said a prejudice against me,' she wrote to Hunt on 8 April 1825. Typically, a letter begun in great indignation ended with assurances of her affection: 'I long to hear from you – & am more tenderly attached to you & yours than you imagine – love me a little & make Marianne love me . . .'

daughter. She was introduced, at her own insistence, as 'Mary Wolstonecraft Godwin, daughter of the celebrated authoress of the Rights of Woman'. This, as we will see, was Mary's way of saying that she now preferred to see herself in a female context, as a woman who preferred the company of women and who, lovingly but not always wisely, preferred to put her trust in her own sex. 'Ten years ago I was so ready to give myself away –' she told Trelawny on 12 October 1835, – '. . . & being afraid of men, I was apt to get *tousy-mousy* for women.'

Among men, scandal was always only a venomous whisper away from the name of a young widow with a disreputable history; among women, she could laugh, flirt and be at ease. Women spoke of her mother with a tenderness and reverence which never failed to move her; women, especially helpless women, could provide an outlet for the love she longed to bestow.

PRIVATE MATTERS

1824–1827

'I happen, as has always been my fate, to have formed intimate friendships with those who are great of soul, generous, and incapable of valuing money except for the good it may do – and these very people are all even poorer than myself, is it not hard?'

Mary Shelley to E.J. Trelawny, 4 March 1827

BY THE TIME SHE MOVED TO KENTISH TOWN MARY WAS AWARE that Jefferson Hogg had become very attached to her pretty friend. Jane still showed no sign of returning his feelings. She seemed, if anything, rather distressed by Hogg's affection; Mary was ready to sympathize.

Hogg had, it was true, made a good living for himself as a lawyer; he was, as Mary knew, conscientious about providing for some of the less successful members of his family. She nevertheless found him a cold, peculiar man. Their friendship had remained awkward ever since the curious period when, as a seventeen-year-old girl, she had allowed Hogg to pursue her because Shelley seemed to wish it. The relationship had become close enough for her to turn to Hogg for comfort after the loss of her first baby girl. 'My dearest Hogg my baby is dead – will you come to me as soon as you can,' she had begged him then; and Hogg had, in his awkward way, tried to console her. That time was long past; even by 1817, she had disliked him enough to dread the occasions of his visits. By 1824, she was prepared to regard him as a useful source of legal advice and a kind, if unworthy, admirer of her friend. She had no idea that Jane had already confided to him all her choicest titbits about Mary's cruel coldness to Shelley; she would have been astonished to know that the two of them were planning to set up home together as soon as a decent period of time had elapsed.

At Kentish Town, much to Mary's satisfaction, her lodgings at 5 Bartholomew Place were only a few minutes' walk from those Jane had already taken in Mortimer Terrace; the two young women were in and out of each other's homes almost every day in the summer of 1824. Still, nothing about the relationship with Hogg attracted suspicion. He was seen as Jane's slightly pathetic suitor, an object for their shared amusement. When one August day, Jane tearfully said that he had upset her with an unpleasant letter, Mary hurried to her defence. 'I think,' she told Hogg, that 'with your great understanding you might contrive to please instead of to annoy "the fair one" – and to make her smile instead of frown . . . do not I entreat you add to her annoyances.'[1] She reminded him that he had a history of worshipping certain ladies and then sulking if they tried to throw off their 'Hogg-bestowed sovereignty'. Well, it was time for him to change his ways – and where, while she remembered, were the letters from Shelley which he had promised to show her?

Hogg must have had a rapid consultation with Jane. He sent Mary a half-hearted apology, and no reference to the letters from Shelley. His tone was found wanting: 'if . . . I cannot obtain the courtesy of your species I will cut their acquaintance for ever,' Mary snapped back.[2] Perhaps this was too rude; she mollified him with a safe account of the ways she and Jane had been amusing themselves. She had gone to the opera and had been thrilled by the intense eyes and passionate acting of the celebrated Milanese soprano, Giuditta Pasta, in the part of Romeo. Then Jane and she had gone 'two or three times' to *Der Freischütz*, the new opera by Weber which had, with its dramatic stage effects and its gloriously creepy scene in the wolf's glen, been an instant success; suitably enough, it was being performed at the theatre where *Frankenstein* had been staged the previous year. 'We liked the music & the incantation scene would have made Shelley scream with delight,' she told Hogg, and listed 'flapping owls – ravens, hopping toads, queer reptiles – fiery serpents skeleton huntsmen and burning bushes' as part of the evening's treats.

Hogg's reassurances and Jane's deceiving reticence had the desired effect; by the autumn of 1824, Mary was ready to make plans for the time when she and Jane might return to Italy, away from the damp embrace of an English November. As the year ended, however, she sank into a deep depression. 'Well did your mother prophecy that I should find England intolerable,' she wrote to Mrs Kenney's daughter, Louisa Holcroft, on 6 January 1825, in a letter wistfully recalling Louisa's visit to London the previous summer. In the closing pages of her fourth journal the same month, Mary unleashed her feelings with a violence which reminds us of how deep the relation was between the raging, outcast creature of her first novel and its creator's darkest, most hidden self. 'I know now why I am an outcast – So be it! I wd. not for worlds do other than I do, & yet – I make not her happiness,' she wrote on 30 January after what had evidently been a painful scene with Jane. But, whereas her creature vented its rage in acts of violence, Mary could only lacerate herself. 'I am a fool –' she wrote in this same journal entry:

> poverty stricken – deformed squinting lame – bald – all every thing – it is quite just that I should be ejected from the sight of man – what a pity that they don't put an end to me at once.
>   I thought I had gained a great deal in learning the cause of my expulsion – I have merely gained a loss – the bitter loss of sympathy & love for my fellow creatures –[3]

The torment of discovering Jane's preference for Hogg has been suggested as the cause of this outburst. It seems more likely that the young women had quarrelled about Mary's low spirits, or about her possessiveness. A whole year later, in the spring of 1826, Mary was still telling Claire how troublesome it was for poor Jane to be 'teazed' by Hogg. Jane was, by December 1826, prepared to risk telling Claire that she had found a kind admirer, identified only as 'Blue-Bag'.* Claire's response was not encouraging: 'Blue-Bag may be a friend to you, but he can never be a lover,' she wrote back from Moscow that month: 'a happy attachment that has seen its end leaves a void that nothing can fill up . . .'[4] This, as Jane was well aware, was a view which Mary shared. Uneasily, she continued to lead a double life.

In January 1825, Mary was miserable about everything. Jane was irritated by her; she couldn't write; she was short of money; it was always raining. Spring, as always, lifted her spirits. They rose still higher when she heard that Hogg was planning to spend the summer in Italy. Glad to be rid of him, Mary nevertheless took care to provide all the help she could give. Keats's friend Joseph Severn, the

---

* 'Blue-Bag' might have been an allusion either to the blue satchels in which lawyers like Hogg carried their papers, or to his pale face. Blue bags of limewash were the commonest way of whitening walls.

British consul at Rome, was one among many who received a letter urging him to be kind to Mr Hogg, he being a friend of Hunt's, of Shelley's, 'and many others of your circle in England'.[5] Hogg left and Mary blossomed as Jane settled into grateful dependence on her friendship.

'Affection for my sweet friend quieted my heart,' Mary noted in an undated journal entry for the summer of 1825. To Leigh Hunt, who was on his way back from Italy to a Highgate cottage large enough to house his eight children, she confessed that 'the hope & consolation of my life is the society of Mrs W[illiams]. To her, for better or worse, I am wedded.'[6] 'Neddy', Dina and Percy played together in the baking fields of hay; the young mothers went on visits to the Novellos, to the Lambs and, when they returned, the Hunts. Supplied with as many free tickets as Mary cared to request from her 'amabil-issimo cavaliere', kind John Howard Payne, they went in tireless pursuit of 'that desperate coquette the opera'[7] and of every role that the great Edmund Kean was ready to offer them. 'Kean! Yes truly – fire & water for him,' Mary wrote excitedly to Payne. '. . . what will he play? Sir G[iles] O[verreach] – Othello – Hamlet – of these I am sure . . .'[8] Acting as each other's chaperones, the young women were up to anything, chattering loudly in Italian as they masqueraded as foreigners in the pit, and giggling when they caught the eye of a handsome Spaniard who tried to follow them home. 'This divine summer has had a most beneficial effect on my spirits,' Mary wrote happily to John Bowring on 31 October. Jane and she had just spent ten days together at Windsor, revisiting the lanes and fields which Mary remembered from her months with Shelley at Bishopsgate and enjoying 'the finest band in the world' every morning as the royal pipes and flutes rehearsed on the terrace at Windsor.

Mary described herself as wedded to Jane; should we conclude that she had entered, or sought, a sexual partnership? A saucy reference in one of her letters of 1827 to Jane about their sexual parts ('our pretty N— the word is too wrong I must not write it') is the only, and by itself, unconvincing evidence we have that the relationship could have been sexual. What it conveys more plausibly is that she was trying to use the same language as her friend. Jane, as Mary noted elsewhere, had no reservation about discussing physically intimate details. In a letter to Hunt of 27 June 1825, in the same paragraph which described her as 'wedded to Jane', Mary wrote that she looked forward to telling him of 'one or two things which will I think surprize and perhaps move you – move you at least to excuse a little what you do not approve'. Was she hinting that her love for Jane was not platonic? The possibility cannot be ruled out. It is more likely that Mary was intending to tell Hunt about her friend Miss Dods. Miss Dods was a lesbian and both Jane and Mary had been seeing a good deal of her that year; this should not lead us to conclude that their own relationship was sexual although it was undeniably intense.

In the meantime, Mary was still being pursued by her own loyal suitor, the provider of all those opera and theatre tickets for herself and Jane. John Howard Payne had admired Mary since their first meeting in the autumn of 1823; his generosity and his readiness to act as an escort to the two young ladies on their long journeys to the Novellos' home at Shacklewell had made him an indispensable part of their life. Godwin liked him; young William was devoted to him; the Lambs thought him splendid. Alone or in company, Payne was reliably cheerful, amusing, unthreatening and kind. Sometimes, it was true, he seemed to be growing a bit sentimental, but it only required a mild reproach, a little reminder of her widowed state, for him to make an embarrassed retreat.

Payne was a patient suitor, but he could not wait for ever. In May 1825, he wistfully told her that she was never out of his thoughts. 'You are perpetually in my presence, and if I close my eyes you are still there, and if I cross my arms over them and try to wave you away, still you will not be gone.'[9] Mary's reply gracefully dismissed the compliment and asked him to be less extreme. 'I truly know how entirely Your imagination creates the admired as well as the admiration –' she told him, 'But do not I entreat you frighten me by any more interpretations.'[10] Towards the end of the month, he pretended to be hurt by her lively interest in everything he could tell her about his friend Washington Irving, who was spending the summer in Paris. So much, Payne jovially wrote, for her fidelity to him! 'Is *ice* a non-conductor?'[11] His bewilderment is understandable, for Mary's letters continued to switch between reproaches ('A part of your present note is very Wrong – very wrong indeed,' on 31 May) and tender invitations to him to come and dine with her at her father's new home in Gower Place ('It is, I think, 20 years since we met,' on 15 June). What was he to understand?

On 25 June 1825, walking Mary home to Kentish Town from a supper with the Godwins, Payne plucked up the courage to declare his feelings. Unluckily for him, he had picked the place and almost the day on which Mary, in the summer of 1814, had declared her love to Shelley.

Mary was in a difficult position. She liked Payne; she had come to depend on his generosity in providing Jane and herself with the chance to see every play, opera and concert that interested them. She did not want to lose this useful friendship, but she had no intention of marrying him. Payne was, as she knew, a romantic man; like a princess in a fairy-tale, she decided to give him a quest. What would really please her, she told him, was the chance to get to know Washington Irving. She had been enchanted by the American essayist's handsome, sensitive face when she saw him at John Gilbert Newton's studio; she had read all his popular works with enthusiasm; she had been allowed to see some of his letters to Payne. This, she gently told her suitor, was the way to please her; Payne was left to conclude that she did not return his love. Her next letter, written on 28 June, supposed that he was 'gay & hopeful' again and wished that he would be as good to himself as he was to other people. Responding the following day, Payne announced that he would put off seeing her until his 'fever' had passed. As regards Irving, he added, 'be assured I will act the hero in this business.'

Payne's heroism took an odd form. Joining Irving in Paris towards the end of the summer, he presented him with a bundle of all the letters Mary had written to him. 'I do not ask you to fall in love,' he wrote in a covering letter of explanation; he added that Mary was, in any case, 'too much out of society to enable you to do so'.[12] This was not what Mary had asked him to do; she had indeed nervously begged Payne to be discreet and not, above all, to make her 'appear ridiculous to one whom I like & esteem'.[13] 'Read Mrs Shelleys correspondence before going to bed,' Irving wrote in his notebook on the night he was handed her letters.[14] That was all he did do. He remained courteous and helpful to Godwin, whose work he admired; he showed no interest in pursuing his daughter.

It seems clear that, although Mary's interest in a friendship with Irving was genuine, she introduced his name chiefly as a way of keeping John Payne at a distance. By November, the subject had become an embarrassment to her and she was tired of Payne's jokes about being a marriage-broker. 'You must really come to an end of bantering me on that subject [Irving] – because after all it is all a mistake,' she told Payne on 29 November 1825. She added, mysteriously, that she could tell him 'a fact or two that would astonish you' to prove it. It is not clear that she told either Payne or Leigh Hunt, to whom she had also dropped mysterious hints of something that would 'surprize' him, just what those astonishing facts were. Most likely, they related to Miss Mary Diana Dods.

Mary had had her first encounter with this unusual lady in the spring of 1822 when she read and admired a collection of verse dramas which Byron had just been sent by his publisher: 'they are works of considerable talent,' Mary had told Thomas Medwin on 12 April, although she thought them greatly inferior to Byron's own works on the same subject. The author of these *Dramas of the Ancient World* was one David Lindsay. By the beginning of 1825, Mary knew that David Lindsay was one of several pseudonyms used by a strange, ardent young Scotswoman with a background which, gradually revealed, had the romance of a gothic novel. David Lindsay and Mary Diana Dods were one and the same.

We do not know how Miss Dods and Mary Shelley met, or even when. The most likely explanation is that they were introduced at the home of Dr William Kitchiner, at whose evening parties Mary was often present after September 1824. (This is the month in which Kitchiner's name first appeared in Godwin's journal; Mary's letters make no reference to him at all.)

William Kitchiner seems, like the Novello family, to have been born to be used by George Cruikshank for one of his Dickens illustrations. Cruikshank did, in fact, sketch one of the doctor's Wednesday dinners, an all-male occasion devoted to the important subject of digestion. A thin, angular man whose usual costume was a long, black, shiny coat, gaiters and a hat as flat as a parson's, Kitchiner had made his name in 1817 with *Apicius Redivivus or Cook's Oracle*, a bizarre collection of dishes with such daunting names as Kitchiner's Peristaltic Persuaders. ('Never affront the stomach!' was the doctor's favourite saying.) Opening his large house in Warren Street, just off the New Road, to mixed gatherings every Tuesday night, Kitchiner hung a sign by the door to remind his guests to 'Come at seven; go at eleven'. His guests included a large number of humorists; one of them sportingly changed the sign to read, 'go it at eleven'.

Mary had been made acutely conscious of her scandalous reputation in her first year at Kentish Town. Few people, other than the hospitable Novellos and the Lambs, were prepared to have her in their homes. Dr Kitchiner, however, was splendidly indifferent to social disgrace. Having inherited a fortune at the age of nineteen from a father who started life carrying coal on the London docks, he had since then lived as he pleased. He was not married to Elizabeth Friend, his mistress since 1804; his son was given the challenging experience of going to Charterhouse and on to Cambridge as their illegitimate child. He was not, in fact, a man who cared much what people thought of him. A few liked him well; regular attendants of his evenings included actors (Charles Kemble, Charles Mathews), journalists (the practical joker Theodore Hook and William Jerdan, editor of the *Literary Gazette*), architects (John Soane), and the celebrated tenor, John Braham. Samuel Rogers, a poet living very comfortably on his income from the family bank, was another occasional visitor to Warren Street.

The only available source we have for Mary's visits to Kitchiner's home are two garrulous articles, both of which were written many years later, by Eliza Rennie, daughter of John the great engineer. From Miss Rennie's descriptions, it is clear that this is where Mary first made friends, not only with the curious Miss Dods, but with the flirtatious and, by general agreement, astonishingly handsome Lord Dillon. Leigh Hunt, who met the literary lord elsewhere, rather liked him: he was, he wrote, 'a cavalier of the old school'.[15] Lord Dillon was reputed to be Eliza Rennie's lover; it didn't stop him trying to thaw Mary's air of cool reserve. He sent her his long and dreadful poem, *Eccelino da Romano, the Tyrant of Padua*, as a mark of esteem and tried to draw her out. She looked so sly, he told her; how was he supposed to put together such wild, imaginative novels as she wrote with such a quiet manner? 'I should have thought you . . . outpouring[,] enthusiastic, rather indiscreet, and even extravagant,' he wrote; 'but you are cool, quiet, feminine to the last degree.'[16] Mary liked talking to Lord Dillon about Italy, where he had lived for ten years, but she refused to be drawn into a correspondence, or whatever else he may have had in mind as a diversion from his marriage.

Lord Dillon was not the only person to be intrigued by the contrast between the modest, appealing figure of Mary and the imaginative achievements of *Frankenstein* and *The Last Man*. His friend Eliza Rennie saw an almost doll-like sweetness of appearance in 'the gentle, feminine, lady-like Mrs Percy Bysshe Shelley, looking the very image of Miss O'Neill's portraits, which she greatly resembles, with her long fair silken ringlets . . .'[17] Rennie's comparison was felicitous or well-informed; Eliza O'Neill was the beautiful young actress whom Shelley had wanted to play the part of Beatrice in his ill-starred verse drama, *The Cenci*.

Lord Dillon was mildly eccentric, preferring to slum it at Warren Street than to be waited on at Ditchley Park, his splendid new home in Oxfordshire. His oddity paled beside the colourful history and bizarre appearance of Miss Dods. She is not identified by name in Eliza Rennie's accounts, but there is no doubt whom she was describing. Rennie presents her, not kindly, as looking like 'some one of the

masculine gender' who has 'indulged in the masquerade freak of feminine habiliments'; her dark curly hair is said to be cut short, like a
man's; her habitual costume is a straight white closely pleated shift
worn under a tight green jacket. Her face is described as pale and
drawn by suffering; this, Rennie hints, was connected to a severe
physical malformation, 'the existence of some organic disease aiding
this materially'. This was the curious young woman who became, at
some point in the winter of 1824, one of Mary Shelley's closest
friends and one whom Rennie went on to praise for 'the charm and
fascination of her manner' and 'the extraordinary talent which her
conversation . . . displayed'.[18]

Miss Dods's story was unhappy enough to intrigue and move a
woman who was always attracted by tales of oppression and hardship.
One of two illegitimate daughters of a Scottish earl, Mary Diana had
been brought up in splendour and then, in 1814, briskly evicted on a
pitiful allowance when her father married a girl slightly younger than
his daughters. Douglases by birth, Lord Morton's daughters received
his meagre financial support on the firm understanding that they
would keep their distance and say nothing about their parentage.
Georgiana, the elder child, married a Captain Carter whose early
death left her struggling to support two young children; Mary Diana
had, since 1821, been trying to keep both her sister and herself by
giving lessons and by writing for anybody prepared to accept her
work.

Although physically unappealing, Miss Dods held out to Mary the
attraction of intelligence and of a life strangely parallel to her own.
Both women were dependent on wealthy and unsympathetic men
who were anxious to disguise any connection to them; both were
struggling hard to make a living by writing; both, at the time they
met, were in desperate need of affection and reassurance. We do not
know exactly what Mary's feelings were for Miss Dods; we do know
that she herself inspired feelings of passionate attachment. Miss Dods's
first (undated) letters address her as 'my Pretty' and 'Miene Liebling';
a gap of five days before they meet is described as a source of intense
pain to her devoted friend. One of the letters is simply signed, 'thine
– D—'.[19] Writing – as David Lindsay – to the Scottish publisher
William Blackwood towards the end of 1825, Miss Dods praised
Mary, 'who is indeed a fine creature', for her combination of 'a very
powerful mind, and with the most gentle feminine manner and
appearance that you can possibly imagine'.[20] Mary returned the
favour the following year, when Miss Dods was away in France, by
doing her best to sell 'David Lyndsay's' latest work to her own pub-

lisher, Henry Colburn, while announcing 'his' intended translation of a German drama.[21] It is likely that Mary was thinking of the Dods sisters and their friend, Charlotte Figge, when she wrote with feeling to Edward Trelawny of having formed 'intimate friendships with those who are great of soul, generous, and incapable of valuing money except for the good it may do – and these very people are all even poorer than myself, is it not hard.'[22]

Mary Shelley remained much too deeply attached to Jane Williams during their years at Kentish Town for it to be likely that she embarked on a sexual relationship with Mary Diana Dods. There may, however, have been rumours. In the autumn of 1825, Mary wrote to Mrs Mason at Pisa, complaining that her stepmother had insisted on being introduced to all her friends and on accompanying her to parties.[23] This sounds like anxious concern, rather than a wish on Mrs Godwin's part to broaden her social horizons. Godwin's laconic journal provides no clues; he had little contact with Kitchiner's circle and none with Miss Dods, although he saw enough of Mary for Mrs Godwin to grumble that he loved his daughter better than his wife. (Nonsense, Godwin responded wearily: 'You are very wrong in saying I do not want your society . . . I see her perhaps twice a week.'[24])

Mary's letters and journal strongly suggest that, intrigued by and fond though she became of poor Mary Diana, her mind was wholly occupied by Jane. Jane was her chosen intimate, her constant companion to operas and plays in the summer of 1825; Jane was on hand to comfort and help when little Percy was taken ill with measles that autumn; Jane was feeling affectionate enough in the spring of 1826, when Hogg was still away, to plan to spend two months with her at Calais. In June, in high spirits, the two young women repeated their bold experiment of going to the theatre alone, in the pit. Jane thought she saw their attentive admirer, the Spaniard; 'he saw not us,' Mary assured Payne, who was again summering in Paris. They had behaved impeccably, 'correct to a miracle'.[25] She was full of good cheer. She had seen and heard her adored Madame Pasta again. She had received the good news that Colburn had not only taken the second volume of her father's *History of the Commonwealth*, but had paid him in advance for two more. She had sold a short story to one of the lucrative new souvenir annuals and had given herself the considerable satisfaction of sending the *Examiner* a passionate defence of Europe's last great castrato singer, Giovanni-Battista Velluti. The audience had, according to Mary, been enchanted; the critics had winced at the spectacle of a man in his fifties shrilling like a choirboy.[26]

Miss Dods and her problems faded from Mary's mind as she planned her summer with Jane. Calais was abandoned in favour of a month at Brighton. Bubbling with happiness, Mary wrote off to Leigh Hunt about Sompting, the pretty Sussex village to which they had removed from the fashionable seaside town. She extolled Jane's perfection. 'She is in truth my all,' she told Hunt on 12 August, 'my sole delight – the dear azure sky from which I – a sea of bitterness beneath – catch alien hues & shine reflecting her loveliness.' It was, she admitted, an 'excessive feeling', but she pleaded with him to understand it, for 'I live to all good & pleasure only through her'.

Jane, still quietly planning when it would be safe to begin her new life with Hogg, was unnerved by such devotion. Mary clung too hard. It frightened her. She drew back. 'I have lived to hear her thank God that it [the holiday] is over,' Mary bleakly noted on 5 September. Her letters that autumn were, for the most part, sombre. She grew low-spirited enough to become plaintive about John Howard Payne's lack of visits.

It is not clear how much Jane had revealed of her plans in the autumn of 1826. By the spring of 1827, she was pregnant and ready to set up home with her lover. Writing to Trelawny on 4 March, Mary tersely announced that her friend's fortunes 'are about to con-clude – differently from mine'. A month later, she struggled to find appropriate words of approval – and failed miserably. Hogg was 'a man of honour', she wrote; nobody could make him happier than Jane. His opinions were liberal, he appeared to be constant and 'if she is happy with him now, she will be so always'. It was fortunate that he had enough money for Jane to 'display her taste and elegance in the way she best likes'.[27] Try how she would, her letter reeked of bitter-ness. She knew by now that Hogg and Jane had been conducting a sexual relationship since his return from Italy, and possibly before his departure. It was hard to suppress the feeling that she had been deceived.

The early summer of 1827 must have been one of the most wretched periods of Mary's life. She had lost Jane, and to a man she despised. She was desperately short of money, thanks to Sir Timothy's capricious forgetfulness. In order to pay her rent at Kentish Town, she was obliged to borrow from Hogg, which must have been humiliat-ing, and from Claire, which must have been worse. Comfort, however, was at hand: she had an opportunity to play guardian angel to a young woman whose situation seemed even more desolate than her own. In May 1827, Mary handed in her notice to Mrs Bartlett at Bartholomew Place. After lingering for another two months, she left

London for Sompting, on the South Coast, the secluded village where she and Jane Williams had stayed the previous summer.

Travelling with Mary on the coach were Percy and little Mary Hunt, on whom Mary had taken pity one day in the Kentish Town stage when Marianne began scolding her daughter. It was in Mary's mind to make use of the child as a companion for Percy, since she did not anticipate having much time to spare for maternal duties. Their other companion in the coach was a young woman with a baby girl. This was Isabel Robinson, not yet twenty, whose affection and beauty had mesmerized Mary from the first time they met.

Isabel's family had already urged Mary to treat their house at Paddington as her own home; there was now every chance that Isabel herself would be ejected from it when her father discovered the fact that she had given birth to an illegitimate child. In planning the future of this young woman, Mary had been working hand in glove with her friend, Miss Dods. Jane Hogg knew what they were planning. All that little Percy and Mary Hunt had been told was that they must take care always to address the lady in the coach as Mrs Douglas.

CHAPTER TWENTY-FIVE

A CURIOUS MARRIAGE

1827–1828

'Our lives are the embodyings of quiet – our only peep at the world is when
we take the children to bathe at Worthing . . . Not one man have we seen,
except an ugly Guardsman one day, who appeared as dropt from the clouds –
& vanished like a meteor. For the rest I read a little Greek, write walk – work
– and the days fly . . .
    I am glad to hear Doddy talks of visiting us soon – Isabel [is] delighted with
her promises of going abroad . . . I wait for my September money . . . Every
blessing attend you – Jeff is included in that prayer now of course – Isabel says
Amen . . .'

Mary Shelley to Jane Williams Hogg, Sompting, 22 August 1827

MARY HAD KNOWN ISABEL ROBINSON AND HER FAMILY SINCE, AT
the latest, the beginning of 1827. Joshua, Isabel's father, was a cultured
man who had made his money out of property development and got
out just before the economic crisis of 1825. By then, he had settled
with his large brood of children in Park Place, Paddington. Although
local records do not reveal the year in which Rosetta Robinson died,
it seems likely that he was already a widower. His house, which was
always called Park Cottage, although it occupied the site of four small
homes, backed on to a nursery garden at the north end of Park Place,
away from the little old church of St Mary's by Paddington Green and
close to the designated route for a new commercial canal. Just to the
east, lying beside the road from London to Kilburn and Edgware, was
Devonshire Place, where a pregnant Jane, now to be known to the
world as 'Mrs Hogg', joined her lover as his common law wife in

September, after a summer spent together in pokier rooms nearby. Later, they made a permanent home in the area, at Maida Place.

Paddington in the 1820s was, despite its proximity to London, a sleepy, semi-rural community. People who groaned at the thought of trailing to Kentish Town from Battle Bridge – as squalid in those days as the renamed Kings Cross area is today – were happy to take a coach from Oxford Street or Tyburn Corner (Marble Arch) for the pleasure of attending one of Mr Robinson's lively, all-male dinners. Conversation at a Park Cottage evening, according to one of the guests, was of 'poetry, philosophy, economy, politics and sometimes religion, but nothing in the way of disputation'. The same guest, Mary's literary friend Cyrus Redding, thought Robinson's evenings were 'the most agreeable I ever remember'.[1] Lord Dillon and Thomas Moore, flirtatious men who had fond memories of Robinson's daughters, 'the Paddington nymphs', and their coaxing ways, shared his view.

The Robinsons, like Eliza Rennie, are elusive figures in contemporary accounts, overshadowed by their famous friends. They can often only be identified by a passing reference to an evening at a charming home in Paddington or to the behaviour of a singularly minxish girl at one of Dr Kitchiner's soirées. This was Mary's friend Isabel, as she was when Mary first knew her in 1826. Below her, and still in their early teens, were Julia, Louisa and Rosa. Ranging from seven-year-old Percy Shelley's age down almost to the cradle were Julian, Charles, Ellen and Eliza. Two older sons were employed and living elsewhere when Mary came into the Robinson family circle.

Isabel, a black-eyed girl with short dark curling hair, had already become a regular guest at Dr Kitchiner's evenings. It was on one of these visits that she had met both Mary Shelley and Mary Diana Dods. Her affair with the American journalist William Grenville Graham had recently been ended by him, leaving Isabel pregnant. Her daughter Adeline was born at some point before June 1827; more probably, late in 1826. It is possible that Isabel accompanied Mary Diana Dods on a visit to France in 1826 in order to give birth to the child without the knowledge of her family. If so, she brought the baby back with her to London. By the time that Mary met her, Isabel had farmed the baby out at a secret address and was contemplating the fact that circumstances might oblige her to abandon it.

Let in on Isabel's secret and concerned by her increasing thinness and nervousness, her female friends took counsel together. Isabel's plan to run off and live in secrecy, alone with her baby in Highgate, seemed to them impractical and unlikely to improve her health.

Instead, they concocted a plan to take her and her child out of London for the summer to rest until she was well enough to travel abroad. It had been decided that she should move to France with the baby. Her escort was to be Miss Dods.[2]

Mary Shelley had not yet left London on 13 July, when she received one of the cruellest shocks of her life. 'My friend has proved false & treacherous!' she wrote in her journal: Isabel Robinson had just opened her eyes to the stories that Jane Hogg had been telling behind her back for the past four years. In normal circumstances, Mary would have demanded an explanation but Jane, as she knew, was suffering acutely in her third pregnancy. That, at least, was the excuse Mary gave herself for saying nothing; a direct confrontation, threatening severance from a woman who had and who still did mean so much to her, was probably more than she could face. She did not hate Jane; she found it impossible to believe that she had behaved with such duplicity. Mary's letters to her became, if anything, more tender and affectionate after Isabel's disclosures.

'Doddy', as she was affectionately known, went up to Scotland in July after learning that her father, the Earl of Morton, had died following a short illness. She hoped, being of an optimistic nature, that he might have made a generous provision which would allow her to live in comfort with Isabel and her baby. Mary, comfortably settled into lodgings at Sompting in Sussex with Isabel, baby Adeline, Percy and little Mary Hunt, suppressed her misery about Jane Hogg's faithlessness as she sent off cheerful descriptions of her rural life. 'We are here calm & I trust contented,' she reported on 28 July. They were waiting anxiously for the news of Lord Morton's will. Neither Doddy nor Isabel seemed to object to the Hunts' daughter having joined them. Worthing, the nearest seaside resort, was dire, full of simpering young ladies in straw poke bonnets and fluttering green crêpe veils. Still, it was delightful to be out of London; perhaps, Mary wrote, she would settle for good in a cottage in the country. Whitton, the lawyer, had indicated that Sir Timothy would approve.

Mary had made up her mind not to refer to Isabel's revelations, yet she could not resist one bitter hint to Jane, 'the prettiest, most graceful blue-eyed Bride the world ever saw – For everybody's sake love yourself tenderly – & think with gentle kindness of her *who for years* has been your devoted Mary S.' She ended her letter with a reminder that her guest was now known as 'Mrs Douglas', and should be so addressed on the outside of letters.

The weather was glorious, the walks sublime, although Isabel was often too weak for more than a short stroll. Every evening, they climbed the upland behind their cottage to gaze out at the sunlit sea and a landscape of villages half hidden among the cornfields. Isabel fretted about the lack of news from Doddy; Mary grieved over the death of the Prime Minister.* George Canning had become one of the most widely loved and respected politicians of his time, both in England and abroad – the one redeeming feature, in Mary's view, of the stagnant Tory government led by Lord Liverpool for too many years. Canning had mentioned her novel in Parliament; she did not forget that mark of esteem, but he was also the only minister to have a sympathetic and intelligent foreign policy. To Jane, she wrote sadly on 15 August of their loss of 'the World's Splendour'; Canning, she told Teresa Guiccioli that month, was a loss not only to England, but to Italy: 'e per voi'.³

Even Sir Timothy, Mary imagined, might share her feelings. Always looking for a way to earn his goodwill, she sent, via the lawyer, her commiseration, at the same time expressing the hope that her allowance would not be delayed. Sir Timothy had deigned to see his grandson for the first time that spring; she imagined he would like to know that Percy was now glowing with health from the sea air. A little wanly, she asked Whitton to thank his employer for all his kindness 'to my poor boy and . . . towards myself'.⁴ She had still never seen or received a word from Sir Timothy Shelley; all was effected through the lawyer's offices.

News had come at last from Scotland. It was not cheerful. Despite the fact that Lord Morton had no son, his entire estate, one of princely size, was left to the male cousin who also inherited the title. His two illegitimate daughters were left a pitiful annuity of £100 each. 'Small indeed is the thing done,' Mary told Jane on 15 August, but 'Doddy' was still grateful not to have been entirely overlooked. Isabel remained frail, but was said to be very excited about their plans for her.

A grasping landlady relet their rooms in Sompting to guests who were prepared to pay her more money. They had been obliged to

---

* Canning, who became Prime Minister in 1827, died within months of taking office, having in the years 1822–7 been one of Britain's ablest foreign secretaries, in the Liverpool administration. A poet as well as a politician, he was the author of 'The Knife-Grinder', which had poked fun at republican ideals in the *Anti-Jacobin Review*, depicting the republican's disappointment when the knife-grinder puts his troubles down to drink, not to the wicked squire, the tithe rent or the attorney. Shelley and Mary must also have loved him as the man who had once fought a duel with their hated Viscount Castlereagh over a military decision of which Canning disapproved.

remove suddenly and '*without milk*' – without funds for new lodgings – Mary wailed to Jane on 26 August, begging a loan of £10. It reached her two days later, at their new lodgings in the village of Arundel where, with the castle above them, a view from their windows of the river Arun and beguiling walks to be taken through woods and rolling parkland, she felt almost grateful for their sudden eviction.

Jane's loan arrived with an intriguing hint which Mary was quick to pick up. 'I am glad for pretty Isabel's sake that D now seriously thinks of les culottes,' she wrote back on 28 August and added, meaningfully, '– I do not expect this person – as Isa names D – for two or three weeks.' Perhaps, writing this, she was struck by how naturally Jane seemed to thrive in an atmosphere of conspiracy. Bitter recollections began to surface. 'I am glad the vision of Kentish Town has past,' she wrote, '. . . I could not return to the like again.'

Mary could brood with the best of them when she chose; fortunately, her time was too occupied for her to indulge in self-pity. Now that Doddy had made her intentions plain to Mary, and her anxiously awaited allowance had arrived from Whitton, it was time to begin creating the web of deception which would protect their dear Isabel. Mary told her first lie of the summer to Teresa Guiccioli, casually announcing that her beloved friend's husband was soon coming to take her to Paris while she herself went 'sorrowfully' back to London.[5] Asking John Howard Payne to share her pleasure at Louisa Holcroft's marriage to John Badams, an eminent chemist, she told her second fib. What a coincidence! Why, her friend at Arundel, 'a sweet little girl', was also married![6] The stage was being set.

The disappointment of being left almost penniless by her father's will initially paralysed Miss Dods. By the last week of August 1827, she had taken a bold decision. Physically and emotionally, she had always felt more of a man than a woman; now, humiliatingly passed over in favour of a male cousin, she decided to reshape her destiny, to become the man who should have inherited, whose place had been usurped. She had initially only planned to go abroad as Isabel's companion and protector. Now, she resolved to transform herself: Isabel would leave England as the wife of Walter Sholto Douglas, father of Adeline. With a false passport to establish her new persona (Mary Shelley was willing to help her obtain one), she could start life again. 'Doddy' had, in a sense, been forced to live in disguise all her life; 'Mr Douglas' seemed closer both to her nature and her noble background than poor, obscure Miss Dods. As Mr Douglas, she could start life afresh.

By 23 September, the transformation was complete. A white-faced and tightly corseted young man knocked at the door of the lodgings in Tarrant Street which Mary Shelley had taken a month earlier. His appearance was unnervingly authentic. Nobody who did not know Miss Dods well would have guessed the truth. 'Nothing can be better than the *arrangements* here. Our friend is absolutely fascinating,' Mary reported excitedly to Jane. 'Mary Hunt is quite delighted – & Percy entertains great respect & great wish to please his new friend. All this is good.'[7]

It was by pure chance that a new player, the emancipated and courageous philanthropist Fanny Wright, wandered into the drama at this moment, knowing nothing of Mary's intrigues, but hoping to carry her off to America as a desirable female companion and helpmate. Fanny, a Dundee girl by birth, had been led by her reverence for Mary Wollstonecraft to expect great things of Mrs Shelley; her young companion, Robert Dale Owen, recently returned from the experimental socialist village of New Harmony which his father had founded in Indiana, had an equally awestruck view of Mary from the older Owen's recollections of visits to the Godwin household. It was inconceivable that the daughter of such a couple should be anything short of remarkable. Encouraged by Dale, Fanny Wright sent off a letter – probably via Skinner Street – inviting Mary to join them.

'You confer on me a very high honour by forgetting for a moment your high & noble views to interest yrself in me,' Mary wrote back on 12 September; she could not hide the pleasure it gave her to be acknowledged as Mary Wollstonecraft's heroic heir, particularly at a time, although she could not say it, when she was acting with a recklessness which might have given even her intrepid mother pause. 'The memory of my Mother has always been the pride & delight of my life,' Mary assured Miss Wright – and hesitated. Her mother might well have embraced the idea of crossing the ocean to live in Fanny's bravely conceived community at Nashoba in Tennessee, where slaves were allowed to earn their freedom through work. She could not imagine herself in America; what, besides, would become of Percy, and of her allowance? Whom would she know there, other than Fanny herself? Admiring the project, she avoided making promises. It was Fanny herself, she flatteringly confessed, who really interested her. Did philanthropic work bring her content? She, for her part, preferred to work for the happiness of a chosen few, 'a narrow circle'. Fanny Wright, at the end of a long and unsatisfactory relationship with the sixty-year-old

Marquis de Lafayette, hero of two revolutions, was staying with her friends the Garnetts in Paris before her return to America. 'Why cannot you come to England?' Mary pleaded. 'I am near the coast – & if you crossed to Brighton, I cd see you. At least I pray you write again.'

Mary's letter, while disappointingly negative about the Tennessee community, was frank and intriguing enough to persuade Fanny that they should meet. In early October, this tall and imposing woman stepped out of her carriage at Arundel and strode through the village to the address given by Mrs Shelley. Here, she was greeted by little Mary Hunt, Shelley's six-year-old son and a smiling, dark-haired couple. They were introduced as Isabel and Walter Douglas, proud parents of a baby girl. Nervousness made Mary hard-edged and inattentive to Fanny's attempts to conduct discussions about the injustices done to their sex. Mildly disappointed, Fanny concluded that Mrs Shelley was somewhat deficient in sensibility and reported as much to her friends in France.[8] Oblivious to the deception being practised on her and hearing that the Douglases planned to settle in France, she obligingly provided them with letters of introduction to the lively Garnett family in Paris.

Fanny's visit was brief, but it had told Mary all she needed to know. The masquerade was entirely convincing; not for a moment had their visitor shown a sign of suspecting the truth about her fellow guests. Writing to John Howard Payne on 13 October, just after Fanny's departure, Mary described her as 'the most wonderful & interesting woman I ever saw'. She had, almost, been tempted to accompany her to America after all, won over by the sheer force of Fanny's personality.

Mary had a reason for keeping up a friendly correspondence with the ever-obliging Payne. A passport was crucial if 'Mr Douglas' was to gain employment in France; not even the intrepid Miss Dods felt ready to present herself for official inspection. Mary had begun her plot to obtain the necessary documents almost as soon as 'Mr Douglas' arrived at Arundel. On 23 September, she wrote off to Payne, who was in London. 'To shew you that I believe you like to serve me, I am about to send you another commission,' she told him. Her next letter explained that her friends, 'the sweet little girl' and her husband, needed passports; unfortunately, they were too ill to come to London to obtain them. Did Payne think he could possibly find two actors ready to impersonate the Douglases, of whom she provided minute descriptions, and to forge the signatures which he would find at the end of the letter? At the bottom of the page, Mary Diana Dods carefully inscribed her own new name, 'Sholto Douglas', beside that of her 'wife'.[9] Payne had never yet let Mary down; a couple of obliging friends were found to masquerade as the Douglases. By 1 October the passports were at Arundel.

A mercury compound she was taking, or perhaps relief at seeing their plans advancing so well, had worked a miraculous improvement on Isabel by October; little Percy, however, became distressingly ill, forcing Mary to revise her plan to travel with the Douglases to France when they left in mid-October. As soon as the child had recovered, she went back with him to London. Mary Hunt, having demonstrated rather too much of the bad temper of which her mother had complained, was returned to her parents.

Alone again with her son, Mary felt tired, triumphant, and a little anxious. Had she done the right thing? Would Isabel be happy in her new life? Would they be safe from discovery? She started making arrangements to visit Paris in the New Year; in the meantime, she stilled her conscience. 'Why may I not hover a good genius round my lovely friend's path?' she asked her journal and decided that the question was rhetorical.[10]

At the end of October, after spending a few days with Fanny Wright at the Harrow home of Frances Trollope (her son Anthony was still only a boy), Mary toyed once more with the idea of sailing to a new life in America, and rejected it. Mrs Trollope – desperate to escape a bullying husband, to make money for the family and to continue her affair with Auguste Hervieu, a French artist whom she smuggled into the party of emigrants at the last moment – couldn't wait to leave. Mary went down to the docks at Gravesend to see them on their way. Fanny Wright squeezed her hand affectionately, full of hopes that they would meet again. 'Dear love,' she wrote fondly as she sat on her berth, 'how your figure lives in my mind's eye, as I saw you borne away from me till I lost sight of your little back among the shipping.'[11]

Only two people remained to remind Mary of the strangeness of the past few months. One was her son, now growing encouragingly tall and strong: 'è bello, grande – forte – buono,' she told Teresa Guiccioli with pride.[12] The other was Robert Dale Owen, who had arranged to follow the two Franceses to Nashoba at the end of the year. Young, sensitive and high-principled, Dale became Mary's regular companion in the days before she and Percy moved to new lodgings near Portman Square. Dale Owen had fallen a little in love with Mary. She was 'gentle, genial, sympathetic, thoughtful and matured beyond her years', he wrote over twenty years later. Animated though she was in conversation, he had noticed how sad she looked when nobody was watching her. Fanny Wright thought she lacked sensibility; Dale feared she might have too much of it to be happy. Encouragement was what she needed, the support of 'a guiding and sustaining hand'.[13]

Mary, writing to Jane Hogg on 23 September, mused on the fact that she was now thirty years old and declared that she would travel a hundred miles for 'one look of true love & sympathy', and almost die for 'that sweet conjunction', by which she meant lovemaking. She craved affection and twenty-six-year-old Dale Owen was ready to offer it. He dropped hints that he would stay, if she wished; he admitted that he sometimes found Fanny Wright a little intimidating.

Owen was a handsome man and a good one; Mary, however, was unable to imagine herself in love with him. Her first loyalty was, she felt, due to Fanny, the woman who had sought her out and who had compared her, so gratifyingly, to her mother. Gently, she encouraged Owen to view Fanny more reasonably; even she, so apparently super-human, might sometimes need comfort. She could have been writing of herself, and was perhaps aware of it:

> Study to please Fanny in all minutia – divine her uneasinesses, & be ever ready at her side with brotherly protection. Do not imagine that she is capable always of taking care of herself: – she is certainly more than any woman, but we have all in us – & she is too sensitive & feminine not largely to partake in this inherent part of us – a desire to find a manly spirit where on {to} lean – a manly arm to protect & shelter us – [14]

'Soeur preçheuse thus finishes her sermon,' Mary concluded playfully, worried that she sounded too solemn. Owen did not forget her words, or her nature. Shelley might have become truly great, he mused in his autobiography, *Threading My Way*, given more time and 'cherished and piloted by his noble wife'.[15] This sense of Mary's benevolent influence was sadly untypical of the general view.

The friendship was affectionately, if sporadically, maintained. 'The Atlantic divides us,' Mary wrote wistfully to Fanny three years later, on 30 December 1830. She wished that their connection was closer. 'Will Fanny never come over? Talk to her of me sometimes Remember me yourself,' she wrote to Dale Owen on the same date. This tells us how slight their contact had become; Owen and Miss Wright had parted ways six months earlier, when she left him to reset-tle herself in France, where she married and lived for the next five years. Fanny had visited England on her way to France; she found no time to make her presence known to Mary Shelley.

Owen left for America early in November 1827 and Mary's life
grew disagreeably empty again. Payne, now meekly returned to his
old role of ticket agent, was obliging and kind; her father was glad to
have her back in London and living close enough for regular meetings. She remained, nevertheless, conscious of the limited circle of her
friendships. Jane Hogg was in the last stages of her difficult pregnancy
and continued unwell; the Hunts were grieving over the loss of a
child, their little Swinburne. In the spring of 1827, Mary had written
to Trelawny in Greece, wondering if he might ever care to return:
'you would not make one of us – you will leave us quickly again . . .
Will you not come?'[16] His answer came in the autumn. He had ended
his brief marriage to a maid of Greece who had spurned native attire
for fashionable French dresses; he was plagued by a 'villainous lawsuit'; yes, he was planning to make his way back to England at last,
when she would find him 'the same unconnected, lone and wandering vagabond you first knew'. He spoke of his unaltered affection, just
as he always did to desolate, faraway Claire; the letter reeked of
discontent and lost illusions.[17]

Talking to Tom Moore at this time during one of their many meetings about his biography of Byron, Mary admitted that she was thoroughly miserable. The cause, she told him, was the discovery of Jane
Hogg's treacherous tale-telling; she was finding it increasingly difficult
to write long, loving letters, as though nothing had happened. The
conversation with Moore took place in February 1828; she had kept
the knowledge of Jane's betrayal to herself for over half a year. Moore,
an outspoken man, pointed out that her excuse – Jane's pregnancy –
was now out of date. The baby – sadly short-lived – had been born
and baptized. He scolded her: she was doing no favour to herself by
this pretence of ignorance. 'By his advice I disclosed my discoveries
to Jane,' Mary wrote in her journal on 12 February 1828. The experience had been excruciating; Jane burst into tears, demanded to know
who had spread this hateful tale and what it was that she was supposed
to have said. She then turned the tables on Mary by accusing her of
being cold and unloving.

We know all this because Mary set it down in the agonized letter
she wrote to Jane Hogg on 14 February, two days after confronting
her. Now, for the first time, she disclosed Isabel as the source of her
information; if Jane really needed to be reminded of all the dreadful
stories she had told, she had only to write to Paris. She wrote, with
dignity and pain, of the damage Jane had done to her reputation by
reporting her to have been a cold wife who had driven Shelley almost
to seek his own death; but the letter did not conceal the fact that what

really hurt was the way Jane had abandoned her for Hogg. 'Often leaving you at Kentish Town I have wept from the overflow of affection – Often thanked God who has given you to me,' Mary wrote.

> Could any but yourself have destroyed such engrossing & passionate love? . . . I have committed many faults – the remorse of love haunts me often & brings bitter tears to my eyes – but for four years I committed not one fault towards you – In larger, in minute things your pleasure and satisfaction were my objects, & I gave up every thing that is all the very little I could give up to them – I make no boast, heaven knows had you loved me you were worth all . . .[18]

The friendship survived, but only because Mary insisted that it must. She made the conditions. The first of them was that Jane should never again try to pretend she had done nothing wrong or expect Mary to forget her past behaviour. Jane's continuing attempts to lay the blame on Isabel's shoulders were received with sorrow and disbelief. 'It is painful to go over old grounds,' Mary wearily told her on 28 June 1828: 'I go only on what you have allowed; long you gave ear to every idle & evil tale against me – & repeated them – not glossed over.' How, when they both knew that this was so, could Jane go on claiming her innocence? Insincerity, to a woman who had grown up in Godwin's household, was among the worst of social sins. 'Do not I earnestly pray you, allude to the past, or the changes which cannot be unchanged –' Mary had sternly warned Jane on 5 June 1828, 'let us begin again.' It was to the credit of them both that their friendship, while never the same, was resumed. Jane would, in her way, make amends for her behaviour over the years. She became one of Mary's staunchest supports.

In 1828, however, much damage had been done and it could not easily be repaired. Isabel, although Mary did not yet know it, was busily spreading the same stories in Paris; in London, there were even rumours that Mary was having an improper relationship with Vincent Novello. Mary decided to do what must be done; she wrote him a little note in Italian enclosing a promised lock of Mary Wollstonecraft's hair and regretting that they would, for some time, be separated by 'circumstances'. Since the only obvious circumstance on the horizon was her plan to make a brief visit to Paris, Mary was plainly referring to the gossip that had been spread. 'This gift . . . will remind you pleasantly of her who loves her friends forever,' she told him, and begged him to 'preserve at least your esteem for Mary Shelley'. She gave no further explanations. The intimacy, harmless though it had been, was at an end.[19]

The spring of 1828 brought news from France that the Douglases were planning to travel to Hanover, where one of Fanny Wright's friends, Miss Julia Garnett, had just begun a new married life, and where Mr Douglas hoped, with the help of Julia's husband, to secure a diplomatic posting on the strength of his forged papers. Percy had now been safely settled at Mr Slater's Academy for young gentlemen in Kensington, an expensive boarding-school recommended by Peacock. Writing to William Whitton, the lawyer, on 8 April, Mary informed him that she intended going to Paris as soon as the Easter holidays were over: 'as I shall be exceedingly anxious to return to him [Percy], I shall not remain away more than three weeks.' Terrified of incurring Sir Timothy's anger, she assured Whitton again a line later that she would be back within the specified time. Both Mary and her son, as she was painfully aware, remained dependent on the goodwill of the lawyer and of the father-in-law she had still not met; if her letters to William Whitton sometimes used a grovelling tone, it was for good reason.

Mary left for Paris in mid-April, taking Isabel's little sister, Julia, for a companion; Julia Robinson was young and innocent enough to be deceived by the false history of her sister's marriage and to accept 'Mr Douglas' for the man he seemed to be. Mary felt giddy and feverish on the crossing to Calais. By the time she had reached the rooms in which the Douglases lived, she was feeling a good deal worse. Meekly, she allowed herself to be taken to her room and put in a hip-bath filled with steaming water. When she tried to get to her feet again, she could hardly stand.[20]

THE HIDEOUS PROGENY

1828–1831

'I am tempted to offer to write a brief outline of Mr Shelleys life if Galignani chose – but then my secret must be kept religiously – & no alterrations made – it would be very short & its chief merit the *absence* of incorrectness –'

Mary Shelley to Cyrus Redding, ?3 September 1829

THE DOUGLASES' FLAT WAS ON THE RUE NEUVE DE BERRY, CLOSE TO the drab municipal park of the Champs Elysées. Here, dazed and feverish, Mary gratefully allowed herself to be put to bed and nursed. Not until the worst of her illness had passed was she told that she had been suffering from smallpox and allowed to look in a mirror. Mary's identification with Frankenstein's creature had never been physical; on the contrary, she knew herself to be a pretty woman, although, at thirty, the bloom had begun to fade. Now, studying a red, encrusted mask and lank, clipped hair, she knew what it was to be a monster. The doctors assured her that the disfigurement was unlikely to be permanent. Her hair would grow, although it never recovered its glorious colour and buoyancy; her delicate skin would not be marked, only robbed of its uncommon transparency and pallor.

She could not hide away. It was bad enough that her illness had put the Douglases and Julia Robinson into quarantine for a fortnight. Isabel, overjoyed to have new company in the claustrophobic rooms she shared with Doddy and her little girl, rattled off a whole list of people who were hoping to meet her. Miss Wright's kind friends, the Garnetts, were going to hold a soirée. Surely she would not miss an opportunity to talk to the great Lafayette? The novelist Benjamin

Constant, now leader of the Liberal opposition, lived with his wife just around the corner. Mary Clarke, a fascinating young Irishwoman who had been taught the art of entertaining by the celebrated Madame Récamier, kept open house in her little rooms on the Left Bank, at rue des Petits Augustins. Doddy, Isabel whispered, bending lower, was a great trial, always watching her and complaining when she so much as looked at a man. The situation was so difficult. The Garnetts, suspecting nothing of the truth, often expressed their pity for her at having such a sullen, demanding husband.

Mary had never been able to resist Isabel in her coaxing mood. She was unaware that her beautiful young friend had wasted no time in passing Jane Hogg's malicious tales about Mary to her new acquaintances in Paris. 'Mrs D[ouglas] has described her [Mary's] character to me & I have seen her letters to her most intimate friends,' Maria Garnett had written to her sister Julia in Hanover on 22 April; she added that she did 'not expect to like her'.[1] Knowing nothing of this, Mary was full of pity for Isabel's situation. Doddy, her body now twisted by the muscular disease from which she suffered, had become demanding and possessive; the marriage which both Mary and Isabel had only seen as a strategy was all too real to her. She could not bear to see Isabel with 'other' men; she was consumed by jealousy and pain. 'What D[oddy] now is, I will not describe in a letter,' Mary wrote unhappily to Jane Hogg after her return to England; '– one only trusts that the diseased body acts on the diseased mind, & that both may be at rest ere long.'[2] In another letter to Jane, she admitted that she now felt overcome with guilt for having helped to put 'the poor child' (Isabel) in this situation: 'as I consider myself in some sort the cause, so I [shall] devote myself to extricate her.'[3]

The Garnetts, prepared by Isabel's accounts for a cold promiscuous woman, were disarmed by the good humour with which Mary displayed her marred looks. 'It was rather droll to play the part of an ugly person for the first time in my life,' Mary lightly wrote later to Isabella Baxter Booth. Her courage had been rewarded: she was 'delighted' by all the people she met, and by the city in which she felt, for the first time, like an inhabitant.[4] The air, unlike that of smutty, smoke-stained London, was as clear as on Richmond Hill; the recently completed Bourse was generally acknowledged to be one of the most magnificent new buildings in Europe; the Palais Royal, lying to the rear of the rue Saint-Honoré, was irresistible to visitors, a shoppers' paradise of hats, china, glass and prints, its arcades crowded from morning to dawn. This was the Paris of Balzac's early novels, where each floor of the grand old buildings offered a different spectacle, from gambling dens in the cellars through the leisured elegance of cafés where nobody frowned at a lady who chose to dine alone, up through the great reception rooms of the bankers, the courtesans and the new aristocracy, into insanitary attics where families lived in crowded poverty.

In Sussex, Mary had been convinced that she wanted nothing more than a country retreat, health-giving walks, a view of the sea. Now, she fell under the spell of Paris. 'The weather is divine,' she wrote dreamily to Jane: 'we are in the open air almost all day, beneath the fresh green chesnuts of the Tuilleries.'[5] The Garnetts, once they had decided to like her, made sure that she was welcomed by their friends in a way that was peculiarly sweet to a woman accustomed to seeing married ladies and young husbands turn their backs when she walked into a London drawing-room. It is possible that she met Stendhal, still smarting at having lost the charming Miss Julia Garnett to the keeper of the royal library at Hanover. More certainly, Mary offered her homage to General Lafayette and endeared herself to Benjamin Constant, 'a venerable benevolent looking old man' with a softly sentimental German wife.[6] While Isabel Douglas, weary of Doddy's possessiveness, flirted with the scholarly linguist Claude Fauriel and drew down on herself the wrath of his mistress, Mary Clarke, Mary found herself being courted by a man she described to Jane Hogg as 'a poet – a creature whose nature is divine'.[7]

The divinity was the twenty-five-year-old Prosper Mérimée. Clever, witty, ambitious but not yet rich, Mérimée lived in as much style as an impecunious writer could hope for in one of the warren of lodgings carved out of the grand old houses flanking the rue Saint-Honoré. A friend of Stendhal, admired by Goethe and Chauteaubriand for his romantic dramas and for the 'translations' of Illyrian ballads he had written himself, Mérimée was still unknown in England. Mary, struck by the resemblance of his new verse-drama, La Famille de Carvajal, to the subject of Shelley's play, The Cenci, promised her support in promoting him. Shortly after her return to England, she wrote to John Bowring at the new Westminster Review and produced a long, commendatory piece for the issue of January 1829, following it up with another in 1830.[8]

Mérimée had quite a way with women; when Mary met him he was still sporting a wounded arm from a duel with his last mistress's husband. His indifference to her blighted looks was as pleasing as his respect for her intelligence. 'What will you also say to the imagination of one of the cleverest men in France, young and a poet, who could be interested in me in spite of the mask I wore,' she boasted to

Isabella Booth on 15 June. Two days before she left Paris in the last week of May, Mérimée wrote her a letter declaring his love. But Mary, by this time, had seen enough of Parisian ways to distinguish between flirtation and passion. Returning his letter with a gracefully expressed wish that he might not live to regret such impetuousness, she offered her friendship: 'vous trouverez en moi une amie simpatisante – compatisante – vraie.'[9]

Nevertheless, sipping tea at the farewell party they gave in her honour that night, the observant Garnetts noticed that the occasion had become 'a flirting party', two of the chief flirts being Mrs Shelley and Mérimée. As for Mrs Douglas, Harriet Garnett drily wrote to her married sister in Germany, she had made herself agreeable to all the other men in the room while poor Mr Douglas looked on, 'sick and disconsolate'.[10] The Garnetts were beginning to get the measure of Isabel, but Harriet's letter is interesting for providing rare evidence of Mary's ability to flirt; her recklessness makes it easier to understand why the stories told by Jane Hogg had so readily been accepted. What looked like flirtation was, in Mary's own view, simply the behaviour of a sexual equal. She flirted to hide the intelligence which, as she was well aware, could make her seem rather intimidating, and because she liked the company of attentive, good-looking men. She did not, it seems, always consider how others might judge her caressing manner.

The first news which greeted Mary on her return to England at the beginning of June was unusually pleasing: Sir Timothy, his wife and his daughters had all paid a call on Percy at Mr Slater's Academy in Kensington: 'I hope he was satisfied with the school and my boy,' Mary anxiously wrote to the lawyer who had given her this information.[11] Perhaps, now that Sir Timothy had seen his grandson again, he might consider raising her allowance, she suggested to Whitton, reminding him that an increase to £300 a year had been mentioned as a possibility. But seeing Percy had not softened Sir Timothy to that extent. If his daughter-in-law wanted more money, she would have to work for it.

Facing strangers in Paris with her 'mask' and short, dull hair was easier than the prospect of being exclaimed at and pitied by her London acquaintances. Told by the doctors that nothing would speed her recovery faster than sea air, Mary rented a cottage for the summer for herself, Percy and Julia Robinson – 'the most amiable little girl I ever knew' – at quiet, unfashionable Hastings on the South Coast. Here, during a glorious summer, she revelled in the sea air and long inland walks. It was very good for Percy as well as herself, she told Jane. His character was beginning to develop: 'without evil – & without sentiment . . . unsocial yet frank – without one ill fold'.[12] As her son grew older, she would note his stubbornness; at eight, he was still as docile as a mother could wish: 'not quite the virtue of his father's family', she could not resist informing William Whitton a year later.

Mérimée sent long, lively letters from Paris, begging for news of her return and, on every possible opportunity, alerting her to the duplicity of Isabel Douglas. How could Mary, the most generous of friends, trust such a creature, he asked indignantly? All her precious Mrs Douglas cared for was turning the heads of foppish young men, an art in which she seemed well-practised.[13] One can't help wondering if Mérimée was writing out of pique; Isabel was an attractive woman, and nearer his own age than Mary herself.

Perhaps his accounts had an effect. Mary's replies have been lost, but she abandoned her idea of rescuing Isabel, while she remained close enough to 'Doddy' to continue offering her work to friendly editors in England. She seems, however, to have lost contact by 1829, the year in which, still masquerading as a man, poor, sickly Miss Dods was sent to a debtors' prison in Paris. The date of her death is not certain, but Isabel felt free to return to London with her daughter the following year. By this time, either from Mérimée or from one of her other Parisian contacts, Mary had been made aware of her true nature. 'I saw Isabel yesterday,' she noted in her journal on 1 December 1830. '– Good heavens – is this the being I adored – she was ever false yet enchanting – now she has lost her fascinations – probably, because I can no longer serve her she take[s] no more trouble to please me – but also she surely is not the being she once was.' It seemed beyond belief that a girl for whom she had risked her own fragile social reputation and even braved the law should have proved as treacherous as Jane Hogg. She could forgive Jane, especially now that Hogg's disgusted family had turned their backs on him, his unwedded wife and illegitimate child. Jane needed her, and the helpless were always sure of Mary's loyalty. Isabel had become capable of making her own way in the world.

Disillusion did not tempt Mary to betray the secret life of the Douglases, but it was not her secret alone. Lord Dillon had already asked her for Doddy's 'donation' in Paris, indicating that he knew of a name change; Jane Hogg knew everything and had no reason to protect the reputation of the woman she hated for betraying her to Mary Shelley. Isabel was probably wise to stay out of England after 1830. Living quietly abroad, the 'widowed' Mrs Douglas became the unlikely wife of a retired clergyman, the Reverend William Falconer, at whose pleasant Italian villa she died, her reputation intact, in 1869. Long before then, the deception had been carried to new heights as Sir Henry Drummond Charles Wolff proudly recorded his marriage abroad to Adeline, daughter of Mr and Mrs Walter Sholto Douglas. The baby for whose sake Mary had embarked on her mission of concocting a false marriage, returned with Sir Henry to become, by the last odd twist in this curious tale, the next-door neighbour and close friend of Mary's son and daughter-in-law on their country estate near Bournemouth. Neither couple were aware of the bizarre chain of circumstances which linked them.

Mary could not resist slipping a few hints at the truth into her work. Disguise plays a large role in *Perkin Warbeck*, the novel she began writing after her return to England in 1828, and in the sentimental stories she produced for the ladies' annuals. 'Ferdinando Eboli' (1829, for the 1830 *Keepsake*) puts the heroine into the costume of a page to escape seduction; 'The False Rhyme' (1829–30) presents a couple who exchange sex by their costumes. 'Transformation' (1830–1), with its story of a misshapen creature who gains possession of a handsome young man's body, owes as much to the history of Miss Dods as to Byron's drama, *The Deformed Transformed*, a work which Mary greatly admired. 'Lift not the painted veil,' Mary insisted in a quotation from her husband which appears countless times in her own work. This particular veil had, after all, been discreetly left in place; who would ever think of searching a lady's annual of love stories for the truth about poor Miss Dods and her romance?

Letters kept Mary in touch with the world during her peaceful summer of exile at Hastings. Jane Hogg sent news of the Hunts' latest disaster; Marianne had taken to drink and the whole family had left Highgate to live in penury near Windsor. Writing back, Mary envied Jane the arrival from abroad of a loving brother and the supportive presence of Hogg, 'a dear Man person'. She had hopes of one herself, she admitted. 'Trelawny in England! – Where – how ardently I desire to see him,' had been her first response to Jane's news of his return from the Continent.[14] 'I long, each day more to embrace the darling again,' she wrote two weeks later on 20 June. 'Tomorrow I hope to know my fate from Trelawny,' she wrote eight days later, '– & I shall then finish this letter – God bless you, my pretty pet!'

The fate Mary was referring to was no more than the news that

Trelawny was prepared to leave London for Hastings to see her; she was sufficiently excited by the prospect not to care what conclusions Jane might draw from her excited notes. Trelawny let her down. He paid a call on Mr Godwin, to whom he became warmly attached. He assured Mary, from a distance, that he loved her: 'my feelings and passions burn fierce as ever – and will – till they have consumed me.'[15] They were not so consuming as to bring him to Hastings. Trelawny liked a handsome woman; having learned of Mary's disfiguring attack of smallpox, he found excuses to stay away. Disappointed, Mary was obliged to comfort herself with the presence of quiet, affectionate Percy, and with visits by Julia Robinson's father and her own.

Mary had told Jane Hogg on 28 June that she hoped, in a few weeks, 'not to be a fright', although her hair was still cropped short and her skin sallow. Godwin was shocked by the change in his pretty daughter when he visited her on 10 August; his unfailing candour would probably have frightened her into staying in seclusion anyway, but events took the decision out of her hands. Julia became seriously ill during his visit. Typhus was suspected. Godwin returned home; Mary, having volunteered to care for Julia while she slowly recovered her health at the Robinsons' Paddington home, gratefully accepted Mr Robinson's suggestion that she should stay there for as long as she wished.

Mary spent the rest of the year at Park Cottage with the Robinsons, working on *Perkin Warbeck*, helping Thomas Moore with his book on Byron and making only rare forays into London. Future visits to the Robinson home in the early summer of 1829 and the autumn of 1830 were made for the pleasure of living in semi-rural surroundings and in the company of this large, friendly family. In 1828, health and vanity were the reasons for her seclusion.

Six years had passed since Claire had set off from Italy to take up a lonely life as a governess in Russia. Mary, when she felt wretched about her own life, reminded herself that Claire's must be even sadder, estranged from all she knew, struggling to please the demanding parents of her pupils, daring to confide in nobody about her past in case she lost her position. The affair with Trelawny had not survived their life in separate countries. She had, it seemed to Mary, little to live for. Since before going to Paris, she had been strenuously urging Claire to give up this drudge's life and come home, if only for a visit. The news that Charles Clairmont and his Austrian wife Antonia had come to London in July 1828 provided Claire with an additional incentive for returning. On 17 October, for the first time since Mary's elopement, the entire family was reunited for a meal at the Godwins' home in Gower Place. Only William, who had fallen out both with his parents and with Mary for reasons which are not clear, was absent. It is possible that he was already involved with Emily Eldred, a young woman of whom all the family, for no known reason, strongly disapproved.

Much of the talk at Gower Place that night must have been of the visitors' lives abroad and of their plans for the future. Godwin, pleased to see his wife reunited with her children, wanted Charles to get work at the new university behind their home, as a professor of German literature and history. Already friendly with several of the academic staff, he could provide all the necessary introductions and recommendations. No such avenues were open to Mary or Claire as females, but Godwin was eager to be of help here also, although not for wholly altruistic reasons. Frederic Mansel Reynolds, an aspiring young writer whom he had met in March that year and who later dedicated his first novel to Godwin, was about to take over the editorship of the new *Keepsake* annual from Harrison Ainsworth. Moore was reported to have been offered a guinea a line for contributions to *The Keepsake*; one could keep a family – or a father, at least – on such generous pay! Smiling at Godwin's incurable optimism, the visitors changed the subject to his own new project.

Cloudesley, the novel on which Godwin began work nine days later, opens like *Frankenstein* with a journey to Russia; the account of life there was supplied from his conversations with Claire. Written from financial necessity, the overlong book was generally dismissed as the work of an old man whose imagination had lost its fire. The warmest appreciation appeared in *Blackwood's Edinburgh Magazine* in May 1830. Other reviewers complained that the novel was tedious; here, readers were urged to imagine that they were listening to some majestic work for the organ, designed to inspire 'new and extraordinary emotions, while we sit soul-enchained by the wonders of his art'. The author of this rapturous account was Mary Shelley; under the cloak of anonymity, she proudly hailed her father as 'one of the wisest men of this or any age'.

Passionate in Godwin's defence, unfailingly loyal in her efforts to support him, Mary had not yet resolved deep-seated feelings of guilt about her father. In *Matilda*, she had painfully described the death of a father and the remorse which drives Matilda to seek her own death. In 'The Mourner', a gloomy story which she wrote for *The Keepsake* in 1829, to accompany a Turner engraving of Virginia Water, Mary again presented a young woman who dies from grief after years of blaming herself for her father's death. Here, Clarice is rescued from a shipwreck while her father is engulfed by the 'murderous Atlantic'. It is possible that Mary's guilt derived from the sense that Shelley had let Godwin down and that this was, in some way, her fault. It is certain that she remained troubled and unhappy about the years of estrangement from her father and that the unfailing devotion she now displayed was, in part, her atonement for the past.

Half foreign as they were by birth, years abroad had completed the sense of alienation from England felt by both Charles and his sister Claire. Made unhappy by Mrs Godwin's treatment of his wife and forced to support himself by taking in boarders from the new London university which declined, for no good reason, to give him a teaching post, Charles took Antonia back to Vienna in the spring of 1830.[16] His relations with Mary were soured for years by the fact that he asked her to pay their travel expenses. Rich only in her distant expectations, Mary was forced to sell some of Shelley's precious – to her – travelling library to raise the necessary sum. Assisting her father was one thing; she felt bitter at being expected to subsidize her step-brother and his wife.

Claire had also had her fill of England by the end of a year. Fretful, ill and kitted out, as Trelawny noted to his disgust when they met, in worsted stockings against the damp English climate, she felt cold, lost and unloved. A New Year's Day note from Trelawny, penned shortly before his departure for Italy in 1829, cannot have done much to raise her spirits. Priding himself on his outspokenness, Trelawny informed her that she had become 'horridly prudish . . . fish-like – bloodless', an 'old Aunt'. This was a jeer at Claire's obsession with her nephew, seen through her adoring eyes as the very image of Shelley.

Claire's enthusiasm for Percy stands in stark contrast to her reaction to Mary, who not only housed her for three months, but lent her the money in September 1829 to rejoin her Russian employers and her pupil at Dresden.[17] Reviewing her thoughts about her stepsister in a private note, probably written at the end of that year, Claire began, glowingly enough, with a tribute to Mary's hair. She described, not her clipped thin locks, but the sunny cloud it had once been, 'so fine, one feared to disturb the beauty of its gauzy wavings with a breath lest the slightest breath should disturb the beauty of its gauzy wavings'.[18] The repetition shows the speed at which Claire was writing; she had now run out of goodwill. Savagely, she berated Mary for having 'given up every hope of imaginary excellence . . . sneaked in upon any terms she could get into the depraved condition of society'. The memory of Shelley – she made an oddly significant reference to 'his ardent mouth' – had been sacrificed to this hunger for 'a share in the corruptions of society. Would to God she [Mary] could perish without note or remembrance,' Claire wrote with a ferocity worthy of Shelley himself; but Claire was always volatile. A sentence later, she forgave Mary all her crimes for 'the surpassing beauty of her mind; every sentiment of her's is so glowing and beautiful, it is worth the actions of another person.'

It is hard to guess what Mary had done to deserve such condemnation. Claire had learned enough about the Douglas business to pass it on to Charles a few years later; she would have wondered why Mary had not joined her lot to that of Fanny Wright in America. Claire would have done so, given half a chance; so, probably, would Mary Wollstonecraft. It was the sense that Mary had betrayed her glorious mother which seems to have fuelled her rage. She herself had taken pride in imparting Mary Wollstonecraft's beliefs to her little Russian pupils; it was beyond her understanding why Mary did not follow her mother's example and adopt a more public role. She had the intelligence, the literary ability, the skill; why did she not put her gifts to use? What was the value of helping oppressed women, if nobody knew about it or could profit from the example? What of the causes which Wollstonecraft and Shelley would have championed, the children being sent out to work themselves to death in mines and factories, the ongoing battle against colonial slavery, the injustice of the electoral system, the horrible conditions in which London's poor were forced to live and die? Claire burned with the political zeal of a female Dickens. And Mary? Mary's attitude seemed to be summed up in a line from one of her essays for the *Westminster Review*: 'A solitary woman is the world's victim, and there is heroism in her consecration.'[19]

The cause for Claire's rage against Mary lay deeper than this and it surfaced towards the end of her long private outburst. She had never been able to forgive Mary for maintaining her friendship with Byron after Allegra's death. Shelley was excused: 'it was his principle never to refuse his countenance even to the most guilty,' Claire wrote understandingly. Mary was beyond forgiveness. Shockingly, Claire compared her behaviour to that of a woman who would hurry forward to shake hands with the executioner of a child. 'I never saw her afterwards without feeling as if the sickening crawling motion of a Deathworm had replaced the usual flow of my Blood in my veins,' Claire wrote.[20]

Claire had never been good at hiding her thoughts. It is inconceivable that she could have spent three months under the same roof as her stepsister without showing her feelings. Writing to Trelawny several years later, in May 1836, Mary acknowledged as much. Claire, she told him dolefully, 'still has the faculty of making me more uncomfortable than any human being – a faculty she, unconsciously perhaps, never fails to exert whenever I see her –'[21] Giving Claire the money for her Dresden passage in 1829, Mary had, perhaps, thought it a small price to pay for getting rid of her stepsister and her reproaches.

Reading Mary's letters from abroad, Trelawny had been moved by her unending sense of bereavement, her devotion to Shelley's memory. Meeting her at last in the autumn of 1828 and wishing to hear what she was doing to promote Shelley's name, he did not hide his disgust at what seemed to him lassitude bordering on indifference. Why did she submit to Sir Timothy's bullying restrictions? If she cared about Shelley's reputation, she should fight for it. 'You distorted my motives,' Mary wrote to him wearily at his home in Florence the following year, '– did not understand my position, and altogether I lost in your eyes during your last visit – You were quite in the wrong.'

Written on 27 July 1829, this was the second letter Mary had sent to explain why she could not comply with Trelawny's request for materials to flesh out the grand tribute to Shelley which he intended to incorporate in his own autobiography. She did not say that a man who had known Shelley for less than six months was not equipped to write about him. She was all for a book about 'the strange wild adventures you recount so well'. But a book of wild adventures was the last place in which she wished the world to read about her husband or herself.

By 1829, Shelley's reputation was just beginning to blossom, largely thanks to the new Galignani edition of his poems introduced by Redding, and to Mary's skill at unobtrusively providing copies of his poems and selective details of his life to any other editor who would agree to conceal her assistance. Alfred Tennyson, who had read everything of Shelley's he could find while he was still at school, began paying tributes to him in his own early works: 'The Poet', published in 1830, was his first homage to Shelley and was recognized as such. His university friend, Arthur Hallam, newly returned from Pisa with a privately published copy of *Adonais* in his baggage, began printing and distributing it to fellow enthusiasts in 1829. Richard Monckton Milnes, a future poet and influential literary figure, was among the band of Cambridge students who felt strongly enough to take the coach from Cambridge to Oxford on a frosty evening towards the end of the year, for the purpose of championing Shelley's

35. Margaret King, later Lady Mountcashell, in the simple costume which rather startled William Godwin in 1800; from an engraving made in Paris by Edmé Quenedey, c.1801

36. (*left*) In Pisa, the Shelleys
spent some time at Casa Galletti
visible here on the far left

37. (*below left*) Casa Prini, the
summer home at Bagni di San
Giuliano rented by the Shelleys
during their time at Pisa. Their
garden bordered on the artificial
canal

38. (*right*) Thomas Medwin,
Shelley's cousin, disliked and
mistrusted by Mary Shelley

39. (*below right*) Francesco
Pacchiani, 'the devil of Pisa',
professor at the university there
on whom Mary drew for some
less likeable aspects of character
in her novel *Valperga*

40. Edward Ellerker Williams:
the self-portrait washed ashore
in the wreckage of the *Don Juan*

41. Jane Williams, by George
Clint. Mary Shelley was also
friendly with Clint, a skilled
miniaturist who captured Jane's
languid beauty

42. Alexander Mavrocordato, in a memorial painting by J. G. Hiltensperger celebrating great liberators; he is shown in 1822, at Missolonghi, where Byron died two years later

43. Edward Trelawny, as he might have looked in 1821, when he first met Shelley and Mary. The drawing is by Edward Duppa

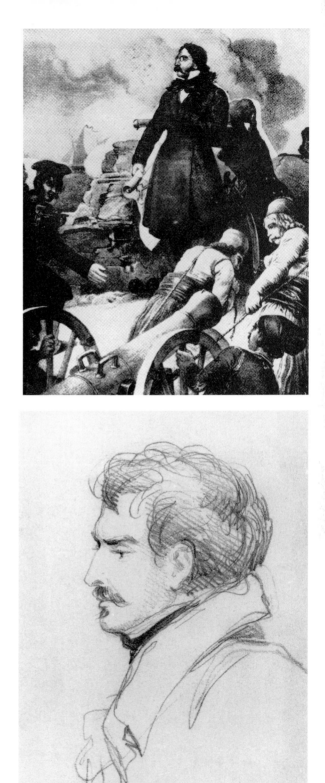

44. (*above left*) These drawings by Edward Ellerker Williams are assumed to represent the *Don Juan* or 'Ariel' and, below it, Byron's boat, the *Bolivar*

45. (*left*) A romantic impression (by Henry Roderick Newman) of the Villa Magni under attack from the sea

46. (*above*) Shelley's cremation through the Victorian eyes of Louis-Edward Fournier. Note Shelley's well-preserved corpse

47. Byron, from a cut-out made by Leigh Hunt's talented wife Marianne when the Hunts and Mary Shelley were Byron's neighbours at Genoa in 1822–3

48. Teresa Guiccioli as a young bride in 1818, after a drawing by John Hayter. She had not yet met Byron

49. The Strand, near Villiers Street, shown by George Scharf. This is where the Godwins were living when Mary returned to London as a widow in 1823

50. (*below left*) John Howard Payne, the actor and playwright who fell in love with Mary in 1825, painted here as Hamlet by Charles Robert Leslie

51. (*below right*) Payne's friend and occasional collaborator, Washington Irving was one of the few men Mary was prepared to marry. The painting is by Gilbert Stuart Newton: Mary saw it being executed

52. (*left*) An evening at Dr Kitchiner's home in Warren Street, by George Cruikshank

53. (*below left*) Thomas Moore, by Sir Thomas Lawrence. Mary saw Lawrence working on this portrait three months before his death in January 1830

54. (*right*) Richard Rothwell, the handsome Irish artist who first painted Mary Shelley in 1831, and thereafter became a good friend

55. (*below*) John Murray, the publisher, to whom Mary Shelley frequently applied for commissions both for her father and herself. The portrait is by H. W. Pickersgill

56. (*below right*) Samuel Rogers, the banker poet who became one of Mary's kindest supporters in the 1830s (caricature bust by Jean Pierre Dantan)

57. (*left*) Harrow on the Hill, where Mary moved in 1833, in order to enable her son to remain at the school as a home-boarder

58. (*below far left*) Trelawny's third wife, Augusta Goring, painted by John Linnell in 1827. Mary advised Augusta to stay with her husband; Trelawny, in due course, left her

59. (*below left*) Godwin at seventy-six, drawn by W. Brockenden. The resemblance to his daughter is noticeable

60. (*right*) Sir Percy Florence Shelley, photographed *c.* 1880 when he was sixty years old

61. (*below*) 'He is a gentleman': Sir Percy Florence Shelley, from a cartoon by 'Ape', for *Vanity Fair*, December 1879

62. (*below right*) Lady Shelley, looking sweetly determined and surprisingly young in her late fifties

63. (*left*) Thomas Jefferson Hogg, sketched by Reginald Easton for Jane and Percy, when he was working on his life of Shelley in the 1850s

64. (*below left*) Mary supports the drowned but draped Shelley: monument by Horatio Weekes, placed by the Shelleys at Christchurch Priory

65. (*below*) Apotheosis: Shelley drawn by Alfred Sourd, *c.* 1913, after Leonardo's head of Christ

66. (*right*) *Frankenstein* in print: the frontispiece of the 1831 edition

67. (*below right*) *Frankenstein* on the stage in 1850: *The Model Man*, a Christmas pantomime

FRANKENSTEIN.

"By the glimmer of the half-extinguished
light, I saw the dull yellow eye of the
creature open; it breathed hard, and a
convulsive motion agitated its limbs.
*** I rushed out of the room."

68. *Frankenstein* on screen in 1931: Bruno Rehak's poster for the film directed by James Whale, and starring Boris Karloff

name at a debate on poetry. Young Edward Bulwer also declared his allegiance to Shelley and drew on him for a rebellious and sensitive young aristocrat in *Pelham* (1828), his first and immensely popular novel.

Mary herself had quietly furnished details for the introduction to a Shelley anthology to be published the following year under the winsome title, *The Beauties of Percy Bysshe Shelley*. Trelawny would have been – and probably was – disgusted to see that this included 'A Revised Edition of Queen Mab Free from All the Objectionable Passages'. Mary did not feel troubled by the omissions. If the objectionable aspects were excluded and the more contentious aspects of Shelley's life were played down, then the poetry would thrive. Changing opinions was a slow and difficult business – and she still had to seem to comply with Sir Timothy's wishes. She would write Shelley's biography herself one day, she told Trelawny in April 1829, but 'it must not be published now – There are too many concerned to speak against him – it is still too sore a subject.'

Trelawny, claiming never to have received an answer to his request, tried again. Mary stood her ground. She would not consent. She had, she told him in July, now decided not to publish anything personal about Shelley until after Percy's death. She had no letters to give him since all early ones had been destroyed 'by an unfortunate mistake' and all later ones were 'purely descriptive'. Trelawny, turning nasty, threatened to publicize the help she had given to Moore unless she did the same for him. In his rage and frustration, he even accused her of having shown more support to Thomas Medwin, who had recently deserted his rich wife after spending most of her fortune, than she was ready to give to him.

'I have ever loved – I do love you,' Mary wrote back to Trelawny in a long defensive letter on 15 December. She reminded Trelawny that she had always disliked Shelley's cousin and praised the kindness he claimed to have shown to poor, abandoned Mrs Medwin. On the subject of a biography, however, she was inflexible. Shelley's private life had, she acknowledged, contained events which were 'hardly for the rude cold world to handle'. His actions, if fully known, might serve as an excuse for 'calumnies and give his enemies a voice'. She disliked Leigh Hunt's approach of 'slurring over the real truth'; silence was her preferred approach. Trelawny could, if he wished, attempt a life of Shelley which contained not a single reference to herself. But, she added with quiet triumph, 'I do not see what you could make of his life without me.'

Intending, perhaps, to inflict a little guilt on a man who was living comfortably in Florence and dining out on tales of his heroic deeds in Greece, Mary went on to remind Trelawny of the troubled situation he had left behind. Britain had not recovered since the crash of 1825; in 1829, economic unrest, unemployment and food shortages were causing riots: 'some change some terrible event is expected,' Mary wrote; 'rents falling – money not to be got – every one poor and fearful.' She added, like the good republican she was, a scornful reference to George IV, 'fishing in Virginia Water and driving about in a pony phaeton – .' Trelawny was not placated by fond messages from 'the pretty Cottagers' of Paddington or by inquiries after Zella, his little daughter by his Greek wife who was living with him in Florence.* Mary heard nothing more from him for almost a year.

Trelawny's threat of publicizing the help she had given to Moore had given Mary a fright: 'it would destroy me to be brought forward in print,' she told him. She was nevertheless proud of the assistance she had given and delighted by the result. Claire, not surprisingly, thought the extracts she had read from Moore's book were 'sad stuff';[22] Mary, meanwhile, told John Murray that she had found the first volume 'accurate to a miracle'. Reviewers made little comment on Shelley's role in Byron's life, but nobody reading Moore's second volume could ignore the role assigned to him as a benevolent and intellectual influence on Byron. At the very least, Mary had ensured that Moore's book did nothing to injure Shelley's growing reputation.

Sir Timothy Shelley had, in the summer of 1829, made a small increase in Mary's allowance to £300 a year; it was, however, insufficiently generous to free her from the need to support herself by writing. The number of proposals which Mary made to John Murray at this time suggests that she was hoping to be given regular employment as an author for his new Family Library, work which would have been adequately paid and more to her taste than producing insipid tales for ladies' annuals.

The range of her suggestions was astonishing. Following Murray's

---

* Mary made a half-hearted offer at this time to adopt Trelawny's daughter, but acknowledged that she would be better off in the Italian climate. Claire also expressed an interest in coming to Florence to bring her up, but Trelawny resisted. (Finally, in 1831, aged three, Zella was adopted by the wealthy, affectionate and childless Marchesa Boccella, an Englishwoman from the West Country who had married and settled in Florence.)

own proposal, which he then dropped, for an 'amusing' life of Madame de Staël, Mary suggested books on Mahomet, on the conquest of Mexico and Peru, on eminent women and on the great philosophers. She was also keen to undertake a history of chivalry and, intriguingly, a history of the earth, 'of the changes on the surface of the Earth, and of the relics of States and Kingdoms before the period of regular history'. She would not be offering controversial opinions, she added nervously, but 'to me these speculations have always been the source of great interest'.[23] Mr Murray preferred her suggestion of a book on philosophers, but in the end took none.

Godwin's approval of his daughter's writings had never been easily obtained. He had praised *Frankenstein* as a remarkable creation, but he had made it clear that *Valperga* was greatly improved by his own revisions, while his commendations of *The Last Man* had been lavished on the Introduction rather than the novel. *Perkin Warbeck*, published in 1830 by Henry Colburn after Murray declined it, earned its author £150 and a friendly, if not ecstatic, reception in the journals and quarterlies. The meagre payment was explicable: these were hard times in the publishing industry and many of the larger firms had gone down. The reward for Mary was in knowing that she had, on this occasion, won her father's wholehearted admiration, although not for the poignant passages in which she unveiled her private thoughts – the description of a mother's agony after losing her child, the account of woman as social outcast, 'fearful of repulse, dreading insult', or the overwrought appeal with which the novel ends. ('Permit this to be, unblamed – permit a heart whose sufferings have been, and are, so many and so bitter, to reap what joy it can from the strong necessity it feels to be sympathized with – to love.') It was not these passages of self-revelation but her scrupulous research which had earned Godwin's respect. Murray might have rejected Mary Shelley as a serious writer; her father was ready to embrace a born historian, a worthy daughter of the author of the four-volume *History of the Commonwealth of England*, the work which had been triumphantly completed in 1828 after several years of labour.

There were other factors than paternal admiration binding Mary to her father in 1830. One was their shared disapproval of the marriage which young William had made at the beginning of the year; another was the future of little Percy. Godwin was fond of his only grandchild – there are several references in his journal to meals and outings with Percy – and Mary doted on him. John Howard Payne was pestered for theatre tickets for Astley's entertainments and for juvenile dramas; in 1829, Mary had extravagantly paid for Percy to have dancing lessons at Mr Slater's Academy and to take drill exercise for the stoop which had, as he grew taller, begun to develop.

Sir Timothy, despite grudgingly raising Mary's allowance in the summer of 1829, had shown no further inclination to meet the boy or, indeed, herself. The time was coming when Percy would need a new school; it would have been astonishing if Mary had not consulted on the subject a man so deeply interested in education as her father. They favoured Eton, and here, for once, it was Sir Timothy who showed more sensitivity. Writing to William Whitton in December 1830, evidently in response to a suggestion made by Mary, Sir Timothy opposed the idea not on grounds of cost but because 'his Poor Father's being there' would cause unpleasantness for a young boy.[24] This, just a month after the old gentleman had been invaded at Field Place by a mob of angry workers, armed with pitchforks and demanding his support, was considerate, even tender.* One wonders, as Mary Shelley often did, how much William Whitton was responsible for keeping the Shelleys at a distance from her and her child.

The principal factor binding father and daughter together, however, was the need for money. A clear indication of their lack of it appears in a hasty note written to Godwin by Mary on 17 January 1830, in which she says that she may be 'driven to borrow' in order to help their old friend James Marshall. Neither Mary nor Godwin could help him; instead, Mary was forced to ask Claire to send home whatever she could spare from her salary.

Supporting each other, Godwin and Mary sought publishers for each other's work. Mary urged John Murray to take her father's new collection of essays and, in May 1830, drew the attention of *Cloudesley's* publisher to an enthusiastic review of it in *Blackwood's* (the review which she herself had written). Godwin, thanking her warmly in July for her kindness to 'a decrepit, superannuated old fellow',[26] responded in kind. Mary was introduced to his new admirer, Edward Bulwer, a clever young novelist with a shrewder sense of the literary market than either Godwin or his daughter.† Although he was not noticeably helpful to Mary in her search for commissions,

---

* Sir Timothy was, in difficult circumstances, courageous: 'he gave them plenty to eat and some good stiff ale to drink. Allowing the stingo time to work the old gentleman then addressed a few words to the men, wishing them well, hoping for better times, etc. and begging to be excused the journey to Horsham . . . "You shall come," shouted one of them striking the table with his stick, "you shall come." Lady Shelley was much alarmed and cried, "Oh! Pray don't hurt Sir Timothy, I hope you won't hurt Sir Timothy." "We won't hurt he," they replied, "but we will have our demands." '[25]

† It is also possible that Moore was responsible for Mary's introduction to Bulwer.

Bulwer's readiness to appear at her social gatherings had its own value. Like many of Bulwer's contemporaries, Mary was intoxicated by his florid style. 'What will Bulwer become? The first author of the age? I do not doubt it,' she wrote in her journal on 11 January 1831 after reading *Paul Clifford*, one of his most dashing novels.

A more fruitful alliance emerged from Godwin's multitude of connections at the new university behind Gower Place. The Professor of Natural Philosophy, an energetic Irish charmer, steamboat enthusiast and preposterous snob called Dionysius Lardner, was superintending two massive projects for a complete *Cabinet Cyclopaedia* and a *Cabinet Library*. A ladykiller in his private life (he ran off with a Mrs Heaviside in 1840 and was successfully sued for £8,000 in damages by her husband*), Lardner had little room for women among his contributors.[27] For Mary, however, an exception was made; in 1833, she was commissioned to undertake an account of the lives of eminent Italian authors, followed, in 1837, by those of the Spanish and Portuguese. Her final collection of essays, on eminent Frenchmen, was published in 1839.

This, on Godwin's part, had been kind; he knew from Mary's fruitless approaches to John Murray how eager she was for work which would stimulate her. He was less high-minded in his readiness to push her into the grim but lucrative world of story-writing for ladies' annuals through his friendship with Fred Mansel Reynolds. The introduction was productive (Mary had been one of the first writers to be commissioned by Reynolds when he began editing the Christmas *Keepsake* albums in 1829). The work was gruelling but well-paid. Composing hectic or sentimental tales appropriate to an engraving of Gulnare, Rosabella, or Medora at her casement window or perched on a rocky shore, Mary's own standards dropped to that of her employer. There was nothing she would not offer to the annuals, if it could bring in a little cash. 'Proserpine', the children's verse drama she had dashed off in the summer of 1820, finally found a home in *The Winter's Wreath* (1832). If 'Midas' had to wait another ninety years, it was not for lack of endeavour.

Mary's correspondence in the early thirties shows her as an able hack. Mindful of the miserable sum she had received for *Perkin Warbeck*, she refused to offer a proposal for her new novel until the economic situation improved: 'things can never be *worse* than now – unless London were on fire,' she wrote glumly to the publisher

---

* Lardner raised the money by giving lectures in the United States and Cuba. Over five years, between 1840 and 1845, his public speaking earned him an impressive £40,000

Charles Ollier at the beginning of 1831. She confessed to Ollier that she was 'full of disquietude for my Father, who depends on his pen'; she hoped to support him by writing an essay a week for Richard Bentley's *Court Journal*, 'on any given subject that was wanted'.[28] The following May, she turned to John Murray again, begging him to consider either Godwin's proposal for a book about famous alchemists or any other of the ideas which he would undertake, so long as he was not expected to write anonymously for periodicals, such as Murray's own *Quarterly Review*: 'a kind of literary pride' kept him from this kind of work, she added defensively and with no sign of resentment that she herself was unable to afford such an elevated attitude.[29] But Murray was not to be enticed and Godwin had to wait another two years to find a publisher for his *Lives of the Necromancers*.[30]

The reputations of both Godwin and his daughter had been made by their early works. (It was *Frankenstein*, not *The Last Man*, which won Mary a place, although at the head of the second rank of writers, in the new *Athenaeum*'s listing of eminent contemporary authors for November 1828.) In June 1830 Henry Colburn and Richard Bentley offered Godwin £50 for the copyright to his best-known novel. *Caleb Williams* was among the first on the list of Bentley's Standard Novels, published in a single volume at six shillings, a fifth of the price of a new book. Shrewdly, Bentley insisted that all Standard Novel authors should revise their texts, thus providing him with a new copyright to their work; within a few years, he had become the owner of most of the great fiction of the Romantic period. Mary, increasingly bold about pushing her own work, offered *Frankenstein* for the series, with a new preface and revisions. Bentley bought himself a bargain for a mere £60; Mary was gratified to learn that 3,000 of the 3,500 copies printed had been sold in the first year.

Mary had written *Frankenstein* in close collaboration with Shelley. The book which appeared in 1831 is the one which should interest us more, for here she was the sole author, acting independently; there is no sign that Colburn had any hand in the changes she made to the text.

Elizabeth Lavenza, Victor's cousin in the original 1818 novel, becomes in 1831 an unconnected orphan whose marriage to him could cause no reader to disapprove. Reduced to a more passive role, she is in line with the sentimental heroines of the annuals to which Mary had become an assiduous contributor. The Frankenstein family's involvement in Victor's career is ruthlessly pruned, emphasizing his solitude and absolving them from complicity. Victor's father, in the first version, had encouraged his interest in science and demonstrated the workings of electric power on a small machine of his own. In 1831, Victor's interest in science is stimulated by a stranger, while Waldman, his second tutor at Ingolstadt, is positioned more powerfully as an evil influence on Victor's ambitious, inquiring mind. 'As he went on I felt as if my soul were grappling with a palpable enemy,' Victor declares in 1831; 'one by one the various keys were touched which formed the mechanism of my being: chord after chord was sounded, and soon my mind was filled with one thought, one conception, one purpose.'[31]

Fate replaces individual choice in the 1831 edition, a revision which is heavily underscored by Mary's enrolment of nature as a giant force, as implacable as the monster. In the 1818 version, Victor saw the glacier at Chamonix only as a wonderful spectacle; in that of 1831, he is aware of 'the blind working of immutable laws'. On a personal level, he is more able to see that he has a parental duty to the Creature he manufactures: 'we are unfashioned creatures, but half made up,' he acknowledges, 'if one wiser, better, dearer than ourselves – such a friend ought to be – do not lend his aid to perfectionate our weak and faulty natures.'[32]

Mary's most striking revisions were directed to strengthening the parallels between Victor Frankenstein and the explorer Robert Walton, whose story encloses his own. Walton's voyage, as has already been suggested, may have stemmed from an earlier novel plan; in the 1818 version, the connections between the two plots were slight. In her 1831 revision, she tightened the links. Walton is shown to share Frankenstein's craving to achieve the impossible. 'There is something at work in my soul, which I do not understand,' he tells his sister.[33] Frankenstein's belief that his man-made creature will mark the beginning of a world free of disease is matched by Walton's hope of making a discovery which will enable him to defeat 'the elemental foes of our race'.[34] Like Godwin's St Leon, Frankenstein and Walton sacrifice family ties to achieve their mission. Frankenstein spells this message out in his warning to Walton: 'you are pursuing the same course, exposing yourself to the same dangers which have rendered me what I am.'[35] In 1818, Walton felt no guilt about the men whose lives he was risking; in 1831, he acknowledges the folly of his 'mad schemes' and the deaths they may cause.[36]

One striking declaration is left unchanged. In the 1831 revision, just as in the original text, Victor Frankenstein dies unrepentant, hoping that another may succeed where his experiment has failed. This, unless we choose to see it as a moment of exquisite irony, should convince us that Mary was on the side of progress. At a time when the worst cholera epidemic in history was ravaging Europe and threatening England, it did not seem wrong to dream of a day when science, by whatever means, might conquer disease, even by the creation of a new laboratory-produced species.

'And now,' Mary wrote in her celebrated Preface to the 1831 edition, 'once again, I bid my hideous progeny go forth and prosper.' She wanted her novel to sell. To help it do so, she presented the tale's conception in a story so romantic, so convincing that it has gripped the imagination of all readers ever since. She had always been given to fantastic dreams, she told her readers; none were stranger than the one which visited her that night at Lake Geneva.

> I saw – with shut eyes, but acute mental vision – I saw the pale student of unhallowed arts kneeling beside the thing he had put together. I saw the hideous phantasm of a man stretched out, and then, on the working of some powerful engine, show signs of life, and stir with an uneasy, half vital motion. Frightful must it be; for supremely frightful would be the effect of any human endeavour to mock the stupendous mechanism of the Creator of the world.

Did any of her readers, remembering Coleridge's explanation of the dream-birth of 'Kubla Khan', pause to question the authenticity of her account? Probably not; even today, Mary's description of the birth of *Frankenstein* is quoted without scepticism. And yet, as we have seen in the affair of Mr and Mrs Douglas, she was, when she chose, a singularly convincing liar.

There is one more important point that we should note about the Preface: it marks the beginning of Mary's revised history of her marriage. She had already, in her Introduction to the Bentley edition of *Caleb Williams*, carefully obscured the date of her parents' wedding, but she had always been open and honest about her own unmarried years with Shelley. No longer. The Preface's readers were given the impression that she had gone to Switzerland in 1816 as a married woman. Shelley was introduced as 'my husband' who was 'from the first, very anxious I should prove myself worthy of my parentage, and enrol myself on the page of fame'. Subsequent references to him maintain the impression that a marriage had taken place before 1816.

Mary's exclusion of Claire's name from her account of the summer at Geneva was understandable; she was well aware of Claire's need as a governess to disassociate herself from scandal. But what had happened to Mary herself since 1829, when she had insisted that Redding's Preface to the Galignani edition should tell the truth about her elopement with a married man? What had changed her mind?

ENTERING SOCIETY

1830–1834

'I have begun a new kind of life somewhat – going a little into society – & forming a variety of acquaintances . . .'

Mary Shelley, Journal, 22 January 1830

TRELAWNY, IN THE MONTHS AFTER SHELLEY'S DEATH, HAD GIVEN Mary a well-intended warning. Of all the people in the world, he told her, she was the most ignorant both of it and of human nature. He was not wrong. She had grown up in the household of a theoretical philosopher, and had spent the next eight years living with an impassioned idealist. She had come home to England determined not to shelter behind lies. She had thought that it was possible to tell the truth about Shelley and herself, to make no pretence that Harriet and he had parted by mutual consent, to publish the fact that she, in 1814, had chosen to live with him and to bear his children. She had innocently supposed that Sir Timothy's heart would soften, that Jane Williams would be grateful for her love and would return it, and that Shelley's fame would grow without the necessity for concealing his personal history.

Six years in England had taught Mary some harsh lessons. Sir Timothy remained obdurate; Jane proved treacherous; Shelley's reputation was growing, but at the expense of the political poetry in which he had so recklessly combined his hopes for the future with savage attacks on the hypocrites and tyrants of the present. This was not to the public's taste, any more than was his atheism, or details of his unorthodox domestic life. Mary did not intend to hide the radical side of Shelley for ever, but at the end of the 1820s she was ready to acknowledge the prudence of suppression. Trelawny, censuring her from abroad for her lack of courage and, as she cautiously began to establish new friendships, for being a social climber, was out of tune with the times.

England entered the Victorian age – with all, both good and bad, that word implies – long before the crowning of an eighteen-year-old girl in 1837. An account of the country's progress during the seven-year reign of Victoria's bluff uncle William could sound exciting. The railway era began; young Charles Darwin decided to join the *Beagle* on its five-year trip of scientific investigation; Ross, in 1831, identified a magnetic site at the North Pole; Michael Faraday discovered the laws of electromagnetic induction, and, with his remarkable 'difference engine', Charles Babbage produced the world's first computer.

In other respects, England seemed to be moving backwards at a time when all the signs from abroad were of liberty and progress. Mary had hailed these signs with delight. Writing an enthusiastic letter to the Marquis de Lafayette on 11 November 1830 and reminding him of their brief meeting in Paris two years earlier, she offered her hearty congratulations on his part in the 'sublime achievements' of the July revolution and on the crowning of a new, republican-spirited king, Louis Philippe. 'How does every heart in Europe respond to the mighty voice, which spoke in your Metropolis, bidding the world be free,' she wrote: '. . . one by one the nations will take up the echo and mine will not be the last. May England imitate your France in its moderation and heroism.' To Fanny Wright, too, she expressed her hopes: 'Will not our Children live to see a new birth for the world!'[1]

'Moderation' is the word to note. This was the autumn in which a mob of agricultural workers had burst into Field Place and demanded Sir Timothy's support for their cause. Newspapers carried regular reports of burnings and riots; the *Quarterly Review* warned its Tory readers to prepare for the day when the tricolore would flutter from village steeples. Reform and the promise of enfranchisement of the voiceless middle class headed the agenda of the new Whig government, led by Earl Grey;* the House of Lords, crowded with

---

* Charles, 2nd Earl Grey (1764–1845) was a politician of whom both Mary and her father could warmly approve. With Charles Fox, he had been among the Whigs who in 1792, following recent events in France, had demanded parliamentary reform for England. In 1797, the year Mary was born, Grey's parliamentary Reform Bill was heavily defeated. Between 1815 and 1830, he advised the Whig opposition without playing an active role in

apprehensive landowners, had no interest in passing a Bill which would give rebel farmworkers the chance to vote against them.

Shelley, or Shelley as he had been in 1822, would have carried the workers' banner; so, once, would Mary. By 1830, however, she had grown more guarded; like her father she now placed her faith in gradual measures. Writing to Lafayette, she had expressed the hope for 'moderation'; writing to Fanny Wright a month later, she accepted the possibility of revolution in England – '[o]ur own hapless country' – but only with extreme reluctance:

> The case seems to stand thus – The people *will* be redressed – will the Aristocrats sacrifice enough to tranquillize them – if they will not – we must be revolutionized – but they intend now so to do – it remains to be seen whether the people's claims will augment with the concessions – Our *sick* feel themselves tottering – they are fully aware of their weakness – long curtailed as to their rents, they humble – How will it all end? None dare even presume to guess.[2]

We should not doubt, although Mary's letters offer scant evidence of her views on the subject, that she welcomed the passing of the Reform Bill in 1832; her letter to Fanny Wright shows that she was sympathetic to the rebellious unemployed, but cautiously so; in a letter written to Dale Owen at the same time, Mary deplored the 'sick destructiveness' of the rioters and rick-burners.

These years of unrest led Mary, increasingly, to become an advocate of slow progress and to oppose the revolutionary measures her husband had espoused. Writing to Maria Gisborne, long settled at Plymouth, on 24 August 1832, she observed that Trelawny 'is too violent in his politics for me – he is radical à l'outrance . . .' It seems likely that Mary herself had already begun to favour the Independents, a significant force in the early 1830s. High-minded democrats, they sought an extended franchise, reduced taxes on the poor, and a new system of national education. They also supported a reduced military presence in Ireland, and the world-wide abolition of Negro slavery. These were reforms which Mary could welcome, all the more so as she had, since 1830, become warmly attached to a man who was hoping to go to the House of Commons as an Independent.

Parliament during the long years of Tory rule under Lord Liverpool, the Duke of Wellington and, very briefly, George Canning. In 1830 the new king, William IV, invited him to form a ministry, following division in the Tory party after the passing of the Catholic Emancipation Bill in 1829. Catholic Emancipation had been part of Grey's vision for a reformed and more egalitarian Britain.

This was Major Aubrey Beauclerk, a near neighbour of Sir Timothy and Lady Shelley's in Sussex.[3]

While the Lords dragged their heels over the Reform Bill, which threatened to undermine their own comfortable way of life, attitudes to women were changing in a way which would also influence Mary's conduct. The time when Lady Caroline Lamb could dress up as a pageboy to catch Byron's attention, when Mary could take pride in living with a married man and bearing his children, were past and regarded by most as best forgotten. The 1830s were years in which only a few reckless women in the middle and upper reaches of English society enjoyed the same sexual freedom as men. Trelawny, returning to London, could boast of his conquests and bawl his contempt for religion and still be asked to dine. Nobody refused to entertain dandyish young Benjamin Disraeli because he was sleeping with Sir Francis Sykes's wife. Edward Bulwer was not punished with social exile for the multitude of affairs which finally caused his wife Rosina to demand a separation. George Norton, the bullying, abusive husband of the playwright Sheridan's granddaughter Caroline, could demand divorce on the grounds of an affair which she may never have had, live on his wife's earnings, claim legacies made to her and obtain custody of her children. A husband could keep a mistress on the side for years and still be granted both his wife's property and their children if she was foolish enough to be caught sleeping with another man.

Wives did, of course, have affairs, and several of Mary Shelley's new friends were among them. What had changed was the need for discretion. London, in the 1830s, shuddered at the boldness of Madame Dudevant for leaving her husband and children in the country to live in Paris, wear trousers, take lovers and – such effrontery! – call herself George Sand. But France had always been decadent, while in England, that wondrous myth, the 'angel of the house', pious, charitable, sexless, was taking shape. Mary had little respect for the new Lady Bountiful, evangelical, tremulously sensitive, and dull, but she recognized her power. For the year 1836, the *Edinburgh Review* appraised a mere six novels among sixty-one religious publications, most of which were specifically addressed to a female audience. Shelley, if he was to gain the admiration of an increasingly devout readership, needed to be purified. And so did his wife.

Mary's readiness to pander to the new, uplifting concept of angelic womanhood is apparent in the way she chose to extend her description of Elizabeth Lavenza in the 1831 edition of *Frankenstein*. 'The saintly soul of Elizabeth shone like a shrine-dedicated lamp in our peaceful home,' she wrote now. 'Her sympathy was ours; her smile, her soft voice, the sweet glance of her celestial eyes, were ever there to bless and animate us.' This was in the new style: Miss Lavenza has become sister to all those Agneses, Ellens and Amelias who never lack a candle or a prayer as they hover in obliging readiness by a penitent's deathbed.

Mary had, when she added this passage, gained a precarious foothold in a circle of sociable, good-natured wives willing to ignore her disgraceful past. No saints themselves, they knew the importance of discretion. Warmed by their friendship and eager to do the best she could for Shelley's reputation and her son's future, Mary began practising reticence. She was pleased when Hogg, publishing his recollections of Shelley at Oxford in the summer of 1832 at her own suggestion, made no allusion to herself. Hogg, she began to think, might be the man to write a life of Shelley, a task which she had herself begun to dread undertaking. In this respect, at least, she and Sir Timothy were drawing closer. Neither of them now wished for Shelley's name to be connected with anything which might seem disagreeable. Sir Timothy's concern, however, remained the reputation of his family name, not his son's status as a poet. Seventy-seven in the year 1830, he seemed unlikely to change his views.

Mary tentatively began a new social life in 1829, shortly after she moved into lodgings at 33 Somerset Street, just off Portman Square. Here, she began to be at home to the wide circle of professional literary acquaintances who did not hold her past against her, to her sociable father, and to a few broad-minded women who, sympathizing with her need for friendship and support, admired her intelligence and independent spirit.

Tom Moore's journal shows him attending two parties at Mary's home, on 10 April and 7 June, at which he met, among others, three of the Robinson daughters, Lady Blessington's sister Mrs Manners-Sutton, the portrait-painter Richard Rothwell, Godwin, a Mrs Coates and Fred Mansel Reynolds. Mary had indeed embarked on a new way of life, although she still found time for quiet evenings at Gower Place with her son and her half-brother, who usually came without his wife. Mary had succeeded also in attracting both Bulwer and Washington Irving to call on her, no mean achievement for a woman who had little to offer beyond her own intelligent company, a cup of tea and some ratafia biscuits carried round by the young maid-of-all-work without whom no London household could survive. (Poor though Mary was, she never had to do her own cooking or washing.)

Some of these visitors became enduring friends. Lady Mary Shepherd, an eccentric old author, Edward Bulwer and his wife Rosina together with Lord Dudley, one of Godwin's patrons, came through her father's wide circle of acquaintance. Bulwer became close enough to be consulted in due course about Percy's career and about assistance for Godwin. The presence of Theodore Hook, a more rackety character who started writing comic operas with his father when he was only sixteen and who had served a two-year prison sentence for embezzlement, shows that Mary was not narrow-minded about the political views of people she liked: a scurrilous, scandalous exuberant character, Hook had for years been the editor of the violently right-wing – and therefore anti-Whig – Sunday newspaper, *John Bull*.

It is not clear how Mary had come to know Lady Blessington's sister Ellen Manners-Sutton, the warm-hearted, twice-married Irish wife of the Speaker of the House of Commons, but this would become a significant friendship. Richard Rothwell's presence is more intriguing. A startlingly handsome young Irishman (one can't help but be struck by the wealth of Irish names which crop up in the journals of both Mary and her father), Rothwell was, by 1830, at the height of a fashionable career. Godwin, who was sitting for his own portrait to Pickersgill that summer, made a note on 18 May 1831 that he had been to visit Rothwell's studio while Mary sat for her portrait. Neither Godwin nor his daughter are likely to have been able to afford the artist's prices as a painter of the aristocracy; perhaps the young man was sufficiently intrigued to paint her for his own pleasure.[4]*

The people who were of most importance to Mary in these long lists of guests were those who seem, at first glance, of least consequence. Among Mary's acquaintances in the English community at Pisa some eight years earlier had been one Emily Beauclerk, then accompanied by a brood of marriageable daughters. Her husband Charles was a retired politician and son of the notoriously profligate Topham Beauclerk, a friend of Dr Johnson's. Mrs Beauclerk was the daughter of the Duchess of Leinster by her second marriage to William Ogilvie.†

---

* If this was the case, he must have kept the canvas; Mary had no portrait for an engraver to copy when John Murray approached her on the subject two years later.

† The Duchess of Leinster, widow of one of the richest men in Ireland, married her children's tutor and lived with him long and happily.

Significantly, the Beauclerks' family home in England was St Leonard's Lodge in Sussex, where they were near neighbours and friends of the Shelleys of Field Place. Here, then, was a connection through which Mary could hope to reach Sir Timothy without having always to approach him through his fiercely protective lawyer.

The connections linking the Beauclerks to two other families of Mary's friends, the Pauls and the Hares, were close but complicated. Mary would, long before 1830, have read and admired *Guesses at Truth* (1827), a widely praised collection of essays on philosophy and poetry written by the intelligent fraternal team of Julius and Augustus Hare. The Hares' third brother Francis, a man known as much for his loquacity as for his wit, his interest in German philosophy and his sallow, mock-lugubrious face, had recently married Anne-Frances Paul whose religious, poetry-writing brother John, a banker, had also just married. His pretty and earnestly philanthropic young bride, Georgiana, was one of the daughters for whom Mrs Beauclerk had been trying so hard to find husbands at Pisa. It was a great loss to Mary when Francis Hare and his wife left England for Italy in September 1830; she was, however, in the same journal entry that lamented their departure, able to record a source of consolation, for 'an intimacy between me & Georgi[a]na is beginning'.

Twenty-six-year-old Georgiana or 'Gee' Paul was her favourite of the Beauclerk clan, but by April 1831 Mary was already on close terms with her friend's siblings, including her eldest brother, Aubrey, heir to both the Sussex and the Irish estates, her 'dear' married sister, Jane Fitzroy, another sister, Caroline, and two of Gee's brothers, Charles and George. Mary's letters make it clear that she was fond of them all and well enough acquainted with their lives to know that Caroline had once been pursued by Edward Trelawny, and that George Beauclerk, still in his mid-twenties, was having an affair with Mrs Wyndham Lewis, an unstoppably vivacious and pretty little woman almost ten years older than himself.*

Many of Mary's inner circle of new friends were of a strongly religious bent. This, too, had its uses. Defending her son's right to be sent to a public school in the summer of 1831, Mary took pride in telling the Shelleys' lawyer to announce that she would be consulting her friend Mrs Hare's brother-in-law Julius, who was both a professor at Trinity College, Cambridge, and a clergyman. These were the friends

---

* Mrs Lewis, courted after her husband's death in 1838 by both Beauclerk and Benjamin Disraeli – for the late Mr Lewis's fortune as much as for her personal charm – chose to marry Disraeli.

who transformed Mary's life and who made it possible for her to accept, almost with equanimity, the fact that Jane Hogg was now wrapped up in her domestic life and that Isabel Douglas, meeting her briefly at the end of 1830, was no longer taking the trouble even to be friendly.

She dined constantly now with Gee and her husband at his parents' home in the Strand, where she admired John Martin's magnificent *Belshazzar's Feast*, the best buy, Sir John Paul liked to say, that he had ever made. She met other members of the large Paul family; she listened with rapture when they invited Gabriele Rossetti, the father of Christina, Dante Gabriel and William Michael, to come and improvise for them in the Italian style, reminding her of the time she had travelled to Lucca to see the great Sgricci perform. Wishing to please rather than to seek comfort in religion, Mary began going to church with the Pauls, attending the twelfth-century church of the Knights Templar, tucked away among the rambling Inns of Court above the Thames. The Master of the Temple, Christopher Benson, was not, which must have relieved her, one of the new charismatic school of preachers; she could sit through his reasoned, elegant sermons without annoyance. The Temple Church was not then famous for the quality of its music, however: the squawks of the two ladies who comprised the choir made sorry listening for a woman who had heard Novello's playing at the Portuguese Chapel in South Street. Mary started bringing Percy to the Sunday services; she hoped that Gee would carry reports back to Sussex which would reach Sir Timothy's ears. Anything was worth trying where Percy's future was concerned. He was, she told Trelawny in March, growing very like Shelley; in the same letter, she casually informed him that her friend Gee Paul was dining with the Shelleys at Field Place that week.

Little Thomas Moore, jotting down rude comments about Mary's gatherings in his journal, especially when he had not been the centre of attention, was insufficiently observant to be struck by the careful exclusiveness of her guest list. Courtly, handsome Lord Dillon was only kept away by ill health as his long-suffering wife nursed him at their great house in Oxfordshire, but Mary asked neither the poor, slightly raffish ladies like Charlotte Figge whom she had met through Mary Diana Dods, nor debt-ridden John Howard Payne. William Godwin saw his sister only at Gower Place or in private; holding a large party the week before Charles Clairmont and his family returned to Vienna, Mary sent them no invitation. She was ready to help Hogg try to find a publisher for his new novel, but he and Jane were not asked to Somerset Street. Establishing a new circle of friends, Mary seemed anxious to keep away anybody who might gossip about her past.

To those who had listened to Jane Hogg's stories about Mrs Shelley, it was intriguing to hear that she had emerged from her retirement. The writer Anna Jameson encouraged her friend Maria Jane Jewsbury to get herself an introduction through Richard Rothwell. Miss Jewsbury's sister Geraldine added a request to Maria's letter, asking for a little sample of Shelley's signature. Admirers of Shelley were always welcomed by Mary; on 18 June, Mrs Jameson was rewarded with a lengthy account of Maria's impressions.

Miss Jewsbury had been fascinated: 'bewitching' was the word she chose before commenting that Mary's combination of 'buoyancy and depth' made her a likely model for Beatrice in Shelley's *The Cenci*. She had liked Mary's 'kind and playful' manner. She was surprised and intrigued by the quality we see least of in Mary's journals and letters, an unforced gaiety, 'simple – natural – and like Spring full of sweetness'. Significantly, Maria ended her account by assuring Anna that Mrs Shelley 'is not one to sit with and think ill of, even on authority'.[5] Stories had obviously reached this group of literary women; what 'authority' did Miss Jewsbury have in mind and what had she heard? Perhaps caution prevailed; no evidence exists of a friendship with Mary having been established before Maria married the Reverend William Fletcher in 1832 and went with him to India, where she died.

Mary's correspondence and journals for 1830–1 show how at ease she felt in this new way of life. The Pauls took her to the opening night of the opera season and invited her to evenings of charades ('tableaux vivants') performed at their home. She heard the singer Davide, much admired by her in Italy, giving his first English performances. She went to the races at Royal Ascot with young Julia Robinson. She raved over the brilliance of Paganini, for one of whose sell-out performances the ever-obliging John Howard Payne had provided her with seats, and decided that she could spend the rest of her life listening to his violin: 'Nothing was ever so sublime.'[6] She sat, thanks to her friendship with the Beauclerks, in the Duke of Norfolk's private row of seats for the coronation of William IV that September, and smothered a grin as she noticed an empty inkwell being tipped for the new king to scratch his signature, and how silly Lord Brougham looked with a coronet perched on his wig.

She should have been happy. Only her continuing financial worries and her own disposition to melancholy prevented her from being so. Writing to Trelawny between 22 and 25 March 1831, she told him that she was 'sinking at last' under the difficulties of her 'wretched' life. Three days later, however, she made a note that she wanted to mark this period as having been 'peculiarly happy', though for no reason she could define. Contentment, she wrote sadly, 'seems to me the dearest blessing of heaven – Yet I cannot command it – it is more various than a lover's moods less controulable than the wind.' In her journal for May, the month in which she sat for Rothwell, she wrote of languor and illness; on 9 September, she followed a miserable out-pouring in verse ('Alas I weep my life away / And spend my heart in useless sorrow . . .') with an optimistic Spanish quotation which might be translated as 'Where one door closes, another one opens.' True, her hopes of placing Percy at a public school that summer were being blocked by Sir Timothy and his lawyer, but this was not enough to explain such violent extremes of emotion. More likely, Mary was telling the truth when she wrote of personal content as something which seemed to come and go at whim, 'without any special cause'. This, as her father sometimes reminded her, was the Wollstonecraft nature; she could do nothing to overcome it.

———

Compensation for the loss of the Hares to Florence in the autumn of 1830 was provided by the discovery of new and equally kind friends. Mary appears to have met Lincoln and Leicester Stanhope through either the Pauls or the Beauclerks; the part they had played in raising money for the Greek cause and, briefly, in Byron's life (Leicester Stanhope had joined him at Missolonghi and brought his remains back to England) linked them to another of her circle, John Bowring. Mary's particular friend became Leicester's madonna-faced wife, Elizabeth, detested by Tom Moore as an intellectual, a 'Blue'. Mrs Stanhope was not so solemn as Moore supposed: 'Write to me like a good girl – & get a very nice set of Beaus for me to flirt with when you give a party or I will flirt with – I won't tell you who,' Mary teased her in 1833.[7]

Mary had moved far from her life as an outcast during the first years back in England, although the sense of a social gap remained, pre-served by her own painful pride. Godwin, blithely indifferent to social niceties, went on a regular basis to the big, noisy gatherings at the home of Elizabeth Stanhope's hospitable mother, Mrs Somerville Wood, where the old lady held forth about her guests from the point of view of their 'phrenology'.* Mary, mortified at having to turn up at the door in a hackney or on foot, preferred to stay away unless she could arrive in style.

In order not to antagonize her new friends, Mary also had to learn to curb her temper. That she was easily roused to anger we know from Hunt's firsthand comments on his experience of it in Italy. Occasional evidence of it slips out, showing a side to her nature of which the Pauls and Beauclerks remained unaware. Pressing for a meeting with Charles Ollier, who often acted as her go-between in publishing negotiations, Mary tartly inquired, on 28 December 1830, if 'your tiresome silence is not occasioned by your being dead'.

Trelawny, too, was given cause to remember that he had once thought Mary quite as prone to ill humour and tantrums as himself. Writing to him over 22–25 March 1831, she seemed to drop a strong hint that she might consider marrying him. 'I do not think that I shall either marry or die this year,' she told him, '– whatever may happen next – as it is only spring you have some time before you.' Was she joking or not? She was in the process of editing and selling his manuscript; cautiously, Trelawny answered that he would not wonder 'if fate, without our choice, united us'.[8] 'Mary Shelley shall be written on my tomb,' she wrote back.[9] Excellent, Trelawny wrote with relief, claiming that nothing in her letter had pleased him so much as this statement and rashly adding that he, too, took pride in his name. Back came a furious letter, rejecting something he had not, in fact, offered. 'My name will *never* be Trelawny,' Mary declared; he belonged 'to womenkind in general – & Mary Shelley will *never* be yours.'[10] He took care after this to avoid both flattery and innuendo.

Ungrateful though he became in later years, Trelawny was much in debt to Mary for her hard work in the autumn of 1830 as the unpaid editor of and agent to his flamboyant naval memoirs. Having told her not to edit, only to add appropriate chapter mottoes from Shelley, Byron and Keats, he was infuriated to be criticized for saying that polygamy was 'not only lawful, but meritorious', and for allowing a bluff sailor to turn down a party of eager, stark naked ladies by telling them that 'I'd rather splice myself to a bit of rotten junk.'[11] 'I, your

---

* Phrenology was much in fashion. Mary herself wrote of 'Spurzheim' and 'bumps' in 1830 in a way that suggests she may have allowed Johann Spurzheim to interpret her character by running his hands over her head. In novels, a sudden spate of references to high or massive foreheads, denoting intellect, shows the spreading craze for phrenology in the 1830s and 1840s. This method of measuring character had been established by Spurzheim's teacher, Franz Joseph Gall (1758–1828).

partial friend, strongly object to [such] coarseness, now wholly out of date,' Mary told him. Booksellers would not like it; no lady would read such stuff. She would, if he allowed it, act as his censor: 'Without this yielding on your part I shall experience great difficulty in disposing of your work.'[12]

Trelawny had not forgotten how Mary had denied him the chance to write about Shelley; back he flung at her in a petulant rage. So she wished to castrate his work as she had done Byron's *Don Juan*? Well, everybody he knew wished she had left *Don Juan* alone.* Lady Burghersh, his friend in Florence, 'aristocratic and proud as a queen', had not objected to his frank and nautical style; why should Mary be so prim? If the book must be edited, let it be by a man, Horace Smith, if need be. Five hundred pounds was the least he expected her to get for his three volumes. But he added that still, whatever she might think of him, 'you every day become dearer to me'[13] – as she very well might, for the efforts she was making on his behalf.

If Mary had been sharp on the subject of marriage, she made up for it by the saintliness of her patience with Trelawny in his new, and nervous, role as an author. The chapter mottoes were supplied and no awkward questions raised about truth. She found him a publisher in Colburn and Bentley's thriving firm and got him the best price she could, £300 with a further £100 for a second edition. Bulwer, Disraeli and Moore might be able to command £100 for a long article, but this was still twice what she had been paid for her own last work. With no thanks from Trelawny, who had wanted it to be called 'Treloen', or, failing that, 'A Man's Life', she even found him a title. *Adventures of a Younger Son* would catch the public interest, she assured him: the hardship of younger sons was much discussed in England.

Trelawny's pleas for anonymous publication were a sham, as they both knew but never acknowledged to each other. He had insisted the publishers be told that the author was a close friend of Shelley and Byron; they had only known one privateer. Every review identified him. The publisher advertised the book as written by an intimate friend of Byron's; the mottoes provided by Mary helped to strengthen his claims to have been the devoted friend, not only of Shelley but of Keats, a poet he had never met.

Gee Paul had done her best to help close the gap between Mary and the Shelleys. Lunching at Field Place, she had been presented with a gold sovereign to be passed on to young Percy who, directed by Mary, sent a letter of effusive thanks to his dear, generous grand-

---

* Mary's changes had been minimal: Trelawny was bluffing.

papa. Sir Timothy, nevertheless, continued to oppose Mary's requests for meetings, and to question that a public school would benefit the boy. 'Not noticed by his own family . . . the forming of friends at school is of importance to him,' she explained via the lawyer in May 1831, but to no avail.

Visiting Gee Paul at her home three months later, Mary could not help noticing that another visitor, Sir Francis Vincent, seemed disagreeably familiar with her friend. 'I do not like him – he is mauvais ton,' Mary noted in her journal. Dining with Gee's parents-in-law that autumn, she was puzzled by their evasive manner. In November, she learnt the truth. Gee was suspected of conducting an affair with Vincent, a married man himself; she was being evicted from her home to live in a secluded village south of London. 'Poor Gee is sent to Norwood – her child torn away – cast away & deserted,' Mary wrote with horror. 'My first impulse is to befriend a woman – I will do her all the good I can.'[14]* Mary spent much of the next two months consoling her friend before agreeing to witness the act of separation. On 9 February 1832, Gee left Norwood for Ardglass, the bleak Irish castle which her brother Aubrey had inherited that month on the death of his grandfather, William Ogilvie.†

Sir Timothy Shelley, already irritated with Gee for interfering in his private affairs, took the worst view of her. Pointedly regretting that Mary had made such an unfortunate attachment, he urged her to move out of London, away from such contaminating company. Gee's parents-in-law, however, were shocked by their son's harsh rectitude and touched by Mary's loyalty to her friend. Already warmly attached to her, they now went out of their way to include Mary in their family circle and to do everything they could to make her life pleasant.

It is from Matthew Arnold and Thackeray's daughter that we have the famous anecdote of Mary being advised by the successful young actress and authoress Fanny Kemble to send Percy to a school where he would learn to think for himself, and of Mary's reply: 'Teach him to think for himself? Oh, my God, teach him rather to think like other people!'[15]

---

* It remains puzzling why Gee should have been sent somewhere so out of the way unless she was pregnant. Mary's response does not suggest that Gee was innocent, only that she intended to stand by her.

† The castle went directly to Aubrey, eldest of the Beauclerk sons, since his mother, the daughter of William Ogilvie, also died that month.

Mary had seen Fanny Kemble on stage; she did not meet her until shortly before Percy went to university. The story is, nevertheless, true to her wish to give her son a conventional education. Faced with Sir Timothy's indifference, she was determined to prove Percy worthy of his inheritance. He seemed such a fine and good boy to her; her letters to Whitton express sad bewilderment that any child should be made to feel so unwanted.

In January 1832, however, Mary had a piece of good fortune. Whitton, who had never tried to help her, retired from old age – he died that summer – and his place was taken by a more open-minded lawyer, John Gregson. Mary had, for some months, been begging for a small increase in her allowance and for a decision about Percy's future; in March, after meeting Gregson, she told him that she had taken action. Percy was due to leave Dr Slater's Academy at the end of the summer. She had enrolled him at Harrow. Benjamin Kennedy, the undermaster with whom Percy was to be lodged since the Headmaster's house had no room, kept thirty boarders. It was a relief to Mary to learn that only two of them were able to exercise the right to use new boys as their fags, or unpaid servants. It was a comfort, too, to know that Sir John and Lady Paul had a cottage nearby, from which they would be able to keep a kindly eye on her son.

Sir Timothy, while expressing no satisfaction at the arrangement, consented to raise her allowance to meet the school costs, estimated by Mary to be no more than £150 a year. Claire, however, was struck only by what seemed to her Mary's continuing and unhealthy obsession with Byron. To send Percy to his old school? Where Allegra had been buried? It was beyond belief, she wrote from Pisa, where she was now teaching from Mrs Mason's home:

> I shudder from head to foot when I think of your boldness in sending him there. I think in certain things you are the most daring woman I ever knew . . . I hope nothing will happen to Percy – but the year, the school itself that you have chosen and the ashes that lie near it, and the hauntings of my own mind, all seem to announce the approach of the consummation which I dread.[16]

'Cholera in Sunderland,' Godwin neatly noted in his journal on 31 October 1831; this was the disease which gave rise to Claire's dark presentiments. It spread down from Sunderland during the winter and into the spring of 1832; by the summer, newspapers were urging city-dwellers to move out of densely populated areas. Mary – trying to supply ideas for her father's new novel, *Deloraine*, urging John Murray to help him while supplying information for the new multi-volume edition of Byron's works, revising a story which Claire wanted her to submit to one of the magazines – had at first no time for precautions. In August, however, more concerned for Percy's welfare than her own, she took him down to spend the rest of the summer by the sea, at sleepy, hilly little Sandgate on the Kent coast.

She had always enjoyed the company of girls she could treat as substitute daughters. She was initially pleased and even flattered when Trelawny sent a honeyed note in May asking her to take charge of his eldest daughter Julia until she could accompany Lady Dorothea Campbell to Italy. Julia came to Sandgate, and here Trelawny joined them.

The reunion was not comfortable. Mary had difficulty in disguising her impatience with Julia, a petulant and demanding featherbrain of eighteen to whom unfashionable Sandgate seemed the worst form of exile, not much improved by the presence of the father she hardly knew. Trelawny, who took lodgings nearby, was in stridently revolutionary mood, roaring for reform and liberty when Mary only wanted peace and leisure. Listening to him misquoting Shakespeare and haranguing her on the dreariness of her life, Mary wistfully compared him to Percy. 'I cannot tell you how much cleverer & more companiable he was than my present companion,' she wrote to Mrs Gisborne.[17] Percy at twelve was a reclusive boy, although essentially steady and affectionate. Trelawny's strangeness was of a different, more troubling kind: there was nothing behind the performance. He is 'destroyed by *being nothing* –' she wrote acutely in her journal, 'destroyed by envy and internal dissatisfaction'.[18] It did not occur to her that much of Trelawny's discomfort was due to the fact that he had, by now, embraced the fantasy of himself as Shelley's lifelong friend and champion. This was not a role he could easily play with Shelley's widow.

Claire's grim forebodings were borne out when their half-brother William fell victim to the cholera in September. The old Godwins, recklessly indifferent to the danger to themselves, helped his wife Emily nurse their son through the rapid last stages of the terrible disease. 'W. dies, half after 5,' his father noted on 8 September; William was still only twenty-nine. They buried him the following day. Trelawny, always capable of kindness, called on Mr Godwin two days later to offer his sympathy, and stayed for supper.

'This is a sad blow to us all –' Mary wrote in her journal before adding, with the sympathy she always felt for widows, 'Most to his unhappy wife.' Claire, musing on his death to Jane Hogg, thought William's chief misfortune had been to lack genius in a family who thought anything less a form of failure.[19] She had a point: Godwin and Mary's idea of a fitting memorial to William was to edit his only and unrevised novel. *Transfusion, or The Orphans of Unwalden* was published in 1835, but no amount of editing could disguise its mediocrity. The best that Godwin could do in his preface was to praise the author as 'a being of the warmest affections and the most entire generosity of temper'.

The unexpectedly high cost of Percy's public school education compelled Mary to move to Harrow village in the spring of 1833; home-boarders were despised, but she could see no alternative. The loss of her son's new clothes in a school fire had added to her problems. It was the worst of times for her disagreeable aunt Everina Wollstonecraft to arrive in London from Ireland, clamorous for support in her needy old age now that her sister Eliza was dead and the Dublin school had closed. Hearing from Jane Hogg that Claire, too, was considering a return to England, Mary was vigorously discouraging. Hard though she worked, she could not provide for them all. It came as a small relief to learn that Everina had a niece in Australia whose husband had prospered and who would be ready to help with her support. This was Elizabeth Berry, a cousin with whom Mary now began to correspond.

Godwin, at least, had become less of a burden. Assiduous visits and appeals to Earl Grey, the Prime Minister, were rewarded in the spring of 1833 when the Whig government granted the old man £200 a year and a home near the Manners-Suttons in New Palace Yard in return for a modest official post. Plans were being made to withdraw this sinecure when the Tories, briefly regaining office in the summer of 1834, restored the position and secured it. It is not, perhaps, surprising that Mary became rather fonder of the Tories after this unlooked-for reprieve.

Trelawny, disillusioned with England, departed on the *Tally-Ho* for America in January 1833, intending never to return. Godwin, who enjoyed Trelawny's rumbustious company, regretted his departure, fearing he would never see him again; Mary, however, expected him to return 'with a whole life of new experiences – the tale of a thousand loves – the same, yet ever new –'[20]

January–Feby March April 1833
I am disturbed by Percy's big bill & resolve on going to Harrow & having him as an home boarder – Trelawny sails to America – Julia &

Rosa [Robinson] spend some weeks with me – the aspect of my life is changed – I enjoy myself yet nothing is certain – Percy & I have both had the Influenza in April – dear Lady Paul dies of it – a sad omen for my going to Harrow – were it not for the change that I anticipate.

Godwin's move to New Palace Yard on 4 May 1833 was marked in his daughter's journal as the beginning of 'the only genial spring I ever knew'; writing to Jane Hogg on 5 May, she hinted that her new cheerfulness was due to more than Godwin's security. 'It is a great addition to happiness,' she wrote, 'to know that there is affection & care for one in one heart, joined to some degree of power to make those things of avail – I hope things will turn out well – *I trust they will* – that is all I know.'

Putting together the scraps of evidence available from Mary's letters and journals, it seems that the change she anticipated was a proposal from her friend Gee Paul's eldest brother, Aubrey. Five years younger than Mary, Major Beauclerk was already the father of two illegitimate children – one by Godwin's friend, the novelist Lady Charlotte Bury – though his relationship with the mothers had not survived. He had retired on half-pay from the 99th Regiment of Foot and was elected to Parliament as an Independent in November 1832. He presented himself as an abolitionist, in favour of electoral reform and, interestingly for an eldest son and heir to two estates, as an opponent of the laws of primogeniture. His views were therefore of the liberal kind most likely to appeal to Mary, and it would be surprising if her warm support for his sister, in the months when she had been hastily dispatched to Norwood, had not won his admiration, or even love.

Mary, certainly, seems to have believed that her tender feelings were returned. By August 1833, though, she was almost suicidal with grief. The official explanation for her dramatic loss of spirits that summer was a savage return of the influenza which had killed her friend Lady Paul. She convalesced at Putney, where she and Julia Robinson walked furiously, up to fourteen miles a day. Walking did not drive away her wretchedness. Approaching her thirty-sixth birthday, she frightened Claire with gloomy reminders that this had been the age at which her mother had died. Surely, Claire deduced, it must be typhus fever and not just influenza which had produced a gloom as black as that which had followed little William Shelley's death.

Mary's hurried and desperate notes in her journal suggest that illness played little part in her anguished state. 'Dark night shadows the world,' she wrote in August, and in September, she dilated on 'frightful calamity' and 'unmerited misfortune'. She must already have guessed or been told what was happening, to write in this way. Aubrey, not noted for his fidelity, was engaged to Ida Goring, the nineteen-year-old daughter of a baronet. Ida's background must have made the betrayal even harder to accept. For all Aubrey's egalitarian talk, his apparent sympathy and respect for Mary's difficult position and straitened circumstances, he had ended by choosing a pretty, conventional girl from his own class.

'I know not what to say, or write,' she wrote in her private book on 14 November as the memory of Jane Hogg's betrayal flooded back with all the bitterness of novelty. On 31 December, staying in London with Trelawny's newly married daughter and drawing faint hope from the news that her octogenarian father-in-law was on his deathbed (he was back on his feet the following year), she received 'un petit billet pour me tourmenter – c'est tout . . .' 'Je pleures,' she added in touchingly bad French, 'je ne sais que faire.' Back in Harrow on 13 February 1834, she wrote only 'Farewel.'

Arguments have been made that the initials 'AB' in Mary's journal may shield some other relationship,[21] but the fact that she wrote 'Farewel' on the very date of Beauclerk's wedding seems conclusive, as does the fact that she recorded the same date the following year as 'An anniversary strange & bitter'.*

Aubrey was a member of the circle that included some of her dearest friends. All of them must have been aware, to some extent, of what she had hoped for, and what had taken place. Humiliation increased her sense of being unable to share her feelings, of having to hide away the shock. 'Loneliness has been the curse of my life,' she wrote in December 1834. 'What should I have done if my Imagination had not been my companion? I must have grovelled on the earth – I must have died – O but my dreams my darling sun bright dreams!'[22] And her thoughts drifted back to the distant days when she sat in St Pancras churchyard by Mary Wollstonecraft's grave, wondering what the future held in store.

---

* The initials which seem to identify Beauclerk appear only once in Mary's journal. 'I have received one little note from A.B. sole testimonial of his existence –' she wrote on 8 July 1834. The fact that not a single letter has survived from Aubrey Beauclerk himself to Mary, or from Mary to him, is significant. Aubrey was a prudent destroyer of incriminating correspondence; he may well have asked Mary to perform a similar service for him.

RELINQUISHING PLEASURE

1833–1836

'My heart & soul are bound up in Percy – My race is run – I hope absolutely nothing except that when he shall be older & I a little richer to leave a solitude, very unnatural to any one, & peculiarly disagreable to me. I like society . . . I enjoy its pleasures . . . & forget sorrow in amusement – *therefore* I suppose I am shut up here where it is impossible to *forget* . . .'

Mary Shelley, Journal, Harrow, 2 December 1834

CLAIRE CLAIRMONT HAD RETURNED TO PISA BY THE BEGINNING OF 1832, working as a day governess from the home of Mrs Mason, the woman she now looked on as a mother. 'With her I am as her child,' she wrote to Mary.[1] Mrs Mason had married George Tighe in 1826, three years after her husband's death, and was as splendid and uncomplaining as ever, although Tighe had become increasingly reclusive and neurotic. Claire, forced outwardly to play the part of a conventional middle-aged spinster for the purposes of her job, was busy with subversive plans for a society of free-loving women who would confer their own names, not those of husbands, on their children. Legitimate children, Claire observed to Mary with her usual tactlessness, could never mean as much to their mothers. How comic that Sir Tim, 'that undying undyable Sir Tim!' was back on his feet again after what had sounded to be a fatal illness in the autumn of 1833. Clearly, he had decided to live for as long as possible, just to spite them. So Mary felt wretched? Well, she should try being a governess. Percy was growing fat, was he? So much the better; she had grown so rosy and buxom herself that she wondered if Mary would recognize her. Percy, she dared swear, was going to become a great philosopher, a prince among men. Now, could Mary stop complaining and mind to send her, for a friend, the autographs of all the fine celebrities among whom she lived?[2]

Out of England, Claire had little grasp of the isolation which preyed on Mary's spirits after her move to Harrow. The coach journey then from London was famously picturesque, rolling past the handsome new cemetery at Kensal Green through the pretty villages of Harlesden and Willesden and alongside the handsome hillside estate of Mr Gray at Wembley Park. Harrow itself was not inviting and few of Mary's friends were tempted to travel the eleven miles either by road or packet-boat, Mary's preferred form of travel. Even Godwin, while lamenting the loss of his daughter, preferred to stay put at New Palace Yard. The Robinsons, who had become almost like a second family to Mary, were settled on the far side of London, having left Paddington when the new Grand Junction Canal transformed it into a noisy goods depot. The girls, it was true, often came to stay with her, but visits were not enough for a woman who wistfully described herself as 'so social – so sympathizing – so easily pleased – & not displeasing'.[3]

In the village itself, Mary was starved for company. Fanny Trollope had returned there for a short period and her fourth son, Anthony, was completing his education at Harrow, but Anthony was several years older than Percy, and Mary, after reading Mrs Trollope's cruelly witty account of the horrors of life with Fanny Wright at Nashoba in her immensely successful *Domestic Manners of the Americans* (1832), had little inclination to resume the friendship. Mrs Trollope's *bête noire*, William Cunningham, vicar of Harrow, was equally uncongenial. Author of a best-seller recounting the history of the Church from the point of view of a hassock, Cunningham was also one of the founders of the relentlessly ardent Clapham Sect which Dickens loved to ridicule. Fanny Trollope pilloried Cunningham, recognizably, in *The Vicar of Wrexhill* (1837), while her son left a memorable portrait of him as the unctuous Obadiah Slope in *Barchester Towers*.

Every morning, Mary could hear the rattle of the oyster-cart being wheeled up the hill, carrying not-so-fresh Billingsgate wares, and the giggles of housemaids at the water pump, before she sat down to work. The lodgings were very disagreeable, she told Mrs Gisborne, and made worse by the fact that she lacked the money to furnish them. 'At the same time I cannot in the least regret having come here. It was the only way I had of educating Percy in a public school – of which institution, at least here at Harrow, the more I see, the more I like –'[4]

Mary's letters suggest that she was unaware of just how little Harrow merited its high fees. Floggings were frequent but random. Masters were hooted when they entered the classroom; boys read the *Satirist* behind their desks and slept through their lessons. In their spare hours, they went beagling, drinking at the weekly fairs at nearby Pinner, swimming in the dirty canal three miles outside the village, and 'toozling' – stoning sitting birds.[5]

Only one pupil, the father of W.B. Yeats's patron, Lady Gregory, won a scholarship to Oxford during Percy's time at Harrow; several others distinguished themselves in the annual Eton *v*. Harrow cricket match at Lords. Percy made his mark neither in sports nor studies. He left before reaching the school's top form, seemingly because of his need for cramming to reach university level. Yet it was not wholly Harrow's fault that Percy failed to do well. By the end of his second year, Mary was beginning to understand that he had no outstanding gift. 'He has the true Shelley hatred of society –' she told Mrs Gisborne; 'he has no ambition & little emulation – yet attentive to his lessons & sufficiently diligent – he is the 20th boy in a form of 50 boys.' She wished that he liked poetry and worked at Latin, although he seemed fond of romances. He had 'a great want of sensibility'. His blue eyes and pink face had been very like his father's at one time, but now, to his mother's dismay, he had become 'excessively fat – his chest would remind you of a Bacchus', she told her old friend.[6] Describing his affection for her, however, Mary could never praise him highly enough. 'One day I said to him – "Suppose when you grew to be a Man – you would leave me all alone" – "O Mamma," he said, "how do you think I could be so shabby: – that would be too bad!"'[7]

It seems strange that Mary, who had always disapproved of Mrs Gisborne's over-protective attitude to her own son, should have taken the same course. 'I think of you & Henry and shrink from binding my life up in a child, who may hereafter divide his fate from mine –' she confessed, 'But I have no resource – Everything earthly fails me but him.'[8] And this was the awful truth of it. Deserted, as she felt in her darkest moods, by everybody, Mary clung to her only child. If he went so much as a mile out of her sight for a swim, she was frantic; if he invited more than two friends to the house, she resented their monopoly of his attention. Was it rebellion of a quiet kind which turned Percy increasingly towards theatricals, which his father had rather disliked, and to the pleasures of rowing, swimming and yachting, activities which filled his mother with black terror when she remembered how Shelley had died? It would not be surprising. We have a brief glimpse of Percy's own unhappiness in a comment which found its way into Mary's journal in December 1834. Percy, she said, had just told her that he wished he had been allowed to stay as a boarder at the school – 'and I who have bartered my very existence for his good', his mother bitterly wrote.

There were other blows. Her aunt, Mary Wollstonecraft's sister Everina, who was now living in north London, took the view that it was Mary's duty to befriend her, since her only other surviving niece, Elizabeth Berry, while ready to give financial help, lived on the other side of the world. Dutifully and wearily, Mary did what she could. She had always sworn to herself to help the poor and needy of her sex; Everina was poor and, being a singularly unpleasant old lady, she lacked friends. 'Everina was never a favourite with anyone –' Mary lamented to Mrs Gisborne, '& now she is the most intolerable of God's creatures . . . she is so disagreable to me, that I know no punishment so great as spending an hour in her Company.'⁹ Hours had, nevertheless, to be spent, for Everina, having nobody else to turn to, became a skilful pricker of her niece's tender conscience.

Her own past brought pain as well. 'I am copying Shelley's letters. Great God! What a thing is life!' she exclaimed in November 1833. Both Shelley and Mary had been in the habit of keeping copies of the letters they wrote; it is possible that she was now reading those in which Shelley had complained of her coldness towards him. The hurt they gave was great; she went on to write of the need to find peace for 'my wounded aching thoughts . . . Why do I ask what is to be – What better than the past? – and that past – it is torture to think upon . . . O that I could forget!'¹⁰

She could not forget. Time after time, the past rose to the surface in her fictions, as it did in those of her father. Publishing his last novel, *Deloraine*, at the beginning of 1833, Godwin had opened his book with a portrait of Deloraine's young wife, who dies, as Mary Wollstonecraft had done, of a fever after childbirth. Painful though it must have been for his wife of thirty years, Godwin could not hide the tenderness he still felt for Mary's mother. 'There was no preparation in any thing she delivered,' he wrote, 'no hint of affectation, no wrinkle produced by any retrospect to herself, her own glory, and the expectation to be admired for what she said, or did. When I sat, or when I walked with her, I saw the thoughts of her mind exactly as they rose. It was all simple, and at the same time all wise.'¹¹

For Mary, too, the past became inescapably present when she sat down to write. *Lodore* was intended as a money-spinner, a novel set in the present, ornamented with the kind of lively social detail in which the so-called 'silver-fork' novels of the 1820s and early 1830s dealt. But in the hands of a woman as intelligent, as thoughtful and as introverted as Mary Shelley, it acquired a resonance untypical of the genre.

The history of the manuscript is not straightforward. Mary claimed that she had completed a version of the book by November 1833. She had not really finished it, for she was still sending off chapters to the printer in March 1834, and suffering the writer's ultimate nightmare of hearing that two fat packets of manuscript had been lost in the post. There was nothing for it but to sit down and rewrite and by June, as she sent off the last recomposed pages, having 'no copy whatever' from which to work, she was ready to snap at an impatient publisher that the misfortune had been 'very disagreable indeed to me as well as to him:

> . . . I did it as soon as ever I could – and tried all I could to do it sooner. The fairies are at work most malevolently if by this time the Printers have not the whole – as I sent the termination of the restoration on Saturday – in two packets . . . I am very sorry, that like Don Quixote, an Enchanter meddles with my affairs.[12]

Mary's rewriting is, however, less intriguing than the fact that she had clearly not finished or even half-completed the novel in November 1833. It was only towards the close of that month that she recorded in her journal the misery it was causing her to copy out Shelley's letters; this was the point at which her relationship with Shelley began to influence the narrative of *Lodore*.

One letter of Shelley's which we know Mary read in November 1833, because she quoted it in her journal, expressed his unhappiness at having left England for Italy. It had been Mary, not Shelley, who had insisted that they travel to Italy in 1818 to return Allegra to her father. She was now made guiltily aware of that fact. In the second and third volumes of *Lodore*, written in the winter of 1833 and early 1834, she turned back the clock and meant it to be seen that she had done so: 'did you recognise any of Shelley's & my early adventures?' she asked Mrs Gisborne eagerly on 8 November 1835. Portraying herself and Shelley in the life of Edward and Ethel Villiers as they cling together in refuge from his creditors, Mary returned to an earlier time when, as it now seemed, their love had been brightest. Fearful and often deserted though she had felt in the first months of her life with Shelley, and correspondingly dark though some passages of the Villiers' lives are, all emphasis is on their happiness.

Ethel's relationship with Villiers is not the only part of the novel to show Mary drawing on experience and familiar events. Ethel has been brought up by her father, Lord Lodore, in the wilds of Illinois and the early chapters of the novel were probably drawn from what Mary had heard or read in Mrs Trollope's book about Fanny Wright's primitive community at Nashoba. Fanny was a Scotswoman; her companion, Mrs Trollope, had gone to Nashoba with an artist who was probably her lover. It cannot be a coincidence that the community in which Lodore raises his daughter is filled with Scots emigrants or that Ethel is loved by a drawing-master there. This was the kind of sly allusive game which Mary enjoyed playing with her readers.

Ethel, as always with Mary's portraits of herself, is an excessively devoted daughter. Her father is Byronically self-willed and dramatic enough in his long exiles from England to have prompted Claire Clairmont to ask when Mary intended to stop drawing on that detestable man for her heroes? For Ethel's heartless English grandmother, Mary fuelled her indignation with thoughts of the woman she had come to believe was the most active and malicious antagonist she and her young son had. 'It is Lady S— who is my bitter enemy —' Mary wrote to Leigh Hunt on 3 February 1835, 'and her motive is the base one of securing more money for herself.' Lady Shelley was the inspiration for Mary's portrait of haughty, unsympathetic Lady Santerre, whose daughter Cornelia marries Lord Lodore at sixteen, the age at which Mary herself had eloped with Shelley.

Reviewing her father's *Cloudesley* in 1830, Mary had warned against 'merely copying from our own hearts'; *Lodore* did, nevertheless, draw on her own experiences. Ethel clearly reflects the difficulties of Mary's situation when placed between Godwin and Shelley. Fanny Derham, the scholarly daughter of Lodore's old schoolfriend, declares with Mary's own passion the importance of championing oppressed women. Young Cornelia Santerre, worldly, silly, fashionable and wholly under the influence of her odious mother, is as far removed from Mary Shelley as one could imagine; but later in the novel her identification with Cornelia as the widowed Lady Lodore becomes striking. She has married Lodore at sixteen; she is just Mary's age, thirty-four, when the novel ends. She wears white dresses, as Mary was noted to do in the 1830s. Repenting of her frivolous life, she makes amends in the third volume by embarking on a lonely retirement, sacrificing everything to the love of her child.

There is one singular phrase which links Mary Shelley especially closely to Cornelia Lodore. Writing up her journal for September 1833, Mary had noted that 'The friendship & gratitude of Gee [Paul] have been very soothing – & from unmerited misfortune my soul rises calm & *free*.' Mary was surely referring here to Gee's kindness at the time of Aubrey Beauclerk's defection. In the second part of *Lodore*, Cornelia learns that her lover, Horatio Saville, has betrayed her to marry a woman of high rank. As Mary struggled to submerge her grief in caring for Percy, so she showed Cornelia's thoughts turn to Ethel, her neglected daughter: 'she felt that in watching the development of her mind, and leading her to love and depend on her, a new interest and real pleasure might spring up in life.'[13] Describing Cornelia's new mood of resolution, Mary wrote: 'She rose calm and free, above unmerited disaster.'

Lodore has suffered from its links to the silver-fork genre; like them, it was for years too easily dismissed because the lively play of the surface disguises the seriousness of the author's intentions. Mary eagerly consumed Edward Bulwer's books while she wrote her novel; she was aiming at a similar audience. What she and Godwin both admired in Bulwer's works was his ability to combine a romantic, somewhat florid, narrative with a strong social message.

The main theme of *Lodore* is love in all its forms, but Mary Shelley also used it to challenge masculine authority over children. She had seen Claire's life destroyed by Byron's fickle treatment of Allegra, the little girl who belonged by law to him. She had seen poor Gee Paul go weeping from her home while her son was taken from her. These cases were not unusual. This was the regular and heartless way in which a child's future was decided. One could wonder if, in pretty, compliant Ethel, Mary Shelley had in mind the kind of girl Byron had wished Allegra to become and whether it had already occurred to her, as it must have done to Claire, that a less strong-willed child might have been kept and indulged, instead of being abandoned in the homes of acquaintances before being finally dumped in a convent.

The publication of *Lodore* was still two years away when Mary noted in her Harrow journal for November 1833 that 'I am going to begin the lives of the Italians.' She needed money for her aunt Everina as well as for her own lodgings, and for the new clothes which Percy must have if he was not to be mocked by his schoolfriends. Writing was also a welcome occupation; the house was empty all day when Percy was at school, and even when he was at home, as she sadly noted to Mrs Gisborne, his 'pleasures are not mine'.[14] Animals were his new passion; she had, with some difficulty, restricted him to keeping one friendly terrier.

She had failed in her attempt to become a regular contributor to

John Murray's *Family Library*, but when, in the autumn of 1833, Godwin's friend at London University, Dr Dionysius Lardner, contracted her to produce almost fifty studies of the eminent men of Italy, Spain, Portugal and France, she was faced with a considerable task. Although she relished the challenge of 'treading in unknown paths & dragging out unknown things',[15] obtaining books for her research was not easy. She hated the idea of working among a crowd of men in the King's Library at the British Museum; Lord Holland, approached by Thomas Moore on her behalf, boorishly refused access to his superb collection of Spanish texts; Harrow lacked a good circulating library. But Mary had prided herself on her power to persevere. As she worked on the lives of Petrarch, Boccaccio, Machiavelli, Metastasio, Goldoni, Alfieri, Monti and Foscolo, her only annoyance was that she had not been allowed more subjects. 'Unfortunately before I was applied to[,] some of the *best lives* were in other hands,' she complained to Leigh Hunt. 'The Omnipresent Mr Montgomery wrote Dante and Ariosto for the present Vol. – the rest are mine.'[16]

Writing the *Lives* was hard work and it took her almost five years to complete them: the final volume of the French *Lives* was published in the autumn of 1839. But Mary realized that this kind of work suited her as well as, and possibly better than, 'romancing'; few readers today would disagree, if they were able to sample her contributions to the Lardner *Cyclopaedia*, long out of print. Godwin, who began by reading his daughter's studies of Foscolo and Goldoni in December 1835, was delighted and impressed. This was the channel into which he had always wanted to direct her; these shrewd and readable studies, enlivened by Mary's candid observations and deepened by her ability to provide her own translations and to make stimulating textual analogies, confirmed the soundness of his judgment. It was an achievement beyond the chosen range of Mary Wollstonecraft. Mary might have inherited her mother's impulsiveness, gullibility and melancholia; she was a Godwin in her scholarship and her desire to instruct.

Not only that: just as her father, in his early works for the Juvenile Library, had smuggled his political and religious opinions into his texts, so Mary used her studies to express her views. This was the period in which the education of a newly literate class of readers was being heatedly discussed and promoted; Mary did not write simply to inform, but to influence. Her essay on Vincenzo Monti, to take one example, became a means of conveying her thoughts on the French Revolution: 'Monti . . . without that ardour of liberty which is so natural to many hearts, and which appears at once senseless and even wicked to those who do not feel independence of thought to be the greatest of human blessings, of course looked on the French revolution as a series of crimes . . .' In the same essay, she forcefully attacked Napoleon as a man who had 'but one idea with regard to liberty, which was a free scope to the exercise of his own will. When that was given him, he could be generous, magnificent, and useful; but when his measures were obstructed, no tyrant ever exceeded him in the combination of a despotism which at once crushed a nation, and bore down with an iron hand every individual that composed it.'

She also seized a chance to defend Shelley: 'no people needs so much sympathy as poets. The interchange of thought and feeling, the fresh spirit of inquiry and invention . . . are with them a necessity and a passion. And though solitude is named the mother of all that is truly sublime, yet this solitude ought not to be that of desolation . . .' Sympathetic to him here, she challenged his ringing proclamation in *The Defence of Poetry* (1821) that poets were 'the unacknowledged legislators of the world': 'a poet,' Mary drily observed, 'makes a bad politician.'

There are passages in these essays which deserve to be celebrated. Who has written more poignantly on remorse than Mary in her essay on Rochefoucauld?

> These are the stings, this the poison, of death. There is no recall for a hasty word . . . the grave that has closed over the living form, and blocked up the future, causes the past to be indelible; and, as human weakness for ever errs, here it finds the punishment of its errors. While we love . . . let all be true and open, let all be faithful and single-hearted, or the poison-harvest reaped after death may infect with pain and agony one's life of memory.

Reading her essay on Goldoni, one of the first she wrote, we can imagine how pleasant and amusing her company must have been when she was in a happy mood:

> The light-hearted rambling life of strolling comedians was alluring beyond measure to a mirthful lad, who loved plays better than any-thing in the world. The company consisted of twelve, besides scene-shifters, mechanists, and prompters; there were eight men servants, and four women, two nurses, a quantity of children, dogs, cats, apes, parrots, birds, pigeons, and a lamb. The prima donna was ugly, clever, and cross; the suicidal drowning of her cat diversified the time; and, after a prosperous and merry voyage, the whole cargo, with the excep-tion of poor puss, arrived at Chiozza.

While Mary wrote, tended her Harrow garden and fretted over her son, her father was enjoying a last sunburst of glory. It was an irony too delicious not to be noted by friends and enemies alike that the celebrated anarchist should have ended as a government employee, with the Tories responsible for his final rescue. Hazlitt's affectionate tribute (in his 1825 collection of biographical essays, *The Spirit of the Age*) had shown the stern political philosopher as a genial old soul, soft as a well-worn glove. Friends, hearing him declare that he no longer believed in giving power to the people, assumed that Godwin had undergone a complete reversal of his views. They were mistaken. Mary, crushed by experience, was slowly becoming more conventional. Her father, in his last and most outwardly placid years, had begun preparing a series of writings on the dangers of orthodox religion.

As a smiling relic of past times, Godwin was visited in droves by people who still kept their distance from his scandal-haunted child. Sheridan's beautiful granddaughter, witty Caroline Norton, was a regular caller, carrying the friendship with her family into a third generation. Harriet Martineau, Anna Jameson, Wordsworth, Macaulay, Disraeli, Lady Blessington, Count D'Orsay, the great, the good and the notorious, all paid their respects to the philosopher who presided at New Palace Yard with the serenity of Mr Dorrit at the Marshalsea. Fashionable Elizabeth Stanhope wrote to beg his autograph for her album. (Godwin courteously declined to oblige.) An old gentleman sent news that his son had hoped to attend Godwin's deathbed in order 'to observe how you would conduct yourself in such an extremity, and how you would die'. Dying prematurely himself, Master Cooke missed his opportunity.[17]

Lamb, grief-stricken by the loss of his old friend Coleridge, died at the end of 1834; taking his place, young Edward Moxon, recently married to Lamb's adopted daughter, came to visit Godwin. Moxon had an ulterior motive for his calls. A publisher of poetry, he had already approached Mary about her husband's poetry, and had been given a polite refusal; next time Godwin saw his daughter, he advised her to think again. Moxon might help her to prevent the regular publication of Shelley's poems in magazines with neither application made nor permission granted; in 1834, Mary had been dismayed by the appearance of two pirated editions of his works, published by John Ascham.

Mary listened to her father. The following year, offered £600 by Moxon for the works and life of Shelley, she began preparing to defy her father-in-law's ban. Quietly, she resumed the task of retrieving her husband's letters of which, in many cases, she possessed only the copies made at the time they were written. Asking Mrs Gisborne for any in her possession, she promised to be the most tactful of censors. 'You know how I shrink from all *private* detail for the public . . . everything *private* could be omitted,' wrote the woman who extolled truth, 'absolute and unshakable', as the 'foundation of our assertions' in her 1837 life of Camoens.[18] Did she already know, one wonders, of the letter to the Gisbornes which Shelley had written in the last month of his life, describing the misery of his marriage? Was it this which she intended to omit? Or was she thinking of the history of little Elena Adelaide and of the fact that Shelley had enlisted the Gisbornes' assistance in sending funds to Naples for the adopted child's support? There was, understandably, a world of difference between publishing such details in letters and in hinting at them, as Mary had recently done, in fiction.*

The last wry joke of Godwin's remarkable career was a good one. One of his official duties was the maintaining of the fire-fighting equipment kept at New Palace Yard. Whatever this equipment may have been and whatever its condition, it proved completely inadequate against the conflagration which smouldered into life on the evening of 16 October 1834, possibly owing to the indoor burning of the old wooden 'tallies' once used to record parliamentary expenses. Godwin, who had been at the theatre, was home again when the fire broke out, but there was never a chance to bring the raging furnace under control as it roared through the timbered buildings of Parliament. 'We saw it here from its commencement blazing like a Volcano – it was dreadful to see,' Mary told Maria Gisborne on 17 November; small Harrovians yelled with excitement, thinking all London was going up in flames. But, while the Manners-Suttons' residence was razed to the ground, Godwin's snug home escaped untouched; rebuilding rather than the fire itself compelled him to move to nearby quarters the following year.

Mary's main worry now was not the Godwins, but the difficulty of keeping Percy in the style to which she was determined he should become accustomed. She could not even afford the tailcoat which, fifteen years old, rather thinner and sporting a small moustache, he had ordered without consulting her for his arrival in the Third

---

* *Lodore* offers one more possible solution to the mystery surrounding that child; Clorinda, a fiery and beautiful Neapolitan, dies in childbirth at the inn at Gaeta where Percy had been conceived in 1819. Did Mary, perhaps, fuse two events and allude here to a young Neapolitan woman whose child Shelley had impetuously decided to adopt after her death?

Remove of the Fifth Form. Embarrassed, she begged Peacock to write to the tailor on her behalf, assuring him that the money would be paid if only the coat could be ready for the first day of term. 'I will do my best to arrange this better hereafter, meanwhile pray assist me on this occasion,' she begged him.[19]

Ill health and money worries kept Mary low in 1835. Her unhappiness was reflected in the efforts of Maria Gisborne and even Claire to rally her, telling her how good a writer she was and that her reward would surely come soon. It had certainly not come yet. *Lodore*, for reasons which have never been entirely clear, was kept back by the publishers until 1835. More warmly received than any previous work, the novel earned her just £100 with £50 more promised if it sold over 700 copies. It did, but Mary was still waiting for her £50 in March 1837. In the meantime, she stoically continued work on the Lardner *Lives*, seeking the advice of Polidori's brother-in-law Gabriele Rossetti for her study of Alfieri, thanking Bowring for helping her to find research books.

Writing to Mrs Gisborne from Harrow on 11 June 1835, Mary fretted because Percy was playing with some friends, out of her sight. She dreaded the thought that Teresa Guiccioli, visiting England, might cause talk by paying her a visit. Castigating herself for a lack of energy and determination, she was even ready to propose that all women were 'wanting in the higher grades of intellect'. In moral feelings, however, she allowed them to be superior to men. Not, she added bitterly, that Jane Hogg would ever allow her to be capable of such feelings; an insensible wife fitted Mrs Hogg's view of Shelley as an injured husband far too well. She felt, she added miserably, 'as one buried alive'.

This letter was written when Mary was on the verge of a nervous collapse, brought on by unrelieved solitude and overwork. The following month, she sent a desperate appeal for help to Jane Hogg. 'Come to me immediately as you love me,' she wrote. '. . . Come – My only Friend Come – to the deserted one – I am too ill to write more.'[20] Alarmed by the fact that Mary had taken the trouble and expense to send a cab for her conveyance all the way from Harrow to the Hoggs' home at Maida Place, Jane obliged. Spending some weeks at Harrow, she nursed the invalid back to health and spirits. It was a reparation for her past behaviour, and was recognized as such. Jane, for all her faults, was always reliable in times of illness, when she showed herself a tender and unselfish nurse.

By September, when Trelawny was back in England and ungratefully blaming Mary for the fact that his book had been republished with neither permission nor payment, she was convalescing at Dover, steeling herself to start work on the Spanish *Lives*. She had become cheerful enough again to tease her old friend about his famously fickle heart; in America, he had devoted himself to Fanny Kemble; back in London, he succumbed to the voluptuous charms and witty tongue of Caroline Norton. Mrs Norton is said to have 'a stony heart withal', Mary told Maria Gisborne on 13 October: '– so I hope she will make him pay for his numerous coquetries with our sex . . .' By November, she had returned to Harrow and was preparing to embark not only on the *Lives* but perhaps, as she told Mrs Gisborne, another novel, but only because 'I want money to get away from here'. The novel had, however, already begun to take shape; a few sentences later, Mary told her friend that it made her happy to hear how affectionate and attentive Mr Gisborne always was to his wife; she intended her new work to display her own view of 'fidelity as the first of human virtues'.[21]

Mr Gisborne, such a model of fidelity to his wife for almost forty years, died in January 1836; 'you must indeed let me hear often of you, if not *from* you,' Mary wrote to the widow on 4 March, knowing Maria's hatred of writing. She herself seemed barely to have stopped that winter; the novel which she had casually referred to in the previous October as a project was now half-finished and she had been busy making arrangements for Percy to go to a private tutor rather than see out his last year at Harrow.

But Mrs Gisborne, bereft, followed her husband after a few months. Mrs Mason had died the previous year; the two women had scarcely known each other but both had played an important part in carrying the memory of Mary Wollstonecraft into the next generation. Claire had taken inspiration for her own work with young girls from Margaret Mason's tales of her bold and delightful governess; Maria Gisborne had done more than anybody else to bring Mary Shelley into contact with the mother she had never known and whose place, for the first weeks of her life, she had lovingly filled.

Mary had already moved with Percy to London, in preparation for sending him to his new tutor, when news came from her stepmother on 2 April that Godwin had been laid low by a chronic catarrhal cough, which was now accompanied by fever. Mary hurried to New Palace Yard. The two women kept vigil by the eighty-year-old philosopher's bed for the next five nights, nodding their encouragement when he occasionally roused himself to express hopes of a speedy recovery. 'What I then went through – watching alone his dying hours!' Mary wrote in June in the journal she had abandoned for over a year. Even now, she could not bear to acknowledge her stepmother's conscientious care; if we had only Mary's diary for evidence, Mrs Godwin's presence in the house would be undetectable.

Godwin died on the evening of 7 April. He had asked to be buried as near as possible to Mary Wollstonecraft at shabby old St Pancras, downgraded to a chapel-of-ease since the arrival of its grander namesake at the north end of the Duke of Bedford's estate. Trelawny had been Godwin's last visitor; remembering his businesslike arrangements for Shelley's cremation and burial, Mary turned to him once more. 'Could you go with the Undertaker to fix on the spot,' she asked on 10 April, adding an apology for trespassing on the kindness of 'the best & most constant of friends'.

Trelawny did his work; the grave was duly opened and Godwin was laid in a coffin above that of his first wife in the presence of a select few, including his sixteen-year-old grandson.* 'I have lost my dear darling Father,' Mary bleakly noted in her journal in June; in the same entry, she expressed her wondering admiration for the calm and cheerful temperament which had sustained him to the end. 'But I! O my God – what a lot is mine.' Godwin, the Gisbornes and Mrs Mason were dead, Percy had gone to a tutor in Warwickshire, and Jane Hogg was absorbed in caring for her baby daughter, an experience which Mary had been ready to tell Mrs Gisborne that she envied her friend, 'even to bitterness'. Claire expressed no inclination to return to England; Charles and his family were also settled abroad. It was not hard to see where the responsibility for the woman Mary had spent a lifetime hating, her own stepmother, was about to fall.

---

* A puzzling entry in Godwin's journal for 5 March 1834 reads: '(Monument, MWG)'. MWG clearly refers to his first wife and not his daughter, who appears as MWS on the same page. Some alteration to the monument in the churchyard of St Pancras was evidently contemplated and, possibly, carried out. Conceivably, Godwin at the same time was making plans for his own burial.

PART V

Keeper of the Shrine

PROBLEMS OF REPUTATION

1836–1838

'Her lively sense of duty was perhaps her chief peculiarity.'

Mary Shelley, *Falkner* (1837)[1]

ATTACHED THOUGH MARY WAS TO THE IDEA THAT SHE POSSESSED prophetic powers, she had not foreseen her father's death when in March 1836 she and Percy moved from Harrow to dingy lodgings on the north side of Regent's Park. Far from it. Having made her plans for Percy to go to Warwickshire the following month, she had been intending to meet her friends the Hares at Brussels, where two of that large and affectionate tribe of Joshua Robinson's daughters were still enjoying themselves after a year abroad. Eight years had passed without Mary's having left England; with Percy safely wrapped in rural solitude, she could lay aside the writing of *Falkner*, and enjoy a little fun. This, until her father's death, had been her scheme for the summer.

Mary's reasons for sending Percy to be tutored by the vicar of Stoneleigh had not been entirely straightforward. Home-boarding caused him social difficulties at school, she told John Gregson, the Shelleys' lawyer, but she also felt that a strapping sixteen-year-old boy should be in a man's company, not his mother's, and at a safe distance from the dangers of London. Percy's sexual development was evidently beginning to discomfort her. Sex was a troubling issue for a widowed mother and Mary felt ill-equipped to deal with the practical business of keeping her son out of danger. In 1837, Trelawny, that genial Lothario, was requested to give young Percy advice on how to keep himself free of disease; travelling with Percy in Europe three years later, Mary was still fretting about the awful consequences of a 'love scrape'.*

If Percy had begun to develop virile impulses at sixteen, he kept silent about them. Quiet, affectionate and once more depressingly stout, he continued his gentle progress through life as if his ambition was to glide to its end without ruffling its surface. Reporting on his first term in Warwickshire, his tutor praised his steadiness; in his spare time, apparently, he was enjoying William Paley's popular work, *Natural Theology, or Evidences of the Existence and Attributes of the Deity*,[3] in which the author proffered his famous explanation of a world designed as if by a blind watchmaker. Mary was not noticeably displeased.

But he must have looked forward to the pleasures of a month in the city before he left for Warwickshire. London had plenty of sights for a boy to enjoy and Percy was, despite his mother's worries, not very mature. ('He is quite a child still – full of theatres & balloons & music,' Mary reported to Trelawny on 3 January 1837.) A tall trio of stuffed giraffes peered down the staircase of the old British Museum; the Strand was a clutter of waxwork and freak shows; an extraordinary jumble of mechanical inventions was on permanent display at the Adelaide Gallery. Charles Babbage was among Godwin's vast circle of friends; perhaps Mary took her son to the reception rooms at his house in Marylebone where the partly assembled 'Difference Engine' had been put on display in the hope of attracting financial support for this advanced form of calculating machine. More to Percy's taste, no doubt, was the curious silver toy on show in another of Babbage's rooms. A mechanical lady on whose finger perched a bird which flapped its wings and opened its beak, it amused visitors who found the workings of the Difference Engine beyond their understanding.[4]

Whatever treats Percy and Mary had been sharing in their first week together in London, Godwin's sudden death in April put an end to them. She had spoken for years as though she stood alone; now, for the first time, it was so. It was impossible to see garrulous old Mrs Godwin as the head of the family; her future rested in Mary's hands.

Mary's feelings towards her stepmother had not softened with time. However unconsciously, they found their way into her work. In 'The Invisible Girl', one of her most intriguing and underrated stories,

* If, as one Shelley authority has suggested, Percy's father had contracted syphilis in his university days, Mary may well have feared the same consequence overtaking her son.[2]

written for *The Keepsake* of 1833, she had painted a savage portrait of 'the odious Mrs Bambridge', a widow who, 'having succeeded in killing her husband and children with the effects of her vile temper, came, like a harpy, greedy for her prey, under her brother's roof'.[5] Just so, in Mary's uncompromising memory, had Mary Jane Clairmont descended on Godwin and his daughter, to make a misery of their lives.

Falkner, the novel which she began planning in 1835 and wrote intermittently throughout 1836, became a vehicle for the secret thoughts she dared allow to the surface only in the fictions or when seeming to comment on impersonal matters as in the *Lives*. Elizabeth Raby, while devoid of the imagination on which Mary prided herself, is immediately linked to her creator by the fact that she first appears, aged about six, weeping by her mother's grave, as Mary had wept by the tomb at St Pancras. Fidelity was the novel's theme; Elizabeth's loyalty is to Falkner, the man with a dark secret who rears her as his child. Mrs Godwin had been quick to discover and make much of the excessive love Mary felt for her father; here, this same love was flaunted. 'Falkner felt a half remorse at the too great pleasure he derived from her [Elizabeth's] society; while hers was a sort of rapturous, thrilling adoration, that dreamt not of the necessity of a check, and luxuriated in its boundless excess.'[6]

Elizabeth's fidelity is echoed in that of her lover, Gerard Neville, set on uncovering the crime which has covered his dead mother's name with disgrace. Did Mary cast Percy as Gerard, dreaming of the day when he would clear her own name of notoriety? Certainly she gave herself the pleasure of castigating the Shelleys again in her portrait of Gerard's father as an unpleasant, pompous baronet and in showing Elizabeth's relations as a family of religious fanatics who are obsessed with the protection of their family name. Following popular convention, Mary underscored the villainy or virtue of her characters by their settings. Neville's unpleasant father lives in splendour, close to the poverty-stricken town of Ravenglass; the selfish Rabys inhabit an old Gothic hall which represents their own outdated feudalism. Neville's kindly sister, by contrast, lives at Fairlight, in the tranquil landscape of which Mary had fond memories from her stay at Hastings in 1828.

Writing at great speed, Mary believed this would be her best novel, but she lacked the health or energy to revise it with her usual care. Published by a minor firm at the beginning of 1837, it was judged principally on the merits of Falkner, the main character. The *Examiner* scolded Mary for showing sympathy to the crimes of adultery and

murder. Several reviewers thought the novel too morbid. None, surprisingly, commented on the hasty inaccuracy of the quotations which
lavishly sprinkled the text and headed the chapters. Only *The Age* was
ready to claim it to be Mary's finest work, worthy in every way of the
author of *Frankenstein*.[7] This, in a period when writers were unblushingly ready to puff each other's work, was hardly a triumphant reception and the novel was faintly praised among her friends. Mary had
already begun to think that she preferred the pleasures of nonfiction;
she showed no regret in announcing *Falkner* as her last novel.

The speed with which Mary wrote had much to do with other calls
on her time in the months after her father's death. Claire, whom she
had been helping to rewrite a short story for one of the Christmas
annuals, was whining from Florence that nobody cared for her and
that her brave public face concealed a broken heart. 'Claire always
harps upon my desertion of her – as if I could desert one I never clung
to – we were never friends,' Mary wrote with understandable but
incautious impatience to Trelawny.[8] (Trelawny maintained a steady
correspondence with Claire.) But she worked over the story and continued to write sympathetic, cheerful letters to her exasperating stepsister. Learning that the Hoggs were short of money and that Jane was
unwell, she passed on a tip from one of Joshua Robinson's sons, a
solicitor, that a new bank was about to open which wanted to employ
'gentlemen of character & yet who will work' as their directors.[9]
When this came to nothing, she tried to persuade Peacock to employ
their mutual friend at the India House and, when he resisted, tried
again. 'A gentleman he [Hogg] is in feeling & conduct,' she kindly
urged. Did it matter if his appearance was a little strange if he had
integrity and some talent? 'What say you? Will you reconsider?'[10]
Peacock declined to do so.

This letter, written on behalf of a man towards whom Mary's feelings remained deeply ambivalent, was generous. The energy of her
endeavours to raise money for the widowed stepmother she had spent
a whole lifetime detesting, was heroic.

Godwin's last diary entry noted that he had paid a visit that day to
John Corrie Hudson, the sole executor of his will. The day after his
death, Mary wrote to Hudson to make arrangements for him to see
her stepmother and, presumably, to discuss her future. The outcome
of this meeting was hardly satisfactory. Fond though Godwin had
been of his wife, the main concern of his will had been with arrangements for his posthumous reputation, a burden he placed in his overworked daughter's hands. Little thought had been given to his
widow's welfare. Mrs Godwin was obliged to leave their government

lodgings to stay with friends and Godwin's magnificent library was sold to raise money for her immediate needs (it fetched £260). Colburn was ready to offer 350 guineas for publishing Godwin's correspondence and a memoir, but only on completion. What was needed in the long term was for Godwin's widow to continue receiving the £300 allowed to her husband from the Royal Bounty by Lord Melbourne, reinstated as Prime Minister since 1835.

Mary's best route to Melbourne was through Trelawny's new friend, Mrs Norton. Beautiful, strong-willed and full of loathing for the husband who made her work like a drudge in order to provide money for his amusements, Mrs Norton was still, in the summer of 1836, very close to both Melbourne and Trelawny. Mary, who knew her only as a handsome presence at Dr Lardner's parties and as the woman who had not given her any commissions during her editorship of *The Keepsake*, was not above joining in the gossip which hummed around Mrs Norton's magnificent shoulders. Tom Moore, visiting her on 21 May, heard an enticing titbit: 'In talking now of Lord [Melbourne's] supposed intrigue with Mrs N. Mrs Shelley said significantly—' but what Mary said we shall never know, because Moore grew uneasy and crossed three lines of gossip out of his diary. Scandal-loving old Samuel Rogers added to the fun that day by telling Moore he had seen Mrs Norton sitting at the theatre between her two lovers.[11]

An appeal to Mrs Norton was written and sent off, via Trelawny, together with one of Claire's most harrowing epistles, probably one which expressed her determination to sacrifice everything for her mother's sake and to become a London housekeeper. (She had written in this vein to Trelawny the previous year, and had been briskly told not to be so ridiculous, since everybody knew she had never liked her mother.) Mrs Norton, however, did not know Claire's gift for self-dramatization; the letter roused her sympathy. She agreed to approach the Prime Minister who, after some prevarication, agreed in turn to an ex gratia payment of £300 to Godwin's widow. It was not a generous concession from a man who had known and admired Godwin all his life and who was fully aware of the family's financial difficulties. But Melbourne had other matters on his mind than a frightened old lady waiting to be evicted from her home; all his thoughts in the summer of 1836 were focused on escaping from a charge which George Norton was preparing to bring against him for adultery with his wife. If Melbourne was found guilty, his resignation would be a foregone conclusion, and the stability of the new Whig government would be under threat.

Melbourne, innocent or not, was cleared of the charge. Caroline

Norton's reputation was ruined by it. Nobody believed that she had been innocent; they thought, probably rightly, that Melbourne had been exonerated because of his position. A year or two earlier, lustrous eyed and resplendently uncorseted on her blue satin sofa in Storey's Gate, Mrs Norton had been the toast of political London, although viewed with suspicion by her own sex. ('I suppose she is very amusing to people who have not much principle,' Melbourne's aristocratic Whig friend, Emily Eden, coldly noted in 1834, perhaps with a touch of jealousy.[12]) Now, deprived of her sons by a law which, for the purposes of inheritance, invariably favoured the father, Mrs Norton moved out of her half-uncle Charles Sheridan's house into shabby rooms in Spring Street, south of the dusty slopes being flattened for the new Trafalgar Square. Mary Shelley was among the few to seek her out and to offer support during this low period, just as she had done to Gee Paul.

Ironically, Mary's own reputation was still, after fourteen years of widowhood, unsavoury enough to make her friendship a mixed blessing; of the older generation, only those who laughed at prudishness, Lady Morgan, Mrs Wood, Samuel Rogers, were ready to entertain her in the years following her father's death. Writing to Trelawny at the beginning of 1837, Mary reassured him that she would 'take very good care not to press myself [on Mrs Norton] – I know what her relations think.'[13] She may have been discreet about their meetings, but the two women were already engaged in a lively correspondence. At the time when Mary allowed Trelawny to think she was keeping a tactful distance from his friend, she was advising on the pamphlet Mrs Norton was preparing: *Observations on the Natural Claim of the Mother.* Mary, who had never forgotten Sir Timothy's threats to separate her from Percy, was strong in her opinions on this matter. 'Perhaps you will not think I have gone *far enough*,' Caroline wrote after sending her a draft of the pamphlet.[14] Mary, who was, in a more devious way, as outspoken as her fine friend, used her essay on the Italian writer, Alfieri, to express her own view:

> There seems something incomprehensible in a state of society that should admit of the propriety, or rather, enforce the necessity, of a boy of nine being separated from all maternal care, and left to struggle as he might, during the precarious season of childhood and adolescence, without a parent's eye to watch over his well-being, and administer to his health and happiness.

Mary's side of the correspondence has not survived, but Mrs Norton's responses show that acquaintance rapidly blossomed into a friendship warmed by old connections. (Godwin, a devoted friend to Caroline's grandfather, the playwright Sheridan, had been one of the few attendants at his pathetically modest funeral and a regular visitor to his grave.) On 7 August 1837, Moore found Mary taking tea with Caroline: 'poor Mrs N. much changed.' Alone with Mary, however, Caroline was her lively forceful self. Mary was scolded for foolish pride in trying to pay for a seat at a theatre when she had been Caroline's invited guest. Worrying over whether she dared take a house in Berkeley Street which had once belonged to a prostitute, she was almost teased into a purchase. She was very silly to worry about the fact that a 'fie-fie' had lived there, Caroline affectionately scolded: 'If you act discreetly and modestly (that is if you paint the rails *dark green*; and *don't* buy a parrot . . .) . . . the barrenness of virtue will be apparent and the house will be as good, as if its face was built out of the sorrowful and remorseful bricks of the Milbanke penitentiary.'[15]*

Mary's finances at this time are somewhat baffling. Godwin had left his daughter little beyond his papers and a couple of paintings; she became anxious whenever her allowance from the Shelleys arrived, as it frequently did, a few weeks late. In January 1837, she was hard up enough to ask Trelawny to lend her £20. Bentley, the publisher of *Lodore*, was reminded that she had been promised £50 when over 700 copies of the novel had been sold, and that she would be glad to have it. By the spring, however, Mary was in a position to inform Trelawny that 'I have plenty at present & hope to do well hereafter.' This suggests that she must have received some unexpected increase in her income. By March, she was living at a good address in South Audley Street; by the late autumn of 1837, having decided against buying the house in Berkeley Street, she had moved to another Mayfair home, 41 Park Street.

Mary was not, however, sufficiently well-off to subsidize her stepmother. She was still living at South Audley Street when she decided to make another appeal to Lord Melbourne, asking him to consider whether Godwin's widow did not merit an annual pension. Caroline Norton was happy to act as her adviser. 'Press *not* on the politics of Mr Godwin,' she warned. Mary must learn to grovel if she was to succeed: 'when *I* beg,' Mrs Norton told her, 'I am a crawling lizard, a humble toad, a brown snake in cold weather.'[16] Too honest and independent to relish fawning, Mary managed, nevertheless, to find

---

* Huge and hideous, Millbank Penitentiary stood on the present site of the Tate Gallery from 1820 to 1890. Caroline's misspelling suggests a mischievous pun on the maiden name of Byron's widow, notorious in the 1830s for her sanctimonious tale-telling.

a tone humble enough for Melbourne to promise support of her request. It was probably as a result of this appeal by Mary that her step-mother was able to settle in the autumn of 1837 at Kentish Town, in a house with a pleasant garden to remind her of old days at the Polygon in Somers Town.

———————

In the summer of 1836, shortly after her father's death, Mary began the task of sorting through his papers and preparing herself for the task of writing his life and editing his letters. Posthumous fame, as she knew, had been a matter of great concern to the old man; his will laid on her the burden of securing it. Dutifully, she wrote off to all his correspondents; to Thomas Wedgwood's surviving brother Josiah, to Hazlitt's son, to Henry Crabb Robinson and – a figure from the distant past – Godwin's former ward and relation, Thomas Cooper, long established as a successful actor in America. The responses were courteous; Cooper, a widower, even suggested that Mary should come and join him and his family. Mary's answer does not indicate whether he was, in fact, inviting her to become his second wife; gracefully, she rejected the invitation. She remained, she told him, dependent on a 'narrow-minded & niggardly' father-in-law whose existence compelled her to live in England. 'While he lives I must remain here . . . Percy is now seventeen – he is all I could wish – but I would not separate from him for the world . . . With such a tie you will perceive that a voyage across the Atlantic is beyond the bounds of possibility.'[17]

Work on Godwin's correspondence and the memoir she was writing to accompany it had to be combined with her continuing researches for the Spanish volumes of the Lardner *Lives*. By the end of the summer of 1836, she was exhausted. Claire, arriving in Paris in October (the family for whom she worked was moving to England), sent an affectionate note scolding her. Of course Mary must not wait in London to receive her: 'your health is the first thing – for Godsake go directly to the sea . . . Pray take care of your health – if you knew what an effect your letter with so bad an account of yourself had on me.' Then Claire gave a lurid account of her own misfortunes, as if Mary's were, after all, slight. 'No pen can describe what I have suffered,' she wrote, and filled a long page with her trials.[18] Perhaps it was not only ill health which caused Mary to decide to spend the rest of the year at Brighton, out of Claire's reach.

Julia, her favourite of the Robinson girls, kept Mary company until

Christmas Eve, and then set off from Brighton for Ardglass Castle to spend a year with Aubrey and Ida Beauclerk, probably in the capacity of governess. The weather became bitterly cold: 'what snow we have had,' Mary wrote to Trelawny on 3 January; 'hundreds of people have been employed to remove it during the last week.' She had been watching them carry it down to the beach after piling it up in the streets in glittering pyramids, and now she was shivering at her desk, and missing Julia, 'the dear entity . . . you know what a dear thing she is.'

Mary had little specific reason for sadness. Claire, she could reasonably hope, might now share the burden of Mrs Godwin; Julia was an assiduous correspondent; Percy had arrived at Brighton in high spirits, showing off his skill at playing the flute, wearing a fine new frock coat and chattering happily of his visits to the theatre. Mary detected a new softness: was her son in love? 'How I dread it,' she confessed to Trelawny. 'I hope you will be useful to me when it begins.'[19]

Perhaps it was only solitude which preyed on her as she stayed on into February at the increasingly empty resort. Certainly, her mood changed, and violently so. Trelawny, writing to ask why she was taking so long to produce her father's letters and the memoir, received a furious response.

Like Claire, Trelawny had a genius for stinging Mary where it hurt. She had already begun to feel oppressed by the responsibility laid on her by her father's will. Caring for him had been, she wrote to Trelawny, 'for many a year a burthen pressing me to the earth'. Now, as she contemplated writing his life, all she could see was the damage it would do to her son. 'This year I have to fight my poor Percy's battle – to try to get him sent to College without further dilapidation on his ruined prospects – & he has to enter life at College – that this should be undertaken at a moment when a cry was raised against his Mother – & that not on the question of *politics* but *religion*, would mar all – I must see him fairly launched, before I commit myself to the fury of the waves.'[20]

It comes almost as a relief to hear Mary at last acknowledging the trial it had been to her to support her old father for the last thirteen years of his life. Now dealing, as she would have to in her book, with Godwin's early opposition to marriage and to orthodox beliefs, views wholly out of fashion in 1837, she was reminded of the damage Godwin's memoir had wreaked on Mary Wollstonecraft's posthumous reputation. That her worries arose not from Godwin's politics but from his religious views is of particular interest. She must, judging by the agitated tone of her letter, have already read her father's unexpected and unpublished last work.

The Genius of Christianity Unveiled, written with all the energy and power of Godwin's most famous book, flew directly in the face of Mary's own wistful hopes of an afterlife. 'What is there behind the curtain?' her father asked his reader before supplying the candid answer: 'Probably nothing.' In a splendid, thundering conclusion, he lambasted a world peopled with fearful, unthinking churchgoers.

> We dare not enquire, we dare not frame propositions, and draw conclusions on the subject. We think it safer to abide in a sort of belief, and to refrain from speculating on so perilous a question. We bow down our faculties in silence, deluding others and deluding ourselves, and subscribing to tenets the most groundless and indefensible.[21]

This view was distressing to a woman increasingly anxious to pay lip-service to conventional religion. She was right to suppose that publication would cause difficulties for Percy when he went to university, particularly since his own father had been sent down for having published an atheistical pamphlet. But, although she did not have the courage to admit this to Trelawny, Mary must also have been concerned for the effect that such a book might have on Shelley's blossoming reputation.

It remained the case that, while Mary was forbidden by Sir Timothy to publish her husband's works, to which she held the copyright, there was nothing to prevent anybody else printing and distributing his poems. Several reviewers and essayists had taken the opportunity of discussing his work in order to quote extensively from it; *The Beauties of Percy Bysshe Shelley*, published by C. Roscoe in 1830 with the approval and assistance of Leigh Hunt and Mary herself, was in its third edition by 1832. Galignani's edition, published in Paris in 1829, also continued to sell. In 1832, with the passage of the Reform Bill, came a national change of mood; for the first time since his death, Shelley's political views became acceptable. His attacks on the oppressive Tory administration could be seen as admirable, honest and far-sighted. Leigh Hunt, who had feared to publish *The Masque of Anarchy* in 1819, the year of the poem's composition, could do so now, and add a preface giving his reasons. Medwin published Shelley items in the *Athenaeum* and *Fraser's Magazine*; Mary, meanwhile, offered her own transcript of Shelley's 'Lines on Castlereagh' to Thomas Kelsall, one of the three men who had backed the short-lived publication of *Posthumous Poems* in 1824; the poem appeared in the *Athenaeum* in 1832. When Bulwer, as editor of the *New Monthly Magazine*, expressed his willingness to publish articles about Shelley, Mary put him in touch with Hogg, whose amiable reminiscences of university days also appeared over a period of six months in 1832.

Shelley's star continued to rise. Robert Browning's poem, 'Pauline', published in 1833, hailed him as 'the Sun-Treader'; Thomas Lovell Beddoes offered an admiring tribute in verse. Shelley's lines to his dead son were widely published in the Christmas annuals of 1834; Ascham published two volumes of the poems in the most widely read of the growing number of pirated editions, while 1835 was marked by respectful accounts of visits to Shelley's grave in Rome by several admiring young poets. His reputation was further enhanced in 1836 when the death of the much-loved poet, Felicia Hemans, reminded the many who mourned her that Shelley, as a sixteen-year-old, had been one of her first admirers. In 1837, marking another step up the ladder, the late Charles Lamb was reproached for his failure to recognize Shelley's genius. Lady Blessington's cooings over a sweet and unworldly poet she had never met did no harm at all. Shelley, by 1837, was widely read and discussed.

This was gratifying to a woman who had worked ceaselessly, if discreetly, to promote Shelley's reputation, giving assistance and, where necessary, her own transcripts of the poems to sympathetic editors, while quoting extensively from his work in her novels. But, while she sought recognition for her husband's work, Mary's unhappy experiences as a widow and her concern for Percy had made her increasingly anxious to shield all personal details of his life with her from view. She liked Hogg's articles, not only for their friendly tone, but for tactfully concluding in 1810.* She could draw comfort from the *Metropolitan* (December 1832), in which an anonymous reviewer of *The Masque of Anarchy* commented that it was better to look at Shelley's poems than to search for details of his private life. The reviewer's opinion was not, it seemed, unique; since the publication of Hogg's articles, there had been no appeals in print for a biography of Shelley.

By 1837, the image of Shelley as a religious sceptic had faded almost entirely from sight. A less financially dependent – and by now cautious – woman than Mary might have jumped at the opportunity which *The Genius of Christianity Unveiled* provided to signal the remarkable link between her father's last work and Shelley's atheism, but these were pious times and such a publication would guarantee

---

* A seventh article, on Shelley's expulsion from Oxford in 1811, was published by the *New Monthly Magazine* in May 1833.

an end to her allowance from Sir Timothy. She had no wish to take the risk, either for her father, for her husband or for her son. Godwin had left a letter with his final manuscript, optimistically valuing it at a thousand pounds and insisting on publication. Mary did not destroy his work; she simply put it away. *The Genius of Christianity Unveiled* first appeared in 1873, more than twenty years after her death.

The project of writing Godwin's life was not abandoned. Her idea seems to have been to produce two separate works, a collection of correspondence linked by biographical notes, and a life which would stop short at the death of her own mother, a period too remote for controversy. Shelley's reputation and her own could suffer no harm from a book which ended at her birth.

Composing the linking passages for Godwin's correspondence was a useful exercise; it afforded Mary an example of how, in time, she might present a life of her husband without angering Sir Timothy or revealing anything injurious to herself. Her notes, prepared between 1836 and 1838, suggest that this was to have been a work of reticence bordering on untruth.[22] The revolutionary nature of the 1793 edition of *Political Justice* was downplayed as she carefully emphasized her father's support of 'the slow operation of change'. Due homage was paid to Godwin's courage at the Treason Trials of 1794 and to the waking of 'a giant's mind' in the heady dawn of the French Revolution. But, coming to the awkward fact of her own conception by an unmarried couple, Mary simply lied. 'At the beginning of this year Mr Godwin married Mary Wollstonecraft. The precise date is not known,' she blandly wrote, although the date and place of the marriage was plainly written in the journals she had in front of her. Should we exonerate her, suggest an oversight, a misreading, in such an important detail as the marriage of her parents? Surely not; she would have scanned the entries twenty times for such a revealing fact. Respectability had become more important than the truth.

A separate project, for a life of Godwin and Mary Wollstonecraft, seems to have been undertaken at the same time. It opened with a poem, 'A Monody on the death of William Godwin', composed by Mary with more feeling than art. 'Godwin was versatile,' she wrote; 'he bore combined / A woman's weakness, a Cato's mind.' The poem continued for another three pages. Reading it, few would disagree with the subject's low opinion of his daughter's abilities as a poet.[23] Mrs Godwin copied out chapters 9 and 10, containing her husband's account of Mary Wollstonecraft's death, perhaps because her step-daughter found this too distressing a task; elsewhere, with the exception of a few allusions to 'the great man', Mary was the principal author. It is not clear why she abandoned it, for a biography which stopped in 1797 offered no threat either to Percy or to Shelley's reputation. It is tempting to suppose that, having sacrificed so much of her life to her father's needs, Mary simply abdicated from a task which threatened to consume the remainder. And who could blame her? She had already done more than enough.*

The regularity of Mary's complaints of exhaustion and ill health in the two years following her father's death were not due solely to her worries about how to carry out his wishes. She was now forty years old and she was driving herself hard. In 1837, she was assessing Godwin's papers, keeping an eye on her stepmother, worrying over whether the Shelleys would be willing to pay for Percy's university education. She was also preparing, after an arduous two years of writing the Spanish *Lives*, to set to work on her third and final set of short biographies, of the eminent French.

Money was the spur. Writing the Spanish *Lives* had interested her, she told Leigh Hunt at the beginning of 1838: 'these do not so much – yet it is pleasant writing enough – sparing one's imagination yet occupying one and supplying in some small degree the *needful*' – by which she meant, money.[25]

As in the earlier volumes, Lardner encouraged her to be as opinionated as she wished – and Mary did wish. She did not, on the whole, care for the French and she let it show.[26] It was a pity, she observed, that Corneille had been born a Frenchman and forced to obey the 'jejune' rules of French verse. Racine's tragedies represented, even at their finest, only 'a dance in fetters'.[27] The best she could say of Molière's work was that he was, among his fellow playwrights, 'the least merely French'.[28] Voltaire was lambasted for cynicism (which did not stop Dr Lardner putting a handsome engraving of him at the front of the book), and Rousseau for hypocrisy. Few exceptions were allowed. Condorcet and Fénelon, so admired by Godwin, received

---

* She seems however to have been working on it still in 1840, since Claire wrote to her that year and urged her to stop: 'Do not think of writing the memoirs – you must on no account use your mind – health is everything.' A letter from Mary in the Abinger collection at the Bodleian Library, dated 6 May 1840, explains to an unidentified addressee that her work 'is not complete & ready for the press, not that there is anything to add – but there are many letters to be reconsidered – all that is here is not to be published – although the exceptions are few.' Shelley's letters had already been published by this date; the obvious conclusion to be drawn is that Mary was still working on her father's life.[24]

almost unstinting praise; Mary's enthusiasm for Rochefoucauld and Mirabeau suggests that she would gladly have extended her chapters on them to twice the length.

Nearing the end of this gruelling enterprise, Mary gives us a hint of the book, rejected by Murray in 1830, which she had wanted to write on celebrated women. Restrained in her accounts of Madame de Sévigné and Germaine de Staël, she made up for it when she came to Madame Roland, the woman young Isabella Baxter had taught her to regard as history's greatest heroine. Mary was less impressionable in her forty-first year than Isabella had been at fifteen. She allowed Manon Roland to have been a trifle vain and thought that a little tact might have saved her husband from hearing 'the ridicule which low-minded men delight in affixing on superior beings of the other sex'. But why, Mary demanded, when Roland himself took pride in his wife's brain and her ambition, should she be criticized for having helped him? Mary's own sense of a wife as partner, not subordinate, emerges clearly here, but this is one of the chief fascinations of her biographical studies. Writing objectively enabled her to reexamine her own life under the cloak of an anonymous chronicler of past events.

'How easy it is in all that is human to spy defects,' was one of the comments that Mary made in her defence of Manon Roland. In 1837, she could still identify with a woman whose name had been unjustly maligned; the sense of being judged and condemned remained as strong as ever. She still feared what was said behind her back; as Shelley's name became increasingly linked to all that was beautiful and gentle and good, her own reputation as the callous wife who had not understood or appreciated him continued to ripple and spread. There were plenty of people who now read Shelley's poetry but still wanted nothing to do with his wife. It was unfair, but it was so. Sir Timothy's injunctions, combined with her own awareness of all the things that could never, for Shelley's sake, be told, guaranteed that no remarkable change in attitude was likely.

She had, nevertheless, made some firm friendships during the 1830s and there is no evidence that any of the women who had become intimate with Mary Shelley during her first timid years of social entertaining had turned against her. Gee Paul, enduringly grateful for the support Mary had given after her separation from her husband, invited her down to Sussex to spend the Easter of 1837 with the Beauclerk family. Against her expectation and much to her delight, the local gentry were rude about the Shelley family and friendly to herself. 'It is they say, & truly, a pleasure to be praised by the praiseworthy – & certainly it is gratifying to find one's enemies unworthy & generally disliked,' Mary wrote to Leigh Hunt on 26 April. She could, for the first time, imagine a future for herself in this pleasant southern landscape when – if ever – Sir Timothy consented to expire. She could not resist reporting that Lady Shelley was considered 'illnatured' by her neighbours, and the daughters thoroughly 'arrogant and disagreable'. Sir Timothy, she had heard, 'though something of a fox, is more of a fool'. It was not yet clear whether he was prepared to meet Percy's college bills.

Back in London for the summer of 1837, she hunted for congenial lodgings. The rooms she had taken at South Audley Street were uncomfortable; still, as she told Hunt in this same letter, 'it is near several people I know & like – & if one is to have *any* society, I find one must tend towards the centre.' Trelawny, always ready to criticize Mary for her social aspirations, allowed that company suited her and that she looked good – for her age. She 'lights up very well at night – and shows to advantage in society', he noted.[29] The American statesman, Charles Sumner, meeting Mary in the late 1830s at a party given by lively old Lady Morgan, remembered that she had been dressed in pure white, a bold touch for a woman over forty; he had thought her 'a nice and agreeable person, with great cleverness'.[30] Here, we have an image of a woman who had stood up to years of hardship startlingly well; this was not an age which favoured cosmetics, and gaslight was not kind to wrinkles. Perhaps Mary's volatile nature was reflected in her appearance, for the descriptions of Trelawny and Charles Sumner stand in striking contrast to the only known portrait of her at this time.

Richard Rothwell had left England for Italy shortly after Mary first sat to him in 1831. Back in England by 1836, he renewed his friendship with Mary, and in the following years often accompanied her in parties to the theatre. By this time, thanks to the influence of that ambitious but unfortunate artist, Benjamin Haydon, he had almost entirely renounced his lucrative career as a portrait-painter to work on large-scale historical scenes; still, he could not resist trying his hand at another portrait of Mrs Shelley. Late in 1839, she sat for him in a low-cut, pinch-waisted black velvet dress which emphasized the fashionably wide slope of her white shoulders. Behind her, Rothwell gracefully alluded to the sustaining spirit of Shelley in a flame-coloured column. Skilled at the art of flattering coarse features and bad skins, he made no such concessions here. Mary looks noble, appealing and all of her years. Her hair, time-darkened and thin, is pulled away from her face; her complexion, while clear of pockmarks, is sallow. The mouth, thin and straight as her father's, carries no hint of a smile; the eyes are tired and a little haunted. It is hard to imagine this woman being tempted to wear a white dress or being praised for the fact that she showed 'to advantage' in society, unless Trelawny meant that she did so by presenting a startling contrast to the worldly women whose company she appeared, increasingly, to enjoy.

The portrait must have been a truthful one; Mary liked it well enough to allow Rothwell to exhibit it in the Summer Exhibition at the Royal Academy in 1840 and without concealing her name.[31] The catalogue entry, for which her permission must have been sought, quoted the lines from *The Revolt of Islam* in which Shelley had hailed her as a 'child of light', glorious by her birth, auspicious in her future. The *Morning Chronicle* critic thought the portrait one of the six finest in an exhibition crowded with sketches and paintings of literary figures; Rothwell's entry was mentioned alongside Maclise's celebrated portrait of Dickens.[32]

'If one is to have *any* society,' Mary had written to Leigh Hunt, as though she would be fortunate to find more than a scant handful of friends in London. Mary always tended to exaggerate the solitude of her life: thanks in part to the success of *Lodore* and in part to the rise in her husband's literary fame, her circle was steadily expanding. Augusta Goring, unhappily married to Ida Beauclerk's bullying, unpleasant brother Harry, became a devoted friend. Sending her consoling letters, Mary urged her to be as cheerful as she knew how and addressed her tenderly as 'dearest little Guss'.

Her acquaintances included several politicians, many authors, and a few who combined both professions. One was Bulwer; another was the dandyish author whose most recent novel, *Venetia* (1837), had drawn on the lives of Shelley and Byron. Mary made no written comment on the book, but she admired Disraeli enough to urge him to strive for something beyond mere dazzle in his maiden speech in the House of Commons in 1837. 'Were your heart in your career it would be a brilliant one,' she wrote, and, because it saved her a little money, she asked him to frank an enclosed letter.[33]

Shared hatred of Italy's Austrian overlords had long ago helped to cement Mary's friendship with the warm-hearted, downright Irish novelist and travel-writer Lady Morgan, who sometimes put her up at her home near Grosvenor Place during Percy's holidays from Harrow and often invited her to attend the literary and political gatherings she held there. By the time Mary had settled into new lodgings in Park Street towards the close of 1837, she was even prepared to give

Lady Morgan one of her most precious relics, a piece of the lock she had cut from Byron's hair in the summer of 1822: 'you may say that I have never parted with *one* hair to anyone else,' she told her in the note which accompanied the gift.[34]

Pride remained an obstacle in some of her new friendships. She did not mind walking out to Brompton to call on Trelawny's mother, Mrs Brereton, and his married sister, Charlotte Trevanion; embarrassed by her lack of a private carriage, she felt unable to call on the actress and author Fanny Kemble Butler after being sent a friendly invitation. Lack of a carriage also kept her from making cross-town visits to the Hunts at their new home by the river in Chelsea village. Now, if Jane Hogg and she were men and wore trousers, she wrote ruefully to Hunt, they would be there in a trice; but how could ladies in their trailing cloaks and lace-trimmed petticoats be expected to toil through the mud?[35] Hunt did not need to be told that it was unthinkable for a respectable lady to hire a hansom.

No transport was needed to make the short journey down to Samuel Rogers's home in St James's Place, just south of Piccadilly. Small, sharp-tongued and with a nose that hooked almost down to his chin, the old banker-poet relished the company of clever women, although he never married. Charmed by Mary, he began in 1837 to issue her with regular invitations to his literary breakfasts, held in the treasure-stuffed house he had built for himself. Urged to hurry to 'the little gate' always open to her there,[36] Mary went almost as often as she was asked, to admire his art collection – Rogers owned a Titian, a Giorgione, a Raphael – and to enjoy his company. 'Rogers' breakfasts are delightful – of such intellectual fascinating society I have had too little in my day,' she wrote in her journal on 30 June 1838: 'how highly I enjoy them when they fall to my share.' It was through Rogers that she met Wordsworth and Keats's friend, Joseph Severn, to whom she had tried to give Hogg an introduction in 1825;[37] it was probably here that she met Leigh Hunt's Chelsea neighbour, Thomas Carlyle, talking nineteen to the dozen, and Richard Monckton Milnes, one of Shelley's warmest admirers among the younger generation. Mouselike, pale and as unquenchably fond of singing as Tom Moore, Milnes was a countryman turned aesthete, his poetically long hair combed down over his velvet collar. The story of his cross-country dash from Cambridge to champion Shelley's name to a group of scornful Oxford men was one he loved to tell.

Milnes would have been able to reassure Mary about her son's new life. Percy had gone to Trinity, Milnes's own former college, in the autumn of 1837; Mary, with memories of Shelley's tales of himself and Hogg at Oxford and of their expulsion for printing an atheis-tical pamphlet, was full of anxiety, although it relieved her to know that her son's closest friend there was Julian, the youngest of Joshua Robinson's sons. Stealthily, she began laying plans for a romance with Peacock's daughter, Mary Ellen, who was kept carefully informed of the dates of Percy's returns home. 'I have very agreable letters from Percy,' she told Aubrey Beauclerk's brother George on 19 March 1838, and added that she had hopes of being 'a happy woman & a lucky one yet'. It must have been very shortly after this date that Mary received the unwelcome news that Percy was in love, not with Miss Peacock but with a girl she had never met. We can note, for it is an intriguing gap, that none of Mary's letters to Percy during this period have survived. It has been generally assumed that Mary's correspondence with her father was destroyed because of the embarrassing degree of affection it may have betrayed; so, perhaps, it was with Percy. It is certainly unthinkable that a mother so pos-sessive as Mary would not have communicated her anxiety; even her letters to Claire on the subject have disappeared. All we have to go on are two letters which Claire wrote back to her in April 1838 from the Windsor household in which she was working as a governess and companion.

Claire's letters, written on 7 and 20 April, make it clear that Mary was extremely uneasy about Percy's affairs and that she had already indicated to Claire that the girl was socially unsuitable ('however unworthy the girl,' Claire wrote back, quoting her). Claire, while pleased to be consulted, was not helpful. She pitied her nephew, she announced in her second letter, 'and all young people of his age, whose heart is opening, who pine to expand themselves, and find insurmountable barriers placed every where'. The barrier to which she referred was, presumably, Mary herself. Happily for Mary's peace of mind, the love-affair seems to have petered out by the autumn of 1838; one can't help wondering whether she assisted it to an end. Having given much of her life to ensuring that Percy grew up to become a fitting heir to the Shelley estate, she had no intention of letting him wreck his prospects by an unsuitable alliance.

This alarm was followed by two pieces of news which would have lasting repercussions. Aubrey Beauclerk's wife Ida, visiting their Sussex estate in the spring of 1838 with her husband and young chil-dren, drowned in a pond, probably the same dark pool which can still be seen outside the hotel since built over the site of the old Beauclerk house, a mile or so from Field Place. Aubrey Beauclerk was if any-thing more appealing to Mary as a griefstricken widower than as the busy political candidate he had been when they first met. 'We shall see,' she wrote in her journal the following year. '. . . We shall see!'

The second piece of news concerned her friend Augusta Goring. 'Mrs Goring has returned to New Street,' Mary had written to Aubrey Beauclerk's brother George in March 1838. This was news which gave her pleasure, not because she thought Mrs Goring's marriage happy, but because she felt it to be preferable to the alternative. 'I rejoice at her return,' she wrote, 'for I think under all the circumstances a separation would have caused her great misery.' On 10 March, she wrote to Augusta, urging her to be 'as kind as you can to Mr Goring'. A few months later, Mrs Goring left home again and went to live south of the Thames, in the isolated village of Barnes. It took a little while for Mary to discover the reasons behind both this decision and the choice of location. It was Trelawny who had introduced Mary to Mrs Goring in 1836; Trelawny, in the summer of 1838, was living in Putney at one of the several houses there owned by his rich radical friend, Temple Leader. His home was barely five minutes' walk up the hill from Mrs Goring's new lodgings at 'the Farm'. A year later, Augusta Goring gave birth to Trelawny's son, Edgar.

A sad undated little note from Augusta to Mary, regretting that they will not be able to meet and regretting the loss of her 'kind [ ] sympathizing friend' suggests that she understood the consequences of her behaviour. Trelawny declined to be so meek. With an odd mixture of defiance and desperation, he wrote off to Claire Clairmont on 17 August 1838, urging her to come and share Mrs Goring's emancipation, living 'free as the winds'. His fury with Mary for abandoning her friend showed up in the lines which followed. She 'is the blab of blabs', he wrote of the woman whose father he had helped to bury only two years earlier: '– she lives on hogs wash – what utter failures most people are!'[38] The word 'blab' makes one wonder if Mary had been careless in talking about Mrs Goring's new life. Mary was not above gossip.

Signs of a rift had been in the air for some time. One could say that they had begun when Mary refused Trelawny the right to publish a life of Shelley. They had certainly been apparent in his attempt to bully her into publishing her father's life and in the scorn which he never hesitated to pour on her choice of friends, although he himself had never been averse to the pleasures of high society. The crux may have been Mary's refusal to admire the radical party to which he was now affiliated, and her unwillingness to contribute to an article on the rights of women which he wrote in 1838, when he was anxious to justify Augusta Goring's desertion of her husband.

We cannot know what Trelawny may have written or said to Mary during the summer when Augusta Goring decided to make her new life with him. Whatever it may have been, it hurt. A long and passionate outburst in her journal, written on 21 October 1838 from her home at Park Street, seems to have been directly prompted by Trelawny's gibes, for she alluded in it to 'the universal abuse of T—' as a prime source of discomfort and unhappiness. Most probably, he had been goading her on the tender subject of her duty, as the daughter of Mary Wollstonecraft, to speak out publicly in the cause of his new hobby-horse, women's suffrage, and, as Shelley's widow, in the cause of political reform. Attacking her, Trelawny could vent the discomfort and unease he must have felt about Augusta.

He struck a tender spot. For the first time and over many pages, Mary embarked on a long examination of what she was and what she might have been expected to become. 'I was nursed and fed with a love of glory,' she wrote. 'To be something great and good was a precept given me by my father: Shelley reiterated it.' With encouragement, she was ready to believe, she might have become what they had wished, '. . . but Shelley died & I was alone – my father from age & domestic circumstances & other things could not me faire valoir – none else noticed me.'

Solitude, poverty and shyness had prevented her from becoming the public figure she might have been; she certainly could not now imagine herself lending support to the radicals: 'rude, envious & insolent – I wish to have nothing to do with them.' Was there, then, another platform on which she could make a stand? She doubted it: 'I have not argumentative powers,' she wrote, remembering Fanny Wright's dogmatic energy.

> I see things pretty clearly, but cannot demonstrate them . . . I am far from making up my mind. I beleive that we are sent here to educate ourselves & that self denial & disappointment & self controul are a part of our education – that it is not by taking away all restraining law that our improvement is to be achieved – & though many things need *great* amendment – I can by no means go so far as my *friends* would have me.

Stung by accusations of 'worldliness' which we may again assume had come from Trelawny, Mary angrily rejected them: 'I never crouched to society,' she wrote, 'never sought it unworthily.' True, she had not written on the rights of women, but she had given them her support, 'befriended women when oppressed – at every risk I have defended & supported victims to the social system – But I do not make a boast . . . and so I am still reviled for being worldly . . . If I write the above,' she concluded, 'it is that those who love me may hereafter know that I am not all to blame – nor merit the heavy accusations cast on me for not putting myself forward – I *cannot* do that – it is against my nature – as well cast me from a precipice & rail at me for not flying.'

Her sincerity is not in doubt. Neither is her pain as she alludes to the misery she felt at discovering how Jane Hogg had betrayed her trust: it is only when she goes on to produce this as her justification for entering society, 'to divert my mind from the anguish inflicted by a friend', that the reader begins to feel a little uncomfortable. Disillusion might serve as a reason for a few months of socializing, but ten years later? The note of truth seems to be rung more clearly when Mary declares, with forgivable rage, that she hates those who oppress her, that she is writing out of irritation and that there are 'some', for which we may silently insert the name Trelawny, 'whom I would gladly never see more'.

Unkindly, the reader feels compelled to pose another question at the end of this tirade. Why, after presenting herself as the champion of oppressed women and knowing, as she did, that Mrs Goring's marriage had been a wretched one, did Mary find it beyond her to make a journey across London to visit a woman who had, for two years, been one of her closest friends? She had no difficulty in going to Putney to stay with her friend Mrs Leicester Stanhope: Barnes was equally accessible.

Trelawny's attacks were churlish and spiteful; they were not wholly unjustified. He was, presumably, much in love with Augusta Goring at this time; to see her cut off by Mary Shelley, the woman who had never stopped telling him how cruel society could be and who now seemed to have found herself a secure place in it, must have aroused feelings of indignation bordering on disgust. Mary had turned her former friend into her enemy.

CHAPTER THIRTY

REPARATION AND RENEWAL

1838–1840

'Irritability of disposition is indeed my great great fault. In the hour of struggle & action it disappears – but in inaction & solitude it frets me unworthily.
Want of animal spirits & liveliness & strength to talk & amuse has been my great
drawback in life both in society & alone. The great thing is I am unequal – If
in favourable circumstances & drawn out I am good company sometimes & am
told I am formed for society – but the cloud comes again . . .'

Mary Shelley, Journal, 21 October 1838

MARY'S RECURRING DEPRESSIONS SUGGEST ILLNESS, AND SHE WAS
living at a time when the condition was neither fully understood
nor curable. As she entered middle age, they were becoming more
pronounced.

Many of the contradictions in Mary Shelley's behaviour, her
sudden impulses towards and away from society, her yearning to be in
the centre of London, followed by sudden moves away from it, her
ability to write in the best of spirits on one day and as though death
would be welcome on the next, can be explained by her depressive
nature. But nothing distressed her more than to be drawn back into
the past.

Sir Timothy was no friend to her. He had, as recently as 1834, been
demanding that she guarantee his wife three years of peace at Field
Place after his death, instead of entering the property which would
rightfully belong to her and her son. He had ordered her to dismiss
Hogg as her occasional legal representative, on the grounds that he
was not a respectable man. (This, presumably, related to Sir Timothy's

belated discovery that Hogg lived with a woman who was not by law his wife.) He had, however unconsciously, done Mary a favour in prohibiting her from publishing her husband's works. Every time Mary began reading Shelley's poems or his letters, the old spectre of remorse was conjured up once more. To read Shelley's works was to be reminded of her coldness and lack of love, and of the horror of poor Harriet Shelley's suicide, for which she blamed herself. 'Poor Harriet,' Mary wrote on 12 February 1839, 'to whose sad fate I attribute so many of my own heavy sorrows as the atonement claimed by fate for her death.'

The time had come, however, when even Sir Timothy could not protect Mary from her strong sense of duty to the dead. In 1834, she had rejected an approach by Charles Lamb's son-in-law, Edward Moxon, for permission to publish Shelley's works. Her explanation then had been that, while believing she held the copyright through her husband's will in all his writings, she was still forbidden to do anything about them. In the summer of 1838, Moxon approached her again. By this time, at least five pirated editions of Shelley's works were in circulation. His reputation stood high; there was no longer any good reason for Sir Timothy to sustain his objections. She obtained his consent for Moxon, Tennyson's publisher, to undertake the task of producing an official four-volume collection of the works, with her editorial control and assistance. Moxon was prepared to pay £500 for the privilege, enough for Mary to move out of London again, to a house in Putney. Sir Timothy's insistence that there should still be no biography was, perhaps, a relief to his daughter-in-law; she, for her own reasons, did not want to invite the public into the murkier corners of Shelley's life.

There was a difficulty here. Moxon was ready to buy Mary's copyrights, but he was a good businessman. Many of the poems had been in print for years; to give them an additional value, he wanted Mary to provide background material. What, without breaking her promise to Sir Timothy, was she to do? Her solution was to turn back to the biographical notes she had intended to accompany her father's works. By writing extended notes of this kind to Shelley's poems and prose-works, she could provide just as much information as she chose while seeming to comply with her father-in-law's wishes. Dividing her material chronologically – 'Poems of 1820', 'Poems of 1821' – she could easily gloss over any aspects of Shelley's life which she wished to suppress.

The energy which Mary brought to the enormous undertaking – the collection of Shelley's poetry was immediately followed by his selected prose and letters and a revised second edition – was remark-able. (She was still working on the two volumes of French *Lives* until the spring of 1839.) Many of the poems had been circulated in a defective form; correcting them, she was forced to work from Shelley's untidy, faded notebooks. The writing was sometimes inde-cipherable, or made so by water damage; her mistakes often origin-ated from a difficulty with the original text. The notebooks did not run in order; she herself had to decide on the chronology and choose whether or not to include a poem which seemed incomplete, as though Shelley had already decided against it. She also had to exer-cise her own judgment in cases where, she was fairly sure, a deletion or alteration had been intended. Above all, she had to write the notes, amounting to the length of a brief biography and forcing her to con-front a past full of tormenting memories. To anyone less determined and industrious, the task might have seemed insuperable; astonish-ingly, Mary had managed to complete the manuscript for the col-lected poems, with notes, by the end of the half year in which she began work.

It was her intention to present Shelley in the best possible light. She nailed her colours to the mast in the introductory note. 'This is not the time to relate the truth; and I should reject any colouring of the truth,' she wrote in the Preface. Since the whole truth was not to be told, compromises could be made. Claire and Allegra were not men-tioned; Shelley was referred to in the singular on every occasion until the date of their marriage. *Epipsychidion* was included, but with no explanatory note; this was one of the poems which Mary noted in her journal that she would gladly have left out. Convinced that Shelley's claim to immortality would depend on his lyrical voice, she used the notes to minimize his political zeal and to stress his unworld-liness, his philanthropy, his delicate health.

The enduring value of Mary's notes is in the context they give to the poems. Biographers and critics remain gratefully dependent on her vivid and accurate descriptions of the places in which they had lived, her glimpses of Shelley dreaming under the trees at Marlow, scribbling in a boat, working in his hot little room at the top of an Italian villa, wandering through the fields. 'It was on a beautiful summer evening,' she wrote in her Note on the Poems of 1820, 'while wandering among the lanes, whose myrtle-hedges were the bowers of the fire-flies, that we heard the carolling of the sky-lark which inspired one of the most beautiful of his poems.' This was her approach, descriptive, evocative, and carefully non-specific. She gave little of Shelley's private life away.

Bitterness crept in only at the end. Concluding with 'The Dirge', the poem she had written as a lament for Shelley's death, Mary expressed dissatisfaction with her own achievement. Ill health and sadness had spread 'their sinister influence' over her notes, she wrote. Touchingly, she apologized 'for not having executed in the manner I desire the history I engaged to give of Shelley's writings'; honourably, she confessed that her recollections had been of 'deep and unforgotten joys and sorrows'. She did not pretend, as she might have done, that her memories were of undiluted happiness.[1]

Queen Mab, of which she had no original copy (her own had been left at Marlow), presented the greatest problems and stirred up the most controversy. Writing in December 1838, to Hogg, to Leigh Hunt, to Moore, to anybody she could think of who might have been supplied with an original text, Mary sought their advice as to what she should do. Richard Monckton Milnes wanted an unexpurgated text but none of the copious notes to the poem in which Shelley had been most outspoken; Moxon, anxious to protect himself, thought that the most atheistical passages of the poem should be excluded; Hogg appeared to agree with the publisher. Mary, while personally opposed to atheism and eerily convinced that Shelley '*now*' felt as she did, still shrank from the idea of publishing a mutilated text. Prudence won: the cutting of tricky passages of *Queen Mab* and a few less significant omissions were Mary's concession to Moxon. Hunt's offer to write part of the Preface with her was firmly rejected. 'The edition will be mine –' she told him on 14 December, '& though I feel my incompetencey – yet trying to make it as good as I can, I must hope [for] the best.'

Mary could hardly have supposed that her approach would win favour with everybody; the reviews were appreciative of Shelley and critical of his widow. The *Examiner* (3 February 1839) felt that she had no understanding of her husband's work; the *Spectator* (26 January 1839) spoke for many in regretting that *Queen Mab* had been published in a truncated form.* The *Athenaeum* (27 April 1839) told its readers that Mrs Shelley's selective editing and excessively concise notes were unlikely to satisfy any true admirer of Shelley's work.

This was hard to bear. It was harder still that the very friends from whom she had sought advice now weighed in with their protests. Trelawny sent his presentation copy back to Moxon with a roar at the omissions: 'How very much he must enjoy the opportunity thus

---

* The widespread awareness of Mary's omissions suggests that complete versions were already known to the authors of these critical reviews.

afforded him of doing a rude & insolent act,' Mary bitterly noted in her journal on 12 February 1839 and added that the omissions were '*almost* worthwhile . . . if only to give him this pleasure'. Hogg was angry that she had left out *Queen Mab*'s dedicatory verses to Harriet and disinclined to believe Mary's assurances that Shelley himself had governed Mary's decision. Shelley had, she recorded in her journal, expressed 'great pleasure' when an earlier edition of the poem had omitted these lines to Harriet: 'this recollection caused me to do the same – It was to do him honour.'[2] They were all, it seemed, against her; Hogg, Peacock, Trelawny, Hunt. Responding to Hogg's reproaches, Mary thanked him for his 'insinuations' and added that the 'poison' of Jane's gossip in the past should have prepared her for this second dose, as big a one as he could mix, 'for which I am proportionately obliged to you'.[3]

Indignant and hurt though she was, the accusations went home. The second one-volume edition of 1839 restored the dedication to Harriet, added two political poems and restored the omitted verses of *Queen Mab*. Mary had the gloomy satisfaction of seeing Moxon's apprehensions come true. He was prosecuted for blasphemous libel in 1841 – it was the last such case held in England – although sentence was never passed and the book remained in circulation.

'I almost think that my present occupation will end in a fit of illness . . . I am torn to pieces by Memory,' Mary wrote in wretched spirits on 12 February 1839. By the time she had settled in her new home at Putney, she was in a state of deep melancholy and exhaustion. 'Illness did ensue – what an illness – driving me to the verge of insanity,' she scribbled in her journal in March. Fortunately, Julia Robinson, always a favourite of Mary's, was able to come downriver from her family's new home on Kew Green to care for her and help to put the house in order. By April, Mary was back at her desk.

The new home on which Moxon's payments had enabled her to take a year's lease was Layton House, hideous on the outside but comfortable and easily habitable, just west of Putney High Street. Percy, recovering from another short-lived romance, one on which Mary had bestowed her blessing in February, liked it for being only a short stroll above the river, since boats now took precedence over the flute as his great obsession; Mary enjoyed living near her friends the Stanhopes, who occupied two handsome houses built on the site of old Putney Palace. The Thames, by the late 1830s, had become the sulphurous, overcrowded, sinister highway of traffic memorably depicted by Dickens in his later novels. Turning her back on it, Mary looked up at a hillside dotted with charming Palladian villas standing on small, pretty estates. London was a leisurely river journey away; as fond of walking as ever, Mary took long strolls across Barnes Common and through Richmond Park as the spring days lengthened into summer and as she felt her spirits beginning to lift. Her strolls did not, however, take her to Augusta Goring, or into the extreme Radical circles which gathered in the houses owned by the prosperous Temple Leader, where Trelawny ranted away with the best of them.

Perhaps Mary was more relieved than she admitted that her son's romance with Gertrude – her second name is not known – was over. In her journal, she wrote of Percy, now in his third year at Trinity, as a blessing to his mother. Mary Ellen Peacock was once again nudged into taking an interest, with suggestions that she might like to visit when Percy was at home or to join him and his young college friends on a boating trip. Old Henry Crabb Robinson, who had become a devoted admirer of the work of both Mary and Shelley, took a dim view of the boy. Percy was 'a loutish-looking youth', he noted after meeting him and his mother on an evening out, 'quite unworthy in his external appearance [of] his distinguished literary ancestors . . . His moral character is highly spoken of. Of his abilities,' he added ominously, 'nothing is said.'[4] Mary, too, fell silent when it came to Percy's academic achievements. In 1838, she had asked Monckton Milnes to look into the matter of getting him some private coaching.

The Robinson family were Mary's most regular visitors as she worked diligently on, preparing Shelley's essays and letters for her final volumes. Taught by her painful experiences over *Queen Mab*, she was determined to censor as little as possible. This did not mean that she was ready to publish everything. 'You see I have scratched out a few lines [of Shelley's *Essay on the Devil and Devils*] which might be *too shocking*,' she wrote to Leigh Hunt on 6 October 1839, 'and yet I hate to *mutilate*. Consider the fate of the book only . . . so many of the religious particularly like Shelley.' In the end, she did not wait for Hunt's advice but decided to defer publication; Shelley's reputation was too precious, too hard-won to be exposed to such a risk. With his translation of the *Symposium* she was ready to be bolder. Hunt was scolded for preferring the bland word 'friendship' to 'love'. The substitution, she rightly told him, simply caused confusion about the genders; besides, she wanted to keep 'as many of Shelley's *own words* as possible'.[5] Publishing the letters, however, she was selective. Leigh Hunt was urged to dig up the originals of six letters he had included in his 1828 publication, *Lord Byron and his Contemporaries*, so that she could fill up his omissions: 'why not – we wish to shew *him* not ourselves – & each word of *his is him*.'[6] This was nobly said, but when it came to publishing Shelley's letters to her father, Mary lost her nerve. Only one, a harmless epistle which gave none of the background away, was sent to Moxon.

Her Preface to Shelley's prose works, published in December 1839, provided a second opportunity for exaltation, and she took it. Shelley's only defect, she wrote, had been to die too young; granting him a faith he had never possessed, she envisaged him risen to a new 'sphere of being, better adapted to his inexpressible tenderness, his generous sympathies, and his richly gifted mind'; here those he had loved would one day join him. Heartfelt though this may have been, it was also an unabashed attempt at sanctification.

The critics, once again, liked the works better than the editing. 'The Examiner was *really* good – *very* – the Athenaeum creditable,' Mary wrote to Moxon on 19 December. In fact, neither of these reviewers had praised Mary's work, and the *Spectator*, with which she was less pleased, had regretted that her own taste appeared to lean towards 'the weakest and most defective parts of his [Shelley's] mind' (14 December 1839). The editor, Mary tartly exclaimed to Moxon, must be 'both a goose and a coxcomb'.*

Leigh Hunt had become a staunch ally in the editorial process, even though Mary did not always agree with his views. Their friendship had faded after Hunt's move to Chelsea; now, while he offered encouragement and suggestions, sometimes rather more than Mary wished for, she deluged him with enthusiastic and encouraging notes about his play, *A Legend of Florence*, due to open in February 1840. Hunt, despite his long career as a theatre reviewer, had never been lucky with his dramas and *A Legend* had already been turned down elsewhere before shrewd Madame Vestris took it for Covent Garden; he was very nervous. 'My fair friends are full of resolution that it *shall* succeed – and I know that it *will*,' Mary reassured him a week before the opening.[8] Three weeks later, she had seen it, read it and was planning to go again. 'Adieu dear successful Dramatic-Poet,' she signed off a letter which informed him that his work was full of 'all the loveliest things of this (when you write about it) lovely world'.[9]† Percy, a young man of few

---

* Another hostile review, on which Mary made no comment, appeared in *The Table Talker, or Brief Essays on Society and Literature* (1840). Here, Mary was criticized for having allowed her own infatuation with Shelley to interfere with her editorial task, and for having produced an incoherent and disappointing collection of the prose.[7]

† Queen Victoria shared her view; writing his autobiography some years later, Hunt proudly remembered that the Queen saw the play four times and then requested it to be privately performed for her again at Windsor.[10]

words, added his own congratulations to Mary's next note: 'Percy says: "Make great thanks to Hunt for his play. I like it very much."'[11]

A less agreeable correspondence with Hunt took place just before the Christmas of 1839, when he sent her a letter from a would-be biographer of Shelley. George Henry Lewes was only twenty-two and his wife Agnes had not yet embarked – with Lewes's approval – on her fruitful partnership with Hunt's eldest son. Perhaps Mary was unaware that Lewes's biography was already partly written and that it had been advertised in four successive editions of the *National Magazine and Monthly Critic* in 1838. Perhaps word had reached her that he was a man of raffish reputation and with progressive views. She brusquely turned down his request for an interview; Hunt was asked to tell the young man that she would not permit a biography.* If anybody was to do it, she would, she wrote, but 'the reasons that prevent me & will prevent me are so tragical – that I could never bring myself to converse on them to my nearest friend – & to a stranger it is quite out of the question.'

It was in this letter to Hunt that Mary was most revealing about the emotional torture she had suffered while working her way through Shelley's poems and letters, some of them for the first time:

> Time may flow on – but it only adds to the keenness & vividness with which I view the past – adds, how much: for when tragedies & most bitter dramas were in the course of acting I did not feel their meaning & their consequences as poignantly as I now do – I cannot write or speak of Shelley to any purpose according to my views without taking a seal from a fountain, that I cannot bring myself yet to let flow.[13]

There were too many things that only she knew, only she could say; even thinking about them plunged her into despair. Mary's reluctance to make revelations did not spring simply from a wish to protect Shelley's reputation, but from knowing how miserable she felt whenever she was forced to remember the past. She did not understand her depressions; she knew that certain things caused them and that those things were better left alone. Nothing, in her experience, affected her more than to confront the chilly, white-faced ghost of herself as she

---

* Lewes's interest in Shelley had drawn him to the family of Leigh Hunt; he and Thornton, Hunt's eldest son, edited the *Leader* together and used its pages to promote Shelley's reputation. Refused permission to continue work on his biography, he used some of the material in two lengthy essays, published in 1841 in the *Penny Cyclopaedia* and the *Westminster Review*.[12] Lewes later became the partner of Marian Evans (George Eliot). His enthusiasm for Shelley never diminished.

was after the deaths of Clara and William; to see herself through Shelley's own unhappy eyes. She was guilty enough, God knew; why must she acknowledge it to strangers, be judged again when none had ever judged her more harshly than she did herself?

If the past could still cause her piercing unhappiness as she read of Shelley's feelings during the bleak months in Naples when he had, perhaps, attempted to adopt a child to compensate for her losses, the present offered hope, and even love. The few poems which Mary wrote in 1838–9 were all on the theme of the healing power of love. On 27 November 1839, she expanded on this theme in her journal:

> Another hope – Can I have another hope? A friendship secure helpful – enduring – a union with a generous heart – & yet a suffering one whom I may comfort & bless – if it be so I am happy indeed . . . I can indeed confide in A's inalterable gentleness & affection . . . but will not events place us asunder – & prevent me from being a comfort to him – he from being the prop on which I may lean – We shall see – If I can impart any permanent pleasure to his now blighted existence, & revivify it through the force of sincere & disinterested attachment – I shall be happy.

Mary's allusions to 'A' and 'his now blighted existence' and to a love she hopes to 'revivify' make it clear that she was thinking of Aubrey Beauclerk.

Mary had stayed on affectionate terms with all the Beauclerk family; it must have been only a question of time before she would meet Aubrey again as a widower with four young children, who had now abandoned his political career to look after his estates in Sussex and Ireland. It seems strange that she should so easily have forgiven a man who had already let her down, but unhappiness was always a magnet for Mary's sympathy. While comforting Beauclerk, she was also caring for another friend. Colonel Jeremiah Ratcliffe, a cultivated and entertaining man with a fine singing voice and high hopes of being made chief Equerry to the newly married Prince Albert, may originally have met Mary through Augusta Goring, who knew him at least as early as 1837. In early March 1840, Ratcliffe was involved – he had seconded the challenger – in a duel between his friend Captain Léon, an illegitimate son of Napoleon, and Léon's cousin, the future Napoleon III. The duel on Wimbledon Common was stopped by the police (duelling was then, as now, technically unlawful, although no statute forbade it) but the story was taken up in the papers and Ratcliffe was widely condemned for his involvement. On 12 March, the *Gazette de France* reported that Ratcliffe had been confined on grounds of insanity.

Mary had been closely involved in these events. The non-duel took place on 3 March. On 5 March, she noted cryptically: 'Ratcliffe taken ill.' Five days later, she confided to Jane Hogg that she had been 'engaged & absorbed by the distress of a friend (no one you know) you know it is my Star to have unfortunate friends.' There was, however, little she could do for poor Ratcliffe after he had been placed in a private asylum, except to defend him to her friends. Thomas Moore had, by 7 April, received a letter from Mary which has not survived but in which she had evidently done her best to present his behaviour in a favourable light. 'Your account of him interested us all very much,' Moore wrote back.

Mary had, as she frankly admitted to Moxon, felt little inclination to write professionally since completing the Shelley editions; the task, although rewarding, had exhausted her. She had moved into temporary lodgings at Richmond in the spring of 1840 after the termination of her year's lease on Layton House at Putney. Confronting the long summer vacation of 1840 and hearing that Percy was planning to spend it in Europe with a couple of fellow undergraduates, she decided that the change and a little adventure would do her good. It was, besides, unthinkable that her son should go abroad without her; Mary found it impossible to imagine that a strapping nineteen-year-old would be able to take care of himself on such a trip. Percy, no youthful rebel, was agreeable to the plan. They determined to sail for France on 13 June.

Sitting on a Brighton balcony a fortnight before their departure, Mary fell under the spell of a moonlit evening and allowed herself to dream of love. 'Amore redivivus' was the heading she chose for her long journal entry of 1 June. Dwelling on the renewing power of love, she thought of Aubrey Beauclerk, and of her good fortune in having a cheerful, affectionate son, who considered it delightful that his mother should accompany him instead of sitting sadly alone at Richmond. 'If I could restore health – administer balm to the wounded heart and banish care from those I love –' she wrote, 'I were in myself happy, while I am loved – and Percy continues the blessing that he is.

Still who on such a night must not feel the weight of sorrow lessened –
For myself I repose in gentle & grateful reverie – & hope for others –

& am content for myself. Years have – how much! cooled the ardent & swift spirit that at such hours bore me freely along. My health impaired by a thousand mental sufferings has cast chains on my soul – Yet though I no longer soar, – I repose – though I no longer deem all things attainable – I enjoy what is – & while I feel that I have, whatever I have lost of youth & hope – acquired the enduring affection of a noble heart – & Percy shews such excellent disposition I feel that I am much the gainer in life.

A little guiltily, Mary compared her own new-found serenity to the wretchedness of poor Jeremiah Ratcliffe, bewildered, friendless and mad: not all private asylums were as civilized as those in which Mary Lamb had allowed herself to be confined from time to time. 'Poor R—' she wrote. '. . . God restore him. God & good angels guard us!'

At peace with herself as she reflected on all that she had done for Shelley in the past two years, Mary toyed with the idea that her labours might have been influenced by the benevolent spirits of the dead. 'Such surely,' she mused, 'gather round one on such an evening, & make part of that atmosphere of love, so hushed, so soft, on which the soul reposes & is blessed.'[14]

CONTINENTAL RAMBLES

1840–1844

'I had thought such ecstacy as that in which I now was lapped dead to me for ever; but the sun of Italy has thawed the frozen stream – the cup of life again sparkles to the brim.'

Mary Shelley, *Rambles in Germany and Italy* (1844)[1]

THE POSITIONS OF THE STEPSISTERS HAD BEEN REVERSED. CLAIRE, as her mother became increasingly incapacitated, went to share the rooms to which Mrs Godwin had moved in shabby Golden Square. Here, the eighteenth-century homes of dead aristocrats had recently come to life again as boarding-houses for the musicians who earned just enough in theatre orchestras to cover rent, meals and cigars. Dickens, taking the square as a setting for Ralph Nickleby's home, wrote of a mournful statue standing guard over a wilderness of shrubs, of swarthy gentlemen smoking at the open windows, of singers from the Opera chorus practising their airs over tinny pianos. It was a world into which Mary had managed never quite to fall, and she stayed away. 'I never see Claire,' she wrote in March 1840 as she began preparing for her continental tour. But Claire's ability to sting her conscience had not diminished. Her health was terrible, she announced that autumn. Her mind was in danger of going. Her whole day was spent rushing from one side of London to the other giving lessons, from Knightsbridge to Richmond. 'That vile Omnibus takes two hours to get to Richmond and the same to come back and so with giving my lessons I am never at home before seven – I get no dinner – nothing within my lips from eight in the morning till seven at night – then the rain fog and cold of this month – I am nearly done for . . .'[2]

Claire had been saying that she was done for almost as long as Mary could remember. Still, the contrast in their present lives was undeniable. 'My birthday – I have felt particularly happy & in good spirits today,' Mary wrote in her journal on 30 August, two months into her holiday. After joining Percy's undergraduate friends, George Defell and Julian, the youngest of Joshua Robinson's sons, at Paris (Robert Leslie Ellis, a brilliant young mathematician, met up with them at a later stage), they had travelled with Mary's maid across France to Coblenz. In 1814, hurrying home with empty pockets from their jaunt to Switzerland, she, Shelley and Claire had travelled north up the Rhine; in 1840, the tourists went south.

Germany had not charmed Mary when she was sixteen; she liked the landscape better now, but the fact that none of the party spoke the language was a drawback. Lack of comprehension had the merit of drawing the companions closer together; at Baden-Baden, however, Mary's age was marked by their disparate reactions. She had not been feeling well during the long journey; the spa's gentle valley offered an invitation to rest. Nothing, to Percy and his friends, could have seemed duller; and nothing, when she reflected on her eagerness to get to Italy, odder to Mary herself than this inclination to dally in a genteel resort when she loved travelling so much. She was, as she readily admitted to herself, looking for excuses to distract the boys from their choice of Lake Como, notorious for squalls and shipwrecks, as the ideal spot in which to settle and revise for their finals. Percy, to his mother's dismay, was already talking of buying a boat there; the past seemed doomed to repeat itself. Her love for Percy was never stronger than when she feared to lose him.

The return to Italy was something she had been imagining and planning for years. Initially, however, the experience was traumatic. She was happy to be praised by the young men for the ease with which she spoke the language; she was startled by the pain, 'amounting almost to agony', which the sight of ordinary objects, window-curtains, the washstand in an inn bedroom, could provoke. The pain was in their familiarity; she felt as if time had pulled her back. She was twenty again, on the brink of life; but the twenty-year-old stood in the shoes of a middle-aged woman whose head had begun, sometimes, to throb so violently that she stood paralysed, or found herself racked by convulsive shudders. She had known illness before, but this was something new and frightening. Work on the collected edition of her husband's works had affected her health, but these new symptoms marked the onset of meningioma, a disease of the brain which would, eleven years later, destroy her.

Como, despite Mary's initial terror of a sailing accident on the lake, calmed her spirits. She looked nostalgically at the Villa Pliniana which she and Shelley had once planned to share with Byron, took out her embroidery, chatted to their fellow guests at the lakeside hotel and wrote a long account of their travels to her aunt Everina Wollstone-craft in her Pentonville lodgings. It was an act of kindness to a crippled old lady whose only journey out of England had been across the Irish Sea; it was also a practical way of recording material for use if she ever wrote another book.

Sitting on the shore at sunset like one of the wistful Gulnares and Rosabellas whose portraits adorned the ladies' annuals, Mary thought about Aubrey Beauclerk, 'his sorrows – his passionate love – his struggles – & how hemmed in & impotent are our powers of sympathy & communication – tears rushed into my eyes.' It was presumably a letter from Aubrey that she was hoping to receive when she made a further private note on the same August day. The mail boat had arrived at the hotel, bringing nothing for her: 'Niente.'[3]

Invitations came from Laura Galloni, Mrs Mason's elder daughter, to visit Venice, where her disagreeable husband was in the French consulate. The prospect of seeing Laura again was tempting, but shortage of money ruled out this extension of the trip. At Milan, much to Mary's distress, Percy left her to return to Cambridge for his finals. Alone with her maid, she decided to pay a return visit, to Geneva, and from there went on slowly by the diligence coach to Paris. Here Aubrey's brother Charles had put his apartment on the elegant rue de la Paix at her service.

Paris had been on Mary's agenda from the first moment of planning an escape from England. Her old friends Lord and Lady Canterbury were there;* Lamartine, an admirer of Shelley's poetry, made arrangements to call on her; Sainte-Beuve, a new acquaintance, was easy and affable. She kept her thoughts to herself after meeting Byron's friend Scrope Davies, who had taken the gentleman's way out of paying his bills in 1820 by moving to France. Later, Mary told

---

* Charles Manners-Sutton had been created Baron Bottesford and Viscount Canterbury in March 1835, to enable him to enter the House of Lords after losing the re-election to his post as Speaker of the House of Commons through, it was commonly agreed, some rather underhand political manoeuvring by the Whigs. 'Nothing can be so shabby as the conduct of the Whigs – to have elected him when they wanted him – to oppose him when it is policy – this is factious in the extreme,' Mary had noted in her journal on 13 February 1834.

Claire that Harriet de Boinville and her large family had been no more than civil, but a warm letter written to Mrs de Boinville shortly after the visit dwelling on the 'happy hours' spent with them all – 'I should *so* like to see you all again' – does not suggest that they had been unwelcoming.[4]

Friendliest of all was Rogers's friend, Richard Monckton Milnes, who was staying in splendour at the Hôtel Meurice. Mary praised his third collection of – not very good – poems; Milnes returned the compliment by making himself her sightseeing companion, showing his comparative youth – he was just thirty – by his eagerness to walk when she preferred to be driven. Visiting art collections, watching, with some sympathy, as King Louis Philippe burst into tears while describing to the hastily convened Chamber of Deputies how an armed man had fired at the royal carriage in the Tuileries, shivering amid the well-muffled crowd gathered outside Les Invalides to see Napoleon's corpse being given a state funeral twenty years after his death, Mary whiled away the time, putting off her return to smoky, fog-drenched London.

'I was not well in Paris – the detestable climate did not agree with me,' she wrote to Milnes's clever lawyer friend, Abraham Hayward, on 14 January 1841. She did not know him well enough to reveal more. A cruel shock had been waiting for her in Paris, delivered with apparent insouciance in a letter from Claire.

The Robinsons had asked her to visit them at Kew, Claire wrote on 30 October. It turned out that they had a piece of news to deliver: Rosa Robinson was going to marry Aubrey Beauclerk. Why such a pretty girl should settle for a gloomy middle-aged widower, Claire could not begin to imagine. Still, she brightly rattled on, his children would have a new mother, Rosa would have money, something the Robinson girls had always lacked, and Mary would be able to stop worrying about them. 'All your acquaintances are glad that you will no longer have to maintain any body but yourself and Percy, though they honour you for the generosity with which you have ever acted towards them.'

It is hard to guess how much Claire knew, but the letter has a slightly artificial tone, as though she was willing Mary to accept the situation with a graceful smile. 'All your acquaintances are glad': how, faced with that, could Mary do anything but meekly assent? Rosa was attractive and, like all the Robinson girls, amusing; why should Aubrey have preferred to unite himself to a low-spirited widow of forty-three? How could she have imagined that he was anything more than grateful for her friendship and sympathy after Ida's tragic death?

Worse news lay ahead. The following year, and again with seeming casualness, Claire reported another choice morsel. Julia, Mary's favourite of the Robinson sisters, was now saying that their friendship with her had been the ruin of her family; Mary's own dreadful reputation had, according to Julia, wrecked their chances of social success.[5]

On 26 February 1841, back in London, Mary made a long wretched entry in her journal. 'I gave all the treasure of my heart; all was accepted readily – & more & more asked – & when more I could not give – behold me betrayed, deserted; fearfully betrayed so that I wd rather die than any of them more' – she broke off in mid-sentence, overcome by her feelings. These were the last words of her own to be written in the journals she had begun with Shelley in 1814, in the summer of their elopement.

The hurt was greater when she remembered all that she had done for the Robinsons. When young Charles had decided to seek his fortune in Australia in the summer of 1839, she had written to Elizabeth Berry, her Wollstonecraft cousin who lived in New South Wales and who, as the wife of a wealthy businessman and landowner, might be able to help him.* She had asked Julia and Rosa to every party she had given, introduced them to every new friend she found, shared her life with them, denied them, so far as she knew, nothing. And yet three sisters, Isabel, Rosa and Julia, had all in their different ways betrayed her.

Mary remained, to her credit, on affectionate terms with Aubrey and Rosa, with Julian, her son's close friend, and with Charles, who returned to England in 1846, after failing to make his way in Australia. Julia's spite continued to sting her as painfully as salt on an open wound. Writing to Claire on 16 August 1842, she claimed that it was she who had 'burst away' from the clinging Robinsons '– & they could not forgive me'. On 1 October, still smarting, she told Claire that Julia's gossip 'utterly prevents my ever associating with her again on terms of friendship – poor thing – what benefit can she see in covering the truth with false tinsel – one cannot guess – but it is nature with some people.' Percy had 'rather a prejudice against her', she added, but this was by the by.

---

* Elizabeth Wollstonecraft, Mary's first cousin, had gone to Australia in 1819 as the wife of her brother Edward's business partner, Alexander Berry. The friendship begun between the cousins in the 1830s through a shared obligation to care for Everina, their only surviving aunt, was maintained by Alexander Berry and Mary after his wife's death in 1845.[6]

There was not much comfort to be taken from the poky new rooms Mary found in 1841 opposite her former lodgings in Park Street, presumably because she wished to keep a good address. (Mayfair, in a period when massive building development caused areas to rise and fall faster than a lady's fashion-conscious waistline, held its own.) Nor could she take much pride in the fact that Percy had scraped through his exams at the lowly level of a 'pass'. Sir Timothy, who remained 'excessively well', was the only and unexpected source of pleasure, when he announced in February that he intended to mark his grandson's twenty-first birthday by presenting him with a personal annual gift of £400 a year.

The news enabled mother and son to contemplate making another journey to the Continent, a prospect which raised Mary's spirits. Wistfully, she dreamed of visiting Egypt, or Sicily, or even Greece, where her old friend Prince Mavrocordato was, for a brief period, Prime Minister. Escape, she fancied, might be a form of renewal, a return to a period which was bathed in a radiant afterglow, as if it had been all happiness: 'what days might pass,' she wrote wistfully in her last, long journal entry of 26 February 1841; 'what hours flow on, radiant with good spirits – teeming with glowing images . . . Then I might live – as once I lived – hoping – loving – aspiring enjoying –'

In the meantime, while Aunt Everina was still able to enjoy a visit and an occasional outing, old Mary Jane Godwin declined, lingered, and finally expired in June. 'Poor Mrs Godwin!' Mary decorously wrote to her cousin Elizabeth in Australia. 'It seemed strange that so restless a spirit could be hushed, & all that remained pent up in a grave.'[7] It was the most, without being hypocritical, that she could bring herself to say to a relation who had no knowledge of her feelings about her stepmother.

Claire, thankful to be released from filial duties, returned to Paris and, helped by the gift of £100 from Mary, announced that she would be staying there. Her reluctance to hand over the letter-filled writing-desk which had passed to her mother after Godwin's death should have given Mary a hint that Claire was a good deal more interested in the history of the family, where it touched upon herself, than she pretended. As time went on, Claire became an obsessive hoarder of correspondence. Mary's letters, however hard she begged for them to be burned, were squirrelled away; Mrs Godwin's were taken out and subjected to copious rewriting for the benefit of posterity.

Mary had moved house once again, to lodgings in Half Moon Street, off Piccadilly, just before her stepmother's death. She was spending a wet summer in North Wales when she read the accounts of Moxon's trial for blasphemy following the publication of *Queen Mab* in Mary's 1839 collected edition. Sergeant Noon Talfourd's speech, in which he movingly argued that the poem represented a stage in the development of Shelley's essentially Christian outlook, had not convinced the jury, but though found guilty, the publisher was subjected to no further penalty and the bolder second edition of the *Poetical Works* remained on sale. It was not, however, with the idea of further publication that Mary now quietly set about retrieving the most potentially explosive of her husband's letters. She had already obtained a loan of all the Gisborne correspondence from their housekeeper in Plymouth. Shelley had been writing to Southey, she knew, in the dangerous year of Elena Adelaide's arrival; Margaret Mason had been one of his chief confidantes; the letters to her father, tucked away in the missing writing-desk, revealed how she and Shelley had defied him in 1814. Protection, not publication, was her aim.

The effects of a twenty-first birthday were wonderful to behold. Timothy Shelley had already announced his financial acknowledgment of the event. Ianthe Shelley, now Mrs Esdaile, invited her young half-brother to spend a fortnight in Somerset in the spring of 1842, an experience which he endured with resignation. (Claire heard from Mary that he had found the Esdailes 'kind & good – but somewhat underbred & not a little bigotted & over pious'.[8]) The Shelleys, not to be outdone, issued invitations to Field Place. Percy, much to Mary's relief, was given a warm welcome by his grandfather; his aunt Hellen, a more temperamental character, flew into a rage when she suspected Percy first of usurping herself and her sister in their father's affections, and then of insufficient gratitude for the social introductions she was good enough to offer. Ianthe had warned Percy that all the Shelleys had dreadful tempers, Mary confided to Claire; still, it was a pity that he was so reluctant to belong to the '"World" – I wish indeed that he did take pleasure in good society – but being angry & scolding him violently will not render it more pleasing to him.'[9]

Percy was always the anxious theme of Mary's letters. How, when he remained so shy and awkward, was he ever to meet anybody? She had ached for a loving daughter after the loss of her own; Percy's wife, if only she could be found, would be her compensation.

Percy, conspicuously failing to find an appropriate bride, remained wedded to boats. In May 1842, Mary was obliged to resign herself to a month at the yachting haven of Cowes, on the Isle of Wight; in June, they spent a pleasant week at nearby Exbury. Rented by a Squire Brett from friends of Gee Paul, Exbury became a favourite visiting place for Mary, a glimpse into the world in which, had the Shelleys shown more kindness, she might have been allowed to lead a happy life. Here, she could sit out on the lawn and look across the Solent, take afternoon drives into the local villages or exclaim with her fellow guests at the courage of the Queen in driving out with her husband just after a botched attack on her life. Victoria was, Mary thought admiringly, 'a brave little thing'.[10]

Mary's sleepy, happy weeks at Exbury and her words of admiration for the Queen mark the distance she had travelled since the impetuous days of her life with Shelley. Victoria was presiding over the biggest colonial and industrial power in the world at a time of singularly ugly social divisions. Shelley, it seems fair to guess, would have matched the outrage of Dickens in *Hard Times* at England's embrace of a chilly utilitarianism which afforded the poor little but the option of voluntary transportation or death of disease or exhaustion. Mary, worn down by years of poverty and social ostracism, was ready to compromise. She would always exert herself in the cause of Italy's freedom from Austrian domination; the social injustices at home which were now being exposed and challenged in the novels of Dickens rated no more than occasional asides in the long letters she conscientiously wrote to Claire, to Elizabeth Berry, to Jane Hogg.

Reform on a large scale was something which Mary was ready to leave to others. Her own chosen contribution to society was, while on a more modest scale, often absurdly generous. Now, as she drew up her plans for a leisurely fourteen-month tour of Europe with her son, she proposed to cover all the travelling expenses of a clever but poor young man called Alexander Knox who had spent much of the summer in her company and who she felt would benefit from such an experience.

It may have been Robert Leslie Ellis, the brilliant young mathematician who once again joined the tourists at a later stage, who guessed that Mary would be enchanted by Knox. Mary's letters show that Percy had only a slight acquaintance with him when they planned the trip. Knox had suffered a breakdown at university in 1841.[11] Ill health, a fondness for writing poetry and lack of money only added to his charms for Mary; 'he is completely incapable of exertion from the tendency to complaint of the heart,' she wrote to Claire from Exbury, adding that Knox's company would be 'a great good for Percy, & for me too'.[12] Knox was socially graceful, able to fit in anywhere. Secretly, she hoped that some of his easy manners would rub off on her dear but depressingly uncouth son.

A few days spent in London before their June departure gave Mary the chance to catch up with Jane Hogg's flurried life. Still a beauty and bored of old 'Dah' – Hogg and she had been 'Mamma' and 'Dah' to each other since the deaths of their parents – Jane had been conducting an indiscreet flirtation with her handsome nephew. Her frantic efforts to hide the fact that her daughter Dina was about to become an unmarried mother seemed, in the circumstances, rather hypocritical, but the father, Leigh Hunt's son, Henry, was not Jane's idea of a suitable husband, being both poor and sexually promiscuous. Her own miserable early marriage had been a harsh education: a bad husband, in Jane's view, was worse than none. Mary, listening to her angry outpourings on the subject of ungrateful daughters, agreed that a short visit to Claire in Paris might be the answer when Dina's baby was born.

The arrangement was eerily close to that made for Isabel Robinson in 1827 at the time when Isabel had disclosed Jane's treachery. Kinder and more discreet, Mary kept Jane's family scandals to herself. Revenge had never interested her.

Jane Hogg's dramas followed Mary abroad as Claire sent transfixing reports of a household seething with resentment, of Jane's love-affair with her nephew having provoked Jefferson Hogg to paroxysms of jealousy, and of an increasingly savage relationship between mother and daughter.

The second tour was not proving to be the rest-cure Mary had hoped for. The heat, when they reached Dresden, was unbearable. 'O the heat – the heat! It is overwhelming – I never felt any thing like it before,' she wailed to Claire on 16 August. Everything seemed unsatisfactory. Knox's expenses were draining her funds, although she was sure that the play he was writing would bring rewards one day. The people all seemed ugly, ill-dressed and dirty. Henry Hugo Pearson, a tall, strange-looking friend of Knox's who had already set several of Shelley's poems to music (Vincent Novello published them), had joined their party and pleased her by offering to harmonize one of her own romantic songs, 'O listen while I sing to thee'.* Pearson was, however, annoyingly reluctant to introduce them to the

---

* The song is dated as having been composed on 12 March 1838, which limits the possibility of giving it an autobiographical reading since Ida Beauclerk was still alive and Mary had no other man – or woman – in her life at that time, or none she chose to acknowledge.

interesting people he claimed to know. As a result, Mary found herself surrounded by bores.

Once settled into comfortable lodgings on the Grand Canal in Venice, they had the benefit of Laura Galloni's large circle of friends. Claire, who heard little but grumbles from Dresden, Prague and Salzburg, was told instead of leisurely morning promenades in St Mark's, of meals with Monckton Milnes who told her that Trelawny had grown dirty and morose, chopping wood all day on Putney common while his mistress cared for their child. Percy was taking lessons on the trumpet, Mary reported; as for herself, she was having her work cut out with two young invalids to care for – Pearson also had a heart complaint – and both, in their different ways, such tricky characters. Pearson had a quick, explosive temper and no understanding of money; Knox was 'proud & sensitive to a fault'. Clever though they both were, their highly strung natures gave her reason to congratulate herself on her son's calm stolidity. Occasionally, Mary felt a twinge of guilt at the knowledge of how much of his money had gone on caring for 'poor dear Knox'. Still, the cause was a good one; she had faith in Knox's brilliance and she remained confident that his company would benefit her son.[13]

Writing up her journey later for publication, Mary played heavily on the melancholy associations evoked by Venice; the letters suggest that her sadness had been short-lived. There had been so much to do, so many people to meet. Company, as she had known when she urged Knox to join them, was always her best defence against grief. Exhausting though it was looking after three young men, two of whom were often extremely demanding, she was never alone.

Settled in Florence for the opening of 1843, at lodgings near the Ponte Vecchio, Mary lapsed into gloom again. Everything had gone wrong. Pearson, resentful of her preference for Knox, had gone off in a temper. Percy had also taken against Knox and was refusing to socialize. Gee Paul had written a silly, skittish letter inquiring about her plans to marry Knox. There was a kind of condescension in Laura Galloni's manner which made it hard to believe that her friendship was sincere.

Mary's own ill health and a depression may well have contributed to the bad feeling which led Pearson to abandon the party. Her letters sound wretched. Laura's nieces and nephews were dismissed as plebeians; the weather was dreadful; their funds were always low. She was cut to the quick when the new Lord Holland, a prominent figure in Florence's social world, refused to be friendly. Her only moment of satisfaction was a brief encounter with Mrs Hoppner which enabled her, just for once, to be vengeful enough to turn her back.

She had searched for Clara's burial place on the Lido in Venice; in Rome, staying on the airy Via Sistina in rooms next to those where Amelia Curran had once lived, she made a pilgrimage to the Protestant cemetery. It was the first time Mary had seen where Shelley's ashes were buried, lying in the shadow of Trelawny's row of young cypresses. But William's grave, to her great distress, was impossible to locate. Like Clara, he was erased, as if he had never existed. There was peculiar pain for a mother in this discovery.

Mary had always loved Rome. Even the appearance of a comet, judged by the Romans to be a warning of evil to come, did not alarm her. Percy, now that Knox had moved out to different lodgings, seemed happy again. In retrospect, she decided that Mrs Mason's daughters meant well enough and suffered only from a lack of exercise. Walking would do wonders for their spirits, announced Mary, whose vigorous explorations had reduced her to bandaging up her aching feet with corn-plasters. Percy flatly refused to be dragged around any more galleries, but his place had been taken by Alexis Rio, a French art critic whose work she had read a decade earlier and whom she had met at one of Rogers's social breakfasts. Rio was her chosen escort and interpreter of art, while his wife, 'a dear good unaffected privitive [sic] Xtian (a pious Catholic)', became Mary's favourite sightseeing companion as she revisited the massive excavated sites. 'I enjoy myself extremely,' she told Claire on 15 April 1843, while continuing to regret Percy's lack of interest in Roman culture. There was no cause for sorrow in the news that Aunt Everina Wollstonecraft, rotting angrily away in a house which she refused to have cleaned, had finally surrendered to a stroke. Dutifully regretful to her fellow niece, Elizabeth Berry, Mary was more candid with Claire, tartly commenting that the wretched old woman had died of 'natural decay aided by her determination to do nothing she was told'.[14] She did not dispute Everina's right to be buried near her sister Mary in the increasingly derelict graveyard at St Pancras.

Memories had tormented Mary less than she anticipated on the journey but when, at the beginning of May, they travelled south again to Sorrento, the view of the bay drew her thoughts back to the last month at Lerici and the horror of the final days there. Percy, desperate to see a remarkable flying machine which was on display in London and a little tired of his mother's attempts to enrich his mind, was ready for England and even for another visit to his stiff relations at Field Place. Mary, uninvited, began making plans for an end-of-summer holiday with Knox. Perhaps, with the opening of a new railroad, they could travel to the Loire valley, or the Rhine, or to one of the French seaside towns or . . . She was still lost in plans when Knox's aunt, on whom he was financially dependent and with whom Mary had stored her furniture while she was on her travels, unexpectedly died.

Poor Knox! Mary wrote to Jane Hogg, not aware of how unsuitably enamoured of the young man she sounded, or of the conclusions her friends were beginning to draw. What was he to do now, with no money and no certain future? It seemed so unfair that young Julian Robinson had married a rich clergyman's daughter while Percy – 'never was anyone so kind & considerate & good' – and Knox remained unattached and 'poor as rats'.[15] There was nothing to be done: home they must go. 'Oh to leave a Paradise –' she wailed to Claire, 'at this moment of loveliness to travel scant of money I know not whither.'[16] Being abroad and penniless had been a thrilling challenge when she was sixteen; at forty-five, the prospect held no charm.

Ever since the previous autumn of 1842, Mary had been urging Claire to join their party; it was unfortunate that she decided to take up this invitation just before Mary had to alter her own plans. Conscious of the disappointment Claire must be feeling, she resolved to make amends by spending August in Paris with her stepsister. The decision, although kindly made, would have unfortunate consequences.

ENTER, THE ITALIANS

1843–1844

'Poor Gatteschi . . . He is mad to join the insurgents in Bologna – and I do not wonder – It is more manly & natural to desire to be in arms & in danger than to be dragging out the miserable life he leads at Paris. I gather from what he says joined to what you tell me that he thinks that he cannot leave Paris with honour while in debt – Poor fellow – for how much better a lot he was made . . . my plan is to make a volume & make a £100 if possible by it for him . . .'

Mary Shelley to Claire Clairmont, 20 September 1843

PARIS IN THE 1840S WAS A POLYGLOT CITY TO WHICH, ALONG with several of the Russian families Claire had known in Moscow, came the Italians whose country was still largely occupied by Austrian troops and controlled from Vienna. Most of these Italians were supporters of Giuseppe Mazzini. Exiled as a dangerous manipulator of anti-conservative feelings, Mazzini had succeeded in giving coherence where there had been only confusion, and in accelerating the process of rebellion. Some sixty thousand patriots had joined his 'Young Italy' movement by 1833, calling for liberation from the foreign rulers and the formation of an independent republic. In 1837, Mazzini had moved to London, where he was perceived as a romantic hero. His connection to the secretive world of the carbonari, from which Young Italy had recruited its hard core of troops, enhanced his Byronic image. Any mention of spies and plots was sure to lead to Mazzini's name; an Italian abroad had only to keep a couple of canaries and look mysterious to be identified as one of Mazzini's conspirators.

Neither Mary nor Claire were impervious to the romance of secret societies; in 1814 both of them had eagerly devoured stories of Adam Weishaupt and the society of the Illuminati. Mary's months in Italy made her unusually responsive to the impoverished Italian exiles who talked of rescuing their country from its foreign overlords. The de Boinville family may have provided the initial introductions (Harriet de Boinville's widowed daughter Cornelia would later form a relationship with one of the Ruffini family who were Mazzini's closest Italian friends). However the connection occurred, Mary was introduced during her month in Paris to a group who had close affiliations with the Young Italy movement. Among them were a married couple from Corsica by the name of Guitera, Carlo Romano, a Count Martini and an unusually handsome would-be-writer employed by him. This was Ferdinando Gatteschi.

Mary, with her weakness for clever, unfortunate young men, had seldom met one whose need seemed so poignant as Gatteschi's. Admiring, chivalrous and respectful, he spoke with passion of the Italian cause, of his literary ambitions, of his own wretchedness – and of his need for money. Hints of an aristocratic past did no harm to his cause, especially as Shelley's patrician status had recently been enhanced by the revelation of links between him and Sir Philip Sidney.* Borrowing 200 francs from Claire, Mary insisted that the money must go to their new friend. 'I am very anxious to hear whether you sent to that poor Unfortunate Gatteschi –' she wrote as soon as she reached London; 'pray let me know – I will pay you faithfully that & all else of money . . . as soon as I can.'[1]

Before leaving Paris towards the end of August 1843, she had promised Gatteschi that she would find him a publisher in England. By 27 September, Mary was ready to tell Edward Moxon that she was writing up an account of her travels. Work was proceeding fast but she wanted money, she admitted, not for herself, but 'for a purpose most urgent & desirable'. A month later, she offered to sell him the

---

* It would be intriguing to know if Mary helped to start this particular hare. William Howitt's *Visits to Remarkable Places* (1840) is the first in print to make the connection between Shelley and the Sidneys of Penshurst Place; the *Monthly Chronicle* picked up the connection in reviewing Howitt's book in February 1840. Three months later, a writer for the *Cambridge University Magazine* produced an essay on 'The Poets of England who have Died Young', in which Shelley and Sidney were again linked and compared. Shelley himself was sufficiently proud of the connection to have called one of his best-known pieces of prose *The Defence of Poetry* after his distant ancestor's *A Defence of Poesie*. A Shelley family tree shows that he was in fact connected to Sidney twice over, through both his mother's and his father's side of the family.

copyright of two books, relating the travels of 1840 and of 1842–3. By January 1844, she had the first book ready to go to press.

It was, she told Moxon, her intention that these books should be light and entertaining, in the style of the little travel book she had published in 1817, *History of a Six Weeks' Tour*. It was in this spirit that she dedicated her new works to the now ageing Samuel Rogers, whose own pilgrimage through Italy in verse, shrewdly shored up by Turner's engravings, had been phenomenally successful in the late 1820s, treading lightly on politics and heavily wherever there was a picturesque scene which Turner could represent. But the Preface acknowledged a change of direction. Here, Mary paid tribute to Lady Morgan, whose outspoken hostility to Italy's subjection either to Austria or the Vatican had earned her a place on the papal list of prohibited books: she had even been accorded the peculiar honour of having her *Italy* burned in the great piazza at Turin. The fury with which her younger friend now attacked Austria as the corrupt and tyrannous gaoler of a country yearning for freedom was stoked by her feelings for Gatteschi. Mary had always stood against the Austrians; she had never before done so with such warmth.

Dissatisfied with her work when she had finished writing, Mary insisted that all the best parts of her second book – she dismissed the first as worthless – had been given to her by Gatteschi. It was, it is true, her political stance rather than her travel-writing skills which won the respect of reviewers, although a primitive few questioned the right of a woman to have a political attitude.[2] As striking to the modern reader is the homage these books paid to her mother.

It is hard to believe that the tribute was unconscious. Describing her journey to Norway on Imlay's behalf, Mary Wollstonecroft had emphasized the fact that she was a mother, travelling with a young child.[3] This, unusually among travel writers of the 1840s, was the role which Mary Shelley adopted. Where she differed from her mother was in representing herself as a figure of respectability; possibly, she stressed this aspect because she was for the first time writing not as 'the author of "Frankenstein"' but as 'Mrs Shelley', the name she had regained when she edited her husband's works. No longer the scandalous Miss Godwin on whose experiences abroad the *Six Weeks' Tour** had been

---

* Even then, however, Mary had not been eager to publish the fact that she was not a married woman. The Preface to the *History of a Six Weeks' Tour* announces that we will be following the adventures of the author, her husband and her sister. Shelley was Mary's husband in 1817, when the work was published; he had certainly not been her husband during their travels in 1814 and 1816, and Claire was not her sister.

based, 'Mrs Shelley' was a devoted middle-aged lady, revisiting scenes
of the past with her son. There was a little egotism in her supposition
that the reader would instantly understand all her mournful allusions
to the significance these scenes held for her; there was none in her
graceful allusions to the mother she knew only through her writings.
Godwin, memorably, had described his wife at the time she was in
love with Imlay as seeming like a serpent grown brilliant and sleek
again with the sloughing of its skin; so Mary, in the first pages of her
book, described the shedding of outworn thoughts as her mind
arrayed itself 'in a vesture all gay in fresh and glossy hues'.[4] Like her
mother, she was happy to contemplate 'the immeasurable goodness of
our Maker', a sentiment which would have caused Shelley and her
father to recoil. Like her mother, she described the joy of losing
herself in a landscape, of seeking out, in solitude, the enduring beauty
of hills, and lakes, and sky. All that she lacked was the spontaneity, the
directness and sad passion which made Mary Wollstonecraft's book so
memorable.

Only one of the many enthusiastic reviewers of *Rambles in Germany
and Italy* made the connection and found the daughter deficient.[5]
Most praised the volumes as entertaining, thoughtful and eminently
readable. Some thought that she alluded too often to her unhappy
past; the *Sunday Times* was more sympathetic in describing the book
as 'a glimpse into the interior of a heart'.[6] Her view of Italy's situation was generally commended. Few of the reviewers spared much
comment for her pages on painting and sculpture. In fact, her belief
that artists had a right to represent love in all forms, both sacred and
profane, was near to Shelley's; her enthusiasm for Greek sculpture
brought her intriguingly close to the attitude of John Ruskin, whose
first volume of *Modern Painters* was also published in 1843.

The London lodgings which Percy had found for them during her
August in Paris proved wholly unsuitable. Shortage of money and a
renewed aversion to living in the city took Mary back to sleepy,
peaceful Putney, now as delightful to her as Leigh Hunt's Chelsea had
become to him. The rent for their new home, White Cottage, lying
on the west side of the village towards Barnes, was 'odiously expensive', Mary told Claire in September 1843 (although Layton House
had cost her even more), and there was no room for entertaining. The
benefits were a garden and easy access to the Thames for journeys into
London – and Percy's boating. Having decided to move elsewhere as

soon as something cheaper became available, Mary grew too fond of her perch between the lively river and the quiet country estates to quit it until circumstances compelled.

Her main concerns, as she began work on the *Rambles*, were not for herself. Kindly, given the way she had been set aside, she commiserated with Aubrey Beauclerk on the death of his eldest daughter by Ida. Gatteschi's letters harrowed her with tales of his poverty; surely, she wrote to Claire, they could pay a governess to pretend to be in need of Italian lessons? Claire's own letters were alarming. Full of dark hints and frantic appeals for Mary's return, they sounded as though she had become emotionally entangled. Was a marriage about to take place, Mary asked? Was she being reckless? Had somebody duped her? 'A person alone is always a victim unless strictly on the defensive,' she wrote, never guessing how painfully apt the advice would soon prove to her own situation.[7] Yes, she wanted to visit Paris again, but only if she could live quite on her own and not be imprisoned by her stepsister's demands and expectations. 'I am sadly & savagely independant . . . I *must* be thoroughly independant,' she wrote and went on to explain that it was only to guard against the 'defect' of her own character that she had reluctantly allowed Joshua Robinson's daughters to live with her from time to time as a 'necessity'.[8]

Perhaps Mary was growing elaborate merely to escape making the simple admission that she did not like Claire well enough to share a home with her; still, the confession that she had needed company because of the 'defect' in her character is intriguing. Mary's letters often now complained of eye fatigue, pains in 'my luckless head' and feelings of weariness and depression;[9] had she taken the Robinsons and, occasionally, Jane Hogg into her home as a way of ensuring that she did not harm herself? Was she sufficiently aware of her mother's suicide attempts to have been frightened that despair might lead her into the same irrational course? In her letters, she says that 'self-violence' was abhorrent to her, which tells us, at least, that the subject was in her thoughts.

Certainly, it now seemed to Mary that she had allowed herself to be bullied by Claire while she was in Paris. If she returned, she said firmly, she would do as she wished, spend much of her time with her old friend Mrs Hare and have no questions asked about her private life. She had seldom asserted herself with such sternness.

Percy's indolence continued to trouble her. She liked his loyalty to Henry Hunt and Jane Hogg's Dina, now married and expecting their second child; she welcomed the visits of his friends to White Cottage. But what was to be the future of a young man who still had no money, who cared nothing for society and whose only occupations were boating and playing the piano? (The trumpet which he had taken up on their second tour abroad had been abandoned as abruptly as the flute before it; Mary had recently acquired a cottage piano for his amusement.) 'I cannot leave him here any time alone,' she told Claire as further entreaties came for her return to Paris.[10] Why, one wonders? Why, when Mary was so fierce about her own need for independence, could she allow none to a steady young man of almost twenty-four? In another letter about Percy, probably written at this time, she expressed anxiety about his fondness for skulking about on his own at night, as if he were a thief or a murderer: 'Percy is waiting for Moonlight,' she told Marianne Hunt. 'I do not like his walks alone on dark nights – He has no finery about him.' She alluded, not to Percy's lack of smart clothes, but to the lack of refinement in such behaviour.

The difficulty was solved when Percy received another invitation to stay with his half-sister Ianthe during December 1843. Consenting, after all her insistence on an independent life, to stay at Claire's lodgings, Mary made a short Christmas visit to Paris.

No marriage was in the offing, despite Claire's hints, but Mary was horrified by her stepsister's state of mind. 'I have serious apprehensions for poor Claire unless she can be rouzed to change the air and scene,' she confided on her return to Marianna Hammond, an ex-governess from the Mason household who had become warmly attached to both women. 'Her health is deplorable – her spirits worse . . .'[11] Paranoia was the word she would have used, had it been in her vocabulary. In the summer, Claire had been obsessed by the idea that the de Boinville family had taken against her; now, she was convinced that one of her Russian acquaintances was spying on her. From 1843 on, there was seldom a period in Claire's life when she was not oppressed by the sense that she was surrounded by enemies. This mild form of mental derangement even led her to believe, towards the end of her life, that Allegra was still alive and that this fact had been kept from her.*

---

* One of Claire's recorded beliefs was that Allegra did not die and that a goat's body had been substituted for her in the coffin sent to England.[12] Trelawny, her equal in the art of imaginative reconstruction, was outraged by such claims. Writing to her on 27 November 1869, he threatened to find an old nun at the convent who could be taught to impersonate Allegra, if that was what she wanted, and 'she should follow you about like a feminine Frankenstein', he added, falling into the usual error of transposing the maker for his creature.[13]

There was no madness in Claire's new, and harsh, perception of Jane Williams Hogg. Claire had always been loyal to Jane, while maintaining an affectionate relationship with Dina, her daughter. Now, for reasons which are unclear, her feelings had grown hostile.* Percy had better be careful, she warned Mary in a long, savage letter; Jane would turn her dangerous tongue against him at the least opportunity, 'get up a little calumny to deteriorate his merit'. She had done it to Mary and now she had done the same to Claire. 'Could I do what is just,' Claire wrote, 'I would have a board stuck up before Mrs Hogg's door, warning anyone who cared for their happiness to have nothing to do with her.' Jane could have all she wanted written on this board, tributes to her beauty, her grace, her generosity, 'and whatever other splendours she would like to have to adorn her, only I would add, that this consummation of excellence has and ever will bring mental ruin to every one she approaches. This is my candid opinion of her.'[15]

Mary, never forgetting how viciously Jane had once slandered her, was ready to agree. Shocked by Jane's harshness to Dina, she had kept her own distance from Mrs Hogg: 'she had better things about her once,' she wrote to Claire and advised her to take the attitude of Dante towards people in Limbo: 'Speak not of them ma guarda e passa.'[16] In Jane's place, she offered herself to her stepsister as a friend in whom to trust.[17]

Claire had turned against the Italian colony, an attitude which Mary put down to her disturbed state of mind. For herself, she remained passionately committed to helping them. 'I have no money,' she told Claire on 23 January 1844 when she could scarcely afford to do more than entertain an occasional friend of Percy's. But Gatteschi had convinced her that his own need was greater than hers; it was in the hope of assisting him that Mary rashly involved herself in trying to sell what now appears to have been a forged painting.

Gatteschi's only source of income, other than herself, was young Count Martini, who retained him on a pittance, being short of funds himself. Martini, during Mary's first visit to Paris in August 1843, told her that he owned and wanted to sell a celebrated painting by Titian. The painting was in Milan, but he showed her an engraving. Mary was sufficiently impressed to promise her assistance. 'Do you know the picture of Titian – the "Woman taken in Adultery" – did you ever

---

* Jane Hogg had apologized to Claire in September 1843 for 'having wronged you, by an unworthy suspicion', planted by a friend she now discredited.[14] This apology had evidently not healed the breach. Perhaps Jane had heard from Mary about Claire's new Italian friends and had taken the opportunity to manufacture a little gossip about Miss Clairmont.

see it?' she wrote from Paris to Joseph Severn, who was helping to form a collection to be displayed at London's new National Gallery. Referring to the print of this picture which had been engraved by Faustino Anderloni, she asked if the original was not worth a great deal? It could, if interest was expressed, be brought to England – what did he think?[18] Severn, not surprisingly, thought that such a work would be of considerable interest.

Late in February 1844, Count Martini arrived in England as Mary's guest. The picture arrived separately by steamer. Its sale would, if it fetched the sum anticipated, solve all Gatteschi's difficulties. Martini, enriched himself, would be able to support him while the National Gallery benefited from a splendid addition to its collection.

Mary's letters make no further reference to Martini's painting. Gatteschi and Guitera continued to solicit her financial assistance; by the autumn of 1845, Count Martini was a ruined man. The likelihood is that the Titian was a forgery and that, as such, it found no purchaser.[19] The story would not, in the 1840s, have been an unusual one. A consequence of the creation of a new national art collection in London was that a large number of forgeries and, in particular, forgeries of Titians, were offered to it. Many were shipped in from the Continent at the time that Martini's picture arrived from Milan.

The silence of Mary's letters on the subject suggests that she knew the painting had failed to find a purchaser; her role, had it been sold, was significant enough for some comment to have been made, either by Claire or herself. Nothing was said. Most probably, she was aware that the painting had been identified as a fake.

This should have alerted Mary to the fact that she was keeping dangerous company. Instead, writing to Claire on 19 April 1844, she told her that Gatteschi was so wretchedly short of money that some had needed to be found at once: 'Nothing *could* I do except send some of what we have in hand – & Percy has complied & helped me in the most Angelic manner – God preserve him!'[20] Such help would not have been required if Martini's painting had realized the thousands they had anticipated.

Mary, as much as Gatteschi, was perilously close to destitution, partly as a result of her reckless generosity. Sixty pounds a year for the rent of White Cottage was more than she could afford; she was committed to giving the Hunt family regular assistance with their own rent; there were servants to be paid, Percy's friends to be entertained and the Italians clamouring as pathetically as a nest of unfed chicks. Sending Claire a loan of five pounds was, she wearily noted, doing the impossible for her only because the impossible had been requested.

Help was in sight from a bereavement which both Mary and Claire had come to believe would never be permitted to transform their lives. (Claire had even, with Mary's approval, taken out a life insurance policy on Percy in case her nephew predeceased his grandfather.) But the ninety-year-old Sir Timothy was ill again. He had risen from his deathbed before now, but the lawyers reported that this time his end was sure. By 20 April, Mary was confident enough of it to send word to Leigh Hunt that, while she and Percy were happy to continue their support after the will was disclosed, they would not immediately be able to produce the £2,000 bequeathed to him by Shelley. Twenty years ago, all had seemed possible, but Sir Timothy had outlived her gloomiest expectations. She herself would first have to repay to the estate, with all the accrued interest, the full cost of Percy's schooling and every penny she herself had been grudgingly allowed: 'In fact,' she nervously confessed, 'I scarcely know how our affairs will be.' Claire also needed warning that she might have to wait some time for her legacy; to Hogg, Mary expressed an uneasy conviction that Lady Shelley and her surviving son, John, would try to ensure that all other beneficiaries received as little as possible.

She had scarcely completed her letter when the news came. 'Poor Sir Tim is gone at last,' she wrote incredulously to Claire on 25 April. She could be glad that his death had been painless; she could not grieve for a flinty old man who had relentlessly opposed every timid overture, who had fought to suppress his son's work, and who had remained convinced until his death that it was Mary herself who had worked to fuel Shelley's contempt for his father and for his inheritance. This had been the one certainty on which Sir Timothy had based his twenty-year refusal to meet his daughter-in-law; the battle did not end with his death. In 1834, the baronet had drawn up a will which ensured that every penny of his personal fortune went to his wife, his daughters and to his second legitimate son, John. Mary and Percy, as Shelley's widow and son, would now inherit the property which would have been his, but only because the entail left no possibility for alternative arrangements.

Mary was not yet aware of the unforgiving nature of her father-in-law's will, although her expectations were not high. Two things, however, were certain and consoling. Her son was now a baronet and she, as Mrs Shelley of Field Place, would at last cease to be an outcast. With good, steady Percy at her side, Mary allowed herself to dream of a tranquil future for them both, of a pleasant country estate like

Exbury, of an affectionate daughter-in-law to give her the grand-children she craved, and above all, of the peace which, nearing fifty and in increasingly frail health, she felt most ready to enjoy. They would help the needy, care for their friends, be good landlords; they would be all, in short, that Shelley might have wished. The dull enduring ache of remorse could at last be assuaged.

BLACKMAIL AND FORGERY

1844–1846

'"Preserve always a habit of giving (but still with discretion), however little, as a habit not to be lost. The first thing is justice. Whatever one gives ought to be from what one would otherwise spend, not from what one wd. otherwise pay. To spend little & give much, is the highest glory a man can aspire to."'

Mary Shelley, Journal, 2 October 1844*

THANKING MARY AT THE END OF 1844 FOR THE RECEIPT OF HIS legacy, complete with the interest that had accrued since Shelley's death in 1822, Jefferson Hogg apologized for the fact that, being less rich than Lord Byron, he could not afford the luxury of forgoing it. Brightly, he offered his congratulations to 'the Baronet-Boy' who, he imagined, would enjoy living in style at Field Place.[1]

Hogg's clumsy geniality had never seemed so misplaced as in the month when, after a dutiful half-year, Mary finally put away the black-bordered stationery she had been using in deference to the late Sir Timothy Shelley. Percy, not she, had been invited to the funeral; if the Sussex estate workers looked favourably on the pink, awkward young man in whose hands their future lay, it was in hope of a change for the better. Sir Timothy's obituary in – where else? – the *Gentleman's Magazine* had praised him as a benefactor and friend of the agricultural labourer.[2] This was true of his early life; in later years, embittered by the prospect of being compelled by the law of entail to

---

* Made shortly after Sir Timothy Shelley's death, this was Mary's last journal entry, and extracts a passage from Edmund Burke's letter to his son, dated 4 February 1773.

leave his house and estate to a daughter-in-law he detested and a grandson he scarcely knew, Sir Timothy had ceased to take any interest in maintenance. The farm buildings were dilapidated; the tenants were anxious for improvements which had not been made; Field Place itself, although pleasant in design, had grown shabby, damp and sad.

It was a 'desperate' house, dull in its position, dull in every way, Mary lamented to Claire after paying a brief courtesy visit there in June. Hellen, the only one of her three sisters-in-law who took some interest in Percy, had been civil; Lady Shelley soon impressed her as 'an active fidgetty old soul clever to boot', her mind fixed on seeing that she received everything to which the will entitled her, and more.[3] Pilfold, Thomas Medwin's lawyer brother, was unexpectedly friendly, offering to do what he could to help the woefully underinformed heirs. The Beauclerks' family solicitor also offered his advice, but Mary, perhaps for reasons of discretion in a gossipy country neighbourhood, decided not to involve him in her worries.

Both Mary and Percy were relieved to learn that Lady Shelley was in no immediate hurry to move out of her home. (She bought herself a new house in Berkshire in October.) Percy fancied the idea of living at Castle Goring, the gigantic mansion his great-grandfather had built near Worthing on the South Coast: 'There is nothing I should like better,' Mary told Claire at the end of the year, although she recognized that her son would need a rich wife to subsidize his life there.[4] For herself, she thought of building a little cottage in the forest of Balcombe which formed part of their shared inheritance. For the present, however, they stayed on at Putney and did their best to calm Claire's suspicions that they were, in their new-found grandeur, planning to exclude her from their lives and prevent her from receiving the £12,000 due to her under Shelley's bequest.* Her demands grew shrill. When was she going to be allowed to visit Field Place? Why did they keep finding excuses to keep her away from Putney? She did not believe Mary's claim that there was no room; she was insulted to be offered rooms over a stationer's shop in the High Street. Suggestions that she should take opiates or try mesmerism for her 'turn of life' did nothing to improve her mood.

Money presented a graver worry than Claire's fretful accusations. Sir Timothy, just as Mary had feared, had left them only what the law

---

* Shelley left no official will that ever came to light. His executors were obliged to proceed according to the informal bequests left among his papers, so far as they could be accommodated under the strict laws of inheritance that governed the entailed estate.

of entail compelled, and it was barely enough for them to survive. An income of somewhere between three and five thousand pounds a year from the estate sounded handsome until she understood the fact that their debts would swallow it all at a gulp. Furthermore, the 'incumbrances', Mary grimly wrote to Claire, amounted to nearly £50,000, all of which must be settled directly; to raise the sum they would be obliged to borrow or take out a mortgage on the estate. Shelley's bequests required £6,000 to be given to Ianthe and a further £22,500 to be divided between Claire, Hogg, Hunt and Peacock. And, as Mary needed no reminding, she was now due to repay Lady Shelley the £13,000 provided, under pressure, for her own and Percy's maintenance. In these circumstances, the best she could do for her widowed sister-in-law, Emily Godwin, was a promise of £50 a year. A less principled woman might have raised the delicate question of Claire's right to £12,000, since half this sum had been intended to benefit Allegra. Mary never made mention of it.

The mid-1840s, the years of agricultural depression, were not the ideal period in which to inherit a run-down, debt-ridden country estate. Advised by the Shelleys' lawyer and by Peacock's kindly friend, Walter Coulson, Mary watched her dreams of comfortable security dwindle into a mere attempt to survive. Even the weather was against them; the torrential rain of 1845 wiped out the crops as effectively as the drought of the following summer. The tenant farmers were unable to keep up their rents, let alone to tolerate a rise; the estate's income shrank to £1,500 in the year 1845. Lady Shelley did not help matters by removing everything bar the fireplace grates, when she left for a more agreeable home near Hungerford in Berkshire. Her conduct, Mary lamented to Claire on 27 October, 'is grasping & mean beyond expression'. Lady Shelley had already been bequeathed the furniture, the linen, the plate and the silver, reducing Mary and Percy's inheritance to little more than the bricks and mortar, now crumbling, of which Field Place was built. The house was in too shabby a state to raise more than £60 a year from the incoming tenant; insult was added to injury when he demanded compensation for the extensive improvements he had been forced to make to render the house habitable. Percy's fantasies of castle life had to be abandoned. Sold at the end of 1845 to the resident lessee, Castle Goring raised £11,250, of which half was instantly swallowed up by one of Shelley's ancient debts.

How much did Percy shoulder of their new responsibilities? Not, although his mother would never admit it, as much as she had hoped. Among his positive contributions, only one comes to mind: in the autumn of 1844, Percy commissioned Joseph Severn to represent his father composing *Prometheus Unbound* in the ruined Baths of Caracalla. But it was Mary who produced the Curran portrait for Severn to work from and Mary who had to correct a nose which was 'anything but right'; Percy, according to Severn, had been perfectly satisfied.

Writing to a biographer who was planning to discuss the lives, among others, of Shelley and Byron, Mary described her son as 'guiless' and 'unworldly'; to Claire, she praised him as 'always cheerful – always occupied, he is the dearest darling in the world – the sheet anchor of my life'.[5] The image was apt enough; in no respect did Percy resemble his father so much as in his passion for boats, if only for the liberty they gave him to float free of cares and commitments; these were left in his mother's charge. She apologized for the parties he forgot to attend; she sought advice from Monckton Milnes on his duties as a country squire; she held her tongue when he splashed out on a new yacht which turned out to be worth half its purchase price. But when Percy, in the autumn of 1845, announced that he was going to read conveyancing law out of sheer boredom, even his mother grew a little exasperated. 'In short,' she told Claire on 25 September, 'his income not being enough to permit him to yacht or to indulge in careless expenditure he feels unoccupied'; loyally, she added that the law would doubtless be good preparation for a political career in the Tory party.

Percy's political ambitions seem to have had more to do with his mother's hopes than his own inclinations. Writing to Milnes in the autumn of 1844, Mary told him that her son had always had 'a great ambition to sit in Parliament' and took his advice about whether Percy might 'come in for Horsham without a contest, in which case I shall urge him to it'.[6] It would not have taken Percy much effort to discover that the only other contestant for the seat was extremely unpopular in the area, but he let himself be put off by the expense of organizing a campaign. In the autumn of the following year, Mary tried again. 'If I can only see him in parliament all will go well,' she told Claire on 1 December, while candidly acknowledging that a parliamentary career would expand Percy's social life. Percy was supposed to be consulting the Duke of Norfolk, the leading local landowner, about his prospects of election; nothing came of it. In 1846, the subject was raised again. Her son's ally this time was Aubrey Beauclerk, who advised him not to risk money on the campaign. The funds which had been set aside for electioneering were used for something much dearer to the young man's heart than campaigning, a new boat.

Percy's behaviour the following year, 1847, makes one rather glad that he did not become a politician. The Reform Act of 1832 had brought no change to the notoriously corrupt Horsham seat; tenants here still voted as their landlord commanded. Appealed to by the local agents for the Whig candidate to allow his tenants 'permission to vote as they please', Percy gave his own vote to the Tory, and forced his tenants to do likewise. The Tory, Sir John Jervis, was subsequently unseated for buying votes.[7]

Mary and Percy became landowners at a time when the agricultural economy was threatened not only by bad harvests and a general recession, but by the mooted repeal of the antiquated Corn Laws of 1815. The Corn Laws ensured that home-grown wheat was kept at a price advantageous to the growers, but impossibly high for the working man. Sir Robert Peel, the Tory Prime Minister, was farsighted enough to support a repeal and the import of cheaper foreign corn; not so, the Tory squires. They, together with Whig landowners headed by the Duke of Norfolk, opposed Peel's arguments. In December 1845, Peel was forced to choose between bowing to their will or offering his resignation. Honourably, he chose to resign.

Where did Mary stand? In principle, she supported the moves towards a repeal. Writing to Claire in the month Peel resigned, she condemned the Duke of Norfolk for his notorious speech recommending a pinch of curry powder in hot water as the labourer's best way of warming an empty stomach.[8] A few days later, she was ready to predict national agitation if the country aristocrats had their way. 'Our Landlords are much to blame,' she wrote, but she was well enough acquainted with them now to recognize the possibility that repeal would ruin them. Why, she sensibly asked, should the repeal not be balanced by a reduction in land tax?

With regard to Ireland in the bleak period after the Great Famine, Mary was less reasonable. Writing to a friend abroad in the spring of 1847, she complained that England had troubles enough of her own without having to send, so she had heard, a million pounds a month to 'people who, in the hopes of money from this country, can scarcely be induced to sow seed for next harvest'.[9] This was an ungenerous attitude, whilst her reasons for supporting repeal in 1845 were hardly altruistic. At a time when she was urging Percy to stand for election at Horsham, a repeal would free him from having to take a stand on the thorny topic of the Corn Laws, which 'form so difficult a bit for a candidate' – especially, although she did not say so, for one who was so slow and inarticulate as her son.

'I am married to Percy,' Mary wrote to Claire in 1847. Certainly, there were striking echoes of her relationship with Shelley. She, as Trelawny had noticed, had always held the purse-strings, run the household, fought off slander. Widowhood had strengthened her sense of control as she decided what should and should not be set in public view. Perhaps, in his amiable readiness to be governed, Percy was adapting himself to his mother's need. Certainly, as she continued to find herself patronized by her husband's relations and cut by such social veterans as Lord Dillon's widow, Percy's stocky and reliable presence was a comfort.

'I am so entirely exiled from the good society of my own country on account of the outset of my life that I *can* care for nothing but the opinion of a few near & dear friends – & of my own conscience,' she had written to Claire on 20 September 1843, in the year before Sir Timothy's death. It was an unpleasant surprise to discover that she was still, by some, considered a disreputable woman. Lady Dillon, living respectably at her late husband's home in Oxfordshire, probably remembered Mrs Shelley as part of the gang of peculiar young women, Mary Diana Dods, Eliza Rennie and Isabel Robinson, with whom Lord Dillon had made friends at William Kitchiner's home. One of them, Eliza Rennie, was thought by many to have been his mistress. Mary, as a part of this group, would not have been a person to whom Lady Dillon felt any need to be polite. Trying in her letters to Claire to hide her hurt feelings, Mary laughed off similar insults as mere 'pieces of impertinence'. In low moments, however, such behaviour was enough to tempt her to forsake society and bury herself in rural seclusion.

Social acceptance mattered less for her own sake than for Percy's. She longed for him to marry; she dreaded his choosing an unsuitable wife. He had, she noted on a visit to Horace Smith's family at Brighton in the autumn of 1845, shown an almost lively interest in the Smiths' sprightly little daughter, Rosalind. Very nice too, Mary told Claire: 'she is a good little thing – & I could not oppose it – but I cannot wish the match.' Two days later, she wrote again. 'I wish I could find a wife for him . . . he is so *right minded* – he ought to be happy.'[10] And so he would be, but, as Mary's comment shows, only when his choice won her approval.

Percy had kept a careful distance from his mother's Italian friends. Awareness of his disapproval may explain why Gatteschi, visiting London shortly after the death of Sir Timothy Shelley, stayed not at

White Cottage but with Alexander Knox. Mary's enthusiasm for the handsome young patriot was undiminished. 'I grieve very much you do not get on better with him –' she reproached Claire on 10 September; 'for the more I see of him the more I esteem his character; which seems to me singularly frank, confiding & true – this is praise for any one – for an Italian very great.' Making what was to be her last journal entry on 2 October, a few weeks after Gatteschi's departure, Mary copied out a favourite passage from one of Edmund Burke's letters. The subject was the importance of generosity: 'To spend little & give much,' she reminded herself, 'is the highest glory a man can aspire to.'

Gatteschi returned to France full of plans to write a play which Mary had promised to translate and offer to the celebrated actor-manager, William Macready; she plotted, meanwhile, to obtain a job with one of the new railroad companies for Gatteschi's friend, Carlo Guitera. Only a few kind words and a little gentle management were required, Mary wrote to Claire; why was she still so determined to think evil of their friends? What if Guitera, despite a pregnant wife, made himself charming to a prospective employer? (Lady Sussex Lennox, half-sister to one of Claire's former pupils, was considering taking him on as tutor for her children.) Gently, Mary reminded Claire of their friend Augusta Goring, living nearby in Putney and bearing Trelawny's children. This, now, seemed scandalous behaviour; was Guitera to be judged more harshly for the small crime of being a flirt?[11]

Claire, once her mind was made up, was not to be budged. By the end of the year, she believed she had proof which would convince even Mary of the danger of these friendships. On 28 December, she reported that Lady Sussex Lennox was heavily embroiled with both Gatteschi and Guitera, that she had taken on Gatteschi's debts of some £400, and that Lord Sussex Lennox, mad with jealousy, had beaten Gatteschi up. The Italians, she added, were meanwhile assuring poor pregnant Madame Guitera that they were doing all they could to stay clear of Lady Sussex Lennox, who was, they ungallantly said, 'too old to inspire love'. Oh, and Oswald Turner, grandson of Harriet de Boinville, had been driven into madness by the fiendish manipulations of Harriet and his mother Cornelia, Claire added as the icing to a letter she astonishingly considered 'a very amusing one'.

Claire's slanderous representation of old Madame de Boinville and Cornelia Turner served to convince Mary that her stepsister had temporarily lost her own wits. Gatteschi had recently told her that he was shocked by Claire's strange appearance; grimly, Mary wrote back to warn her against blackening the character of their mutual friends. 'I imagine you are scarcely aware how shocking and discreditable to her [Lady Sussex Lennox] are your details – let us draw a veil over them in mercy to our sex & forget them.'[12]

Peace was made during Claire's visit to Putney at the beginning of 1845. With quiet success, Mary proved a point she had been striving to make for some time. When Claire was lodged above the stationer's shop, not under her roof, they could enjoy each other's company; it was only when they lived together that quarrels broke out. Returning to Paris in April, Claire expressed a gratitude which amounted almost to an apology. It had been, she wrote with customary exaggeration on 7 May, 'the only bright episode in my life'. Mary's company had been 'charming', her conversation 'so wise and so universal' as to benefit all who had the pleasure of knowing her. With more warmth than she had shown for years, Claire sent fond wishes to Mary's two dogs and added her hopes that Percy's formal presentation at court by Lord de L'Isle and Dudley had gone well.

Mary had already discouraged Claire from sinking her legacy into Austrian land, presumably because she wished to join her brother Charles and his family in Vienna. It was during this honeymoon period after the visit to Putney that Mary put forward another idea: might Claire be interested in joining her scheme to buy and rent out an opera box? There was only one opera house in London; Mary had been told that the box would hold or increase its value while being rented out for £300 a year. Perhaps it was the theatrical connection which so enchanted Claire; certainly, she was determined to ignore the warnings which followed Mary's discovery of the riskiness of such an investment. Mary chose instead to put her modest savings into the railways which were being spun over the countryside as fast as a spider's web; Claire, by the end of June 1845, had decided to invest £4,000, a third of all she had been bequeathed, in a box on the Grand Tier. It was to prove a disastrous venture.

Claire's visit had shown her that Mary was not living in such state as she had enviously supposed; as the summer of 1845 made a mockery of its name, she received increasingly doleful reports. Shelley's surviving creditors were calling for payment; the Sussex tenants, their harvest ruined, were unable to pay the rents; Mary had been obliged to dismiss her manservant and could not even afford to stay in Cowes, where Percy was sailing his yacht with Aubrey Beauclerk's nephew and namesake. It was a little humiliating, when she visited the Sussex estate in August, to be obliged to live with the Beauclerks at South Lodge because she had no home to call her own.

'To spend little & give much . . .' So she had written and she was determined to follow Burke's precept. Some causes, however, seemed worthier than others. Richard Monckton Milnes was begged to request Sir Robert Peel to fulfil his predecessor's promise of £100 to Isabella Booth, nursing a violent and now deranged husband; Mary's sympathy for Gatteschi began to wane at last as he once again drew on her for funds while making no attempt to find employment. Charles Clairmont, who was visiting Claire in Paris with his family in the summer of 1845, seemed more deserving: Mary told Claire to turn a debt of £10 into gifts for Charles's children. Heartily thanked, she had no idea of how harshly the Clairmonts were scrutinizing her life behind her back. Charles shuddered at the thought of Mary's long association with such a ghastly tribe as the Robinsons of Paddington; Claire sniped at her superior manner and mournfully declared that Mary had always hated her. Young Wilhelm Clairmont, listening attentively, stored the gossip away, wondering what strange kind of woman this quasi-aunt in England must be.[13]

Mary's plans to economize and recover her health by spending the autumn of 1845 on the Continent were arrested by a bombshell from Paris. Gatteschi's pride had been stung by criticism of his relationship with Lady Sussex Lennox, his pocket by Mary's increasing reluctance to subsidize his needs. As the summer ended, his letters changed their tone; Guitera dropped strong hints that only money would prevent use being made of the letters in which Mary had unguardedly poured out her heart to Gatteschi. 'I cannot fathom his designs,' she wrote in bewilderment to Claire on 15 September; her friends were on hand to explain that she was being subjected to blackmail. Alexander Knox, alerted either by Guitera or by Claire, was all for immediate action. To this, Mary was at first vigorously opposed. Yes, the shock had been terrible, but caution warned her against being precipitate. 'Knox must not get it talked of among the English – my name wd get wind at least – the English are the people to avoid.'[14]

Claire, maliciously and inaccurately noting on the envelope of this letter that Mary had referred to 'my Knox', confirmation of a love-affair which she had long suspected, shared his unequivocal view of Gatteschi as a villain. Mary, pathetically, clung to the hope that his intentions were not so very wicked. Nevertheless, before the end of September, she had agreed to let Knox and a legal adviser take what-ever steps were necessary to recover the damaging letters. 'They were written with an open heart –' she confessed, '& contain details with regard to my past history, which it wd. destroy me for ever if they ever saw light.'[15] Distraught by the savage unpleasantness of Gatteschi's latest demands, she gladly promised Knox to stop writing defensive replies. Instead, she asked him to send back a portrait of Gatteschi which she had treasured, not least for the young man's exceptional beauty, 'just done up & directed & sent without a word'.

Handsomely repaying all Mary's past generosity to him, Knox became her chief guide and support in this nightmarish affair. The old *cabinet noir* system, allowing for the interception and examination of suspicious correspondence, still operated in France; it was notoriously employed in England in 1844 when the letters of Mazzini were seized and opened. Here, in Knox's opinion, lay their only chance of getting the incriminating letters out of Gatteschi's hands. He was a member of a revolutionary party; this would be a sufficient reason for the French police to take an interest in his mail. Mary, wishing no harm to the man who was now trying to blackmail her, shuddered at the possible consequences for him; Knox was both persistent and persuasive. Nothing could be done without authority from England; reluctantly, Mary agreed to see if the necessary letter could be obtained from Lord Brougham, the former Lord Chancellor and noted legal reformer. She reached him by asking Trelawny to apply to Temple Leader, one of Brougham's closest friends; by the end of September, Knox was in a position to enlist help from the formidable Gabriel Delessert, French Prefect of Police. The £250 which Mary guiltily sent Knox from the meagre income shared between herself and Percy was presumably the estimated cost of a complicated undercover operation.

'Oh what an easy dupe I have been – & worse,' Mary lamented on 1 October, in one of the many letters which Claire swore were being burned, just as she requested. Sick with apprehension and terrified that Percy might discover what was going on behind his back, she accompanied him to Brighton on a fortnight's visit to see Horace Smith and his family. Here, while Percy flirted with young Rosalind and the Smiths expressed concern at his mother's wan appearance, Mary fretted over Gatteschi's betrayal. Perhaps Knox was right; the man was an out-and-out villain; she almost wished that Lord Sussex Lennox would go and beat him up again. Anything was better than the thought of the vengeance he might take: 'we must not forget that he is vindictive unprincipled, & when desperate will stick at nothing he *can* do,' she wrote to Claire on 9 October. In another letter written on the same day, her imagination ran riot among the possibilities. Gatteschi would use daggers instead of threats if he had the chance, she wrote; only terror of the guillotine or the galleys could subdue him now. 'My letters must be got somehow – either by seizure or purchase – & then he must be left – As to helping him – there are others starving – but enough of that he must be crushed in the first place.'

Her wish was granted. On 11 October, two French newspapers announced in tones of strong disapproval that the homes of two Italian exiles (Gatteschi and Guitera were named) had been visited by the police and many of their private papers removed. Sceptical of the official reason, suspicious of an involvement in an Italian insurrection, the journalists expressed their disgust at such treatment of impoverished refugees.[16] *Le Messager*, on 12 October, carried a defensive piece for which Delessert was probably responsible. Mary's letters, safely returned to Knox's keeping, were destroyed.

That, as far as Mary was concerned, marked the end of her connection to the Italian circle in Paris. There is a curious postscript to the story. Many years later, when Claire Clairmont and her niece were living in Florence, an after-dinner caller knocked at the door. Pauline (Paula) Clairmont found the visitor an entertaining companion, 'clever – amiable and cultivated', although a little deaf. His name, he told her, was Luigi Gatteschi; he was an old acquaintance of her aunt's. Reminding her that they had met once before, when he had called and found her aunt out of the city, he demanded an interview with Claire. Paula may have missed the significance of his remark that he still possessed an excellent memory; Claire did not. Refusing to see him, she warned her niece that she would be thrown out of the house if she ever dared communicate with Gatteschi again. There, infuriatingly, the trail ends. Paula obeyed her aunt; no further mention of the old blackmailer has yet been found.[17]

It took Mary some time to recover her equilibrium. The possibility of a reprisal terrified her; what if Gatteschi discovered the part she had played? By the end of October, while bitterly reproaching herself for her folly – 'to have wasted so disgracefully so much of Percy's money – to have been so intimate with such a villain' – she was eager to put the whole horrid business behind her. 'I feel I shall never be the same person again after this,' she told Claire. 'God grant I may be a better one – for there is ample room for improvement.'[18] Claire herself had never appeared in a better light; unaware of how diligently her revealing letters had been squirrelled away, Mary expressed her gratitude to 'you who have ever shewn me so much kindness & whom I have so ill requited throughout'.[19]

It was a bad moment for Mary's old friend Mrs Kenney to write and ask if her son Thomas Holcroft might be given some of Godwin's letters for publication. Mary had never liked Holcroft and reticence, not publicity, was her preferred course after the Gatteschi incident. Sending as a sop the letters which Thomas Holcroft's father had written to her own, Mary gave a hesitant answer to Mrs Kenney's inquiries about the long-anticipated memoir of Godwin. Yes, she still regarded it as 'a sacred task devolved on me'; no, she could not say when she would feel strong enough to undertake it.[20] The probability is that she had already decided that non-publication was the wiser course.

———

'O what a dupe I have been,' Mary had wailed during her autumn of disillusionment. She was about to be duped again, and within days of congratulating herself on a fortunate escape. Protecting the reputations of those she loved had always been her vulnerable point. She had for some years been endeavouring to recover any correspondence which might damage Shelley's now almost blameless reputation. Hearing from his publisher and friend Thomas Hookham that a large number of letters had come into the possession of a visitor to his Bond Street premises, she was quick to respond.

Hookham's visitor was a personable, intelligent and unscrupulous forger who had presented himself to John Murray several years earlier as Byron's legitimate son, the child of a secret marriage in Cadiz in 1809, when Byron was twenty-one. Byron was said to have acknowledged this son in a conveniently lost letter written from his deathbed to Augusta Leigh. Major George Gordon de Luna Byron had impressed Murray with his elegance and plausibility; his claims of birth acquired additional credibility in 1844 when he met Byron's half-sister and was rewarded with an encouraging note about his plan to collect materials for a life of his father. Armed with what amounted almost to a guarantee from Augusta, the Major gained access to many of Byron's original letters and became skilled at copying his hand; he also obtained possession of some of the letters which Mary and Shelley had written to each other in the early years and which had been lost after their departure from Marlow. Here, too, the Major had been practising his copying skills. Too shrewd to part with originals when copies could fetch a good price, he became an artful concocter of plausible fakes.

Mary was easily persuaded that the letters Major Byron had acquired were authentic. Scarred by her experience with Gatteschi, she mocked Hookham's credulity in believing that the letters would be freely given. 'He wont *give* any letters – of that be assured,' she told him on 30 October. She was ready to offer £20 for a batch, much though it angered her to pay for what she regarded as stolen property. On 10 November, the Major acknowledged receipt of £30 for an unspecified number of letters. Peacock, asked for advice, scolded her for being so gullible; Mary refused to listen. Hookham was told that she would pay a pound for any letter from Shelley to her and half a crown for whatever others Major Byron had for sale. Doubtful of the authenticity of the documents she had already purchased, she hoped by patience to obtain the originals. By March 1846, at least eighteen letters were in her hands, several of which she could identify as copies. Sick with worry that the Gatteschi experience was to be repeated, she scrawled a distraught letter to Hookham.

> *I am sure* this man has *many more letters* – in time I hope to get them – he will come again – & you can say – that there were *many* more of Shelley's letters. I cannot write more. Don't raise the mans hopes about money or he will become impracticable – at first he hoped for hundreds had he got those he would have grasped at thousands – now he is obliged to content himself with units he has *many more* manage to get them.[21]

A six-month silence ensued.

Mary was holidaying in Baden-Baden in September, together with her friend Mrs Hare, when Hookham sent word that a certain 'Mr Memoir' – this was one of Byron's aliases – had advised him that the Major was ready to sell some more of his collection. He had also demanded the return of the letters Mary had already bought; his intentions were unclear.

Given courage by distance, Mary decided to let him do his worst. If the Major wanted his forgeries back, let him take them, and make as many more copies as he liked. She urged Hookham to discuss the situation with her dear friend Alexander Knox, who would, she was sure, support her decision. And no, she did not want Thomas Holcroft to feel he needed to do anything about 'Mr Memoir' on her behalf. She sent her thanks to Mr Holcroft for his offer and his letter, 'disgusting' though its contents had been.* She did not want Mr Holcroft to meet Mr Knox. She did not, above all, want to be drawn into a scandal. 'The great thing will be [to] avoid police reports & police Magistrates.' It was only a year since newspaper accounts of the raid

---

* The nature of this 'disgusting' letter remains unclear, although her wish 'to relieve Mr Holcroft from all onus on the subject' suggests that he may have been professionally connected as a lawyer to Hookham or Byron, or even both.

on the homes of Gatteschi and Guitera; she was afraid that the old story would be raked up as soon as any public investigation of a new blackmailing plot began.[22] She did, as a precaution, send Hookham a letter of authority by the same post, stating her wish that he should take possession of any copied letters which legally belonged to her: 'they are mine by law & cannot in any way be published by anyone else,' she wrote, identifying her main source of worry, that Byron would carry out his threat of publishing whatever she refused to buy at the price he named.

Almost two years later, at the beginning of 1848, Mary's worst fear seemed about to be realized when the *Athenaeum* advertised a new life of Lord Byron. It promised to contain 'numerous letters', the free use of all manuscripts and, most alarmingly, 'a mass of anecdotes' provided by, among others, Mrs Shelley.[23] A week passed before Major Byron's publishers, discovering that much of his material had been unofficially obtained from John Murray, returned it and agreed, in the face of legal action, not to proceed with the book.

Nobody could accuse the Major of lacking perseverance. A few months later, a credulous London bookseller, William White, was visited by a pretty lady calling herself Mrs Byron. She had, she tearfully said, been compelled by circumstances to make occasional sales from literary letters collected by her late father. Like the Major, for whom she was of course acting, Mrs Byron preferred to sell one or two letters at a time; they fetched more money when presented in isolation. White bought all he was offered and, in good faith, passed on the news to Mrs Shelley that he had some interesting correspondence for sale. But Mary had been duped for long enough. Writing his own account in 1852, White was still smarting at the memory of her answer, given 'in so angry and coarse a tone as to leave no doubt that she thought my only motive was to extort money'.[24] Most probably, she recognized the White letters as being ones of which she had already purchased copies.[25]

Given this response, it is surprising to find Mary, acting through a third party, as the purchaser of five Shelley letters and the manuscript of a poem from a sale held in December 1848. Among these was a letter – it is not clear at what point, if at all, she recognized it for a copy – which Shelley had written to her on 11 January 1817. Mary would have been easily able to identify it and recognize its significance from the extract printed in the catalogue. This was the letter in which Shelley had eagerly reported Godwin's news of 'evidence' of Harriet's infidelity in the period leading up to the 1814 elopement. Mary, for whatever reason, had been desperately anxious to acquire it. The purchase price was six guineas. Having obtained her prize, she put it carefully away with the rest of her hoard.

The Gatteschi affair had left Mary feeling emotionally drained and deeply indebted to Claire for her support and for her restraint. (Claire had, after all, warned her against both Gatteschi and Guitera almost from the beginning.) Anxious to express gratitude, Mary could not repress the habit of disapproval. Claire's efforts to find her just the right French cloak and bonnet were met with a regret that she had chosen bright colours, not an appropriate black; she was scolded for maintaining her friendship with scandalous, dangerous Lady Sussex Lennox; she was told not to bring her odious French maid when she next came to Putney. When Claire complained about the lack of income from her opera box, she was reminded that Mary was too poor even to give a dinner party, that she kept no horse and paid no visits in town: only Knox's agreeable company kept her from a life of complete solitude at Putney.[26]

Claire had never expressed any great enthusiasm for Alexander Knox; she certainly did not expect to be invited to contribute to his support. This, on 1 December, just two months after the Gatteschi letters had been recovered and destroyed, was what Mary invited her to do. Knox had, while living in Paris that autumn, recklessly purchased a luxurious flat which he could not afford to maintain. (Had a part of Mary's £250, intended for the cost of recovering letters, gone towards its purchase?) Mary could only 'darkly guess' why he might have bought it; Claire was invited to arrange its sale. A week later, Mary had a better idea. Claire's own modest home cost her 800 francs a year; why should she not pay an extra 200 and rent Knox's rooms? They were, she added encouragingly, in a better and more sociable part of the city: 'I cannot help feeling that you would be a gainer.'

We should not, perhaps, blame Claire for assuming that she was being exploited again. The next letter, dated 11 December, informed her that Mary had just given Knox the considerable sum of £100. She did not feel good about it: 'my poor poor Percy wd he had no Mother to rob him in this wicked manner,' she scrawled inside the envelope, and added a black wish: 'a thousand times wd I were dead.' She wrote again the following day, in similar vein: '*I can do no more* – & he – what can become of him –' A deletion of two separate three-line entries in the last paragraph was followed by the usual request that the letter be burnt.

Claire put the letter away. A week later, on 17 December, she sent

Knox a curious coded message in an otherwise insouciant letter to Mary. 'Tell Knox,' she wrote, 'that Annie Farrer says Mr Howard sees little of his young wife but is always at his Club playing cards. This is Annie's version of the result of the beautiful Miss McTavishe's marriage – it will amuse him and he knows how much credit to give to Annie's versions.' As a response to Mary's distraught requests and outbursts of contrition, this verged on the bizarre. Had Knox been having an affair with the beautiful Miss McTavishe? Did Claire know precisely why he had been so recklessly extravagant, and wish to punish him with news of the sequel? It seems a plausible explanation.

Mary had often complained of Claire's genius for stinging her conscience. This gift was well employed in the following months. Planning her arrival in England, Claire wrote bravely of the pleasure it would give her to live near them, 'particularly as I have not long to live'. She had, she went on, spent the winter making her dear nephew a hearthrug of every colour except black, 'an emblem of his fate, past, present and future'. Whatever Claire might think in private of Mary and of her relationship with Knox, her faith in her nephew's remarkable abilities remained undimmed: 'now if he goes into Parliament and if he falls in love,' she wrote, 'and to boot is as he is, a musician and a metaphysician and a good boater, in a little time he will be a universe of a man comprehending all things.'[27]

ANXIOUS TIMES

1845–1848

'It is terrible to write such words half in jest – but these are awful times.'

Mary Shelley to Alexander Berry, 28–30 March 1848

'WHAT YEARS I HAVE SPENT! –' MARY SIGHED TO CLAIRE AT THE end of 1845; 'the years in Somerset Street alone in London – the years at Harrow – quite alone – Well it is over now – & with years comes liking for quiet – All I ask is to be free from care . . .'[1] Cares stuck like burrs. Relief at the news that Knox had found regular and reasonably well-paid employment writing on politics for the *Morning Chronicle* was swept away in preparing for Claire's arrival, wondering what unpleasant use Major Byron might be planning for the letters she had failed to obtain, and struggling to furnish a new London home.

The house was Percy's choice. A handsome, brand-new building in Chester Square, on the south side of Belgravia, it had been bought with some of the proceeds from the sale of Castle Goring. Percy, backed by Alexander Knox and Gee Paul, was delighted by it; Mary, longing for country air and a pretty cottage on part of the Shelley estate, was less enthusiastic. It was 'a pretty & cheerful' house, she told Claire on 11 December, shortly after the purchase had been made. A month later, worn down by the business of finding servants, buying furniture from the sales and worrying about the cost of upkeep, she was ready to declare that 'I hate [it] with all my heart.' Her only comfort was that it would be convenient for

Percy, if he succeeded in the Horsham election and went into Parliament.

A minor but hurtful source of distress at this time was a gratuitous attack on Shelley's poetry by Edward Bulwer, a man Mary had always looked on as a friendly supporter, someone who shared Monckton Milnes's enthusiasm for promoting her husband's work. But Bulwer introduced his new translation of Schiller's poems with an attack on 'young poets [who] vie with each other who can write the most affectedly'; Shelley was singled out as a bad influence, an example of writers who use showy and fantastic language to disguise their ideas from the reader, 'if, indeed, any general idea is to be found buried amid the gaudy verbiage'.[2] Bulwer had mistaken the spirit of the times if he thought this would win him friends, Mary wrote indignantly to Edward Moxon; he 'casts an indelible stain on his own name, as long as it survives'.[3] Bulwer was not, in fact, alone in making this point. Reviewing Tennyson, a poet of the younger generation, in 1842, Hunt had criticized his language as excessively flowery and sensual, and warned him to steer away from the influence of Keats and Shelley, Tennyson's schoolboy idol.[4]

Mary's annoyance is understandable, however. She had seen little adverse criticism of her husband in the last few years. Her edition of the *Poetical Works* had been steadily reprinted throughout the 1840s and her notes, however scornfully received at the time, had exercised the influence she had intended. Shelley was a poet 'whose genius and virtue were a crown of glory to the world – whose love had been the source of happiness, peace and good', she had written.[5] In 1844, Elizabeth Barrett had written quiveringly of a life sacrificed to the quest of Beauty, while George Gilfillan's account of Shelley in his celebrated series of literary portraits that year eulogized his prophetic power and his selfless benevolence.[6] (Reviewing Gilfillan's portraits in 1845, Thomas de Quincey, excusing Shelley's anti-Christian views, had added his own memorable image of the poet as 'an angel touched by lunacy'.) It was small wonder, after such tributes, that Mary grew indignant at any criticism of a Shelley who had almost become her own creation.

Still unaware of any specific cause for her increasingly severe bouts of ill health, Mary was near to collapse by the time the house in Chester Square was ready for occupation. The geologist and physician Gideon Mantell, a man who had known and liked her for several years, was just leaving his own house in Chester Square on the evening of 12 March 1846 when he received an urgent request to visit a patient at No. 24.[7] The alarm must have been considerable: John

Ayrton Paris, President of the Royal College of Physicians, was also
called in. The diagnosis they made was 'neuralgia of the heart' and
the best cure they could suggest was a quiet convalescence. Percy, naturally, thought that nothing would help his mother's recovery so well
as a holiday at Cowes, where he could spend his spare time yachting.
'I returned no better,' Mary told Leigh Hunt sadly in June, although
she was anxious to let him know that Percy had been 'unspeakably
attentive to & careful of me'. The doctors could do nothing for her.
Still 'a complete invalid', she planned to spend the rest of a scorch-
ingly oppressive summer away from London.[8]

It was not a good time for her to hear from Thomas Medwin that
he had completed and was preparing to publish a full-length life of
Shelley. Medwin was staying with his brother Pilfold at Horsham
when he approached Mary in May 1846; it may have been Pilfold, a
lawyer, who pointed him towards the Record Office and the
Chancery papers of 1817–18, in which mention was made of Shelley's
atheism as a reason for withholding his paternal rights of custody.
Mary was horrified. She herself had written all that needed to be said,
she wrote back hastily: 'I vindicated the memory of my Shelley and
spoke of him as he was – an angel among his fellow mortals – lifted
far above this world – a celestial spirit given and taken away . . .' An
account of the kind Medwin might wish to give, 'the account of the
Chancery Suit above all', would undermine all that she had achieved.
Forbearance was what would serve Shelley's memory best now, she
pleaded, 'forbearance – and reserve'.[9]

Medwin's answer confirmed her worst fears about the book he
claimed to have finished. Scorning Gilfillan and De Quincey for 'their
accursed Cant – their cold false conventionalities – their abominable
Claptrap', he accused Mary of cowardice in not having published the
'History of Christianity' which Shelley had allowed him to read. Her
objections came too late; his book, he untruthfully boasted, would be
published in six weeks, 'at latest'.[10] Hearing no more, Medwin invited
Mary to buy his manuscript and the guarantee of his future silence.
The Chancery proceedings would be an 'indispensible' part of the
book, he threatened, as would other unidentified passages 'whose discussion you would not approve of'. He named £250 as the payment
a publisher had offered and warned her to act quickly, as 'we are going
to press immediately'.[11]

This was blackmail, and was seen as such; it took Mary a year to
discover that Medwin's manuscript had already been turned down by
several publishers; Colburn had rejected it on the very day of
Medwin's threatening demand. Even without this information, she

was sceptical of his claims. Sending the letter on to Jane Hogg on 30 May, she ridiculed the idea that anybody would have offered such a sum: 'had he said £100 there had been a semblance of truth.' She had not bothered to answer his last letter, she added; 'nor of course shall I this'. But her experiences with Gatteschi and Major Byron had taught her caution; Hogg was requested to examine all of Medwin's correspondence with a lawyer's eye before returning it to her safe-keeping.[12] She had another year to wait, anxiously, before learning what Medwin might choose to say about the delicate subject of the Chancery case.

Going abroad provided an escape from worry. Mary had fallen in love with Baden-Baden on her travels with Percy and few spas had such a reputation for curing nervous complaints. In July, as the temperature in London drove everybody away who could afford the luxury of escape, she set off for the German spa, then at its zenith as one of the most fashionable in Europe. Kind, cheerful Mrs Hare and her sister Miss Paul were there to keep her company as she dutifully sipped the waters, walked out for her daily bath and sighed at the relentless heat. (John Leech's cartoons for *Punch* in the summer of 1846 showed London cabbies stripped down to hats and underwear; holidaying on the Rhine, Charles Dickens was feeling ready to melt.) Roulette in the stifling candle-lit rooms of the casino was less tempting than cool evening carriage drives out to the great ruins of Caracalla's baths, reminding her of Rome, or slow walks along the bank of the river Oos. The doctors were being most kind and helpful, she told Claire; it still took only one extended stroll to prostrate her.

There was no point in feigning grief at the news that old Lady Shelley had died of gastroenteritis at Elcott, her new home in Berkshire, in August. Courteous visits had been paid to Elcott, the last of them only a few months ago, but it had been hard to maintain an affectionate manner, especially after Lady Shelley's ungenerous behaviour over Field Place; writing to the recently widowed Alexander Berry in Australia, Mary commented without sentiment that her mother-in-law's death was a benefit to Percy. (Lady Shelley's annual allowance had already cost him a thousand pounds.) She was far more distressed by Claire's passionate objections to being evicted from her roost in Chester Square at the end of the summer.

It had suited Mary, who never liked to think of Percy being alone, that he should have his aunt's company while she was away. But Percy, lovingly urged to come and undertake a cure for an ailment of his own at the spa, was ready to take up the invitation by the end of a baking August in the city. Surely, Claire could not expect them to keep a full household running for a solitary visitor's benefit in the season when all large London homes were asleep in their dustsheets? But Claire's pride was easily wounded. 'I fear I worded my letter about shutting up my house unkindly,' Mary wrote to her on 5 September in soothing tones:

> for you seem hurt – & I am so, *so* sorry – God know[s] I am the last person who ought to inflict the smallest pain on you – I to whom you have ever been so kind – forgive me if it is so – I entreat you – When I wrote I was very ill . . . I was in hopes from Percy that your spirits were better – but you do not write so. This opera house &c must weigh on them . . . Adieu dear Claire pray forgive me . . .

The damage had been done. Claire was not to be comforted by friendly words on her new relationship with charming, elusive Walter Coulson, the Cornish-born newspaper editor whom Mary had often seen at the Novellos' home in the 1820s. Sulkily, Claire moved back to the house she had rented earlier that summer on Osnaburgh Street, within earshot of the mangy lions in the Regent's Park zoo and the wheeze and creak of trains being cranked up the last steep incline from Camden into the new station at Euston. The area was neither fashionable nor pleasant; the contrast to quiet, elegant Chester Square was hard to ignore. So was Mary's reluctance to visit. True, her health was unimproved when she returned from Germany in the late autumn; to a touchy stepsister with rheumatic complaints of her own to worry about, Mary seemed to use illness as a convenient reason for staying clear of a less genteel area than her own.

Sick, fretful and worried as always about Percy's future – 'He is told he must look out for an Heiress,' Mary informed Alexander Berry, a man who now took an affectionate interest in his late wife's relations on the other side of the world – she was ready to admit that the appearance of an heiress ready to marry an easygoing young baronet would be 'a desirable event'.[13]

The sale of Castle Goring and the death of Lady Shelley persuaded Mary's friends that she must by now be a wealthy woman. She was not. She gladly applied to the Royal Literary Fund in December for assistance to Isabella Booth in her grim role as nurse and keeper to a lunatic invalid. But an appeal from the Novello family, perhaps for a contribution to the Italian school begun by Mazzini and energetically supported by them, was rejected; a guinea was all she could afford, she told Novello, and she imagined that a guinea was 'giving nothing'.[14] The Hunts chose that same month, January 1847, to remind Mary of the fortune they had saved her by producing the letter in which Byron had renounced the £2,000 due to him as Shelley's executor.[15] But when Marianne boldly called at Chester Square to ask for a reward, she was told that Mary was not at home. Mary did not pretend that the statement had been true: 'beg Marianne to forgive me – but I could not see her,' she wrote to Hunt.[16] She could see less demanding friends: 'I am always at home by ½ past 4,' she told Edward Moxon that same week and then reproached him for staying away.

Mary's wish to see Moxon probably had something to do with a small, three-volume edition of Shelley which was brought out with her approval, plus a reprint of the uncut 1839 edition, in 1847. Here, after all the trouble she had experienced over the cutting of blasphemous passages from *Queen Mab* in 1839, Mary chose the easy option of printing only the innocuous first two cantos. It had, she noted in her introduction, been 'deemed advisable'; did she hope to draw the general reader's attention away from the controversial passages in the later cantos and the notes, which were also omitted? Perhaps. 'The opening of Queen Mab is the most striking part of the poem,' she wrote defensively. 'It is the boy's dream of beauty and love. [The verses] bear the impress of earnest, daring, fearless youth. Shelley's angelic nature breathes in every line, and these cantos must always be pre-eminently valued by those happy few who understand and love him.' It was as near as she dared go to dismissing all that made the poem a treasure to Shelley's radical audience; another brick had been laid in the wall she was protectively creating around her husband's reputation.

The stepsisters had always competed when it came to pre-eminence in suffering; a return of Mary's illness in the opening months of 1847 was sufficiently grave to put her well ahead in this grisly game. Sick though she evidently was, Claire was still suspicious enough to see her as a rival in love. When Mary, with the kindest intentions, invited Walter Coulson and Claire to dinner together, intending to spend the evening quietly resting upstairs, Claire instantly detected a plot. Mary had asked Coulson only because she was in love with him herself! 'Take my word for it, dear Claire, I shall never marry anyone,' Mary reassured her after apologizing for any unlucky vagueness in her invitation. She added affectionate hopes that Claire would win such 'an excellent husband', one who would be 'too happy to have a clever accomplished wife fond of & taking care of him . . . I wish with my whole heart he were yours.'[17]

Mary's wishes were heartfelt. Convalescing at Brighton in June, she sent Claire an affectionate letter of praise for her courage, her ability to make friends wherever she went, her willingness to shoulder her troubles alone; who could not want to see her rewarded? Advising against another friendship with someone identified only as 'B', she set herself to thinking how Coulson could be coaxed into marriage.

Mary's advice to Claire was, she assured her, only 'theoretical'. Coulson must be made to feel utterly comfortable and at home when he visited Osnaburgh Street. No man could resist having life made easy for him; it was up to Claire to offer peace, to become 'a benign and gentle influence'. Self-control was the secret, Mary added:

> All my experience tends to prove that a Man's affections once engaged are much more easily kept if a woman can show attachment without passion & affection & devotion with a self-controul with regard to the greatest happiness, most difficult – yet most desirable to attain – This makes a woman all powerful with a man – He must believe in your affection yet know that you can resist him – & then . . . his attachment takes deep roots & is never changed . . .[18]

It is possible to interpret Mary's reference to 'the greatest happiness' as marriage; it is as likely that she was warning Claire not to sleep with Coulson until she was sure of him. The second explanation, given the impetuousness of Claire's past relationship with Byron, seems more convincing. Mary's letter did not help bring about the desired match; it does raise the intriguing question of whether her advice was based on her experience of being loved and rejected by Aubrey Beauclerk. Had Rosa won him by showing a restraint which Mary herself had failed to exercise and which she now decided to use as a warning to Claire?

The illness which kept Mary in bed in the opening months of 1847, when she invited Claire to dine with Walter Coulson, was as severe as it had been after the scare she had given the doctors in March 1846. 'I hope & trust I am getting better at last,' she wrote to Vincent Novello on 5 January; a month later, she wistfully told Edward Moxon that she hoped to be 'entirely restored to health before *very* long'; by May, she could only report that she was 'nearly well', having been confined to her sofa for almost four months. Dr Mantell, an agreeable neighbour who was always ready to lend books and to come round for talks about geology,* a subject in which Mary took a keen

---

* The Mantell collection of fossils was sold for £5,000 to the British Museum *c.* 1840.

interest, had retired from practising medicine; instead, Mary placed herself under the care of a Dr Smith.* This doctor, judging from his recommendation to Claire of soapy washes as a cure for rheumatism, was a man of eccentric views. The several operations he performed on Mary in February produced little improvement, although she was correctly informed that a small growth which Smith had discovered, seemingly on her spine, would disappear of its own accord. Still too weak to sit up without support, she was advised to take a holiday by the seaside: 'change of air is the best remedy,' she wrote to Leigh Hunt just before setting off for the South Coast.

A change of air was always welcome if it meant escaping from 'odious' London, but Mary was quick to regret having chosen to visit noisy Brighton and not peaceful, congenial Sandgate for her summer convalescence. Percy was away, sailing his yacht among the Norwegian fjords with – a thoughtful gift from his mother – Mary Wollstonecraft's *A Short Residence* at his side, but Aubrey Beauclerk's sister Gee was staying nearby and Mary, still 'sadly bored', was feeling well enough by August to ask Isabella Booth and then Claire to join her. (Her anxious attempts to separate their visits suggests that the two women had little in common.) 'I like to see young people,' she told Claire in her letter of invitation;[20] she was rewarded by visits from Alexander Knox and from Jane Hogg's daughter, Dina Hunt.

Dina and her husband Henry were as poor as the rest of the Hunts and just as hopeless at providing for themselves, although Dina had some skill as an artist. Mary, urging her to try to earn some money by this means, was again dismayed by the fecklessness of Hunt and his tribe. Marianne had long ago found solace in drink; Hunt, chattering delightfully on every subject under the sun, remained as incapable as his wife of keeping hold of the money he shamelessly took from anybody willing to support him. Carlyle left out gold sovereigns on his mantelpiece when expecting a visit from Hunt; Dickens, in 1847, raised £440 for him with a theatrical benefit. The Whig government were less generous, granting a reluctant annual pension of £200. They were 'shabby' not to have given more, Mary told him on

---

* Dr Smith is not to be confused with the better-known Dr Southwood Smith. The distinction is made clear in a letter from Mary to Claire of 28 July 1847 in which Mary wrote that 'tho' I was not acquainted with him', she had commended Southwood Smith to their mutual friend Emily Dunstan as 'both clever and liberal'. Miss Dunstan, who may have been a former servant, was in prison, although the charge against her is not known. Seriously ill, she was allowed home before the end of July. Mary, who had reluctantly sent £10 to her sister, was relieved to hear that the Dunstans had borrowed more successfully from another quarter. Later in the summer, she made excuses to prevent Emily from joining her at Brighton.[19]

29 June; tactfully, she forbore to mention that she was still struggling to repay the last £200 she had borrowed on his behalf.

Hunt's chance to show his gratitude followed almost directly on the happy report of his pension from the Whigs. Early in July, Medwin wrote that he was working on the last proof of his book about Shelley, that he expected it to cause a great stir and that he was indifferent to anything the critics might choose to say. Mary had barely put his note in the post to Hogg for legal advice when she saw the book advertised in the press. Immediately, and with touching faith in the ageing Hunt's influence in the world of journalism, she begged him to exert his power to suppress any reviews that might already have been written. 'I most earnestly desire that it may fall dead born,' she told him on 11 July; Hunt gallantly promised to see that it did.

Five days later, Mary renewed her campaign. Conscious by now that Hunt's eldest son Thornton was better placed as a journalist to work on her behalf, she concentrated on supplying him with a sense of the high importance of his mission. Think, she urged his father to instruct 'dear good Thornton', of the harm Medwin might do to poor Claire who 'never injured any one – suppose *she* were mentioned'; think of the damage he might do to Harriet Shelley's name, and to Ianthe – '& who knows how many whom the wretch with what he calls his slashing may inflict misery upon'. If the book could be suppressed before publication, 'a triumph in evil' would be vanquished, an achievement 'worthy of Thornton's best endeavours – God speed him in it – the bad seldom succeed in open wickedness –'[21]

Thornton's endeavours came too late. Medwin's life of Shelley was published that autumn and widely reviewed. The critics, one of whom inadvertently praised Medwin as the author of Hogg's 1832 recollections of Shelley at Oxford, were friendly; a few smiled at his eagerness to push himself to the front of the story. (Thackeray, borrowing from Medwin for the character of Captain Sumph in *Pendennis* in 1849, allowed the captain to boast that his schoolfriend Shelley had been expelled 'for a copy of verses, every line of which I wrote, by Jove'.[22]) The anecdotal, rambling style, similar to that employed by Medwin's friend Captain Jesse in an 1844 life of the late Beau Brummell, was appealing and entertaining; the copious inaccuracies and misquotations counted for less with readers than Medwin's affection and respect for his subject.

Mary, if she ever read the book – she begged for it not to be sent to her – was probably torn between relief and exasperation. Medwin had, after all, been more tactful than she had anticipated. Generous to Jane Williams, he had given a sympathetic portrait of Claire, while not disguising the fact that she had been pregnant when she arrived at Geneva in 1816. No mention was made of the fact that Harriet was with child when Shelley eloped with Mary and no attempt was made to suggest that Shelley's first marriage had been suitable or happy. It was, Medwin observed, only remarkable that he should have continued for so long 'to drag on a chain, every link of which was a protraction of torture'.[23] Less use had been made of the Chancery papers than he had threatened; the story of little Elena Adelaide was transformed into a romantic tale of a lady who, having followed Shelley from Geneva to Naples, met him, told her history, and died. No child was mentioned; Medwin may never have known more than he breezily related.

Concerning Mary, Medwin displayed a mixture of respect and boorishness. 'It could not have been her personal charms that captivated him [Shelley],' he wrote, 'for to judge of her in 1820, she could not have been handsome, or even what may be denominated pretty.'[24] He hinted at 'substantial reasons' for Mary's having 'thrown herself on his [Shelley's] protection', a phrase which could only be taken to mean that she had become pregnant. *Frankenstein*, however, was stoutly defended as the work of Mary alone and *Valperga* was praised for its 'eloquence and beauty and poetry'. Medwin was not being wholly unfair when he regretted her lack of skill in 'delineation of character – and dialogue –; she had not seen enough of the world – or mixed enough in society to anatomize mankind.'[25] It is not the criticism but the tone which grates; Medwin wrote as one who could do it all so much better. Not unexpectedly, he called on her to publish the 'Essay on Christianity'; it did not seem to him that Shelley's views would shock a mid-nineteenth-century audience.

Mary did not share Medwin's confidence and she felt no obligation to heed his request. Writing a short article on her at the end of the year, George Gilfillan, one of Shelley's most ardent admirers, sighed for the life which only she could write;[26] Florence Marshall, Mary's first biographer, claimed that she now began gathering papers for this purpose.[27] There is no evidence that this was so. Mary had not shifted her view since May 1846, when she told Medwin that she had already done all that could be done, 'with propriety'.

Percy, rosy and cheerful after his summer sailing trip around the coast of Norway, returned in September to take his mother on a visit to his Shelley aunts, now living at their late mother's house near Hungerford. Percy gallantly escorted the aunts on riding expeditions; Mary, after purchasing Lady Shelley's open carriage, an object she had coveted for some time, proposed that she and her son might use it for an excursion to Wales. Visiting the Vale of Usk, she grew conscious that Trelawny and Augusta, who had moved to Wales some time after Goring divorced her in 1841, were nearby. Writing to Augusta the following year, Mary gave ill health as her excuse for not calling;[28] in 1850, she claimed not to have known that they lived in Wales. The truth was that she had been anxious to keep Augusta at a distance ever since her friend had begun living with Trelawny; she did not, perhaps, know that they had at last, in 1847, become a married couple.

In November, however, Trelawny came to London on his own. Mary had often confided her worries about Percy to him in the past; she did so again now, seemingly unaware of how little of his affection she had retained since their disagreement in 1838 over his relationship with Augusta and Mary's refusal to share his political views. Percy had become involved with a young woman – too young, in his mother's view. He was not suited to the role of a tutor or guide; that, at least, was the reason Mary gave for opposing a match. It is not known what Trelawny said, beyond urging Mary to resume her friendship with his wife. Percy's romance was short-lived and it may well have been his mother's interference which nipped it in the bud. Much though she loved her son, her desire to control his life is difficult to condone. He was, after all, almost twenty-eight, seven years older than Shelley had been when Mary and he eloped to Switzerland.

The unexpected death of her friend Gee Paul in that December was felt deeply by Mary. Gee's reclusive father, Charles Beauclerk, was already dead; Aubrey and Rosa were living at Ardglass in Ireland. The death of Gee broke her last link with a family whose kindness – Aubrey had long ago been forgiven for his betrayals – shone in contrast to the social slights and cuts over which Mary still often brooded. It was only occasionally now that she acknowledged her own bold flouting of convention to have been the first reason for her exclusion; all she remembered, in a bitter letter warning Isabella Booth about the unfriendliness of London society, was that people had refused to help her when she most needed friends.[29] The year 1840, when Percy had turned twenty-one, and when she had hoped most for kindness and received none, was especially vivid in her memory of life as an outsider. To us, remembering her friendships with the Hares, the Manners-Suttons, the Beauclerks, Lady Morgan, Mrs Norton, Samuel Rogers – the list could fill a paragraph – it does not seem that her exclusion had been so absolute and enduring as she imagined, but Mary's depressive nature caused her to dwell on the darker aspects of her life, until they obscured the existence of these affectionate and enduring relationships.

Shelley's 'child of light' was now past fifty and becoming increasingly conservative in her views. Mary Wollstonecraft had been twenty years younger when she went to Paris, burning with enthusiasm for the high ideal of a revolutionized, egalitarian society. Mary, always more cautious than her mother, had grown up during the hardship and disillusionment of the post-revolutionary years. Travelling with Shelley through a ravaged France in 1814, she had been shocked by the deserted villages, the derelict countryside. The Creature of *Frankenstein* had been shaped, in part, as her response to this, its burning of the de Lacey family's cottage a warning of the monstrous potential for damage which was released when revenge took precedence over justice. 'I am not for violent extremes,' she had written in 1838, when she refused to join Trelawny and his friends among the Philosophical Radicals in supporting agitation by the Chartists for a reformed electoral system; if she had sensed any injustice in the transportation of two rebel Chartists to Australia the following year, she failed to express it.

A final test of Mary's political views came ten years later when Europe burst into rebellion against military oppression and antiquated monarchies. In February 1848 came the news from France that Louis Philippe had been replaced by a provisional government; by the end of March, revolutions had taken place in Sicily, where the Bourbons had been overthrown, and in Hungary and Lombardy. The 'five glorious days' of Milan marked the ousting of Austria's military force from that city. The King of Piedmont-Sardinia was challenged and defeated. From Paris, as a flood of French emigrés made their way to England, news filtered through of terrified English families who had seen their homes ransacked and burned. The Chartists, marking the tenth anniversary of their claims with plans for a mass march on London, were perceived as evidence that the revolutionary spirit had spread to England.

Mary's initial response to the changes in France was indignant. Writing to Peacock's widowed daughter she expressed her despair that so many French had abandoned their country instead of staying to fight for order: 'the worst feature in all French changes is, that all people of any birth, station fortune or influence fly at once.' She nevertheless passed on her secondhand news that Lamartine, appointed head of the new provisional government, was warning English residents to leave Paris and withdraw their property; Mary Ellen was urged to stay with her father in England until things calmed down.[30]

Things did not calm down and Mary, by the end of March, had

become both angry and frightened. These were 'awful times', she wrote to Alexander Berry in Australia. 'There is no doubt that a French propaganda is spread among all the nations – they are rousing the Irish & even exciting the English Chartists.' Ireland was locked in religious battle, one half detesting the other; in England 'the Chartists are full of menace – covert & secret'. So complete was her terror that she was ready to ask Berry whether, if the worst came to the worst, they could take refuge with him. 'We would make fight first – but if Percy & I ran to Australia would you allow us to *squat* on your land?' They would pay rent, she forlornly added, by raising and selling crops.[31] She made this request at a time when Percy was canvassing for the Horsham seat, but Mary had ceased to feel any faith in her son's ability to become an effective political figure. The most she could say to Berry was that she expected him to win respect, if he gained the seat, for 'stainless integrity & uprightness'.

Mary's fears of revolution in England were calmed by the extraordinary measures taken on 10 April to defeat the Chartists' plan to march on Parliament with a monster petition signed, it was inaccurately rumoured, by almost six million names. Some 170,000 special constables were enrolled; the Bank of England and other public buildings were prepared against attack; the military, headed by the aged Duke of Wellington, were concealed at strategic points along the projected route to Westminster. The march was prudently reduced to a meeting and disbanded after a promise that the petition would be conveyed to Parliament for scrutiny and consideration. Mary, who had been worried that Claire's home might be attacked by a riotous mob, was much relieved.

The year of revolutions marked the culmination of 'the hungry Forties' in England and widespread unrest on the Continent among the rural and urban poor. Mary, as she heard of Germany, too, breaking down into anarchy, with rents unpaid and peasants making war against their landlords, reacted with terror and disgust. Her own celebrated novel and its message of political warning was surely in her mind as she wrote to Alexander Berry in June of the 'fearful events' in Europe: 'Countless uncivilized men, long concealed under the varnish of our social system, are breaking out with the force of a volcano & threatening order – law & Peace.'[32] However readily Mary championed individual causes, cared for former servants, raised or gave money to needy friends, she had little sympathy for revolutionaries. Her father's daughter, she continued to place her trust in gradual, peaceful measures for reform.

It was Charles Clairmont who now showed himself the truer

heir to Mary Wollstonecraft, for whom he had always felt a profound admiration. Writing from Vienna to scold Claire for her increasingly reactionary views, he made a passionate defence of Italy's right to free herself from Austrian domination, despite the fact that his own employers were the imperial family. Were the heroic rebels to be 'crushed by the heel of a Metternich', he demanded? How dare Lord Brougham tell the House of Lords that Austria was asserting her ancient right to rule! What right? No, it would not do to say that Austria had been quiet and happy until revolution came: 'it was not a happiness suitable to the dignity of the human race . . . it was the contented torpor of the herd grazing and fattening for next week's market . . .'[33] Even Charles, however, was alarmed when his young son Wilhelm showed signs of joining the rebels. Eagerly though he championed the rights of the oppressed, Charles did not want any Clairmont blood spilt in the cause. Wilhelm was shipped over to England to join his aunt Claire and take a course in farm management.

Comfort, and the prospect of financial security, were on hand at last for a weary middle-aged lady who was increasingly at the mercy, not of dangerous revolutionaries, but of her own rapidly deteriorating health. On 22 June, at St George's, Hanover Square, Mary witnessed her son's marriage to a woman of whom she wholeheartedly approved, a woman who frankly admitted to a later biographer that she had lost her heart, not to Percy, but to his mother.[34] Her name was Jane St John and she came into Mary's life as a loving daughter, ready to share her burdens and, so Mary devoutly hoped, to give her the grandchildren she longed for. Percy was a disappointment; who could tell what his son or daughter might not be raised to achieve?

THE CHOSEN ONE

1848–1851

'. . . she is to us as the dearest portion of ourselves.'

Mary Shelley to Augusta Trelawny, 24 September 1849

THE NEW LADY SHELLEY LIKED IT TO BE THOUGHT THAT SHE WAS a clergyman's daughter. Her father, Thomas Gibson, was in fact a Newcastle banker who never married Ann Shevill, the mother of his nine children. Gibson, who died when Jane was twelve, left each of his children £5,400; Jane, sent off to live with an aunt and uncle in the Lake District, received her portion in 1841, when she married Charles Robert St John, a younger son of Lord Bolingbroke. Ann, her sister, married his first cousin.

Jane's husband, an invalid throughout their childless marriage, died three years later, leaving his twenty-four-year-old widow a legacy of £15,000 and the guardianship of his nine-year-old illegitimate son, Charles. His eldest brother, patron of a Dorset living, probably owned or helped find the small house nearby which became her main home. Tempting though it is to draw comparisons with Mary's unconventional background, they are slight. Jane had not been stigmatized by her mother's unmarried status; she herself never broke society's rules.[1] The illegitimate child to whom her husband appointed her guardian had been born six years before they met.

Jane first enters Mary's letters on the eve of the dreaded Chartist meeting on 10 April 1848. Writing to Claire two days earlier, Mary told her that 'Mrs St John is still with us – She stays longer than I expected.' This rules out a story that Percy cancelled his plan to stand for Horsham on 24 March because he became engaged that day;[2] Mary would not have written so coolly to his devoted aunt two weeks after such an announcement.

Jane, as a loquacious old lady, was happy to give a fuller account. Talking in 1894 to young Maud Brooke (Maud really was the daughter of a clergyman, a devoted Shelleyite), she gave away nothing of her parentage. The story, in her version, began in the autumn of 1847, when she came up from Dorset to stay with a sister who lived in Chester Square and who one day pointed out the house with 'the Frankenstein curtains' on the opposite side. Percy, she learned, was interested only in boats, but friends urged Jane to make friends with his mother. 'You should know Mrs Shelley; you would suit each other so well.' Visiting Baden-Baden, she met a friend of Percy's who thought that she and Percy, too, would make a perfect couple.

It was, in Jane's recollection, Mary who initiated the friendship. Jane was staying with another member of the family in Bayswater and resting after 'one of my bad headaches' when a visitor was announced. Jane, who was short and plump, fondly recreated Mary for Miss Brooke's attentive ears as a creature of almost ethereal grace. She had been 'tall and slim' with 'the most beautiful deep-set eyes I have ever seen'. Mary's spiritual looks were enhanced by the information that she always dressed 'in long soft grey material, simply and beautifully made'.[3] Jane's voice can also be heard in the last pages of Florence Marshall's 1889 life of Mary as she describes the same meeting: 'a fair, lovely, almost girlish-looking being, "as slight as a reed", with beautiful clear eyes . . . put out her hand as she rose, saying half timidly, "I'm Mary Shelley."'[4]

The details had been coloured by memory, but there is no doubt that Mary and Jane took to each other. Jane was invited to stay at 24 Chester Square and here, with his mother's warm encouragement, Percy eventually proposed. On 30 March, Mary was still telling Alexander Berry that she hoped Percy would win his seat; by 10 June, she could inform Augusta Trelawny that her son had won instead 'the sweetest creature I ever knew . . . all goodness & truth'. They were married twelve days later by Jane's clergyman brother-in-law: 'Please God, you will be happy together,' Mary wrote to Jane that morning. A week later, while the couple honeymooned in the Lake District, Mary allowed herself to paint a happy picture of the future. Jane cared only for others, she told Alexander Berry; now that Percy had given up politics, the three of them would live together at Field Place where, helped by his wife's modest fortune, they would devote themselves to the care of the estate and the tenants while, she hoped, improving their own income. Perhaps Mr Berry might wish to know that the nearest railway station was only three miles from the house, should he ever wish to visit England?[5]

A month later, ensconced at her favourite seaside resort of Sandgate with Knox for company, Mary was trembling at the cost of compensating the Field Place tenant for his renovations (£500) while paying interest on their 'odious mortgages' on the estate (£1,500): 'where we are to get it I don't know,' she wailed to Claire who, having been excluded from the wedding, was now angrily accusing Mary of saying unpleasant things about her. 'The phrase you quote certainly does not look pretty all by itself,' Mary admitted, but how could Claire suppose she would permit gossip, or indulge in it herself? 'Talking over one's friends to other friends is a practice I have in abhorrence . . .'[6] Claire was unconvinced; had Trelawny not described Mary to her as 'the blab of blabs'? She also took note that, after the move to Field Place in August, there was scarcely a letter of Mary's in which she did not refer to Knox as a guest. Already suspicious, Claire drew the worst conclusions.

Twenty-six years after Shelley's death, Mary arranged her modest possessions, her writing-desk, her dressing-case, her books, in his old room on the first and uppermost floor of Field Place. From the windows, she looked out across the lawn to a handsome group of cedar trees. The estate was run-down; the house, while 'any thing but a country seat of any mark whatever', seemed more agreeable than she remembered from her first visit shortly after Sir Timothy's death. It had a more relaxed atmosphere than she could have guessed from the pompous attitude of the Shelleys.[7]

The thing which told against Field Place for two ladies who were such martyrs to their health as Mary and her daughter-in-law was the fact that the house stood on cold clay soil, and in a low position. In warm weather, Field Place would seem delightful. Arriving in a summer of torrential rain, Mary was appalled by the damp. The fires smoked; the drawing-room steamed like a laundry behind its long windows. It was 'the dampest isle in Xendom', she told Claire; '. . . the whole place is a swamp – Nothing can be so bad for me.' Forbidden to bring even one maid when she visited because of lack of room, Claire was invited to sympathize with Mary's own difficulty in this respect. 'The number of Maids one must keep in the country is a trouble – & yet I always feel it is one of the best ways in the world of doing good – giving work to the industrious.'[8]

Such startling lapses in tact, together with repetitions and nervous apologies for her forgetfulness, are a sad testimony to Mary's increasingly confused state as the undiagnosed tumour on her brain began to affect her mind as well as her body. Neuralgia caused her spine to tingle as though it was on fire; the bouncing movement of a carriage was unbearably painful; even a short walk had become an endurance test. Dr Smith was unable to suggest anything beyond calomel, cod liver oil and rest as a cure for the nervous headaches and periods of semi-paralysis which afflicted his patient. Staying at Field Place at the beginning of 1849, Mary was too depressed and ill to join in conversation; the worst part of living in London during the previous autumn had been the lack of a room in which she could shut herself away in solitude. And still nobody could tell her what was wrong. She was puzzled when Mrs Mason's elder daughter, the Italian-speaking Laura Galloni, now embarked on a writing career, declined her offer to act as a translator; Laura's refusal was probably well meant, since Mary's letters now frequently described writing as a great effort.*

Life was not being kind to Mary. Jane was often as much of an invalid as herself and as impossible to diagnose. One month, the doctors would announce that she was cured; the next, Mary would hear that Jane was on the verge of death. Longing for some of her son's calmness, or lack of imagination, she resigned herself to the fact that the damp at Field Place would always be dangerous to her daughter-in-law, that expensive journeys abroad would become a regular feature of her beloved children's life, and that her substitutes for the longed-for grandchildren were to be a pack of amiable house-dogs and Charles or 'Carlo' St John, the loutish young ward who paid them occasional visits when he was home from a career in the navy. (Reluctant to own up to the fact that Jane's first husband had fathered an illegitimate son, even though the boy had been born in Corfu in 1832, long before Jane's first marriage, Mary preferred to disguise him as a 'near relative' of the late Mr St John.)

Jane's illness is intriguing. Mary had seen no hint of it before the marriage; is it too far-fetched to wonder if, childless in her first and second marriages, Jane used illness as a way of keeping Percy out of her bedroom? Such situations have occurred; Mary, not Percy, was the

---

* 'I walk very well – but must not use my head – or strange feelings come on –' Mary told Claire on 5 February 1849; six days later, she told Claire that 'writing is the one thing, that makes me uncomfortable.' She had already made a stab, in 1846, at translating Laura Galloni's *Inez de Medine*, a story which was published in Italy that year. The two chapters which survive in the Abinger collection do not make one regret the absence of more. Laura's florid style and unconvincing characters, when married to Mary's banality as a translator, would not have gladdened a publisher's heart.[9]

great love of Lady Shelley's life. Marrying the son, she had chosen the mother.

Shelley's tongue had been in his cheek when he nicknamed his hot-tempered Mary 'Pecksie' after a singularly obliging and docile little bird in a children's book. Percy was equally wry in giving Jane the name 'Wren' or 'Wrennie'. Jane's cocked head and rotund shape did give her a slight physical resemblance to this shy bird; not so, her nature. As Mary, worn out by life, became an increasingly shadowy figure in their triangular relationship, Jane, despite her mysterious ailment, became increasingly formidable. 'To live with Mary Shelley was indeed like entertaining an angel. Perfect unselfishness, selflessness indeed, characterized her at all times,' she informed Mary's biographer.[10] But Mary's submission, when allied to Percy's biddability, underlines the degree to which her daughter-in-law had taken the reins into her own capable hands. Mary wanted always to be with her beloved 'children'; Jane, allowed full authority, was happy to give her that pleasure.

To Claire, watchful, excluded and poor, it was apparent that her own tenuous role as confidante and near-relation had been usurped. The new Lady Shelley now ruled the roost at Field Place; Mary had been swallowed up by her and what Claire scornfully called their *super-fine set*. Occasionally, she showed her claws. How lucky that Lady Shelley was so economical! she exclaimed to Mary in one letter: 'for she told me she did not care for the luxuries of Life, and wanted only Bread and Cheese.'[11] The jeer is impossible to miss. A storm, where two such characters were concerned, was bound to brew. Nobody could have anticipated its ferocity.

In the spring of 1849, Charles Clairmont's young son Wilhelm was joined in England by his pretty sister Clara; Claire, full of goodwill, made plans to settle her niece as a teacher in a select ladies' school, perhaps at Brighton, an hour's journey on the new railway from the lodgings which she had taken for them all in a village near Maidstone in Kent. The trouble, as she candidly owned in an appeal to Mary for help that April, was that she was so poor. 'I suffer so much in all ways from want of money.' There were times, Claire wrote, when she simply sat down and cried. 'I must say that I think –' she went on ominously, but Mary or perhaps her daughter-in-law destroyed the rest of the letter;[12] all we know is that Mary was 'grieved & even shocked' by Claire's observations.[13]

Answering in what she hoped was a soothing way, Mary apologized for being unable to send any money when they were struggling to pay bills for repairs and for Jane's doctors. The bad harvest of 1848 had resulted in unpaid rents. It was all they could do, she explained, to keep up the interest on their mortgage on the estate. Of course, she wished to help little 'Clairkin' and Willy. If Claire would only consider settling near them, Willy could be taught agriculture by their bailiff: 'but you have objections to his seeing much of us – as unsettling him'. Afraid of triggering one of Claire's outbursts, she scribbled an anxious afterthought inside the envelope, a hope that she had not, in her haste, written anything which might seem 'vain & presuming'.

'I fear so much to offend you,' Mary wrote to Claire a month later, embarrassed by the fact that a pre-arranged visit by Percy's Shelley aunts could not be undone and that all the bedrooms would be occupied when Claire visited. Would she, perhaps, be willing to stay in a local inn? She would not, but a compromise was reached. Wilhelm would not visit. Clara ('Clari') would come alone, after the aunts, 'les tantes', had left. Claire, who had expressed a strong wish not to be in the house at the same time as Jane Shelley, promised to join them later.

Clari's visit to Field Place, lasting several weeks, overlapped with one by Alexander Knox, recovering from an unhappy romance the previous year. Clari was young, gentle and apprehensive of her future as a teacher in a country she had only known for a month. Knox, lonely and sorry for her, fell in love. Lady Shelley gave the couple her enthusiastic support. Mary, despite mild anxiety at letting her dear Knox ally himself to a member of the hot-blooded Clairmont family, sent off a cheerful account of Clari's engagement to Charles in Vienna. Nobody, it seems, had thought to tell Claire of these developments before her own arrival at Field Place was announced.

Relating a bare outline of the drama to Florence Marshall, Jane Shelley remembered that, having disliked Claire from the first time they met, she was preparing to leave Field Place for London when Mary 'burst out in a vehement manner, not usual to her: "Don't go, dear; don't leave me alone with her. She has been the bane of my life since I was two!" I gladly stayed.'[14]

The next part of the story demonstrates Jane Shelley's forceful nature. She had, she later recalled, already decided that the engagement was an excellent thing for both young people. But Claire, when she arrived, 'began in a half-mad way to say all kinds of horrid things', probably concerning her belief that Knox was Mary's lover. Confronted by a weeping Clari, a hysterical Claire and a distraught

Mary, Jane took prompt action. Mary was escorted to her bedroom and left there behind a locked door. A groom was then summoned and told 'in a loud voice . . . to go instantly for the doctor, and to tell him that Miss Clairmont was very ill and excited and that he must bring some drug to cure her'.[15] The effect of this sinister threat was gratifyingly prompt; Claire left for Maidstone as soon as a carriage could be called to take her to the station. Shortly afterwards, she learned that Clari had gone quietly to London with Knox on 16 June and married him at the church where Percy had wedded Jane. The Shelleys, crowning arrogance with impudence, had given a ball to celebrate the occasion. Clari, seemingly unaware that she had done anything outrageous, sent her aunt a charming note to thank her for the gift of a cap and to report having received 'a most kind and affectionate letter' from her parents.[16] In the year when *Jane Eyre* offered a grim warning against the horrors of girls' schools and when the best recommendation Mary Shelley had been able to offer was for a teaching job in distant Liverpool, Clari must have felt that marriage, and to a loving, clever man, offered a happy alternative.

Claire's response to her niece's behaviour was strange indeed. Charles, questioning the terms of abuse she now applied to his daughter, was grimly informed that Clari had married a monster of infamy. Accepting that Claire must have sound evidence for her allegations, he was astonished when, a month after the wedding, she suggested that this villain might be the ideal person to find a good husband for Clari's sister, Pauline. It amazed him still more that Claire thought Willy should ask Knox for financial help. Living with the Knoxes in the autumn of 1849, Willy did receive support for his agricultural training, and when he visited Vienna after his father's death there of a stroke in February 1850, Knox paid his fare for the round trip.

Jane and Percy, it became increasingly clear, were the prime targets of Claire's hatred. In March 1850, Claire wrote a letter of furious reproach to Willy for his ingratitude to friends of hers with whom he lodged after his return. So he thought them dull? Perhaps he would prefer Field Place, where 'the new married wife feels far deeper interest in her husband's male friend than in her husband himself; [where] the young men who frequent the House, run a muck with the young women; if they are married, they dance riga-doon with them; if they are unmarried they fetch a Bull and carry off the young lady on its back . . .'[17] Ordered to write to Sir Percy and accuse him of having been an unappreciative grandson to Mrs Godwin, a subject on which he was ill-equipped to form an opinion, Willy refused to obey his aunt. His sister Pauline, however, after

KEEPER OF THE SHRINE

being shown the letters which Claire had hoarded as precious evidence of Mary's love-affair with Knox, was persuaded to write a reproach in the summer of 1850, an act which won her aunt's approval.[18] Antonia Clairmont, Charles's widow, was lambasted for having dared to send Mary a polite little note that July. An ultimatum was promptly issued from Claire's new London lodgings: communication with the Knoxes was – just – permissible, but there could be none with the Shelleys:

> Until they have made reparation for their insolence to us, it stamps
> with dishonour any member of our family, who holds any intercourse
> but a hostile one with them, and my resolution is taken and I will part
> from any of my relations who do. I have not words to express the
> shame I feel at your conduct.[19]

Words were not something Claire had ever been short of when she was enraged and her unfortunate sister-in-law continued to be deluged with reminders of the Shelleys' wickedness. As far as Mary was concerned, however, Claire kept her vow: all communication was terminated. Two years after Mary's death, Claire started to rewrite history again. In 1850, she had been ready to tell Antonia that 'Mrs Shelley, a mother herself, instigated Clary to outrage every law of natural tenderness, every filial duty, every family tie.' Now, it seemed that she had been innocent; it was all Clari's fault. Clari, poisoned by Lady Shelley's evil stories of her aunt Claire, had 'torn the old friend of my youth from me after five and forty years that we had stood together, sent that poor friend to a too early grave, and done all she could to make me insane with grief'.[20] Only a threat by Antonia Clairmont to send all of Claire's letters on to Alexander Knox put an end to her crazy diatribes in 1854. She expressed no grief when her twenty-nine-year-old niece died of pulmonary consumption in 1855. Years later, Claire had the gall to suggest that Knox, who had married again, should ask the Shelleys to send her some money; not even she had the nerve to make a direct appeal to the family she had slandered with such viciousness.[21]

Mary's own letters disclose nothing of this. Perhaps, as her health grew steadily weaker, she was relieved to be estranged from Claire. Grateful though she had been to her stepsister during the period of the Gatteschi fiasco, admiring though she was of the courage with which Claire had survived her long hard years as a governess, there had never been much love lost between them. As a child, she had usurped Mary's place; as an unwelcome third in her life with Shelley, she had been a trial and an embarrassment; as a voluble espouser of

Mary Wollstonecraft's beliefs, she had become a living reproach to Mary Shelley, her daughter and perceived heir. Bitterest of all, however, to a woman who had always done everything she could to shield Claire's reputation, was to find herself accused of keeping a lover young enough to be her son. No evidence has ever been found for believing that Mary had an affair with Knox; Claire's consisted only of the affectionate terms in which Mary often alluded to him in her letters, a single misread phrase – 'my Knox' where Mary had actually written 'beg Knox' – and the fact that he had once written her a note on the inside of one of Mary's envelopes.

The furore and its repercussions destroyed what should have been a pleasant summer for Mary at Field Place, but there was comfort in watching Shelley's reputation continue to flourish. A new publication, the *Stage Manager*, praised him in a series of essays published in the spring and summer of 1849. One reviewer of contemporary poetry respectfully noted his mounting influence, while another called his poems the most musical in the language. Exonerated and even apologized to from the pulpit of Eton College Chapel by the Conduct (the senior chaplain) in the same year, Shelley was discovered to have been a truly Christian poet, solaced in his darkest days by the gentlest and most understanding of wives. Mary herself was made the subject of a poem, honouring the love and compassion which she had shown.[22] Lady Shelley, hearing her mother-in-law 'constantly refer to what he [Shelley] might think, or do, or approve of, almost as if he had been in the next room', was easily persuaded of the poet's virtue and benevolence, and that his second marriage had been one of unusual compatibility.[23]

In September 1849, Percy and Jane left England for a climate more beneficial to Jane's health. Joining them at the end of the month, Mary made her first visit to the south of France, where she dutifully followed Jane in taking 'little sips' as a homoeopathic cure, having found no help in conventional medicine. Occasionally, she felt well enough to be taken out on a donkey to admire the sea from the hills behind Nice; for the most part, she lay on a sofa, conserving her energy to write an occasional letter. Peacock's daughter, widowed in 1844 when her husband, like Shelley, was drowned, was congratulated on her forthcoming marriage to young George Meredith. Augusta Trelawny was reminded that Mary wished to reclaim the little Curran portrait which Trelawny had kindly collected on her behalf and, less kindly, kept.* She felt a little uncomfortable when Augusta meaning-fully asked how Mrs Paul had felt about returning to spend her last years with a husband she no longer loved; Mary, who had strongly urged Augusta to follow the same course, was forced to admit that the reconciliation had not been a great success. It seemed to her now that the long estrangement from Augusta had been against her own wishes: 'I had always, so to speak, a natural inclination for you,' she told her.[25]

Home again after nine months abroad, Mary felt well enough to make a little visit to the Knoxes and another to Shelley's sisters at Elcott, their Berkshire home. The vicar of Elcott had been both 'amiable & agreable', she wrote to John Hastings Touchet, a pious country gentleman who often visited Field Place. Reassured that Jane was now 'quite herself again – as plump as a partridge & as gay as a lark, no headaches & no pains', Mr Touchet was also treated to an account of a 'sad piece of domestic history', the unlooked-for preg-nancy of Brenda, one of the house-dogs at Field Place. Wishing that Brenda would be a little less fecund, Mary longed for Jane to produce a child: 'we have our dogs & our doves & our birds –' she wrote to Isabella Booth, a proud grandmother, '& wish that we had our babies – but we must wait till Jane is yet better than she is now.'[26] Grandchildren would, she felt, help to compensate for all those chil-dren of her own that she had buried; they would love her uncrit-ically, undo the sense of superfluousness which sometimes overcame her as Jane's friends and relations filled the house.

Her hopes were not rewarded. 'Jane's health is our only real evil,' Mary wrote sadly to Augusta Trelawny on 12 August. 'When she is well all is bright & gay . . . I wish they had a family – & as her health improves & she becomes strong, we hope it will arrive.' But the only thing which appeared to strengthen Jane was absence from Field Place, and even this did not have the desired result.

While Mary worried about grandchildren, Jane and Percy were becoming increasingly concerned about her own state of health. The dampness of Field Place was, they were convinced, as deleterious to her as to her daughter-in-law. Plans for a move to England's Riviera, the sunny south coast, were already in progress.

It is unclear whether Mary was told that Jane, in 1849, had decided

---

* The picture was not returned. Trelawny maintained that Mary had thought it unflattering and had been happy for him to keep it. He acknowledged that Mary had once asked for the portrait of herself to show to a friend: 'To this verbally or in writing I refused, and she never afterwards alluded to it.'[24]

to purchase 'the admired seat of Boscombe Lodge', a pleasant if unremarkable white house standing on the cliffs a mile east of Bournemouth's unspoilt village.[27] This was the home which the Shelleys planned for Mary's last years as it became increasingly evident that full recovery was unlikely. Perhaps, knowing her love for the 'cascine', the beautiful pine forest which separated Pisa from the sea, they thought that Boscombe's woods and sea breezes would bring back happy memories.

The house stood ready, but Mary, by the autumn of 1850, was no longer well enough to be subjected to any radical changes in her life. Instead, Jane and Percy took her back to Chester Square, where she could be attended by the doctors of their choice. Sitting up in bed on 15 November, she made a last appeal to the Royal Literary Fund to help her old friend Isabella Booth. Mrs Booth's poverty was most 'bitter & pressing', Mary wrote weakly; her sacrifice in looking after her husband had been great. 'His Malady demanded a care & courage in nursing, which for a woman to undertake & go through with alone, demanded heroic exertion – She persevered to the last, at the sacrifise of her own health.'[28] Her letter reveals how strongly, even now, Mary Shelley felt for women to whom society offered no help or support. The description could as well have been applied to herself.

The Royal Literary Fund declined to help Mrs Booth again, however unfortunate her circumstances might be. Mary's response to their apparent indifference was to take matters into her own hands. Percy was asked to guarantee Isabella an allowance of £50 a year for the rest of her life, a promise which was dutifully kept.[29]

Mary's last letter was a tender little note to Peacock's daughter, begging her and her father to try to find time for the visit they had failed to pay to Field Place that summer. She looked forward to being introduced to Ellen's fiancé, Mr Meredith, and to reading the poems he hoped to publish.[30]

Years had passed since Mary had enjoyed more than a few weeks of continuous good health. Operations, homoeopathy, long periods of rest; all remedies had failed to cure a mysterious and painful illness which she imagined must be connected to her nervous and melancholy temperament. In the last cold weeks of 1850, confined to her bed at Chester Square and attended by a homoeopathic doctor who, Percy irritably observed, 'did not do her the least good', she felt her left leg turning numb. Partial paralysis followed but, by 3 January, her son felt hopeful enough to inform a worried Isabella Booth that their new doctors looked on the patient's chances of recovery 'very favourably'. A week later, he wrote again to thank Mrs Booth for offering to come and nurse his mother, and to refuse, since 'there is no danger now'.

Percy's optimism was short-lived. On 23 January, Mary had a series of fits, after which she lapsed into a coma. The last and most astute of her physicians, Richard Bright, deduced that the paralysis had been caused by some form of brain damage. Her case was now recognized to be hopeless. The coma lasted for eight days, during which no signs of suffering were apparent to her attendants. She died shortly after dusk on 1 February. Mary Anne Henry, the maid who had faithfully attended her for more than ten years, was in the room to draw down the blinds and close the curtains. Percy and Jane were by the bed: 'her sweet gentle spirit passed away without even a sigh –' Jane told Alexander Berry in one of the letters she wrote to give out the news.[31]

No medical records have survived but the death certificate confirmed what Dr Bright had already deduced from his patient's symptoms. Mary Shelley's illness stemmed from brain damage: a 'supposed tumour' in the left cerebral hemisphere was noted to have been 'of long standing'.

The house in Chester Square was sold a month after Mary's death. Moving promptly to Boscombe, Jane and Percy rented out Field Place. The estate was gradually parcelled out and sold off to raise revenue for its absentee landlord. In private hands today, Field Place makes no outward advertisement of its connection to the Shelley family;* at Boscombe, a small museum in the much-altered house, the names of the local roads – and, bizarrely, the Sir Percy Florence Shelley pub – keep the connection alive. Even though Mary Shelley never saw the pleasant view from the manor-house windows, of pine trees and lawns spreading out high above the sea, it is easier to imagine her here, a small resolute figure marching into the wind which gusts along the cliff path on a bright afternoon, than in the woods and low flat fields which enclose Shelley's old home.

Mary's death, mourned by the few old friends who survived and had stayed in touch with her son, was marked by a few trite verses and, on 15 February 1851, by a bland obituary in the *Athenaeum*. Shelley's dedication to *The Revolt of Islam* was quoted here as evidence of 'a real affection and the confidence of a real companionship'. All details of their early life together were omitted: if Shelley's story could

---

* A brass commemorative plaque was placed in Shelley's birth chamber in the 1870s on the instructions of Richard Garnett, who had become closely involved with the Shelleys and their archive. The interior has been meticulously restored by the present owner.

not yet be told, the anonymous writer argued, then the same discretion should be extended to his wife. Commended for her 'singular elegance of tone', Mary Shelley was reproached for the 'pervading melancholy' of her contemporary fiction and for the 'oppressive' languor of her historical novels. Her accounts of travels in Italy were praised; those of her travels in Germany were dismissed. Her editing of Shelley's works and her intelligent, opinionated essays for the *Cabinet Cyclopaedia* were passed over as mere literary hackwork. Only for *Frankenstein* was the obituarist unreserved in his enthusiasm. Mrs Shelley had here achieved 'a wild originality unknown in English fiction', he wrote; *The Last Man* had been unjustly neglected, but 'her "Frankenstein" will always keep for her a peculiar place among the gifted women of England'.

AFTERLIFE

'What a Set! What a World!'

Matthew Arnold, *Essays in Criticism* (1888)

DAYS AFTER MARY'S DEATH, PERCY AND JANE DECIDED TO EXHUME her parents' bodies. Mary, so Jane told Maud Brooke years later, had authorized the deed herself. 'I would like to rest at Bournemouth near you, but I would like to have my father and my mother with me.' Jane probably made this up; during the same conversation, she said that 'it would have broken my heart to let her loveliness wither in such a dreadful place.'[1]

Their intentions were good. The old borough of St Pancras had been vandalized by the railway companies. Streets, gardens and manor-houses were being pulled down to make way for the new lines. The directors of the new Midland railway had their sights trained on the neglected churchyard; in the 1860s, Thomas Hardy, then a young architect, uneasily presided over the nocturnal excavation of the east part of the graveyard and the removal of inconvenient tombstones, monuments and coffins. One old tree is still enclosed by the evidence, mossy tablets propped in rows around the base of its trunk.

The coffins of Mary Wollstonecraft and Godwin were hastily dug up and taken away in a private carriage; Everina Wollstonecraft and Godwin's second wife were left to take their chances.* An American

---

* Since Everina Wollstonecraft's burial place has disappeared, it must have been close to the grave of her sister and Godwin in the eastern part of the churchyard. A monument to Godwin and his two wives was erected at a later date in the diminished graveyard.

minister, visiting a neighbour of the Shelleys in 1868, was given the
bizarre details of the sequel.[2] Jane was determined that the bodies
should be reburied in St Peter's Church at Bournemouth; the vicar,
having heard nothing to suggest that these were suitable candidates,
was equally determined that they should not. He had not reckoned
with Lady Shelley's forceful nature. Bringing the coffins with her, she
sat in her carriage outside the churchyard's locked gate until the vicar,
fearing the scandal in a tiny village, surrendered. A large common
grave was dug on the high slope behind the church and, under cover
of night, Mary's parents were unceremoniously dropped into the pit.*
The commemorative slab mentioned, despite the vicar's protests, the
most famous writings of Mary's parents, but not *Frankenstein*. Even
Jane stopped short of desecrating hallowed ground with the name of
that blasphemous work, whatever the literary critics might say in its
praise.†

Claire was outraged. She had already written Sir Percy a strongly
worded complaint about his failure to inform her of Mary's death.
'Because I am myself dying I will speak my mind,' she announced in
her habitual style before dragging out the well-gnawed bone of
Knox's marriage to her niece.[3] To learn from the lawyers that her own
mother had been left to moulder alone at St Pancras, while Godwin
and Mary Wollstonecraft were spirited away to join their daughter,
was an insult she could scarcely credit. The news was indeed horrifying, Willy Clairmont agreed: 'it is so atrocious a deed that it can not
escape the notice of the public.'[4] Willy was mistaken. Uninformed,
the public failed to react.

Lady Shelley, having successfully stormed the gates of St Peter's,
was ready for the next stage in the process of sanctifying the adored
'Madre'. She was inspired, perhaps, by the last lines of a sentimental
homage to Mary which appeared in the *Leader* a month after her
death ('Happy departed ones! A brief farewell, / Till friend clasps
friend upon the silent shore').[5] A sculptor, Horatio Weekes, was

---

* Today, one can regret the Shelleys' decision. St Peter's churchyard stands on a busy corner,
overlooked by a hideous Stakis Hotel and confronted by the boarded-up windows of Berlin's
Wicked Fun Bar.
† The parish council of St Michael's Church, Chester Square, took the same view in 1977,
when application was made to put up a plaque to Mary Shelley on the exterior of her own
home, then the rectory. A plaque was permitted, but without any reference to *Frankenstein*.
The house is now in private hands, and the plaque has been adjusted to mention *Frankenstein*.
The present occupants have also commissioned murals for the interior, depicting scenes from
the Shelleys' lives.

commissioned to produce a monument which, denied room in St Peter's, was granted a discreet place in Christchurch Priory, by far the most beautiful and ancient religious building in the vicinity of Boscombe. Modelled after Michelangelo's *Pietà*, the marble bas-relief shows Mary as the Mater Dolorosa, barefoot and tastefully dressed in a toga, sitting by some seaweed-draped rocks with her husband reclining on her knees in the position of the dead Christ. Very much in keeping with the new style of Victorian church sculpture, it was unusual in representing parents, rather than a spouse or children. But Mary and her husband had, for the childless Shelleys, filled that gap.

Mary, in her final days, had apparently given many 'longing and beseeching' glances towards the small locked writing-desk which she always kept near her.[6] A year after her death, Percy reluctantly agreed to open it. Inside, they found his mother's journal and a copy of *Adonais* with a page folded to make an envelope. 'We opened it reverently,' Jane told Maud Brooke, 'and found ashes – dust and we then knew what Mary had so longed to tell us: all that was left of Shelley's heart lay there.' The discovery gave Jane her next idea, for a household shrine devoted to the memory of Shelley, Mary and their friends.

Boscombe, over the next few years, became a museum for the dead and a stage for the living. Actors, neighbours and friends were invited to evenings of theatricals. As a boy, Sir Percy had always loved going to plays; as a man in his late thirties, he began writing his own. A talented amateur whose ambition was only to entertain, he also composed the music and painted the scenery, including a drop cloth representing the Bay of Lerici and the Villa Magni. (One friend to whom Percy taught his technique and who went on to become a professional artist, left Boscombe in disgrace after painting white ribs on his host's Italian greyhounds and getting them to run through the garden like a pack of spectres.[7]) Jane, possessed of a good speaking voice and stage presence, was told by the silver-tongued Sir Henry Irving that she was the worthy heir to Mary Wollstonecraft's friend Mrs Siddons and presented with a ring which the great actress had once owned.

There was more than a touch of theatre in the shrine which Jane created at the opposite end of the house. A recessed corner of the drawing-room was chosen for 'the Sanctum' and given a blue ceiling studded with gold stars. Crimson curtains and dim red lighting created a suitably devotional atmosphere. Apricot satin cloths kept daylight from the glass display cases containing manuscripts, a mass of hair bracelets, miniatures and – a gift from Trelawny – the Sophocles found in the jacket Shelley was wearing when he drowned.* Over the fireplace, Rothwell's grim portrait of Mary in her forties looked down on a copy of the Weekes monument.† One impressionable young visitor remembered being shown an urn in which, her mother whispered, the ashes of the poet's heart were kept. Another was more struck by a glimpse of the Shelleys on their way to Boscombe in a carriage emblazoned with the family coat-of-arms and driven by two splendid gentlemen in crimson livery, white cockades fluttering from their hats.[8]

Here, at the beginning of 1857, Jane decided to bring together Hogg, Peacock and Trelawny to discuss the writing of a biography of Shelley. Percy had already visited Trelawny at Usk; he came away with the battered copy of Sophocles, but without the portrait of Mary which Trelawny now claimed had been given to him. Asked to Boscombe, Trelawny refused on the grounds that he had grown too old and crabbed to sit around telling tales of the past.[9] The Shelleys, mistrustfully aware that he had begun his own version of Shelley's last years, decided to waste no time. On 24 February, Jane informed Edward Moxon that Hogg was prepared to undertake the book; she believed that Mary, who had helped Hogg to publish his articles on Shelley at Oxford, would approve the choice.[10]

Hogg, a regular visitor to Boscombe in 1857, seemed the perfect candidate. He talked with lawyerly enthusiasm about the importance of giving accurate evidence: 'To falsify documents would be to injure the faith of history, and to destroy the credit of our book,' he told Jane.[11] Encouraged, and anxious that his account should seem in every way superior to anything Trelawny might offer, the Shelleys introduced him to the aunts and allowed him to take away boxes of

---

* Many of the relics from the Sanctum are preserved in a walnut dressing-case which belonged to Mary Shelley and which is now in private hands. The most moving of its contents, tucked away in the velvet-lined lid, is the tarnished mirror in which Mary's face was once reflected. The box also contains an oval amethyst ring once belonging to Mary Wollstonecraft which Mary and Jane wore after her, and Mary's own little seal with her initials in Gothic letters.

† Lady Shelley commissioned the little-known artist Reginald Easton to copy Amelia Curran's portrait of Shelley; at the same time Easton painted two miniatures as twin portraits. One was a copy of a painting done of Shelley as a child by the Duke of Montpensier; the other, allegedly taken from a death mask, was of Mary Shelley. The miniatures were probably done in 1857, when Easton was staying at Boscombe and sketching Hogg's portrait for inclusion in the shrine. The miniature of Mary shows her wearing the circlet of the Rothwell portrait and a shawl which, mantling her hair, confers the religious status of the figure on the Weekes monument. One could guess that the suggestion came from Lady Shelley.

letters, including the notes Mary had made for a life of Shelley. Jane invited Hogg to call her 'Wrennie'; he signed himself her 'Dah'. In March 1858, the first two of four projected volumes, ending on the eve of the 1814 elopement, were proudly delivered to Boscombe and, with rising dismay, perused.

Hogg's main crime against Mary had been to adapt her notes towards a life of Shelley for his own use and to omit the fact that she had asked his advice about whether or not to cut sections from *Queen Mab* for the 1839 edition. His account of his first glimpse of her at Skinner Street, pale and piercing-eyed in a tartan frock, is vivid enough to have been gratefully used by all biographers. Percy and Jane, not having seen Shelley's letters to Hogg, were unaware of how ruthlessly the biographer had manipulated their contents. (A letter in which Shelley reproached Hogg for trying to seduce Harriet appeared, but as a fragment of an unpublished novel.) What they could not fail to see was that Hogg's ego had wrecked the project; everywhere they looked, Shelley appeared as the simple-minded dependant of his cleverer and more interesting friend. And that this monstrosity, dedicated to herself, should have been 'called into life by me', Jane Shelley lamented to Peacock, seeing herself as an innocent version of Mary's Frankenstein.[12]

Percy, prodded by Jane, wrote to demand censorship rights over the next volumes; Jane, aware that Hogg still had a good deal of Shelley material at his home, was more diplomatic. Writing from 'my own Sanctum' a few days later, she apologized for Percy's letter. He must not mind it. She had read the book three times now, and really, with a few trifling exceptions, it 'is all we could wish; & many a good laugh it gave me'. He must promise to come and visit them soon.[13]

Jane was playing a double game. While soothing Hogg, she was calling on everybody who had known her parents-in-law to speak out against his work. One friend needed no inviting. Writing to reassure Claire that she had not even been mentioned in Trelawny's *Recollections of the Last Days of Shelley and Byron* (1858), Peacock told her that the author had, if anything, been too discreet.[14] But Hogg had infuriated Peacock with his condescending denigration of Harriet ('the good Harriet') Westbrook. Having refused to lend moral support to Jane Shelley by coming to Boscombe in the summer of 1858 when Harriet's daughter Ianthe had been invited to stay, Peacock began preparing his own soberly corrective account of the past.

Ianthe Esdaile did come; it was her first and last visit. She came and, according to Lady Shelley, wept after being shown a selection of letters and memorabilia. Peacock, keeping his distance, published his objections in an article for *Fraser's Magazine* that June; Hogg, uncrushed, continued writing. Loftily, he ignored the Shelleys' request that they should be allowed to inspect and censor as they wished. In the summer of 1859, he was taught a cruel and public lesson. Lady Shelley, respectfully assisted by a young man from the British Museum, a twenty-four-year-old Shelley enthusiast called Richard Garnett, presented her own version of the past.

The *Shelley Memorials* opened with a ferocious indictment of Hogg's incomplete biography. The editor, while taking the opportunity to warn her readers against forged letters and to sound a good deal more expert in this area than she in fact was, addressed herself first to the 'fantastic caricature, going forth to the public with my apparent sanction' to which readers of Hogg's first volumes had been subjected. It was this, Lady Shelley explained, which had compelled her to 'clear away the mist' of inaccuracy, and to give 'a truthful statement of long-distorted facts'.[15] A legal letter to Hogg meanwhile coolly informed him that Sir Percy would take him to court if he attempted to publish without consent any correspondence of his father's or mother's.[16]

Without permission, Hogg's hands were tied. All he could do was to copy Jane's affectionate note of the previous year to anybody who might wish to support him. Writing to Monckton Milnes, he added that Lady Shelley should be forgiven, 'on the grounds of insanity', her family being 'low' and 'somewhat crazy'.[17] Hogg had always been his own worst enemy and vindictiveness undid him now. His friends did not rally. The remaining two volumes were still unpublished when he died three years later. The manuscript does not appear to have survived.

It is impossible not to sympathize with poor Ianthe Esdaile at this time. Hogg, in a sniggering allusion to her mother's 'rosy' complexion, had hinted that Harriet had a drink problem. (Hogg's view of Harriet's intemperance, shared by Lady Shelley, seems to have been based on the fact that her father had owned a tavern as well as a coffee-house which served liquor.) The *Shelley Memorials*, by a dexterous chapter-break, managed to kill Harriet off and leave Shelley grieving over 'the self-sought grave of the companion of his early youth' before allowing Mary to appear in the guise of his comforter. It was admitted that they had not immediately married; the blame was laid on Godwin's teaching rather than on the embarrassing truth, that Shelley already had a living wife.

The Esdailes, hating publicity, kept their heads down. Shelley's two surviving sisters, so far as is known, said never a word. Peacock, with whom Sir Percy was convinced Harriet had slept during her marriage to Shelley, sprang again to her defence. In January 1860, he published another article in *Fraser's Magazine*, in which he bluntly related the sequence of dates so skilfully disarranged in the *Memorials*. He rejected Lady Shelley's statement that the separation had been by mutual consent. Harriet was described with great cordiality; Shelley's passion for Mary, and that alone, had in Peacock's view separated him from a cheerful and affectionate wife.[18] This was war and Lady Shelley took up the cudgels with relish. Richard Garnett was employed to write a public response. Only discretion, he announced in June 1860, had so far prevented the Shelleys from publishing documents which would demolish Mr Peacock's 'allegations'.[19] Two years later – why did he wait so long? – Peacock defiantly published further pertinent dates, and extracts from the Chancery suit, in *Fraser's Magazine*. This time, in March 1862, he included Shelley's damaging statement to Eliza Westbrook that Mary's 'union' with himself had been 'the cause of her Sister's Ruin'.

Spiritualism, imported from America in the 1850s, was a great comfort to Lady Shelley at such times. Mary sent a message from the beyond that Peacock would soon be gone. (He died in 1866.) Having deleted an inconvenient mention of enduring guilt about Harriet from Mary's journals, Jane prepared a letter about her parents-in-law for the Esdailes to study: 'not the slightest feeling of remorse had ever touched either of these most sensitive natures on Harriet's account,' she unblushingly informed them. Hogg's references to Harriet's 'habits of intemperance' and her growing indifference to her husband were brought forward.[20] The obliging Garnett was recruited to help prepare a further volume of defensively edited materials. This became the infamous *Relics of Shelley* of 1862. Peacock had been quite wrong to suggest that Mary had helped destroy a happy marriage, Garnett wrote; to prove it, he quoted a letter in which Shelley, before meeting Mary, described his wife in terms of 'disgust and horror'.[21] A treacherous blank concealed the fact that Shelley had been describing, not Harriet, but her sister Eliza.

Lady Shelley was not the only woman who was busily rewriting the past and talking to spirits. The widowed Marquise de Boissy, formerly Teresa Guiccioli, moved to a house near Florence shortly after Claire Clairmont took up residence there in 1859. Claire, keeping up with old friends through Jane Hogg, satisfied herself with an occasional shaft aimed at Lady Shelley's domination of a weak husband; Teresa, informed by chatty apparitions that de Boissy and Byron had now become the best of friends, decided that the great love-affair of her life had been no more than a tender friendship. Busily writing her recollections, Teresa destroyed or rewrote any letters that interfered with her own version, scribbled furious annotations all over Moore's biography of Byron and, wherever she found the word 'love' applied to herself, altered it to 'devotion'.[22] Tempting though it is to berate Jane Shelley, she was acting in the spirit of the times. Reverence, in the Victorian biographer's mind, was paramount. Truth was less important than defending the dead from scandal.

A refuge to Claire, Italy was to Percy and Jane a country for pilgrimages. In 1863, they made a tour of hallowed sites. At Rome, they were pleased to find Shelley's grave being tended and smothered in violets by a future poet laureate, young Alfred Austin; at Lerici, the locals were quick to tell them just what they wished to hear. A fisherman announced that Shelley had been as beautiful as Christ, a pleasing confirmation of the Shelley represented by Weekes's sculpture. He allowed them to copy a drawing of Mary which he had found in the deserted villa.* Jane, hoping for a visitation, spent a cold and disappointing night in Shelley's bedroom.

Frankenstein, or rather, the Creature, had by now settled into the role of all-purpose bogeyman in English politics. During the Crimean War, he was brutish Russia; in 1866, he was the working-class man; in 1843 and again in 1869, he provided a useful image for rebellious Ireland. As the Creature became increasingly savage and unsympathetic, portraits of his creator became equally distorted. Eliza Rennie, describing Mary in 1860, remembered a genteel ex-governess with a beautiful voice whose dearest wish had been to conceal her professional career and whose life had been unfairly haunted by 'calumnies'. (These were presumably the stories of Mary's supposedly scandalous summer as part of the 'league of incest' at Geneva in 1816, although Rennie may also have been alluding to gossip spread by Jane Hogg.[23]) Thornton Hunt, relying on anecdotes told by his late father, described a clever, handsome slattern, a careless mother with a sharp, querulous temper. The fact that he believed Mary, not Mrs Novello, was known as 'the Wilful Woman', gives a hint of the casual nature with which he threw his piece together. But Thornton was among many who had been shocked by Lady Shelley's readiness to believe the worst of Harriet. She had been entirely innocent when the marriage ended, he wrote; he did Harriet no favour, however, by offering 'evidence' that she had come near to prostitution in her last years. Shelley's own increasingly pristine image was not helped by Hunt's hints of 'rude

---

* See Appendix 3.

trials' to his constitution during his brief spell at Oxford, never discussed in public but revealed, Thornton believed, in some discreet allusions to classical authors made in Mrs Shelley's novels.[24] No reader could doubt that Hunt was referring to a sexual infection. This was not what Lady Shelley had anticipated when she invited him to champion the cause.

Among the readers of Hunt's account was William Michael Rossetti, who had his own connection to the Shelleys. His father had known both Godwin and Mary; his uncle, John Polidori, had flirted hopefully with Mary in Geneva during the summer of 1816. The first British editor of Whitman's poetry, Rossetti had not yet become a reverent acolyte himself. That period lay far ahead, after the deaths of his more famous brother and sister. As a left-wing bachelor moving in Bohemian circles in the 1860s, Rossetti saw no reason why the flaws in a great poet should be concealed. He was shocked when Richard Garnett coolly informed him that the lengthy preface to his new edition of Shelley's poems was not satisfactory, either to Garnett himself or to 'the family'. Rossetti held his ground, despite a long friendship with Garnett. All he was prepared to do, after hearing that it would distress Ianthe, was to delete the 'fact' that her mother had, in her last years, taken up with a 'very humble' man and that Shelley, at least, believed she turned to prostitution.[25]

The Shelleys did their best to divert this tiresome lover of truth by letting it be known that he would never have their approval or be invited to view the Sanctum. Swinburne, another admirer, urged Rossetti to stick to his guns: 'Do root things up,' he wrote, 'for I am sure the closer we get to facts the greater and purer he [Shelley] will come out.'[26] A month later, on 29 June 1869, Rossetti had a long, enthralling conversation with Trelawny who, having broken with his wife Augusta and the mistress who replaced her, was back in London and living close to his mother's old Brompton home.

Claire Clairmont had, by a fluke of timing, just written to Trelawny after a gap of decades, to ask if she was mentioned in Teresa Guiccioli's memoirs. She was surprised and touched to receive back a long and affectionate letter in which, while reassuring her about Teresa's book – it was a shallow, harmless work, Trelawny comforted her, containing no reference to herself[27] – he urged her to write down all she could remember. Claire was ready to oblige him.

This was the point at which Mary Shelley's reputation, lovingly protected by her daughter-in-law, came under fire. Rossetti, who shared most of the information that came his way with Richard Garnett, was the beneficiary of the combined energies of two mischievous old storytellers with time on their hands. Reports from Garnett that there had been a great burning of documents relating to Harriet at Boscombe in 1870 strengthened Rossetti's sense of the importance of gathering evidence from another, less partial quarter. Dazzled by Trelawny's gifts, a relic (Trelawny had a suspiciously large number of these ready for visitors) of the poet's charred remains, a sofa on which Shelley had slept at Pisa,* Rossetti failed to smell out the prejudice in the reports he was being given.

Trelawny's old affection for Mary Shelley had soured long before her death. Now, persuaded by his own narratives that he alone had been Shelley's cherished friend, he became her most censorious judge. 'Mary Shelley's jealousy must have sorely vexed Shelley –' he wrote to Claire on 3 April 1870; 'indeed she was not a suitable companion for the poet – his first wife Harriett must have been more suitable – Mary was the most conventionable slave I ever met – she even affected the pious dodge, such was her yearning for society – she was devoid of imagination and Poetry . . .' And so on. Claire, while unwilling to condemn Mary on religious grounds (she had herself become an ardent Catholic) was ready to comply in other respects. Warmed by Trelawny's affection for his 'dear old friend', as he now fondly addressed her, she deluged him with recollections, presenting herself as the innocent victim of circumstances. Mrs Godwin's letters of 1814 to Lady Mountcashell were taken out and copied, with many emendations and careless rewritings, causing even the gullible Rossetti to wonder why the name 'Claire' appeared with such regularity in letters written by a mother who had always firmly addressed her daughter as Jane.

Claire's references to Mary were garrulous and sometimes inaccurate. They were not vindictive. Her main concern was to clear her own name of scandal and to find a buyer for her collection of Shelley letters in order to raise money for Pauline, the niece who now lived with her in Florence, and for Pauline's illegitimate daughter, who also shared her home. (Trelawny's offer of £50 was rejected as insufficient.) One wonders, however, if Claire would have written with quite such readiness had she known that Trelawny was planning a further volume of reminiscences.

To Rossetti, pleased to find that Trelawny shared his own eagerness for the truth, the project seemed an admirable one, a complement to

---

* The sofa, given to Rossetti by Trelawny, is still in his family's possession. Visiting Helen Guglielmini in Rome, I sat on it, rather nervously. Handsome but frail, it seems unlikely to have been used as a bed, except in emergencies.

the edition of Shelley letters which he prepared between 1872 and 1879. And then, Trelawny was so generous with his introductions. In 1871, Rossetti met Jane Hogg, deaf but still handsome in a wig of brown curls; in 1873, he went to see Claire in Florence and came away impressed by this small white-haired lady, her bright-eyed stare belying her age.[28] Claire, fortunately for him, had not yet read his Memoir. In 1875, listing to Trelawny the mistakes Rossetti had made, she innocently sealed his view of Mary as a religious fanatic by telling him that they had both received a most correct upbringing, including weekly visits to church followed by questions on the sermon.[29]

The Shelleys, knowing nothing of all this, had begun with the deaths of Hogg and Peacock to feel that the reputations of Percy and Mary were secure. An agreeable ex-cleric, C. Kegan Paul, had been enlisted by them to write a life of William Godwin. The result, published in 1876 after careful examination by Sir Percy, contained nothing scandalous. Ianthe's death that year reduced the likelihood of any further trouble from the Esdailes on the score of Harriet. Percy and Jane were free, for a short time, to enjoy monitoring the progress of the theatre they had begun building as an enhancement to their new London home, Shelley House, on the Chelsea Embankment. (Oscar Wilde mischievously named his own home nearby 'Keats House' in competition.) And then, in 1878, Trelawny brought back to life his twenty-year-old book, rewritten and retitled as *Records of Shelley, Byron, and the Author.*

Shelley was glorified. The victim of Trelawny's vivid, vitriol-dipped pen was Mary. The book's appendix stripped her naked of dignity, of virtue, of intelligence and, above all, of the right to be admired as Shelley's wife. She was a hypocrite, Trelawny wrote. She was cold. She was obsessed with society. She understood nothing of her husband's nature or his work. *Frankenstein* was the work of Shelley's brain, not hers; widowed, she had sunk back to her 'natural littleness'. Shelley's marriage to her was described as 'the utmost malice of fortune', endured with saintly resignation by a man who had never recovered from the loss of his first wife. Trelawny, in this vigorous reconstruction of the past, had been Shelley's chosen companion and confidant. Even the story of Shelley's heart was turned around. Mary, disgusted by such a relic, had given it to Hunt, according to Trelawny, who conveniently forgot that he himself had given it to Hunt on the beach and that Jane Williams had been forced to beg it back for the widow.

Garnett, summoned to the defence again, only succeeded in rousing the old man's love of battle. Trelawny had, besides, his own reputation to defend. His name had, by dint of his own efforts, become linked to those of Shelley and Byron in the public imagination. His response to Garnett, published by the *Athenaeum* in August 1878, was malevolent enough to provoke Jane Shelley into asking whether, at his bidding, she might give herself the pleasure of taking his portrait and lock of hair out of the Sanctum.[30] Trelawny's answer, if he sent one, has not survived. Curiously, Amelia Curran's portraits of Mary and Claire were still proudly displayed on his wall.

Sir Percy, now almost sixty and happiest with his boats, his theatricals and his dogs, had had his fill of shrine-guarding, having long since made up his mind that Harriet Westbrook's low background and weak nature explained his father's defection to a finer woman. A gentle character, Percy lavished affection on young relations ('Shelley-boy', his cousin John's second son, was a favourite) and his own adopted daughter, Bessy Florence, a motherless niece of Jane's. His unpublished diary shows him experimenting with photography, joining the local bicycle club, skating on Sunday mornings (but only after attending church) and gravely timing himself with a pedometer as he strolled out to a London lunch at the Beefsteak or the Garrick. In London, his literary background made him a figure of interest; he dined out with actors, painters and poets who asked him once because he was Shelley's son and again, because he was such a cheerful, easygoing guest. If he was, as Trelawny once told Rossetti, a 'degenerate', he was a most discreet one. At Boscombe, he loyally supported local activities and was pleased by the number of neighbours ready to come and applaud his plays. Unaware of the bizarre link resulting from his mother's friendship with raffish Isabel Douglas, he made friends with her illegitimate daughter, Adeline Drummond Wolff, who was now living with her husband at the neighbouring country estate. A brief but more intense friendship formed when Robert Louis Stevenson settled at 'Skerryvore' in Bournemouth before frail health and a restless spirit took him to the drier heat of Samoa.

Stevenson, who dedicated one of his finest novels, *The Master of Ballantrae*, to the Shelleys, affectionately evoked all that was best about Percy in a letter written to Jane shortly after her husband's death. It was his innocent eccentricity and pleasure in fantasy that most charmed Stevenson. 'Do you remember coming once to call on us, you two together,' he wrote to Jane, 'on a day of a high wind? and how, as you drove on, he made a romance that you were driving through a forest, and would come presently to an old ruined abbey . . .'[31] Being Stevenson, he couldn't resist spinning out the tale, but the story was clearly of Percy's own making. As Stevenson noted, there was 'a deal of his father' hidden behind the bluff exterior, the pink cheeks and beaky nose of the country squire.

Jane, rallying from Trelawny's treacherous assault, spent the 1880s in a whirl of Shelleyan activity. Her main task was to edit the Boscombe collection of letters into four volumes, privately published as *Shelley and Mary* in 1882. Many letters were committed to the flames at this time; alterations took place wherever Lady Shelley found something that displeased her. Amelia Curran was turned into the author of a letter written by Claire about nursing little William Shelley in his last days; Shelley's mention of the fact that Mrs Hoppner had accused him of urging Claire to take 'violent medicines' to terminate her supposed pregnancy in Naples was omitted. Linking passages threw blame, wherever it might be supposed to fall on Mary's coldness, on to Jane Hogg. This was all of a piece with Lady Shelley's willingness, at Garnett's suggestion, to remove anything from public view which reflected badly on the Shelleys' marriage. One letter from Shelley to the Gisbornes, in which he described his marriage as hell, went missing; another, from Hogg to Jane Williams about Mary's failings as a wife, was destroyed. The strength of Jane's obsession shows up most clearly in the fact that, threatened with libel by Harriet's grandson if she made any more slanderous allegations, she found a way out by writing her own view of Harriet's character and behaviour in a long note placed in the flyleaf of every copy of *Shelley and Mary* which was sent out from Boscombe. It is not easy to reconcile this unforgiving old lady with the 'out and out stunner of a delightful woman' by whom the artist Edward Lear was so entranced when one of the Shelleys' yachting trips brought them to Corfu and, briefly, into his life.[32]

Jane was ready, at last, for the lives of Shelley and Mary to be presented to the world. The official biographers were carefully picked and were given the heavily edited correspondence presented in *Shelley and Mary* for their source-work. The Dublin scholar Edward Dowden, selected for Shelley – his own great love was Wordsworth – fought hard to paint an honest picture. Sweetening Jane with assurances that he saw Mary as 'the best influence, for man & poet, of all his life',[33] he was willing to paint Harriet black as a coal-scuttle, but only with the documents to substantiate the claim. It would, he smoothly assured her, be indeed 'a great point' to vindicate Mary, but he could not do it without proof.[34] The arrival in Dowden's hands of the miserable, bewildered letters Harriet had written to Miss Nugent in 1814–15 was not good news for the Shelleys; neither was Garnett's reminder to them that Dowden 'is not writing as an advocate, as I did in the *Relics*, but as an historian . . .'[35] Dowden did not take kindly to suggestions that his new findings might be reshaped or suppressed by the Boscombe censors; his readiness to 'arrange' the light in which Shelley's passionate letters to Claire should be presented was small comfort.[36]

Dowden's first pleas to be shown more than a handful of the Boscombe letters had been refused. In the autumn of 1885, with his research almost finished, he was finally granted a peep at the riches tucked away there during a one-night visit to the Shelleys' home. He was shocked to discover how many of the texts he had been given to work from were mutilated or inaccurately transcribed; a fascinating record of his reactions exists in the form of his own annotated *Shelley and Mary*, passed via Richard Garnett to the British Museum. Purchasing the right to see the letters which Mr Buxton Forman had bought from Claire before her death in 1881, Dowden had another shock. The Shelleys had disguised her birthdate, encouraging him to see Claire as a mature woman capable of exerting a powerful influence on an impressionable girl, and old enough to have known just what she was doing in her flirtation with Shelley. Now, for the first time, he realized that Claire had been the youngest of the three.[37]

Given the trying circumstances in which Dowden worked, his book was impressively truthful and informative. Tact was maintained, however; members of the newly formed Shelley Society (this was an age besotted with Keats, Browning, Tennyson and Shelley, all of whom had their own societies) could read his book without anguish. The Esdailes pronounced themselves content (Claire's recollection that Harriet's last relationship had been with a respectable army officer was incorporated); Garnett praised the biographer's self-restraint.

Dowden's book was published in 1886 and was modestly success-ful: two thousand copies sold during the first two years. In 1889, thus offering no competition, Florence Marshall's life of Mary appeared.* The musical and conscientious daughter of a clergyman, Florence Marshall had come with high recommendations, probably from Garnett or the Shelleys' literary neighbour at Boscombe, Sir Henry Taylor. Lady Shelley had been a little cowed by Dowden's academic qualifications; she felt confident of controlling a timid lady biog-rapher. Woman to woman, she advised Florence on how best to approach her subject. She must be wary of Harriet ('worldly &

---

* An American biography of Mary published in 1886 by Helen Moore appears to have escaped the Shelleys' attention or to have been judged unworthy of interest; Moore's book relied heavily on Trelawny's *Records*.

frivolous, hard to her husband') and sympathetic to Mary ('truthful, modest & unselfish').[38] It was not expected that she should look too deeply into anything that might prove unpleasant. Lady Shelley helped her along by destroying the letters written by Mary's mother to Fuseli, which she had acquired in 1884.

Florence Marshall was content to be led. Mary, as wife and widow, was painted in just the colours Lady Shelley could have wished, muted, respectful. Trelawny and Hogg were rebuked for having published inaccurate accounts of her (interestingly, Mrs Marshall considered Hogg's 'ironical' eulogies of Mary's talents more shocking than Trelawny's hostile comments). No mention was made of the recently discovered letters from Mary to Claire about Gatteschi. Mary was defended for not having written Shelley's life (her own part in it had been too large, too influential, Mrs Marshall explained, for objectivity) and lauded as a devoted mother. Almost the only criticism Mrs Marshall was prepared to make concerned her subject's writings; she admired *Frankenstein*, and that was all. As a way out, she offered the novel idea that Mary's literary genius had been arrested by her attachment to Shelley; the comet had become an unadventurous satellite.

Jane Shelley did not object to Marshall's approach; moral reputation was of more importance than literary status, after all. Just as in Shelley's case, she was happy to see the fiery, more dangerous side of his nature overshadowed by examples of his gentleness and by emphasis on his least radical works; she was well-pleased by Mrs Marshall's desire to emphasize Mary's religious nature, to defend her reluctance to write a life of her husband as having been prompted by a kindly wish to protect the 'erring' – that is, Claire – from publicity, and to see both Claire and Jane Hogg roundly condemned. Mrs Marshall's overworked analogy between Mary and the girl in the Hans Andersen tale who tortures her hands weaving nettle shirts for the salvation of her brothers seemed wholly appropriate to this history of a life of sacrifice.

Percy died shortly after Marshall's anodyne portrait of his mother was published. He was buried in 1889 in the family grave at St Peter's, together with the ashes of his father's heart.* Resourceful Jane, comforted by Robert Louis Stevenson's tribute to Sir Percy's fine soul, 'honest as a dog's', ordered her own name to be engraved below her husband's in preparation for her own demise.

She was alone now; even Trelawny had gone. (His last attachment, Miss Taylor, took his ashes to Rome in 1880 in a small walnut box.

* See Appendix 1.

After some altercation over whether she should be fined for importing the remains of a body without permission, they were laid in the grave beside Shelley's, just as Trelawny had wished.[39]) Zealous as ever, Jane continued with what had become the high purpose of her life. Sweetened with the promise of £500 and the news that Shelley's admirers would pay for the cost of installation, University College, Oxford, accepted a statue of the poet in 1893; the Bodleian, in the same year, agreed to become a repository for a third of the Boscombe collection of Shelley manuscripts and letters, with certain restrictions imposed. (These included a box of letters which were not to be examined until 1922, the centenary of Shelley's death.*) Admirers like young Maud Brooke and Edward Woodberry, editor of a new collection of Shelley's poetical works, were rewarded with glowing accounts of Mary; letters continued to be diligently sought and purchased, including those which Mary had written to Jane Williams shortly after Shelley's death. Sadly, since it appears to have been lost, Lady Shelley never saw the painting of her mother-in-law by 'Cleobulina' Fielding which Richard Garnett, visiting Jane Hogg's grandson in 1903, thought 'the best I had seen'.[40] There can be little doubt that Jane Shelley, had she been shown the portrait, would have bought it and saved it for posterity.†

Dying, after several years of ill health, in 1899, Lady Shelley was given short shrift by the *Athenaeum*. Her wish to show Shelley as 'a faultless hero of romance' had won only one unflinching defender in Richard Garnett, the obituarist wrote; that approach 'has been abandoned by all unprejudiced investigators. The whole matter forms a curious episode in literary history.'[41]

The *Athenaeum's* snappish response suggests that Lady Shelley's endeavours had not been entirely successful; George Bernard Shaw, paying a visit to the Shelley chapel at University College in the 1890s, wondered when they were going to put up a relief of the poet 'in a tall hat, Bible in hand, leading his children on Sunday morning to the church of his native parish'.[42]

Tempting though it is to lay all the blame for the reconstruction of Shelley on Jane Shelley's shoulders, Mary herself has to share the burden. It was Mary, not her daughter-in-law, who had used her notes and prefaces of 1839 to suggest that Shelley's political zeal would, with maturity, have waned and to plead his case by claiming that 'the stamp

---

* The contents, when examined, proved disappointingly tame.
† See Appendix 3.

of such inexperience' was on all he wrote. It was Mary who had assured the readers of *Queen Mab* that Shelley had never wanted to see the poem published. Printing a letter he had written to this effect for publication when a pirated edition appeared in 1821, she suppressed the fact that Shelley had written privately that its appearance was rather amusing and that he had asked to be sent copies of it by Leigh Hunt and Horace Smith.

Shelley's reputation as a radical poet had survived in spite, not because of Mary's efforts. She had been friendly with Robert Dale Owen in the late 1820s, but it was no thanks to Mary that the Owenite workers of the early to mid-nineteenth century treated Shelley's *Queen Mab* as their Bible. The poem's influence is apparent from the fact that it was constantly reprinted and quoted from in radical journals and advertised in Chartist pamphlets and papers. Thomas Medwin had noticed this and commented on the fact in his life of Shelley; Trelawny regarded it as cause for celebration. Mary did not.

'I have no wish to ally myself to the Radicals,' Mary had written firmly in October 1838, while acknowledging that she now differed in this respect from both her husband and her father. It was probably her awareness of George Lewes's radical politics which prompted her decisive rejection of his request to write Shelley's life in 1839. It will not do as an excuse to say that Sir Timothy did not wish a life to be written; Mary had, by 1839, become adept at slipping copy into editors' hands and at providing anonymous information; her connection to Lewes need never have been declared, especially since he was a close friend of Leigh Hunt's.

Lewes's magnificent extended tribute to Shelley, published in the *Westminster Review* in April 1841, tells us the kind of biography he would have written, had he been allowed. Praised, in the year after Thomas Carlyle had given a celebrated talk on heroes and hero-worship, as 'the original man, the hero', Shelley was presented by Lewes not as a quivering sensibility or a frail martyr, in the style increasingly favoured by Mary herself, but as a political reformer, a champion of the oppressed. It is not that Mary did not say this in her own prefaces; she constantly alluded to Shelley's zeal for reform and for social improvement, but she did everything she could, however unconsciously, to make him sound more like a lady philanthropist than a political rebel. She drained him of all sense of risk and danger, the very thing which made him such an exciting and inspiring poet to the working man or the middle-class radical. Lewes, not Mary, was ready to celebrate Shelley as a voice springing straight from the white heat of the French Revolution. We should not, then, be too hard on Jane; in her diligent promotion of Shelley as wistful dreamer, cruelly misunderstood by those who did not know him personally, she was only pursuing the course already marked out by Mary.

'That's her final give-away for me,' Katherine Mansfield wrote indignantly to John Middleton Murry in December 1920, after reading an inaccurate report of Mary Shelley as having carried Shelley's relics home from Italy under a glass case perched on her knees. 'Did everybody know? Oh didn't they just? I've done with her.' Mansfield was always excitable in her reactions, but she was not alone by 1920 in reacting against Jane Shelley's loving portrait of Mary as the supreme example of devoted widowhood. William Michael Rossetti's wife Lucy, thirty years earlier, had written a sharply critical life of Mary, a life which, while it drew directly on Trelawny's *Records*, was probably also fuelled by the Rossettis' long-standing friendship with George Lewes. Lucy Madox Rossetti disliked the way Mary had played down Shelley's radical nature; Katherine Mansfield was writing in the postwar years when there were widows and mothers whose tragedies eclipsed Mary's loss.

Eleven years after Jane Shelley's death, Edison made the first *Frankenstein* film. Another, now lost, was made in 1915, but 1931 was the year in which Boris Karloff, directed by James Whale, gave Mary's uncherished creature new life and, for the first time, the pathos of his original. The films spawned; the author dwindled. Rosalie Glynn Grylls's excellent biography of 1938, wedged between *The Bride of Frankenstein* (1935), with Karloff, and *Son of Frankenstein* (1939), with Karloff again, aroused modest interest. Muriel Spark's short life, marking the centenary of Mary's death, sensibly gave considerable space to the one great work which now entirely overshadowed the author. But the view expressed by Richard Garnett in his 1897 essay on Mary for the *Dictionary of National Biography* continued to stick: she must, Garnett wrote, have been 'magnetized' by her husband to produce a novel so far beyond her normal reach. *Frankenstein*, although little read, had become a work of mythic power, an allegory flexible enough to be adapted to almost any contemporary situation; Mary, colourless, mournful, pliant, seemed less convincing than Shelley as its author.

Mary's letters, first published in 1944 from copies which had often been scrubbed of vitality for the sake of decorum, did little to rescue her. Neither did it help that Richard Holmes gave this 'darkly handsome' woman such a poor write-up in his scintillating life of her husband. *Shelley: The Pursuit* (1974) memorably identified Shelley as a man in flight from responsibility, a free-loving anticipator of the commune-loving 1960s, mismatched to a sulky, bad-tempered wife. (Holmes was more lenient towards Mary in a later work, *Footsteps* (1985). Professor Jean de Palacio's brilliant and enlightening *Mary Shelley dans son oeuvre* (1969), a work which sadly remains untranslated, was directed at the specialist reader.

The last thirty years have seen a dramatic change in Mary Shelley's status. Much of this has been due to the feminist critics and biographers who have, in rescuing her from the Victorian view, discerned a writer of high ambition and considerable talent, if not genius. *Matilda*, published in 1959 after lying untouched for years among the Shelley archives (Garnett first saw it at Boscombe in 1905 and was unsure which of the Shelleys was its author), has been subjected to intensive scrutiny and praised as a work of courageous self-revelation; *Valperga* has become one of the most widely discussed of Mary Shelley's works, seen by one recent editor as a brilliant riposte to Sir Walter Scott's *Ivanhoe*, praised by others for its subversive criticism of masculine power and for its interpretation of Italy's contemporary problems through her past. Betty T. Bennett's indispensable three-volume edition of Mary's letters (1980–4) has been complemented by an admirable edition of the *Journals* (1987) by Paula Feldman and Diana Scott-Kilvert. Emily Sunstein, publishing an authoritative biography of Mary in 1989, regretted that, in a period of re-evaluation of her work, the woman remained overlooked. Sunstein's Mary was a passionate, impetuous woman, cast in her mother's mould, a ready challenger of the conventions, a great editor, a major literary figure. Challenging Rosalie Glynn Grylls's presentation of Mary as, in Emily Sunstein's words, 'a morbid moper', she offered a new vision:

> Aspiration, enthusiasm, challenge, active mind and spirit, and optimism were among her cardinal qualities, contrary to the impression that she was temperamentally cool, quiet and pessimistic, and it was her incapacity for resignation to cold reality that eventually wore her down.[43]

Eight years later, in the bicentennial celebrations of her birth, Mary's life was of less interest than her varied literary career, as historian, editor, travel-writer, novelist and poet. Judging by the number of papers on it, *Lodore* threatened to eclipse the popularity of *Valperga*, although strikingly little attention was paid to the novel's autobiographical content. The *Keepsake* stories, even, had become worthy of scholarly examination and debate. Her mother, while sharing in the celebrations, was almost as thoroughly overshadowed as Godwin and Percy Shelley.

Given this new-found veneration it is not surprising that the news, in 1997, of the discovery of a 'new' manuscript by Mary Shelley was greeted with high excitement. (It was new to English readers; Italians had already read excerpts of *Maurice* in a book on Lady Mountcashell which was published by Mario Curreli that year.) A lost Ode by Keats could hardly have prompted more jubilation. Claire Tomalin's researches into the family in whose possession the little manuscript had remained added to the charm and interest of the find.

Maurice, while engaging, was no great work. Why, then, the excitement? It was not, on this occasion, limited to a few knowledgeable professors. The public responded to the discovery with an interest not shown, for example, towards recently found letters of Shelley and Byron, or, from another well-loved era, an unpublished poem by Siegfried Sassoon.

The answer to this seems to be twofold. Mary's literary standing is now such that any work by her, however slight, is of interest to those scholars who regard her as a major figure in the Romantic canon. As Mary's works become increasingly accessible (several of her novels are now available in paperback editions), so too the general reader is drawn to her in part because her story is better known and in part because her name is so frequently invoked as the author of *Frankenstein*: no discussion, for example, of genetic engineering in the popular press fails to mention the name of *Frankenstein* and its author.

This is both a good and a bad thing. It has helped to draw attention to Mary Shelley's name, but without deepening our knowledge of who she was. On the contrary. While the newly canonized Mary is placed increasingly beyond the grasp of the general reader, her role as 'the wicked stepmother' of genetic science, in the memorable phrase coined by Professor Lewis Wolpert, threatens to lead her larger but underinformed audience into new misconceptions both of the author and the intentions behind her most celebrated work. Fascinating though it is to explore the novel's evident connections to both Mary and her husband's knowledge of galvanism and of contemporary discussions of vitalism, to the stories Mary may have heard as a child of experiments being made on the 'resurrected' bodies of criminals, this is not where her own interest lay. The making of the Creature, so enthralling to film directors, concerned Mary Shelley less than the idea of parental alienation from a manufactured child, a laboratory product. The story at the heart of *Frankenstein* is of a monstrously selfish scientific experiment, monstrous because Victor, having made a living, loving son for himself (we remember how the Creature reaches towards him), rejects it. Love is the message at the heart of Mary's novel; only when her creature is denied affection does he become a monster and turn on the species which gave him life in its image.

We invoke Frankenstein – always taking the name of the creator, not his creature – whenever science dares to improve on nature. The book has a more important warning to deliver and one which brings us closer to understanding its author. No parent, under whatever conditions, has the right to deny love to a child. Mary herself wrote out of a deep sense of personal hurt, as a girl whose rebelliousness had been punished with exile by the father she loved too well to share. If our sympathy is always with the Creature, it is because his is the voice of pure pain, the voice outside the Garden of Eden, outside the circle of family affection, outside society. *Maurice*, as Claire Tomalin perceptively observed in her introduction to the story, offers a more hopeful view, of a child whose nature cannot be altered by harsh treatment, who is incapable of revenge. Somewhere between the Creature's bitter misanthropy and Maurice's trusting gentleness, we can look for Mary herself.

Mary wrote her one great work when she had only begun to taste the bitterness of rejection. The most harrowing aspect of her life is to see how, through no fault of her own, it began to mirror her novel. Mary, like her creature, became a pariah. When Shelley died, his friends had already been made aware that his marriage was on the rocks, and that the fault was Mary's. Disgraced by her connection to him, tortured by the sense of her own inadequacy as a wife, publicly disowned by his family, Mary in her widowhood was thrust into the icy regions of solitude to which she had banished the Creature of her imagination. Hounded, persecuted and vilified, she taught herself how to survive. She remained, until the end of her life, generous, forgiving, tolerant and hopeful. The depression which she voiced in her journals was, we always need to remember, hidden from her friends. Her father was one of the few people who saw, and pitied, the disposition to melancholy which she had inherited from his wife. One wonders how much more sympathy she might have gained if she had been a little less fiercely reserved.

Remorse is at the heart of Mary's life after Shelley's death and the key to her recreation of him. Her journal tells us that she firmly believed she was condemned by fate to pay for the suffering and death of his first wife, the young woman Shelley abandoned for a greater love. Shelley himself died during a period of estrangement, the worst of emotional situations in which to lose someone you love. The terrible combination of guilt and remorse impelled Mary to dedicate herself to an act of literary atonement. Her recreation of Shelley as a man who was, if not Christian, Christlike, allowed her to repossess him, to give him in death what she felt she had wrongly withheld in life, an absolute and unconditional devotion. The cruel irony of her achievement was that, in elevating her husband, she had once again forfeited the sympathy of his admirers. They saw increasingly, as the nineteenth century wore on, a man who had been manipulated to fit his widow's conventional views. They had read, and had believed, Trelawny's brutal indictment of a woman he had never fully understood and whose place he was intent on usurping. They did not see that Mary was, however unconsciously, crucifying herself. The Shelley she set before them was a man of whom she could never have been worthy. Believing that she had failed him, she encouraged the world to share her view. And the world, reacting against the heroic but misguided efforts of Jane Shelley to set Mary on a pedestal at her husband's side, became increasingly ready to oblige her.

Mary Shelley is not the active, enthusiastic, optimistic woman described by recent biographers. She is a woman who struggled all her life against the unpredictable volatility of her own nature, who never knew when the black cloud of depression would settle around her, who was tormented by the sense of her own inability to become what she felt the world expected her to be, a second Mary Wollstonecraft, who tortured herself with the thought that every misfortune that came to her was directed by fate, as her punishment for having taken Shelley from his first wife, for having failed him herself. The most admirable thing about Mary is that, feeling as she did, she never surrendered, seldom revealed her unhappiness and continued, until the end of her life, to work to win Shelley, never herself, the honour that she felt was his due.

AN ACCOUNT OF THE BURIAL
OF SHELLEY'S HEART

The following note was written by E. Gambier Parry at the end of his personal copy of Trelawny's *Records of Shelley, Byron and the Author*. The details given in this text modify the usual account of the burial of Shelley's heart. The Canon St John referred to here is a member of the family of Lady Shelley's first husband.

Shelley's Heart

My old friend Canon Ferdinand St John (Canon of Gloucester Cathedral) told me that he was Trustee of the Shelley family, Lady Shelley then living at Boscombe. St John paid Lady Shelley periodical visits, and on one of these occasions he came to see me at Sou[th]bourne, where we then were owing to Tom's illness. Our conversation turned on Shelley, & I referred to the fact that his, St John's, brother Canon at Gloucester, Canon Harvey, had been Shelley's fag at Eton. St John said – 'Yes, & I buried Shelley's heart! Lady Shelley had it, & it was enclosed in a silver case. She asked me what she had better do with it, & I said – "bury it." So it was arranged that this should be done: The heart in its case was conveyed to Christchurch Abbey, where it was duly buried, and I read the Service.'

E Gambier Parry [undated]

SOME UNPUBLISHED
LETTERS

To John Murray from Mary Shelley

11 Bartholomew Place Kentish Town
13 January 1827

Sir,
    I have heard that you contemplated endeavouring to purchase the copy-right of a selection of Mr Shelley's works – and that you even applied to my father-in-law Sir Tim. Shelley on the subject. I write merely to say that these copy-rights are mine and that if you still wish to make such a purchase I should be happy to enter into a negotiation with you upon it.
    I am, Sir,
    Your ob[edien]t servant
    Mary Shelley*

To Constantine Henry Phipps, First Marquis of Normanby from Mary Shelley

Layton House Putney
8 December 1839

Dear Lord Normanby
    It was a great comfort & relief to me, that Lord Melbourne was good enough to give the sum in question to Mrs Godwin. I am grateful to

---

* The last sentence only has been previously cited in *The Letters of Mary W. Shelley*, ed. Frederick L. Jones (University of Oklahoma Press, 1944) and *The Letters of Mary Wollstonecraft Shelley*, ed. Betty T. Bennett (Johns Hopkins University Press, 1980), vol. 1.

you for the kindness you express; you have ever shown a munificent spirit with regard to deserving literary persons.

I have told the Bookseller to send you some volumes which I think will please you. We can none of us forget that you too are an author* & one we delight to read –
 With many thanks, I am
 Ever Yrs truly
 Mary Shelley

To Joseph Severn from Mary Shelley, n.d.

Mr Hogg is a friend of Leigh Hunt, of Mr Shelley, and many others of your circle in England. Permit me, therefore, to introduce him to your acquaintance.†

---

* Mary Shelley's grateful tone can be explained by the fact that Lord Normanby's name often appeared on subscription lists for Godwin. She also, by 1839, knew him as a cousin of her late friend, Lord Dillon. She had read Lord Normanby's *The English in Italy* (1825) without guessing the author's identity. It is 'very clever amusing & true', she wrote to Leigh Hunt on 12 August 1826, adding that since she had also seen books about Italy by Lady Oxford and by Lady Charlotte Bury (the same Lady Charlotte who had a child by Aubrey Beauclerk), she thought she would review them in a single article. 'The English in Italy', published without signature in the *Westminster Review* that October, discussed Lord Normanby's work together with Mrs Jameson's *Diary of an Ennuyée* and the anonymous *Continental Adventures: A Novel*. Normanby also published two companion volumes, *The English in France* (1828) and *The English at Home* (1830). *Matilda: a Tale of the Day* was published in 1825 and has nothing in common with Mary's then unpublished novel, *Matilda*. Lord Normanby also occasionally contributed to the *Keepsake* albums.

† Extract cited in a sale of autographs and letters advertised by John Weller, bookseller, 1871. Despite the reference to Shelley as though he was still alive, this was evidently written by Mary when Hogg was about to make his first visit to Italy in 1825. Severn was then living at Rome. Hogg reached Rome that autumn and was dismayed to find that Teresa Guiccioli knew all about his affair with Jane Williams and that Jane was still a married woman: 'without telling her an actual untruth, I induced her to believe that was a mistake, & that you were free,' Hogg reported. In the same letter, written from Naples on 6 December, he told Jane that he had met Severn. 'Mr Severn has finished the portrait of Trelawny; it is said to be a good likeness; I will not forget it.' On 6 January 1826, he confirmed that he had collected Severn's portrait and was bringing it back to England 'safe in my bag'. (*After Shelley: The Letters of Thomas Jefferson Hogg to Jane Williams*, ed. Sylvia Norman (Oxford, 1934).)

T. J. Hogg to Richard Monckton Milnes, incorporating Hogg's copy of
a letter to him from Lady Shelley

London 12 September, 1859

Dear Sir,

I have placed in the hands of some of my friends, who take an
interest like yourself, in 'The Life', the letter of which I send you a
copy, for I think you ought to see it, & you may make any use of
it you please. The least painful refutation of the extraordinary statements contained in the Preface to the 'Memorials' is to be found in
the belief, that there was a touch of madness in the Editor's race: they
were rather low people, & moreover somewhat crazy. I will consent
therefore to the humane Verdict, 'Not Guilty, on the ground of
Insanity'.

I am just about to start for the North, doomed to wander, like an
unburied ghost, over the county of Northumberland, until the end of
October. If you should desire further information I shall be happy to
supply it; in that case address me as below.

I am ever, Dear Sir, faithfully yours,

T Jeffn. Hogg,

Revising Barrister, to the care of Mr John Elliot, Clerk of the
Peace, Newcastle upon Tyne

[copied out in TJH's hand: Lady Shelley to TJH]

'For the last three days, Dear Dah, you have never been out of my
thoughts, & I am very glad to sit down in my own Sanctum to write
& tell you, how grieved I was to have caused you so severe a disappointment.

Hellen [Shelley] promised to tell you this, & she seemed to think,
when she left us, that she had comforted us all. I have read the book
three times since then, & I find that merely the letters H.G. [Harriet
Grove] in the margin of some of those letters without date make all
the difference in the world. But for some of these letters, & the way
in which he spoke occasionally of his father, I think the book is all we
could wish; & many a good laugh it gave me, even in the midst of my
distress. You know, dear Dah, that even the very sight of this long
desired book put me in a horrible state of agitation, & the first reading
of course was very different to both Percy & myself, than it could possibly be to anyone else. I had been so unwell too for a long time, that
my brain once set to work seemed to be on fire: – my distress too to
grieve you was very great. I want to know when you think you can
come to us. In three weeks again I must go to town, to see my doctor,
who is making me quite well & strong; but after that, I think, you
might settle your own time within the next two months. We shall
probably have the house full of people, somehow or another, but you

won't dislike that. Let me hear from you very soon; neither Percy, nor myself, can be quite happy & comfortable until we do. Believe me always, Dear Dah, very affectionately yours, Wrennie.

Percy says – "Do say to Dah how sorry I was to flurry him with my note, but then you know, Nin, you were in such a way that I did not know what to do!"

By the bye – Shd I get you a better bedroom candlestick? – for the stern hour of ten, when Chips & every other attraction fails to keep womankind from their beds & a scurvy bedroom candlestick.

Postmark. Christchurch, April 15 1858)'*

Byron to Mary Shelley, Genoa, 1823, n.d.

Dear Mrs Shelley

I have received the enclosed notice through Murray from London – which I can't help feeling a little premature as well as public. It was not my intention to make my name stand forth so dramatically; will you ask Hunt whether *he* has any news from England on the subject? – I have h[ad] a long letter from M[urray] complaining bitterly about Mr John H[unt] whose behaviour he [says was] very rude to him. Have you anything on y[our] affairs?†

---

* This letter, printed with the kind permission of the Wren Library, Trinity College, Cambridge, is in the Houghton Papers, 12/37. It was probably one of several which Hogg wrote after Lady Shelley's attack on him in the *Shelley Memorials*. It certainly suggests that the Shelleys had decided to take a conciliatory attitude, perhaps because they knew that Hogg had already completed the material for further volumes which they wished to secure, and because they were eager to retrieve the letters which Hogg had been loaned. The mystery of what happened to the rest of Hogg's work has never been solved. Hogg, if he retained it, would surely have decided to publish and be damned. It is not impossible that Lady Shelley obtained possession of the manuscript by this show of friendship, and then destroyed it.

† This unpublished letter is now in the library of the University of Pisa, Ms 775.232. It was displayed as part of the 'Paradise of Exiles' exhibition at Pisa in 1985 and has been printed by Mario Curreli in *Una certa Signora Mason* (Edizioni ETS, 1997). Byron's discomfort seems to have concerned the fact that his name was being pushed to the top of advertisements for the *Liberal*. The letter shows how heavily Byron depended on Mary to act as a go-between in his dealings with Leigh Hunt, and that he felt able to treat her in a professional but friendly way.

PORTRAITS OF
MARY SHELLEY

The earliest alleged portrait of Mary Shelley was first seen in the edition of her journals prepared by Paula Feldman and Diana Scott-Kilvert and published in 1987. A miniature from a privately owned Irish collection, it is enclosed in a circle of plaited hair with the words 'Mary Shelley 1815' superimposed in gilt wire on the reverse. It shows a youngish woman – Mary was twenty at the time – with short, light curling hair and with a long nose and thin mouth which give it a passing, but not striking, resemblance to the oil portrait of her by Richard Rothwell. Against its authenticity stands the fact that Mary was not yet married to Shelley in 1815. Hers was not an unusual name; it is possible that the miniature is of Percy Bysshe's sister Mary, who was also born in 1797 and who, confusingly, was physically similar to her namesake.

Rosalie Glynn Grylls, whose biography of Mary Shelley was published in 1938, was the first to publish 'Mary Shelley at nineteen'. This was another miniature, allegedly painted at Geneva in the summer of 1816 and given to E.J. Trelawny, who in turn presented it to William Michael Rossetti. Here, Mary is shown with dark hair which is coiled into untidy shells over her ears. Doris Langley Moore, an authority on the history of costume as well as on Byron, has cast doubt on this portrait by pointing out that the leg-of-mutton sleeves of Mary's dress are more appropriate to the year 1825. It is worth remembering, however, that Trelawny, who lived in Geneva shortly after Mary's visit there and knew her well by 1821, never doubted that the portrait was authentic.

Mary was also painted in 1819 by Amelia Curran, when she was living in Rome. Left with Miss Curran in Rome, this portrait was eventually retrieved on Mary's behalf by Trelawny. He kept it, asserting that Mary had never liked the picture, although she had made several requests for its return.

This picture disappeared after Trelawny's death. A further portrait of Mary in 1819, by Signor Delicati, has also been lost. So, regrettably, have the portrait and miniature which Edward Williams painted of her in 1821. Shelley, on 15 August, wrote to thank his wife for the birthday gift of a miniature to wear 'upon my heart, this image which is ever present to my mind'.

A portrait of Mary seated behind a desk and looking wistfully conscientious, painted by S.J. Stump, has now been discredited.

The miniature reproduced on the jacket of this book was executed by Reginald Easton. Easton was staying with Sir Percy and Lady Shelley at Boscombe in 1857, during which year he drew Thomas Jefferson Hogg and painted miniatures of Sir Percy's late parents. The portrait of Mary was alleged by Lady Shelley to have been made from a death mask, but the evident intention was to combine the image of her as a young woman with a hint of her widowhood, conveyed by draping a dark lace mantilla over her hair and shoulders. She wears a spray of pansies, for remembrance, at her breast.

In 1863, making a tour of Shelley sites in Italy, Sir Percy and his wife were allowed to copy a drawing of Mary which a Lerici fisherman told them he had found in the deserted Villa Magni. They did not question the portrait's authenticity. There is, in the archives of the National Portrait Gallery, a reproduction of a drawing of Mary, looking haggard and unhappy, her hair loosely pinned up into a cluster of curls. It is, quite possibly, a self-portrait dating from the summer of 1822: Mary had trained as an artist and kept up her lessons when she was living at Bath in the autumn of 1816. Her journals record her sketching and painting in Rome three years later. I have been unable to establish contact with the portrait's owner, but I am indebted to Adrian Hemming for passing on the information that Dr Marcello Pelligrini, a Florentine, inherited this picture from a relation whose great-aunt was given it by Mary Shelley when she was living at the Villa Magni. The drawing is reproduced here for the first time.

In 1902, Richard Garnett was visited by Jane Williams Hogg's grandson, Colonel Leigh Hunt, who had brought over from his home in Brussels a picture of Mary Shelley. Describing it after Colonel Hunt's death to Edward Dowden on 8 January 1903, Garnett wrote that the artist was one '"Cleobulina" Fielding (whom I have not traced, but suspect to have been a member of Copley Fielding's family).' He added that the portrait, painted in 'about 1833', was 'the best I had seen'. In 1903, he was still waiting for Hunt's widow to communicate with him about the portrait, but no further mention of it has been traced.

Richard Rothwell had become a celebrated portrait painter, able to command eighty guineas for a commission, when William Godwin noted on 18 May 1831 that he had visited Rothwell's studio while Mary sat for her portrait. In 1833, Mary confidently informed John Murray that she had no portrait of herself suitable for his engraver, Finden, to work from and that she would not, therefore, be available for inclusion among the gallery of friends who were to adorn his new luxury edition of Moore's Life of Byron. Either Mary was lying or Rothwell had kept a portrait for which she could not afford to pay. There are references during this period to a portrait of her having been executed by George Clint, a well-known miniaturist who lived close to the Godwins' home in Gower Place, but this work has been lost.

Mary's friendship with Rothwell was resumed when the Irish artist returned from Italy in the late 1830s. In April 1840, his portrait of her was shown in the Summer Exhibition at the Royal Academy.

It is usually assumed that this was the portrait on which Rothwell was working in 1831, when Mary was thirty-three years old. Since the Royal Academy only exhibited recent work in the Summer Exhibition, the likelihood is that Mary sat for him again, probably in the autumn of 1839, when she was forty-two. This is a more convincing age for the face of the woman whose portrait now hangs in the National Portrait Gallery. Mary either bought or was given the painting after the exhibition. It was hung in the Boscombe shrine after her death.

In 1958, a new portrait of Mary Shelley turned up in a South Kensington saleroom, stowed away in a box of theatrical props and costumes which sold to a private buyer for 18 shillings. Put up for sale again in 1998, the painting was withdrawn because of insufficient authentication.

A label on the back of this mysterious work announces it to be of Mary Shelley by Rothwell. The portrait is strikingly unlike any other of Rothwell's works and can, I think, be assumed to be by another hand. But is the sitter Mary Shelley? The long, Godwinian nose and thin lips, together with the thin gold head circlet which also appears in the authenticated Rothwell portrait, suggest that this may be the case. The historical costume department of the Victoria & Albert Museum has dated the sitter's off-the-shoulder dress of pale blue satin with short puffed sleeves to between 1835 and 1843. A shawl of dark lace loosely draped over the arms is evidently intended to be admired and may possibly be the lace mantilla which Claire brought over from Paris in the mid-1840s.

Against this, we must set the fact that, although Mary wore two rings, she is not known to have worn other jewellery. The sitter for this portrait wears two handsome bracelets. It is possible that the sitter was Mary's sister-in-law and namesake, but it is also tempting to see this as a portrait of Mary, intended to acknowledge the dignity of her new role in society following the death of her father-in-law in the spring of 1844. If this was the case, we would need to ask why Lady Shelley, a devoted daughter-in-law and preserver of Mary's possessions, would have allowed such a treasure to pass unnoticed. Another possibility is that the painting was commissioned in 1833, when John Murray first approached Mary Shelley to ask if she would be willing for an engraving of her by Finden to be included in the new Byron edition. 'I could not make up my mind to be exhibited among the portraits, I have such a dislike of display,' Mary told Murray on 10 February 1835. But perhaps a portrait had been commissioned, which Finden then

decided was unsuitable for the purposes of engraving or which Mary
decided should not be used. In the 1830s, Mary was still apprehensive of
being publicly identified as Mrs Shelley, since such publicity had been
expressly forbidden by Sir Timothy.

More tenuous likenesses can be mentioned here. A portrait of Beatrice
Cenci which was, in Mary Shelley's lifetime, attributed to Guido Reni, was
thought by some of her friends to have been very like her; others thought
she resembled the tragic actress Eliza O'Neill who Shelley had hoped would
play the part of Beatrice in his drama. Leigh Hunt gave a hint of Mary's slyly
elusive expression when calling her, as a young woman of twenty-two, 'the
nymph of the sidelong looks';* while his son Thornton, writing on Shelley
in the *Atlantic Monthly* in February 1863, made an intriguing observation on
Mary's resemblance to a marble bust in the Towneley Collection, now at the
British Museum:

> If the reader desires a portrait of Mary, he has one in the well-known
> antique bust sometimes called 'Isis' and sometimes 'Clytie': a woman's
> head and shoulders arising from a lotus flower. It is most probably the
> portrait of a Roman lady, and is in some degree more elongated and
> 'classic' than Mary; but, on the other hand, it falls short of her, for it
> gives no idea of her tall and intellectual forehead, nor has it any trace
> of the bright, animated, and sweet expression that so often lighted up
> her face.

* Leigh Hunt–Mary Shelley, 9 March 1819, *Shelley and Mary* (1882), pp. 366–71.

NOTES

The following abbreviated forms have been used for those works most frequently cited in the textual notes. All quotations reproduce the spelling and punctuation of the published texts.

BL&J   *Byron: Letters and Journals*, 12 vols. and supplement, ed. Leslie A. Marchand (John Murray, 1973–94)

CC   *The Clairmont Correspondence: Letters of Claire Clairmont, Charles Clairmont, and Fanny Imlay Godwin*, 2 vols., ed. Marion Kingston Stocking (Johns Hopkins University Press, 1995)

CCJ   *The Journals of Claire Clairmont*, ed. Marion Kingston Stocking (Harvard University Press, 1968)

CTS   *Mary Shelley: Collected Tales and Stories*, ed. Charles E. Robinson (Johns Hopkins University Press, 1976)

Godwin   C. Kegan Paul, *William Godwin: His Friends and Contemporaries*, 2 vols. (1876)

G&M   *Godwin and Mary: Letters of William Godwin and Mary Wollstonecraft*, ed. Ralph M. Wardle (Lawrence, 1966)

G&S   William St Clair, *The Godwins and the Shelleys* (Faber, 1989; 1991)

Marshall, MWS Florence (Mrs Julian) Marshall, *The Life and Letters of Mary Wollstonecraft Shelley*, 2 vols. (1889)

MWSJ   *The Journals of Mary Wollstonecraft Shelley*, ed. Paula Feldman and Diana Scott-Kilvert (Oxford University Press, 1987)

MWSL   *The Letters of Mary Wollstonecraft Shelley*, 3 vols., ed. Betty T. Bennett (Johns Hopkins University Press, 1980–8)

PBSL   *The Letters of Percy Bysshe Shelley*, 2 vols., ed. Frederick L. Jones (The Clarendon Press, Oxford, 1964)

PW   *The Poetical Works of Percy Bysshe Shelley*, 4 vols., with notes by Mary Wollstonecraft Shelley (1839)

R&R   Emily Sunstein, *Mary Shelley: Romance and Reality* (Little, Brown, New York, 1989)

S&M   Shelley and Mary, ed. Lady Shelley, 4 vols. (privately printed,
             1882)*
Shelley's Friends   Maria Gisborne and Edward E. Williams: Shelley's Friends, Their
             Journals and Letters, ed. Frederick L. Jones (University of
             Oklahoma Press, 1951)
Shelley and His   Shelley and His Circle, 1773–1822, 8 vols., ed. Kenneth Neill
Circle   Cameron (vols. 1–4) and Donald H. Reiman (vols. 5–8) (Harvard
             University Press, 1961–86)
Talks   Maud Rolleston, Talks with Lady Shelley (1897)

Reference is also made to the following collections, where papers relating to Mary
Wollstonecraft Shelley (MWS) are deposited:

Abinger   The Abinger Papers, Bodleian Library, Oxford (the principal
              archive, its holding includes MWS's notes on Shelley's poems, her
              edited version of Godwin's autobiography, and her notes towards
              a biography of her parents, as well as most of her letters to Maria
              Gisborne, Jane Williams Hogg, Edward Trelawny and Leigh and
              Marianne Hunt)
BL   The British Library (containing the journals of Claire Clairmont,
              Maria Gisborne and Edward Williams)
Huntington   Huntington Library, San Marino, California (containing most of
              MWS's letters to Claire Clairmont, originally acquired by H.
              Buxton Forman)
Murray   The John Murray Archive, Albemarle Street, London (contain-
              ing MWS's letters to Byron)
Pforzheimer   The Carl H. Pforzheimer Collection, New York Public Library
              (containing among other items over 400 letters, notes and tran-
              scripts by MWS)
Silsbee   The E.A. Silsbee Collection, James Duncan Phillips Library,
              Peabody Essex Museum, Salem, Massachusetts (containing the
              notebooks of Edward Augustus Silsbee recording his conversa-
              tions with Claire Clairmont in the 1870s)

---

* According to Sir Percy Shelley's preface to S&M, all four volumes are said to have been
prepared by Lady Shelley, and to 'comprise all the letters and other documents of a biographical nature at present in the hands of Shelley's representatives' (1 January 1882). For this
biography, use has been made of the annotated personal copy of Edward Dowden, donated
to the British Library, the first volume of which contains this note:

These volumes – of which Lady Shelley had given duplicates to the Bodleian Library
– are by her direction to be kept private until I think 1922 (the centenary of Shelley's
death).
      In this copy I have copied many passages from Jane Clairmont's papers, which I
obtained the use of from Mr Forman.

The following shortened forms are used for several of the principal persons in the narrative:

CC	Claire Clairmont	MJG	Mary Jane Godwin
Ch.C	Charles Clairmont	MW	Mary Wollstonecraft
CL	Charles Lamb	MWG/MWS	Mary Wollstonecraft
EJT	Edward John Trelawny		Godwin, later Shelley
EW	Edward Williams	PBS	Percy Bysshe Shelley
FI	Fanny Imlay	PFS	(Sir) Percy Florence
HS	Harriet Shelley		Shelley
JHP	John Howard Payne	STC	Samuel Taylor
JG	John Gisborne		Coleridge
JS	(Lady) Jane Shelley	TG	(Countess) Teresa
JW/JWH	Jane Williams, later		Guiccioli
	Hogg	TJH	Thomas Jefferson Hogg
LH	Leigh Hunt	TLP	Thomas Love Peacock
MG	Maria Gisborne	WG	William Godwin
MH	Marianne Hunt		

CHAPTER ONE: *The Age of Prometheus*

NOTE: Unsourced material in this chapter is taken from the autobiography of William Godwin and the biography of him by his daughter, Mary Shelley. Neither work was completed. Both are in the Abinger collection as Dep. b. 226/1, Dep. c. 606/1–5, Dep. c. 532/8 and other folders. Also in the same collection is Godwin's Journal, comprising 32 small notebooks, Dep. e. 196–227.

1. William St Clair, *The Godwins and the Shelleys* (Faber, 1991), pp. 51–2 (hereafter *G&S*). Written by Robert Merry, who wrote under the pen-name Della Crusca and founded a poetry school under that name. He was the first poet with whom Godwin had a close friendship.

2. A lucid account of Godwin's philosophy is given by John Passmore in *The Perfectibility of Man* (Duckworth, 1970), ch. 9, 'Governmentalists, Anarchists and Geneticists'.

3. Mary Shelley (hereafter MWS) was wrongly informed by her father that the book had been priced at three guineas (C. Kegan Paul, *William Godwin: His Friends and Contemporaries*, 1 (1876), p. 80 (hereafter *Godwin*). But £1 16s. still placed it far beyond the reach of the working man. Like many influential works of the period, it was more discussed than read.

4. 'Godwin . . . attended the trials every day, though he knew himself to be a marked man, had his friends been found guilty,' Mary Shelley wrote in the biography of her father which she never completed. Quoted by Kegan Paul, *Godwin*, 1, pp. 134–5, but see also the headnote to this chapter.

5. William Godwin (hereafter WG)–Joseph Gerrald, 29.1.1794. Quoted in *Godwin*, 1, p. 128. Gerrald, a wealthy radical passionately committed to

the cause of reform, was sentenced to be transported for fifteen years after attending a dinner, perceived as a subversive meeting. Mary Shelley's account (see note 4) does not conceal her indignation at the injustice done to him.

6. William Hazlitt, *The Spirit of the Age* (1825), Oxford World Classics, p. 20.

7. WG (Abinger, Dep. b. 226/1).

8. Andrew Kippis, *A Vindication of the Protestant Dissenting Ministers, with regard to their Late Application to Parliament* (1772), p. 26.

9. *Godwin*, 1, p. 19.

10. WG, *An Account of the Seminary* (1783), reprinted in *Political and Philosophical Works of William Godwin*, 5, ed. Pamela Clemit (Pickering & Chatto, 1993) (hereafter *Works*). The prospectus offered tuition in Greek, Latin, French and English to twelve pupils.

11. Ann Godwin–WG, 29.5.1788 (*Godwin*, 1, pp. 55–6).

12. Ibid., p. 39.

13. Amelia Alderson–WG, 1 November 1796 (Abinger, Dep. b. 210/6).

14. *Godwin*, 1, p. 40.

15. William Dunlap, *A History of the American Theatre* (New York, 1832), p. 182.

16. WG, *Memoirs of the author of 'The Rights of Woman'* (1798), ed. Richard Holmes (Penguin Books, 1987), p. 245.

17. Godwin, who destroyed it, noted in the *Memoirs* that the autobiographical elements of the play had been treated seriously.

18. *Godwin and Mary: Letters of William Godwin and Mary Wollstonecraft*, ed. Ralph M. Wardle (Lawrence, 1966), p. 2 (hereafter *G&M*).

19. See St Clair, *G&S*, pp. 155–6, for an account of the relationship between Godwin and Maria Reveley (later Gisborne) at this period.

20. WG, *Memoirs*, ch. 8, p. 249.

21. Mary Wollstonecraft (hereafter MW)–WG, 1.7.1796 (*G&M*).

22. WG–MW, 13.7.1796 (*G&M*).

CHAPTER TWO: *A Birth and a Death*

1. *Godwin*, 1, p. 276.

2. Ann Godwin–WG, 3.5.1797 (Abinger, Dep. c. 516/1).

3. MW–WG, 11.4.97 (*G&M*, as for all similar citations in this chapter).

4. MW–WG, 3.6.1797.

5. WG–MW, 17.6.1797.

6. MW–WG, 19.6.1797.

7. WG–MW, 5.6.1797.

8. MW–WG, 6.6.1797.

9. *Memoirs*, ch. 7, p. 242.

10. MW, *A Vindication of the Rights of Woman* (I have used the excellent Cambridge University Press 1995 reissue, edited by Sylvana Tomaselli), p. 246.

11. MW, *A Short Residence in Sweden, Norway and Denmark*, ed. Richard Holmes (Penguin Books, 1987), p. 183.

12. WG, *The Enquirer* (1797), p. 1.

13. Ibid., p. 130.

14. MW, *Lessons* (Abinger, Dep. f. 65). These originally appeared in the posthumous edition of Mary Wollstonecraft's works, published by Godwin in 1798. (A copy of the printed pages, bound as a separate booklet with the signature 'E Wollstonecraft – 1798', is preserved in the Abinger collection, Dep. f. 65. This suggests that Mary's aunt had a copy bound as a first reading book for the baby girl.)

15. *Gentleman's Magazine*, LXVII, noted on 2.8.1797, p. 203.

16. MWS, 'The Choice', written in 1822–3: *Journals of Mary Shelley*, ed. Paula Feldman and Diana Scott-Kilvert (Oxford University Press, 1987), p. 704 (hereafter *MWSJ*).

17. MW–WG, 30.8.1797.

18. Ibid.

19. J.F. Clarke, *Recollections of the Medical Profession* (1874), p. 293.

20. Anthony Carlisle–Richard Owen, 12.3.1834 (Library of the Royal College of Surgeons, Carlisle Mss).

21. Eliza Fenwick–Everina Wollstonecraft, 12.9.1797 (*Godwin*, I, p. 283).

22. WG, *St Leon* (1799), ed. Pamela Clemit (Oxford World's Classics, 1994), ch. 28, pp. 293–4. Godwin described his sensation of devastated bereavement with less passion but as much eloquence in one of his last novels, *Deloraine* (1833).

23. WG–George Tuthill, 13.9.1797 (*Godwin*, I, p. 284).

24. WG–Anthony Carlisle, 15.9.1797 (ibid., p. 285).

25. William Nicholson–WG, 18.9.1797 (ibid., pp. 289–90). The impressive size of Godwin's own forehead was often cited by phrenologists as proof that the intellect was reflected by external dimensions. He may, in the desolate weeks following his wife's death, have been temporarily inclined to catch at straws for comfort. But common sense prevailed. In his collection of essays, *Thoughts on Man* (1831), ch. 20, Godwin rejected the science of phrenology, while gleefully reminding his readers that one of the most cold-blooded murderers in history had been discovered to have an unusually large 'organ of benevolence'.

26. WG, 'Note', 1798 (*Godwin*, I, p. 295).

27. *Gentleman's Magazine*, LXVII, October 1797.

28. *Monthly Review*, XXVII, September–December 1798.

29. *Anti-Jacobin Review*, I, 1798.

30. Hannah More, *Strictures on Female Education* (1799), I, pp. 48–9.

31. Quoted in Claire Tomalin, *The Life and Death of Mary Wollstonecraft* (revised edition, Penguin Books, 1992), ch. 19.

32. 'The Vision of Liberty' was published in the *Anti-Jacobin Review*, August 1801. The author was anonymous.

33. I am indebted for this information to the series of lectures on reading in the Romantic period given by William St Clair at Trinity College, Cambridge, in 1998.

34. *Quarterly Review*, 1833. The work under review was Allan Cunningham's six-volume *Lives of the most eminent British Painters, Sculptors and Architects* (1830–3).

35. MWS, *Frankenstein, or The Modern Prometheus* (1818), I, iv.

36. Ann Mellor, *Mary Shelley: Her Life, Her Fiction, Her Monsters* (Routledge, 1988), is one of the liveliest and most stimulating, whether or not you agree with Mellor's interpretations.
37. MWS, 'The Elder Son' (1835). Reprinted in *Mary Shelley: Collected Tales and Stories*, ed. Charles E. Robinson (Johns Hopkins University Press, 1976) (hereafter *CTS*).
38. MWS, 'An Eighteenth Century Tale: A Fragment', reprinted in *CTS* and dated by Robinson as preceding 1824.

CHAPTER THREE: *Father and Daughter*
1. MWS, 'The Mourner' (1830), *CTS*.
2. MWS, 'The Elder Son' (1835), *CTS*.
3. MWS, *Lodore* (1835), I, iii.
4. MWS–PBS, 18.10.1817.
5. WG–Harriet Lee, June 1798 (*Godwin*, I, pp. 303–4).
6. WG–Mrs Cotton, 24.10.1797 (ibid., p. 281).
7. Samuel Taylor Coleridge (hereafter STC)–WG, 8.9.1800, and hereafter, in *Collected Letters of Samuel Taylor Coleridge*, 6 vols., ed. E.L. Griggs (Oxford University Press, 1956–71).
8. STC–WG, 6.12.1800.
9. STC–WG, 21.5.1800.
10. WG–James Marshall, 11.7.1800 (Abinger, Dep. c. 214).
11. Margaret Mountcashell–WG, 9.9.1800 (Abinger, Dep. c. 516).
12. Margaret Mountcashell–WG, 6.8.1800 (Abinger, Dep. c. 516).
13. WG–James Marshall, 11.7.1800 (Abinger, Dep. c. 214).
14. WG–James Marshall, 6.8.1800 (Abinger, Dep. c. 214).
15. The event was reported in the *Annual Register* for 1803 (February). The significance of Aldini's experiments was more sceptically assessed in the *Edinburgh Review*, III, 1803, pp. 193–8. Aldini was then the Professor of Experimental Philosophy at Bologna University. In the Library of the Royal College of Surgeons, there is a handwritten account by a witness to Aldini's experiments on frogs, rabbits and a mastiff in 1802 (275.h.17). Aldini's own account, in *General Views of the Application of Galvanism to medical purposes principally in cases of suspended animation* (1819), describes another experiment made by a colleague on 5 July 1804 on a drowned boy, resulting in a violent expulsion of bodily fluids (water, saliva, shit); an allusion to the fact that his galvanic piles were on sale in Leicester Square suggests that a certain amount of home-experimenting went on.
16. 'You are placed in the situation I longed to occupy at the commencement of my public life,' Carlisle wrote to the anatomist Richard Owen on 12 March 1834. Carlisle provided many notes to Owen for the influential series of thirty lectures on generation and anatomy which he delivered that year to an audience which included Charles Darwin, just returned from his travels on HMS *Beagle*.

CHAPTER FOUR: *A Shared Life*

1. Henry Crabb Robinson, *On Books and Their Writers*, ed. Edith Morley (1938), 1, p. 235.
2. *Godwin*, 2, p. 58. Mary's son, Sir Percy Shelley, read the proofs and probably supplied this account; her daughter-in-law advised. The description of Mrs Clairmont's garden monologues comes from Maud Rolleston, *Talks with Lady Shelley* (1897), p. 35 (hereafter *Talks*).
3. Herbert Huscher, *Keats-Shelley Memorial Bulletin*, VIII (1957) and XI (1960). See also *G&S*, ch. 18 and nn. 27, 28 and 30 to that chapter.
4. Eliza Fenwick–WG (Abinger, Dep. c. 214), undated but evidently related to John Fenwick's letter to WG of 24.11.1801 in the same file. Here, Fenwick refers to a row between his wife and Mrs Godwin (hereafter MJG). Later letters from Eliza show that Mrs Godwin's well-meant bossiness continued to infuriate her.
5. Charles Lamb (hereafter CL)–John Rickman, 16.9.1801, and hereafter, in *The Letters of Charles Lamb to Which are Added Those of His Sister Mary Lamb*, ed. E.V. Lucas (1935), 3 vols.
6. CL–T. Manning, 29.3.1809.
7. CL–William Hazlitt, 28.11.1810.
8. Mary Lamb–Mrs Hazlitt, 7.11.1809.
9. Crabb Robinson, *On Books and Their Writers*, 1, p. 235.
10. Quoted in Don Locke, *A Fantasy of Reason: The Life and Thought of William Godwin* (Kegan Paul, 1980), pp. 206 and 235. Locke notes (p. 235) that someone has drawn a blue pencil through Place's reference to Mrs Godwin.
11. Aaron Burr–Theodasia Burr, 21.11.1808, in *The Correspondence of Aaron Burr and his daughter, Theodasia*, ed. Mark van Doren (New York, 1929), p. 264.
12. Harriet Shelley (hereafter HS)–Catherine Nugent, October 1812, in *The Letters of Percy Bysshe Shelley*, 2 vols., ed. Frederick L. Jones (The Clarendon Press, Oxford, 1964), 1, p. 327 (hereafter *PBSL*).
13. Ann Godwin–WG, 15.11.1803 (Abinger, Dep. c. 516/1).
14. *A Picture of the New Town of Herne Bay, By a Lady* (John Macrone, 1835), identified by William St Clair as the work of Mrs Godwin, who knew the area well.
15. MJG–WG, September 1805 (Abinger, Dep. c. 523).
16. WG, *Thoughts on Man* (1831): Godwin, *Works*, 6, ed. Mark Philp (Pickering & Chatto, 1993), pp. 21–3.
17. WG–MWG, 24.9.1812 (BL, Ashley 3267). Published as Appendix A in volume 2 of *The Clairmont Correspondence*, 2 vols., ed. Marion Kingston Stocking (Johns Hopkins University Press, 1995) (hereafter *CC*).
18. MWS–Maria Gisborne (hereafter MG), 30.10–17.11.[1834] as dated in *The Letters of Mary Wollstonecraft Shelley* (hereafter *MWSL*), 3 vols., ed. Betty T. Bennett (Johns Hopkins University Press, 1980–8), vol. 2.
19. WG (as William Scolfield), *Bible Stories* (Philips, 1803), Preface, reprinted in Godwin, *Works*, 5, ed. Pamela Clemit (Pickering & Chatto, 1993), p. 312.
20. MWS, as Mrs Shelley, *Maurice, or The Fisher's Cot* (1820), unpublished in

her lifetime. On 10 October 1821, her father rejected it for the Juvenile Library as unworthy of being expanded to publishable length; Mary herself appears to have given it no further thought. Professor Mario Curreli, *Una certa Signora Mason* (Edizioni ETS, 1997), p. 31, quoted from the original manuscript which he had read in the Dazzi-Cini archive; *Maurice* was published the following year with notes and an introduction by Claire Tomalin (Viking).

21. WG–Mrs Fordham, 13.11.1811 (Abinger, Dep. b. 214/3). This was written when Mary had been five months away from home; Godwin might have been unusually sensitive to any imagined criticism of him as a parent at this time.

22. MJG–Lady Mountcashell, 15.11.1814 (Pforzheimer). This comes from one of the copies made by Claire Clairmont (hereafter CC) of her mother's letters, partly printed in previous works but without this section. To those who share my doubts about the stability of Claire's mental state when she scratched out, rewrote and expanded her mother's letters, it must remain questionable whether Trelawny, to whom the copy was to be dispatched, was receiving Mrs Godwin's words or Claire's.

23. WG, *History of England* (Hodgkins, Hanway Street, 1806), p. 114.

24. The collaboration between W.F. Mylius, of Red Lion Square, and Godwin remains puzzling. This British Library copy is bound in leather as 'Class Book: Godwin', but the preface, although unsigned by Mylius, refers to his previous success with the Junior Class Book and to subsequent discussions with other teachers. References to the pleasures of watching a child's imagination at work sound like Godwin's. The collection ranges across his whole circle of friends and includes the banker-poet Samuel Rogers, 'Perdita' Robinson, Thomas Holcroft, Coleridge, M.G. Lewis, Helen Maria Williams, Erasmus Darwin and Humphry Davy. There is a youthful contribution from Byron. A generous selection of Charlotte Smith's sonnets are also included; so is an extract from John Ford's play *Warbreck*, much admired by Godwin. [?]Philips's 'Winter at Copenhagen' helped feed Mary's imagination in *Frankenstein*; it contains striking descriptions of frozen billows, glassy plains and moonlit, ice-locked ravines. Old favourites, Cowper, Thomas and Young, are also given space. The book's influence on Mary at a formative period would repay further study.

Anybody interested in tracing Godwin's publishing career might note that an 1819 edition of Mylius's *School Dictionary of the English Language*, published together with Baldwin's *A New Guide to the English Tongue*, claimed that 25,000 copies had been sold since the first printing in 1809!

25. Charles and Mary Lamb, *Tales from Shakespeare* (1807). These were initially published as separate booklets under Charles's name.

26. For a full account, see Emily Sunstein, 'Young Mary Godwin', *Keats-Shelley Journal*, 45, May 1996. The poem is printed as an appendix in MWS, *The Novels and Selected Works of Mary Shelley*, 8, ed. Jeanne Moskal (Pickering & Chatto, 1996) (hereafter *Selected Works*).

27. Emily Sunstein, in her biography *Mary Shelley: Romance and Reality* (Little, Brown, New York, 1989) (hereafter *R&R*), was the first to suggest that Mary wrote these two books. I am not convinced. Mrs Barnard writes livelier dialogue

and has none of Mary's interest in descriptive passages. Several critics have been impressed by the fact that *The Prize* is set near Marlow where Mary herself lived in 1817; the use of the phrase, 'I must have a little patience', in Mrs Barnard's *The Parent's Offering* has been thought significant. The context, of somebody waiting to be paid a shilling, is less than persuasive. Finally, the fact that Barnard wrote a story for Godwin called 'The Fisherboy of Weymouth' while Mary offered him *Maurice*, also about a fisherboy who had Weymouth connections, refutes the suggestion that Mrs Barnard was a pseudonym used by Mary.

28. Skinner Street was then and remained a street of booksellers and publishers. This is a comprehensive list: John George Barnard, 57 Skinner Street, 1802–24; Bumpus, 23, and then 3 Skinner Street, 1828–33; Sampson Low, 57 Skinner Street, 1837–?; John Major, 17 Skinner Street, 1817–22; George Richmond, 53 Skinner Street, 1849–?; Thomas Sharpe, 15 Skinner Street, 1845–8; Wallis & Son, 42 Skinner Street, 1814–26; William Wilson, 57 Skinner Street, 1840–56. M.J. Godwin's Juvenile Library was at 41 Skinner Street, next to Wallis & Son, from 1807 to 1825. (Wallis, a publisher of children's games and jigsaw puzzles, complemented the Juvenile Library rather than offering serious competition.)

CHAPTER FIVE: *Tensions*

1. CC–Edward John Trelawny (hereafter EJT), April 1871 (*CC*, 2).
2. Aaron Burr, *Private Journal*, facsimile edition (New York, 1903).
3. *R&R*, ch. 3, p. 47.
4. MWG–Lady Mountcashell, n.d. (Pforzheimer). This reference appears in a previously unpublished extract from one of Claire's heavily revised copies of her mother's letters. It may be connected to the fact that Claire herself was later diagnosed as scrofulous, when the glands in her throat were noticed to have swollen. The fact that Mary was for some time incapable of using her arm certainly suggests something more serious than the eczema for which soothing poultices were applied.
5. MJG–WG, 10.6.1811 (Abinger, Dep. c. 523).
6. MWS–Jane Williams (hereafter JW), 10.3.1823 (*MWSL*, 1).
7. MWS–Percy Bysshe Shelley (hereafter PBS), 28.10.1814.
8. MWS, in her notes towards a life of her father, quoted by Kegan Paul, *Godwin*, I, pp. 36–7. (The memoir is in the Abinger Papers, Dep. c. 606.)
9. WG–MWG, 18.5.1811 (Abinger, Dep. c. 523).
10. WG–Mrs Fordham, 13.11.1811 (Abinger, Dep. b. 214/3).
11. WG–MJG, 4.6.1811 (Abinger, Dep. c. 523).
12. MJG–WG, 10.6.1811 (Abinger, Dep. c. 523).
13. Scott, *Marmion* (1811), canto vi.
14. MJG–Lady Mountcashell, 15.11.1814 (abstract by Richard Garnett, Bodleian, Ms Shelley c. 1, fol. 556).
15. WG–PBS, 30.3.1812, and hereafter, in *PBSL*. Some of Godwin's letters to Shelley and copies of them are in the Abinger collection (Dep. c. 524).
16. WG–PBS, 4.3.1812.
17. WG–PBS, 4.7.1812.

18. PBS–WG, 10.1.1812 and 24.2.1812.

19. PBS–WG, 24.2.1812. Fleetwood grows up in Wales and later meets Ruffigny in Switzerland, which Shelley was eager to visit.

20. PBS–WG, 26.1.1812.

21. PBS–WG, 11.6.1812.

22. MWS–CC, 15.12.1844 (*MWSL*, 3).

23. WG–W.T. Baxter, 8.6.1812, in Mrs Julian Marshall, *The Life and Letters of Mary Wollstonecraft Shelley*, 2 vols. (1889), 1, pp. 27–9 (hereafter Marshall, *MWS*); *Shelley and His Circle*, 3, ed. Kenneth Neill Cameron (Harvard University Press 1970), pp. 100–2.

CHAPTER SIX: *A Glassite Household*

1. From MWS's Preface to the 1831 edition of *Frankenstein*.

2. MWS and PBS–W.T. Baxter, 30.12.1817. Here she assured Baxter that his daughter's 'are not below me in station'. For information on the Baxters, I am much indebted to the present head of the family, Normaile Baxter.

3. WG–MWS, 10.10.1821 (Abinger, Dep. c. 524).

4. The description of Isabella and the observation on her similarity to Shelley derive from a book by her grandson, James Stuart, *Reminiscences* (1911).

5. Charles Clairmont (hereafter Ch.C)–MWS, 18.9.1822 (*CC*, 1).

6. Stuart, *Reminiscences*, see note 4, above.

7. See note 1, above.

8. Ibid.

9. Elizabeth Hitchener's view is reported on 4 August 1812 in Harriet Shelley's letter to her Irish friend Catherine Nugent: Harriet's letters to Catherine Nugent are given in chronologically placed footnotes to *PBSL*, 1.

10. HS–Catherine Nugent, [?] October 1812.

11. Francis Place–WG (BL Mss 35, 145 f.44).

12. This was quoted angrily back to Fanny in a letter from Shelley, 10.12.1812 (*PBSL*, 1).

13. Richard Holmes, *Shelley: The Pursuit* (1974; Penguin Books, 1987), p. 172.

14. HS–Catherine Nugent, 16.1.1813; she made her allusion to Mrs Godwin on 22 June 1813.

15. The anecdote about Lamb is given in *Forfar's Pastime Papers* by the Reverend John Stirton (Forfar, 1917), pp. 98–9; see also *Dundee Advertiser*, 7.9.1897, reproducing Christina (Christy) Baxter's recollections.

16. Marshall, *MWS*, 1, pp. 30–4. Marshall, whose biography was published in 1889, is probably a more reliable source than Christy in her long interview about her connection to Mary, given eight years later. Marshall's account may give a more accurate reflection of Mary's own recollections, as given to Lady Shelley, with whom Florence Marshall was in close contact. I have failed to discover the whereabouts, if it still exists, of the diary Christy Baxter kept in 1812–13.

17. William Hazlitt, *Conversations of Northcote* (1830). Northcote and his sister were among Godwin's closest friends.

18. Mary Wollstonecraft, *Maria* (1798), ch. 7. It is not clear when Mary first read

her mother's novel but it is reasonable to suppose that the Baxters had copies of her work.

19. Diary, quoted in A.H. Millar, 'Some Unpublished Facts', *Dundee Advertiser*, 2.12.1911.

CHAPTER SEVEN: *Love and Confusion*

1. Edmund Blunden, *Shelley: A Life Story* (1946), p. 113, quoting an unidentified contemporary annalist.

2. Mrs de Boinville–T.J. Hogg (hereafter TJH), 18.4.1814, in T.J. Hogg, *The Life of Percy Bysshe Shelley* (1858), 2 of a projected 4, p. 533.

3. William Godwin, *Political Justice*, Book 8, ch. 8, Appendix: 'Of Co-operation, Cohabitation, and Marriage'.

4. Hogg, *Shelley*, 2, p. 538.

5. PBS–TJH, 4.10.1814.

6. MWS, 'Life of Shelley' (1823?) Bodleian, Ms Shelley adds. c. 5, f. 113v: facsimile and transcript ed. A.M. Weinberg, *The Bodleian Shelley Manuscripts*, 22, pt 2 (1997), pp. 266–87, at pp. 266–7.

7. PBS–TJH, 4.10.1814.

8. HS–Catherine Nugent, 20.11.1814 (see Chapter 6, n. 9).

9. *Shelley Memorials*, ed. Lady Shelley (1859), p. 68.

10. W.M. Rossetti, *Memoir of Shelley* (1886), p. 77.

11. PBS–HS, 14.7.1814.

12. HS–Catherine Nugent, 20.10.1813.

13. Described by Edward Dowden to Richard Garnett, 6.12.1883, in *Letters about Shelley*, ed. R.S. Garnett (1917), p. 84.

14. The original book is in the Huntington Library, San Marino, California (RP 114869).

15. MJG–Lady Mountcashell. Letter dates from variant copies are 2 September, 16 August and 20 August. For further warnings against believing Mrs Godwin's letters in the only form we have them, transcribed and then rewritten by Claire, the reader may wish to read the wise words of Professor Marion Kingston Stocking in her edition of the Clairmont correspondence, especially p. 659, n. 19. We can enjoy the liveliness of Mrs Godwin's letters; we cannot place our faith in them.

16. Godwin's letter to Shelley exists only in an extract, cited in a Sotheran's sale catalogue (1923), cat. 784, no. 841. St Clair (*G&S*, p. 550) notes that the whereabouts of this letter and an earlier one to Shelley, of 10 July, sold in the same lot, are unknown.

17. PBS–HS, 13.8.1814. Here he urged her 'to come to Switzerland, where you will at least find one firm & constant friend . . .'

18. PBS, writing on 2 August 1814 in the journal which he and Mary had decided to keep together on their travels. Godwin's journal entry starkly records the hour and date of the runaways' departure.

19. MJG–Lady Mountcashell, 15.11.1814, in Dowden's paraphrase, *Life of Percy Bysshe Shelley*, 2 (1886), Appendix, pp. 546–8.

CHAPTER EIGHT: *Six Weeks in Europe*

1. *The Journals of Claire Clairmont*, ed. Marion Kingston Stocking (Harvard University Press, 1968) (hereafter *CCJ*).

2. MWS, 'The English in Italy', a review of three travel books for the *Westminster Review*, October 1826.

3. PBS, 2.8.1814 (*MWSJ*).

4. PBS–HS, 13.8.1814.

5. *CCJ*, p. 61, translated by Professor Kiffin Rockwell. The gender of the embracer is not, in fact, identified by Shelley's Latin.

6. Hogg, *Shelley*, 1, p. 257.

7. *CCJ*, 20.8.1820. In later life, Jane (as Claire Clairmont) rewrote part of the 1814 journal, incorporating details, such as Mary's refusal to bathe naked, which had not been in the original. These are published in full in *Shelley and His Circle*, 3, pp. 342–75. The original journal is in the British Library (Ashley 394).

8. WG, *Fleetwood* (1805), ed. Pamela Clemit (Pickering & Chatto, 1992), p. 72.

9. This was *The Assassins*, later recalled by Mary as having been inspired by a French book which Shelley had bought in Paris.

10. *CCJ*, 25.8.1814.

11. Ibid., 27.8.1814.

12. *MWSJ*, 28.8.1814; *CCJ*, 5.9.1814.

13. Further details can be found in Christopher Frayling, *Nightmare: The Birth of Horror* (BBC Books, 1996), pp. 35–6. Mary herself never alluded to Dippel or to Castle Frankenstein as sources of inspiration.

14. *MWSJ*, 28.8.1814.

15. MWS, *Rambles in Germany and Italy in 1840, 1842 and 1843* (1844), in *Selected Works*, 8, ed. Jeanne Moskal (Pickering & Chatto, 1996), p. 163.

16. *MWSJ*, 8.9.1814; *CCJ*, 9.9.1814.

17. See Marion Kingston Stocking in *CCJ*, pp. 40–1, n. 38.

18. *CCJ*, 11.9.1814.

19. MWS–Marianne Hunt (hereafter MH), 6.6.1840 (*MWSL*, 2).

CHAPTER NINE: *Experiments in Living*

1. The first date given for Mrs Godwin's letter was 7 August. This is made most unlikely by the fact that Lady Mountcashell was with the Godwins on that day. Edward Dowden, printing extracts from her letters in an appendix to his biography of Shelley, noted that Mrs Godwin's next letter refers to another sent on 14 August, in which she has given details of the elopement. The various dates offered in Claire's copies of her mother's letters remain puzzling; so does Mrs Godwin's source of information for the runaways' purchase of a donkey in Paris. Her daughter, presumably, had made contact.

2. WG–John Taylor, 27.8.1814, in *The Elopement of Shelley and Mary as related by William Godwin*, ed. H. Buxton Forman (1911).

3. PBS–HS, 15[14].9.1814.

4. PBS–HS, 3.10.1814.

5. PBS–HS, 5.10.1814.

6. MWG, *MWSJ*, 6.12.1814.

7. I have used the text of *Lodore* (1835) edited by Lisa Vargo (Broadview, 1998). Elements of Shelley's character can be found here in Henry Derham, Edward Villiers and Horatio Saville; Mary drew on herself for aspects of Fanny Derham, Ethel Villiers and Ethel's mother, Cornelia Lodore.

8. *Lodore*, p. 339.

9. Ibid., p. 337.

10. PBS–MWG, 4.11.1814.

11. PBS's entry in the shared journal, Friday, 7.10.1814.

12. Ibid., 14.10.1814.

13. *CCJ*, 14.10.1814.

14. PBS–MWG, 24.10.1814.

15. MWG–PBS, 28.10.1814 (*MWSL*, 1).

16. MWS–CC, 10.7.1845 (*MWSL*, 3).

17. MWG, *MWSJ*, 28.10.1814.

18. MWG–PBS, 28.10.1814.

19. See St Clair, *G&S*, ch. 29, or the earlier biographies by Roger Ingpen (1917) and Newman Ivey White (1947) for detailed accounts of Godwin and Shelley's financial transactions.

20. MWG–PBS, 3.11.1814.

21. MWG–PBS, 28.10.1814.

22. PBS–MWG, 27.10.1814.

23. Ibid.

24. TJH–Thomas Love Peacock (hereafter TLP), 8.9.1817, in *Shelley and His Circle*, 5, ed. Donald H. Reiman (1973), p. 284.

25. PBS, 'Letter to Mrs Gisborne', 1819.

26. T.J. Hogg, *Memoirs of Prince Alexy Haimatoff, translated from the original Latin mss. under the immediate inspection of the prince, by John Brown, Esq.* (T. & E.T. Hookham, 1813; Folio Society, 1952), p. 131.

27. Anonymous nine-page review, convincingly identified by Edward Dowden in his *Life of Shelley* (1888) as by PBS: *Critical Review*, VI, 6 (December 1814).

28. MWG–TJH, 1.1.1815.

29. MWG–TJH, 24.1.1815.

30. MWG–TJH, 2.3.1815.

31. MWG–TJH, 6.3.1815.

32. Cline's achievement is mentioned in a review of *An Enquiry into the Probability and Rationality of Mr Hunter's Theory of Life, being the subject of the first Two Anatomical Lectures, delivered before the Royal College of Surgeons of London by John Abernethy, FRS, Professor of Anatomy and Surgery to the College*, in *Edinburgh Review*, XXIII, 1814, p. 385.

33. MWG–TJH, 25.4.1815.

34. MWS and PBS–CC, 20.3.1822.

35. PBS–Byron, 11.9.1816.

36. MWG, *MWSJ*, 23.3.1815, as reported by Charles Clairmont.

37. CC–Fanny Imlay (hereafter FI), 28.5.1815 (*CC*, 1).

CHAPTER TEN: *Retreat from London*

1. MWG–PBS, 27.7.1815.
2. Ibid.
3. William Lawrence, FRS, had been appointed second professor at the Royal College of Surgeons in 1815; his inaugural lectures, *An Introduction to Comparative Anatomy and Physiology*, were delivered in March the following year. His *Lectures on Physiology, Zoology, and the Natural History of Man* were published in 1819. Marilyn Butler, introducing and editing *Frankenstein* (Oxford World Classics, 1993) has also emphasized the link between Lawrence and the Shelleys; where I see Mary reacting against Lawrence's views on the Negro as manlike but lacking in man's feelings, Professor Butler sees in Lawrence's lectures a source for Mary's interest in the subject of vitalism. A materialist, Lawrence argued that the divine spark was not required to create moral feelings in man. Butler also points out, interestingly, that in 1815 Lawrence was studying and caring for 'a monster', a boy born with part of his brain missing (Butler, Introduction, pp. xli–ii).

   It is reasonable to suppose that, even if Mary and Shelley were not present at Lawrence's inaugural lectures, they were familiar with their content as a result of their friendship with him. Among the subjects Lawrence discussed in detail was the story of 'Peter the wild boy', a mute discovered near Hamelin in 1724 and much discussed as an example of man in his original state; Peter may have contributed something to *Frankenstein* as well as to Browning's poem about the children led by a vengeful magic ratcatcher into a mountain near Hamelin. Mary was still consulting and meeting Lawrence in the 1840s.
4. PBS–MWG, 24.10.1814.
5. Mungo Park, *Travels in the Interior Districts of Africa performed under the direction and patronage of the African Association, in the years 1795, 1796 and 1797* (1799). Mary could already have heard admiring reports of Park from his friend, Anthony Carlisle.
6. *MWSJ*, 14.12.1814.
7. CC–MWS, 2.6.1835.
8. Ch.C–CC, 13–20.9.1815.
9. Thomas Love Peacock, *Melincourt* (1817), ch. 5.
10. PBS–TJH, 22.9.1815.
11. MWS, Note on *Alastor*, in *The Poetical Works of Percy Bysshe Shelley* (1839) (hereafter *PW*).
12. CC–Byron, 29.9.1816. The review was by Josiah Condor in *Eclectic Review* (October 1816), p. 132.
13. PBS, *Alastor*, lines 182–9.
14. PBS–WG, 6.3.1816.
15. Ibid.
16. WG–PBS, 7.3.1816 (*PBSL*).
17. PBS–WG, 3.5.1816.
18. Sarah Inchbald ('Mrs Perfection')–WG, 11.11. 1816 (Abinger, Dep. b. 509).

CHAPTER ELEVEN: *Storms on the Lake*

1. See Silsbee Papers (hereafter Silsbee), box 7, file 3. Silsbee recorded his interviews with Claire Clairmont and her niece in small memorandum books which have been preserved in the Silsbee family papers at the Peabody Essex Museum in Salem, Massachusetts. Many of his comments are published in the two volumes of *The Clairmont Correspondence*, ed. Marion Kingston Stocking (Johns Hopkins University Press, 1995), abbreviated here to *CC*, 1 and 2.
2. I have accepted the convincing conjectures of Marion Kingston Stocking (*CC*, 1, p. 25, n. 1) on Claire's likely whereabouts and the ordering and dates of her letters to Byron. Byron's half-sister, Augusta Leigh, was living at Devonshire House until mid-April.
3. WG–John Murray, 21.5.1814 (Murray). Coleridge did get £100 from Byron; Murray discouraged Byron from making a similar gift to Godwin and Maturin.
4. CC–Byron, 21.4.1816 (see note 2 above).
5. *Collected Letters of Samuel Taylor Coleridge*, ed. E.L. Griggs (Oxford, 1956–71), 4, pp. 628–9; Richard Holmes, *Coleridge: Darker Reflections* (HarperCollins, 1998), ch. 9, p. 426.
6. Thomas Babington Macaulay, *Letters*, 1, ed. Thomas Pinney (Cambridge University Press, 1974).
7. CC–Byron, 21.4.1816.
8. Ibid.
9. CC–Byron, 6.5.1816.
10. MWG–FI, 17.5.1816. This, the only extant version, was published in *History of a Six Weeks' Tour* (1817).
11. Ibid.
12. FI–MWG and PBS, 29.5.1816 (*CC*, 1).
13. 'J.S' [St Aubyn?] to 'Stuart', 6.6.1816. This letter, held at the Horsham Museum, is printed in *The Letters of Bysshe and Timothy Shelley*, transcribed and annotated by Susan Cabell Djabri and Jeremy Knight (Horsham Museum Society, 2000), pp. 119–22.
14. Thomas Moore, *The Life of Lord Byron, with his Letters & Journals* (1830 and 1831), ch. 27 in the one-volume edition (1838).
15. *Quarterly Review* (July 1819); William Lawrence, *An Introduction to Comparative Anatomy and Physiology being the two Introductory Lectures delivered at the Royal College of Surgeons on the 21st and 25th March, 1816*.
16. Cornelia A.H. Crosse, *Memorials, Scientific and Literary, of Andrew Crosse, the Electrician* (1857).
17. *Fantasmagoriana*, pp. 152–3. *Fantasmagoriana, ou Recueil d'Histoires de Spectres, Revenans, Fantômes etc* was translated from German to French 'par un Amateur' in 1812. When the Geneva party read it in this form, the book was already available in an English version, translated by Mrs Utterson as *Tales of the Dead*. Mary's recollection of the details in 1831 was a little vague; their influence in 1816 should not be discounted.
18. Preface to *Frankenstein, or The Modern Prometheus* (1831). The Preface to the first 1818 edition was written by Shelley, as if by the [anonymous] author.

19. The diary of Dr J.W. Polidori, 18.6.1816 (Polidori's diary was eventually published from a family-edited copy in 1911 by his nephew, W.M. Rossetti).

20. See Gavin Beer, 'An Atheist in the Alps', *Keats-Shelley Memorial Bulletin*, IX (1958). The entry mentioned here for 23 July 1816 was first recorded on 26 June 1817, by Humphrey Senhouse, when he, Edward Nash and Robert Southey were on an alpine visit. Mary was also bold enough to announce that she was en route to 'l'enfer' from London, which suggests a defiant awareness of her reputation as a fallen woman.

21. The will is printed in *Shelley and His Circle*, 4, pp. 702–18; *MWSJ*, p. 122, n. 1.

22. MWS, Preface to *Frankenstein, or The Modern Prometheus* (1831).

23. Ibid.

24. Byron–John Murray, 15.2.1817, in *Byron: Letters and Journals*, 12 vols. and supplement, ed. Leslie Marchand (John Murray, 1973–94) (hereafter *BL&J*).

25. Byron, *Manfred* (1817), lines 112–15.

26. Byron, 'Darkness' (July 1816), lines 2–5.

27. *Frankenstein* (1818), 2, viii.

28. CC–Byron, ?29.8.1816.

29. *MWSJ*, 28.5.1817.

CHAPTER TWELVE: *Distressing Events*

1. PBS–Byron, 29.9.1816.

2. FI–MWG, 3.10.1816 (*CC*, 1).

3. Claire, in the 1870s, recalled having been a witness to this scene, but Claire's memory was notoriously unreliable (*CC*, 1, p. 86). Claire's account is in Silsbee (box 7, folder 2).

4. *The Cambrian*, 12.10.1816, reprinted in *CC*, 1, p. 87.

5. Maria Gisborne, Journal, 9.7.1820, *Maria Gisborne and Edward Williams: Shelley's Friends, Their Journals and Letters*, ed. Frederick L. Jones (University of Oklahoma Press, 1951), p. 39 (hereafter *Shelley's Friends*).

6. WG–MWG, 13.10.1816 (Dowden, *Shelley*, 2, p. 58).

7. FI–MWG, 3.10.1816 (*CC*, 1).

8. MWS–Leigh Hunt (hereafter LH), 14.12.1838.

9. MWG–PBS, 5.12.1816.

10. Henry Crabb Robinson, Diaries, 17.11.1817 (Dr Williams' Library, Gordon Square, London).

11. PBS–MWG, 16.12.1816.

12. MWG–PBS, 17.12.1816.

13. As can be seen in the original letter in the Murray archive.

14. PBS–CC, 30.12.1816.

15. Quoted by St Clair in *G&S*, p. 417.

16. PBS–MWS, 11.1.1817.

17. WG–W.T. Baxter, 12.5.1817 (Pforzheimer).

18. Edward Dowden–Lady Shelley (hereafter JS), 12.5.1884 (Abinger, Dep. c. 769/3, fols. 36v–44r).

19. Lady Shelley's zealously protective attitude towards her parents-in-law is discussed in greater detail in the final chapter.

Chapter Thirteen: *At Albion House*

1. MWS–MH, 13.1.1817.
2. PBS–Eliza Westbrook, 18.12.1816. Shelley's observation was quoted in Miss Westbrook's deposition of 10 January 1817. Although it is not certain that Mary saw this, Shelley shared most of his anxieties over the Chancery proceedings with her.
3. Leigh Hunt, 'To TLH During a Late Sickness', *Examiner*, 1.9.1816.
4. MWS–MH, 2.3.1817.
5. MWS–LH, 5.3.1817.
6. LH–Vincent Novello, 17.4.1817, in Charles and Mary Cowden Clarke, *Recollections of Writers* (1878), pp. 198–9.
7. PBS, 'To Constantia, Singing' (1817), stanza 4.
8. G.H. Lewes, *Westminster Review* (April 1841), p. 310, reviewing Shelley's letters and poems. Since Lewes was a close friend of Leigh Hunt's son, Thornton, who had been at Marlow in 1817, the allusion to Shelley's companion is probably accurate.
9. Dowden, *Shelley*, 2, pp. 121–3. Dowden's account was based on interviews with surviving Marlow residents.
10. *Talks*, pp. 66–7.
11. MWS–PBS, 16.10.1817.
12. MWS–MH and LH, 30.6.1817.
13. LH–MWS, 16.11.1821 in *Shelley and Mary*, 4 vols. (privately printed, 1882), 3, p. 705 (hereafter *S&M*).
14. Henry Crabb Robinson, Diaries, 23.12.1817 (Dr Williams' Library) notes Kenney's comment.
15. LH–MWS, 16.11.1821, in *S&M*, 3, p. 705.
16. PBS, 'Dedication to Mary' in *The Revolt of Islam*, first published under this title in January 1818.
17. *The Prose Works of Percy Bysshe Shelley*, 1, ed. E.B. Murray (Oxford University Press, 1993).
18. MWS–Christina Baxter, 4.1.1817.
19. PBS–Byron, 9.7.1817.
20. MWS–PBS, 5.10.1817.
21. MWS–PBS, 26.9.1817.
22. Ibid.
23. MWS–PBS, 24.9.1817.
24. W.T. Baxter–Isabella Booth, 3.10.1817 (*Shelley and His Circle*, 5), pp. 339–40.
25. W.T. Baxter–PBS, 29.12.1817 (ibid., pp. 380–1).
26. David Booth–Isabella Booth, 9.1.1818 (ibid., pp. 390–2).
27. MWS–PBS, 5.10.1817.
28. MWS–PBS, 16.10.1817.

29. *A Shelley Library*, ed. T.J. Wise (1924), p. 56. The reference here is to an edition published in 1840, supposedly from a 'fac-simile' reprint of one of twenty copies printed by Charles Ollier for Shelley.

30. WG–MWS, 14–18.2.1823 (Abinger, Dep. c. 524).

31. TLP–PBS, August 1818 (*S&M*, 2), p. 327.

32. St Clair, *G&S*, p. 444.

33. John Timbs, *Curiosities of London* (1855), p. 16.

34. Godwin's journal gives 'Tea' as the time of the meeting; tea equated to our after-dinner coffee.

35. MWS–LH and MH, 22.3.1818.

CHAPTER FOURTEEN: *Joys and Losses*

1. Since the records of Elise's family, first identified by Emily Sunstein in 'Louise Duvillard of Geneva, the Shelleys' Nursemaid' (*Keats-Shelley Journal*, XXIX, 1980, pp. 27–31), show no record of her having had a daughter, it is usually assumed that Aimée Romieux, born on 20 January 1816, is the child of Elise's mother's second marriage. Mary and Claire's letters provide convincing evidence that Aimée was, in fact, Elise's child. Writing to the Hunts on 6 April 1818 just after meeting Elise's family, Mary gave them a lengthy description of Aimée. She is said to be 'very beautiful with eyes something like but sweeter than William's – a perfect shaped nose and a more beautiful mouth than her Mothers expressive of the greatest sensibility'. No description is given of any other member of the nursemaid's family, but the Hunts would naturally have been interested to hear about a child of Elise's after spending several weeks in her company at Marlow. Mary's description of Aimée as having a mouth more beautiful than her mother's would make sense to the Hunts only if she was talking of Elise; they had never met Madame Romieux, who lived in Switzerland. Three weeks later, on 26 April 1818, Claire told Byron that Elise was 'a mother herself'. We can conclude that Elise, when the Shelleys decided to employ her at Geneva in 1816, probably had an illegitimate baby which was given the name of her stepfather and brought up as a member of his family while she returned to England with the Shelleys.

2. CC's retrospective journal entry for 8.4.1818.

3. MWS–LH and MH, 6.4.1818.

4. MWS, *The Last Man* (1826), 3, p. 266. The villa is here envisaged as it might have become had Shelley and Mary been rich enough to restore it; when they visited Lake Como in 1818, the villa was in a state of great dilapidation.

5. CC–Byron, 27[26?].4.1818. (The original is in the Murray archive, in a box entitled – though not by Byron! – 'Letters from the Ladies'.)

6. MWS–MH and LH, 13.5.1818.

7. MG–MWS, 21.6.1818, in *Shelley's Friends*, p. 52.

8. MWS–MG, 17.8.1818.

9. MWS–MG, 15.6.1818. Paolo Foggi may have been taken on in Livorno; Mary writes as if Mrs Gisborne already knew of his existence.

10. WG–PBS, 8.6.1818 (*S&M*, 2).

11. MWS, Note on 'The Cenci' (*PW*).

12. Richard Holmes, *Shelley in Love* (Anvil Press, 1980), p. 98.

13. Ibid., p. 106.

14. PBS, 'One Love', *Shelley and His Circle*, 6, pp. 633–5 (also Bodleian, Ms Shelley adds. e. 11, pp. 1–9). Titled 'One Love' by PBS, it is better known as 'On Love'. Mary transcribed it in 1829 for a sentimental Christmas annual, *The Keepsake*, to which she became a regular contributor.

15. Thomas Moore, *Byron*, p. 389. The 'informant' here, although not named, was almost certainly Teresa Guiccioli or possibly Mrs Hoppner herself. Mary would not have wished to denigrate a girl she had herself sent to care for Allegra.

16. Elise's letters for this period have not been preserved. Claire's letter to Byron was written on 15 or 18 May 1818. In the 1870s, she repeated this accusation in a letter to Trelawny (*CC*, 2).

17. CC–Augustus Silsbee (Silsbee Papers, box 7, file 2).

18. MWS–MG, 17.8.1818.

19. PBS–MWS, 18.8.1818.

20. PBS–MWS, 23.8.1818.

21. Mary, writing in 1839, was probably drawing on Shelley's own description of Este as 'an extensive Gothic castle, now the habitation of owls and bats' (PBS–TLP, 8.10.1818).

22. MWS, 'Petrarch', *Lives of the Most Eminent Literary and Scientific Men of Italy, Spain and Portugal*, 1 (1835).

23. MWS, *Rambles in Germany and Italy in 1840, 1842, and 1843* (1844), Letter VI (1842).

24. WG–MWS, 27.10.1818 (Abinger, Dep. c. 524).

25. Nora Crook and Derek Guiton, *Shelley's Venomed Melody* (Cambridge University Press, 1986), discuss this possibility. Had Shelley been infected, neither he nor Mary would have imagined that the disease could be a danger to her.

26. *Rambles*, Letter VI.

CHAPTER FIFTEEN: *A Mysterious History*

1. CC–Byron, 12.1.1818.

2. Mary's opinion that there 'was not much in them' was given in a letter to Trelawny, 28.7.1824. Her view is partly confirmed by the strikingly unscandalous nature of Byron's later journal notes, published in *BL&J*, vol. 8.

3. PBS–TLP, 9.11.1818.

4. *MWSJ*, 18.11.1818.

5. PBS, 'The Coliseum: A Fragment of a Romance', in *Essays, Letters from Abroad, Translations and Fragments*, ed. Mrs Shelley, 2 vols. (1840), 1, pp. 168–82.

6. PBS–TLP, 17/18.12.1818.

7. Alphonse Lamartine, *Twenty-five Years of My Life* (1872), Bk 4, ch. 1.

8. Anna Jameson, *The Diary of an Ennuyée* (1826).

9. MWS–Sophia Stacey, 7.3.1820 (date amended from 5 to 7 by Betty T. Bennett in 'Newly Uncovered Letters and Poems by Mary Wollstonecraft Shelley', *Keats-Shelley Memorial Bulletin*, XLVI, July 1997).

10. MWS–MG, 22.1.1818.

11. MWS–Isabelle Hoppner, 10.8.1821 (Murray).

12. The information paraphrased here comes from Richard Belgrave. In his letter to Byron of 16 September 1820 (Murray), Hoppner gave Elise Duvillard Foggi as his source.

13. The revealing Hoppner correspondence is in the Murray archive.

14. Elise Foggi–MWS, 27.7.1821 (Murray).

15. Thomas Medwin, *Conversations of Lord Byron* (1824), p. 314.

16. *Medwin's Revised Life of Percy Bysshe Shelley* (1847), ed. Henry Buxton Forman (1913), pp. 205–8. (This was published as 'A New Edition printed from a copy copiously amended and extended by the Author and left unpublished at his death'.)

17. See Marion Kingston Stocking in *CC*, 2, pp. 645–53. It should be added that if, as Professor Stocking suggests, a 'scrape' meant that the lady became pregnant at Naples, the problem is deepened, but not solved.

18. John Polidori, as the anonymous author of *Sketches illustrative of the manners and costumes of France, Switzerland and Italy* (1820).

19. Marianna Starke, *Travels on the Continent* (1819), p. 440.

20. *MWSJ*, 2.3.1819.

21. *CCJ*, 28.3.1819.

22. MWS–LH, 6.4.1819.

23. Ibid.

24. Isabelle Hoppner–MWS, 6[?].1.1819 (Abinger, Dep. c. 811/3). A hint of Mrs Hoppner's grim tone can be given here: 'Cette pauvre petite enfant souffre du froid dans une manière vraiment effrayante, elle est toujours gelée.' She also drew unfavourable comparisons between Allegra and her own child.

25. MWS, 'Valerius, the Reanimated Roman', *CTS*, p. 341. Not published in Mary's lifetime, the story is generally assumed to have been written in 1819.

26. E.J. Trelawny to the *Athenaeum*, 1878, in *Letters of Edward John Trelawny*, ed. Henry Buxton Forman (Oxford University Press, 1910), p. 263.

27. MWS–MG, 30.5.1819.

28. MWS, 'The English in Italy', a review, *Westminster Review*, VI (October 1826), p. 335.

CHAPTER SIXTEEN: *A Loss and a Gain*

1. MWS–MH, 29.6.1819.

2. CC–Byron, 16.3.1820.

3. Dr Bruce Barker–Benfield, in *Shelley's Guitar* (Bodleian exhibition guide, 1992), p. 118, gives a detailed account of this poem's appearance. Being a pencil draft with some ink insertions, it is extremely faint; the last line was only recovered (by Judith Chernaik) and printed in 1972.

4. Byron, amused by the caricature of himself as Mr Cypress in *Nightmare Abbey*, sent Peacock a gold locket as acknowledgment.

5. MWS–MH, 28.8.1819 and to LH, 24.9.1819.

6. WG–?, 1.12.1820 (Abinger, Dep. c. 607/6 [partial transcript in MWS's hand]).

7. MWS–Amelia Curran, 18.9.1819.

8. WG–MWS, 9.9.1819 (Abinger, Dep. c. 524). It looks as though the light cancellation, a single pen line, was done by Godwin at the time of writing but left, as if he wished his thoughts to be read.

9. *Matilda* (first published 1959; ed. Pamela Clemit, Pickering & Chatto, 1996), 2, ix, p. 48.

10. Ibid., x, p. 56.

11. Ibid., x, p. 55.

12. Mrs Gisborne's journal, 8.8.1820 (*Shelley's Friends*).

13. *Matilda*, xii, p. 67.

14. No attempt was made to publish either *Matilda* or its draft version, *The Fields of Fancy*, until over a hundred years after Mary's death.

15. PBS, *The Mask [Masque] of Anarchy*, 1819; 1832.

16. MWS (*PW*). Here, Mary argued that Shelley was calling on the many to unite passively to establish their rights. This seems rather a tame interpretation.

17. Charles had published an account of the insurrection in the *Morning Chronicle*, 13.2.1819, and signed it with his own initials. His mother, impressed by Charles's fluent style and political commitment, tried hard to get him a job on *The Times* through Crabb Robinson who was a friend of the proprietor, John Walter.

18. MWS–LH, 24.9.1819.

19. Marion Kingston Stocking gives a detailed account of the family in *CC*, 2, p. 134.

20. MWS–MG, 9.11.1819.

21. MWS–MG, 13.11.1819.

22. Sophia Stacey, in Helen Rossetti Angeli's transcription of her diary in *Shelley and His Friends in Italy* (1911), pp. 97 and 104.

23. *The Prose Works of Percy Bysshe Shelley*, ed. Richard Herne Shepherd (1888), 3 vols., 1, pp. 402–5 and 407–8.

24. MWS–MH, 24.3.1820.

25. Ibid.

26. *CCJ*, 8.2.1820.

27. PBS–MG, 11.3.1820, in David Mackenzie Stocking and Marion Kingston Stocking, 'New Shelley Letters in a John Gisborne Notebook', *Keats-Shelley Memorial Bulletin*, XXXI (1980), pp. 1–9.

28. Mrs Mason (Lady Mountcashell)–MWS, [8].10.1819 (Abinger, Dep. c. 517/2).

29. Ibid., 15.1.1820.

30. MWS–MH, 24.3.1820.

31. MWS–WG, 14.3.1820. The only surviving sentence from this letter is included in *MWSL*, 1.

32. WG–MWS, 30.3.1820 (*Godwin*, 2, p. 271).

33. Hoppner MSS (Murray).

34. MWS–MG, 8.5.1820.

35. CC–Byron, 1 and 4.5.1820. The letter of 4 May survives only in draft form

(*CC*, 2). Byron may have remained unaware that he was being slandered by a servant of the Shelleys.

36. CC–Byron, 15[?18].5.1819.
37. MWS–MG and John Gisborne (hereafter JG), 18.6.1820.
38. PBS–MG, 19.7.1820.

CHAPTER SEVENTEEN: *In Absentia Clariae*

1. This verse was probably written in 1816 (draft in notebook, Bodleian, Ms Shelley adds. e. 16, p. 66), but was not published by Mary until 1839.
2. *Maurice, or The Fisher's Cot* was published by Viking in 1998, with an introduction by Claire Tomalin. Mary sent a fair copy (now lost) to her father, evidently hoping that it might bring revenue to the ailing Juvenile Library. Godwin was dismissive. 'If you were disposed to add more – enough to make up a volume – I should be very happy to publish it,' he wrote, 'but I would not have you give yourself trouble about it; such books do not make ready money.' WG–MWS, 10.9.1822 (Abinger, Dep. c. 524). I have found no evidence that Mary tried to publish it elsewhere.
3. MWS, Note to *The Witch of Atlas* (*PW*).
4. It is worth noting that even in the laudatory prefaces written for the collected edition of 1839, Mary was prepared to say that Shelley's talents remained underdeveloped in 1821, a year before his death.
5. PBS, Introductory verses, 'To Mary', *The Witch of Atlas* (1820; 1824), stanza 3.
6. MG, Journal, 28.8.1820 (*Shelley's Friends*).
7. PBS–TLP, 8.11.1820.
8. Mary used the recently published second edition of J.C.L. Simonde de Sismondi's *Histoire des républiques italiennes du moyen âge* (Paris, 1818). It had not yet been translated into English.
9. MWS–LH, 7.8.1823.
10. MWS, *Valperga* (1823), 3, xii.
11. *MWSJ*, 22.10.1820.
12. *Valperga*, 1, iii.
13. PBS–CC, 29.10.1820.
14. MWS–CC, 14–15.1.1821; Medwin himself gave a detailed account of the meaning and origin of the word 'seccatura' in his life of Shelley; the word evidently held no personal significance for him.
15. Lady Morgan, *Italy*, 2 (1821), p. 230.
16. *Medwin's Revised Life of Shelley*, ed. H. Buxton Forman (1913), p. 270.
17. MWS, Note to 'Poems of 1820' (*PW*).
18. PBS–CC, 29.10.1820.

CHAPTER EIGHTEEN: *Life on the Lung' Arno*

1. This description is based on Mario Curreli's account of Pisa in *Una certa Signora Mason* (1997) and Lady Blessington's *The Idler in Italy*, 2 (1839 edition), pp. 483–505.
2. MWS, *Valperga*, 2, x (ed. Stuart Curran, Oxford University Press, 1997), p. 280.

3. Ibid., 3, iv, p. 348.
4. MWS–CC, 14–15.1.1821.
5. MWS–CC, 21.1.1821.
6. Jules Blancard, *Etudes sur la Grèce contemporaine* (Montpellier, 1886), p. 331. See also Marion Kingston Stocking's extract from J. Millingen, *Memoirs of the Affairs of Greece* (1831), in *CCJ*, pp. 473–6.
7. PBS–CC, 8.6.1821.
8. MWS, 'The Bride of Modern Italy' (1821), *CTS*, p. 33.
9. *Epipsychidion* was first published in 1822 with a revised introductory note by Shelley explaining that the (deceased) author's poem did not require 'a matter-of-fact history of the circumstances' to be understood by 'a certain class of readers', to whom it was directed. It is unusual in not carrying any commentary by Mary in her 1839 edition.
10. I have quoted from the letters in Newman Ivey White's *Shelley*, 2 vols. (Secker & Warburg, 1947). The Italian originals can be read in Enrica Viviani della Robbia, *Vita di una donna* (Florence, 1936).
11. MWS–MG, 7.3.1822.
12. MG–MWS, 9.2.1822 (*Shelley's Friends*, p. 77).
13. John St Aubyn–MWS, 10.6.1826 (Abinger, Dep. c. 516).
14. Henry Reveley's account of the accident on 16 April 1821 is in *S&M*, 3, pp. 605–6.
15. MWS–MG, 30.6.1821.
16. PBS–Charles Ollier, 21.7.1821.
17. In 1824, Mary dated the untitled poem to 1814, thus implying an address to Harriet; by 1839, she had set the date as 1821. Emily Sunstein, in *R&R*, p. 437, notes that Mary's correction would have been made after she considered the fact that the earliest poem in this notebook dated from 1816. It seems improbable that Mary read the poem in Shelley's lifetime.
18. MWS–Isabelle Hoppner, 10.8.1821.

CHAPTER NINETEEN: *Don Juan among the Ladies*
1. PBS–MWS, 15.8.1821.
2. MWS–MG, 6–10.5.1822.
3. MWS–MG, 30.11.1821.
4. CC–MWS, 31.10.1821.
5. *The Autobiography of Leigh Hunt*, ed. Roger Ingpen (Dutton, 1903), p. 289.
6. E.J. Trelawny, *Records of Shelley, Byron and the Author* (1878; Penguin Books, 1973), ch. 2, p. 63.
7. Ibid., pp. 64–5.
8. *MWSJ*, 19.1.1822.
9. Trelawny, *Records*, ch. 3, p. 68.
10. Mary went to services on at least four occasions in Pisa, besides the baptism of the Williamses' daughter.
11. MWS–MG, 7.3.1822.
12. *MWSJ*, 7.2.1822.

13. MWS–MG, 9.2.1822.

14. PBS–Edward Williams (hereafter EW), 26.1.1822. (Six words have been deleted.)

15. EW, Journal, 8.1.1822 (*Shelley's Friends*). The original journal is in the British Library (adds. 36622).

16. Elise's letters are in the Murray archive. Both are dated 12 April 1822, but Claire's journal suggests that they were completed on 18 April.

17. Examined with infra-red, it still proves virtually unreadable. Claire's wish to hide her entry – the pen is certainly hers – tells us that there was something worth concealing.

18. MWS–CC, 20.3.1822.

19. PBS–CC, 24.3.1822.

20. PBS–CC, 31.3.1822.

21. The guitar was sold in 1898 by Jane's grandson, on condition that the purchaser, E.A. Silsbee, should give it to a public institution in Great Britain. Silsbee presented it to the Bodleian Library, through Richard Garnett, in the same year. The poem is also at the Bodleian (Ms Shelley adds. e. 3, fols. 2v–3r).

22. EW–PBS, n.d. (Bodleian, Ms Shelley adds. c. 12, fol. 24).

23. MWS–JW, 31.5.1823.

24. EW, Journal, 24.3.1822.

25. MWS–Byron, 12.4.1822.

26. EW, Journal, 1.5.1822.

CHAPTER TWENTY: *At the Villa Magni*

1. Anna Jameson, *Diary of an Ennuyée* (1826), p. 314.

2. Henry James, 'Italy Revisited' (1877), *Collected Travel Writings* (Library of America edition, 1993), p. 399.

3. MWS, Notes to the 1822 poems (*PW*).

4. MWS–MG, 15.8.1822.

5. MWS, 'The Choice', in *MWSJ*, p. 491. Thought to have been written at the beginning of 1823.

6. Claire Tomalin, *Shelley and His World* (Penguin Books, 1992), p. 104. This remains the best short guide to Shelley.

7. MWS–MG, 2.6.1822.

8. Emily Sunstein, *R&R*, p. 217.

9. EW, Journal, 15.5.1822 (*Shelley's Friends*). This journal was with Williams when he drowned. Mary was the first to read and transcribe large tracts of it, with the intention of drawing on it for her planned life of Shelley.

10. EW, Journal, 12.5.1822.

11. MWS–MG, 2.6.1822.

12. EW, Journal, 13.6.1822.

13. Joseph A. Dane, 'On the Instability of Vessels and Narratives: A Nautical Perspective on the Sinking of the *Don Juan*', *Keats-Shelley Journal*, 47 (1998).

14. EW, Journal, 14.5.1822, 28.5.1822.

15. MWS–MG, 15.8.1822.

16. PBS–JG (surviving only in JG's transcript), 18.6.1822.
17. See Appendix 3.
18. *MWSJ*, 7.7.1822.
19. MWS–MG, 15.8.1822.
20. LH–PBS, 21.6.1822 (*PBSL*, 2, p. 439).
21. PBS–LH, 24.6.1822.
22. MWS–MG, 15.8.1822.
23. EW–JW, 6.7.1822 (*Shelley's Friends*), pp. 162–3.
24. MWS–LH, *c.* 30.6.1822.
25. PBS–MWS, 4.7.1822.
26. Agnes M. Clarke, 13.7.1822 (Clarke Journal, Houghton Library, Cambridge, Mass.).
27. EW, Journal, 6.6.1822.
28. MWS–MG, 15.8.1822.
29. Ibid.
30. Ibid.
31. MWS–MG, 27.8.1822.
32. MWS–WG, [?]19.7.1822. These sentences were quoted by Godwin in a letter he sent to his friend John Taylor on 16 August 1822; they survive in an extract copy at Duke University, S.C. See also St Clair, *G&S*, p. 555. Unfortunately Mary's letter was delayed; Godwin heard of Shelley's death on 4 August from a third party. I conjecture the date of her writing from the evident effect of Trelawny's revelation and the fact that no mention is made of plans for burial or cremation.
33. The startling effects of incandescent lime were discovered shortly after this and put to dramatic use on stage. An experiment on the Thames on a moonless night showed that a man's hand, lit up by lime, could be seen from a distance of ten miles. Trelawny was much struck by the brilliance of the flames which consumed the bodies of his friends.
34. MWS–MG, 15.8.1822.
35. PBS, *Adonais*, stanza xlii.
36. The heart's survival in intense heat is hard to explain, even if it had been in an advanced state of calcification. It is possible that the object snatched from the flames was the poet's liver.
37. *MWSJ*, p. 424. A later holograph draft of this account by Trelawny is in the British Library (Add. Mss 39168.S). Trelawny expanded and altered the account of the cremations in his later reminiscences.

CHAPTER TWENTY-ONE: *Bitter Waters*

1. MWS, 'The Choice', dated July 1823 in her journal. Mary left a copy of this poem with the Hunts and asked them to transcribe it for her.
2. MWS, 'Life of Shelley' (Bodleian, Ms Shelley adds. c. 5, fol. 117v, 276–7).
3. MWS–Thomas Medwin, 29.7.1822.
4. LH–Elizabeth Kent, 26.9.1822 (Pforzheimer).
5. See Chapter 20, note 32.

6. WG–Everina Wollstonecraft, 4.10.1822 (Pforzheimer).

7. WG–MWS, 6.8.1822 and 9.8.1822 (Abinger, Dep. c. 524).

8. TLP–MWS, 19.10.22: *The Works of Thomas Love Peacock*, ed. H.F.B. Brett-Smith and C.E. Jones (Halliford edition, Constable, 1934), vol. 8.

9. Byron–W. Webb, 2.9.1822, *BL&J*, vol. 10.

10. Mrs Mason–MWS, n.d. (*S&M*, 4, p. 922).

11. Byron–John Murray, 3.8.1822 (*BL&J*).

12. MWS–John Murray, *c*. 26.1.1830.

13. MWS–Byron, 21.10.1822 (*Don Juan*, XI, lvi–lxi).

14. MWS–Byron, 30.3.1823 (*Don Juan*, XV, xlv).

15. *MWSJ*, 19.10.1822.

16. MWS–MG, 27.8.1822.

17. MWS–Byron, dated by the arrival of Godwin's letter, referred to here, on the same date. Mary also omitted to mention that Trelawny's friend Captain Roberts was a regular visitor; Roberts–MWS, 1.5.1823 (Abinger, Dep. c. 516).

18. *MWSJ*, 15.5.1824.

19. William White, *The Calumnies of the 'Athenaeum' Journal Exposed* (privately printed, 1852), pp. 11–12.

20. MWS–JW, 15.10.1822.

21. MWS–TJH, 9.9.1822.

22. Charles Dickens, *Pictures from Italy* (1846), ch. 5.

23. Marianne Hunt, Journal, 20.9.1822 and 7.10.1822 (Keats-Shelley Memorial House, Rome).

24. EJT–CC, 22.11.1822 (*Letters of Edward John Trelawny*, ed. H. Buxton Forman (1911)).

25. EJT–MWS, 2.4.1823 (*S&M*, 4, pp. 930–2).

26. MWS–CC, 19–20.12.1822.

27. MWS, 'Life of Shelley', p. 281 (see note 2, above).

28. WG–MWS, 15.11.1822 and 14–18.2.1823 (Abinger, Dep. c. 524).

29. Ibid.

30. WG–MWS, 6.5.1823 (*S&M*, 4, p. 940).

31. Mrs Mason–MWS, n.d. (*S&M*, 4, pp. 918–19). Jane Shelley substituted the name of Gisborne for Godwin, but the contents of the letter make it clear that Mrs Mason was referring to the Godwins. The anticipated advance was £400, for 'when the entire edition is sold'. See also Mrs Mason–MJG, 25.2.1823 (Abinger, Dep. c. 517).

32. MWS–MG, 3–6.5.1823.

33. Ibid.

34. MWS–LH, 3–5.8.1823; *Examiner*, 2.3.1823.

35. MWS–Charles Ollier, November–December 1839.

36. Sir Timothy Shelley–Byron, 6.2.1823, in Doris Langley Moore, *Accounts Rendered* (John Murray, 1974), pp. 404–5.

37. See Dr James Bieri, 'Shelley's Older Brother', *Keats-Shelley Journal*, 39 (1990). On 17 April 1821, Horace Smith had told Shelley that Whitton's daughter was on the point of marrying 'Captain Shelley'. For further details see S.C. Djabri,

A. Hughes and J. Knight, *The Shelleys of Field Place: The Story of the Family and Their Estates* (Horsham Museum Society, 2000), p. 114.

38. Sir Timothy Shelley–William Whitton, 8.8.1822 (Pforzheimer).
39. Sir Timothy Shelley–Byron, 6.2.1823.
40. MWS–JW, 10.4.1823.
41. Ibid.
42. JW–MWS, 27.3.1823.
43. CC–MWS, 11.4.1849 (*CC*, 2).
44. TJH–JW, 10.9.1824 (Abinger, Dep. d. 565, fols. 13r–15r. The letter survives in John Gisborne's book of copied correspondence to Jane from Mary and Hogg. Jane evidently supplied him with originals.
45. TJH–JW, 17.4.1823 (Abinger, Dep. c. 211).
46. LH–Elizabeth Kent, October 1822 (Pforzheimer).
47. MWS–JW, 30.7.1823.
48. LH–Vincent Novello, n.d. but evidently written shortly before Mary's arrival in England (Brotherton Collection, Leeds (Novello Cowden Clarke Papers)).
49. MWS–JW, 23.7.1823. The details which follow are taken from the same letter.
50. John Cam Hobhouse, Diary, 1.5.1829 (BL Add. Mss 43744–43765). This was noted after Hunt had published a derogatory portrait of Byron in *Lord Byron and His Contemporaries* (1828).
51. MWS–Teresa Guiccioli (hereafter TG), n.d. (quoted in Iris Origo, *The Last Attachment* (Jonathan Cape and John Murray, 1943; rev. edn 1962)). The following letter was transcribed into French by the Countess Guiccioli for her unpublished seventeen-hundred-page manuscript memoir 'La Vie de Lord Byron en Italie' and was written between 2–10.7.1823.
52. Marchand, *Byron*, 3, p. 1085.
53. Ibid., p. 1086.
54. Mrs Mason–MWS, 19.7.1823 (Abinger, Dep. c. 517/2).
55. MWS–JW, 23.7.1823.
56. MWS–MH and LH, 30.7–1.8.1823.
57. MWS–LH, 3–5.8.1823.
58. The Thomas revision is now in the Pierpont Morgan Library, New York (PML 16799). Mary's revision was done in December 1818 and shows few points of correspondence with Godwin's revisions. This suggests that Godwin had not sought permission or suggestions from his daughter for his own alterations. A helpful account of the background is given in Nora Crook's introduction to her edition of the novel for MWS, *Collected Works*, 1, p. xcvi. Godwin's journal notes that the second edition of *Frankenstein* was published on 11 August 1823.

    Mary's own revision (Thomas) made Henry Clerval more poetical, more Shelleylike, and intensified the gloom of Frankenstein, as noted in Walton's letter to his sister of 13 August. The Creature's non-human aspect was stressed by her addition, in the first description of its appearance, of 'the contortions that ever and anon convulsed and deformed his unhuman features'.
59. MWS–LH, 13–14.8 and 18–19.8.1823.

60. Ibid.
61. MWS–LH, 18–19.1.1823.

CHAPTER TWENTY-TWO: *Fame, of a Kind*

1. MWS–Louisa Holcroft, 2.10.1823.
2. These details are given in advertisement form at the back of an 1823 reprint of *The Parent's Offering*, also by Mrs Barnard (BL 12806r3). Mrs Fenwick's new story, priced at 1s. 6d. was *The Mouse Trap*.
3. Lady Caroline Lamb–WG, September 1823 (*Godwin*, 2, p. 285). She had been taking Godwin's literary advice for some months on her novel, *Ada Reisz* (1823).
4. WG, Will, 12.2.1827 (Pforzheimer). He stipulated that the portrait of himself by Northcote must eventually pass to his grandson, but left it first to his wife.
5. MWS–LH, 9–11.9.1823.
6. Ibid.
7. *Theatrical Observer*, 9.8.1823.
8. The combination of humour and terror has remained strong in *Frankenstein* productions. *Dracula*, which had its first stage reading at the Lyceum, was later combined with the Frankenstein story in a 1971 film and in *The Rocky Horror Show* (1973). Neither of these stories would have achieved their extraordinary grip on popular imagination without the help of the theatre (in *Frankenstein's* case) and of the cinema (in *Dracula's*).
9. *Hansard Parliamentary Debates*, 2nd Series, 16.3.1824.
10. MWS–LH, 9–11.9.1823.
11. WG–MWS, 27.2.1824 (*S&M*, 4, p. 1016a–c). He also noted writing this letter in his diary. Godwin's words hurt, but Mary had already sensed her failure: 'my labours are futile,' she wrote in her journal on 30 January 1824; ' – how differently did I commence an undertaking with my loved Shelley to criticize and encourage me as I advanced – I can in no way reconcile myself to my solitude.'
12. WG–Henry Colburn, 23.12.1823 (V&A, Forster archive).
13. MWS (anonymous), 'Rome in the First and Nineteenth Centuries', *New Monthly Magazine*, March 1824.
14. MWS (anonymous), 'The Bride of Modern Italy', *London Magazine*, April 1824.
15. MWS (anonymous), 'A Visit to Brighton', *London Magazine*, XVI, December 1826.
16. MWS–JW, 7.8.1827.
17. MWS–LH, 20.10–3.11.1827.
18. Henry Crabb Robinson, Diaries, 16.11.1823 and 22.12.1824 (Dr Williams' Library).
19. Ibid., 8.4.1838.
20. MWS–LH, 18.9.1823.
21. *MWSJ*, 3.9.1824. It is not certain that it was Procter who paid these 'long tho rare visits' but since Beddoes was in Italy that summer, Mary would hardly have questioned his reasons for not visiting her. Beddoes had been given the com-

mission of bringing back Amelia Curran's portrait of Shelley. He did not fulfil it: two years later, William Millar, in his *Biographical Sketches of British Characters Recently Deceased*, regretted that there was still no known portrait of Shelley.

22. *Examiner*, 13.6.1824, p. 370; *Edinburgh Review*, XL, 24.7.1824, p. 499; *Literary Gazette*, 17.7.1824, p. 452. The last of these gives a rare hint of the way gossip was spreading about Mary's having been an unloving wife; the writer of this review had evidently heard something to make him question the sincerity of her grief.

23. Payne was first mentioned by Godwin in an 1817 letter to one of his young protégés, James Ogilvie; he was at Godwin's home on 25 August, 26 September, 5, 12 and 26 November 1823.

24. John Howard Payne (hereafter JHP)–Henry Harris, 3.5.1817 (Payne Notebooks, 1815–1817, Houghton Library, Mass., Ms Am. 1972).

25. JHP–MWS, 1825, in *The Romance of Mary W. Shelley, John Howard Payne and Washington Irving* (The Bibliophile Society, Boston, 1907), pp. 28–31.

26. MWS–TJH, 3.10.1824.

27. Isabella Baxter Booth–MWS, 1.11.1823 (Abinger, Dep. b. 211/2(a)); MWS–LH, 9–11.9.1823. Isabella spent some time living apart from her husband, but by 1828 they were both in London and Isabella hoped to travel abroad with Mary, the trip Shelley had planned for her in 1817. She remained deeply unhappy: 'I glide here and there like a restless ghost,' she told Mary on 24.6.1828 (Abinger, Dep. b. 211/2(a)). Mary's occasional letters to her are affectionate, loyal and concerned. They are never in the passionate key of those written to the women she loved.

28. LH–Vincent Novello, 24.7.1823 (Brotherton Collection, Leeds (Novello Cowden Clarke Papers)).

29. MWS–MH, 13.6–18.6.1824.

30. The description given here is compiled from published letters written by Mary to the Hunts in October and November 1823.

31. MWS–Mary Sabilla Novello, 27.12.1824.

32. MWS–LH, 25.10 and 3.11.1823.

33. MWS, *The Last Man* (1826), 3, vii.

34. Mary and Charles Cowden Clarke, *Recollections of Writers* (1878), pp. 37 and 41–2. These entries were written by Mary, who was named not for Mary Shelley but for Mary Lamb, who taught her Latin when she was a child. Her husband also recalled the raptures which Edward Holmes, Vincent Novello's devoted pupil, went into about the young widows. 'He used to be unmercifully rallied about his enamoured fantasies with regard to both . . .' (ibid., pp. 39–40).

35. *MWSJ*, 18.1.1824.

CHAPTER TWENTY-THREE: *Literary Matters*

1. *Morning Chronicle*, 15.5.1824.

2. EJT–MWS, 30.4.1824 (*S&M*, 4, pp. 1006–9). Colonel Leicester Stanhope received a similar claim, written two days earlier.

3. MWS–EJT, 22.3.1824.

4. MWS–TG, 16.5.1824, trans. Ricki B. Herzfeld (*MWSL*, 1). Mary's article, sent to the *London Magazine*, was not published.

5. MWS–EJT, 28.7.1824.

6. MWS–LH, 9–11.9.1823.

7. Thomas Medwin–MWS, 10.7.1824, in Ernest J. Lovell, Jr, *Captain Medwin: Friend of Byron and Shelley* (Austin, Texas, 1962), pp. 160–70.

8. *MWSJ*, 2.7.1827.

9. MWS–EJT, see note 5.

10. MWS–John Cam Hobhouse, 18.11.1824.

11. This copy is in the Athenaeum Library, London.

12. CC–MWS, 15.3.1836. The novel of which Claire had heard was *Falkner* (1837). It is not known whether Claire discovered a resemblance to Byron in the complex and passionate Rupert Falkner.

13. MWS–TG, 10.12.1827.

14. An extract from this letter, dated 1829, appeared first in Teresa Guiccioli's unpublished 'La Vie de Lord Byron en Italie' (see Chapter 21, note 51).

15. The particular source of Teresa Guiccioli's ire was the poem 'Lines on a Hindoo Air' which is always published as Byron's. The proof she demanded was a copy of it in his handwriting (TG–John Murray, December 1832). Since Moore's book was already published, the Countess's concern relates either to the three-volume edition of 1833 or to the seventeen-volume edition of Byron's works which Murray began publishing in 1832.

16. TG–John Murray, October 1832 (Murray).

17. R. Glynn Grills, *Mary Shelley: A Biography* (Oxford University Press, 1938), pp. 200–5.

18. Ibid. (TM–MWS, 24.1.1830).

19. MWS, *The Last Man*, 1, vi.

20. *MWSJ*, 8.6.1824.

21. Ibid., 30.1.1825.

22. MWS–JHP, 27.9.1825.

23. MWS–JHP, 29.11.1825.

24. WG–Henry Colburn, 7.1.1826 (V&A, Forster archive).

25. *London Magazine*, IV, March 1826, p. 422.

26. *Monthly Review*, March 1826, pp. 333–5.

27. William Hazlitt, 'Essay on a Sundial', *New Monthly Magazine*, October 1827. This sentence was published for the first time since 1827 in Hazlitt, *Selected Essays*, ed. Duncan Wu (Pickering & Chatto, 1998).

28. MWS–MH, 10.10.1824.

29. MWS, 'Roger Dodsworth, the Reanimated Englishman', *CTS*.

30. *The Biographical Keepsake* (1827), p. 226.

31. MWS–EJT, April 1829.

32. MWS–Cyrus Redding, September–November? 1829.

CHAPTER TWENTY-FOUR: *Private Matters*

1. MWS–TJH, 30.8.1824.

2. MWS–TJH, 3.10.1824.

3. *MWSJ*, 30.1.1825.

4. CC–JW, December 1826 (*CC*, 1).

5. MWS–Joseph Severn, n.d. (see Appendix 2). I am indebted to William St Clair for drawing this to my attention.

6. MWS–LH, 27.6.1825.

7. MWS–JHP, 15.6.1825.

8. Ibid.

9. *The Romance of Mary W. Shelley, etc.*, op. cit., pp. 34–5.

10. MWS–JHP, ?4.5.1825.

11. *The Romance*, p. 51.

12. JHP–Washington Irving, 16.8.1825 (*The Romance*, pp. 18–19).

13. MWS–JHP, 29.7.1825.

14. Washington Irving, 16.8.1825: *Journals and Notebooks*, 3, ed. Walter A. Reichart (University of Wisconsin, 1969–70), p. 510; MWS–JHP, 28.6.1826, 29.6.1825.

15. Hunt, *Autobiography*, ed. Roger Ingpen (1903), 2, p. 51.

16. Viscount Dillon–MWS, 18.3.1829 (Abinger, Dep. c. 516).

17. Eliza Rennie Walker, 'An Evening at Dr Kitchiner's', *Friendship's Offering* (1842), pp. 243–9.

18. Eliza Rennie, *Traits of Character; Being Twenty-Five Years of Literary and Personal Recollections* (1860), 2, pp. 207–8.

19. Mary Diana Dods–MWS, n.d., but all letters are addressed to Bartholomew Place or Terrace, which dates the letters to before the summer of 1827 (Abinger, Dep. c. 516/11).

20. 'David Lindsay'–William Blackwood, November–December 1825 (Blackwood Papers, National Library of Scotland).

21. MWS–Henry Colburn, 30.10.1826.

22. MWS–EJT, 4.3.1827.

23. As rephrased in Mrs Mason–MWS, 13.11.1825 (Abinger, Dep. c. 517).

24. WG–MJG, 6.4.1826, quoted in *Godwin*, 2, pp. 296–7.

25. MWS–JHP, 11.6.1826.

26. MWS's first letter about Velluti was published in the *Examiner*, 11.6.1826, under the name 'Anglo-Italicus'; her second was not published.

27. MWS–EJT, 8.4.1827. (Leigh Hunt added to this letter.)

CHAPTER TWENTY-FIVE: *A Curious Marriage*

1. Cyrus Redding, *Memoirs of Thomas Campbell* (1860), 2, pp. 175–6.

2. Details of Mary Diana Dods's life and her early relationship with Isabel Robinson largely follow Betty T. Bennett's engrossing account in *Mary Diana Dods, A Gentleman and a Scholar* (William Morrow, New York, 1991).

3. MWS–TG, 20.8.1827.

4. MWS–William Whitton, 15.8.1827.

5. MWS–TG, 20.8.1827.

6. MWS–JHP, 30.8.1827.

7. MWS–JWH, 23.9.1827.
8. Frances Wright–Harriet Garnett, March 1828 (quoted in Bennett, *Dods*, p. 114).
9. MWS–JHP, 25.9.1827.
10. *MWSJ*, September 1827.
11. Frances Wright–MWS, 9.11.1827 (*S&M*, 4, p. 1103).
12. MWS–TG, 4–10.12.1827.
13. Robert Dale Owen, 'Frances Wright, Lafayette and Mary Shelley', *Atlantic Monthly*, October 1873.
14. MWS–Robert Dale Owen, 9.11.1827.
15. Owen, quoted in Marshall, *MWS*, 2, p. 178.
16. MWS and LH–EJT, 8.4.1827.
17. EJT–MWS, 24.10.1827, in *Letters of E.J. Trelawny*, ed. H. Buxton Forman (Oxford University Press, 1910).
18. MWS–JWH, ?14.2.1828.
19. MWS–Vincent Novello, 11.3.1828.
20. MWS–JW, 27.4.1828.

CHAPTER TWENTY-SIX: *The Hideous Progeny*

1. Maria Garnett–Julia Garnett Pertz, 22.4.1828 (Payne-Goposchkin Papers, Houghton Library, Cambridge, Mass.).
2. MWS–JWH, 28–29.6.1828.
3. MWS–JWH, 5.6.1828.
4. MWS–Isabella Baxter Booth, 15.6.1828.
5. MWS–JWH, 16.5.1828.
6. Ibid.
7. MWS–JWH, 5.6.1828.
8. MWS, 'Illyrian Poems and Feudal Scenes', *Westminster Review*, January 1829, pp. 71–81. Her second appreciation of Mérimée was written in October 1830.
9. MWS–Prosper Mérimée, 24.5.1828.
10. Harriet Garnett–Julia Garnett Pertz, 25.5.1828, see note 1 and Bennett, *Dods*, p. 40.
11. MWS–William Whitton, 4.6.1828.
12. MWS–JWH, 28.6.1828.
13. Prosper Mérimée–MWS, 5.10.1828.
14. MWS–JWH, 5.6.1828.
15. EJT–MWS, 8.7.1828 (Abinger, Dep. c. 510).
16. Godwin's Journal, 30.3.1830: 'Clairmonts for Vienna.' (Bodleian)
17. Godwin's Journal, 18.9.1829: 'Jane C[lairmon]t. for Dresden.' The Godwins never called her Claire or Clara.
18. *CCJ*, although written as a separate note, dated by Marion Kingston Stocking to after 1828 by virtue of allusions to Dresden.
19. MWS, reviewing 'The Loves of the Poets', *Westminster Review*, 2, October 1829, pp. 472–7.

20. See note 18.
21. MWS–EJT, 14.5.1836.
22. CC–MWS, 28–30.3.1830.
23. MWS–John Murray, 8.9.1830.
24. Sir Timothy Shelley–William Whitton, in R. Ingpen, *Shelley in England* (1917), p. 613, dated to end of 1830.
25. Account given by John Browne, a Horsham draper (Horsham Museum, HM Mss Cat. No. 813–14).
26. WG–MWS, 22.7.1830: *Godwin*, 2, p. 309, but dated in *S&M*, 4, to 15.4.1830.
27. As recorded in Lardner's entry in the *Dictionary of National Biography*.
28. MWS–Charles Ollier, January–February 1831.
29. MWS–John Murray, 4.5.1832.
30. Godwin's *Lives of the Necromancers* was finally published by the obscure firm of Frederick Mason in 1834, after being rejected by Murray, Colburn and Lardner. Published in the US the following year, possibly through the support of Washington Irving, it was much admired by Edgar Allan Poe, who wrote an enthusiastic appreciation in the *Southern Literary Messenger*, 2 (1835), p. 65. An interesting study could be made of the fascination with alchemy, magic and superstition which Mary shared with her father. An obsession with specific and significant dates in her novels clearly relates to this interest. In *Frankenstein*, for example, dates are used both to draw parallels between the story and the nine-month gap between conception and childbirth, and to allude to the birth of Mary herself. This aspect of *Frankenstein* has been ably discussed by Anne K. Mellor, *Mary Shelley*, op. cit.
31. *Frankenstein* (1831 edn), 1, iii.
32. Ibid., 1, Letter IV.
33. Ibid., 1, Letter II.
34. Ibid., 1, Letter IV.
35. Ibid., 1, Letter IV.
36. Ibid., 3, vii.

CHAPTER TWENTY-SEVEN: *Entering Society*
1. MWS–Fanny Wright, 30.12.1830.
2. Ibid.
3. *Morning Chronicle*, 5.11.1832, for a report of Major Beauclerk's opening address to the electorate as the candidate for East Surrey. He was elected by them on 8 November 1832.
4. See Appendix 3.
5. Maria Jane Jewsbury–Anna Jameson, 18.6.1830, in *Anna Jameson: Letters and Friendships*, ed. Mrs Stewart Erskine (1915).
6. *MWSJ*, 18.7.1831.
7. MWS–Elizabeth Stanhope, 17.5.1833.
8. EJT–MWS, 8.4.1831.
9. MWS–EJT, 14.6.1831.
10. MWS–EJT, 26.7.1831.

11. The manuscript of *Adventures of a Younger Son* is at the Houghton Library (Cambridge, Mass.), carrying deletions and alterations by Horace Smith, Mary Shelley and possibly Hogg. The criticisms by Mary referred to here are to pages 394–5 of the original manuscript.

12. MWS–EJT, 27.12.1830.

13. EJT–MWS, 19.1.1831.

14. *MWSJ*, 18.11.1831.

15. Matthew Arnold, *Essays in Criticism* (1888), pp. 205–6. In Arnold's celebrated essay on Shelley, he quoted Mary as saying: 'Teach him to think for himself? Oh my God, teach him rather to think like other people.' Arnold's essay, a review of Edward Dowden's *The Life of Shelley* (1886), was highly supportive of Mary Shelley. Anne Thackeray, Lady Ritchie, *Chapters from Some Memoirs* (1894), pp. 205–6, gave the mother's passionate answer as: 'Ah! No, no, bring him up to think like other people.'

16. CC–MWS, 26.10–8.11.1832 (*CC*, 1).

17. MWS–MG, 24.8.1832.

18. *MWSJ*, June–September 1832.

19. CC–JWH, 1.2.1833.

20. MWS–EJT, 11.1.1833.

21. *Shelley and His Circle*, 6, p. 665.

22. *MWSJ*, 2.12.1834.

CHAPTER TWENTY-EIGHT: *Relinquishing Pleasure*

1. CC–MWS, 26.10.1832 (*CC*, 1).

2. Paraphrased from Claire's letters to MWS, 1832–4.

3. *MWSJ*, 2.12.1834.

4. MWS–MG, 30.10.1834.

5. See H.J. Torre, *Recollections of School Days at Harrow, 1831–1836* (1890).

6. MWS–MG, 17.7.1834.

7. Ibid.

8. Ibid.

9. MWS–MG, 19.8.1834.

10. *MWSJ*, 23.11.1833.

11. WG, *Deloraine*, 3 vols. (1833), 1, v.

12. MWS–Charles Ollier, 10.6.1834.

13. *Lodore*, 3 vols. (Richard Bentley, 1835), 2, iv.

14. MWS–MG, 17.7.1834.

15. MWS–John Bowring, 3.10.1835.

16. MWS–LH, 3.2.1835.

17. W. Cooke–WG, 5.12.1834 (*Godwin*, 2, p. 323).

18. MWS–MG, 9.2.1835.

19. MWS–TLP, 13.1.1835.

20. MWS–JWH, June–July 1835 (as dated by Bennett, *MWSL*, 2, p. 249).

21. MWS–MG, 8.11.1835.

CHAPTER TWENTY-NINE: *Problems of Reputation*

1. *Falkner*, 3 vols. (Saunders & Otley, 1837), 1, ix. A two-volume edition was published by the same firm in the same year, without alterations to the text.
2. Crook & Guiton, *Shelley's Venomed Melody*. See chapter 14, note 25, above.
3. The Revd A.C.H. Morrison–MWS, 27.3.1836 (Abinger, Dep. c. 516).
4. Doran Swade and Simon Schaffer contribute fascinating essays on Babbage and his salon in the 1830s to *Cultural Babbage*, ed. Francis Spufford and Jenny Uglow (Faber, 1996). It is likely that Mary, even if she did not visit Babbage, knew of his invention and had heard of the Silver Lady from her father, who had regular meetings with Babbage at this period.
5. MWS, 'The Invisible Girl' (1833), *CTS*, p. 196.
6. *Falkner*, 1, v.
7. *The Age*, 2.4.1837, p. 106.
8. MWS–EJT, 14.5.1836.
9. MWS–TJH, 18.1–2.4.1836.
10. MWS–TLP, 6.6.1836.
11. Moore, *Journals*, 5, ed. Wilfred S. Dowden (University of Delaware Press, 1984–9). The mention of Rogers's piece of gossip was recorded on the same date, 21 May 1836.
12. Emily Eden, 4.1.1834, Durham University Library (Grey Mss).
13. MWS–EJT, 26.1.1837.
14. The Hon. Mrs George [Caroline] Norton–MWS, 5.1.[1837] (Abinger, Dep. c. 538).
15. Caroline Norton–MWS, 29.?9.[1837] (Abinger, Dep. c. 538).
16. Caroline Norton–MWS, n.d. (Abinger, Dep. c. 538).
17. MWS–Thomas Abthorpe Cooper, February–March 1837.
18. CC–MWS, 19.10.1836.
19. MWS–EJT, 3.1.1837.
20. MWS–EJT, 26.1.1837.
21. WG, 'The Genius of Christianity Unveiled', *Works*, 7, ed. Mark Philp (Pickering & Chatto, 1993), p. 239.
22. The Abinger collection, Dep. c. 606/1–5 contains Mary's editorial notes; Dep. b. 226/11 contains her edited version of Godwin's autobiography; Dep. c. 532/8 contains more of her notes towards a biography of her parents. On 18 December 1837, Harriet de Boinville asked her to help Francisco Solano Constancio prepare a brief memoir of Godwin, which she probably did. It appeared as by Constancio et Z in *Biographie Universelle*, XVII, pp. 40–2. (See *CC*, 2, p. 364 for a fuller account of these details.)
23. MWS–MG, 11.6.1835. Here, Mary told Maria Gisborne that Jane Williams Hogg and Godwin had mocked her praises of Mary's poetry and that they thought nothing of her personal favourite, 'The Dirge', which she here copied out for Mrs Gisborne to read.
24. CC–MWS, 30.10.1840. MWS to [?unidentified] (Abinger, Dep. c. 606/4), published in *Lives of the Great Romantics*, 1, ed. Pamela Clemit (Pickering & Chatto, 1999), p. 95. Dr Bruce Barker-Benfield, Senior Assistant Librarian at

the Bodleian, feels that this, the traditional explanation for the letter, 'doesn't seem unreasonable' (letter to author, 30.7.1999).

25. MWS–LH, December 1837–March 1838 (date conjectured by Professor Bennett in *MWSL*, 2).

26. *Lives of the most Eminent Literary and Scientific Men of France*, 2 vols., The Cabinet of Biography, ed. the Revd Dionysius Lardner (1838–9).

27. Ibid., 1, p. 327.

28. Ibid., 1, p. 97.

29. EJT–CC, 23.3.1836.

30. Charles Sumner, *Memoir and Letters*, ed. Edward L. Pierce (Boston, 1893), 2, p. 21.

31. See Appendix 3. Since the exhibition opened in April 1840, the latter part of the previous year seems a reasonable date. Paintings for the Summer Exhibition were seldom accepted unless of very recent date. They were always on sale. Mary's, presumably, failed to sell and was presented to her by Rothwell at the end of the summer.

32. *Morning Chronicle*, 8.5.1840.

33. MWS–Benjamin Disraeli, 15.11–7.12.1837 (date conjectured by Betty T. Bennett in *MWSL*, 2).

34. MWS–Lady Morgan, December 1837–March 1839, dated by the fact that she wrote her letter from her home at Park Street (*MWSL*, 2).

35. MWS–LH, December 1837–March 1838.

36. Samuel Rogers–MWS, letters of 1838–44 and n.d. (Abinger, Dep. c. 768).

37. See Appendix 2.

38. The reference to Mrs Goring was omitted from the published text in H. Buxton Forman's edition of Trelawny's letters. Letters from Augusta Goring to Mary Shelley in 1837 and n.d. are at the Bodleian (Abinger, Dep. c. 510).

CHAPTER THIRTY: *Reparation and Renewal*

1. Notes on Poems of 1822 (*PW*).

2. *MWSJ*, 12.2.1839.

3. MWS–TJH, 11.2.1839.

4. Henry Crabb Robinson, Diaries, 4.3.1839 (Dr Williams' Library).

5. MWS–LH, 10.10.1839.

6. MWS–LH, 15.11.1839.

7. William Johnstone, *The Table Talker, or Brief Essays on Society and Literature* (1840), 2, pp. 274–9.

8. MWS–LH, 3.2.1840.

9. MWS–LH, 27.2.1840.

10. Hunt, *The Autobiography of Leigh Hunt*, ed. Roger Ingpen, 2 vols. (E.P. Dutton & Co., New York, 1903), ch. 25.

11. MWS–LH, 12.3.1840.

12. Lewes, signed as G.H.L., *Penny Cyclopaedia of the Society for the Diffusion of Useful Knowledge* (1841), XXI, pp. 374–6; *Westminster Review* (1841), 35, pp. 303–44.

13. MWS–LH, 23.12.1839.

14. *MWSJ*, 1.6.1840.

CHAPTER THIRTY-ONE: *Continental Rambles*

1. MWS, *Rambles in Germany and Italy in 1840, 1842 and 1843* (1844), 1, Letter VIII, in *Selected Works*, 8, ed. Jeanne Moskal (Pickering & Chatto, 1996), p. 124.
2. CC–MWS, 30.10.1840.
3. *MWSJ*, 18.8.1840.
4. MWS–Harriet de Boinville, March–May 1841.
5. MWS–CC, 1.10.1842, quoting from a lost letter written to her by Claire at an unspecified but evidently fairly recent date.
6. Additional details about Alexander Berry, an outstandingly successful self-made man, are given by Betty T. Bennett in *MWSL*, 3, p. 20. The Berry–Shelley correspondence is in the State Library of New South Wales, in the Alexander Hay Collection.
7. MWS–Elizabeth Berry, 14.1.1842.
8. MWS–CC, 9.5.1842, reporting Percy's description.
9. Ibid.
10. MWS–CC, 2.6.1842.
11. The details come from Cornelia Crosse, *Red-Letter Days of my Life* (Bentley, 1842), vol. 2, p. 150. In later life, Mrs Crosse recalled, Knox still retained 'a joyous out-of-school boy look in his face'. Her book also provides descriptions of Leslie Ellis, whose discoveries in the field of botanic science are claimed here to have anticipated the work of Charles Darwin.
12. MWS–CC, 2.6.1842.
13. MWS–CC, 1–2.10.1842.
14. MWS–CC, 23.3.1843.
15. MWS–JWH, 9.7.1843.
16. MWS–CC, 19.7.1843.

CHAPTER THIRTY-TWO: *Enter, the Italians*

1. MWS–CC, 30.8.1843.
2. Jeanne Moskal, editor of the *Rambles* (Pickering & Chatto, 1996), provides an excellent summary in MWS, *Selected Works*, 8, pp. 49–56. Professor Jean de Palacio's observations and summarized reviews in *Mary Shelley dans son oeuvre* (Paris, 1969) are indispensable.
3. Fanny, 'my Fannikin', 'my little frolicker', was left at Gothenburg near the Swedish-Norwegian border while Mary Wollstonecraft undertook the most dangerous part of her journey. Compare Letter 16, in which she speaks of 'my babe, who may never experience a father's care and tenderness', with Mary Shelley, in *Rambles*, 1, Letter VI, fretting over the possible loss of her son in a sailing accident: 'A tragedy has darkened my life: I endeavour, in vain, to cast aside the fears which are its offspring; they haunt me perpetually, and make too large and too sad a portion of my daily life.'
4. *Rambles*, p. 76, letter dated 18.6.1840.
5. *Tait's Edinburgh Magazine*, XI, November 1844, pp. 729–40.

6. *Sunday Times*, 25.8.1844, p. 2.

7. MWS–CC, 11.9.1843.

8. MWS–CC, 20.9.1843.

9. Ibid. Mary wrote here of trying homoeopathy or cold-water cures.

10. MWS–CC, 7.10.1843.

11. MWS–Marianna Hammond, 22.1.1844.

12. As noted in *CC*, 2, p. 608, quoting the note made by E.A. Silsbee in the 1870s (Silsbee, box 7, file 2).

13. EJT–CC, 27.11.1869 (Pforzheimer).

14. JWH–CC, 4.9.1843 (BL, Ashley 5036).

15. CC–MWS, 28.1–11.2.1844.

16. MWS–CC, 23.1.1844.

17. MWS–CC, 16.2.1844.

18. MWS–Joseph Severn, 15.12.1843.

19. The editor of Mary Shelley's letters (Bennett, *MWSL*, 3, p. 108, n. 2) and her most recent biographer (Sunstein, *R&R*, p. 363) identify Martini's painting as *The Adulteress brought before Christ*, purchased on a date prior to 1855 by the Scottish collector Archibald MacLellan, and subsequently presented by him to the Glasgow Art Gallery and Museums. Identified as a Giorgione by 1864, this is a work of great importance. Its background has been extensively researched and discussed. No provenance details connect it to Count Martini or to a sale in 1844. The likelihood of its being Martini's 'Titian' on the same subject is ruled out by its size. According to Mary's letter to Joseph Severn of 15 December 1843, Martini's painting measured 11 feet by 5 feet. The Glasgow Giorgione was at one point trimmed by 4 inches. (A precise copy of the untrimmed original by another artist, Cariani, hangs beside it.) Before trimming, the Giorgione measured 7 feet 10 inches by 4 feet 6 inches. It seems unlikely that the painting which Count Martini brought to England was authentic. The original work, as Mary observed in her letter to Severn, would have been worth 'several thousand pounds'. Martini's circumstances remained straitened. (I am indebted to Hugh Stevenson and his colleagues at the Glasgow Art Gallery for information and advice regarding the Giorgione painting in their collection.)

20. MWS–CC, 19.4.1844.

CHAPTER THIRTY-THREE: *Blackmail and Forgery*

1. TJH–MWS, 16.12.1844 (Abinger, Dep. b. 211/3(b)).

2. *Gentleman's Magazine*, XXII, August 1844, p. 206.

3. MWS–CC, 7.12.1844.

4. MWS–CC, 23.12.1844.

5. MWS–Rose Stewart, 1.5.1844; MWS–CC, 27.10.1844.

6. MWS–Richard Monckton Milnes, 11.11.1844.

7. See S.C. Djabri, A. Hughes and J. Knight, *The Shelleys of Field Place*, op. cit., p. 143.

8. MWS–CC, 11.12.1845.

9. MWS–Alexander Berry, 29.3.1847.

10. MWS–CC, 14.10.1845.

11. MWS–CC, paraphrased from her letters of 10–14 September 1845.

12. MWS–CC, 8.1.1845.

13. Wilhelm Clairmont–CC, 17.8.1849. Trelawny's wife, formerly Augusta Goring, is a possible source for the hostility sensed by Claire; Mary had been free in expressing to Trelawny her dislike of Claire, and Claire herself alluded to Augusta in these conversations with her brother. For Charles's view of the Robinsons, see Ch.C–CC, 14.7.1849 (*CC*, 2).

14. MWS–CC, 15.9.1845.

15. MWS–Andrew Alexander Knox, 16–24.9.1845.

16. *Le Constitutionel* and *Le National*, 11.10.1845. Sunstein notes that no reference to either Gatteschi or Guitera survive in the records of the Préfecture in Paris (*R&R*, p. 454, n. 11).

17. *CCJ*, p. 220, n. 56.

18. MWS–CC, 22–23.10.1845.

19. MWS–CC, 8.10.1845.

20. MWS–Louisa Kenney, 22.10.1845 (date conjectured by Betty T. Bennett, but evidently before 1846).

21. MWS–Thomas Hookham, 11.3.1846.

22. MWS–Thomas Hookham, 12.9.1846.

23. *Athenaeum*, 18.3.1848.

24. William White, *The Calumnies of the 'Athenaeum' Journal Exposed* (privately printed, 1852). A full and fascinating account of the Major's career is given by Theodore G. Ehrsam in *Major Byron: The Incredible Career of a Literary Forger* (John Murray, 1951). See also Richard D. Altick, *The Scholar Adventurers* (Macmillan, New York, 1960).

25. Some of White's collection was bought for Mary's son and daughter-in-law at auction on 12 May 1851. Subsequently discovered to be forgeries, these letters were nevertheless retained in the Shelley collection. Exposed as an impostor, the Major fled the country. In 1867, he visited the Marquise de Boissy (the former Teresa Guiccioli) and again announced himself as Byron's son. He later sent her the bills for his hotel. Two monthly numbers of *The Inedited Works of Lord Byron* were published in New York in 1849–50; from then on the Major's life became increasingly Walter Mittyish. He was, on various occasions, introduced as an aristocratic exile, a British naval officer, a journalist and a mining prospector. His wife, meanwhile, worked as a housekeeper. The date of his death is uncertain. Altick, op. cit., pp. 164–5, n. 22, gives further details. Additional information is supplied by T.J. Brown in 'Some Shelley Forgeries by Major Byron' (*Keats-Shelley Memorial Bulletin*, June 1963).

26. MWS–CC, 20–22.11.1845.

27. CC–MWS, 19.1.1846.

CHAPTER THIRTY-FOUR: *Anxious Times*

1. MWS–CC, 29.12.1845–3.1.1846.

2. For Edward Bulwer's translations, see *The Poems and Ballads of Schiller*, 2 vols. (1844). The reference to Shelley is in the Introduction; MWS–LH, 30.1.1846.

3. MWS–Edward Moxon, 30.1.1846.

4. Leigh Hunt, 'Poems of Alfred Tennyson' (*Ainsworth's Magazine*, 1842), anthologized in *Leigh Hunt: Selected Writings*, ed. David Jesson Dibley (Carcanet, 1990), pp. 119–27. Tennyson's debts to Shelley are particularly apparent in the poetry written before 1840 at a time when many younger poets were acknowledging Shelley, Keats and Wordsworth as sources of inspiration.

5. MWS, Notes on 'Poems of 1822' (*PW*).

6. Elizabeth Barrett Browning, *A Vision of Poets*, 2 vols. (1844), 2, pp. 3–59; George Gilfillan, 'Percy Bysshe Shelley', *A Gallery of Literary Portraits* (London, Edinburgh, Dublin, 1845), pp. 71–105. The collection also appeared in separate articles in *Tait's Edinburgh Magazine*.

7. *The Journal of Gideon Mantell, Surgeon and Geologist*, ed. E. Cecil Curwen (Oxford University Press, 1940), p. 202.

8. MWS–LH, 3.6.1846.

9. MWS–Thomas Medwin, 13–16.5.1846.

10. Thomas Medwin–MWS, 17.5.1846 (*MWSL*, 3, p. 285).

11. Thomas Medwin–MWS, n.d. (ibid., p. 287).

12. MWS–JWH, 30.5.1846.

13. MWS–Alexander Berry, 12.11.1846.

14. MWS–Vincent Novello, 5.1.1847. The Novello family were not importunate. Novello was approaching Mary at the suggestion of his daughter, Mrs Clarke, who also took an interest in the Italian school.

15. MH–MWS, 26.1.1847 (Berg Collection, New York Public Library).

16. MWS–LH, ?26.1.1847 (date conjectured from Mary's allusion to Marianne's letter and visit on this date).

17. MWS–CC, 19.3.1847.

18. MWS–CC, 22.6.1847.

19. MWS–CC, 1.8.1847. *MWSL*, 3, p. 325 prints the letter from Sarah Dunstan to Mary dated 23.7.1847, first published in *The Letters of Mary W. Shelley*, ed. Frederick L. Jones (1944), 2, p. 304.

20. MWS–CC, 14.7.1847.

21. MWS–LH, 16.7.1847.

22. Quoted by Sylvia Norman, *Flight of the Skylark: The Development of Shelley's Reputation* (University of Oklahoma Press, 1954), p. 175.

23. *Medwin's Revised Life of Shelley*, ed. H. Buxton Forman (1913), p. 123. Forman's edition includes the Chancery papers and additions and corrections made by Medwin for an unpublished second edition.

24. Ibid., p. 121.

25. Ibid., p. 374.

26. G. Gilfillan, 'Mrs Shelley', *Tait's Edinburgh Magazine* (December 1847), pp. 850–4. This was the third of a series on female authors.

27. Marshall, *MWS*, 2, p. 308.

28. MWS–Augusta Trelawny, 10.6.1848.

29. MWS–Isabella Baxter Booth, 16.4.1847.
30. MWS–Mary Ellen Peacock Nicholls, 15.3.1848.
31. MWS–Alexander Berry, 28–30.3.1848.
32. MWS–Alexander Berry, 30.6.1848.
33. Ch.C–CC, 7.6.1848 (*CCL*, 2).
34. Marshall, *MWS*, 2, p. 310.

CHAPTER THIRTY-FIVE: *The Chosen One*

1. Information about Lady Shelley is based on Betty T. Bennett's notes to *MWSL*, 3, pp. xxiv–v and pp. 334–5. I do not share Professor Bennett's belief that Jane was 'especially dear' to Mary because she was in need of social protection. Jane was wealthy, respectable and surrounded by devoted relations, including those from her late husband's family. Nothing demonstrates this so strongly as the fact that Mr St John's eldest brother took the service for her second marriage.
2. This was alleged by William Albery, *A Parliamentary History of the Ancient Borough of Horsham, 1290–1885* (1927), p. 404.
3. *Talks*, pp. 25–8.
4. Marshall, *MWS*, 2, p. 310.
5. MWS–Alexander Berry, 30.6.1848.
6. MWS–CC, 28.7.1848.
7. MWS–Augusta Trelawny, 24.2.1850.
8. MWS–CC, 28.8.1848.
9. Abinger, Dep. c. 767/3. For further discussion of Laura Galloni's work, see Claire Tomalin's excellent introduction to *Maurice, or The Fisher's Cot* (Viking, 1998), pp. 49–52; Betty T. Bennett, *MWSL*, 3, p. 282, lists several of Galloni's novels, including the posthumously published *I due castelli* (1881). Laura Galloni's letters to Mary Shelley, written between 1848 and 1850, express affection and gratitude for Mary's kind encouragement in her literary endeavours (Abinger, Dep. c. 517/3).
10. Marshall, *MWS*, 2, p. 311.
11. CC–MWS, 11.4.1849.
12. CC–MWS, 1.4.1849.
13. MWS–CC, 6.4.1849.
14. Marshall, *MWS*, 2, p. 312.
15. *Talks*, pp. 40–2.
16. Clara Clairmont–CC, 18.6.1849 (*CC*, 2, p. 509, n. 2).
17. CC–Wilhelm Clairmont, 10.3.1850. Late in life, Claire gossiped to Silsbee that Lady Shelley had shocked these friends of hers and of Mary's – a Colonel and Mrs Pringle – by going with Knox to Brighton after her marriage to Percy (Silsbee Papers, box 7, file 3). Claire was probably recalling Knox's visit to Mary at Sandgate shortly after the marriage. There is no evidence that Lady Shelley had any special interest in Alexander Knox.
18. Antonia Clairmont–CC, 18.9.1850, refers to 'the letter you made Pauline write Mrs S' (*CC*, 2, p. 534, n. 2.).
19. CC–Antonia Clairmont, 1.8.1850.

20. CC–Antonia Clairmont, 6.9.1853.

21. Claire recalled a confused version of the quarrel in the 1870s when Silsbee came to Florence to play the traveller to her ranting mariner.

22. *The Stage Manager: A Weekly Journal of Dramatic Literature and Criticism*, 10.3.1849, p. 29; 31.3.1849, p. 52; 28.4.1849, p. 84; 5.5.1849, pp. 90–1; 12.5.1849, pp. 100–1; 30.6.1849, p. 154; E.C. Hawtrey, *Sermons and Letters delivered to Eton College Chapel 1848–9* (Eton, 1849), p. 112; W.G. Clark, 'Cor Cordium', *A Score of Lyrics* (Cambridge, 1849), pp. 20–1; P.P., 'On the Poetry of the Modern Age', *London University College Magazine* (April 1849), pp. 140–7. The affectionate portrait painted of Shelley by Leigh Hunt in his *Autobiography* (1850) helped to sustain the new image of a poet much slandered and misunderstood. So did a review of Matthew Arnold's poems in which William Michael Rossetti, Polidori's nephew, praised Shelley as 'the heir of Plato' (February 1850): *The Germ: Thoughts towards Nature in Poetry, Literature and Art*, ed. Robert Stahr Hosmon (University of Miami Press, 1970), p. 88.

23. Marshall, *MWS*, 2, p. 312.

24. E.J. Trelawny to the editor, *Athenaeum*, 3.8.1878.

25. MWS–Augusta Trelawny, 24.9.1849 and 24.2.1850.

26. MWS–Isabella Baxter Booth, 30.6.1850.

27. *Guide to Bournemouth* (1842). Major Stephenson had been the previous owner of the house, which later became a school. The grounds have now been converted to tennis courts, a bowling green and a children's play area.

28. MWS–Octavian Blewitt, 15.11.1850.

29. Sir Percy Shelley (hereafter PFS)–Isabella Baxter Booth, ?6.2.1851.

30. Nicholas A. Joukovsky, 'Mary Shelley's Last Letter?', *Notes and Queries* (September 1977), p. 338.

31. Jane Shelley (hereafter JS)–Alexander Berry, 7.3.1851.

CHAPTER THIRTY-SIX: *Afterlife*

1. *Talks*, p. 90.

2. M.D. Conway, 'South Coast Saunterings in England', *Harper's New Monthly Magazine* (March 1869), p. 463.

3. CC–PFS, 2–5.2.1851.

4. Wilhelm Clairmont–CC, 3.3.1851 (*CC*, 2, p. 537, n. 1).

5. E.W.L., 'Lines on the Death of Mrs Shelley', appeared in the *Leader*, 24.2.1851, edited by Thornton Hunt and G.F. Lewes. Lady Shelley liked the poem enough to reprint it in *Shelley Memorials* (1859).

6. *Talks*, pp. 30–1.

7. R. Glynn Grylls, from an account given to her by Mrs Bray, *Mary Shelley* (1938), p. 255.

8. Albinia Locke in Sylvia Norman, *Flight of the Skylark*, op. cit., pp. 214–15; Mrs Bray to R. Glynn Grylls, *Mary Shelley*, pp. 253–4; Agnes Mott, *Shelleyland* (1930).

9. EJT–JS, February 1857 (Grylls, *Mary Shelley*, p. 285).

10. JS–Edward Moxon, 24.2.1857 (Pforzheimer).

11. TJH–JS, 20.4.1857 (Abinger, Dep. c. 813/3).

12. JS–TLP, 10.6.1858 (Houghton, Cambridge, Mass. Ms Eng. 1205.1[9]). A copy of Hogg's second volume, liberally annotated by Lady Shelley, is in the London Library where it arrived after being bought as a replacement volume. This has not been previously identified.

13. JS–TJH, 15.4.1858, quoted by Hogg in a letter to Richard Monckton Milnes, 12.9.1859 (Houghton Papers 12/36, Trinity College, Cambridge).

14. TLP–CC, 12.5.1858 (BL, Ashley 1614).

15. JS, Preface to *Shelley Memorials* (1859). A first draft is in the Abinger collection (Dep. c. 812/1). The Shelleys paid Smith Elder £326 15s. 5d. to produce the first private edition of 1,000 copies, which sold slowly. It was republished in 1875.

16. Messrs Durville & Lawrence (solicitors)–TJH, 3.2.1859 (Abinger, Dep. c. 766/6).

17. See note 13.

18. TLP, *Fraser's Magazine*, January 1860.

19. Richard Garnett, 'Shelley in Pall Mall', *Macmillan's* (June 1860).

20. JS, n.d. and with no signature, in two drafts (Abinger, Dep. c. 767/5(b)).

21. Richard Garnett, *Relics of Shelley* (1862), p. 153.

22. Iris Origo, *The Last Attachment*, pp. 416–17. The thought of Teresa and Claire living in such proximity but never meeting adds piquancy to the events made famous by Henry James in *The Aspern Papers* (serialized in 1888). James based it on the story he heard of an American (Silsbee) paying court to an aunt and her niece in order to obtain the love letters once written to the aunt by a poet. Marion Kingston Stocking, in an appendix to volume 2 of the Clairmont letters, gives a detailed account of Silsbee's pursuit and his connection to Shelley circles in England, *CC*, 2, pp. 654–8.

23. Rennie, *Traits*, 1, pp. 106–9.

24. Thornton Hunt, *Atlantic Monthly* (February 1863). The story of Shelley's having contracted a sexual disease during his years at Oxford originated in this article; my own view is that Mary's allusions to Ovid do not signify a shared secret. Would a woman so anxious to defend Shelley's name have been so reckless? Would Shelley himself have told the gossip-loving Leigh Hunt something which he considered too private to reveal to Peacock, Hogg or Williams? I doubt it, but see also Crook & Guiton, *The Envenomed Melody*, op. cit.

25. W.M. Rossetti–Richard Garnett, 11.6.1869, 18–21.6.1869, 29.6.1869, in *Letters about Shelley*, ed. R.S. Garnett (1917), pp. 21–6. Thornton Hunt was Rossetti's source and even Rossetti thought that Hunt had gone too far.

26. Algernon Swinburne–W.M. Rossetti, 22.5.1869 (BL, Ashley 1621).

27. EJT–CC, 17.9.1869. (*My Recollections of Lord Byron* was translated into English earlier that year by Hubert Jernyngham.)

28. W.M. Rossetti, *Some Reminiscences* (1906), p. 386.

29. CC–EJT, 30.5.1875 (*CC*, 2).

30. JS–EJT, August 1878 (Abinger, Dep. c. 812/3, retained copy in JS's hand). An

unpublished draft letter from Lady Shelley in the same collection alludes to the earlier *Recollections* (1858) and suggests that Trelawny was influenced by an enemy of Mary's, someone 'who may have had a grudge against her son'. Lady Shelley was thinking of Claire. She was wrong to see her as a malevolent adviser; Claire's letters were voluble, but never vicious, about Mary. Percy, writing to Dowden in November 1885, told him that Claire had been extremely clever but never truthful. He blamed this on the fact that she was 'not quite sane'. Trelawny, during his first meeting with Rossetti in 1869, told him that 'Miss Clairmont has been mad, and in an asylum' (W.M. Rossetti–Richard Garnett, 29.6.1869, in *Letters about Shelley*).

31. R.L. Stevenson–JS, 15.1.1890 (Grylls, *Mary Shelley*, p. 292).
32. Sylvia Norman, *Flight of the Skylark*, p. 241.
33. Edward Dowden–JS, 19.10.1883 (Abinger, Dep. c. 769/5).
34. Edward Dowden–JS, 11.11.1885 (Abinger, Dep. c. 769).
35. Richard Garnett–[?unidentified] n.d. (Abinger, Dep. c. 812/4, transcript by Sir Percy Shelley). It is possible that Garnett was writing to Sir Henry Taylor, a friend and neighbour of the Shelleys who had recommended Dowden to them; the letter discussed the problematic chapter 7 of Dowden's book in which Shelley's defection from Harriet to Mary was discussed.
36. Edward Dowden–PFS and JS, 17.11.1885, reminded them that this was beyond their power, and an 'unwise' wish (Abinger, Dep. c. 769/4, fols. 57v–59v).
37. Edward Dowden–JS, 22.10.1886 (Abinger, Dep. c. 769/5, fols. 44v–46v).
38. JS–Florence T. Marshall, n.d. (Abinger, Dep. c. 767/5(b)). A pencil draft.
39. Account by John Frucchi, Director of Cemeteries at Rome, 28.2.1910 (Keats-Shelley Memorial House, Rome).
40. Richard Garnett–Edward Dowden, 8.1.1903 (*Letters about Shelley*).
41. Anonymous, *Athenaeum*, 1.7.1899.
42. Newman Ivey White, *Shelley*, 2 (Secker & Warburg, 1947), p. 416.
43. *R&R*, p. 402.

BIBLIOGRAPHY

WORKS BY MARY SHELLEY

Novels

Frankenstein; or, The Modern Prometheus, 3 vols. (Lackington, 1818);
revised one-volume edition with new preface (Colburn & Bentley,
1831)
Matilda, 1819–1820; first published as *Mathilda*, ed. Elizabeth Nitchie
(University of North Carolina Press, 1959)
Valperga; or, The Life and Adventures of Castruccio, Prince of Lucca, 3 vols.
(Whittaker, 1823)
The Last Man, 3 vols. (Colburn, 1826)
The Fortunes of Perkin Warbeck, A Romance, 3 vols. (Colburn & Bentley, 1830)
Lodore, 3 vols. (Bentley, 1835)
Falkner: A Novel, 3 vols. (Saunders & Otley, 1837)

Plays

'Proserpine, a Mythological Drama in Two Acts', *The Winter's Wreath* for
1832 (1831)
'Midas!', *Proserpine & Midas*, ed. André Henri Koszul (Humphrey Milford,
1922)

Stories

Mary Shelley: Collected Tales and Stories, ed. Charles E. Robinson (Johns
Hopkins University Press, 1976). Robinson includes 'The Pole',
although this was in fact written by Claire Clairmont, with Mary
Shelley's revisions, and 'The Pilgrims', about which he records strong
reservations. The story is included because Richard Garnett had
published it in a collection of Mary Shelley's stories in 1891 and, as
Professor Robinson notes, 'he possibly had access to a letter or MS by
which to determine her authorship'.

Children's Stories
Maurice, or The Fisher's Cot, ed. Claire Tomalin and first published in 1998
  (Viking)

Travel Works
(with P.B. Shelley) *History of a Six Weeks' Tour through a Part of France,
  Switzerland, Germany and Holland: with Letters Descriptive of a Sail round
  the Lake of Geneva, and of the Glaciers of Chamouni* (Hookham & Ollier,
  1817)
Rambles in Germany and Italy, in 1840, 1842, and 1843, 2 vols. (Moxon, 1844)

Editorial Works
Posthumous Poems of Percy Bysshe Shelley (John & Henry Leigh Hunt, 1824)
The Poetical Works of Percy Bysshe Shelley, 4 vols. (Moxon, 1839); one-volume
  edition, with added postscript (Moxon, 1840)
Essays, Letters from Abroad, Translations and Fragments, By Percy Bysshe Shelley,
  2 vols. (Moxon, 1840 and 1841)

Bibliographical Essays
Lives of the Most Eminent Literary and Scientific Men of Italy, Spain and Portugal,
  3 vols., forming part of Lardner's *Cabinet Cyclopedia* (Longman, 1835
  and 1837). In volume 1, Mary wrote all the lives with the exception
  of Dante and Ariosto; in volume 2, it is beyond doubt that she wrote
  the lives of Pietro Metastasio, Carlo Goldoni, Vittorio Alfieri,
  Giambattista Marino, Vincenzo Monti and Ugo Foscolo. In volume 3,
  a recently published letter suggests that she may have written the life
  of Alonzo de Ercilla, the only one of the twenty-one essays which had
  hitherto been in doubt. The rest had already been attributed to her.
Lives of the Most Eminent Literary and Scientific Men of France, 2 vols., forming
  part of Lardner's *Cabinet Cyclopedia* (Longman, 1838 and 1839). All the
  essays in these two collections appear to have been written by Mary
  Shelley.

This list is not comprehensive. For a longer, more speculative catalogue of
Mary's works, including many anonymously published articles, reviews and
poems, the reader is referred to Emily W. Sunstein, *Mary Shelley: Romance
and Reality* (1989), Appendix B.

FURTHER READING

For a full background reading list, see *The Letters of Mary Wollstonecraft
Shelley*, 1, edited by Betty T. Bennett (Johns Hopkins University Press,
1980), pp. xxix–xxxvi and *The Clairmont Correspondence*, 1, edited by
Marion Kingston Stocking (Johns Hopkins University Press, 1995), pp.
xlix–lvii.

The following works were especially useful and/or stimulating in researching the present biography.

Betty T. Bennett, *Mary Diana Dods, A Gentleman and a Scholar* (Johns Hopkins University Press, 1994)

Edmund Blunden, *Shelley* (Collins, 1946)

Marilyn Butler, *Romantics, Rebels and Reactionaries: English Literature and Its Background 1760–1830* (Oxford University Press, 1981)

John Buxton, *Byron and Shelley: The History of a Friendship* (Macmillan, 1968)

David Crane, *Lord Byron's Jackal* (HarperCollins, 1998)

Mario Curreli, *Una certa Signora Mason* (Edizioni ETS, 1997)

Jane Dunn, *Moon in Eclipse: A Life of Mary Shelley* (Weidenfeld & Nicolson, 1978)

Eleanor Flexner, *Mary Wollstonecraft* (Coward, McCann, 1972)

Celina Fox (ed.), *London: World City 1800–1840* (Yale University Press, 1992)

R.S. Garnett, (ed.), *Letters about Shelley* (Hodder & Stoughton, 1917)

Elizabeth Grant, *Memoirs of a Highland Lady*, 2 vols. (1898; Canongate, 1988)

R. Glynn Grylls, *Claire Clairmont: Mother of Byron's Allegra* (Murray, 1939)

——*Mary Shelley: A Biography* (Oxford University Press, 1938)

——*William Godwin and His World* (Odhams Press, 1953)

Alethea Hayter, *A Sultry Month: Scenes of London Literary Life in 1846* (Faber, 1975)

Richard Holmes, *Shelley: The Pursuit* (Weidenfeld & Nicolson, 1974)

Leigh Hunt, *Autobiography*, ed. Roger Ingpen (Dutton, 1903)

Don Locke, *William Godwin: A Fantasy of Reason* (Routledge, 1980)

Peter H. Marshall, *William Godwin* (Yale University Press, 1984)

Ann Mellor, *Mary Shelley: Her Life, Her Fiction, Her Monsters* (Routledge, 1988)

Sylvia Norman, *Flight of the Skylark* (University of Oklahoma Press, 1954)

Julian Offray de la Mettrie, *L'Homme Machine* (1645), *L'Homme Plante* (1648), intr. Justin Leiber (Hackett, 1994)

Cecilia Powell (ed.), *Italy in the Age of Turner* (Merrell Holberton, 1998)

William St Clair, *The Godwins and the Shelleys* (Faber, 1989)

Carla Sanguinetti, *Mary Shelley, Dialogo d'amore* (Edizione Giacche, 1997)

Iain Sinclair, *Lights Out for the Territory* (Granta, 1997)

Muriel Spark, *Mary Shelley, Child of Light* (1951; revised edition, Constable, 1988)

Francis Spufford and Jenny Uglow (eds.), *Cultural Babbage* (Faber, 1996)

Emily Sunstein, *Mary Shelley: Romance and Reality* (Johns Hopkins University Press, 1989)

Janet Todd, *Mary Wollstonecraft: A Revolutionary Life* (Weidenfeld & Nicolson, 2000)

Claire Tomalin, *Shelley and His World* (Thames & Hudson, 1980)

——*The Life and Death of Mary Wollstonecraft* (Penguin Books, revised edition, 1992)

Newman Ivey White, *Shelley*, 2 vols. (Secker & Warburg, 1947)
Lewis Wolpert, *The Unnatural Nature of Science* (Faber, 1992)
Jonathan Wordsworth, *Ancestral Voices* (Cassell, 1991)
——*Visionary Gleam* (Cassell, 1993)
——*The Bright Work Grows* (Cassell, 1997)

ACKNOWLEDGEMENTS

Special thanks are due to the editors and general staff at John Murray, who have been exemplary in balancing help with restraint. I would especially like to thank Grant McIntyre, Gail Pirkis, Caroline Westmore and Howard Davies. Thanks to Dr Bruce Barker-Benfield at the Bodleian Library and to Doucet Fischer and Stephen Wagner at the Pforzheimer Collection at the New York Public Library, to Christopher Fletcher at the British Library, to Marilyn Brooks, Peter Cochran, Clarissa Campbell Orr and Nora Crook at Anglia University, to William St Clair, Diana Scott-Kilvert, Claire Tomalin and Janet Todd for all their advice and help, to members of the Byron Society, to the curators of Keats House in Hampstead and to Catherine Payling at the Keats-Shelley Memorial House in Rome. I am grateful as always for the patience, advice and good humour of all at the London Library. Thanks too to Douglas Matthews for elevating the index to a work of art. Anybody working on the lives of the Shelleys is indebted to Lord and Lady Abinger, whose family continue to add to the magnificent collection of manuscripts preserved as the Abinger collection at the Bodleian Library.

Thanks are also due to Mr and Mrs Normaile Baxter, Professor Massimo Bacigalupa, Elaine Benedetti, Mrs Katy Bedford, to Adrian Blunt at the Inner Temple Library, Philippa Gregory, Jane Ridley, Stella Tillyard, and to Carl Stead for intriguing thoughts on the 'Neapolitan charge'. Thanks also to Denise Chantrey and Colin Johnson for research undertaken in the Bath Record Office and local newspapers. I am much indebted to Mario Curreli at the University of Pisa, to Richard Conrad for musical advice, to the staff of the Dundee Library, Ian Flett, to Graham Dennis, to Miss Dugan at Cupar Library, to the Dazzi family, to Susan Djabri, to Christopher Edwards and, with huge gratitude, to Margaret Elston. I am grateful for being introduced to Mary Shelley's Rome by Helen Guglielmini and her husband. Thanks to Enid Foster at the Garrick Theatre Museum, to Hugh Stevenson at the Glasgow Art Gallery, to Ann Hardie at the Wellcome Institute, Harriet Cullen, Richard Holmes, to Jeremy Knight at the Horsham Museum and to the staff at the Houghton Library, Cambridge, Mass., and of the Wren Library, Cambridge. Thanks, too, to the staff at the Guildhall Library, Holborn Library and at the Museum of London and the Victoria & Albert Museum. The Library of the Royal College of Surgeons was a haven and an invaluable source of information. Thanks to Deborah Jenkins at London Metropolitan Archives. At the Lerici Museum, I owe thanks to Carla Giunchi and to Tyler Lincoln for introducing me to the pleasure of reading Mary Shelley in Italian. Abbie Mason gave me food for thought about Fanny Imlay; Diane Middlebrook and Ann Mellor contributed and added to the pleasure of my research. Jacob Simon was very kind in advising on the research into some mystery portraits; Charles Robinson offered some dazzling insights into *Frankenstein* in his lecture inaugurating the chair in Byron Studies at Nottingham University. Sam Stych was wonderfully hospitable at Bagni di Lucca, Gabriella Tealdi brightened life at Pisa. Special thanks to Oliver Morton and Nancy Hynes, for reasons they will know. Thanks, too, to Bill Zachs for sharing some fascinating material with me. Thanks, as always but never with more warmth, to Anthony Goff, for being everything a perfect agent could be, and to Anthony Gottlieb, for being everything a perfect husband could be. And thanks to all the friends and family, God bless them, who kept me entertained and reassured throughout what has often seemed a dauntingly ambitious project.

The faults are all my own.

INDEX

BIO
SHELLEY   Seymour, Miranda.

            Mary Shelley.

                        33910020776317
$35.00   08/27/2001

<table>
<tr><td colspan="4">DATE</td></tr>
<tr><td></td><td></td><td></td><td></td></tr>
<tr><td></td><td></td><td></td><td></td></tr>
<tr><td></td><td></td><td></td><td></td></tr>
<tr><td></td><td></td><td></td><td></td></tr>
<tr><td></td><td></td><td></td><td></td></tr>
<tr><td></td><td></td><td></td><td></td></tr>
<tr><td></td><td></td><td></td><td></td></tr>
<tr><td></td><td></td><td></td><td></td></tr>
<tr><td></td><td></td><td></td><td></td></tr>
<tr><td></td><td></td><td></td><td></td></tr>
<tr><td></td><td></td><td></td><td></td></tr>
<tr><td></td><td></td><td></td><td></td></tr>
</table>